Handbook of East Asian Entrepreneurship

With the shift of the global economic gravity toward emerging economies and the roaring economic growth of the past three decades in China, East Asian catching-up growth strategies have profound implications for latecomer economies. While there are many handbooks on entrepreneurship in general, there is nothing on East Asian entrepreneurship. This is the first of its kind on the market.

The volume provides a useful reference for those who want to know of East Asian entrepreneurship and business systems. It also provides many excellent cases and illustrations on the growth of entrepreneurial firms and the rise of branded products in East Asia. Policy-makers or scholars who are interested in entrepreneurship, small and medium-sized enterprises, Asian business systems, international business, innovation and technology management, economic development, strategic management and East Asian studies would benefit from this volume.

Written by experts in their respective areas, the *Handbook of East Asian Entrepreneurship* is an excellent review of theories, policies and empirical evidence on important topics in entrepreneurship in East Asian economic development. The book is both a superb teaching tool and a valuable Handbook in development economics.

Fu-Lai Tony Yu obtained his PhD from the University of New South Wales (ADFA). He has taught at Hong Kong Baptist University, Hong Kong Polytechnic University, Monash University (Australia) and Feng Chia University (Taiwan). He is currently Professor of Economics at Hong Kong Shue Yan University. His research interests include entrepreneurship, small and medium-sized enterprises, Austrian economics, governmental economics and Asian business systems.

Ho-Don Yan is a Professor in the Department of Economics, Feng Chia University, Taiwan. He received his PhD in economics from the State University of New York at Albany. His research fields include open macroeconomics and entrepreneurship.

Handbook of East Asian Entrepreneurship

Edited by Fu-Lai Tony Yu and Ho-Don Yan

LONDON AND NEW YORK

First published 2015
by Routledge
2 Park Square, Milton Park, Abingdon, Oxon OX14 4RN

and by Routledge

605 Third Avenue, New York, NY 10017

First issued in paperback 2020

Routledge is an imprint of the Taylor & Francis Group, an informa business

British Library Cataloguing in Publication Data
A catalogue record for this book is available from the British Library

Library of Congress Cataloging-in-Publication Data
Handbook of East Asian entrepreneurship / edited by Fu-Lai Tony Yu and Ho-Don Yu.
pages cm
Includes bibliographical references and index.
1. Entrepreneurship—East Asia. 2. Corporations—East Asia. 3. Industrial management—East Asia. I. Yu, Tony Fu-Lai, 1950– II. Yu, Ho-Don.
HB615.H26 2014
338′.04095—dc23
2014001678

ISBN 13: 978-0-367-36245-4 (pbk)
ISBN 13: 978-0-415-74323-5 (hbk)

Typeset in Bembo and Stone
Sans by Apex CoVantage, LLC

Contents

Figures

Tables

Contributors

Kevin Au is Associate Professor in the Department of Management, The Chinese University of Hong Kong, Shatin, Hong Kong.

Michael Carney is a Research Chair in Strategy and Entrepreneurship, Concordia University, Canada.

Shu-Ting Chang is a graduate of the Management Science Department, National Chiao Tung University, Taiwan.

Chyong Ling Judy Chen is Associate Professor in the Department of Economics, Feng Chia University, Taiwan.

Liang-Chih Chen is Assistant Professor in the Graduate Institute of Building and Planning, National Taiwan University, Taiwan.

Charlie Z.W. Chiang is a Chief of the Industrial Development Division in the Economic Bureau of Taichung City Government, Taiwan.

Eugene K. Choi is Associate Professor, Graduate School of Technology Management, Ritsumeikan University, Japan.

Myeong-Kee Chung is Professor of Economics in the Department of Chinese Studies and Economics in Hannam University, South Korea.

Ming Dong is Lecturer in the School of Economics and Management, Xidian University, China.

Antony Drew is Lecturer in International Business and MBA Program Director at the University of Newcastle, Australia.

Charles E. Eesley is Assistant Professor in the Department of Management Science and Engineering, Stanford University, USA.

Ramzi Fathallah is a PhD student in International Business and Strategy at the Richard Ivey School of Business, Western University, Canada.

Nerys Fuller-Love is Lecturer in the School of Management and Business, Aberystwyth University, UK.

Eric R. Gedajlovic is the Beedie Professor of Strategy and Entrepreneurship at the Beedie School of Business, Simon Fraser University, Canada.

Richard A. Gershon is Professor and Co-Director of the Telecommunications and Information Management Program at Western Michigan University, USA.

Stephen Grainger is Senior Lecturer in International Negotiation and Asian Business at Edith Cowan University, Perth, Australia.

Mark J. Greeven is Associate Professor in the School of Management, Zhejiang University, China.

Mei-Chih Hu is Professor at the Institute of Technology Management, National Tsing Hua University, Taiwan.

Kathryn Ibata-Arens is Director of Global Asian Studies and Associate Professor of Political Economy at DePaul University, USA.

David F.K. Ip is Associate Professor and Associate Head of Department of Applied Social Sciences at the Hong Kong Polytechnic University.

Sung Wook Joh is Professor at the Business School, Seoul National University, South Korea.

Nobuo Kawabe is President, Bunkyo Gakuin University and Professor Emeritus, Waseda University, Japan.

Pekka Kess is Professor of Industrial Engineering and Management at the University of Oulu, Finland.

Anton Kriz is Senior Lecturer at the University of Newcastle, Australia.

Diana S. Kwan is Project Coordinator at the Office of Educational Services, the Chinese University of Hong Kong, Shatin, Hong Kong.

Adrienne La Grange is Associate Professor in the Department of Public Policy, City University of Hong Kong.

Richard Cheung Lam is Assistant Professor of Department of Economics and Finance at Hong Kong Shue Yan University, Hong Kong.

Janet Tai Landa is Professor of Economics, Emerita, at York University, Canada.

Seung-Joo Lee is Professor of Management at the KDI School of Public Policy and Management, South Korea.

Tzong-Ru (Jiun-Shen) Lee is Professor in the Marketing Department at National Chung Hsing University, Taiwan.

Jian Bai Li is a PhD candidate in the Department of Management Science and Engineering, Stanford University, USA.

John Lie is C.K. Cho Professor of Sociology at the University of California, Berkeley, USA.

Jeffrey K. Liker is Professor of Industrial and Operations Engineering at the University of Michigan, USA.

John A. Mathews is Professor of Strategic Management at Macquarie Graduate School of Management, Macquarie University, Sydney, Australia.

Matti Muhos is Research Director of Micro-Entrepreneurship at the University of Oulu, Finland.

William R. Nash is Professor Emeritus of Educational Psychology at Texas A&M University, USA.

Ingyu Oh is Professor of Hallyu Studies at the Research Institute of Korean Studies, Korea University, South Korea.

Terutomo Ozawa is Professor Emeritus of Economics, Colorado State University, and a Research Associate, Center on Japanese Economy and Business, Columbia Business School, USA.

Hun Joo Park is Professor at the KDI School of Public Policy and Management, South Korea.

Frederik Pretorius is an Honorary Fellow of the Asian Institute of International Law at the University of Hong Kong, and Adjunct Professor, Urban Finance, Urban and Regional Economics at the University of Canberra, Australia.

Gordon Redding is Professor of Asian Business and Comparative Management at INSEAD, France.

Bing Ren is Professor in the Department of Business Management of Nankai University, China.

Daniel Shapiro is Dean of the Beedie School of Business at Simon Fraser University, Canada.

Jianfu Shen is a teaching fellow in the Department of Accounting and Finance, Hong Kong Polytechnic University, Hong Kong.

Na Shen is Lecturer in the Department of Business Administration, Hong Kong Shue Yan University, Hong Kong.

Solee I. Shin is a Postdoctoral Researcher at the Center of East and South-East Asian Studies at Lunds University in Sweden.

Peter St. Onge is Assistant Professor in the Department of Marketing, Feng Chia University, Taichung, Taiwan.

Zhongjuan Sun is a Research Fellow at the Research Center for Technological Innovation (RCTI), School of Economics and Management, Tsinghua University, Beijing, China.

Hao Tan is Senior Lecturer in International Business at the University of Newcastle, Australia.

Kuanrong Tian is a PhD student in the Department of Innovation, Entrepreneurship and Strategy, School of Economics and Management, Tsinghua University, Beijing, China.

Yanyu Wang is a PhD student in the Department of Innovation, Entrepreneurship and Strategy, School of Economics and Management, Tsinghua University, Beijing, China.

Jong Hyun Wi is Professor at Chung-Ang University Korea, and Visiting Professor of CRESST (National Center of Research on Evaluation, Standard and Student Testing) UCLA, USA.

Ching-Yan Wu is Assistant Professor at the Department of Finance and International Business, Fu-Jen Catholic University, Taiwan.

Wei Xie is Professor in the Department of Innovation, Entrepreneurship and Strategy of Tsinghua University, Beijing, China.

Fangqi Xu is Professor in the Faculty of Business Administration and Director of the Institute for Creative Management and Innovation, Kinki University, Japan.

Ho-Don Yan is Professor in the Department of Economics, Feng Chia University, Taichung, Taiwan.

Fu-Lai Tony Yu is Professor in the Department of Economics and Finance, Hong Kong Shue Yan University, Hong Kong.

Introduction

Fu-Lai Tony Yu and Ho-Don Yan

The gravity of the world economy is shifting toward emerging economies. According to the International Monetary Fund (IMF) (2012), the GDP weight of emerging and developing countries has jumped from 30 percent in 1990 to 48 percent in 2010 in just 20 years.[1] Global foreign direct investment (FDI) flows have been teetering toward the developing world as well. In 2012, the United Nations Conference on Trade and Development (UNCTAD) (2013) reported that developing countries absorbed more FDI than developed countries for the first time ever, accounting for 52 percent. McKinsey Global Institute (MGI) also estimated that by 2025 annual consumption in emerging markets will rise to US$30 trillion, up from US$12 trillion in 2010, and will account for nearly 50 percent of the world's total, up from 32 percent in 2010 (Atsmon *et al.*, 2012). How emerging economies, particularly China, can grow so fast in so short a period of time has become the interest of study on the development economics and growth strategies for catching-up, such as import substitution, big push, and flying-geese theories (Radelet and Sachs, 1997) over the past half-century, and the recent new structural economics (Lin, 2012a).

The economic growth theory, chiefly designed for developed countries that have a similar industrial structure and technology capability, predicts that lower-income countries eventually will converge or catch up to higher-income countries (Solow, 1956; Barro, 1997). For most emerging and developing economies with the disadvantage of backwardness in their technology, the growth model postulated by mainstream economics, either the neoclassical or new classical growth models, is unsuitable (Lin, 2004). Given the co-existence of advanced and backward nations, the latter could skip several stages that the former had to go through by adopting the advanced technologies of the former as Gerschenkron (1962) argued. Lin (2004) postulated that latecomer nations can turn this "backwardness" into an advantage by adopting a competitive advantage-following strategy, in lieu of a competitive advantage-defying strategy. Emerging economics can benefit from developing labor-intensive production and borrowing incumbent and tested technologies invented by advanced countries. As observed by the World Bank (2008), though developing countries lack advanced technological competencies, technological progress can occur through the adoption and adaptation of pre-existing but new-to-the-market or new-to-the-firm technologies.

Apart from the national level of the above-mentioned growth strategy, it is important to investigate the growth strategies from the firm level. After all, the creation of a nation's wealth consists of the summation of each individual firm. However, the intellectual tyranny of the neoclassical firm theory over-emphasizing efficient resource allocation comes at the cost of assuming that goods and services are given and the economy becomes production-less (Coase and Wang, 2011; Coase, 2012). A production-less economy overlooks the importance of the role of clever ruses, ingenious schemes, and brilliant innovations of the outstanding entrepreneurs who dedicate themselves towards product development and the organization of production. Indeed, the gathering pace of globalization and the convergence of the trio of information, communication, and technology have intensified competition and simultaneously democratized entrepreneurship at a cracking pace. Entrepreneurs have been touted as "global heroes," and entrepreneurship is an indispensible component of growth and prosperity (Bygrave and Zacharakis, 2008: 1; *The Economist*, 2009; Wright and Zahra, 2011).

Like the growth theories on the macro-level, from the perspective of the firm level, the research paradigm of entrepreneurship studies is inherently based on developed economies, in which the focal emphasis is how to lead the market through creative innovation and dominant market strategies (Hobday, 2000). As latecomer firms lag behind in knowledge of technology, marketing, and management, it is hard for them to compete head-to-head with the multinational corporations (MNCs) of advanced economies. Instead, over the past four decades, many successful latecomer firms wanting to upgrade their technology normally followed a catch-up path. First, they start practicing original equipment manufacturing (OEM), which is making products that are sold abroad and bear the brand name of another company (mostly MNCs), as a way to link to the global production network and to learn new technologies, managerial skills, and global market practices (Hobday, 1995; Mathews, 2002; Yan *et al.*, 2014). An OEM strategy could help accumulate a large amount of wealth and capabilities for firms, thereby helping to transform OEM firms into establishing their own brand manufacturing (OBM), which is producing and selling products with the firm's own brand, and this requires more innovation-driven business practices. Many latecomer firms have gone through this transforming process and eventually forge ahead of those MNCs from advanced economies. Examples include Sony, Toyota, and Samsung, to name but a few.

The unusual speed of technological progress in post-war East Asian countries (Japan, South Korea, Taiwan, China, and Hong Kong) has been praised as a good example of the catching-up growth model (Page, 1994; Hobday, 1995; Mathews, 2002; Lin, 2004). The implications of the East Asian catching-up experiences are profound and have become an active area of investigation. East Asia has heterogeneous capitalism structures, with Hong Kong as a nearly complete *laissez-faire* market economy and the other four economies marked under different types of government-directed capitalism (Baumol *et al.*, 2007). Taiwan is noted for its abundant small and medium-sized enterprises (SMEs), South Korea's economy is dominated by business conglomerates (*chaebols*), Japan's businesses are known for industrial networks (*keiretzu*), and China is replete with emerging multinational manufacturers. There have also been different levels of economic development within the region, not to mention large differences in population, culture, industrial structures, and economic policy. However, a common feature shared by these five economies is that they all either have experienced or are experiencing rapid catching-up growth. The sequential, yet in-tandem growth pattern of the East Asian region is known as the "flying-geese," led by Japan, followed by South Korea, Taiwan, Hong Kong, and Singapore, and with China as the tail (Akamatsu, 1962; Ozawa, 2009).[2] Through technology dissemination and emulative learning, East Asian countries sequentially and successfully have built their skills and upgraded their industrial structures.

What is the role of entrepreneurship in the catching-up growth strategies? Variant entrepreneurial activities are defined, such as in Kirchhoff (1994) and Wenneker and Thurik (1999), among others, and entrepreneurial behavior can be divided into two types: adaptive entrepreneurship (or Kirznerian entrepreneurship) and revolutionary entrepreneurship (or Schumpeterian entrepreneurship) (Yu, 2001), or are similarly known as replicative entrepreneurship and innovative entrepreneurship by Baumol *et al.* (2007). The former refers to *opportunity discovery* focusing on those producing or selling a good or service already available through other sources, while the latter refers to *opportunity creation* focusing on those who produce new products and have new methods of production (Alvarez and Barney, 2007).

The mainstream growth theory emphasizes that the way for firms to lead in the market is through intensive R&D investment (or Schumpeterian entrepreneurship) in order to advance technology progress. With relative lower capabilities, this is not a viable strategy for firms in developing countries, particularly in the early stage of development. Rather than seeking new product innovation, which requires costly research, innovation, marketing, and branding capabilities, accompanied by a higher risk of product failure, Bolton (1993) argued that the merits of imitation help firms to benefit from the experience of pioneers. The imitators can focus on developing process capabilities by mastering the latest technologies for low-cost, high-quality product replication. The theoretical argument and the success of the catching-up experiences of East Asia indicate that for latecomer economies, an effective catching-up growth strategy hinges upon adaptive entrepreneurship.

This volume is divided into two parts. Part I presents the key themes related to the concept of adaptive entrepreneurship and East Asian catching-up growth strategies. Part II presents cases of entrepreneurial firms and their founders in East Asia, including Japan, Taiwan, South Korea, China, and Hong Kong.

Part I Key concepts

Many business practices and academia are nowadays inadvertently associated with entrepreneurship. Entrepreneurship has become a common platform enabling communication for variant research fields, such as economics, strategic management, organizational behavior, leadership, etc. As Shane and Venkataraman (2000) noted, entrepreneurship is a broad label that houses a hodgepodge of research studies.

Stevenson and Jarillo (1990) divided studies of entrepreneurship into three key questions: (1) *what* happens when entrepreneurs act; (2) *why* they act; and (3) *how* they act. The first question relates to the economics field and emphasizes the impact of entrepreneurial activities on the economy (Schumpeter, 1934; Kirzner, 1973). The second question is closely related to psychology and sociology. *Who* entrepreneurs are has been the question often asked. An entrepreneur is perceived as an individual, and the general viewpoint concerns the role of personal characteristics and social network (Hoang and Anoncic, 2003; Shane, 2003: 96–117). The third question of *how* usually refers to management and mostly includes issues of competitive advantage, dynamic capabilities, and leadership (Porter, 1990; Teece *et al.*, 1997). Separating the focus into three target questions—what, who, and why—in the research of entrepreneurship is certainly helpful, though one cannot deny that most studies spontaneously touch on two of them or all three.

This Handbook is about East Asian entrepreneurship and the issues of focus relate to catching-up growth strategies and adaptive entrepreneurship. The key concepts found in the three different questions involve 15 chapters, with five chapters on each of the three subjects contrived for this Handbook. The first subject encompasses catching-up and growth strategies, the second involves social factors and entrepreneurship, and the third involves incubation and types of entrepreneurship.

Catching-up and growth strategies

In Chapter 1, Terutomo Ozawa reasserts the relevance of the prominent "flying-geese" theory, proposed originally by Professor Kaname Akamatsu (1897–1974) in the mid-1930s. The economic environment has changed enormously since Akamatsu's seminal concept, and some of his core concepts are outdated in light of the rapid changes in technology, commercial knowledge, economic structures, institutions, and international relations in the global economy. In order to adapt this theory to the current economic situation, Terutomo Ozawa updated and reformulated the "flying-geese" theory. Extending the framework of Mathews (2002), John A. Mathews and Hao Tan in Chapter 2 apply it to the recent case of global expansion by Chinese renewable energy firms in the wind power and solar photovoltaic (PV) sectors. Under this framework (called the LLL framework), latecomers can overcome competitive disadvantages and enhance their dynamic capabilities by linking up with the global market, leveraging their resources by means of relatively lower labor costs, and learning through repeated linkages and leveraging.

Ming Dong provides a catching-up strategy in Chapter 3 by using a case study of imitative entrepreneurship in China. This chapter presents a new term of catching-down, or *shanzhai,* which in a sense is avoiding technology over-shooting, yet in fact it is highly profitable for a firm to adapt and modify newly-invented goods to serve local needs. The meaning of *shanzhai* ranges from pure imitation (counterfeit or copycat) to very good innovation (new product development). Ming Dong used two cases (the Subor learning machine and the *shanzhai* Samsung handset) to illustrate how *shanzhai* flourishes in China's markets.

Entrepreneurial behaviors are conditional not only on firms' internal capacity, but also the structures in which they are embedded. In Chapter 4, Solee I. Shin examines entrepreneurial innovations in various national settings within the context of divergent economic structures and competition, by studying large retail conglomerates of three East Asian economies: Daiei (Japan), Shinsegae (South Korea), and the Uni-President Group (Taiwan). Whether a newly born company can survive or grow to the mature stage is a critical question for strategic management.

Chapter 5 offers the growth strategy for an existing firm. Differing from other studies, Matti Muhos, Tzong-Ru Lee, Shu-Ting Chang, and Pekka Kess focus particularly on the early-stage firm and develop a four-stage framework—conception and development, commercialization, expansion, and stability/renewal—to anatomize what the exact challenges are at each stage that confront the early-stage firm, through intensive interviews at different management levels of companies. Three Taiwanese SMEs are investigated in order to evaluate the effectiveness of their growth strategies.

Social factors and entrepreneurship

In Chapter 6, Janet Tai Landa establishes a model for the Chinese middleman, which provides a theoretical foundation for Chinese entrepreneurs, who then take advantage of superior information in the social network to reduce the transaction costs from contract uncertainty. In a precarious institution, economic exchange could rely upon invisible codes of ethics that are embedded in the personalized exchange relations among the members of the ethnically homogeneous middleman group (EHMG), which function as constraints against breach of contract and hence facilitate exchange among Chinese middlemen. The EHMG reveals itself to be a low-cost club-like institutional arrangement. This chapter also lays a foundation for those studies of Chinese *guanxi* and the bamboo network.

Stephen Grainger in Chapter 7 examines the definition, base development, and importance of *guanxi* in business and at the organizational level of China. In order to develop and maintain *guanxi* relationships, four essential strategies are analyzed: tendering favors, nurturing long-term mutual benefits, cultivating personal relationships, and cultivating trust. A specific form of *guanxi*, the "bamboo network," primarily refers to overseas ethnic Chinese who have built up influential family business conglomerates in Southeast Asia.

In Chapter 8, Bing Ren, Kevin Au, and Na Shen examine in particular the ongoing phenomenal bamboo network in China, which provides a fast-growing thicket of bamboo capitalism and might be the source of China's vigorous economic growth (*The Economist*, 2011). The analysis of Ren *et al.* emphasizes three characteristics: being opportunity-driven, flexibility, and cooperativeness.

By comparing the Western perception of paternalism, Antony Drew, Anton Kriz, and Gordon Redding in Chapter 9 examine how this systematic constraint will affect entrepreneurial spirit in China's transition economy. Paternalism in the Chinese context is a state and familial patriarchal system of coercion and obligation centered around implicit or explicit moral responsibility, benevolence, and the consequential accepted norms and methods of behavior. Helping the society as a whole is more important than worrying about individuals, groups, towns, and/or regions in China.

In Chapter 10, Michael Carney, Ramzi Fathallah, Eric R. Gedajlovic, and Daniel Shapiro focus on the issue of how ethnic Chinese family firms (ECEF) internationalize. The authors offer four different perspectives of the internationalization of ECEFs. Given that Asia is undergoing rapid social and economic growth, the emergence of a prosperous population of firms owned and controlled by Chinese entrepreneurs, including many diaspora and returnees working in Western societies, usually defies ethnic stereotypes. The role of the ethnic Chinese family firm becomes less prominent in the wave of internationalization.

Incubation and types of entrepreneurship

In order to revitalize its three decades-old moribund economy, both Japan's public and private sectors have endeavored to foster new venture creations. Kathryn Ibata-Arens in Chapter 11 studies a revolution in new business incubation in Japan. To specifically address how each incubator is implemented, she presents three case studies: Kyoto Mikuruma (the network model), Sguga Cikkabi 21 (the training model), and Venture Generation (providing international networks for firms).

Chapter 12 studies the role of *chaebols* in South Korea. Sung Wook Joh argues that using internal capital markets (ICMs) is the key to help facilitate *chaebols*' diversification strategy through channeling resources from one affiliated firm to another one. The 1997–1998 Asian financial crises helped cull uncompetitive *chaebols*, and the surviving ones changed their management style and marketing strategies. In Chapter 13, Hun Joo Park argues that though the story of South Korea's economic development has been dominated by big businesses (*chaebols*), the role of both old and new small and medium-sized entrepreneurs has become more crucial over time. Even though South Korea's undemocratic *dirigisme* had largely slighted SMEs, both first- and second-generation small entrepreneurs threw all their energies into making something of their enterprises, working endlessly and incrementally increasing efficiency and productivity gains.

In Chapter 14, Charles E. Eesley and Jian Bai Li study how technology entrepreneurs succeed in China's transitional economy. Eesley and Li observe that technology entrepreneurship in China is a curious fusion of patrimonial control and market economy. Eesley and Li argue that technology entrepreneurship in China is still hindered by factors related to the lack of political and legal reforms relative to the progress in economic reforms.

Nerys Fuller-Love in Chapter 15 discusses variant perspectives of what supposedly deters more female entrepreneurs, such as traditional norms and cultural factors that make it more difficult for women to start and build a business. Social and cultural factors play an important part in shaping attitudes towards women. Many female entrepreneurs choose industries with low barriers to entry, thus making it difficult for them to develop and grow the business.

Part II East Asia cases

In Part II of this Handbook, we include 20 cases from five East Asian economies: Japan, Taiwan, South Korea, China, and Hong Kong. The spectrum of the industries included in these cases is wide, ranging from traditional manufacturing firms, such as bicycles (Giant of Taiwan) and automobiles (Toyota of Japan; Hyundai of South Korea), to high-tech and electronics products' brands, such as Samsung (South Korea), ASUS (Taiwan), and Alibaba (China), and even down to firms from service industries, such as convenience stores (7-Eleven, Japan), catering (Maxim's, Hong Kong), and beverages (Wahaha, China).

Japan

Following the collapse of Japan's financial markets in the late 1980s, the myth of "Japan as Number One" (Vogel, 1979) lost its luster, and the country's economy has languished ever since. The success of the big firms born during Japan's great post-war entrepreneurialism later discouraged graduates from joining new business ventures. Japan's vital signs on entrepreneurship have been dire ever since then. In 2012, the Global Entrepreneurship Monitor, a survey by a group of universities, put Japan tied for last place out of 24 developed nations for levels of entrepreneurial activity (*The Economist*, 2013).

However, one should not be fooled by Japan's three lost decades, as various vibrant entrepreneurial corporations are alive and kicking. In Chapter 16, Jeffrey K. Liker writes of the innovative spirit of Kiichiro Toyoda, the founder of Toyota Automobile, by researching his family, education background, the influence of his father Sakichi Toyoda, known as "King of Inventors," and his learning of factory operations from on-site observations. It is well known that Kiichiro fermented the Just-In-Time (JIT) principle in the automobile industry, which became the foundation of the well-known Toyota Production System (TPS). People are less aware, as Jeffrey Liker explains, that the original idea of eliminating all "slack time in our work process" came from an idea when Kiichiro missed a train at a station in England.

While people celebrate successful firms, failure can be more educational. Peter St. Onge in Chapter 17 examines the downfall of one of the world's largest toy firms, Takara Toys, when it was simultaneously hit by leadership and industry transitions. Peter St. Onge demonstrates that the dark side of entrepreneurship results from misjudgment in passing the baton to unsuitable successors. The firm's demise is an educational example of how emotional family ties can obstruct judicious judgment for CEO succession.

As a failure case, Takara Toys is not alone. Founded by Masaru Ibuka in 1945 after Japan's defeat in World War II, Sony, with its innovative capability, was a fierce competitor in global consumer electronics from the 1960s to the 1990s. From 2002, Sony started a decade-long decline in major product development. In Chapter 18, Richard A. Gershon directs attention to what led to Sony's decline by specifying five contributory reasons: (1) the tyranny of success; (2) executive leadership failures; (3) the challenges of a disruptive technology; (4) a risk-averse culture; and (5) lengthy development times and poor coordination.

Before UNIQLO launched its flagship shop on Fifth Avenue, New York, in 2011, few people thought Japan could lead the market for world-wide fashion brands, which have been dominated by Paris, Milan, or New York. In Chapter 19, Eugene K. Choi explains the fast growth path of this Japanese fashion giant, Tadashi Yanai and the company he established, Fast Retailing, along with the brand UNIQLO. Aspiring to prove that top quality can be found at a reasonable price, Tadashi Yanai has created a kingdom for this fashion brand.

In Chapter 20, Nobuo Kawabe illustrates the commercial spirit of two influential figures in the history of the Seven & I Group, Masatoshi Ito with his general merchandise stores (or superstores) and Toshifumi Suzuki with his convenience store operations. With the rapid development of e-commerce since the mid-1990s, 7-Eleven has become an expedient platform for services such as paying electric power bills, package tours, and event tickets, and later has expanded to meal services and banking services.

Taiwan

The plethora of "*lao-bans*" (bosses) of small and medium-sized enterprises (SMEs) is one of the influential factors in Taiwan's economic development (Shieh, 1992; Numazaki, 1997). While Taiwan's abundance of SMEs provides vibrant entrepreneurial activities, those SMEs are mostly embedded in various densely interwoven clusters. One of the main competitive advantages of Taiwan's economic dynamism can be ascribed to its sophisticated cluster industry (World Economic Forum, 2008, 2013).[3] According to Taiwan's Ministry of Economics, around 70 industrial clusters are scattered in the northern, center, and southern plain areas of western Taiwan.[4] The northern part of Taiwan encompasses mostly high-tech clusters, the central part comprises machine tools and traditional industry, and the southern part makes up heavy industries (such as steel and shipping) (Ching and Chou, 2007). Industrial clusters offer opportunities for an entrepreneur to organize a firm inside the cluster.

Drawing upon the concept of absorptive capacity to explain the entrepreneurial actions of one of Taiwan's most prominent electronics corporations, ASUS, in Chapter 21 Chyong Ling Judy Chen examines how ASUS has created competitive advantages through accumulating its absorptive capacity. The focal points are: (1) CEO Jonney Shih's leadership style and organizational culture in building ASUS' absorptive capacity; and (2) R&D and apprentice-style on-the-job training in building up ASUS' absorptive capacity.

Liang-Chih Chen in Chapter 22 studies one of Taiwan's key clusters, machine tools, and four key entrepreneurs during the different development stages in Taiwan's machine tool industry in the central part of Taiwan. Liang-Chih Chen argues that to understand the dynamics behind the development of this cluster, it is necessary to examine critical issues regarding how the localization of machine tools' production emerged, how the production networks were formed, and how the relevant industrial structure within the cluster evolved.

In Chapter 23, based on the concept of strategic entrepreneurship, Mei-Chih Hu and Ching-Yan Wu examine the growth of one of Taiwan's two big bicycle corporations, Giant, and its founder King Liu. Mei-Chih Hu and Ching-Yan Wu proffer an archetypical case of how one Taiwanese firm started from practicing OEM and thereby learned the technology from industrial countries and eventually accumulated its own innovative capability to transform itself into practicing OBM.

In Chapter 24, Charlie Z.W. Chiang and Ho-Don Yan study the growth and transformation of the biggest corporation in Taiwan, Foxconn. Specifying a three-stage model of a firm—namely, formation, growth and transformation—Chiang and Yan designate the main focus of each stage, such as entrepreneurship of opportunity discovery and firm creation in the formation stage, strategic management in the growth stage, and leadership in the transformation stage. This chapter provides a view of the emergence of CEO Terry Gou and how he has led Foxconn to become a truly global giant.

South Korea

South Korea's *chaebols* are the product of a government-directed industrialization policy in the 1970s and 1980s. The term *chaebol* has grown to include a broad range of industrial and service businesses protected from foreign competition and enjoying implicit government risk sharing and guarantees (IMF, 2010). In the early days, South Korean corporations were perceived as low-end producers of imitative products struggling with a poor quality image. Since the 1990s, South Korea started to forge ahead by taking the lead in computer industries, such as DRAM. In the 2000s, Samsung TV became the world's largest producer of TVs, surpassing Japan's Sony. In 2012, Samsung overtook Apple and Nokia to be the world's largest smartphone maker. Many corporations from South Korea currently not only have surpassed Japan either in the technology level or marketing, but also compete in the global market with advanced economies.

In Chapter 25, Myeong-Kee Chung portrays a legendary entrepreneur, the founder of the Hyundai Group, Chung Ju Yung (1915–2001). This chapter summarizes seven principal management strategies adopted by Chung Ju Yung: to create a new growth engine ahead of the trend; to create new markets; to keep promises and respect contractors; to emphasize the spirit of self-reliance; to stress the importance of human resources and encourage each employee's self-development; to provide leadership with positive thinking; and to care about corporate social responsibility.

Noting that South Korea has led the world in technology development in online gaming, Jong Hyun Wi explains in Chapter 26 how South Korean online games have created a different business model from other online games. The country's games have created a system of micro transactions, which game companies around the world have adopted. Jong Wi looks in particular at four prominent figures, Jake Song and Jung Ju Kim (Nexon), Taek Jin Kim (NCsoft), and Bum Su Kim (NHN), to describe how South Korea has taken a leading role in the online gaming business through disruptive innovation.

Seung-Joo Lee in Chapter 27 analyzes Samsung's transformation into a global giant corporation from the perspective of dynamic capabilities, focusing on three elements: (1) entrepreneurial insights and bold investment by top management; (2) rapid technology catch-up through dynamic learning and resource leverage; and (3) relentless innovation in products and processes to achieve global market leadership.

In 2012 when "Gangnam Style" became a big music recording hit globally, it reminded the world that South Korea not only can lead in the high-tech industry, but also in the entertainment industry. In Chapter 28, John Lie and Ingyu Oh describe the rise of K-pop, along with SM Entertainment and its founder, Soo Man Lee. John Lie and Ingyu Oh argue that the eventual emergence of the current K-pop formula rests less on his innovative and far-sighted conception. Rather, it has relied more on his willingness to make incremental improvements and to learn from his rivals and competitors.

Mainland China

Thanks to its phenomenal double-digit annual growth over the past three decades, China has become the world's second-largest economy and in many ways the most dynamic. Less obvious is what the secret is to its success. It is often vaguely attributed to "capitalism with Chinese characteristics," typically taken to mean that bureaucrats with heavy, visible hands work much of the magic. Coase and Wang (2013), along with others (Huang, 2008), predicate that the triggering force of China's strong market economy is from the marginal forces, namely, private farming, township and village enterprises, private business in cities, and the Special Economic Zones.

These "marginal revolutions" have brought entrepreneurship and market forces back to China during the early period of reform. A revolutionary change in a political or economic sphere opens up many opportunities (Shane, 2003).

In Chapter 29, Zhongjuan Sun, Wei Xie, Kuanrong Tian, and Yanyu Wang study the case of Lenovo, a leading IT company and a rising global multinational corporation from China. Founded in 1984, the Lenovo Group is the leading IT company in China. In less than three decades, its current CEO Yang Yuanquing and his predecessor Liu Chuanzhi have spearheaded Lenovo's ascent to be the second largest PC provider in the world. This chapter links entrepreneurship with capability accumulation to explain the success of Lenovo.

Fangqi Xu and William R. Nash in Chapter 30 study the Wahaha Group, founded by Zong Qinghou in 1987, which is the number one maker of soft drinks in China. Based on literature research and interviews, Fangqi Xu and William R. Nash explain how Zong Qinghou led Wahaha through various growth stages by creating effective management innovations that included innovations in product development, marketing, and managerial methods.

Mark J. Greeven describes in Chapter 31 how the Alibaba Group succeeded in creating sustainable value to suppliers, partners, and customers within a short time frame. This chapter analyzes the entrepreneurial spirit of its CEO, Jack Ma, such as his wisdom, passion, and perseverance, and provides rich insights and possibilities for research into business model innovation, knowledge sharing, innovation capability, strategy in emerging markets, and leadership.

In the case study of Haier in Chapter 32, Diana S. Kwan and Fu-Lai Tony Yu argue that the Haier Group, as a latecomer firm in China, went through three stages in its technological path: stage 1, acquiring basic production skills; stage 2, consolidating production capabilities; and stage 3, enhancing innovative capabilities. This case shows that through a process of entrepreneurial learning, manufacturing firms in China can "go global" and catch up with firms in advanced countries.

Hong Kong

Hong Kong was ceded to Great Britain through the Treaty of Nanking in 1842. With a land area of around 1064 square kilometers that was considered as useless granite, it is devoid of any natural resources and relies on outside sources for its fuel and raw materials. Although it went through a precarious period during its transition of returning back to China, Hong Kong is one of the most developed economies in Asia. Various studies have attempted to explain the reasons for Hong Kong's economic success, such as a favorable location with a good harbor, a pool of hard-working labor, the inflow of capital and entrepreneurs from China, and the system of *laissez-faire* capitalism. Yu (1996) was the first to argue that Hong Kong is an entrepreneurial society and examined how entrepreneurial activities enabled Hong Kong to catch up with early industrialized nations, providing examples of the textile and electronics industries. Three cases included in this Handbook are Hongkong Land Holdings, Maxim's Group, and the Li & Fung Group.

Hongkong Land Holdings Ltd (HKL) is a leading real estate investment, management, and development company in Hong Kong, with a substantial real estate portfolio concentrated in the prime commercial areas of Hong Kong. In Chapter 33, Jianfu Shen, Adrienne La Grange, and Frederik Pretorius illustrate the important facts of HKL: the state of business, governance, strategy, and the influence of governments. HKL has worked steadily since the late 1990s to reposition itself and to renew and partially redevelop its portfolio of prime commercial property assets in Hong Kong. HKL has adapted to the business environment and overcome the political problems in post-handover Hong Kong.

Maxim's Group, founded in 1956, has been a successful food and beverage cum restaurant chain in Hong Kong. In Chapter 34, David F.K. Ip and Richard Cheung Lam study how S.T. Wu and James Wu discovered the market opportunity for Western-style restaurants, through their entrepreneurial spirits in sensing, grasping, and exploiting opportunities. The two brothers have created a business kingdom with a wide array of services and products, including Chinese, Asian, and European restaurants, fast food outlet, bakeries, and cafés under their own brand.

Chapter 35 explores how Li & Fung is now one of the largest providers of consumer goods in the world, though it hardly owns or hires any workers, raw materials, machineries, or factories for making household products. By linking up and coordinating with the most efficient and cheapest manufacturing processes in different parts of the world, as Fu-Lai Tony Yu and Diana S. Kwan illustrate, Li & Fung is able to gain pure entrepreneurial profit.

Implications: praise for adaptive entrepreneurship

This Handbook provides a large array of cases to explain the growth of entrepreneurial firms in East Asia. Topics covered range from entrepreneurship in small and medium-sized enterprises, Asian business systems, international business, innovation and technology management, to economic development, strategic management, and East Asian studies. Cases selected include a large spectrum of industries, such as the largest beverage company, Wahaha (China), well-known global automobile brands, Toyota (Japan) and Hyundai (South Korea), and the electronics product manufacturers of Sony (Japan), Lenovo (China), ASUS (Taiwan), etc. Most of these successful firms arrived on the scene after World War II.

Although Schumpeterian, or heroic, entrepreneurship brings breakthroughs to the economy, it is very rare in economic history. This volume emphasizes that the driving force for catching-up growth strategies is adaptive entrepreneurship. Most entrepreneurs are adaptive. Adaptive entrepreneurship is associated with the discovery of profitable discrepancies, gaps, and mismatches of existing knowledge and information, which others have not yet perceived and exploited (Kirzner, 1973; Cheah and Yu, 1996). It is important to note that the gist of adaptive entrepreneurship is not only about imitation, it is more to do with learning and adapting. No invention ever comes out from the vacuum. Moreover, most of the greatest scientists would admit that their findings would not be possible without them "standing on the shoulders of giants." Japan has been deemed the leader of industrial upgrading in East Asia. Ozawa (2009) rightly asserted that the factual leader of the flying-geese theory is the USA, with Japan benefitting from US-led global capitalism. In the cases of Sony, UNIQLO, 7-Eleven, or Toyota, all these Japanese firms show that their founders were frequent visitors to the USA and Europe in order to learn technology and knowledge at the earlier stage of industrialization. The lesson is clear. Behind the leadership of Japan in automobiles or consumer electronics products or South Korea in mobile devices, entrepreneurs all started from emulation and learning.

With the twin forces of technology and economic liberalization, economic catch-up can be achieved quicker than before for emerging and developing countries. First, given that goods and services are traded in fragmented and internationally dispersed production, multinational corporations (MNCs) are more able to take advantage from creating the production model of a global supply chain (GSC) (Baldwin, 2012; Cattaneo *et al.*, 2013). By allowing poor nations to join supply chains rather than investing decades of time in building up their own, GSCs have transformed the world. Second, Ferguson (2011) articulated the easier accession to the six killer apps of Western power: competition, medicine, science, property rights, consumerism, and work ethics. It is thus expected that latecomer nations and firms can learn to catch-up much more expeditiously.

With the majority of potential consumers living in emerging and developing countries, the growth potential of the world economy will be pinned down there, as can be witnessed by the many MNCs of emerging markets that have been created there, such as Lenovo and Haier of China (*The Economist*, 2008). Starting as emulative learners, Lenovo and Haier have grown and accumulated wealth and capabilities at a dazzling speed. With their comparative advantage in adapting to local needs, Lenovo and Haier not only have achieved the dominant respective market share of PCs and white goods of China, but they also are able to compete in global markets. MNCs of developed countries will lose their edge if they are unable to adapt their production to the needs of the majority of global consumers, or the so-called reverse innovation that Govindarajan and Trimble (2012) aptly argued. The catching-up strategies and the adaptive entrepreneurship championed by East Asian economies in general, and through each individual firm in particular, provide useful lessons not only for the latecomer firms of Africa, Latin America, and Southeast Asian countries, but also for MNCs of developed countries.

Notes

1 This measure is based on the purchasing power parity. Emerging and developing countries encompass 150 countries out of the world's 184 countries (34 advanced countries), with 4 newly industrialized Asian economies (Hong Kong, South Korea, Singapore, and Taiwan) excluded (IMF, 2012).

2 The first theoretical framework of linking these five economies as a closely-connected developing group was through the "flying-geese" theory of economic development, proposed by Akamatsu in the 1930s. With Japan as the leader of the flying-geese, followed by South Korea, Taiwan, Singapore, and Hong Kong, and then China, Thailand, Indonesia, the sequential development pattern resembled an inverted V-shaped flying formation of wild geese. There are three sub-patterns of the flying-geese theory: the intra-industry dimension, the inter-industry dimension, and the international division of labor dimension (Lin, 2012b).

3 Since 2004, Taiwan has been ranked highly in this index. From 2004 to 2007, Taiwan was in second place, in 2007 it moved up to first place, and thereafter it fell back down to second place until it climbed back to first place in 2012 again.

4 For instance, Taipei has digital content and ceramics clusters; Hsinchu has optical disk, automobile, and glass clusters; Taichung has bicycle, precision machinery, and musical instrument clusters; Changhua has knitted hosiery and bicycle clusters; and Tainan has TFT-LCD, IC, and knitted sweater clusters.

Bibliography

Akamatsu, K. (1962) "A historical pattern of economic growth in developing countries," *Journal of Developing Economies,* 1(March–August): 1–23.

Alvarez, S.A. and Barney, J.B. (2007) "Discovery and creation: alternative theories of entrepreneurial action," *Strategic Entrepreneurship Journal,* 1: 11–26.

Atsmon, Y., Child, P., Dobbs, R. and Narasimhan, L. (2012) "Winning the $30 trillion decathlon: going for gold in emerging markets," *McKinsey Quarterly,* McKinsey Global Institute, August.

Baldwin, R. (2012) "Global supply chains: why they emerged, why they matter, and where they are going," *CEPR Discussion Paper,* No. 9103, London.

Barro, R.J. (1997) *Determinants of Economic Growth: A Cross-Country Empirical Study,* Cambridge, MA: MIT Press.

Baumol, W.J., Litan, R.E. and Schramm, C.J. (2007) *Good Capitalism, Bad Capitalism, and the Economics of Growth and Prosperity,* New Haven, CT: Yale University Press.

Bolton, M.K. (1993) "Imitation versus innovation: lessons to be learned from the Japanese," *Organizational Dynamics,* (Winter): 3045.

Bygrave, W. and Zacharakis, A. (2008) *Entrepreneurship,* Chichester: John Wiley & Sons, Inc.

Cattaneo, O., Gereffi, G., Miroudot, S. and Taglioni, D. (2013) "Joining, upgrading and being competitive in global value chains: a strategic framework", *Policy Research Working Paper Series,* No. 6406, The World Bank.

Cheah, H.B. and Yu, T.F.L. (1996) "Adaptive response: entrepreneurship and competitiveness in the economic development of Hong Kong," *Journal of Enterprising Culture,* 4(3): 241–266.

Ching, C.-H. and Chou, T.-L. (2007) "Differentiations in Taiwan's regional industrial clusters: the impacts of China effects," *Journal of Geographical Science,* 49: 55–79.

Coase, R.H. (2012) "Saving economics from economists," *Harvard Business Review,* December.

Coase, R.H. and Wang, N. (2011) "The industrial structure of production: a research agenda for innovation in an entrepreneurial economy," *Entrepreneurship Research Journal,* 1(2): 1–11.

Coase, R.H. and Wang, N. (2013) "How China became capitalist," *Cato Policy Report,* Cato Institute, 35(1): 7–10.

Ferguson, N. (2011) *Civilization: The Six Killer Apps of Western Power,* Harmondsworth: Penguin Books.

Gerschenkron, A. (1962) *Economic Backwardness in Historical Perspective: A Book of Essays,* Cambridge, MA: Belknap Press of Harvard University Press.

Govindarajan, V. and Trimble, C. (2012) *Reverse Innovation: Create Far from Home with Everywhere,* Boston: Harvard Business Review Press.

Hoang, H. and Anoncic, B. (2003) "Network-based research in entrepreneurship: a critical review," *Journal of Business Venturing,* 18: 165–187.

Hobday, M. (1995) "East Asian latecomer firms: learning the technology of electronics," *World Development,* 23(7): 1171–1193.

Hobday, M. (2000) "East versus Southeast Asian innovation systems: comparing OEM- and TNC-led growth in electronics," in L. Kim and R.R. Nelson (eds) *Technology, Learning, and Innovation: Experiences of Newly Industrializing Economies,* Cambridge: Cambridge University Press, pp. 129–169.

Huang, Y.S. (2008) *Capitalism with Chinese Characteristics: Entrepreneurship and the State,* Cambridge: Cambridge University Press.

IMF (2010) "People in economics: the unlikely revolutionary," *Finance and Development,* June, pp.18–20.

IMF (2012) *World Economic Outlook,* April, Washington, DC: International Monetary Fund.

Kirchhoff, B.A. (1994) *Entrepreneurship and Dynamic Capitalism,* Westport, CT, Praeger.

Kirzner, I.M. (1973) *Competition and Entrepreneurship,* Chicago: University of Chicago Press.

Landa, J.T. (1981) "A theory of the ethnically homogeneous middleman group: an institutional alternative to contract law," *The Journal of Legal Studies,* 10(2): 349–362.

Lin, J.Y. (2004) "Developing strategies for inclusive growth in developing Asia," *Asian Development Review,* 21(2): 1–27.

Lin, J.Y. (2012a) "New structural economics: a framework for rethinking development," in *New Structural Economics: A Framework for Rethinking Development,* Washington, DC: World Bank, pp. 11–47.

Lin, J.Y. (2012b) "From flying-geese to leading dragons: new opportunities and strategies for structural transformation in developing countries," *Global Policy,* 3(4): 397–409.

Mathews, J.M. (2002) "Competitive advantages of the latecomer firm: a resource-based account of industrial catch-up strategies," *Asian Pacific Journal of Management,* 19(4): 467–488.

Numazaki, I. (1997) "The Laoban-led development of business enterprises in Taiwan: an analysis of the Chinese entrepreneurship," *The Developing Economies,* XXXV(4): 440–457.

Ozawa, T. (2009) *The Rise of Asia: The 'Flying-Geese' Theory of Tandem Growth and Regional Agglomeration,* Cheltenham: Edward Elgar Publishing.

Page, J. (1994) "The East Asian miracle: four lessons for development policy," in S. Fischer and J.J. Rotenberg, (eds) *NBER Macroeconomics Review,* 9: 219–282.

Porter, M.E. (1990) *The Competitive Advantage of Nations,* New York: Free Press.

Radelet, S. and Sachs, J. (1997) "Asia's reemergence," *Foreign Affairs,* 76(6): 44–59.

Schumpeter, J.A. (1934) *The Theory of Economic Development,* New York: Oxford University Press.

Shane, S. (2003) *A General Theory of Entrepreneurship: The Individual-Opportunity Nexus,* Cheltenham: Edward Elgar.

Shane, S. and Venkataraman, S. (2000) "The promise of entrepreneurship as a field of research," *Academy of Management Review,* 25(1): 217–226.

Shieh, G.S. (1992) *"Boss" Island: The Subcontracting Network and Micro-Entrepreneurship in Taiwan's Development,* New York: Peter Lang Publishing.

Solow, R.M. (1956) "A contribution to the theory of economic growth," *Quarterly Journal of Economics,* 70(1): 65–94.

Stevenson, H.H. and Jarillo, J.C. (1990) "A paradigm of entrepreneurship: entrepreneurial management," *Strategic Management Journal,* 11: 17–27.

Teece, D.J., Pisano, G. and Shuen, A. (1997) "Dynamic capabilities and strategic management," *Strategic Management Journal,* 18(7): 509–533.

The Economist (2008) "Emerging-market multinationals: the challengers," January 10.

The Economist (2009) "A special report on entrepreneurship: global heroes," March 29.

The Economist (2011) "Entrepreneurship in China: let a million flowers bloom," March 10.

The Economist (2013) "Entrepreneurs in Japan: time to get started," August 31.

UNCTAD (2013) *World Investment Report 2013: Global Value Chains: Investment and Trade for Development,* United Nations Conference on Trade and Development, New York: United Nations.

Vogel, E. (1979) *Japan as Number One: Lessons for America,* Cambridge, MA: Harvard University Press.

Wenneker, S. and Thurik, R. (1999) "Linking entrepreneurship and economic growth," *Small Business Economics,* 13: 27–55.

World Bank (2008) *Global Economic Prospects: Technology Diffusion in the Developing World,* Washington, DC: World Bank.

World Economic Forum (2008) *Global Competitiveness Report 2008–2009,* Geneva: World Economic Forum.

World Economic Forum (2013) *Global Competitiveness Report 2013–2014,* Geneva: World Economic Forum.

Wright, M. and Zahra, S. (2011) "The other side of Paradise: examining the dark side of entrepreneurship," *Entrepreneurship Research Journal,* 1(3): 1–5.

Yan, H.-D., Chiang, C. and Chien, C.S. (2014) "From original equipment manufacturing to branding: entrepreneurship, strategic leadership, and Taiwan's firm transformation," *International Entrepreneurship and Management Journal,* 10(1): 81–102.

Yu, T.F.L. (1996) "Entrepreneurship and economic development in Hong Kong," PhD dissertation, University of New South Wales, Canberra, Australia.

Yu, T.F.L. (2001) "An entrepreneurial perspective of institutional change," *Constitutional Political Economy,* 12(3): 217–236.

Part I

Key concepts

Entrepreneurship, innovation and growth strategies in East Asia

Catching-up and growth strategies

1

The "flying-geese" theory of catch-up growth and international business[1]

Terutomo Ozawa

Akamatsu's original theory

The "flying-geese" (FG) theory of economic development is now well known the world over, having gained respectability in academia and popularity in the news media—especially against the backdrop of a string of successful economic catch-ups that have occurred across East Asia since the end of World War II. In particular, the speech delivered by Saburo Okita, former Japanese Foreign Minister, referring to the theory at the fourth Pacific Economic Cooperation Conference in Seoul in 1985, further made policy-makers and the mass media aware of it. It is the only theory of Japanese origin that has so far been well recognized outside Japan. It is, for example, considered a major doctrine of development strategy, along with the "big-push" theory and the "import substitution" approach (Radelet and Sachs, 1997).

The FG theory was originally set out by Professor Kaname Akamatsu (1897–1974) of Hitotsubashi University, Tokyo, in the mid-1930s. He studied in Germany for two years (1924–1926) and was strongly influenced by the German Historical School and Hegelian dialectic. Akamatsu's theory of trade-driven structural change and growth in catching-up economies explains how emerging economies emulate and learn from more advanced ones in their attempts to industrialize. It is basically built on the stages-of-growth theories advanced by German historical School economists, especially Friedrich List (1789–1846) who conceptualized a catch-up sequence from import dependence to import substitution to export expansion. Akamatsu also drew on the ideas of Alexander Hamilton (1757–1804) and Henry Carey (1793–1879), both Americans, who along with List, advocated infant-industry protection in order to promote national industrial development. In Akamatsu's original theory, therefore, nationalism plays a key role in motivating and managing *national* industrial development.

Three patterns of FG formation

When the FG theory is mentioned, this usually conjures up the image of a regionally clustered group of economies advancing together in leader–follower relations. This image has been popularized by the media in particular. Yet, this is not the pattern that Akamatsu considered "basic." In fact, it is just one of three patterns that he identified:

> The wild-geese-flying pattern . . . includes three subpatterns. The first *basic* pattern is the sequence of import–domestic production–export. The second pattern is the sequence from consumer goods to capital goods and from crude and simple articles to complex and refined articles. The third pattern is the alignment from advanced nations to backward nations according to their stages of growth.
>
> *(Akamatsu, 1961: 208, emphasis added)*

Thus, what Akamatsu considered "basic" is: a three-step progression of import (M) → domestic production (P) → export (X) (hereafter MPX). And this is exactly the sequence conceived by List ([1841] 1956). On the other hand, the second pattern describes a process of *industrial upgrading*, and the third *a hierarchy of economies* operating at different stages of growth that facilitates knowledge transfer from the more advanced to the less developed countries.

Although there is no clear explanation of why he called the Listian MPX pattern basic, we can surmise that it is the very pattern he empirically discovered in the development histories of many Japanese manufacturing industries over the period of 1870–1939 (such as woolen goods, cotton yarn, cotton cloth, spinning and weaving machines, general machinery, bicycles, and industrial tools), for which he made inter-temporal statistical analyses. His discovery confirmed List's original idea. Akamatsu plotted the time-series trend lines of imports, domestic production, and exports for each industry. These lines showed a consistent wave-like pattern of three orderly steps of industrial development, in which imports first rise and then decline, while domestic production begins to take over, gradually substituting for imports, and finally exports emerge successfully (Akamatsu, 1935). He then dubbed this pattern the "flying-geese formation" because "wild geese fly in orderly ranks forming an inverse V, just as airplanes fly in formation" (Akamatsu, 1962: 9). In other words, the MPX mechanism served as the powerful engine of development for *each* Japanese manufacturing industry, kick-starting and enabling initially protected industries eventually to produce domestic substitutes for imports and then to develop into export-competitive industries. And such progress in each manufacturing industry, one after another, gave a strong and continual impetus to Japan's entire economy to move up the ladder of growth, tracing out the sequence of industrial upgrading. And Japan's catch-up, in turn, impacted and altered the "alignment of countries" along the way. In other words, the second pattern was the *outcome* of trade-driven industrial development, while the third one was the *parametric* conditions under which Japan initiated industrialization and which its catch-up itself altered in the end. Thus, the MPX progression was the main driver, though the three patterns functionally interacted with each other in propelling catch-up growth. (For other important features of Akamatsu's FG theory, see Ozawa, 2009).

Updating and reformulations needed

Given the fact that Akamatsu constructed the FG theory on the basis of his statistical studies of the development experiences of Japanese industries in the late nineteenth century through the early twentieth century, some of his core concepts are naturally outdated in the light of rapid changes in technology, commercial knowledge, and economic structures, institutions, and international relations in the global economy. Hence his original theory definitely calls for an update and restatement.

First of all, in Akamatsu's conceptualization, trade was the *only* driver of catch-up industrialization (as envisaged in the MPX progression). Most importantly, therefore, *the role of today's ubiquitous multinational enterprises (MNEs) as a catalyst to structural change and growth* was not taken into consideration. MNEs are the innovators, knowledge disseminators, and prompters of structural change. Prior to his death in 1974, however, Akamatsu had only begun to see the beginning of the MNEs' meteoric rise, and was unable to fully comprehend and take account of their role in his analysis. As a consequence, in his model, the MPX progression is driven solely by the conventional strategy of infant-industry protection that builds *nationally* owned/managed industries at home, *fending off* any incursion of foreign interests as business investors/owners in home industries. Nowadays, however, the three-step sequence of MPX can be time-compressed and carried out *simultaneously* by foreign MNEs which can set up both import-substituting and export-oriented local production in emerging markets—practically overnight.

Indeed, this is the new strategy of foreign direct investment (FDI)-fueled industrial take-off which is a more expedient alternative to the conventional strategy of infant-industry protection. And such an open-economy, inclusive approach has increasingly been adopted by emerging economies in kick-starting industrial take-off (Ozawa, 2011). In other words, the conventional closed-economy strategy is giving way to the FDI-fueled strategy as an initiator of catch-up industrialization. From the MNEs' point of view, this means that their initial exports (X) are quickly replaced by outward FDI (OFDI) in their formerly export markets (i.e., export-substituting FDI in overseas markets). And simultaneously, these MNEs often end up importing their own offshore-produced goods back home, thereby creating new exports (M*) from their host economies. As a consequence, international production (overseas output by MNEs) is becoming larger and larger in value and ever more important as an engine of industrialization in the host economies than the conventional type of international trade.

In addition, intra-company trade has increasingly been replacing arm's-length trade. In this connection, cross-border supply chains have become ubiquitous, combining overseas production and intra-company trade under the management and governance of MNEs. This is the latest global business model adopted by MNEs, a phenomenon that was hardly discernible in Akamatsu's day. Given these recent developments in globally connected production, moreover, there is no longer much room left for economic nationalism as a motivational tool for catch-up (i.e., the nationalism-colored approach stressed by Akamatsu) in the emerging world. Emerging markets have increasingly been opening up and joining the global community of freer trade and investment that can help trigger and boost their growth.

Moreover, Akamatsu also left the key notion of structural change rather vague. He merely stated, in a rough manner, that production structure evolves "from consumer goods to capital goods, and from crude and simple articles to refined and complex articles." After all, the essence of economic development is nothing but structural upgrading. Therefore, structural change needs to be carefully described and defined in detail. For that matter, the notion of the "ladder of economic development" is often casually used without concrete specifications in the discipline of economics. In what follows, all these issues will be addressed, as we update and restate the original FG theory.

MNEs as a creature of structural transformation

MNEs from any market (advanced and emerging alike) are basically *creatures of structural transformation* at different growth stages in their home economies. Historically, structural upgrading (a result of establishing brand-new goods/industries and shedding existing old ones through the Schumpeterian process of creative destruction) has been driven by major breakthrough innovations (each of which entailed a cluster of incremental technological supplements and refinements, resulting in a paradigmatic shift of industrial structure). And innovation is spurred by entrepreneurs and R&D-focused enterprises, many of which eventually are destined to expand abroad as MNEs in pursuit of business opportunities to exploit their firm-specific advantages.

Ever since the Industrial Revolution and Britain's unilateral adoption of economic liberalism (free trade and capital flows), overseas business operations have become more industrially-oriented, more market-driven, and more private-profit-focused than ever before. Above all, in the wake of the Industrial Revolution a series of rapid technological and structural changes began to occur in a number of countries—first across Europe, then the United States, and later Japan and Russia. And each stage of industrial transformation entailed *a different set of needs and opportunities for overseas business expansion*. The overseas commercial activities of those early industrializers were initially *aligned with* the national interests of their home economies. But more recently, there has been a growing chasm between national and private interests, notably in advanced countries, concerning domestic employment and technology transfer among others.

A "leading-sector" stages model *à la* Schumpeter: an overall analytics

Given the causal links between structural change and the emergence of MNEs, we must understand the historical process and patterns of industrial structural transformation. Here, a comprehensive perspective can be obtained by the "leading-sector" stages model *à la* Schumpeter (Schumpeter, 1934; Ozawa, 2005, 2009). This model is built on a historical sequence of growth that is punctuated by stages (that can be captured as "structural breaks" in econometrics), and in each stage a certain industrial sector and technological thrust can be identified as the main driver of structural transformation. This perspective is in line with what Schumpeter (1942) stressed in terms of "the perennial gale of creative destruction" that drives the process of industrial upgrading under capitalism. Also, the same idea was re-emphasized by Rostow (1960) in his view of "economic history *as a sequence of stages rather than merely as a continuum*, within which nature never makes a jump" (ibid.: 16, emphasis added).

So far, the world economy has witnessed five tiers of leading-sector industry emerge in wave-like progression since the Industrial Revolution—and currently a new tier is in the making (see Figure 1.1). The five tiers have been: (I) endowment-driven industries (represented by textiles and other light industry goods in labor-abundant countries and by extraction of minerals and fossil fuels in resource-rich countries); (II) resource-processing industries (represented by steel and basic chemicals); (III) assembly-based industries (exemplified by mass-produced automobiles); (IV) R&D-driven industries (such as computers, electronics, and pharmaceuticals); and (V) information-technology (IT)-enabled industries (e.g., digital telecoms, operating platforms, search engines, and social media). And (VI) a new tier consisting of what may be called green-technology (GT)-based industries (such as energy-saving and pollution-abating devices, new cleaner energies (solar, wind, geothermal, etc.) and a healthier living environment (both public and personal health and medical services)). The new tier is in the making as the advanced world strives to promote a "green economy" and "sustainable growth."

The above chronological model of leading-sector industries means that diverse types of MNEs have been born, *each as a creature of a specific stage of structural transformation*. This perspective thus analyzes the rise and changing nature of MNEs as an evolutionary vicissitude of structural transformation—that is, as a theory of economic development.

The series of tiers described above simply traces out a broad historical sequence in which different leading sectors have transformed the industrial structure in presently advanced economies. In this regard, it should be noted that the concept of the "ladder of economic development" is often and casually used in economics—but so far without any clear-cut definition and specification. The "leading-sector" stages model gives a meaningful definition to this hitherto unspecified notion. The tiers described correspond to the "rungs" of the ladder. Moreover, the concept of

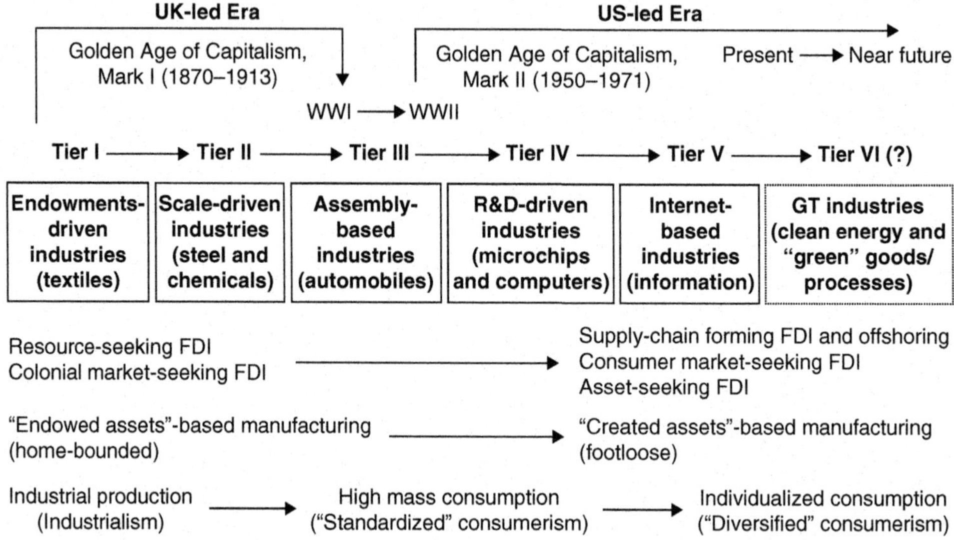

Figure 1.1 The ladder of economic development: historical industrial upgrading under UK- and US-led global capitalism

Source: Based on Ozawa (2009).

the ladder itself applies to the historical progression and dynamics of innovation and structural transformation—that is to say, the ladder of technological (industrial knowledge) development. This view is thus based on the causes for structural change and development. In this respect, modern-day MNEs are not only *innovators* who contribute to structural renewal in their home economies but also are *cross-border transplanters* of industrial and institutional knowledge inherent in different growth stages to the rest of the world. And because of the ever-faster pace of resultant knowledge diffusion, emerging markets are in an ever-more favorable position to catch up at a rapid pace by borrowing innovations from advanced markets—and also because many more MNEs from the advanced world are now eagerly entering the emerging economies in pursuit of larger markets.

Structural changes under British—and then American—hegemony

The ladder of economic development described above has been built by global capitalism, initially under British and then under American hegemony. Endowment-driven (Tier I) and scale-driven (Tier II) industries were basically introduced under British hegemony before World War I, and were centered on industrial goods, representing the age of industrialism. Overseas operations of national firms as early MNEs were once conducted largely in the national interests of their home countries—that is, on the whole, no mismatch between public and private interests. Overseas investments in resources extraction were intended to support Tier II industries and employment at home—and basically to exploit Ricardian rents (i.e., profits from securing the cheaper supply sources of resources). And for these two tier industries the doctrine of comparative advantage (based on factor endowments) was the dominant principle of international trade.

In contrast, other tiers (Tiers III–VI) have been largely engendered under American hegemony, especially since the end of WWII. All these upper tiers are mass-consumption oriented, ushering in the age of *consumerism*. This is no surprise, since consumer spending has represented the lion's share of demand in the US economy, the leader of global capitalism, since 1929 when this measure was adopted by the Commerce Department (it now accounts for no less than 70 percent). Furthermore, US-led industrial upgrading has become increasingly more knowledge-driven, making R&D and engineering play a pivotal role in industry competitiveness—hence in trade and MNEs' global investment. In other words, trade now stems increasingly more from *"created" competitive advantages* rather than from *"endowed" comparative advantages.*

Here, the monopolistic (scale-based) theory of trade (Helpman and Krugman, 1985) can explain competitive-advantage-based trade better than the Ricardian doctrine of comparative advantage. It should also be noted that these higher-tier MNEs are in pursuit of Schumpeterian rents (profits gained from an outward shift in demand functions by exploiting their firm-specific advantages) in overseas consumer markets, as well as of Ricardian rents in overseas labor and talent markets. In short, the major configurations of MNEs themselves have metamorphosed over time—in lockstep with their home countries' structural transformations.

Customized, indigenously crafted catch-up approach: a caveat to stages theory

Given the above stages model that traces out a broad historical pattern of structural transformation as its key contour, however, this does *not* mean that late industrializers need to replicate exactly the same sequence of growth trail-blazed by earlier industrializers. In fact, latecomers are totally free to jumble it, take short-cuts by leapfrogging, or enter all stages even simultaneously—though normally from the *low* end (that is the labor-intensive or low-quality segment, as will be seen below), depending on their catch-up strategies, capabilities, and circumstances. In other words, they can emulate advanced countries' growth patterns in a broad manner but always customize their own catch-up processes in adaptation to their country-specific circumstances. As Gerschenkron puts it, "In every instance of industrialization, *imitation* of the evolution in advanced countries appears in combination with *different, indigenously determined elements*" (1962: 20, emphases added).

It is important to note, however, that Gerschenkron's celebrated analysis, presented as a critical commentary on Rostow's stages theory of growth (1960), was focused *solely* on European industrialization in the nineteenth century and did not—could not—take into consideration the epoch-making emergence of MNEs in the twentieth century, and their role as a powerful agent of structural transformation and homogenization in the global economy. Their operations make the world economy grow more homogeneous in characteristics than ever—that is, an overall convergence tendency in industrial production, consumption behavior, and institutions.

A growth curve and transitional bottlenecks

Economic growth proceeds along an S-shape trajectory. It accelerates up to an inflection point in the early stages of catch-up and then decelerates during the maturing stages. In this regard, what is relevant is a distinction made by Krugman (1997) between two modalities of growth: "input/perspiration-driven" and "efficiency/inspiration-driven." Growth acceleration occurs under the first modality of growth (corresponding to endowment-enabled Tier I growth and investment-based Tier II growth in our model). For instance, China's growth has operated in the input-driven modality in the recent past but is now slowing down. On the other hand, growth deceleration begins under the second modality of growth (involving the knowledge-based, higher-tier industries, from Tier III onward, in our model) as an economy begins to mature.

The "input-driven" early stages of catch-up growth are considered relatively "easy" to achieve, since what is required is to mobilize basic factors of production—unskilled labor (from rural areas) to set up export-focused Tier I industries (i.e., for low-wage, perspiration-based manufacturing) and a large chunk of capital and land to establish scale-based Tier II industries (e.g., steel, cement, chemicals, and the like). The latter, as an input supplier, can assist to build much-needed infrastructure (for transportation, communications, public sanitation, education, etc.) in the early stages of growth when industrialization and urbanization gather momentum. And a successful "input/perspiration-driven" phase quickly enables a catching-up economy to attain a middle-income status. In contrast, the "efficiency/inspiration-driven" phase requires sophisticated industrial knowledge, advanced technology, and a highly skilled labor force, all of which cannot be acquired overnight. In other words, the economy may face the risk of falling into the middle-income trap.

True, emerging markets enjoy a latecomer advantage. They are able to catch up at a faster pace than earlier industrializers—due largely to continual increases in the cross-border flows of modern technology, industrial knowledge, and investment capital. That is to say, the whole S-shape growth curve itself has been becoming steeper, thereby making the catch-up process all the more time-compressed. The downside of such a shortening catching-up time is, however, that catch-up growth encounters transitional bottlenecks more quickly and more often in a magnified manner. For example, shortages of factory workers occur toward the end of successful Tier I (labor-driven) growth. And a host of environmental problems accompany resource-processing activities and fossil fuel consumption under Tier II growth (heavy and chemical industrialization). Being on the cusp of graduating from the "input/perspiration-driven" phase of growth, China is currently facing these two bottlenecks. These are the transitional challenges any catching-up economy must confront and deal with, if it is to further climb the ladder. In fact, such bottlenecks prompt strategic decision-making and problem-solving at both the national policy and enterprise business strategy levels. In this sense, an emerging economy's "challenge and response" mechanism (Toynbee, 1962) plays a key role in turning any adversity into an opportunity. Japan, for example, turned the problems of labor shortage and pollution into opportunities for robotics and pollution-preventing innovation respectively.

The "double-helix" ladder of growth: side-ladders added

In addition to the *inter*-industry ladder of structural upgrading, each stage has produced a *vertical* concatenation of *intra*-industry sub-sectors, the upper end of which is highly capital-intensive and technologically sophisticated, while the lower end is labor-intensive and technologically standardized (see Figure 1.2). This *intra*-industry (often *intra*-firm or *intra*-product) vertically integrated (hence, divisible) structure of production may be called "a side-ladder." Particularly in recent years, the side-ladder has come to be actively used by MNEs to outsource activities in their supply chains. Consequently, the progression of industrial upgrading (of the *inter*-industry type) and the vertical chains of value-added (of the *intra*-industry type) together have opened up structural opportunities for firms in both advanced and emerging markets to pursue a new division of labor in production across borders.

Also, the side-ladder is a focus of technological innovation in, and for, emerging markets. Local companies are now striving to "innovate on the cheap," while foreign MNEs similarly try to introduce the low-end lines of products suitable for local consumers' pockets in emerging markets. The low-priced Nano mini-cars produced by Tata Motor, India's recently innovated stripped-down medical devices, and its low-end outsourcing services (e.g., call centers and back-office works) are representative examples of the former, and Nissan's latest plan to dust off and reintroduce its once-discarded old Datsun brand at as low a price as $3,000 illustrates the latter. In electronics, too, Apple, the high-end iPhone maker, started to produce a less expensive model

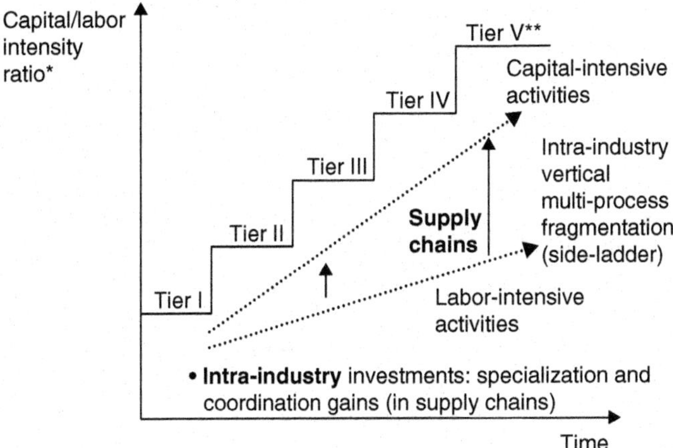

Figure 1.2 The "double-helix" ladder of economic development and supply chains

Notes:

*Capital includes intellectual capital (industrial knowledge).

**Given the nature of "green technology," Tier VI (in the making) is not likely to develop a vertical division of labor, unlike parts-intensive, assembly-based manufacturing. Hence, tier VI is not shown above.

Source: Based on Ozawa (2009).

as a way to introduce emerging markets to the brand. Similarly, global beer brewers, such as SAB-Miller, are capturing the lower-income consumers in Africa with a new cheaper brand.

The evolution of cross-border manufacturing in a hierarchy of economies

Comparative advantage recycling in labor-intensive Tier I industries

In East Asia, labor-intensive Tier I industries (e.g., garments, toys, and other sundries) have repeatedly transmigrated, in a relaying fashion, from Japan to its lower-wage neighboring economies (initially to the newly industrializing economies (NIEs) then, from the NIEs to the ASEAN-4, from whom most recently to China). This has culminated in what may be called "comparative advantage recycling" (Ozawa, 2009), since emerging economies have a comparative advantage in low-wage production but eventually lose it as they each succeed in industrialization. When labor-abundant countries attract and host low-wage manufacturing, on a significantly large enough scale, their wages are most likely driven up, as is presently evidenced in China. The outcome is nothing surprising. Since labor is most intensively used in producing labor-intensive goods, wages are expected to rise more than any other factor prices. This wage-magnification effect is envisaged in the well-known Stolper–Samuelson theorem (1941).

Actually, another round of comparative advantage recycling is now in the making. Because of wage increases and labor strife in China and the yuan's appreciation, foreign MNEs, as well as Chinese enterprises, have begun to relocate to China's neighboring countries such as Vietnam, Cambodia, Bangladesh, and Myanmar in search of low-cost labor. In fact, sensing this new round of industrial transmigration, Robert Zoelick, former President of the World Bank, called on China in 2009 to invest in Sub-Saharan Africa's manufacturing base other than in infrastructure and resource-extractive projects in which China is already heavily involved. Although there are some signs of Chinese manufacturers (mostly small and medium-sized firms) investing in Africa, it still remains uncertain how much China really can transplant labor-intensive manufacturing there, thereby helping jumpstart industrial modernization in the vast continent (Ozawa and Bellak, 2011).

Interestingly, on the other side of the Pacific, Mexico, a still labor-abundant, relatively low-wage country, is involved in comparative advantage recycling. In light of the huge wage difference vis-à-vis its rich northern neighbors, in 1965, the Mexican government initiated the Border Industrialization Program (BIP), which has come to be much better known as the Maquiladora (or Maquila) Program, to attract labor-intensive manufacturing and create jobs for the unemployed along the border. The program proved successful in hosting foreign MNEs' investments, especially after Mexico joined the North American Free Trade Agreement (NAFTA) in 1994, despite some serious environmental problems it faced. Yet the country was soon losing in competition with then low-wage Asian economies (initially the NIEs, then the ASEAN countries, and more recently China and India), and the Maquila Program started to decline toward the end of the 1990s. In the past few years, however, it has begun to regain outsourcing jobs and attract U-turn investments from China, whose labor costs are expected to top Mexico's in a few years' time. One estimate says that China's average wage has risen from 60 cents an hour in 2000 to about US$2.50 including benefits, while Mexico's is about US$3.50 in 2012 (*Wall Street Journal*, Sept. 17, 2012). China's rising yuan is another factor making Mexico even more favorable a location for low-cost manufacturing. Nevertheless, Mexico itself is similarly moving away from low-wage-based manufacturing to higher-skill production. In fact, its foreign MNC-driven auto industry is fast thriving, creating higher-wage jobs and expanding the middle class, which now accounts for about a half of the households in Mexico.

Cross-border supply chains

The side-ladder enables a vertical division of labor across borders, resulting in global supply chains. These chains can be established within a multi-layered hierarchy of economies operating at different stages of growth—hence, their technologies, skills, and wages of different levels to be used as joint inputs in a complementary manner. Thus, the chains are set up within a company on the intra-industry side-ladders of development. The recent IT revolution has made supply-chain management all the more effective and reduced transaction costs, as seen in the popular phrase "the death of time and distance." MNEs normally produce high-end upstream inputs in the advanced world, procure lower-end intermediate goods in middle-income countries, and subcontract final assembly operations in low-wage countries—and control and govern procurement and marketing along the way. Supply chains can geographically spread far and wide so as to capture an array of location-specific comparative and competitive advantages around the world, depending on the nature of the product involved.

It was America's low-tech industry, branded apparel/garment that pioneered in establishing cross-border supply chains, mostly through outsourcing, as early as the 1950s, shifting apparel making from the USA to Japan and Central American countries at that time (Bonacich and Waller, 1994). Given the nature of this standardized traditional industry, its vertical chains were—and still are—rather short and simple, normally involving designers, yarn and fabric suppliers, apparel makers, and distributors/retailers. The supply chains of low-end apparel are, in general, dispersed geographically across borders—with final retailers (retailing MNEs from advanced markets) who govern the whole operations. The upstream segments of production are usually located in a particular region (e.g., a region comprised of China, Hong Kong, Singapore, and

Taiwan, and a region surrounding Turkey in the Mediterranean). In contrast, supply chains for high-fashion apparel stay close to the final customers in the advanced countries because of the short-cycle-fashion nature of the merchandise and the need to satisfy the fast-changing consumer tastes.

Automobiles are an assembly-based, parts- and components-intensive industry, involving tens of thousands of parts, components, and accessories. The auto production process is vertically fragmented with the final assembly operations at the end of the process, giving opportunities for a cross-border vertical division of labor. However, with a few exceptions (the supply chains of automakers in the ASEAN region and in the NAFTA region), global automakers' supply chains are located mostly within a close radius of a particular locality where final assembly takes place due to the *just-in-time* delivery orientation of parts procurement. Automobile MNEs entering the emerging world usually start out by investing in kit-assembly operations and later gradually move to local parts production. The middle-income countries with relatively large domestic markets (notably the BRIC (Brazil, Russia, India and China) countries) have seen the rapid development of supply chains mostly within their borders or across their neighboring countries.

In East Asia, for example, regional networks of automobile production and marketing have been pioneered extensively by Japanese automakers in search of markets and under pressure from the rising value of the yen. Their "lean (flexible) production" system (Ohno, 1978; Womack *et al.*, 1990) relies heavily on the closely-knit cohorts of core-parts suppliers at home—with the outsourcing ratio as high as roughly 80 percent (whereas Detroit automakers used to produce in-house about 70 percent of parts and components). This particular Japanese feature of networking has necessitated—and facilitated—the formation of regional supply chains as Japanese automakers strove to capture other East Asian markets (Ozawa, 2005).

Consumer electronics has turned out to be most suitable for this new type of division of labor, since the components and parts outsourced are small in size, light in weight, and high in value—suitable for air freight at low costs. American electronics MNEs are the most active users of supply chains. Apple's production chains for iPad and iPhone illustrate *cross-regional* operations, involving East Asia and the United States. Compared with textile supply chains which are open to any MNEs, electronics supply chains are set up in a more company-specific (or even more product brand/model-specific) fashion—and more short-term-oriented (i.e., more location-wise shifting) than their automobile counterparts.

In aircraft production, the Boeing 787 Dreamliner jet has an expansive global supply chain network, which suddenly found itself publicized because of the problems (overheating and fires) of lithium-ion batteries wired with its high-capacity electrical system. Batteries are produced by Japan's GS Yuasa Technology, while battery chargers are made by a unit of British aerospace supplier Meggitt PLC, but are connected with the batteries by its subcontractor Thales SA of France. The French company is responsible for the job of integrating "batteries made on one side of the Pacific with chargers made on the other side of the ocean" (*Wall Street Journal*, Jan. 23, 2013). Dreamliner production involves as many as 45 big companies, though they are mostly American, supplying the main components such as the fuselage, the engine, the airframe, and the tires. In general, about 70 percent of all the parts for Boeing aircraft are supplied by American companies and 30 percent are outsourced from foreign companies (*CNNMoney*, Jan. 18, 2013). Similarly, Airbus jets production has its core supply chains for its main components, spreading across France, Germany, Britain, and Spain—but depends overall on some 1,500 suppliers in 30 countries.(www.airbus.com/tools/airbusfor/suppliers, 5/27/2012). Most recently, in fact, the company began to assemble some of its A320 family of aircraft in China and the United States. Thus, Airbus production is more globally dispersed, involving many more countries as suppliers than Boeing production.

As seen above in Boeing's battery incident, cross-border supply chains' operations are often disrupted by problems that arise with far-away suppliers. Japanese multinationals were adversely affected by natural disasters (e.g., Japan's earthquake and tsunami in 2011 and Thailand's floods in 2012). Apple had a problem with its Chinese assembler Foxconn in a labor dispute when the iPhone 5 went into production and its launch was consequently delayed. In April 2013, the tragedy of a factory building collapse at Rana Plaza, a major supplier of clothes for global retailers, near Dhaka, Bangladesh, killed more than 1,120 workers. This prompted a voluntary international labor pact to pay for inspections, building upgrades and training. Despite all these recent problems, nonetheless, the current trend of establishing supply chains continues unabated, since the long-term benefits of the new geographical division of labor are considered much greater than the short-term costs of supply disruption. In summary, global supply chains are built on the intra-industry side-ladders in search of efficiency—but with all those accompanying problems.

Conclusion

We have updated and reformulated the original FG theory in such a way that it is applicable to the present-day global economy. Structural changes as the essence of economic development and the role of MNEs as a key promoter of structural upgrading have been emphasized, the oft-used, nebulous notion of the ladder of development has been specified in terms of the double-helix ladder, and comparative advantage recycling and supply chain development have been examined in terms of the reformulated FG theory. However, we have so far told only a supply-side story due to lengths limitation. The financial and demand-side dimensions of FG-style growth are explored elsewhere (Ozawa, 2011, 2013).

All said and done, nonetheless, one may still ask: how relevant is the restated FG theory to international business scholars—and practitioners? In essence, the theory can serve as a window to look at future economic opportunities and bottlenecks in emerging markets, especially those still underdeveloped but already on track to industrial modernization—and the possible future difficulties that are likely to confront the manufacturing sector of advanced economies which is increasingly exposed to relentless competition from fast-catching up economies. This is because the FG pattern of catch-up growth follows the aphorism "history repeats itself." Catching-up economies basically follow in the footsteps of more advanced ones in their attempts to move up the ladder of development, replicating the latter's earlier experiences. A particular industry inherent in a given stage of growth thus comes into existence in a staggered manner in one emerging market after another. So, one can anticipate where economic activities and opportunities are migrating. And a particular kind of bottleneck occurs similarly in a stage-specific fashion. In this regard, for example, the recent labor shortages and wage hikes in China are what should have been anticipated well in advance, since exactly the same bottleneck was earlier experienced by Japan and the NIEs during the course of their labor-driven phase of catch-up. The same applies to the pollution problem associated with the heavy and chemical industrialization phase. These predictable trends are highly relevant to—and in fact, create critical decision factors for—the practitioners of global business. In short, the FG theory offers broad predictions (if not specific ones due to the idiosyncratic circumstances of each economy) and hence, useful leads for business decision-making.

Note

1 This chapter is based on a book manuscript in progress by T. Ozawa, *The Evolution of the World Economy: The 'Flying-Geese' Theory of Multinational Corporations and Structural Transformation,* Cheltenham: Edward Elgar (copyright © T. Ozawa, forthcoming).

Bibliography

Akamatsu, K. (1935) "Wagakuni Yohmokogyohin no Boheki Suisei" [The trend of Japan's trade in woolen goods], *Shogyo Keizai Ronso,* 13: 129–212.

Akamatsu, K. (1961) "A theory of unbalanced growth in the world economy," *Weltwirtschaftliches Archiv,* 86: 196–215.

Akamatsu, K. (1962) "A historical pattern of economic growth in developing countries," *Developing Economies,* preliminary issue 1 (Mar.–Aug.): 1–23.

Bonacich, E. and Waller, D.V. (1994) "Mapping a global industry: apparel production in the Pacific Rim Triangle," in E. Bonacich *et al.* (eds) *Global Production: The Apparel Industry in the Pacific Rim,* Philadelphia, PA: Temple University Press.

Gerschenkron, A. (1962) "Economic backwardness in historical perspective," in B.F. Hoselitz (ed.) *The Progress of Underdeveloped Areas,* Chicago: University of Chicago Press.

Helpman, E. and Krugman, P. (1985) *Market Structure and Foreign Trade,* Cambridge, MA: MIT Press.

Krugman, P. (1997) "Whatever happened to the Asian miracle?" *Fortune,* 136(4): 26–29.

List, F. ([1841] 1956) *The National System of Political Economy,* Philadelphia, PA: Lippincott.

Ohno, T. (1978) *Toyota Seisan Hoshiki: Datsu-kibo no Keiei o Mezashite* [Toyota Production Formula: Toward Non-Scale-Based Management], Tokyo: Daiyamondo.

Ozawa, T. (2005) *Institutions, Industrial Upgrading, and Economic Performance in Japan: The 'Flying-Geese' Paradigm of Catch-up Growth,* Cheltenham: Edward Elgar.

Ozawa, T. (2009) *The Rise of Asia: The 'Flying-Geese' Theory of Tandem Growth and Regional Agglomeration,* Cheltenham: Edward Elgar.

Ozawa, T. (2011) "The role of multinationals in sparking industrialization: from 'infant industry protection' to 'FDI-led industrial take-off'," *Columbia FDI Perspectives,* 39 (June 6).

Ozawa, T. (2013) "How do consumer-focused multinational enterprises affect emerging markets?" *Columbia FDI Perspectives,* 95 (May 20).

Ozawa, T. and Bellak, C. (2011) "Will the World Bank's vision materialize? relocating China's factories to Sub-Saharan Africa, flying-geese style," *Global Economy Journal,* 11(3): 1–16.

Radelet, S. and Sachs, J. (1997) "Asia's reemergence," *Foreign Affairs,* 76(6): 44–59.

Rostow, W.W. (1960) *The Stages of Economic Growth: A Non-Communist Manifesto,* Cambridge: Cambridge University Press.

Schumpeter, J.A. (1934) *The Theory of Economic Development,* New York: Oxford University Press, originally published in German.

Schumpeter, J.A. (1942) *Capitalism, Socialism and Democracy,* London: Unwin.

Smith, A. ([1776] 1908) *An Inquiry into the Nature and Causes of the Wealth of Nations,* London: Routledge, reproduced New York: E.P. Dutton.

Stolper W.F. and Samuelson, P.A. (1941) "Protection and real wages," *Review of Economic Studies,* 9: 58–73.

Toynbee, A.J. (1962) *A Study of History,* New York: Oxford University Press.

Womack, J. P., Jones, D.T. and Roos, D. (1990) *The Machine that Changed the World,* New York: Macmillan.

World Bank (1991) *World Development Report,* Washington, DC: World Bank.

2

Entrepreneurial strategies in Asian latecomer firms

Linkage, leverage and learning

John A. Mathews and Hao Tan

Introduction

What are the distinctive features in entrepreneurial strategies that East Asian firms have adopted to pursue their growth and prosperity? And what theoretical framework can be employed to account for those features? In this chapter, we explore these two questions and provide some preliminary answers. Our examples come from the Chinese wind power and solar photovoltaic (PV) industries, which have emerged and internationalized extremely rapidly, rising to world dominance in less than a decade (Mathews and Tan, 2012). While these firms and their accelerated internationalization are of interest from many perspectives (not least their contribution to the greening of international business), we emphasize in this chapter the challenge they pose for conventional theories of internationalization.

The emergence and growth of entrepreneurial firms from East Asia has been the subject of intensive research for the past several decades. Previous studies have focused on entrepreneurial firms from the region, ranging from family businesses from Hong Kong, high tech firms in Taiwan, Korean business conglomerates (*chaebols*), Japanese business networks, to emerging multinational manufacturers from China. There has also been great heterogeneity across the environments of firms within the region. The region encompasses the second largest advanced economy (Japan), newly industrialized economies (NIEs), including Taiwan, South Korea and Hong Kong, and the largest emerging economy (China). Not only are economies in the region at various levels of economic development, there also exist large differences in their political systems, cultures, and industrial structures.

Despite wide-ranging differences among firms and their environments in the region, some remarkable features have emerged in strategies of many entrepreneurial companies. Those features are certainly most profound in firms from latecomer economies such as South Korea and Taiwan, and now China; but they could also be observed in some Japanese firms especially when Japan itself was a latecomer. Common features shared by many latecomer firms include rapid growth and accelerated internationalization, innovation, reliance on personal and organizational networks, leverage on foreign technologies, as well as the strong role of the state in those firms' success.

We apply a theoretical framework that one of us has developed to account for the entrepreneurial strategies of East Asian latecomer firms, namely the linkage, leverage and learning (LLL) framework (Mathews, 2002, 2006a, 2006b). The LLL framework was originally introduced to explain the internationalization strategies and international success of what were dubbed 'Dragon Multinationals' from the Asia Pacific region, as an alternative and complementary framework to the dominant OLI (ownership, locational, internalization) account in International Business.

The OLI framework outlines three types of advantages as the driving forces of foreign direct investments by multinationals (Dunning, 2000). The OLI framework suggests that the multinational companies enjoy certain *a priori* microeconomic advantages in host markets over domestic rivals. These are: (1) they can invest overseas and compete with local companies despite the liabilities of foreignness that lie in their ownership-specific advantages (O) over local firms such as brand, superior technologies or returns to scale; (2) they enjoy locational attractions (L) of the host countries such as cheaper factors of production; and (3) they benefit from internalization advantages (I) that the company can enjoy by engaging in producing abroad rather than through trade in the open market (ibid.). Note that these are all concepts deriving from microeconomics (with its unrealistic assumptions based on equilibrium), whereas the alternative framework of LLL is based on strategizing, where firms are held to take decisions in conditions of uncertainty, disequilibrium and market dynamics. A comparison and contrast between the LLL and the OLI frameworks in accounting for advantages of multinationals over local firms is reproduced in Table 2.1.

In this chapter, we extend the LLL framework along three interrelated fronts. First, we examine the growth and success of firms from East Asia, whether in their domestic or international domains. We apply the LLL framework to capture both international expansion as well as domestic growth strategies of firms. Second, we focus on entrepreneurial firms, especially those that were founded relatively recently when the region has been increasingly integrated into the global economy and the region itself has undergone phenomenal economic and institutional transitions.

Table 2.1 OLI and LLL frameworks compared

Criterion	*OLI*	*LLL*
Resources utilized	Proprietary resources	Resources accessed through linkage with external firms
Geographic scope	Locations established as part of vertically integrated whole	Locations tapped as part of international network
Make or buy?	Bias towards operations internalized across national borders	Bias towards operations created through external linkage
Learning	Not part of the OLI framework	Learning achieved through repetition of linkage and leverage
Process of internationalization	Not part of the OLI framework: MNEs' international reach assumed	Proceeds incrementally through linkage
Organization	Not part of OLI framework; organization could be multinational or transnational	Global integration sought as latecomer advantage
Driving paradigm	Microeconomics: transaction cost economics	Strategy: capture of latecomer advantages via resource leverage
Time frame	Comparative static observations, comparing one point in time with another	Cumulative development process

Source: Adapted from Mathews (2006a, p. 21).

We argue that this is the group of firms for which the LLL framework is best suited. Third, we articulate the dynamic nature of the framework, highlighting the mutual reinforcements among linkage, leverage and learning processes, and how firms without substantial initial resources can build advantages through the LLL processes in a disequilibrium setting. We then apply the framework to the important recent case of global expansion of Chinese renewable energy firms, in the wind power and solar photovoltaic (PV) sectors.

In particular, we take the perspective of *entrepreneurship* in our analysis. Stevenson and Jarillo (1990: 23) define entrepreneurship as 'a process by which individuals—either on their own or inside organizations—pursue opportunities without regard to the resources they currently control'. Stevenson and colleagues further contrast and compare the entrepreneurial approach and the administrative approach in management behaviour along eight dimensions, as summarized by Brown *et al.* (2001) (Table 2.2). An entrepreneurial approach is not exclusive to small and medium-sized enterprises (SMEs) but is also applicable to large firms (Stevenson and Jarillo, 1990). From a Schumpeterian entrepreneurial perspective, we argue that East Asian entrepreneurial firms use the LLL strategies not so much to reduce 'transaction costs' as neoclassical economists would argue, but rather for the purpose of discovering and creating opportunities, and then taking advantage of them through sustained programmes of investment.

In the following sections we will first examine linkage, leverage and learning as three entrepreneurial strategies of East Asian latecomer firms, and briefly outline the dynamic, interacting processes that drive growth and success of the firms. We will then provide some recent evidence regarding firms in the Chinese renewable energies sector to illustrate and test those points.

Table 2.2 Entrepreneurial vs. administrative focus in management

Entrepreneurial focus		*Conceptual dimension*		*Administrative focus*
Driven by perception of opportunity	←	Strategic orientation	→	Driven by controlled resources
Revolutionary with short duration	←	Commitment to opportunity	→	Evolutionary with long duration
Many stages with minimal exposure at each stage	←	Commitment of resources	→	A single stage with complete commitment out of decision
Episodic use or rent of required resources	←	Control of resources	→	Ownership or employment of required resources
Flat, with multiple informal networks	←	Management structure	→	Hierarchy
Based on value creation	←	Reward philosophy	→	Based on responsibility and seniority
Rapid growth is top priority; risk accepted to achieve growth	←	Growth orientation	→	Safe, slow, steady
Promoting broad search for opportunities	←	Entrepreneurial culture	→	Opportunity search restricted by resources controlled; failure punished

Source: Adapted from Brown *et al.* (2001, p. 955).

Linkage, leverage and learning as entrepreneurial strategies of East Asian latecomer firms

We adopt a strategic approach to birth, growth and internationalization of East Asian entrepreneurial firms, and in so doing utilize the fundamental concept of 'resource leverage' introduced to the management literature by Hamel and Prahalad (1993). In place of the traditional emphasis on strategy as 'fit' between a firm's activities and the business environment, Hamel and Prahalad emphasized that successful firms initiate strategic actions that change the environment, and where they take actions is based not on what they already have but on what they aim to achieve. The leverage of resources (such as technologies, patents, knowhow) through such strategic actions as creation of joint ventures, making acquisitions or licensing technologies are central to such a view of strategy. These concepts were applied by Hamel and Prahalad to cases of business success in leading economies, mainly Japan and the USA—but the concept also fits the needs of latecomer firms that start with little but are able to catch up quickly to incumbents through judicious use of resource leverage strategies. From the perspective of entrepreneurial strategies, the process of resource leverage (RL) proceeds through three stages—linkage, leverage and learning.

Linkage

Linkage as an entrepreneurial strategy involves the efforts of entrepreneurial and latecomer firms to establish formal and informal connections with others in order to access external resources. Resource leverage always has to begin with some form of linkage. Linkage can be effected through strategic alliances, partnerships, and joint ventures; and through informal connections that take such forms as *guanxi*. Linkage can also be reflected at different levels, including personal and organizational networks (Hoang and Antoncic, 2003).

The importance of linkage via strategic networks to firm performance has been widely recognized in the strategy literature in general (Gulati *et al.*, 2000) and for Chinese entrepreneurial MNEs in particular (Peng, 2012). Compared with the networking of more established firms, entrepreneurial networking is considered to be more urgent for the survival of start-ups; to be more intensive as entrepreneurs tend to make more efforts to establish, develop and maintain strong ties with stakeholders; and to have a larger impact on firm performance.

The entrepreneurial strategy of linkage seems particularly relevant and significant in the context of East Asian latecomer firms. Inter-linkage of firms has long been regarded as 'the most important organizational feature' of Asian businesses, and to some extent, Asian capitalist systems (Hamilton, 1996: 2). Networks of firms from different countries in East Asia are formed through various mechanisms and show different characteristics (Hitt *et al.*, 2001, 2011). For Chinese entrepreneurs, the focus has been on informal social networks, or *guanxi*, derived from 'personal relationships bounded in geographical, social or institutional space' (Zhou *et al.*, 2007: 674). Social network ties are regarded as a key determinant for Chinese entrepreneurs to discover, evaluate and exploit opportunities (Tang, 2010); and to gain performance benefits from growth and international expansions (Zhou *et al.*, 2007). Given the strong role that the state plays in the economy, entrepreneurs not only need to develop and maintain interpersonal ties with managers in other firms but sometimes more importantly with government officials (Peng and Luo, 2000).

Linkage plays a vital role in the emergence and growth of new high-tech ventures in East Asian countries such as Taiwan (Lin *et al.*, 2006). As described in Mathews (2006c), the Taiwanese electronics industry was made possible largely because of the opportunities created by the vertical disintegration of the global PC industry in the 1980s, and the position of Taiwanese firms as OEM carriers. On the other hand, Taiwanese firms also benefited from the linkages among themselves that were strengthened by the birth of high-tech parks and the resulting cluster effects. Further, analyses of more recently emerging industries in Taiwan such as solar PVs based on patent citation data reveal that Taiwanese firms have largely benefited from international technology diffusion (Wu and Mathews, 2012).

Leverage

Entrepreneurship is 'the process of discovering new ways of combining resources' (Sobel, 2007). In view of this, what is important to entrepreneurs and entrepreneurial firms is not what they 'possess', but what opportunities they can 'discover' and how they may take advantage of them. This notion departs from the traditional resource-based view of the firm, which emphasizes 'existing' resources and capabilities of the firm as the source of its sustained competitive advantages, and which evaluates strategic effectiveness of the resources based on whether they are valuable, rare, costly to imitate and well organized (Barney, 2002). As has been observed in many successful entrepreneurial firms from the region, they may not appear to be distinguished from others, at least initially, in terms of the resources.

In his commentary on the original paper by one of us where the LLL framework appeared (Mathews, 2002, 2006a), Narula (2006) states:

> [i]f the dragon MNEs did not have some kind of superior ownership advantage, it is inconceivable that they would be able to leverage networks and international partnerships with 'incumbents' to acquire complementary resources if they had nothing to offer in return!

We argue that the statement misses an important point in relation to entrepreneurship in general and to the leverage strategy deployed by latecomer entrepreneurial firms in particular. The process of entrepreneurship is not necessarily based on exchange of resources with equivalent economic values, but rather on the leverage of opportunities that have arisen and the entrepreneur's willingness to take the risks involved (Stevenson and Jarillo, 1990). In the case of white goods industries, this process has been analysed for cases of emerging market MNEs such as Mabe from Mexico, Arcelik from Turkey and Haier from China, where each company demonstrates accelerated internationalization and innovative strategies when compared with earlier incumbents (Bonaglia *et al.*, 2007).

Latecomer firms may leverage opportunities they have discovered to 'leapfrog' in technology and access the market. Discussions of such leapfrogging strategies, as outlined in Lewis (2007), are found in several streams of research, including technology transfer, national innovation systems and/or learning networks. First, the leapfrogging is likely to be enabled by technology transfer, especially from advanced to developing economies. Technology transfer can take place through a range of channels, including licensing, R&D collaboration, FDI, joint ventures, trade of capital goods, and recruitment of skilled employees. Second, the national innovation system of the receiving country (see e.g. Lundvall, 1992) forms an essential condition in determining the absorptive capability of the latecomer firm, or the receiver in a technology transfer. Finally, technology transfer is likely to be initiated in the learning networks of the latecomer firm, which is termed as linkage strategies above.

Learning

Many Asian firms have undergone a transformation from emulators to innovators (Chittoor *et al.*, 2009; Luo *et al.*, 2011). A learning strategy seems to be the key driver in this process. However, compared with that of established firms from Western advanced economies, the learning process of many East Asian latecomer firms has several features. First, the State has been a key force in driving the learning process of many East Asian latecomer firms. As discussed in Mathews (2006c), government agencies in East Asian countries, and their interaction and mutual support, have played an important role in fostering technology breakthroughs in key areas as identified to be critical to industrial development of the countries. Especially important among the government agencies are various public research institutions, such as the Industrial Technology Research Institute (ITRI) in Taiwan, the Korea Institute for Industrial Economics and Trade (KIET) and the Electronics and Telecommunications Research Institute (ETRI) in Korea, and the Institute of Microelectronics (IME) in Singapore. The role of such institutions in fostering and guiding the processes of learning in East Asia is shown in Figure 2.1.

The learning behaviour of many East Asian latecomers has distinctive characteristics. Many of them are quick learners ('fast followers'), and underpinning the learning pattern of those entrepreneurial firms is the strong market pressure they face to catch up and compete with their Western counterparts in the same market, whether it is the domestic market in the home country or the international market. On the other hand, as latecomers, entrepreneurial firms from the region have the learning advantages of 'newness' because they face less technological and market uncertainties in choosing what to learn and also 'because they possess fewer deeply embedded routines' (Luo *et al.*, 2011: 39).

Why are the LLL strategies so pronounced among East Asian entrepreneurial firms? While it is not our intention here to provide a thorough discussion, we would like to explore two possible roots of those strategies. First, the region has been deeply influenced by the Confucian philosophy which emphasizes that 'individuals are not isolated entities but a part of a larger system of

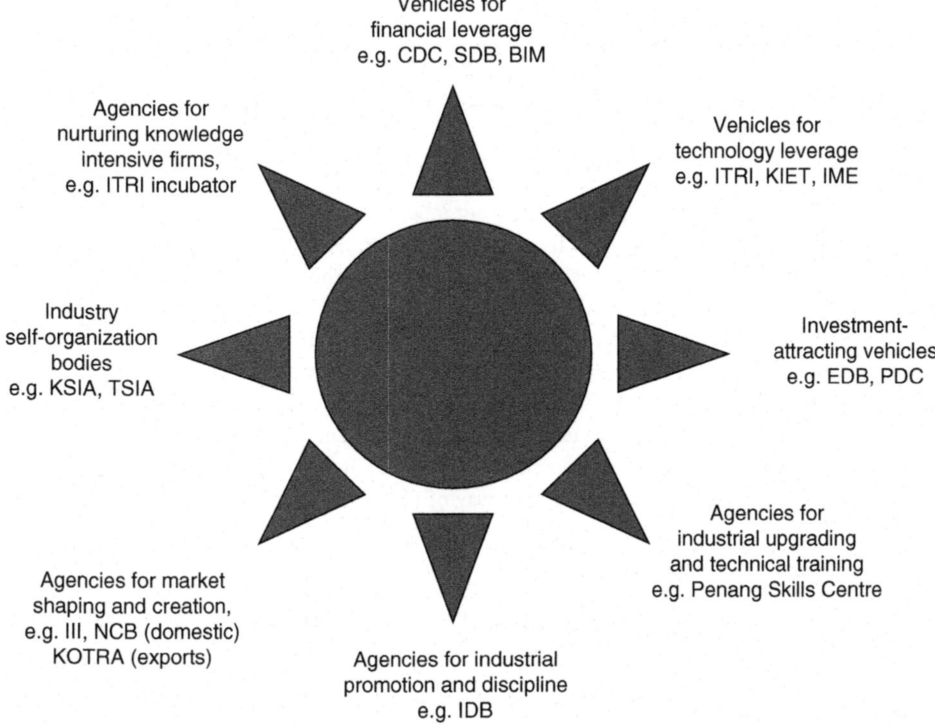

Figure 2.1 National system of economic learning in East Asian countries

Source: Adapted from Mathews (2002).

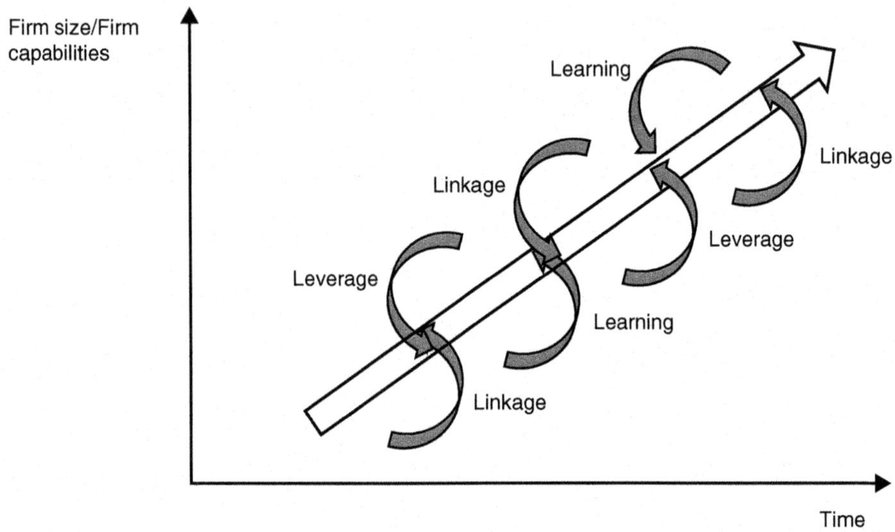

Figure 2.2 The dynamic process of LLL

interdependent relationships' (Hitt *et al.*, 2001: 358). Embodied in this culture, Asian firms seem more skilful and willing to link with others in their business dealings based on trust. Second, the environment that entrepreneurial firms face in the region is more volatile than that in Western countries. Those firms face greater competitive pressure, more regulatory uncertainties and more rapid industrial changes; and thus conventional strategies based on linear analysis seem less likely to work for those firms. The latecomer firms have no alternatives but to engage in LLL.

The dynamic nature of the LLL framework

The linkage, leverage and learning strategies are not independent, rather they interact and mutually reinforce each other. The dynamic LLL framework (Figure 2.2) suggests that the capabilities of the firm are built up through the mutual reinforcement process of the three strategies which drive the growth of the firm. Social capital built through linkage can help the company both leverage its needed resources and access knowledge (learning) (Hitt *et al.*, 2001). The process can be repeated in a never-ending sequence, with fresh linkages creating further opportunities for leverage of resources and the L&L steps being accomplished with greater efficiency and effectiveness in a process of learning, or what might be called collective entrepreneurship (Mathews, 2009).

LLL is a process that brings latecomer firms into greater and greater levels of integration into the global economy, which is the most useful way of thinking about the process of internationalization in a global era.

Applying the LLL framework to the Chinese renewable energy sector

In this chapter, we take the Chinese renewable energy sector as a test case for the discussion above. We specifically focus on entrepreneurial initiatives in two industrial segments of the sector, namely the wind and solar PV industries, which provide evidence for the applicability of the LLL framework to entrepreneurial strategies. The creation, expansion and internationalization of those renewable energy industries in China have been phenomenal.[1]

The competitiveness of Chinese indigenous firms from those industries in both the domestic and international markets has been evident. In the wind power industry, Chinese wind turbine manufacturers took four places in the list of Top Ten wind turbine manufacturers in the world (Table 2.3). Chinese turbines have now been sold in more than 19 countries, and exports of Chinese wind turbines have increased from a mere 2.3 MW in 2007 to 430 MW in 2012 (GWEC, 2012).[2] Similarly, Chinese PV manufacturers supply about half of the world solar PV modules; and nine of the top 15 solar PV module manufacturers in the world are currently from China (and 10 out of 15 if Canadian Solar is counted as a Chinese company, which it is in all but name) (Table 2.4).

Table 2.3 Market shares of top 10 wind turbine manufacturers, 2011

Rank	*Wind turbine manufacturer*	*Country of origin*	*Global market share (%)*
1	Vestas	Denmark	12.9
2	Goldwind	China	9.4
3	GE Wind	USA	8.8
4	Gamesa	Spain	8.2
5	Enercon	Germany	7.9
6	Suzlon Group	India	7.7
7	Sinovel	China	7.3
8	United Power	China	7.1
9	Siemens Wind Power	Denmark	6.3
10	Ming Yang	China	2.9
	Others		21.5
Total Sales > 40 GW			

Source: REN21 (2012).

Table 2.4 Market shares of top 15 solar PV module manufacturers, 2011

Rank	*Firms*	*Market share*	*Country of origin*
1	Suntech Power	5.8	China
2	First Solar	5.7	USA
3	Yingli Green Energy	4.8	China
4	Trina Solar	4.3	China
5	Canadian Solar	4	Canada
6	SunPower	2.8	USA
7	Sharp	2.8	Japan
8	Tianwei New Energy	2.7	China
9	LDK Solar	2.5	China
9	Hanwha-SolarOne	2.5	China
9	Hareon Solar	2.5	China
12	JA Solar	2.4	China
13	Jinko Solar	2.3	China
14	Kyocera	1.9	Japan
15	REC	1.9	Norway
	Other	51	
Total Sales => 40GW			

Source: REN21 (2012).

Most significant players in both the Chinese wind and solar PV industries were only founded in the early or mid-2000s. Compared with incumbents in the USA, Europe and Japan, many Chinese firms had little technological inventories and knowledge specific to those industries. The question then arises: How did China manage to build those industries so quickly? And how did Chinese entrepreneurial firms in those industries develop their competitive advantages in both the domestic and international markets? Let us examine their emergence in light of the LLL framework.

Linkage

The linkage strategy of Chinese firms in those industries is reflected in their efforts to partner with others and quickly build the capacity to tap into sources of technological knowledge using licensing, joint ventures and foreign company acquisition, as well as purchase of equipment—leading ultimately to Chinese indigenous innovation. In the wind power industry, Chinese wind turbine manufacturers formed linkages with foreign partners to enable technology transfer from companies in a handful of countries as early wind turbine innovators including Denmark, The Netherlands, Germany and the USA (Lewis, 2007, 2011). The channels of forming linkages include joint R&D, mergers and acquisitions (M&As) licensing (Figure 2.3). Figure 2.3 reveals that some of the Chinese wind power firms have embedded themselves in the global learning networks of wind turbine technologies. For example, *Goldwind*, the largest Chinese wind power company, started its wind turbine manufacturing based on a licence to the 600 kW turbine from Jacobs, a small German firm, and the 750 kW turbine from German firm REPower. The company was engaged in R&D collaboration on the 1.2 MW turbine technology with the German firm Vensys, resulting in joint development of the innovative Permanent Magnet Direct Drive (PMDD) technology (see below). Vensys was subsequently acquired by Goldwind and became a subsidiary focusing on R&D. By doing so, the company has been able to access technologies of other foreign companies such as Enerwind, CKD NOVE Energo, Eozen, IMPSA, and REGen Powertech; and has eventually transformed itself from being an importer of foreign technologies to being an indigenous innovator.[3]

Another Chinese wind turbine manufacturer, *Sinovel* worked closely with Windtec (a subsidiary of AMSC) to develop leading-edge 3 MW and 5 MW turbines (bypassing the kilowatt stage), and by 2010 it had supplied all 34 offshore turbines to the Donghai Bridge project with its own MW-power machines. Since then, Sinovel has internationalized rapidly, opening sales and production points in several countries including the USA, Brazil, Sweden, Turkey, India and South Africa. In the USA, Sinovel won a contract to supply a 1.5 MW turbine for a pumping station in Charleston, Boston. However, in 2012, Sinovel and Windtec fell out; Sinovel has subsequently been embroiled in an IPR infringement suit with Windtec.

Ming Yang is a private-sector firm that launched into the wind turbine manufacturing industry relatively late in 2006, based in Zhongshan in the southern Guangdong province (Pearl River Delta). Previously a relatively small manufacturer of electrical transmission and distribution equipment, the company became the first Chinese wind turbine exporter to the US market in just two years. Since 2010, it has been listed on the NY Stock Exchange—the first Chinese wind power company to do so. It has collaborated with the German firm Aerodyn Energiesysteme to jointly develop turbines which have won German technical quality certification. Ming Yang has leapfrogged to the lead technologically, through its alliance with Aerodyn, and now offers 1.5 MW three-blade turbines and 2.5 MW as well as 3.0 MW Super Compact Drive (SCD) advanced two-blade turbines, while it has announced that larger 5 and 6 MW turbines are due for release in 2013, and an even larger 12 MW model is said to be under development.

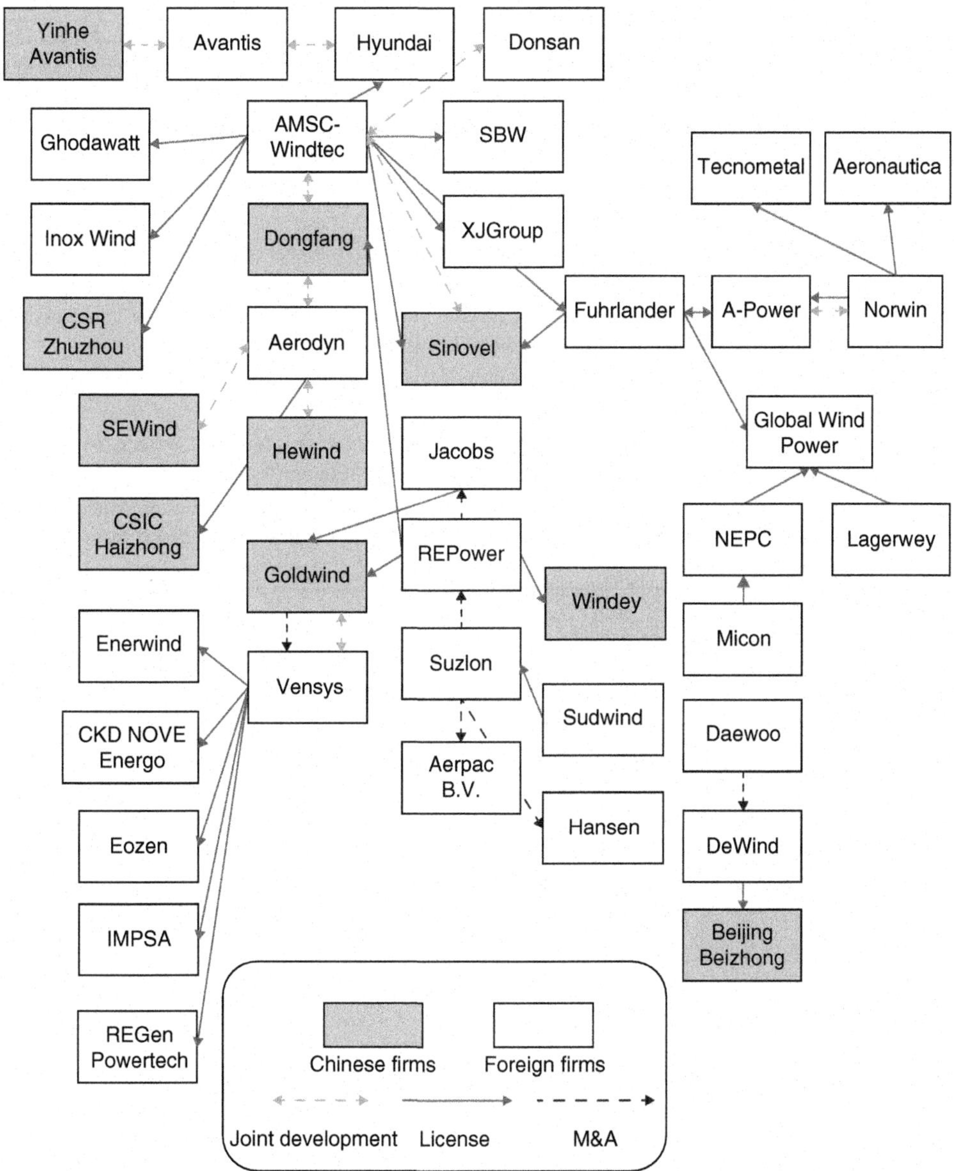

Figure 2.3 Wind power technology transfer networks

Source: Based on Lewis (2011, p. 297).

Ming Yang has established a strong manufacturing base and associated supply chain cluster at Zhongshan.

Similarly, *PV manufacturers* in China have also largely built on foreign technologies initially. De la Tour *et al.* (2011) studied the international technology transfers to the Chinese solar PV and found that, in contrast to the wind power industry, the Chinese solar PV firms rarely utilized licensing in accessing technology. Instead, imports of manufacturing equipment and labour mobility are identified as two main channels through which Chinese solar PV firms have

Table 2.5 FDI activities of Suntech up to 2012

- In March 2008, the company acquired an 11.7% equity interest in Hoku Scientific (a Nasdaq-listed company based in Idaho, US) for a total consideration of approximately $20 million
- In March 2008, the company acquired a total of 14.0% equity interest in Nitol Solar for a total consideration of approximately $100 million. Nitol Solar is a privately held company incorporated in the Jersey Islands and is in the process of operating a polysilicon manufacturing facility near Irkutsk, Russia
- Acquisition of Suntech Japan (formerly MSK) which is a leading manufacturer of BIPV systems based in Japan
- Invested in Global Solar Fund, S.C.A, Sicar, or GSF, an investment fund created to make investments in private companies that own or develop projects in the solar energy sector
- Acquisition of EI Solutions, Inc., a commercial PV systems integration company based in the United States, now part of Suntech
- Acquisition of KSL-Kuttler Automation Systems GmbH, or KSL-Kuttler, a leading Germany-based manufacturer of automation systems for the printed circuit board industry
- Acquisition of a majority interest in CSG Solar AG, or CSG Solar, a German company engaged in developing, producing and marketing PV cells on the basis of crystalline silicon on glass technology

acquired the necessary technologies and skills at the initial stage of the development (ibid.). For the latter, for example, Chinese diaspora and foreigners make up a large number of the boards and management of most large Chinese PV companies.

Chinese solar PV firms seem to have taken a more aggressive approach to acquire technologies from overseas by actively engaging into technology-seeking type of FDI activities. For example, Suntech, the largest solar PV manufacturer in the world until its partial implosion in 2012, launched a number of downstream and upstream acquisitions, in order to acquire foreign strategic assets to complement the manufacturing and design, as summarized in Table 2.5. It is through such linkages that Suntech, Canadian Solar and other Chinese PV firms were able to leverage knowhow, technologies and market access.

Leverage

Formation of linkages with foreign companies may provide latecomer firms with the opportunities to participate into global supply chains; but that will not guarantee the conversion of the opportunities into the companies' capabilities. A number of leverage strategies have been adopted by Chinese wind and solar PV companies to consolidate technological, financial and institutional opportunities.

In the wind power industry, Lewis (2007) observes that, facing great technological barriers by leading wind turbine companies, Chinese companies such as Goldwind managed to establish licensing agreements with second-tier foreign companies in the industry. Those smaller companies are more likely to share their technologies because 'they have less to lose in terms of international competition, and more to gain in license fees' (Lewis 2007: 226).

In the Chinese PV solar industries, companies such as LDK Solar, Hanergy and Giga Solar have all utilized typical latecomer strategies to focus on a dominant technology (in this case, on crystalline silicon for LDK and Giga Solar and on CIGS thin-film technology for Hanergy), and were able to develop advantages based on standardization, mass production and cost reduction, utilizing the largest possible market for their product, namely, the global market. In this, Chinese solar PV firms like Suntech and LDK Solar have been very successful—if over-stretched financially, which is currently a major source of concern for them.

In order to leverage financial resources, a large proportion of Chinese companies in those two industries have launched IPOs (initial public offerings) on stock markets soon after they were founded to raise expansion capital; this is a phenomenon not commonly seen in traditional industries. By the end of 2011, no fewer than 11 Chinese PV companies had been listed on the stock exchanges in the USA, 8 companies were listed on Hong Kong stock exchanges and 14 companies were listed on stock exchanges in China (Greenpeace, 2012)—no doubt the concerns over global warming played a role in facilitating this process.

The Chinese government has provided strong support in the industrial development of the two industries. One policy that the Chinese wind companies have particularly benefited from is concerned with the support and requirement of the government for local content. China required 70 per cent of the turbine content in concession wind power projects to be made locally (Lewis, 2007). In order to meet this requirement, foreign companies wishing to access the market had to choose to set up manufacturing subsidiaries in China rather than export products. During this process, technology diffusion took place and local competitors were able to absorb and localize the technologies. The strategy was discontinued after vigorous foreign protest was mounted—but after it had achieved its intended outcome.

Learning

These processes of L&L have been repeated over and over again, with the companies gaining efficiency and effectiveness with each iteration—best described as a process of learning. For example, in the case of the Chinese wind power firm Ming Yang, after its initial resource leveraging forays into international markets, the company was confident enough to invest in knowledge acquisitions. The company began to tap into global knowledge networks through establishing R&D centres in both Denmark (near Vestas) and in the USA. In 2012 Ming Yang announced a strategic partnership with India's Reliance group to develop wind turbines for the Indian market and beyond into SE Asia. This South-South pattern of joint development is surely one of the characteristics of the 'emerging' MNEs from emerging markets. Ming Yang now has R&D centres in both Denmark and the USA, demonstrating its capacity to leverage knowledge resources from the developed world.

The aim of the repeated application of L&L strategies is to raise the technological capabilities within firms, so that they approach the technological frontier, in a process described memorably by Kim (1997) as moving 'from imitation to innovation'. This is clearly seen in the case of PMDD (Permanent Magnet Direct Drive) technology, as introduced by Goldwind, based on its joint venture with Vensys. PMDD is an advanced form of turbine traction that dispenses with gearing, and thereby provides more a reliable operation as well as greater efficiency (Sun and Yang, 2013). Goldwind turbines are now exclusively PMDD machines, both 1.5 MW and 2.5 MW. The innovative technology was developed jointly with the firm Vensys, which started as a partner and eventually became a subsidiary of Goldwind. So this is a clear case of LLL—a link is made by Goldwind with Vensys, which is then consolidated into a permanent arrangement; knowhow and technology are leveraged from the link, and assimilated within Goldwind; and finally the technology is transformed into world-cutting edge in a process of learning.

Conclusion

The fundamental reason why LLL matches the strategies of latecomers (as illustrated here in the case of the international expansion of Chinese wind power and solar PV firms) is that it is a strategic framework, based on the notion of resource leverage. It is formulated in terms of the actual practices of firms as they deal with uncertainty, disequilibrium and market dynamics. By contrast, the traditional OLI framework is based on micro-economic reasoning, where the (hidden) assumptions are that firms encounter each other in conditions of equilibrium and where they comply with economic assumptions such as marginal pricing, full information and universal, free access to technology. It is worth emphasizing the point that these conditions are rarely (if ever) found in real-world circumstances in international business. We stress these differences, because in our view an approach to internationalization strategy should be based on strategic reasoning. Obviously micro-economic principles are important, but they are not the whole story.

Notes

1 A recent case from the Harvard Business School (Vietor, 2012) examines China's successes in wind power, solar PV and lithium-ion batteries, in each of which sectors it leads the world, and concludes:

> The government of China, its renewable industries, its engineers and its workers have labored incredibly hard during the past decade to replace carbon-fuels and to build industries that are globally competitive. In wind, solar and electric vehicles, the country's manufacturers now lead the United States and Europe in the global market place . . . China is now a major exporter of solar cells and modules, of towers and lattice masts for wind projects, and of lithium-ion batteries. Its firms have begun exporting wind turbines and electric vehicles—the first signs of successful industrial policy. As Wen Jiabao has pushed China to move up the value-chain in exports, it is clear that renewable energy technologies will be at the leading edge.
>
> *(ibid.: 10)*

2 Specifically in the wind power sector, the international political economy scholar Joanne Lewis comments:

> It took firms in China, India and South Korea less than 10 years to go from having no wind turbine manufacturing experience to having the ability to manufacture complete wind turbine systems that are state-of-the-art and either already available or soon to be available on the global market.
>
> *(2011: 301)*

3 Since then, Goldwind has been nominated twice by MIT's *Technology Review* magazine as one of 'The 50 Most Innovative Companies in the World' in 2011 and 2012.

Bibliography

Barney, J. (2002) *Gaining and Sustaining Competitive Advantage,* 2nd edn, Upper Saddle River, NJ: Prentice Hall.

Bonaglia, F., Goldstein, A. and Mathews, J.A. (2007) 'Accelerated internationalization by emerging multinationals: the case of the white goods sector', *Journal of World Business,* 42: 369–383.

Brown, T.E., Davidsson, P. and Wiklund, J. (2001) 'An operationalization of Stevenson's conceptualization of entrepreneurship as opportunity-based firm behavior', *Strategic Management Journal,* 22(10): 953–968.

Chittoor, R., Sarkar, M., Ray, S. and Aulakh, P. S. (2009) 'Third-world copycats to emerging multinationals: institutional changes and organizational transformation in the Indian pharmaceutical industry', *Organization Science,* 20(1): 187–205.

CWEA (2012) *Statistics of Chinese Wind Power Installation,* Beijing: Chinese Wind Energy Association.

de la Tour, A., Glachant, M. and Ménière, Y. (2011) 'Innovation and international technology transfer: the case of the Chinese photovoltaic industry', *Energy Policy,* 39(2): 761–770.

Dunning, J. H. (2000) 'The eclectic paradigm as an envelope for economic and business theories of MNE activity', *International Business Review,* 9(2), 163–190.

Dunning, J.H. (2006) 'Comment on dragon multinationals: new players in 21st century globalisation', *Asia Pacific Journal of Management,* 23: 139–141.

Greenpeace (2012) *Clean Production of Solar PV in China,* Beijing: Greenpeace (in Chinese).

Gulati, R., Nohria, N. and Zaheer, A. (2000) 'Guest editors' introduction to the special issue: strategic networks', *Strategic Management Journal,* 21(3), 199–201.

GWEC (2012) *Global Wind Energy Outlook 2012,* Global Wind Energy Council. Available at: www.gwec.net/publications/global-wind-energy-outlook/.

Hamel, G. and Prahalad, C.K. (1993) 'Strategy as stretch and leverage', *Harvard Business Review,* 71(2): 75–84.

Hamilton, G.G. (ed.) (1996) *Asian Business Networks,* New York: Walter de Gruyter.

Hitt, M.A., Ireland, R.D., Camp, S.M. and Sexton, D.L. (2001) 'Strategic entrepreneurship: entrepreneurial strategies for wealth creation', *Strategic Management Journal,* 22(6–7): 479–491.

Hitt, M.A., Ireland, R.D., Sirmon, D.G. and Trahms, C.A. (2011) 'Strategic entrepreneurship: creating value for individuals, organizations, and society', *Academy of Management Perspectives,* 25(2): 57–75.

Hoang, H. and Antoncic, B. (2003) 'Network-based research in entrepreneurship: a critical review', *Journal of Business Venturing,* 18(2), 165–187.

Hobday, M. (1995) 'East Asian latecomer firms: learning the technology of electronics', *World Development,* 23(7): 1171–1193.

Kim, E.M. (1996) 'The industrial organization and growth of the Korean chaebol: integrating development and organizational theories', in G.G. Hamilton (ed.) *Asian Business Networks,* New York: Walter de Gruyter, pp. 231–254.

Kim, L.S. (1997) *Imitation to Innovation,* Boston: Harvard Business Press.

Lewis, J.I. (2007) 'Technology acquisition and innovation in the developing world: wind turbine development in China and India', *Studies in Comparative International Development,* 42(3–4): 208–232.

Lewis, J.I. (2011) 'Building a national wind turbine industry: experiences from China, India and South Korea', *International Journal of Technology and Globalisation,* 5(3): 281–305.

Lin, B.-W., Li, P.-C. and Chen, J.-S. (2006) 'Social capital, capabilities, and entrepreneurial strategies: a study of Taiwanese high-tech new ventures', *Technological Forecasting and Social Change,* 73(2): 168–181.

Lundvall, B.-Å. (1992). *National Systems of Innovation: Towards a Theory of Innovation and Interactive Learning.* London: Pinter Publishers.

Luo, Y. (2003) 'Industrial dynamics and managerial networking in an emerging market: the case of China', *Strategic Management Journal,* 24(13): 1315–1327.

Luo, Y., Sun, J. and Wang, S. L. (2011) 'Emerging economy copycats', *Academy of Management Perspectives,* May: 37–56.

Mathews, J.A. (2002) *Dragon Multinational: A New Model of Growth,* New York: Oxford University Press.

Mathews, J.A. (2006a) 'Dragon multinationals: new players in 21st century globalization', *Asia Pacific Journal of Management,* 23: 5–27.

Mathews, J.A. (2006b) 'Response to Dunning and Narula', *Asia Pacific Journal of Management,* 23: 153–155.

Mathews, J.A. (2006c) 'Electronics in Taiwan: a case of technological learning', in V. Chandra (ed.) *Technology Adaptation and Exports: How Some Developing Countries Got it Right,* Washington, DC: The World Bank, pp. 83–126.

Mathews, J.A. (2009) 'China, India and Brazil: tiger technology, dragon multinationals and the building of national systems of economic learning', *Asian Business & Management,* 8: 5–32.

Mathews, J.A. and Cho, D.S. (2000) *Tiger Technology: The Creation of the Semiconductor Industry in East Asia,* Cambridge: Cambridge University Press.

Mathews, J.A. and Tan, H. (2012) 'The transformation of the electric power sector in China', *Energy Policy,* 52: 170–180.

Mathews, J.A. and Zander, I. (2007) 'The international entrepreneurial dynamics of accelerated internationalisation', *Journal of International Business Studies,* 38(3): 387–403.

Narula, R. (2006) 'Globalization, new ecologies, new zoologies, and the purported death of the eclectic paradigm', *Asia Pacific Journal of Management,* 23(2), 143–151.

Peng, M.W. (2012) 'The global strategy of emerging multinationals from China', *Global Strategy Journal,* 2(2): 97–107.

Peng, M.W. and Luo, Y. (2000) 'Managerial ties and firm performance in a transition economy: the nature of a micro-macro link', *Academy of Management Journal,* 43(3): 486–501.

Redding, G. (1996) 'Weak organizations and strong links: management ideology and Chinese family buiness networks', in G.G. Hamilton (ed.) *Asian Business Networks,* New York: Walter de Gruyter, pp. 27–42.

REN21 (2012) *Renewables 2012 Global Status Report.* Paris: Renewable Energy Policy Network for the 21st Century.

Sobel, R.S. (2007) 'Entrepreneurship', in D.R. Henderson (ed.) *The Concise Encyclopedia of Economics.* Available at: www.econlib.org/library/Enc/Entrepreneurship.html.

Stevenson, H.H. and Jarillo, J.C. (1990) 'A paradigm of entrepreneurship: entrepreneurial management', *Strategic Management Journal,* 11(5): 17–27.

Sun, S.L. and Yang, X. (2013) 'The rise of Chinese wind turbine manufacturers', in P.P. Li (ed.) *Disruptive Innovations from China and India: The Strategic Implications for Local Challengers and Global Incumbents,* London: Routledge.

Tang, J. (2010) 'How entrepreneurs discover opportunities in China: an institutional view', *Asia Pacific Journal of Management,* 27(3): 461–479.

Vietor, R.H.K. (2012) 'Low-carbon, indigenous innovation in China', Harvard Business School Case 9–712–061.

Wu, C.-Y. and Mathews, J.A. (2012) 'Knowledge flows in the solar photovoltaic industry: insights from patenting by Taiwan, Korea, and China', *Research Policy,* 41(3): 524–540.

Yang, M. and Pan, R. (2012) 'Harvesting sunlight: solar thermal industry in China', in M. Yang and R. Pan (eds) *China's Industrial Development in the 21st Century,* Singapore: World Scientific.

Zhou, L., Wu, W. and Luo, X. (2007) 'Internationalization and the performance of born-global SMEs: the mediating role of social networks', *Journal of International Business Studies,* 38(4), 673–690.

3

Catch-down innovation, imitative entrepreneurship and *shanzhai* production in China

Ming Dong

> It is by imitation, far more than by precept, that we learn everything; and what we learn thus, we acquire not only more efficiently, but more pleasantly. This forms our manners, our opinions, our lives.
>
> *(Edmund Burke, 1729–1797)*

Before starting the discussion on innovation, entrepreneurship and *shanzhai* production, let's first look at two cases.

Case 1 Family Computer and the Subor learning machine

The Nintendo Entertainment System (also abbreviated as NES or simply called Nintendo) is an 8-bit video game console that was released by Nintendo in North America in 1985, in Europe in 1986 and Australia in 1987. In Japan (where it was first launched in 1983), it was released as the Family Computer, commonly shortened to either the Famicom, or abbreviated to FC (Figure 3.1).[1] The console can be used with a variety of gaming cartridges produced by Nintendo or other third parties. It soon became a very popular gaming system for both teenagers and adult gaming fans. Meanwhile, personal computers (PCs) started to become more a part of family life in the 1990s though at a very high price. In terms of technological complexity and use, the PC is much more complicated and has more advanced functions. At that time, the FC and PC were similar to two cars driving on different roads, using different levels of technologies and targeting distinctly different markets. People would not normally expect a product with both PC and FC functions (although this did become possible decades later with intelligent consoles such as the Xbox and PS3).

However, several Chinese entrepreneurs saw the opportunity to converge the two roads, to meet the needs of those families who wanted some of the basic functions from a PC while also having the opportunity to play FC games. Accordingly, they produced another product—the Subor learning machine SB-486D (Figure 3.2). It has a keyboard, two game controllers and a cartridge slot. By plugging in different cartridges (gaming or learning programmes), it can be used either as an FC or as a learning machine. The model name '486D' reminds people of the

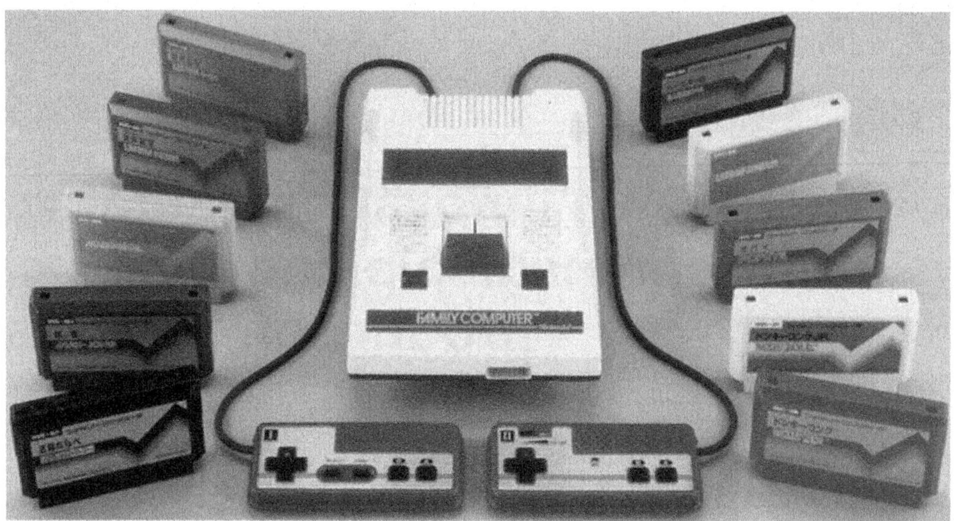

Figure 3.1 The Family Computer system

Figure 3.2 The Subor learning machine SB-486D

very popular 486 DX PCs at that time. It is compatible with all Nintendo game cartridges so it is possible to switch seamlessly between the gaming and learning functions. The price of the Subor learning machine is much less than a real 486 PC and is similar to the price of a genuine FC.

Case 2 the genuine Samsung N7102 and the *shanzhai* Samsung handset

Samsung has been highly successful in the smart phone field in recent years. The N7102 was one of the high end models introduced in 2012, with a 5.5-inch HD screen (1280*720 HD Super AMOLED), a four-core CPU (Samsung Exynos 4412), 2G RAM and 16G ROM, two sim slots (supporting GSM and/or WCDMA) and an Android OS (4.1). This model aptly represents the current trend in smart phone technology: larger screen, more powerful CPU and slimmer shell. The genuine Samsung N7102 is sold at a price of RMB 4000 + (this may vary a little depending on the dealer). Not long after the introduction of the N7102, a Chinese *shanzhai* manufacturer introduced their version: a 5.5-inch HD screen (1280*720 HD screen from SHARP), a four-core CPU (MTK6589), 1G RAM and 4G ROM, two sim slots (supporting GSM and/or WCDMA) and an Android OS (4.1). Figure 3.3 shows these two products.

The biggest difference between the two is the CPU/chip set manufacturer, and size of memory. Unless the system information in the operating system is thoroughly checked, nobody knows which is which, and differences between the two are not noticeable to the extent that there is not an obvious performance gap in everyday use. They also look identical. The MTK6589 platform has a very similar performance compared with the other four-core platforms, but with much less energy consumption.[2] The most attractive fact is that the *shanzhai* handset only costs RMB 1500, about one-third of the genuine Samsung.

Figure 3.3 The Samsung N7102 (left) and the *shanzhai* version (right)

Case 1 was one of the early examples of technology imitation, functional innovation and *shanzhai* production. It successfully combined two technologies into one new product to meet the needs of a new market segment. Although no public conflicts and disputes were recorded between Subor and Nintendo, it is now believed that there are indeed technological imitations (legal or illegal) and even pirating in this case. Case 2 was a more recent example of a *shanzhai* product. It has an identical industrial design to its prototype product, including the screen, the shell, the buttons and even the brand label on the products. It also has very similar functions with its prototype but is sold at a much lower price.

What can be understood from these two cases? This chapter presents the reader with the unique phenomenon—*shanzhai*—across a wide range of products in China. It can be seen in the electronics and mobile industries from Cases 1 and 2 and can be observed in other industries too (i.e. shoes and clothes). The increasing appearance of *shanzhai* elements in the market has pushed research attention towards this area. Scholars have attempted to produce different theories to explain the emergence and development of *shanzhai*. As a very brief summary to the work in the area, the use of the term '*shanzhai*' and the characteristics of *shanzhai* products will be examined, then the phenomenon will be interpreted from two aspects: the perspective of technological catch-down (as opposed to the widely known technological catch-up process in many developing countries), and the wider perspective of imitative entrepreneurship (as opposed to innovative entrepreneurship). One question will be asked: Why is *shanzhai* production so common in China but not in other countries? The answer to this question is very complex and requires years of work, however, it is hoped that this chapter can provide the readers with some of the important aspects of the *shanzhai* phenomenon through the lens of innovation and entrepreneurship, while leaving enough room for further discussion and inspiration.

Characteristics of *shanzhai* products

Shanzhai is always associated with imitation and intellectual property violation. One of the problems with the term *shanzhai* is that people tend to use it interchangeably with imitation, copycat or even counterfeit. The meaning of the term '*shanzhai*' can range from purely imitation (counterfeit or copycat) to very good innovation (new product development). Such confusion and ambiguity lead to bias as many people do not see the potential of *shanzhai* but view it only as bad imitation as well as an IP violation.

Shanzhai products, though varying in brand names, functions, price and quality, do share some common characteristics:

- *Low cost and short lead time:* For the mobile phone industry, for example, not only has the cost of designing and manufacturing a phone been lowered, the time to get the products onto the market has been greatly shortened. In the traditional model, large phone makers such as Nokia will need about 6 months to bring a new design to market. However, for *shanzhai* phone producers, this time has been shortened to only 45 days. This is a vast improvement and the phone producers rely heavily on this 'fast track' mode to respond to the customers' needs in time. The short lead-time also helps the producers keep some of their loyal customers.

  Three factors contribute to the short lead time in *shanzhai* production. First, as the upstream design function has been produced by the prototype product that the *shanzhai* product is imitating, the time and money spent during this period has been saved. Second, the suppliers who provide ready-to-use or make-on-order parts enable *shanzhai* companies to further save time on sourcing and fabrication. Finally, *shanzhai* products do not have long testing and quality monitoring processes, something that further reduces the overall cost and lead time. As a result, *shanzhai* products have shorter fabrication cycles and lower prices and can therefore reach the end user much faster, as well as getting feedback from end users in a much more time-efficient manner.

- *Acceptable quality for the price:* Although one of the commonly cited criticisms of *shanzhai* products is their low quality, many *shanzhai* users do cite 'acceptable quality for its price' as one of the main reasons for their choice of buying a *shanzai* product. The trade-off between quality and price is often ignored by many people. From the user's point of view, an 'acceptable' quality level actually helps to overcome the so-called 'technology over-shooting' problem. The concept of 'technology over-shooting' suggests that firms try to keep prices and margins high by developing products with many more features than customers can actually absorb or really require. In Case 1, it is very reasonable to imagine that many of the advanced functions in PCs will never be used by a teenage user whose primary reason for using a PC is to facilitate learning at school. Therefore, the over-shoot advanced functions will be discarded and elementary functions will be retained and integrated with an FC, bringing the price down to an acceptable level. In Case 2, the degrading of the CPU and memory size also does not really affect the user's experience in the mid-to-low end customer range. Leaving aside the obvious IP violation, the *shanzhai* version of the N7102 has overcome this technology over-shooting by taking out those expensive and unnecessary components.
- *Functional innovation:* People may think that *shanzhai* products have nothing competitive to offer other than their low price. However, as Case 1 has illustrated, apart from the cost and price advantages, *shanzhai* products are actually often quite innovative in terms of the product functions that can create distinctive advantages. In Case 1, functional innovation is reflected in the combination and cross-over of gaming and learning. In other cases, functional innovation may be found in the form of the installation of extra function modules, for example, outdoor speakers/a TV receiver module or three available SIM slots on mobile phones. Evidence shows that many people buy *shanzhai* products not only because their prices are low, but also because the products provide functions that are not provided by mainstream producers.

Explaining *shanzhai* production

Catch-down innovation in shanzhai *production*

The 'catch-up' theory explores the ways in which developing countries build their capabilities to move from doing simple, knowledge-using production activities, to more complex, knowledge-creating production activities, before finally competing at the technology frontiers (Hobday, 1995). In this process some regions stop at possessing only production capacities while some others move on to more innovative capabilities. By continuing to build capacities for production, firms learn by doing and accumulate the necessary knowledge to move up (catch-up). The catch-up takes time while the production capacity is gradually transformed into technological capabilities (Bell and Pavitt, 1993, 1995). From a technological development perspective, this means learning from the technologies possessed by more advanced countries/regions/organizations, and adopting and adapting such technologies to serve the unique needs for production of certain products.

This path implies adoption of the Schumpeterian philosophy of distinctive advantage in innovation, which aims to create something new and is only possessed by one party. To become an innovator, one has to at least acquire resources that are unique in many ways (Barney *et al.*, 2001), and in most cases, one has to acquire further capabilities to deal with the dynamic nature of the environment (Teece and Pisano, 1994; Eisenhardt and Martin, 2000). After production capacity has been accumulated, firms will have to move up the technology ladder in order to innovate. In this argument, a hidden premise exists in the fact that the learners often target more advanced technologies. However, there are also possibilities that firms can move in the opposite direction: after production capacity has been accumulated, firms can focus on relatively mature technologies and head down towards the low end of the technology spectrum, learning how to better manage mature technologies to exploit more value out of the utilization process of such technologies. They research and develop normally integrated mature technologies in order to harness the value of existing technologies, rather than apply new technologies. This is known as 'catch-down' innovation.

Together with this is the expansion of the low-end market that has created a considerably large demand for mature technologies, simply because they are affordable. This low end of the market is called 'the bottom of the pyramid' (BOP) (Prahalad, 2009). The demands from this market act as a strong engine to sustain the high-speed growth of technological catch-down activities. In examining catch-down innovation, both the supply side (heading down the technology spectrum) and demand side (meeting needs from BOP market) need to be considered.

In the case of catch-down innovation, *shanzhai* products provide similar functions by using mature and readily available technologies instead of cutting-edge technologies. These mature technologies require very little or no R&D investment as it is mature and 'imitates' others. For example, in the case of *shanzhai* mobile phones, *shanzhai* companies invest very little in their own R&D, therefore it is unlikely that they will develop new technologies. However, this does not affect the process whereby they conduct the following activities: (1) adopting technologies (technological designs) provided by third party upstream suppliers (here, MTK[3]); and (2) adopting existing technologies (industrial designs) from leading firms. As a result, they adopt mature technological innovation from leading firms without investing heavily in developing such technologies in-house. This strategy has created two advantages: (1) the price of the final product is greatly reduced due to less spending on R&D; and (2) the *shanzhai* companies are pushed to innovate in areas other than cost in order to attract users.

However, it is important to understand how innovations become operational. Shi and Rong (2010) took the *shanzhai* handset industry as an example to explore the systems and operational mechanisms of the industry. Their study has revealed the specific structural elements and their roles in the industry but they did not really answer the question why a network looks like it does and how it impacts the technological choices of *shanzhai* companies. Network thinking can be extended to a more general level and draw a generic supply network for *shanzhai* production (Figure 3.4).

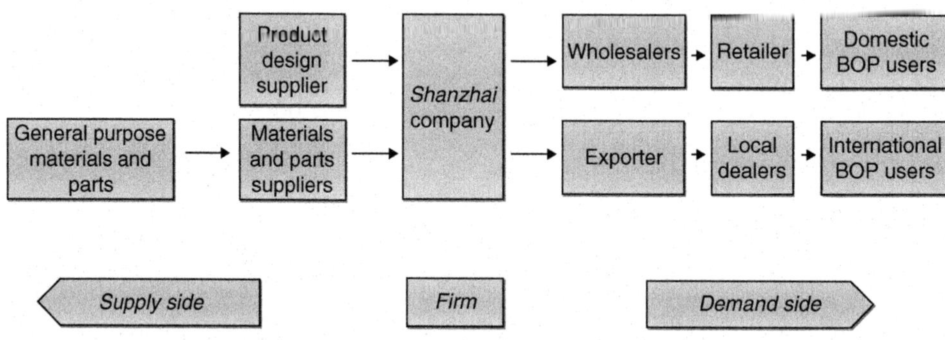

Figure 3.4 A generic supply network for *shanzhai* production

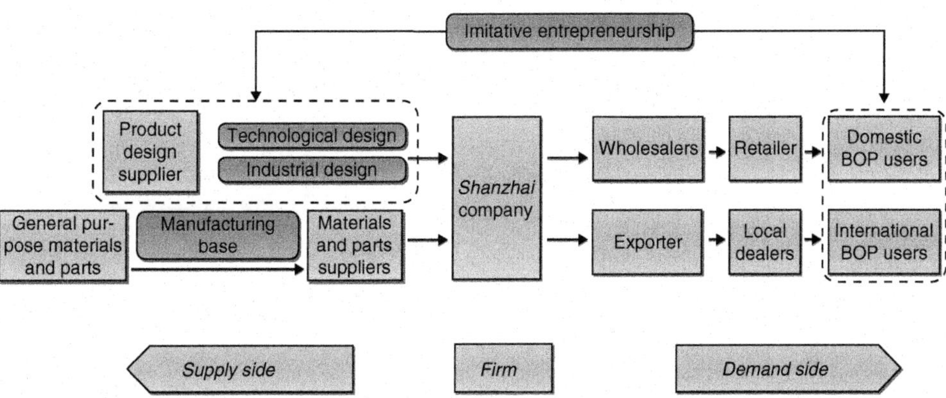

Figure 3.5 *Shanzai* production and imitative entrepreneurship

Not a great deal of information can be extracted from Figure 3.4 on the mechanism for both supply and demand sides of catch-down innovations. However, if we add four new boxes, namely, technological design, industrial design, manufacturing base and imitative entrepreneurship, it will appear as in Figure 3.5.

In Figure 3.5, product design has two dimensions—the technological dimension deals with technologies used in the product while the industrial dimension deals with the appearance of a product. These two dimensions are the key to understanding technological catch-down in *shanzhai* production. Examining the mechanisms behind these boxes will enable us to answer the questions proposed at the beginning of the chapter.

To complete the product design with no or little R&D investment, *shanzhai* firms need to find the most cost-efficient way to develop both the core technology design and industrial design. By imitating prototype products, they complete the industrial design. This needs to be conducted by people who are capable of analyzing, dissecting and replicating the inventions of others (Baumol, 1988). Now this may not be very difficult with the help from some modern reverse engineering techniques. However, this approach has its constraints. Either there are some people who can provide holistic technology design solutions (as MTK does in the case of *shanzhai* phones), or there are some with basic knowledge on how to break the design down into several easier-to-replicate modules. The latter will require that the technology used is not too new otherwise modularization would be extremely difficult (as difficult as hackers fully cracking newly released OS). On the other hand, user needs help to coordinate the design process. Primary needs from the BOP market will be reflected in the designs: those technologies that can meet the basic, sometimes unique needs will be favored (and such needs have not been met due to the fact that mainstream producers have overlooked the BOP users).

Drawing upon these two dimensions, a typology of *shanzhai* products can be proposed. Such a typology distinguishes the *shanzhai* product from its similarity with the industrial design of its prototype product. In summarizing the different *shanzhai* products on the market, and how we might identify, perceive and manage the process of fabricating them we use a simple quadrant map (Figure 3.6). The vertical axis refers to the similarities in the technological dimension of product innovation while the horizontal axis refers to the identification of the products—how people distinguish the *shanzhai* product and the original prototype product. Increased similarity means more potential IPR issues may exist. For example, a counterfeit product is placed at the top-right corner with the highest degree of imitation in both dimensions. It has to be noted that

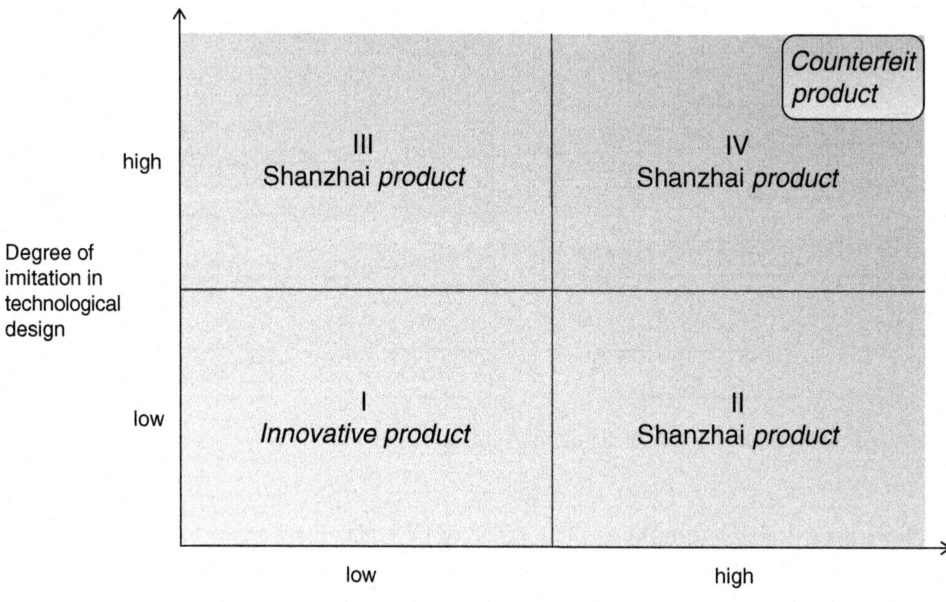

Figure 3.6 A simple quadrant map of degree of imitation

the quadrant-based map is used to simplify the categorization, in reality, a product may be placed in any of the two quadrants simultaneously in Figure 3.6.

In such a typology, presuming the existence of prototype products, all other products fall into the broader scope of *shanzhai* products except for those new products developed with very little imitation in both technological and industrial design. It can be argued that in fact *shanzhai* production is much more widely seen in China. At the same time, the high level of innovation has not been captured and fully understood by scholars in quadrants II, III and IV (i.e. Case 1).

The examination of the demand side of *shanzhai* requires a different lens—imitative entrepreneurship plays an important role in identifying the demands, responding to the demands, and bringing about innovations.

Imitative entrepreneurship in *shanzhai* production

In terms of the behavioral perspective, the core spirit of entrepreneurship is the never-ending pursuit of new market/profit opportunities (Peneder, 2009). This includes the identification of demands from both existing and new market segments. To transform market opportunities into profit, entrepreneurs will also have to translate demands into product design and produce such products. Innovative entrepreneurs do this in the form of inventing while imitative entrepreneurs do this through following and imitating.

The distinction between imitative and innovative entrepreneurship has long been a topic of debate among scholars. Exploration and investigation were conducted to link the types of entrepreneurship to the innovations in firms. However, in the context of *shanzhai* production, it is hard to assign either imitative or innovative characteristics to the entrepreneurial activities, as it contains both. Judging from the sources of product designs, *shanzhai* definitely belongs to 'imitative entrepreneurs' as the degree of innovativeness in core technologies is very limited and the uniqueness of the industrial design is largely missing. Judging from the structure and content in the supply network of *shanzhai*, we may consider them to be the so-called 'innovative nascent entrepreneurs' as they start their business with routines, competencies or offers significantly varying from those of existing organizations (Koellinger, 2008).

It is important not to become overly involved with the complicated debate on the 'innovative or imitative' dichotomy. The primary aim here is to make clear the meaning of entrepreneurship in the context of *shanzhai* production. We take and extend the position put forward by Baumol more than two decades ago: 'an imaginative act of imitation—of technology transfer from its place of origin to new and fertile ground—is also very much an entrepreneurial act' (Baumol, 1988: 4). Entrepreneurs in *shanzhai* production link the place of origin (prototypes) with its fertile ground (demands from BOP market) via imitations in product designs and innovation in the supply network to realize such designs. In this sense, imitative entrepreneurial behaviors can at the same time be innovative.

In the supply network illustrated in Figure 3.5, imitations in *shanzhai* production primarily take place in the product design process. Suppliers of materials and parts are flexible enough to match their supply volume to the needs of *shanzhai* companies (the next section will provide more information on the supply of materials and parts for mobile phones). In this sense, parts suppliers and the *shanzhai* company co-evolve over time, collaborating to meet customer needs from the BOP market. This is also the reason why we choose product design similarity to construct the typology: imitation takes place in product design process in the form of similar technological design and similar industrial design. A higher degree of imitation in these two dimensions always means more potential IPR issues.

Looking at the landscape of *shanzhai* production—imitation in product design and innovation in supply network—we agree with the statement that entrepreneurship is the 'introduction of new economic activities' (Davidsson, 2005; Koellinger, 2008). Accordingly, the follow-up question is: what do entrepreneurs need to introduce such new economic activities here, imitating product design and co-evolving with their parts suppliers? Is the entrepreneur's prior knowledge in the industry relevant?

According to Shane (2000), systematic training and previous experiences in a particular field are relevant to the entrepreneur's ability to sense and take new business opportunities. However, from the analysis of supply network structure we see no significant relevance between an entrepreneur's ability to produce *shanzhai* products and his previous knowledge in the area. Because of the minimum level of technological knowledge required in the product design, entrepreneurs do not necessarily require relevant experience to enter into business.

The manufacturing base and its role in shanzhai production

It is now important to touch on the manufacturing process in *shanzhai* production. After the firm has acquired the necessary product designs, they still face the challenge of sourcing parts and fabricating the parts into the final products. This is often over-looked when examining the *shanzhai* phenomenon. People tend to focus on whether/how the *shanzhai* product is different from its prototype and the design for its core technologies. They also tend to assume that after overcoming the product design barrier, firms can easily transform the design into products. In reality, it can be argued that the sourcing of available parts is even more important and is the primary reason why the copycat phenomenon exists everywhere but the majority occur only in China. In this section we will discuss the supply of *shanzhai* iPhone parts as evidence to support our argument.

Shanzhai electronic parts and accessories

The iPhone is one of the most popular smart phones on the market and is designed by Apple Inc. The demands for Apple parts and accessories are high due to this popularity. Taking the USB data cable as an example, on one hand, the data cable for the iPhone has worn over time and, on the other hand, original parts from Apple are very expensive. This has pushed the emergence of cheap *shanzhai* cables for the iPhone. Figure 3.7 shows two *shanzhai* cables and the genuine one. The comparisons of these products are summarized in Table 3.1.

From Table 3.1 we can see that the performances vary only very little among these three cables. If we assume the durability and life expectancy for these cables are different, would that be a 25 times difference (149:6)? Therefore, for price-sensitive customers *shanzhai* cables would be a much better choice.

There are even more choices in the market, with the price range from ¥6–49, depending on the quality of the materials used. For example, it is possible to find a cable with genuine dock plug but a *shanzhai* connecting cable; it is also possible to find a cable that is made from all or

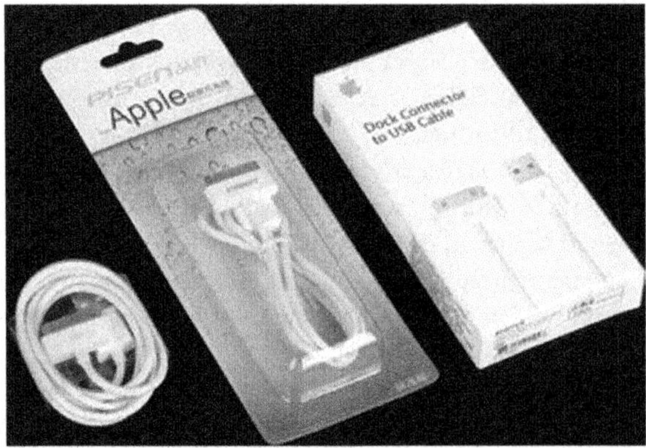

Figure 3.7 Two *shanzhai* cables and the genuine one

Table 3.1 Comparison of *shanzhai* parts and genuine parts in Figure 3.1

	Shanzhai *cable 1 (left)*	Shanzhai *cable 2 (middle)*	*Genuine Apple cable (right)*
Price	¥6	¥12	¥149
Package	No package	Simple package	In box
Plug dimension	2.5mm	2.4mm	2.4mm
Cable length	101mm	79mm	101mm
Transmitting speed	27.137MB/s (write) 21.338MB/s (read)	27.114MB/s (write) 21.399MB/s (read)	27.025MB/s (write) 21.382MB/s (read)
Charging time	2h 30m	2h 25m	2h 25m

Note: Data from independent reviewer and elaborated by author.

no genuine materials. However, it is more of a challenge to find genuine materials, such as a dock. We interviewed several owners of small parts stores in Huaqiang North, Shenzhen:

> You can buy anything you need in this market; [the market] is so capable [of finding what you need]. Technological problem? We don't really worry about that. They say they have the materials from the OEM factories and we don't really care. We buy parts and we fabricate the parts into the product we want. We pay higher price for better parts, as simple as that.
>
> *(Parts store owner A)*

> They have their own channels; they have contacts in the OEM factories. You don't want to know the details and they won't tell you neither. You negotiate the wholesale price with them and they supply what you need.
>
> *(Parts store owner B)*

There are hundreds of parts stores like this in Huaqiang North market. Their annual sales range from RMB 600,000–1,200,000 while the initial investment is around RMB 150,000.

The case of phone accessories reveals one very important fact: the prior production capacity accumulated in OEM manufacturing has enabled Chinese firms to source almost anything that has and has not been manufactured in China. People can now source from raw materials to any middle products in the market. The reasons for this are based on the fact that Chinese manufacturing firms can make good use of their prior learning experience and the knowledge accumulated to enter the supply network for *shanzhai* production (as a parts supplier). Such experiences and knowledge can be easily turned into capacities to supply the parts in demand and components for *shanzhai* products. Regarding the illegality, Chinese manufacturing firms may supply the market with surplus OEM products or middle products on an under-the-table basis. Such surplus products will be bought by *shanzhai* producers and be used in *shanzhai* products.

In either case the supply network relies heavily on the large manufacturing base in China. It is very difficult to replicate the supply network as no other country has a comparable manufacturing base. This existence of a significant production capacity and of the manufacturing base contributes to the fact that shanzhai production is common in China but not in other countries.

A final note

The ethical and governance aspects of *shanzhai* have deliberately been left out of the picture in our discussion. As Baumol *et al.* (2009) pointed out, the relationship between innovation, entrepreneurship and these aspects is important to the development of enterprise culture. However, as a relatively new phenomenon, exploration of the structural elements of *shanzhai* (innovation and entrepreneurship) has higher priority over the contextual elements of *shanzhai* (institutional and governance factors). A good understanding of how *shanzhai* products are produced can form the basis for further research. For research into the contextual issues, see Cheung (2012), Xuesong and Weijie (2010), Mitra and Chunlin (2010).

Conclusion

This chapter has attempted to categorize *shanzhai* products in China and contextualize the phenomenon using technological catch-down and imitative entrepreneurship theories. These theories are not randomly selected. Analysis of the *shanzhai* supply network highlights the relevance of these theories. The discussions are suggestive rather than conclusive in nature, partly because the phenomenon has yet to be fully examined in the same way that has been attempted here. The typology of *shanzhai* products helps overcome the confusion and ambiguities when citing the term '*shanzhai*'. By analyzing the generic supply network for *shanzhai* production, we have identified the fact that the product design process is where most imitation takes place. Further analysis has shown that *shanzhai* production primarily imitates its prototype in technological design and industrial design. In order to reduce costs, *shanzhai* companies normally do not conduct product design, rather, they use turnkey solutions from upstream suppliers (i.e. the turnkey solution from MTK for *shanzhai* mobile phones), or they 'borrow' designs from other prototype products (i.e. *shanzhai* iPhone parts). To do this, they focus on mature technologies, which have lower entry barriers and are easier to modulate. As such, the technological choices of *shanzhai* companies are determined by their imitative product design strategy. What is innovative in this process is that the *shanzhai* companies often re-combine or add functional modules to their product, to enable better services for their customers. Such innovations involve prompt responses to the ever-changing consumer demands, and active and sensitive entrepreneurs are required to make these responses. Many entrepreneurs do imitate others in the product design domain. However, they innovatively insert their companies into the supply network, and co-evolve with the network by creating demands for raw materials, parts and component suppliers. The last and the most important point is that the *shanzhai* product also has cost competitiveness over normal products. As a result, the whole *shanzhai* industries are growing at an extremely fast rate.

Notes

1 Description taken from Wikipedia and edited by author, see https://en.wikipedia.org/wiki/Nintendo_Entertainment_System.
2 If interested, detailed reviews and comparisons of MTK6589 and other chip family can be easily found on any mobile technology forums.
3 MediaTek Inc. is an IC design firm in Taiwan. MTK 6589 is one of its turnkey solutions for downstream mobile phone manufactures.

Bibliography

Barney, J., Wright, M. and Ketchen Jr., D.J. (2001) 'The resource-based view of firms: ten years after 1991', *Journal of Management,* 27(6): 625–641.

Baumol, J.W. (1988) 'Entrepreneurship: productive, unproductive and imitative; or the rule of the rules of the game', Economic Research Report, Chesterton, MD: C.V. Starr Center for Applied Economics.

Baumol, J.W., Litan, R.E. and Schramm, C.J. (2009) *Good Capitalism, Bad Capitalism and the Economics of Growth and Prosperity,* New Haven, CT: Yale University Press.

Bell, M. and Pavitt, K. (1993) 'Technological accumulation and industrial growth: contrasts between developed and developing countries', *Industrial and Corporate Change,* 2: 157–210.

Bell, M. and Pavitt, K (1995) 'The development of technological capabilities: trade, technology and international competitiveness', World Bank Paper, Washington, DC: World Bank, pp. 69–101.

Cheung, M. (2012) 'Shanzhai phenomenon in China: the disparity between IPR legislation and enforcement', *International Review of Intellectual Property and Competition Law,* 43(1): 3–20.

Davidsson, P. (2005) *Researching Entrepreneurship,* New York: Springer.

Eisenhardt, K.M. and Martin, J.A. (2000) 'Dynamic capabilities: what are they?' *Strategic Management Journal,* 21(10–11): 1105–1121.

Hobday, M. (1995) 'East Asian latecomer firms: learning the technology of electronics', *World Development,* 23(7): 1171–1193.

Hobday, M., Rush, H. and Bessant, J. (2004) 'Approaching the innovation frontier in Korea: the transition phase to leadership', *Research Policy,* 33: 1433–1457.

Koellinger, P. (2008) 'Why are some entrepreneurs more innovative than others?' *Small Business Economics,* 31: 21–37.

Mitra, J. and Chunlin, S. (2010) *Innovation, Entrepreneurship and Governance: The Shanzhai Handset Business,* Washington, DC: International Council for Small Business (ICSB).

Peneder, M. (2009) 'The meaning of entrepreneurship: a modular concept', *Journal of Industry, Competition and Trade,* 9: 77–99.

Prahalad, C.K. (2009) *The Fortune at the Bottom of the Pyramid: Eradicating Poverty Through Profits,* 5th edn, Harlow: Pearson Prentice Hall.

Shane, S. (2000) 'Prior knowledge and the discovery of entrepreneurial opportunities', *Organization Science,* 11(4): 448–469.

Shi, Y. and Rong, K. (2010) 'Shanzhai manufacturing and its network behaviours', in *Proceedings of IEEE International Conference on Industrial Engineering and Engineering Management,* pp. 2183–2187.

Teece D.J. and Pisano, G. (1994) 'The dynamic capabilities of firms: an introduction', *Industrial and Corporate Change,* 3: 537–556.

Xuesong, Y. and Weijie, Z. (2010) 'Talk about the protection of intellectual property rights of industrial design in China from the phenomenon of "Shanzhai"', in *Proceedings of 11th International Conference on Computer-Aided Industrial Design and Conceptual Design,* 2: 955–958.

4

Entrepreneurship and Asian business systems

Solee I. Shin

Introduction

"Economic progress, in capitalist society, means turmoil," wrote Schumpeter in 1942, as he laid out his conception of capitalism (1942: 32). His idea of capitalism is revolutionary. Constant changes and turmoil characterize the capitalist process of growth. Furthermore, economic growth, according to Schumpeter, is not merely a function of capital accumulation or continuous business activities, nor is it due to external changes in the environment. Instead, he believes a combination of factors such as business expansion, heightened competition, and rise in wages will work to cyclically undermine and devalue wealth and profit, factors that enable the functioning of the system yet are constantly eliminated by the very working of the system (ibid.: 49).

Schumpeterian growth rather occurs through a series of innovative practices that disrupt and destroy the existing system, and bring revolutionary changes.

> These revolutions periodically reshape the existing structure of industry by introducing new methods of production such as the mechanized factory, the electrified factory, chemical synthesis and the like; new commodities such as the railroad service, motor cars, electrical appliances; new forms of organization such as the merger movement; new sources of supply such as La Plata wool, American cotton, Katanga copper; new trade routes and markets to sell in, and so on.
>
> *(ibid.: 68)*

The introduction of new methods in production, new forms of organization, new models of supply by capitalist entrepreneurs, these are the processes that "incessantly revolutionize the economic structure from *within,* incessantly destroying the old one, incessantly creating a new one" (ibid.: 83). This is the process he labeled "creative destruction."

However, the Schumpeterian model of entrepreneur-driven growth, while placing innovation and entrepreneurial activities at the center of capitalist dynamics, does not fully elaborate on the source of those innovations. The changes that are effected become incorporated into the new system, and destroy the old and are conceived as truly "revolutionary," with their origins completely divorced from the structures in which they were created.

A more recent reworking of his ideas provides a clearer conception of innovation and its sources. Abernathy and Clark (1985) develop a framework to categorize various innovations.

They argue that innovations are not unified, and while "some innovations disrupt, destroy, and make obsolete established competence [in a Schumpeterian way, by completely redefining the requirements needed to gain competitive advantage]; others refine and improve [by providing continuous advancements, efficiency, solutions to existing problems]" (ibid.: 4). However, what they consider crucial in the firms' capacity to innovate is the "fundamental internal reality" of the firm, which "rests on a set of material resources, human skills and relationships, and relevant knowledge" (ibid.: 5).

In examining the US auto industry, Abernathy and Clark point to factors that exist within the firms—their internal reality—as well as its interaction with the immediate outer environment as providing foundations for innovation. This is a useful starting point to consider the sources of entrepreneurial innovation, but also needs reworking if we are to consider innovation and entrepreneurship in cross-national contexts. To examine entrepreneurial innovations in various national settings, we will have to situate them within the context of divergent economic structures and competition, where there are high levels of variation not only in the firms' internal capacity and structures, but also in how competition is structured economy-wide.

Conceptualizing innovations in East Asia

The aim of this chapter is to examine the sources of entrepreneurial innovation in divergent institutional settings. For the purpose of this chapter, the cases will be limited to the three East Asian economies of Japan, Korea, and Taiwan. It is argued that innovation in East Asia has been varied by location, and how it varied has depended upon the institutionalized ways of conducting business and the historical trajectory of economic development. While viewing entrepreneurial innovation as activities situated within the divergent business systems, I will examine how entrepreneurial activities will have to fit within the context of each system, as within the existing recipes for conducting business, in order to be successful. To demonstrate the point, examples are given of various entrepreneurial activities, which brought innovative changes in the retail sector within the three economies, and show how the very ways changes happened fit well with the overall context of the business system.

The main insight here is that even revolutionizing ideas and innovations need to use elements from and build on the existing platform or "package" (Becker, 1995) to gain traction within the system, and especially to become incorporated as standard practice. Acknowledging this continuity of innovation with the system of its origination is not in any way to deny the "newness" of the ideas and practices that were introduced. Rather, it is to situate the practice within a larger context, in which the practice is perceived as new and appealing to those who are accepting it. Socially advancing innovation is not devoid of context, but rather happens as the entrepreneurs grapple with the available ingredients surrounding them, while referring to the elements within the system to come up with new ideas.

Becker (1995) makes this point clear by referring to the available set of interconnected practices and relationships in a given system as a "package." Giving an example of the music world, he discusses various co-dependent elements of the system, such as systems of musical notation, instruments, music theory, artists, composers, audiences, concert halls, and recording studios. He also mentions that since "each piece in the package presupposes the existence of all the others" (ibid.: 304), when one chooses to use one of the elements in creating music, it is easy to take other elements within the system. This way, the package exerts a kind of an inertial force, a type of hegemony that maintains a certain level of stability in the social world.

It is extremely difficult to start from scratch when creating innovations in a world where there are already well-established ways of doing things. Consider Becker's example of Harry Partch, a composer who developed music for a 42-tone scale. Because no 42-tone scale had previously existed, along with inventing the scale, Partch had to invent musical instruments to play it, as well as train a generation of Partch instrumentalists. The training time for a two-hour concert for these students averaged months, compared to the six to nine hours a major orchestra will put in for similar amounts of music. Despite how unconventional Partch's work seems, he still had to rely on various social elements to continue his work: he relied on conventional music halls and distribution channels to perform and sell his products.

The point here is that it is extremely expensive and difficult to create innovations that do not relate to the existing social context, not to mention to make the practice gain wide acceptance. Most innovations, and particularly successful innovations, are rather incremental in the sense that they happen through processes of reworking existing elements within the context of, and in reference to, what is already in place. This not only makes innovation less expensive than starting completely from scratch, but also makes it relatable to the recipients who are already well positioned in the current configuration of the system, of which they are inseparable parts. So the successful innovators are most likely not Harry Partches, but active participants within the system.

So how does this insight regarding incremental and contextual innovation relate to the Schumpeterian idea of "creative destruction"? The experiences in Asian retailing suggest that even if the entrepreneurs referred to and built on the existing elements within each system for innovation, as the practices become incorporated, multiple elements of the old system were destroyed in the end. Innovative entrepreneurship incrementally builds on elements of the system in which it develops, but the changes that follow as adopters of the new practice restructure their behavior surrounding the practice, can in fact bring about "revolutionary" transformations in the system in the way that Schumpeter predicted.

Asian business systems and entrepreneurs

To understand how new innovations relate to the existing social context in Japan, Korea, and Taiwan, we can follow Becker and think of the combination of elements and practices contained in the business world of the three countries as a kind of a "package." In each package, we see entrepreneurs, producers, suppliers, distributors, consumers, retail infrastructure, as well as other often followed methods of building relationships, getting supply deals, assembling products, and running and structuring a business. There are also pronounced inter-country differences in what is contained in the "packages" of different economies. Using Whitley's words, we can also think of the differences in terms of "Asian business systems" (Whitley, 1992).

At the center of the business systems' literature is an examination of how variations in institutional contexts differently affect market practices. Particular combinations in authority structures, firm types, and inter-firm relations produce a set of differences that structure not only the organizational forms of the dominant businesses in different contexts but also strategies at the individual participants' level. This means that managerial practices, and recipes for achieving economic success vary, as well as how entrepreneurs and business people in different contexts "achieve control over major economic entities and so the ways in which they understand the business world and set priorities" (ibid.: 5). Thus, it will be beneficial to briefly summarize the specific inter-country differences, especially the difference in forms and capacity, to examine how the recent innovations in retailing have built on the system characteristics that were already in place.

The most prominent differences between the three countries revolve around the organization of the dominant firms in the production sector. While there are undeniable within-country variations in Japanese, Korean, and Taiwanese economies, the dominant businesses of the three countries show a level of cohesion in how they are structured as well as how they control and coordinate their activities (Whitley, 1992; Hamilton, 1996). The differences in the configuration of business groups as well as practices clearly distinguish one economy from another (Hamilton, 1996; Hamilton and Biggart, 1988), and have developed concurrently as the firms have gradually defined their core activities and how to coordinate them.

For example, in Japan, business groupings called horizontal *keiretsu* dominate the industrial sectors. *Keiretsu* are clusters of firm networks, where the affiliated firms cluster themselves coherently across various markets from finance and capital, production of component parts, as well as general trading (Gerlach, 1992; Lincoln and Gerlach, 2004). Unlike the Korean and Taiwanese business groups, Japanese *keiretsu* are not family-owned groups. Instead, the *keiretsu* are jointly owned and characterized by high level of mutual dependence and subcontracting relationships between the individual firms that belong to the given group cluster, without clear delegation of authority between firms (Lincoln and Gerlach, 2004). The network of firm relationships operates beyond these formalized groupings and pervades much of the Japanese industrial economy through subcontracting relationships, making production a largely cooperative process between affiliated and networked firms with various capacities.

Despite their overwhelming presence in the Japanese economy, the recent growth prospects of these horizontal *keiretsu* have been rather low. Webs of tangled relationships without a central authority structure have made diversification and business expansion a much slower and conflict-laden process for the *keiretsu*. Their relative rigidity in structure and slow decision-making have allowed firms with faster decision-making skills to enter the under-developed sections of the Japanese economy.

In Taiwan, while there are diversified business groups with the capacity to work across multiple sectors, the most representative form is the Chinese family firm. These overwhelmingly small and medium-sized enterprises (SMEs) are the backbone of Taiwan's export-oriented manufacturing economy, responsible for the majority of consumer goods produced in Taiwan for export. These firms have over time formed highly specialized and flexible production networks while maintaining their relative small size and centralized-decision making structure (Feenstra and Hamilton, 2006).

As small and medium-sized family firms, most Taiwanese firms lack cross-sectoral abilities but are well qualified to undertake highly flexible and specialized production of a component part. Since it takes collaboration between multiple firms, each of which specialize in different parts of a product, to produce the final product, the overall export-driven manufacturing system is highly dependent upon external collaboration between the various firms with different specialized capacity.

Contrasting sharply with Taiwan, the firms that dominate the Korean economy are the highly diversified and large family-run business groups, called *chaebols*. The groups control a large number of subsidiaries, which, in the case of the largest group, amount to hundreds in total. A small number of the top business groups are involved in virtually every industrial sector and show high levels of concentration within each sector. The top *chaebols* fiercely compete against each other for a larger share of the overall market, and each group attempts to vertically control the entire production process. Inter-group collaboration is rare and business groups show high levels of diversification, and vertical integration.

These internal patterns in how production activities are coordinated and controlled in the three Asian economies are the foundation, on which subsequent economic changes can build in times of immense changes. As will be shown in the empirical discussion below, entrepreneurs depend on these principles of organizations and patterned responses to them when creating new ideas and practices.

The development of retail markets in Asia

The economic focus of these countries before their respective "retail revolutions" was predominantly production, and primarily for export. Domestic markets were left largely under-developed with the majority of retail sales coming from individually owned mom and pop stores. However, as the series of economic successes led to the internal accumulation of wealth, a richer population, and higher standards of living, while rising costs of production and various economic crises had led to unpredictable overseas sales of domestically produced goods, the future success of the traditional growth strategy that relied solely on export-driven manufacturing became uncertain. At the same time, to the domestic business groups and entrepreneurs, it was gradually becoming clear that vast opportunities lay in the domestic economies of Asia, which were largely "up for grabs."

The retail transformations happened first in Japan, starting sometime during the late 1950s, followed by Taiwan in the late 1980s, and happened last in Korea in the late 1990s. Since the onset of their respective retail revolutions, entrepreneurs in these three countries have introduced new retail formats and technologies that have dramatically reorganized their respective retail sectors. Of course, not all of the introduced technologies and formats worked, and it was not necessarily the first technologies and retail formats that were introduced that became the most successful, disproving the idea of the "first mover advantage" often espoused by business and retail analysts. Instead, the most successful were those entrepreneurs who used the already existing recipes for running successful businesses and making money to apply to a new playing field called modern retailing. These entrepreneurs understood well how to do business in their respective countries, brought in innovations that well suited the pre-existing contexts rather than ones that were completely "out of context," and flexibly modified their retail strategies as the competition changed.

In the next section, I provide examples from three retailers that had a leading role in the respective retail revolutions in the three economies: Japan's Daiei, Taiwan's Uni-President, and Korea's Shinsegae were the first retail market players to introduce the idea of discount retail stores in their countries. The discounter played a crucial role in the retail revolutions of all three economies yet how they came about differs considerably by country.

Japan: Daiei's Isao Nakauchi

Large scale retail transformation in Japan was led by independent retailers who gained influence during the 1960s and 1970s. They were independent from the existing retail structures of primarily mom and pop stores as well as the modern department stores affiliated with the horizontal *keiretsu*. At the time, department store chains, such as Mitsukoshi, Takashimaya, Isetan, and Matsuzakaya, operated as part of *keiretsu* groupings, as the most dominant modern retail format, but showed limitations as they were run largely on a consignment-based system and did not have much control over their floor space. The department stores did not have much influence over the products that were sold and the manufacturer-driven system allowed the suppliers to control sales space and staff as well as pricing (Sternquist *et al.*, 2000; Larke and Causton, 2005).

The emergence of independent retailers such as Daiei and Ito-Yokado led to large changes in the traditional retail sector as they started to introduce previously untried retail formats and technologies. Although the formats they introduced—discounters and hypermarkets—were ideas originating from the West, the retail strategies were modified to fit the context of the Japanese business landscape.

Particularly well known are the entrepreneurial activities of Isao Nakauchi of Daiei. Daiei's Nakauchi, though he is blamed extensively for excessive diversifications that led the debt-laden company to the brink of bankruptcy, did introduce revolutionary changes to Japanese retailing early on and grew Daiei into one of the earliest and most successful retail enterprises that Japan has ever seen.

Nakauchi founded Daiei as a drugstore in 1957 in Osaka. He adopted the motto of "good products, cheaper and cheaper" (Foreign Press Center Japan, 2002), and used various strategies to pass on lower prices to the customer by purchasing overstocks and paying cash for the goods for lower prices. In the manufacturer-driven system of distribution, cartels between store-owners, as well as the multi-layered structure of distribution kept the prices of goods artificially high, so these retail strategies of bulk purchases and price-cutting were highly revolutionary business strategies. Initially started as a drugstore chain, Daiei quickly expanded to sell various types of other consumer goods and by the 1970s had established itself as a chain with a nation-wide presence, exceeding sales of the largest department stores at the time.

Nakauchi's strategies that challenged the existing market power of manufacturers were only made possible from his position as an entrepreneur, independent from the horizontal *keiretsu* clusters, yet as someone with insights into the Japanese consumer market. As an independent retailer, Daiei was able to bypass wholesalers, who were usually part of *keiretsu* networks, and was free to choose the suppliers with whom it wanted to deal and bargain with. This independent position enabled the retailers to undercut the large mark-ups that usually get added to the product after it goes through multiple wholesale layers. Despite numerous attacks by and disputes with large manufacturers[1], Daiei continued its cost-cutting efforts, however, without compromising the quality of the products. They were also the first retailer to introduce and develop private brand products and such market-making efforts led them to become a trusted and a very popular retailer in the early stages of Japan's retailing revolution.

Isao Nakauchi's entrepreneurial activities can be summarized best as identifying a niche. He focused on making assessments of the current state of the Japanese retail market, and devised various strategies to provide alternative models of retail. The innovative practices he introduced were not completely devoid of context but rather derived from his effort to provide solutions to the issues of ubiquitously high prices and an inefficient and convoluted distribution system led by the horizontal *keiretsu*.

These efforts resonated well with the Japanese consumers and were not only followed by many other retailers—notably Ito-Yokado and Jusco—who adopted these strategies and improved upon them, but also set the standards for domestic discount retailing. The particular format over time had gained popularity in the Japanese market place and led to a sharp decline in traditional retail formats.

Taiwan: Uni-President Group and Carrefour

Taiwan's retail development has primarily been led by joint ventures and technology transfers between multinational retailers and domestic business groups. With the overwhelming entry and success of foreign retailers such as 7-Eleven, Carrefour, and Costco, the names of foreign retailers have quickly spread in a country without much local competition. The market share of foreign retailers accounts for a much larger share of the Taiwanese market than that of Korea or Japan, where foreign retailers like Wal-Mart and Carrefour have had trouble expanding.

The reason Taiwan's retail revolution has proceeded through collaboration between local and multinational retailers, rather than by indigenous retail brands[2] is connected to the organization of its production economy. As mentioned above, a large proportion of Taiwan's firms are SMEs, with a strong focus on export-oriented manufacturing. With a high level of specialization and limited cross-sectoral capacity, these firms have not been incentivized to diversify into retailing. This uneven focus on manufacturing in the economy has left the task of domestic market development largely in the hands of a small number of semi-diversified domestic business groups.

However, only a handful of Taiwanese business groups have ever tapped into the retail sector, and most of them ran limited operations as department store retailers. As most business groups did not possess expertise in food and general retailing, they opted for tie-ups with foreign firms as a strategy to develop their retail operations.

Starting with 7-Eleven in 1979, foreign retailers have entered the Taiwanese market through technology transfers with domestic partners. After the Taiwanese government liberalized the retail market in 1986, other business groups[3] have also teamed up with foreign retailers to run retail joint ventures (Hitoshi, 2003). The resulting operations directly reflect the collaborative dynamics in technology and information sharing, as well as the mutual learning process, through which the Taiwanese entrepreneurial activities to develop retailing have unfolded.

The case of Uni-President Group's development into the largest retailer in Taiwan through various foreign partnerships illustrates how Taiwanese entrepreneurs have built on their market characteristics to bring innovations to their market. Uni-President Group was the largest processed food manufacturer in Taiwan, but started developing retail operations in late 1979. Initially, they introduced 7-Eleven stores in Taiwan through a technology transfer agreement with Southland Corporation (Liu, 1992). While relying on foreign branding and know-how in retail technology, Uni-President used their core competency in food manufacturing to supply the 7-Eleven stores. The venture, after a few years, became tremendously successful and positioned itself as the largest retailer in Taiwan.

In 1989, Uni-President also established a joint venture with Carrefour to be the second company in Taiwan to run hypermarkets. This partnership was beneficial for both sides as Carrefour's expertise allowed Uni-President to expand into a new retail segment, while Uni-President's local ties and knowledge proved beneficial for Carrefour's entry into Taiwan. The two sides blended their expertise, to run the stores under the globally recognized Carrefour brand while introducing various innovations that fit the local context. They localized ideas first derived from France such as the "shop-in-shops" concept that combines shopping areas with specialty vendors and food service businesses, to attract local customers, and also used a mix of global and locally inspired promotion strategies such as product promotions and coupon systems (Chinomona and Sibanda, 2013).

The adoption of the localized yet global strategies of Uni-President Group in running both 7-Eleven and Carrefour reflects how the newly introduced retail innovations utilize the readily available "recipes" within the Taiwanese business system. Most local business groups, rather than trying to develop the retail market from scratch by experimenting solely with their own capacities, used their pre-existing connections to foreign retailers and opted for foreign tie-ups. As seen in bids to hire local managers to decide on the various promotions and vendors, they have also attempted to relate the newly introduced retail models to the existing social context by modifying various strategies to something more easily recognizable by the Taiwanese consumers.

These efforts gained wide acceptance within Taiwan over the course of the next two decades, bringing a complete change in the organization of the retail market. Taiwan has developed into an economy with a modern retail sector, yet one with the most international characteristics, an economy with the strongest presence of global retailers in Asia.

Korea: Shinsegae Groups' E-Mart

The *chaebols* are formidable market players, exerting vast influence in nearly every sector of Korea's economy. Previous research shows the important role they have played in Korea's export economy (Amsden, 1992). The retail sector also has been largely organized through the *chaebols*' market-making activities in recent decades. The top *chaebols* were able to use their centralized decision-making structure and large market power to develop the once inefficient retail sector. Shinsegae, a retail *chaebol*, which was a spin-off from the Samsung Group, opened Korea's first hypermarket, E-Mart, in 1993. Shortly after, other *chaebol* groups developed their own hypermarket chains copying Shinsegae. In 1996, LG opened the first location of LG Mart, in 1997, Samsung started operating Homeplus, and in 1998, Lotte Group introduced Lotte Mart. Each of these groups have focused on aggressively expanding their locations and market share vis-à-vis others, and have multiplied in numbers in a short period of time.

As the hypermarket sector was nearing saturation, the same set of *chaebol* retailers also expanded into other retail businesses such as catalog and online sales, specialty retailing and mall operations. Most notably, they systematized neighborhood corner stores, which used to be primarily mom and pop stores, by introducing a retail format called "enterprise-class supermarkets" (or SSMs; Super Supermarkets).[4]

The dramatic change to organized retailing has brought complete change to the Korean retail sector. Between 2000 and 2010, the total traditional market sales nationwide halved (*Hankyoreh*, 2011); a large number of traditional distributors, wholesalers, and merchants were displaced. Hundreds of traditional markets disappeared, and neighborhood supermarkets run by families were largely replaced with standardized SSMs. By the end of 2009, discount stores accounted for 35 percent of all formal retail sales in Korea (Coe and Lee, 2013).

At the center of these changes are the entrepreneurial activities of *chaebols* that introduced innovative store formats and retail technology. The example of Shinsegae's entrepreneurship reflects how the *chaebols* utilize their organizational capacity to bring innovations.

Once a Samsung subsidiary and a department store retailer, Shinsegae has become a leading retailer in Korea. Since 1993, Shinsegae has used their market position as a large *chaebol* and market competitor to thwart competition and introduce novel retail innovations that transformed the retail sector. Their most notable market innovation has been the Korean-style hypermarket called E-Mart, currently the largest and most successful hypermarket retailer in Korea. Over the course of the years, they not only have expanded their operations rapidly, but also have actively taken part in restructuring distribution channels and adopting new technologies. E-Mart was the first to establish their own state-of-the-art distribution center in 1996, and the first to introduce private brand products, which were often processed in their distribution centers' production facilities. The retailer also directly worked with suppliers to cut costs and reduce the length of the product chain.

Shinsegae used their large market power and subsidiaries in various related sectors to develop their retail formats. The Shingsegae group's large-scale capacity allowed the *chaebol* group to internally coordinate its activities and their innovations to gain wide acceptance in Korea in a short period of time. They used their own subsidiaries in construction to build retail locations, and to choose suppliers. Sometimes they blatantly went against the guidelines set by the Fair Trade Commission to give discounts to affiliated suppliers or ones with network ties.

Conclusion: the consequences of the retail revolutions and creative destruction

Successful innovations often bring revolutionary changes in the societies where they are adopted. In all three Asian countries discussed above, the huge success of the discount retailers has led to a rapid transformation of the entire domestic retail sector. Standardized retail supported by innovative technologies became the platform on which Asian populations consumed a diverse range of products.

As Schumpeter's idea of creative destruction predicted, the new retail structures that were adopted necessarily brought destruction to the old structures that had governed the previous systems. To be clear, none of the entrepreneurs who introduced the idea of the discounter and modern chain retailer intended to destroy the existing structure. The destruction rather happened as a necessary consequence of the enterprising activities. In all three countries, traditional wet markets, mom and pop stores, and various wholesale and distribution points disappeared as the locus of distribution and retail shifted to the new structures that had been introduced.

The innovations in retailing did in fact build something new and brought transformative changes, but they are not without context. As seen by the comparisons in how they were adopted across different systems, the process of innovation itself is contained in an inertial system. Within each country, the entrepreneurs used the established ways of doing business, as well as the readily available capacities of their businesses to introduce innovations. While the Japanese Daiei used their market position as a non-horizontal *keiretsu*-affiliated firm to bypass wholesale layers and introduced the idea of discount retailers, the Taiwanese Uni-President Group, aware of their limited capacity to diversify as well as their own retail experience, hooked up with reputable global retailers to bring innovation. Finally, the Korean Shinsegae used their huge market power and vertically-integrated group structure to rapidly spin out retailers that would hegemonically redefine the rules of retailing in Korea.

These respective patterns of innovation and entrepreneurship are not merely coincidental. They reflect long-standing organizational principles that are societally embedded and historically constructed, which guide the actions of even the most innovative entrepreneurs and businesses.

Notes

1 Most notable is the dispute with Matsushita electronics that famously lasted for 30 years after Matsushita found out Daiei was selling their products at a discount price (t'Hooft, 2004).
2 This trend has nonetheless happened but without posing a big threat to the global retail entrants, as can be seen in the case of RT Mart.
3 For example, Makro entered through a joint venture with Holmsgreen Holdings, Carrefour teamed up with Uni-President, Costco entered through a joint venture (JV) with President Group, and French Promodes through a JV with Far Eastern Group.
4 These are medium-sized food retailers measuring between 1,000 and 3,000 sqm. The largest SSMs are HomePlus Express (Samsung-Tesco), LotteSuper (Lotte), and EmartEveryday (Shinsegae).

References

Abernathy, W. and Clark, K. (1985) "Innovation: mapping the winds of creative destruction," *Research Policy*, 14(1): 3–22.

Amsden, A.H. (1992). *Asia's Next Giant: South Korea and Late Industrialization*, Oxford University Press.

Becker, H. (1995) "The power of inertia," *Qualitative Sociology*, 18(3): 301–309.

Chinomona, R. and Sibanda, D. (2013) "When global expansion meets local realities in retailing: Carrefour's glocal strategies in Taiwan," *International Journal of Business and Management*, 8(1): 44–59.

Coe, N. and Lee, Y. (2013) "'We've learnt how to be local': the deepening territorial embeddedness of Samsung-Tesco in South Korea," *Journal of Economic Geography*, 13: 327–356.

Feenstra, R. and Hamilton, G. (2006) *Emergent Economies, Divergent Paths*, Cambridge: Cambridge University Press.

Foreign Press Center Japan (2002) "Troubled supermarket giant Daiei announces three-year management reconstruction plan," January. Available at: www.fpcj.jp/old/e/mres/japanbrief/jb_242.html (accessed 29 May 2013).

Gerlach, M. (1992) *Alliance Capitalism: The Social Organization of Japanese Business*, Berkeley, CA: University of California Press.

Hamilton, G. (ed.) (1996) *Asian Business Networks*, Berlin: de Gruyter.

Hamilton, G. and Biggart, N. (1988) "Market, culture, and authority: a comparative analysis of management and organization in the Far East," *American Journal of Sociology*, 94(Supplement): S52–S94.

Hankyoreh (2011) "10 nyŏn sa'i jŏntongsijang maechul 'pant'omak" [Traditional market sales halve over the last ten years], 20 September. *Hankyoreh News*. Available at: http://m.hani.co.kr/arti/politics/politics_general/497097 (accessed 17 July 2012).

Hitoshi, T. (2003) "The development of foreign retailing in Taiwan," in J. Dawson (ed.) *The Internationalisation of Retailing in Asia*, London: Routledge, pp. 35–48.

Larke, R. and Causton, M. (2005) *Japan: A Modern Retail Superpower*, Basingstoke: Palgrave Macmillan.

Lincoln, J. and Gerlach, M (2004) *Japan's Network Economy: Structure, Persistence, and Change,* New York: Cambridge University Press.

Liu, S.-S. (1992) "7-Eleven in Taiwan," in N.-T. Wang and A. Amsden (eds) *Taiwan's Enterprises in Global Perspective,* Armonk, NY: M.E. Sharpe, pp. 297–308.

Schumpeter, J. (1942) *Capitalism, Socialism, Democracy,* New York: Harper and Brothers.

Sternquist, B., Chung, J. and Ogawa, T. (2000) "Japanese department stores: does size matter in supplier–buyer relationships?," in M. Czinkota and M. Kotabe (eds) *Japanese Distribution Strategy: Changes and Innovations,* London: Thomson, pp. 67–77.

t'Hooft, W. (2004) *Japanese Contract and Anti-Trust Law: A Sociological and Comparative Study,* New York: Routledge.

Whitley, R. (1992) *Business Systems in East Asia,* London: Sage.

5

Growth strategies in early-stage technology-intensive firms

Matti Muhos, Tzong-Ru Lee, Shu-Ting Chang and Pekka Kess

Introduction

The growth and development of companies have been extensively studied over the past few decades, and the literature in this area includes multiple perspectives, such as the static equilibrium theory (Coase, 1937), stochastic models (Gibrat, 1931), transaction cost theory (Williamson, 1975), economics of growth theory (Penrose, 1959), resource-based theory (Penrose, 1959), evolutionary theory (Nelson and Winter, 1982), organizational ecology theory (Hannan and Freeman, 1977), strategic adaptation theory (Sandberg and Hofer, 1982), motivational theory (McClelland, 1961) and configuration theory (Greiner, 1972). Most of these perspectives are concerned with the factors leading to organizational growth. However, configuration (or company lifecycle or stages of growth) perspectives (Muhos *et al.*, 2010; Muhos, 2011) have attempted to clarify managerial challenges and priorities during the early stages of a company development (e.g. Greiner, 1972; Churchill and Lewis, 1983). This perspective relates to the contribution of growth to a company and the manner in which a growing company should be managed (Wiklund, 1998; Davidsson and Wiklund, 2006). The growth configuration literature reveals diverse managerial problem configurations specific to the different growth stages.

Based on recent reviews (see Levie and Lichtenstein, 2010; Muhos *et al.*, 2010; Phelps *et al.*, 2007), numerous models have attempted to clarify the early stages of a company's development. However, there is a need for more focused and context-specific viewpoints to clarify the early stages of technology-intensive companies in different business cultures. The East Asian context remains unexplored from this perspective.

This chapter bridges the above described gap by answering the following research questions: According to the recent empirical literature, what challenges are faced by early-stage technology-intensive companies? How do the experiences of managers in early-stage technology-intensive companies relate to the assumptions of stage frameworks? Which perspectives should be considered when using stage frameworks in the East Asian context?

This retrospective multiple case study seeks to analyse the early stages of technology-intensive companies in East Asia, particularly in the Taiwanese business context. Finnish, Thai and Californian contexts have preliminarily been explored by the authors (see Muhos, 2011; Muhos *et al.*, 2013) with similar methodology. The sequential incident technique (SIT) (Fisher and Oulton, 1999; Edvardsson and Roos, 2001) is used. SIT is a specific type of critical incident technique (CIT) (Flanagan, 1954). Three perspectives were analyzed in each case company for triangulation purposes, that is, one perspective each from company management, operations management and marketing management.

This study devises a four-stage framework, which describes the early stages of technology-intensive companies and demonstrates these stages through three case studies. The main findings of the 14 recent empirical stage models focusing on technology-intensive companies are synthesized into a self-evaluation framework (Muhos, 2011). To test the findings, empirical cases in the Taiwanese context are studied. This will permit an analysis of the gaps between the reality of selected Taiwanese companies and the framework, and will highlight the potential paths for further development of the stage models. In this study, the applicability of the framework is preliminarily tested and context-specific viewpoints analyzed.

This chapter addresses scholars who are interested in the process perspective on company growth and development. The study may also function as a useful guide for those responsible for company growth and development policies, those considering investing in a defined group of companies, and the owners and managers of growing companies.

The results of the study may be effectively used in intermediary organizations as a framework for predicting the early growth stages of technology-intensive companies. The context-specific viewpoints and their impact on the early growth stages of companies have not been widely studied. This study considers the context and provides new insights into the growth and management of technology-intensive companies in the studied context. It is necessary to recognize context-specific viewpoints when the stages of growth frameworks are used.

The following definitions figure prominently in this analysis: First, a technology-intensive firm is an independently owned research- and product development-intensive company whose continuous aspiration to gain valuable, rare and inimitable technological knowledge leads to the creation of new or enhanced products and services (Salonen, 1995; Tesfaye, 1997). Second, the term 'early' refers to the newness of the firm; according to Storey and Tether (1998), a new firm is not more than 25 years old. Third, the term 'stage' corresponds to a unique configuration of variables, for example, strategies, problems and priorities that growing firms are likely to face (Miller and Friesen, 1984; Hanks *et al.*, 1991; Coad, 2007).

The self-evaluation framework

The framework described in Table 5.1 functions as a reference framework for this study. We use this framework to reflect on and analyze the experiences of managers during the stages of early growth.

Table 5.1 Early stages of technology-intensive companies: assumptions of the self-evaluation framework

Stage	*Stage description/assumption codes*
1. Conception and development	A newly established firm is owner dependent (1-A1). At this stage, the objective of the firm is product and/or technology development (1-A2) and the establishment of an early customer base (1-A3). The main activities relate to the business idea (1-A4), identification of a market (1-A5) and resource mobilisation (1-A6). The development of a working prototype is initiated in this stage (1-A7). The management is informal, flexible and creative (1-A8); face-to-face communication is used (1-A9), and the owner makes all the decisions (1-A10). The organization functions as a product development team (1-A11). The cash flow falls into the red due to a lack of product at this point (1-A12).

(Continued)

Table 5.1 (Continued)

Stage	*Stage description/assumption codes*
2. Commercialization	This stage begins with early reference customers (2-A1). At this stage, the objective of the firm is the creation of business and commercialisation of the product (2-A2). The stage is characterized by early manufacturing (2-A3), marketing (2-A4) and initial technical challenges (2-A5). The company learns to produce the product (2-A6). The management style is participative (2-A7) and coordinative (2-A8). The owner and/or a few partners dominate the nucleus of the administrative system (2-A9). Resource generation and survival are key issues (2-A10). The amount of negative cash flow decreases (2-A11).
3. Expansion	At this stage, manufacturing and technical feasibility and market acceptance lead to high growth (3-A1) and constant change (3-A2). The main objective of the firm is to ensure company growth and increasing market share by marketing and manufacturing the product efficiently and in large volumes (3-A3). The company needs to produce, sell and distribute products in large quantities (3-A4), while ensuring efficiency and effectiveness through structures and processes (3-A5). New customers and new market channels require constant attention (3-A6). High growth leads to personnel problems (3-A7). Although the owner and/or entrepreneurial team are central, a sense of hierarchy increases (3-A8). Moderate budgets are allocated and used for communication (3-A9). More specialized functions are considered and added (3-A10). Positive cash flow increases rapidly (3-A11).
4. Stability/renewal	The company faces a slowing growth rate (4-A1) and intense competition in the maturing product market (4-A2). Attempts need to be made to launch a second generation of the product and efficiency issues must be addressed (4-A3). The identification of new markets is essential for company renewal (4-A4). However, cost control and productivity are main concerns in this stage (4-A5). Resulting product generation and profitability improvements enable the firm to maintain growth and reasonable market share (4-A6). The owner is usually supported by or replaced by a professional manager or a management team, and professional management systems are added (4-A7). Strategies, rules, regulations and procedures are standardized and formalized (4-A8). Employees become specialized, but they are non-risk takers (4-A9). Specialized functions are added (4-A10). This stage is characterized by decreasing cash flow (4-A11).

Source: (Muhos, 2011).

Methodology

The present research takes the form of a retrospective multiple case study. According to Yin (1989: 23), 'A case study is an empirical inquiry that investigates a contemporary phenomenon within its real-life context when the boundaries between phenomenon and context are not clearly evident and in which multiple sources of evidence are used.'

In this study, we analyzed three case companies in East Asia, particularly in Taiwan, using sequential interviewing technique (SIT) and semi-structured interviews conducted during the Spring of 2013. Three managerial perspectives were examined for each case company for triangulation purposes, that is, one each from company management, operations management and marketing management. The case study follows the guidelines stipulated by Yin (1989). In an overview of critical incident technique (CIT) methods, Gremler (2004) recognizes several variants of CIT, including SIT, which have been created to consider the sequential character of the process studied (Stauss and Weinlich, 1997). Case studies using SIT elucidate the main sequences of the process under analysis prior to the collection of data. This is advantageous if the process has already been defined empirically. The critical incidents are reflected in the sequential framework presented in the theoretical part of the study. The case reports are based on three separate case studies.

Case studies in Taiwan

The selected case companies are located in Taiwan. According to the Global Entrepreneurship Monitor (2012), within the Asia Pacific and South Asian category, Taiwan is considered an innovation-driven economy, together with Japan, Singapore and the Republic of Korea. Among the innovation-driven economies, the level of early-stage entrepreneurial activity is the highest in Taiwan. Moreover, according to the entrepreneurial framework conditions, Taiwan is a positive example among Asia Pacific and South Asian countries in terms of internal market dynamics, physical infrastructure and social/cultural norms.

The key data on the three case companies is summarized in Table 5.2. The companies Colorful Ninbo International Corporation, Genton Corporation, and I-Hsiang Food Corporation are referred to in the later parts of this chapter as Case A, Case B, and Case C.

Company A

Company A focuses on the development of healthy food products. The concise growth history of company A is presented in Figure 5.1. According to the self-evaluation of the managers, the company was at stage 4 at the end of 2008.

Table 5.2 The key characteristics of the three case companies

Case company	*Established*	*Technology*	*No. of employees, year 2012*	*Sales (million NT$), year 2012*
A	2002	Healthy food products and technology	14	15.8
B	2009	High-tech distributor	8	40.0
C	1999	Catering technology and service	93	168.7

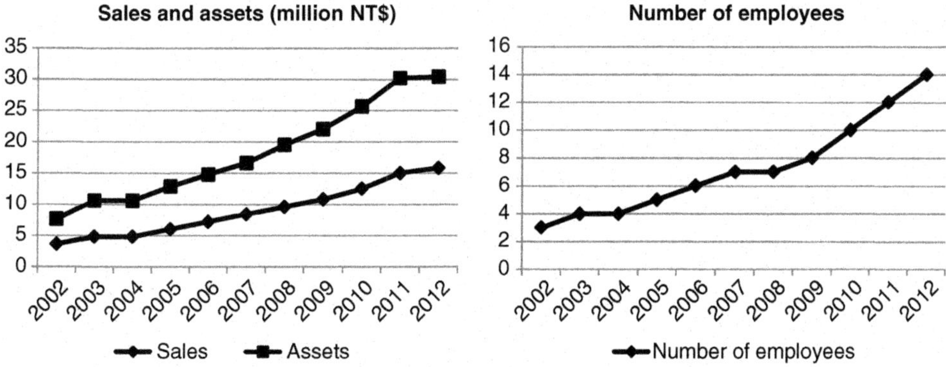

Figure 5.1 Key growth characteristics of case company A

Company A was established in 2002. The company underwent the conception and development stage (S1) between February 2002 and February 2005, the commercialization stage (S2) between March 2005 and March 2010, and the expansion stage (S3) between April 2010 and December 2012. Based on the self-evaluation of the managers interviewed, the company was in the stability/renewal stage (S4) in January 2013. The company had been in this stage for less than one year before the end of the investigation period.

The majority (31) of the incidents (42 recalled altogether) recalled by the interviewees were parallel to the self-evaluation framework. However, 11 contradictory aspects were found in this case. The summary of the parallel incidents related to case company A are presented in Table 5.3.

The summary of the contradictory (fresh) viewpoints collected from company A are presented in Table 5.4.

Table 5.3 Summary of the parallel aspects of company A

Stage	*Parallel aspects*
Stage 1	The owner started the business as a vendor. The company initially developed healthy pot stickers; the owner developed this initial product independently. The early business-to-business customer base of the company comprised newly established firms. Subsequently, the owner decided to develop dishes that were both healthy and delicious. The relatives of the owner financed the company. The owner directly interacted with the employees and customers and took all the business decisions independently. The healthy pot sticker did not become a mature product during this stage.
Stage 2	The business reputation developed during the first stage led to the creation of a customer base for this stage. The owner developed various healthy food products. The target market comprised customers seeking healthy dishes. The owner established his restaurant near a hospital. The company developed new flavours and dishes, and attempted to cook these dishes using less oil and salt. The owner used local raw materials to prepare dishes and learned cooking skills from local chefs. The owner managed the entire business independently. Because there were only a few employees, the owner used emotional management to manage employees. The owner needed more money for expansion; therefore, he financed the business through bank loans. The owner lacked a long-term vision and borrowed money at a high rate of interest, leading to a high financial leverage.
Stage 3	The business had cumulative food production experience. The high feasibility product and efficient production led to high market acceptance of the product and efficient business performance. Because of the initial help extended by the government, the business matured rapidly. It was a good business with a government brand, and it received continuous government help, which generated a positive cycle for the business. The owner expanded the restaurant to increase the number of customers and turnover rate. A central kitchen was established to respond to increasing demand. The owner began focusing on the souvenir market to create a new business line. New employees were hired due to an increase in the number of customers. The company also hired new employees, including professional and experienced chefs, an assistant and restaurant manager with professional skills. The owner faced some personnel problems; he considered hiring a professional manager, but he continued to remain the key figure managing the business during this stage. The owner continued to handle the interaction and communication with employees, customers and educational circles. The cash flow increased rapidly due to the business expansion.

(Continued)

Table 5.3 (Continued)

Stage	*Parallel aspects*
Stage 4	Recently, the topic of health has been receiving widespread attention. Increasing numbers of restaurants near hospitals have started selling healthy dishes. The company developed souvenirs as a second-generation product. The owner intended to add the production of this second-generation product to the original production line, and extend the effectiveness and efficiency of the original production line for another product. The second-generation product (souvenir) enabled the business to increase its market share and promoted the growth cycle of the business. The owner standardized many processes, such as the production process, employee training and development process, to reduce costs. At this stage, the owner was ready to hire a professional manager. The concept of a professional management system matured during this stage. Employees became more specialized; for example, there were employees who served as specialized restaurant managers and specialized chefs.

Table 5.4 Summary of the contradictory viewpoints of company A

Stage	*Fresh viewpoints*
Stage 1	Because company A was a micro-sized company, it did not have an operational model, and at the time, the owner did not think that there was a need to develop such a model.
	Besides the owner, there were only three employees. The owner did not need to focus on managing employees.
	The cash flow was not in the red. The costs of the micro-sized business were low; therefore, it was not difficult to recover costs. The company had a positive cash flow.
Stage 2	According to the owner, the cash flow is rarely in the red during the commercialization stage in this type of business in Taiwan.
Stage 3	The owner developed a unique cooperation relationship with the education circles to reduce the cost of university–industry cooperation.
	There was no need to increase the production volume by outsourcing the production process. The company chose to produce all the products internally.
Stage 4	The growth of cash flow did not become more flat; however, this may happen later because the business has just entered stage 4.
	The owner did not add any specialized functions to the business. The owner did not assign business functions, such as product development, management or marketing, to specialized teams or employees. The owner was deeply involved in these functions and managed them independently.
	The owner continued to improve the original products.

Company B

Company B focuses on the distribution of high-tech products. The concise growth history of company B is presented in Figure 5.2. Company B was established in 2009. The company underwent the conception and development stage (S1) between April 2009 and June 2010 and the commercialization stage (S2) between July 2010 and November 2011. The company entered the expansion stage (S3) in January of 2012 and it had been in this stage for over one year when the analysis began.

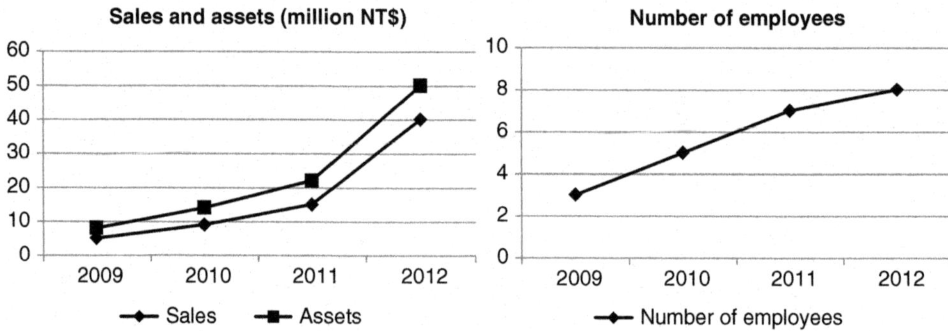

Figure 5.2 Key growth characteristics of case company B

The majority (18) of the incidents (30 recalled altogether) recalled by the interviewees were parallel to the self-evaluation framework. However, 12 contradictory aspects were also found in this case. The summary of the parallel incidents related to company B are presented in Table 5.5.

The contradictory viewpoints collected from company B are summarized in Table 5.6.

Table 5.5 Summary of the parallel aspects of company B

Stage	*Parallel aspects*
Stage 1	Three people were involved in this business and the owner closely cooperated with his two friends (partners). The owner started the business as an agent of foreign technology rather than as a producer of this technology. The owner was only responsible for the branding and distribution functions of the business. A flexible management style was used. In stage 1, the owner managed the business independently. The owner assigned work to his partners according to their past job experience. The company received financing from relatives. The owner directly contacted customers and enterprise partners.
Stage 2	In this stage, the owner handed over the authority to manage the business to his partners. The owner started lowering the proportion of agent business and began planning his own product line. The owner extensively communicated with the current customers to seek their feedback for the new product line. If a customer wanted to try the new product, the owner provided free test samples to get early feedback and to increase customer involvement.
Stage 3	In this stage, the sales volume, market share and market acceptance of the business increased. The company hired a technical consultant to provide technical advice and education to its customers, thereby differentiating the business in the market. The company relocated its factory to China to lower production costs. Owing to language similarities between Taiwan and China, it was easier for the owner to communicate with the Chinese employees than the employees of other comparable markets. The company explored foreign markets (new markets) to increase their market share. As a part of this initiative, they hired foreign employees; however, this created some human resource problems, including training of foreign employees and communication barriers. The business was profitable and the cash flow increased rapidly. Owing to the nature of the business, the owner needed to carefully monitor the laws; however, it was difficult to track all the foreign laws. The company implemented a marketing model for the sales staff and began expanding its portfolio of products and services. Because of business expansion, the company began facing the need for additional financial resources.
Stage 4	*Not applicable because the company has not reached this stage yet.*

Table 5.6 Summary of the contradictory viewpoints of company B

Stage	*Fresh viewpoints*
Stage 1	The early customer base was accumulated by the owner's past work experience; therefore, he did not need to create a new customer base.
	Because the owner identified himself as an agent, he did not need to manufacture and develop products. The owner had outsourced the manufacturing.
	The owner had assigned responsibilities to each of the partners during the initial stage of the business.
	The owner believed that the business should be systematized at this stage itself.
	The partners had strong past work experience and the owner used their experience to establish the business.
	The business was already profitable at this stage. Owing to his previous work experience, the owner knew how to avoid losses.
	Venture capital firms have a short-term vision, making it difficult to persuade them to invest in new businesses. Therefore, the owner sought financing from relatives.
Stage 2	Although the owner started to improve the standards of the products, he continued to play the role of a distributor rather than a producer.
	The business was already profitable in this stage; therefore, the cash flow was not in the red.
Stage 3	The manner in which the owner managed the business did not change from stage 2 to stage 3.
	The owner continued to run the business as a distributor; therefore, no products were manufactured by the company.
	The owner had already standardized the processes of the company although the business had not entered stage 4 yet.
Stage 4	*Not applicable because the company has not reached the stage yet.*

Company C

Company C focuses on catering service and technology. The concise growth history of company C is presented in Figure 5.3. According to the self-evaluation of the managers, the company was at stage 4 when the interviews were conducted.

Company C was established in 1999. The company underwent the conception and development stage (S1) between January 1999 and August 2005, the commercialization stage (S2) between September 2005 and December 2009 and the expansion stage (S3) between January 2010 and December 2012. Based on the self-evaluation of the managers interviewed, the company was in the stability/renewal stage (S4) in January 2011. The company had been in this stage for over two years when the investigation started.

The majority (19) of the incidents (28 recalled altogether) recalled by the interviewee were parallel to the self-evaluation framework. However, nine contradictory aspects were also found in this case. The parallel incidents related to company C are summarized in Table 5.7.

The contradictory viewpoints collected from company C are summarized in Table 5.8.

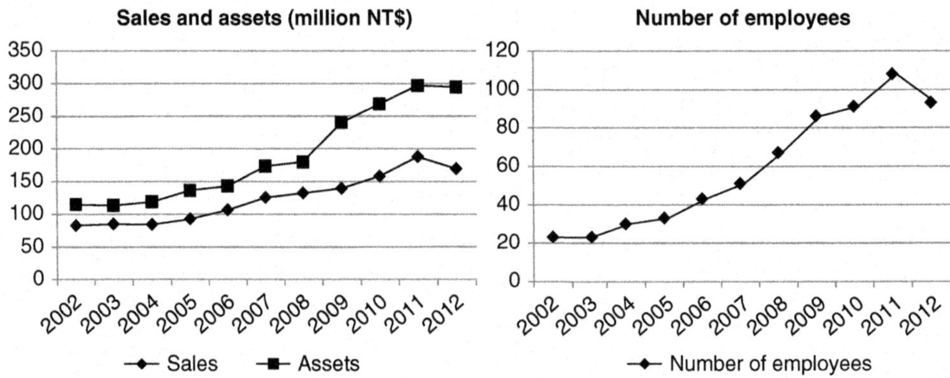

Figure 5.3 Key growth characteristics of case company C

Table 5.7 Summary of the parallel aspects of company C

Stage	*Parallel aspects*
Stage 1	The catering service and technology company was established and financed by a parent company by acquiring a competitor's equipment and factory. The target customers of the company were students, including elementary school, junior high school and senior high school students. Despite the existence of a management structure, the owner had to communicate with the employees of the original company and new customers. The owner had to make decisions independently.
Stage 2	The company had to deal with both the old customers of the acquired company and its new customers. The government invited bids for build-operate-transfer (BOT) projects, in which the owner saw a significant business opportunity for the company. The owner used new and innovative ways to market its service (e.g. educating students about nutrition at every school and playing games with students). BOT projects became a new domain for the company; therefore, the owner needed to learn how to produce food products and train new dieticians. Dieticians and the hygiene management staff worked together to manage the manufacturing process. The government is concerned about the quality of food that is served to students. The owner found an effective way to address this issue by developing a unique inspection technology, thereby providing the business with a competitive advantage.
Stage 3	The owner assembled a group of dieticians and combined nutrition information with the marketing of their service. These initiatives attracted the leaders of schools. The owner established new factories to attract customers and win their confidence. This enabled the company to increase its market share. The technological and manufacturing processes became mature and the business grew steadily. The company expanded its factories to increase the efficiency of the manufacturing process and to monitor quality easily. The company began developing frozen products and built an internet platform as a new sales channel. Producing new products by using old equipment enabled the company to raise capacity and lower costs.
Stage 4	Undoubtedly, there are periods of slack in the student market and the company could make losses during such periods. Therefore, the owner needed to explore other markets. Before developing new products, the owner focused on developing a special selection of dishes for the new years on lunar calendar. Subsequently, the owner developed frozen foods as the second-generation product. The manufacturing process was standardized. During this stage, the owner required the employees to develop professional skills further.

Table 5.8 Summary of the contradictory viewpoints of company C

Stage	*Fresh viewpoints*
Stage 1	The owner was originally an employee of the parent company, and this parent company acquired another company, company C. The owner was assigned to manage the new business. The company was not established from scratch. The owner used the management structure of the parent company to manage the new business. Because of the acquisition, the owner received the employees and technology from the original company. He did not need to hire and train new employees or develop new technology. The company had already started earning profit during this stage.
Stage 2	The company was already earning profit; therefore, the cash flow was not in the red.
Stage 3	There was no serious human resource problem because the employees originally belonged to the parent company. The management structure of the parent company was already established; therefore, there were no structural management problems.
Stage 4	Owing to the characteristics of this industry, the competition in the BOT market is not as severe as that in the catering service market. The second-generation products only improved the growth rate marginally; therefore, it could not be treated as a new business line.

Cross case analysis

In Table 5.9, the number of parallel and contradictory incidents is analyzed based on the three cases. Overall, 100 critical incidents relating to early stages of growth were collected and analyzed. Of the total number of incidents, 68 were parallel to the self-evaluation framework and 32 were contradictory to the assumptions of this framework. In other words, the majority of the incidents supported the self-evaluation framework; this finding partially supports the applicability and further development of such a model in the East Asian context.

Table 5.9 Number of parallel and contradictory incidents

Case	*No. of parallel incidents on stage 1*	*No. of parallel incidents on stage 2*	*No. of parallel incidents on stage 3*	*No. of parallel incidents on stage 4*	*Total no. of parallel incidents*
A	8	6	10	7	31
B	5	4	9	*not applicable*	18
C	3	6	6	4	19
Total	16	16	25	11	68
	No. of contradictory incidents on stage 1	*No. of contradictory incidents on stage 2*	*No. of contradictory incidents on stage 3*	*No. of contradictory incidents on stage 4*	*Total no. of contradictory incidents*
A	3	3	2	3	11
B	7	2	3	*not applicable*	12
C	4	1	2	2	9
Total	14	6	7	5	32

However, in relative terms, more contradictory aspects were found in this study than in those in the three previously studied contexts in Thailand, Finland and the USA. In these contexts, the proportion of the parallel aspects was higher. Moreover, the descriptions of the framework in this study matched the experiences of the managers less well than those in the earlier contexts. The results indicate that there are many context-specific issues that need to be considered in the East Asian context when using the self-evaluation framework presented in the theoretical part of this study.

Conclusion

In this chapter, the four-stage framework that described the early stages of technology-intensive companies was created and preliminarily tested. In this study, the applicability of the four-stage self-evaluation framework and the context-specific viewpoints were investigated. It is necessary to understand these viewpoints when using the framework in East Asia. The main findings are presented in the following paragraphs.

First, through the meta-analytical synthesis, a four-stage self-evaluation framework for early-stage technology-intensive companies was developed. These four stages included conception and development, commercialization, expansion and stability/renewal. Table 5.1 of this study details these stages. This study employed the synthesis as a set of assumptions that were tested using three case studies.

Second, three cases from Taiwan were analyzed to test how the experiences of the managers related to the assumptions of the framework in the East Asian context. The applicability of the framework was preliminarily tested by investigating the number and content of parallel aspects in relation to the assumptions of the framework. The majority of the incidents supported the self-evaluation framework; this finding provides partial support for the applicability and further development of such a model in the East Asian context. However, in relative terms, more contradictory aspects were found in this study than in those in the three previously studied contexts in Thailand, Finland and the USA, and the descriptions of the framework matched the experiences of the managers less well than those in the contexts studied earlier.

Third, the contradictory (fresh), context-specific viewpoints of the stage framework in the East Asian context were clarified. Tables 5.4, 5.6 and 5.8 summarize the stage-specific fresh perspectives. The following types of contradictory incidents were found: In the *conception and development stage*, Taiwanese companies often do not need to start from scratch. This is because some companies may have the backing of multi-generation family businesses, some may be established as spin-offs by the parent company and the owner-manager of a new company may have other existing businesses. These backgrounds provide significant support in terms of human and financial capital, market-ready technologies, existing customer bases and other types of resources that enable the company to become profitable during the first stage of growth. Some of the case companies in our study already had a positive cash flow in the first stage of growth. Moreover, Taiwanese firms seem to prefer resource generation through families as compared to other sources; family-based funding is considered to be more reliable, cost-efficient and patient than venture capital firms and banks.

In the *commercialization stage*, the most common contradiction relates to positive cash flow and the profitability of the business. New firms aim to become profitable from the beginning by obtaining financing from families and friends and support from existing businesses. The establishment of a new business seems to be part of a long-term plan of a broader network of people (and generations). In the *expansion stage*, the company may achieve growth through a multifaceted network, that is, the company may be able to, for example, rapidly develop tested managerial structures and systems with the network's support. The feeling of belongingness to the broader network may increase loyalty and minimize problems among employees. The owner may retain managerial authority during this stage.

Finally, in the *stability/renewal stage*, the company may create a dominant position for itself in the market, which may result in decreased competition. The owner-manager may retain managerial authority and continue to be deeply involved in the management of business operations. Instead of developing new types of product categories/generations, companies may focus on the continuous improvement of the existing products.

In conclusion, we created and preliminarily tested the four-stage framework that described the early stages of technology-intensive companies. The three cases that were evaluated in the study primarily supported the assumptions of the framework. The empirical stage framework is an effective tool for reflecting on and predicting the challenges faced during the early development of a company. Moreover, this study revealed numerous context-specific viewpoints that were contradictory to the framework; companies in different contexts face culture- and context-specific issues in early stages of their growth. Growth is a multidimensional phenomenon, and each early-stage technology-intensive company is unique. Based on the proportion of contradictory aspects, special attention should be paid to further analyzing the development of stage 1 (conception and development), in the Taiwanese context and in the broader East Asian context.

The case-study strategy using SIT proved effective for the open-ended analysis of early growth, considering the sequential character of the process. The construct validity of the study was based on a sound research plan, multiple sources of evidence, synergy between quantitative and qualitative data and an established chain of evidence. Analytic generalization (generalization to a theory) of the findings is possible to build context-specific frameworks that are applicable to the Taiwanese context. The findings of the study cannot be generalized to other countries or business contexts and are based on the time of data collection. Case-study protocol was followed and a database was established, permitting further testing of the findings. In future studies, additional East Asian business contexts could be evaluated by taking advantage of the research strategy presented in this study. Moreover, the Taiwanese context should be studied further using more cases and in-depth analyses of different industries and sectors.

Bibliography

Churchill, N.C. and Lewis, V.L. (1983) 'The five stages of small business growth', *Harvard Business Review,* 61(3): 30–50.

Coad, A. (2007) 'Firm growth: a survey', *Max Planck Institute Papers on Economics and Evolution,* 6: 1–72.

Coase, R.H. (1937) 'The nature of the firm', *Economica,* 4(16): 386–405.

Davidsson, P. and Wiklund, J. (2006) 'Conceptual and empirical challenges in the study of firm growth', in *Entrepreneurship and the Growth of Firms,* Cheltenham: Edward Elgar Publishing.

Edvardsson, B. and Roos, I. (2001) 'Critical incident techniques', *International Journal of Service Industry Management,* 12(3): 251–268.

Fisher, S. and Oulton, T. (1999) 'The critical incident technique in library and information management research', *Education for Information,* 17(2): 113–125.

Flanagan, J.C. (1954) 'The critical incident technique', *Psychological Bulletin,* 51(4): 327–358.

Gibrat, R. (1931) *Les inégalités économiques,* Paris: Recueil Sirey.

Greiner, L. (1972) 'Evolution and revolution as organizations grow', *Harvard Business Review,* 50(4): 37–46.

Gremler, D. (2004) 'The critical incident technique in service research', *Journal of Service Research,* 7(1): 65–89.

Hanks, S.H., Watson, C.J. and Jansen, E. (1991) 'Toward a configurational taxonomy of the organization life cycle', in G. Hills and R. LaForge (eds) *Research at the Marketing/Entrepreneurship Interface,* Chicago: University of Illinois Press.

Hannan, M.T. and Freeman, J. (1977) 'The population ecology of organizations', *The American Journal of Sociology,* 82(5): 929–964.
Levie, J.D. and Lichtenstein, B.B. (2010) 'A terminal assessment of stages theory: introducing a dynamic states approach to entrepreneurship', *Entrepreneurship Theory and Practice,* 34(2): 317–350.
McClelland, D.C. (1961) *The Achieving Society,* Princeton, NJ: Van Nostrand.
Miller, D. and Friesen, P.H. (1984) 'A longitudinal study of the corporate life cycle', *Management Science,* 30(10): 1161–1183.
Muhos, M. (2011) *Early Stages of Technology Intensive Companies,* Oulu: University of Oulu.
Muhos, M., Kess, P., Phusavat, K. and Sanpanich, S. (2010) 'Business growth models: review of past 60 years', *International Journal of Management and Enterprise Development,* 8(3): 296–315.
Muhos, M., Kess, P., Rasochova, L. and Foit, D. (2013) 'Early stages of technology-intensive companies in Southern California', in *Proceedings of Technology Innovation and Industrial Management Conference* (TIIM 2013), Phuket, Thailand, 29–31 May, pp. S5 193–199.
Nelson, R.R. and Winter, S.G. (1982) *An Evolutionary Theory of Economic Change,* Cambridge, MA: Belknap Press.
Penrose, E.T. (1959) *The Theory of the Growth of the Firm,* New York: John Wiley and Sons.
Phelps, R., Adams, R. and Bessant, J. (2007) 'Life cycles of growing organizations: a review with implications for knowledge and learning', *International Journal of Management Reviews,* 9(1): 1–30.
Salonen, A. (1995) *International Growth of Young Technology-Based Finnish Companies,* Helsinki: Finnish Academy of Technology.
Sandberg, W.R. and Hofer, C.W. (1982) 'A strategic management perspective on the determinants of new venture success', in K.H. Vesper (ed.) *Frontiers of Entrepreneurship Research,* Wellesley: Babson College, pp. 204–237.
Stauss, B. and Weinlich, B. (1997) 'Process-oriented measurement of service quality', *European Journal of Marketing,* 31(1/2): 33–55.
Storey, D.J. and Tether, B.S. (1998) 'Public policy measures to support new technology-based firms in the European Union', *Research Policy,* 26(9): 1037–1057.
Tesfaye, B. (1997) 'Patterns of formation and development of high-technology entrepreneurs', in D. Jones-Evans and M. Klofsten (eds) *Technology, Innovation and Enterprise: The European Experience,* London: Macmillan, pp. 61–106.
Wiklund, J. (1998) *Small Firm Growth and Performance: Entrepreneurship and Beyond,* Jönköping: Jönköping International Business School.
Williamson, O.E. (1975) *Markets and Hierarchies: Analysis and Antitrust Implications, a Study in the Economics of Internal Organization,* New York: Free Press.
Xavier, S.R., Kelley, D., Kew, J., Herrington, M. and Vorderwülbecke, A. (2012) *Global Entrepreneurship Monitor 2012 Global Report,* London: GEM.
Yin, R.K. (1989) *Case Study Research: Design and Methods,* Beverly Hills, CA: Sage Publications.

Social factors and entrepreneurship

6

A theory of the ethnically homogeneous middleman group: an institutional alternative to contract law (with an Afterword)*

Janet Tai Landa

Introduction

Central to the economics of property rights-public choice theory[1] is the recognition that laws and institutions are important in promoting the efficiency of an economy. One of these institutions is the law of contracts. Contract law, via its role in constraining traders from breach of contract, reduces transaction costs and hence facilitates exchange.[2] But how do traders cope with the problem of contract uncertainty in an environment where the legal framework is nonexistent or poorly developed? The work of anthropologists such as Alice Dewey (1962) on Chinese traders in Java, and Cyril Belshaw (1965) on traders in "traditional" markets suggests that traders *personalize* or *particularize* exchange relations as a way of coping with contract uncertainty.

Since the details of how personalistic exchange relations function as substitutes for contract law have not been discussed by these writers nor by others working in this field, first-hand fieldwork was necessary. Questionnaire surveys of and interviews with Chinese middlemen engaged in the marketing of smallholders' rubber in Singapore and West Malaysia in 1969[3] revealed that (a) the marketing of smallholders' rubber—through the various levels of the vertical marketing structure—was dominated by a middleman group with a tightly knit kinship structure consisting of four clans (Tan, Lee, Ng, Gan) from the Hokkien-Chinese ethnic group; (b) that mutual trust and mutual aid formed the basis for the particularization of exchange relations among Chinese middlemen; and (c) that within the Chinese economy, transactions among middlemen were based on credit, while Chinese middlemen used cash transactions with indigenous smallholders to reduce contract uncertainty.

The fieldwork, the subsequent analysis of data, and the findings revealed that Chinese middlemen were not just a random collection of Chinese traders. Rather, they were linked together in complex networks of particularistic exchange relations to form an ethnically homogeneous middleman group (EHMG). But the real significance of the visible, surface structure of the EHMG lies in its underlying deep structure: the invisible codes of ethics, embedded in the personalized exchange relations among the members of the EHMG, which function as constraints against breach of contract and hence facilitate exchange among Chinese middlemen.

The EHMG thus reveals itself to be a low-cost club-like institutional arrangement, serving as an alternative to contract law and the vertically integrated firm, which emerged to economize on contract enforcement and information costs in an environment where the legal infrastructure was not well developed.

Two recent studies confirm my findings. Clifford Geertz (1978) rationalizes the "institutional peculiarities" of the bazaar economy (e.g., "clientalization," the pairing off of buyers and sellers in recurrent transactions) in terms of the bazaar's function in reducing information costs under contract uncertainty. Richard Posner (1980, p. 26), in his insightful paper on institutions of primitive societies, discusses alternative responses for coping with the costliness of contract uncertainty:

> Another response to market transaction costs is the transformation of an arms-length contract relationship into an intimate status relationship. In some primitive societies if you trade repeatedly with the same man he becomes your blood brother and you owe him the same duty of generous and fair dealing that you would owe a kinsman. This "barter friendship" resembles the pairing of buyers and sellers in bazaars that Geertz noted. It is a way of bringing reciprocity into the exchange process and thereby increasing the likelihood that promises will be honored despite the absence of a public enforcement authority.

Independent of the work of Geertz and Posner, this chapter develops a theory of the EHMG, using a property rights-public choice approach and drawing on the economics of signaling. The second section of the chapter develops a theory of the emergence of the EHMG as a result of individual choices, on the part of many interdependent traders, to join a network of personalistic exchange relationships. The third section develops a theory of codes of ethics, embedded in kinship/ethnic relations, as a functional equivalent to the law of contracts. The fourth section develops a theory of the EHMG as an efficient institutional arrangement for economizing on information costs in an environment characterized by imperfect information. The concluding section will suggest some implications of our theory for further research.

A theory of the formation of the ethically homogeneous middleman group: an analysis of particularistic exchange under contract uncertainty

Standard theories of exchange (Edgeworth and Walrasian models) depict competitive trade as an impersonal process of exchange, because these theories refer to a zero transaction costs economy with no contract uncertainty. In such an economy, there is no need to identify trading partners nor any reason for the institution of contract law since trading partners can be regarded as homogeneous with respect to contract behavior. Thus, impersonal market forces alone determine the pairing of buyers and sellers. Under conditions of contract uncertainty with positive transactions costs, on the other hand, a rational trader will not indiscriminately enter into impersonal exchange relations with anonymous traders. At any particular point in time, an individual is embedded in a "social structure"[4] with "rules of the game" that serve to constrain his behavior. Hence, a rational trader will enter into particularistic exchange relations with traders bound by institutional constraints whom he knows to be trustworthy and reliable in honoring contracts.

In order to choose a particularistic network of trading partners that will minimize the out-of-pocket costs of protection of contracts, a rational trader will equip himself with a "calculus of relations" (Fortes, 1969). Such a calculus allows the trader to rank all traders in a market according to a small number of categories corresponding to different "grades" of traders, in descending

Table 6.1

	Categories of social relations	Grades/ranking
A. (Insiders)	1. Near kinsmen from family	1
	2. Distant kinsmen from extended family	2
	3. Clansmen	3
	4. Fellow villagers from China	4
	5. Fellow Hokkiens	5
B. (Outsiders)	6. Non-Hokkiens (Teochews, Cantonese, etc.)	6
	7. Non-Chinese (Malays, Europeans, etc.)	7

order of trustworthiness.[5] Consider the system of discriminatory rankings established by a typical Hokkien trader (call him "Ego") as shown in Table 6.1.

The system of discriminatory rankings of traders can be represented by the use of a von Thünen series of concentric circles to depict differences in grades of trading partners, with the best grade located at the center. Assume smooth differences in the grades of trading partners up to the first ethnic boundary separating Hokkiens from non-Hokkiens; thereafter assume a significant change in the grade of partners after crossing the Hokkien-Chinese boundary and an abrupt change as the major ethnic boundary is crossed. See Figure 6.1.

Assume that Ego, equipped with this subjective calculus of relations, begins his choice of a least-cost network of trading partners. The cost implications of five homogeneous trading

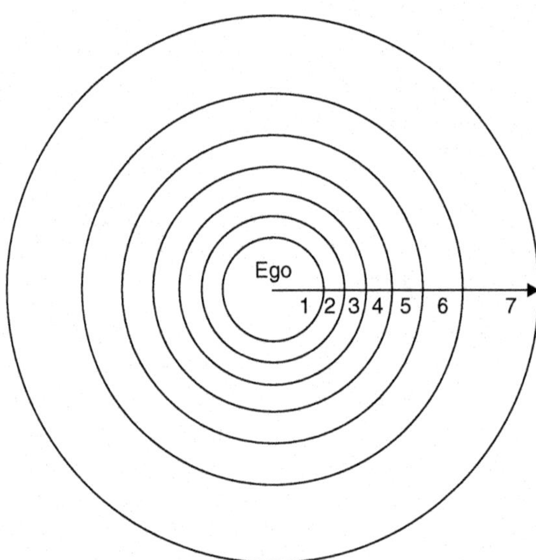

1. Near kinsmen from family
2. Distant kinsmen from extended family
3. Clansmen
4. Fellow-villagers
5. Fellow-Hokkiens
6. Non-Hokkiens
7. Non-Chinese

Figure 6.1 Von Thünen concentric circles to depict seven grades of trading partners

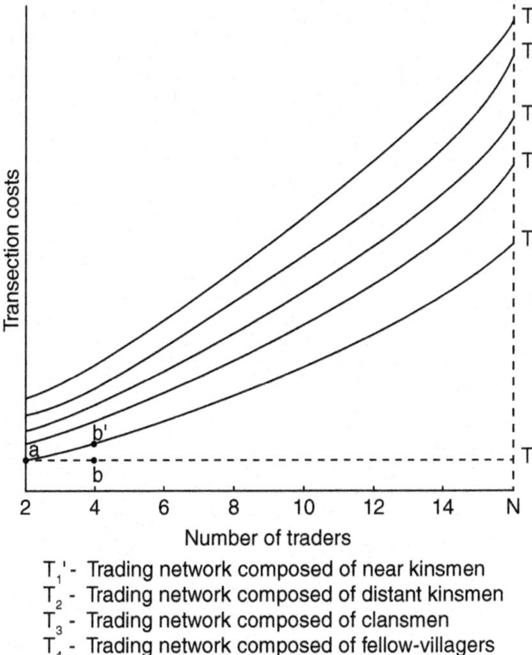

Figure 6.2 Cost implications of five homogeneous trading networks composed of different grades of traders

networks of size *N*, each composed of a different grade of traders, are illustrated in Figure 6.2. Note that each transactions-cost curve rises as the size of the trading network increases. The rising transaction-cost curve is due to two kinds of costs: (a) coordination costs of interdependent traders rise as the network increases in size, because the coordination costs of two isolated pairs of traders are lower than the coordination costs of two pairs of traders connected in a network. If we start from two traders at point *a*, the movement will not be from *a* to *b* on the horizontal transaction-costs curve T_1, as the size of the network increases from two to four traders. Rather, the movement is from *a* to *b′* on the rising transaction-cost curve T_1'; (b) costs of contract enforcement rise as the number of interdependent traders in the trading network increases. As a trading network increases in size, it is increasingly vulnerable to the antisocial behavior of even one trader who, in breaking his contract, may cause "chain reaction" effects of a breach (Landa, 1976).

Faced with five trading networks of size *N*, a rational trader will choose the least-cost trading network, $T'_1(N)$ since $T_5(N) > T_4(N) > \ldots T'_1(N)$. With a larger network of trading partners, with fixed group size *K*, Ego will choose all his trading partners from category 1 before moving outward to the next category. As Ego moves outward from the center, members of his trading network or "club" will be chosen from ever-widening circles with the result that "club" members become increasingly more heterogeneous as more than one grade of trading partners are included. The transaction-cost implications of two trading networks, T_1 and T_2, for a fixed group size *K*, each with a different "mix" of trading partners, are illustrated in Figure 6.3. T_1 is drawn with a discontinuity at *Y* to denote that beyond *Y*, costs rise abruptly as trading partners are chosen from a different ethnic group (outsiders). Such a discontinuity manifests itself by Ego's choice of a well-defined ethnically homogeneous middleman network, with membership size *Y*. The relevant transaction-costs curve

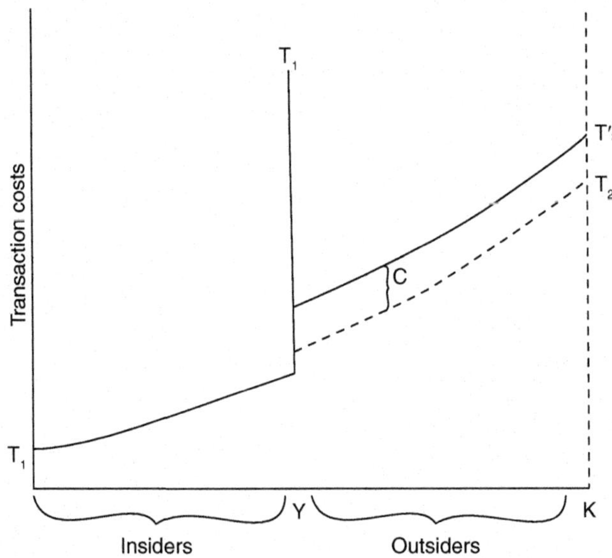

Figure 6.3 Cost implications of two trading networks with differences in the "mix" of trading partners

for the homogeneous network is T_1, which has a sharp kink at the group boundary. For transactions outside the ethnic boundary, Ego resorts to the use of cash to reduce contract-enforcement costs to zero. Were there no opportunity costs in using cash, the relevant transaction-cost curve for the heterogeneous trading network with membership size K would be T_2. But since there are opportunity costs associated with the use of cash transactions, the relevant transaction curve is T'_2, which exhibits a discontinuity at Y. The vertical distance, c measures the opportunity costs incurred by Ego in using cash transactions with outsiders. For some traders, T'_2 is the relevant transaction-cost curve associated with a heterogeneous trading network. This would involve a situation where the Chinese middleman, in his role as village dealer, has to enter into exchange relations with a large number of smallholders belonging to a different ethnic group. If the Chinese middleman refuses to trade with "outsiders," he must incur the opportunity costs of exclusion, the costs of foregone profits. So long as the opportunity costs of excluding outsiders from trade exceed transaction costs, a trader has an incentive to cross ethnic boundaries to incorporate outsiders into his trading network. The importance of Ego's *subjective* calculus of relations in determining the *objective* optimal "mix" of trading partners therefore depends upon the number of members in the constituent concentric circles, the degree of heterogeneity of the population, and a balancing off, at the margin, between transaction costs of including outsiders and the opportunity costs of exclusion of outsiders. The outcome of Ego's discriminatory choice of trading partners is the formation of a particularistic trading network comprising members who share the same (Confucian) code of ethics. Given a nondecomposable middleman economy, the structural effect of many individual Chinese middlemen's discriminatory choice is the formation of an EHMG.[6]

Code of ethics as the functional equivalent of the Law of Merchants or Law of Contracts

Under conditions of contract uncertainty, kinship/ethnic status embodying the Confucian ethics is a valuable intangible asset for a potential trading partner because of the "priority rights" Ego confers upon his trading partner; kinship/ethnic status is an essential input in the middleman's transaction technology. But the costs of obtaining this valuable input is zero for the trading partner possessing a kinship/ethnic status. Kinship or ethnic status is not a "right" that can be purchased by those who do not possess the requisite status.[7] Status is acquired by virtue of a person being born into a particular kinship/ethnic group. Kinship/ethnic rights may therefore be regarded as a species of "status rights" (Dales, 1972), the set of rights lying between the subset of private property and common property rights. These rights are equivalent to rights of citizenship, including preferential access to job opportunities, but are accessible only to subsets of the total population.

Since status rights, as an essential input, are nontransferable and nonmarketable by nature—it is a human capital (*in personam*) assignment—the opportunity sets of traders are *not* the same in markets dominated by a particular kinship/ethnic group. Only those "insiders" who can marshal all the essential inputs, including kinship/ethnic status, can become middlemen. The "outsiders," being de facto without status rights, are excluded from middleman roles because they cannot obtain an essential nonmarketable input necessary for middleman-entrepreneurship under conditions of contract uncertainty. If industry conditions are favorable for expansion of middlemen activities, the value of status rights as an entry ticket into personalistic markets rises. Thus, under conditions of contract uncertainty, "insiders" have a differential advantage vis-à-vis outsiders in appropriating new middleman roles for themselves. To neutralize somewhat the unequal access to trading opportunities, outsiders may substitute reputation for kinship/ethnic status. But, acquisition of reputation is not costless.[8] The transaction costs of an outsider, in the role of middleman, are higher than his counterpart who is an insider. The higher transaction costs of outsiders constitute an entry barrier into personalistic markets. Because of the low costs of entry into one's own trading community in contrast to the high costs of entry into another ethnic trading community, a partner has a strong incentive to remain loyal to his own trading partner and the kinship/ethnic group of which he is a member. Furthermore, the economic sanctions facing a trader who violates group norms take the following forms: (a) withdrawal of credit so that the trader has to deal on a cash basis; (b) exclusion from future dealings; and (c) "expulsion" from the group via bankruptcy proceedings. The code of ethics, embedded in kinship/ethnic networks, functions to deter Ego's trading partner from breach of contract and hence may be seen as the functional equivalent of the Law of Merchants or modern law of contracts.

Once the code of ethics emerges in a Chinese middleman economy, all externalities are internalized.[9] The existence of an ethical code of conduct helps to achieve efficiency in several ways. First, Chinese middlemen are able to appropriate profit expectations as intangible assets with a high degree of certainty, thereby facilitating middleman-entrepreneurship. Second, Chinese middlemen are able to reduce out-of-pocket costs of private protection of contracts; this shifts the total transaction-cost curve of a middleman firm downward. Third, middlemen are able to economize on the holding of commodity inventories and money by the creation of an efficient forward market in goods and money within the boundaries of the Chinese middleman economy. The result is the creation of "dual markets": the existence of forward markets and credit transactions within the Chinese middleman economy side by side with spot markets and cash transactions within the indigenous economy.

The "calculus of relations," informal social networks, and mutual aid associations: efficient information screening and mobilizing devices

To this point, we have proceeded on the implicit assumption that Ego possessed the requisite nonprice information about the trustworthiness of a potential trading partner. This assumption must now be relaxed to include Ego's search for nonprice information and the strategies Ego invents for economizing on information costs. An ingenious strategy Ego can use is to equip himself with the "calculus of relations" (Fortes, 1969). The calculus of relations, as will be shown, is an informationally efficient screening device because it enables Ego to pick up nonprice market signals directly from social characteristics of the potential trading partner (such as kinship distance, ethnic identity, etc.), and hence predict the contractual behavior of his potential trading partner with a high degree of accuracy.

To equip himself with an informationally efficient calculus of relations, Ego must be able: (a) to establish a system of discriminatory rankings of all traders in a market into a small number of categories corresponding to "grades" of traders, in descending order of reliability; and (b) to identify his potential trading partner at low cost. It may be inferred from a typical Hokkien trader's system of discriminatory rankings that Ego uses four basic structural principles to classify all traders into seven categories of traders: kinship, clanship, territory, and ethnicity; the general classificatory principle being based on the degree of "social distance" (Sahlins, 1965) between Ego and his potential trading partner. Ego's discriminatory system of ranking of trading partners reflects the *content* and the *limits* of the Confucian code of ethics.[10]

Confucian ethics, in overseas Chinese society, prescribes differences in the patterns of mutual aid obligations between people with varying degrees of social distance within a well-defined social structure—near kinsmen, distant kinsmen, clansmen, fellow villagers, and fellow Hokkiens. Kinship relations, in which social distance is at a minimum, are strong ties that involve the severest degree of constraint in dealings among kinsmen. Kinship relations are the irreducible jural and moral relations, and kinsmen are thus the most reliable people with whom to trade. Because of differences in the degree of behavioral constraint, each of the five categories of members occupies a special place within the overall social structure of the Hokkien ethnic community. This implies that different behavioral patterns can be predicted for each category of members corresponding to their location in the social structure. The most orderly or reliable pattern of contractual behavior is predicted for close kinsmen and the least reliable or most disorderly behavior is predicted for fellow Hokkiens. This, then, forms the basis for Ego's internal differentiation of Hokkien traders into five different categories of traders.

The limits of Confucian ethics form the basis for Ego's classification of all traders into two categories: (a) the "insiders" (the Hokkien traders) who, by virtue of their shared code of ethics, form a "moral community" of reliable traders; and (b) the "outsiders," not constrained by the Confucian ethics, who are perceived by Ego to be unreliable. Since non-Hokkien Chinese traders are socially closer than non-Chinese traders, the former are perceived to be more reliable than non-Chinese traders and hence non-Hokkien traders are assigned to category six. Between Ego and a non-Chinese trader, social distance is at a maximum. Ego perceives cooperation with a non-Chinese to be difficult since an outsider may withhold cooperation or may even exhibit "negative reciprocity" (Sahlins, 1965, p. 144) behavior. Thus, non-Chinese traders are assigned to category seven.

In a society in which members adhere strictly to the code of conduct of the group and have a clear idea of who is an "insider" and who is an "outsider": (a) consistency in subjective discriminatory rankings of trading partners is to be expected of members of the group;[11] and (b) consistency in behavior is expected of different categories. This being the case, Ego is able to establish a small number of categories of social relations for the discriminatory ranking of all traders in a market.

Having established his system of ranking of traders, it remains for Ego to identify a potential trading partner in order to place him in the proper category. To do this efficiently, Ego looks for certain relational attributes of his potential trading partner. The ethnic attribute of a non-Chinese trader is highly visible and distinguishable to a Chinese trader. This means that Ego, when encountering a non-Chinese trader, needs to acquire only one piece of information by a mere glance to completely remove uncertainty regarding the identity of the non-Chinese trader and hence assign him to the proper category (i.e., category seven). To correctly identify a Chinese trader and hence assign him to his proper category, Ego needs to acquire at most only four pieces of information—what dialect he speaks, his place of origin, his surname, and his relationship to Ego. Ego can acquire information necessary to identify all his potential trading partners at a very low or virtually zero cost. Kinship/ethnic attributes are thus non-price market signals that convey valuable information to Ego about the reliability of his potential trading partner at low cost.[12] The trader's calculus of relations may be regarded as a *low-cost screening device.* Once a trading partner is identified, he is assigned to his proper category and hence "graded." Ego then proceeds to use the calculus of relations as a tool of action for the actual choice of his trading partners in the manner discussed in the second section.

There are additional reasons why Ego prefers to choose potential trading partners from his own ethnic community. First, the existence of dense person-to-person informal communication networks within Ego's ethnic community makes it possible for Ego to pool information regarding the contractual behavior of a potential partner. The exchange of non-price information among members without charge economizes on information costs. This contrasts with the higher information costs Ego may expect to incur when he searches for information regarding an "outsider" across ethnic boundaries where the withholding of information is always a possibility. Second, members of Ego's own ethnic community, being "insiders" with strong ties to Ego, are perceived to be more trustworthy than "outsiders."[13] Information acquired from insiders is therefore considered by Ego to be more *reliable;* hence he can economize on the quantity of information he collects. Third, by knowing the background of the potential trading partner—his clan, his place of origin in China—Ego can acquire information from the networks of mutual aid associations within his own community or from the community leaders who maintain extensive networks of contacts throughout the community.

Confining choice of a potential trading partner within Ego's own community therefore greatly economizes on information costs. Conceptually, however, Ego's problem does not end with searching for information regarding his potential partners. In a vertical market structure, where traders are linked directly and indirectly together by long chains of mutual interdependence, Ego needs to acquire information not only about his own set of potential trading partners but also his partner's partners. Information costs would be prohibitive. This, however, implicitly assumes impersonal networks of traders. In personalistic middleman markets, where traders are linked together by kinship or ethnic ties, if v_1Tv_2 (read: v_1 trusts v_2) and v_2Tv_3, then v_1Tv_3. Mutual trust, via "transitive trust," becomes *collective trust,* a public good because it enables Ego to decompose the complex network of traders into his own subset of traders and confines his search to this subset.

Finally, by choosing trading partners from one's own ethnic community, Ego minimizes the presence of "semantic noise" between senders and recipients of price information, thereby creating an efficient communication channel for the acquisition and transmission of fast and reliable price information.[14] This contrasts with an alternative setting in which Ego does not speak the language of the "outsiders" and must make an initial investment in learning to speak the language if he chooses a network of "outsiders" as trading partners.[15] Because of the high degree of dependence of Chinese traders on the spoken word for information, and because of the mutual unintelligibility of the different Chinese dialects, traders who speak the same dialects are thus drawn together into networks of exchange relations to form an ethnically homogeneous middleman group.

Conclusions

In this chapter, we have developed a theory of the ethnically homogeneous middleman group in the context of an exchange economy characterized by contract uncertainty. We have argued that the EHMG may be viewed as a club-like structural arrangement, an alternative to contract law and to the vertically integrated firm, which emerged to economize on contract enforcement and information costs.[16] The theory has broad applications and lends itself readily to extensions for further research, only two of which will be noted here:

1. *A general theory of homogeneous entrepreneurial groups engaged in either illegal or legal activities.* We may develop a theory of the ethnically homogeneous (Italian) Mafia group as a low-cost club for the enforcement of contracts since Mafia entrepreneurs, by the very nature of their illegal activities, operate outside the legal framework.[17] Similarly, the theory may explain why successful trading groups operating in other underdeveloped economies characterized by contract uncertainty are *socially homogeneous groups*: the East Indians in East Africa, the Syrians in West Africa, the Lebanese in North Africa,[18] the Jews in medieval Europe, and the Medici merchant-bankers in fifteenth-century Florence. This general theory of homogeneous trading groups would examine: (a) the assignment of property rights, the structural principles—kinship, clanship, caste, ethnicity, religion—for the delineation of the *boundaries* of groups (Carr and Landa, 1980), and the institutions for facilitating exchange among members and between members and outsiders[19] as well as (b) the dynamics within the homogeneous trading group as the group responds to the development of the economy. The function of the homogeneous trading group as a low-cost arrangement for contract enforcement may become increasingly redundant as the economy evolves a more developed legal infrastructure. Consequently, the particularistic exchange networks based on mutual trust will gradually be replaced by impersonal exchange networks based on contract.
2. *The economic theory of optimal jurisdictions.* Our theory of the EHMG may be extended to include the spatial dimension in which ethnic boundaries coincide with political boundaries.[20] It may be used to explain, for example, why standard marketing areas in traditional China were organized in hexagon-shaped areas where boundaries were coterminous with the existence of distinct homogeneous communities[21] and why the policing of each standard marketing community was provided by private protective agencies in the form of secret societies. That theory may also be used to explain why nation-states tend to be organized along *ethnic* lines.[22]

Notes

* This chapter was originally published as an article in *The Journal of Legal Studies,* 10 (2), (June, 1981): 349–362. I thank Professors Fu-Lai Tony Yu and Ho-Don Yan, editors of the *Handbook of East Asian Entrepreneurship*, for inviting me to contribute a chapter by reprinting my 1981 paper, thus making it possible for my paper to be read by readers who are previously unaware of my 1981 paper, and to give me an opportunity to write an "Afterword" accompanying the reprint of my paper.

1 For the literature on the economics of property rights, see Furubotn and Pejovich (1972). For the literature on public choice theory, see Mueller (1976).

2 See Posner (1977, Chapter 4), Landa (1976). Contract law, however, does not deter "efficient breach" where a trader can compensate the victim and himself be made better off by breach. See Goetz and Scott (1977). See also Clarkson *et al.* (1978).

3 The details of the study are contained in Chapter 3, Landa's (1978b) unpublished Ph.D. dissertation.

4 "Social structure" is a key concept used by sociologists to describe the pattern of recurrent and regularized interaction among two or more persons, hence implying the existence of norms for regulating behavior. See, for example, Blau (1975).

5 For a theory of clubs that explicitly incorporates discrimination in the choice of consumption· sharing partners, see Tollison (1972). Tollison's theory is an extension of Buchanan's (1965) theory of clubs.

6 Ego (v_1) chooses his trading partners, v_2 and v_3 on a kinship or ethnic basis; v_2 and v_3, in turn, choose their trading partners on the same particularistic basis; then the result is the emergence of an EHMG.

7 But some of these rights may be acquired by marriage or conversion.
8 For a discussion of the costs of acquiring reputation, see Landa (1976).
9 The types of exchange externalities associated with breach of contract in the context of smallholder rubber are: (a) supply-breach externalities (failure to deliver); (b) quality-externalities (delivering an inferior grade of smallholder rubber, smallholder rubber being divided into five grades); and (c) debt-default externalities.
10 For a discussion of the limits of morality, see Buchanan (1978).
11 For a discussion of this, see White (1963).
12 For the economics of signaling and screening in the context of a job market paradigm, see Spence (1974), and Akerlof (1976). For an anthropological discussion of classificatory kinship systems as signaling devices for the creation and maintenance of social order in primitive societies, see Morgan (1970), Fortes (1969), and Colson (1974).
13 For a discussion of the role of strong and weak ties in transmission of job information, see Boorman (1975).
14 For a discussion of the importance of creating an efficient communication channel, see Marschak (1968).
15 For a discussion of the difficulties of communication across nations, see Arrow (1969).
16 Our theory of the EHMG may be regarded as an extension of Alchian and Demsetz's (1972) theory of the firm: rather than *ex post* monitoring of team members, emphasized by Alchian and Demsetz, we emphasize *ex ante* discriminatory choice or screening of team members so that the efficient *form* of economic organization itself can be designed. The Alchian–Demsetz theory is an extension of Coase's (1937) classic paper on the nature of the firm.
17 This linkage was suggested to the writer by Francis X. Tannian, commenting on an early version of the paper presented at the Public Choice Society meetings, April 15–17, 1976, Roanoke, VA.
18 The major exception to our theory is the absorption of Lebanese traders into the dualistic economy of Brazil.
19 For some of these institutions which facilitate exchange between different ethnic groups, see Landa's (March 1980) unpublished paper on the Kula Ring.
20 Tiebout (1965) points out that urban areas can be efficiently organized in a system of many small homogeneous communities whose populations have similar tastes for public goods. Tiebout's "voting-with-the-feet" theory relies on the ability of people to move, in fact, to choose one's jurisdiction of residence.
21 See Landa's (1978a) unpublished paper.
22 Singapore provides an excellent example. Although Singapore and West Malaysia form an economic entity, Singapore, with its predominantly Chinese-merchant community, pulled out of the Federation of Malaysia on August 9, 1965, to form an independent nation-state (the Republic of Singapore) within the Commonwealth.

References

Akerlof, G. (1976) "The economics of caste and of the rat race and other woeful tales," *Quarterly Journal of Economics,* 90(November): 599–617.

Alchian, A. and Demsetz, H. (1972) "Production, information costs, and economic organization," *American Economic Review,* 62(December): 777–795.

Arrow, K.J. (1969) "Classificatory notes on the production and transmission of technological knowledge," *American Economic Review,* Papers and Proceedings, 59(May): 29–33.

Belshaw, C.S. (1965) *Traditional Exchange and Modern Markets,* Englewood Cliffs, NJ: Prentice-Hall, Inc.

Blau, P.M. (ed.) (1975) *Approaches to the Study of Social Structure,* New York: The Free Press.

Boorman, S.A. (1975) "A combinatorial optimization model for transmission of job information through contact networks," *The Bell Journal of Economics,* 6(Spring): 216–249.

Buchanan, J.M. (1965) "An economic theory of clubs," *Economica,* 32(February): 1–14.

Buchanan, J.M. (1978) "Markets, states, and the extent of morals," *American Economic Review,* 68(May): 362–368.

Carr, J. and Landa, J.T. (1980) "The economics of symbols, clan names, and religion," unpublished paper presented at the Southern Economic Association Annual Meetings, Washington, DC, November 5–7, 1980, and at the Law and Economics Workshop, Faculty of Law, University of Toronto, November 26, 1980.

Clarkson, K.W., Leroy Miller, R. and Muris, T.J. (1978) "Liquidated damages vs. penalties: sense or nonsense?" *Wisconsin Law Review,* 4: 351–390.

Coase, R.H. (1937) "The nature of the firm," *Economica,* 4(November): 386–405.

Colson, E. (1974) *Tradition and Contract: The Problem of Order,* Chicago: Aldine.

Dales, J.H. (1972) "Rights and economics," in G. Wunderlich and W.L. Gibson, Jr. (eds) *Perspective of Property,* State College, PA: Institute for Land and Water Resources, Pennsylvania State University.
Dewey, A.G. (1962) *Peasant Marketing in Java.* New York: Free Press of Glencoe.
Fortes, M. (1969) *Kinship and the Social Order: The Legacy of Lewis Henry Morgan,* Chicago: Aldine.
Furubotn, E.G. and Pejovich, S. (1972) "Property rights and economics theory: a survey of recent literature," *Journal of Economic Literature,* 10(4): 1137–1162.
Geertz, C. (1978) "The bazaar economy: information and search in peasant marketing," *American Economic Review,* Papers and Proceedings, 68(May): 28–32.
Goetz, C.J. and Scott, R.E. (1977) "Liquidated damages, penalties and the just compensation principle: some notes on an enforcement model and a theory of efficient breach," *Columbia Law Review,* 77: 554–594.
Landa, J.T. (1976) "An exchange economy with legally binding contract: a public choice approach," *Journal of Economic Issues,* 10(4): 905–922.
Landa, J.T. (1978a) "Central-place theory, social distance costs, and Nozickian minimal states," paper presented at the Public Choice Society Annual meetings in New Orleans, LA, March 3–5.
Landa, J.T. (1978b) "The economics of the ethnically homogeneous middleman group: a property rights-public choice approach," unpublished PhD dissertation, Virginia Polytechnic Institute and State University (June 1978).
Landa, J.T. (1980) "Primitive public choice and exchange: an explanation of the enigma of the Kula Ring," unpublished paper presented at the Public Choice Society Annual meetings, San Francisco, California, March 14–16.
Marschak, J. (1968) "Economics of inquiring, communicating, deciding," *American Economic Review,* Papers and Proceedings, 62(May): 1–18.
Morgan, L.H. (1970) "Systems of consanguinity and affinity of the human family," Volume 21 of *Smithsonian Contributions to Knowledge. Anthological Pub.*
Mueller, D.C. (1976) "Public choice: a survey," *Journal of Economic Literature,* 4(2): 395–433.
Posner, R.A. (1977) *Economic Analysis of Law,* 2nd edn, Boston: Little, Brown.
Posner, R. (1980) "A theory of primitive society with special reference to law," *Journal of Law and Economics,* 23(April), 1–53.
Sahlins, M.D. (1965) "On the sociology of primitive exchange," in M. Banton (ed.) *The Relevance of Models for Social Anthropology,* London: Tavistock Publications.
Spence, A.M. (1974) *Market Signalling,* Cambridge, MA: Harvard University Press.
Tiebout, C. (1965) "A pure theory of local expenditures," *Journal of Political Economy,* 64(October): 416–424.
Tollison, R.D. (1972) "Consumption sharing and non-exclusion rules," *Economica,* 39(August): 276–291.
White, H.C. (1963) *An Anatomy of Kinship,* Englewood Cliffs, NJ: Prentice Hall.

Afterword (Written December 2, 2013)

My theory of the ethnically homogeneous middleman group (Landa, 1981) was based on my six months of fieldwork on Chinese middlemen involved in the marketing of smallholders' rubber in Singapore and West Malaysia in 1969. The article, published in *The Journal of Legal Studies*, and reprinted here in this Handbook, is a slightly revised version of a core theoretical chapter from my Ph.D. dissertation on overseas Chinese middlemen success (Landa, 1978), written under the direction of James M. Buchanan.

The results of my fieldwork in 1969 revealed that Chinese smallholders' rubber merchants were linked together in *particularistic or personal* networks of exchange to form an ethnically homogeneous *Hokkien-Chinese* middleman group. Since standard or Neoclassical economic theories of exchange depict exchange as an *impersonal* exchange between *anonymous* traders, existing economic theories of exchange cannot explain the phenomenon of the EHMG. I developed a new exchange paradigm—incorporating the concept of transaction costs from New Institutional Economics pioneered by Ronald Coase (1937), as well as incorporating some concepts from sociology and anthropology—to explain the empirical reality of the embeddedness of the Confucian code of ethics/social norms, which promote mutual trust among the merchants linked in particularistic networks/EHMG, which serve as an institutional alternative to contract law for enforcing contracts in economies lacking well-developed legal infrastructure. In doing so, I introduced *trust* and *identity—personal identity and group identity*—into economics (Landa, 1981), as well as informal institutions into the "new law-and-economics of social norms" literature (Landa, 2005).[1]

Because of the originality of my theory of the EHMG, my paper was widely cited by law-and-economics scholars. However, my paper was ignored in mainstream economics journals. Mainstream economists have, instead, given credit to economist Avner Greif (1993) for pioneering a theory of the homogeneous "Jewish Maghribi traders' coalition," in eleventh-century Mediterranean trade, as an institution arrangement which substituted for formal contract law for enforcement of contracts among themselves. Because there were many other scholars—albeit less well-known than Greif in terms of citation counts—who, like Greif, in the 1990s, developed theories of ethnic/social trade networks very similar to mine, without acknowledging my 1981 paper, Charles Rowley (2009)—a former long-time editor-in-chief of *Public Choice,* and hence an obvious "citation enforcer"—published a paper setting the priority/citations record straight. Similarly, sociologist Mark Granovetter's (1985) theory of the embeddedness of personal relations in social networks functioning to mitigate malfeasance, was credited by sociologists with launching the New Economic Sociology. But, as I pointed out, Granovetter's theory is very similar to my 1981 theory of the EHMG (Landa, 2001), but without incorporating the concept of transaction costs, and without using rational choice theory.

Note

1 For further extensions of my theory of the EHMG/economics of identity to other homogeneous trading groups, preliterate societies and non-human societies, see my book (Landa, 1994) and my survey article (Landa, 1996).

References

Coase, R.H. (1937) "The nature of the firm," *Economica,* New Series, 4(16): 386–405.

Granovetter, M. (1985) "Economic action and social structure: the problem of embeddedness," *American Journal of Sociology,* 91(3): 481–510.

Greif, A. (1993) "Contract enforceability and economic institutions in early trade: the Maghribi traders' coalition," *The American Economic Review,* 83(3): 525–548.

Landa, J.T. (1978) "The economics of the ethnically homogeneous middleman group: a property rights–public choice approach," unpublished PhD dissertation, Virginia Polytechnic Institute and State University.

Landa, J.T. (1981) "A theory of the ethnically homogeneous middleman group: an institutional alternative to contract law," *The Journal of Legal Studies,* 10(2): 349–362.

Landa, J.T. (1994) *Trust, Ethnicity, and Identity: Beyond the New Institutional Economics of Ethnic Trading Networks, Contract Law, and Gift-Exchange,* Ann Arbor, MI: The University of Michigan Press.

Landa, J.T. (1996) "Doing the economics of trust and informal institutions," in S.G. Medema and W.J. Samuels (eds) *Foundations of Research in Economics: How Do Economists Do Economics?* Cheltenham: Edward Elgar, pp. 142–162.

Landa, J.T. (2001) "Coasean foundations of a unified theory of western and Chinese contractual practices and economic organisations," in R.R. Appelbaum, W.L.F. Felstiner, and V. Gessner (eds) *Rules and Networks: The Legal Culture of Global Business Transactions,* Portland, OR: Hart Publishing, pp. 347–362.

Landa, J.T. (2005) "Bounded rationality of *Homo classificius*: the law and bioeconomics of social norms as classification," in C.A. Hill (ed.) *Symposium: Must We Choose Between Rationality and Irrationality? Chicago Kent Law Review,* 80(3): 1043–1329.

Rowley, C.K. (2009) "The curious citation practices of Avner Greif: Janet Landa comes to grief," *Public Choice,* 140: 275–285.

7

The Chinese market economy and its effect on *guanxi* in the twenty-first century

Stephen Grainger

Introduction

Chinese society has long been known for its emphasis on *guanxi* as a guiding principle of economic and social organization (Fried, 1953; Walder, 1986) and many seeking to do business in China have found *guanxi* is important in achieving success (Xin and Pearce, 1996; Blackman, 1997; Tsang, 1998; Lovett *et al.*, 1999; Standifird and Marshall, 2000). Chinese executives have utilized their *guanxi* to enhance financial outcomes (Luo and Chen, 1996), market benefits (Davies *et al.*, 1995), competitive advantage (Yeung and Tung, 1996; Tsang, 1998), as an efficient marketing tool (Luo, 1997b) and to secure resources, information, contracts, equipment, better prices, technical assistance, public services, economic exchanges and to overcome administrative interventions with local, provincial and national governments (Brunner *et al.*, 1989; Ambler, 1995a; Farh *et al.*, 1998; Park and Luo, 2001; Zhang *et al.*, 2012).

Debate among researchers and practitioners has ranged from the significance of *guanxi* being in decline (Guthrie, 1998; Fan, 2002) to it growing in importance (Standifird and Marshall, 2000; Yang, M.M., 2002). The majority of recent findings support *guanxi* continuing to play an important role in business in China, however, questions remain as to whether its significance will be maintained in the future. Further debate has focused on whether the changing dynamics of *guanxi* and China's evolving market economy are also affecting the practices of nepotism in Chinese organizations.

In this chapter we examine the definition, base, development and importance of *guanxi* in business and at the organizational level and its likely significance in the future. Further we discuss the resultant changes occurring to nepotism as market forces continue to impact the level and quality of human resource performance as companies search for greater effectiveness and efficiency. Let us first look at two examples that highlight the utility of *guanxi* and its nepotistic benefits to get a taste of the complexity, sensitivity and benefits of these phenomena.

Example 1

Despite having a signed 20-year contract with Beijing officials, the US fast food giant, McDonald's was evicted from its prime location in the heart of Beijing's premier shopping district after only two years. The businessman who wanted to build on the site and who was able to engineer McDonald's eviction was Li Kashing, one of Hong Kong's wealthiest businessmen. Li had a plan to develop a US$2 billion project; the Oriental Plaza, in central Beijing and in 1994 the development of his project hit an obstacle when McDonald's refused to move from the site Li had earmarked for the vast compound. With a 20-year contract signed by the government, McDonald's were not moving, however, Li used his *guanxi* with the Chinese authorities to secure their eviction. This occurred because Li had strong trusted connections with senior city officials and politicians, whereas, by contrast, McDonald's had not kept its *guanxi* in good condition (Ambler, 1995a; Luo, 1997a).

Throughout Li's business career he had 'produced' *guanxi* (Kipnis, 1997) by developing long-term relationships with those in power, many of whom he had grown up with and worked with over a long period of time. The relationship favours he had granted to his government friends and connections over the years made him an insider and resulted in him gaining a distinct advantage in developing his business initiatives and profiting from return favours. One example was when former President Jiang Zemin visited Hong Kong for the hand-over from British to Chinese rule in 1997 and for the opening of the Chek Lap Kok Airport in 1998. On both these occasions, he was a complementary guest at Mr. Li's premier five-star hotel. Furthermore Li's partner in developing Beijing's newest commercial complex was his personal friend and Chief Executive of Hong Kong at that time Mr. Tung Chee-Wah. Not many could boast the same influential connections in China as Mr. Li. The success of his negotiations in developing the Oriental Plaza in Beijing confirmed his reputation as the Territory's premier tycoon and master of *guanxi* (Polin, 2000). Conscious of preserving McDonald's face or *mianzi*, the authorities gave McDonald's permission to open six more restaurants in Beijing in return for vacating the Plaza site. With McDonald's gone, Li gained permission to develop his vast shopping complex.

Example 2

In 1986, Ms. Zhou, formerly a train conductor with the Tianjin Railway, used her *guanxi* to gain a position as an accountant for a motor cycle repair shop, a difficult move that required several months of *guanxi* work. Her problem was that Ms. Zhou had a baby that could no longer travel with her on the train in her position as conductor; her mother-in-law could not take care of her baby while she went to work and she did not have any *guanxi* with those who could help to enroll the baby in the overnight nursery. To solve this problem required some sensitive *guanxi* work.

The Director of the local Labour Bureau was the elder brother of an 'old friend' of her respected uncle. When the Director heard about Ms. Zhou's situation through her uncle, he used his power to intervene to grant Ms. Zhou the official documentation granting her permission to search for a new job. This would have been almost impossible without this assistance from a higher authority. To gain her new position at the motor cycle repair shop near her home also required sensitive *guanxi*. The daughter of the Director of the motor cycle shop was an old high school friend for whom Ms. Zhou had once purchased some clothing for on a trip to Shanghai. This was done as a favour and the Director returned the favour by giving Ms. Zhou a position in his shop thus maintaining the *guanxi* of his daughter and his family (Bian and Ang, 1997).

These examples highlight the diversity and variety of *guanxi* involved in the spectrum of real-life interactions. Many wise Chinese have turned the art of *guanxi* into a carefully calculated science and there are people who live entirely on their *guanxi* (Butterfield, 1983). Even outside mainland China the advantages of good *guanxi* can be found at all levels in the Chinese Commonwealth (Kao, 1993).

Guanxi

Defining guanxi

As seen in these two examples, *guanxi* exists in many different situations, develops in many different ways and each *guanxi* relationship carries its own connotations and history. Pye's (1992) description of *guanxi* as 'friendship with continued exchange of favours' and King's (1991) as a 'network of personally defined reciprocal bonds' highlight the reciprocal exchange of favours that characterize this phenomenon.

In general, *guanxi* refers to the establishment of a connection between two individuals to enable a bilateral flow of personal favours or social transactions (Yeung and Tung, 1996; Luo, 1997a). Chinese people both consciously and unconsciously use *guanxi* to guide daily activities and it is so deeply rooted in Chinese society that it is reasonable to expect that a person brought up in a Chinese community would be aware of and have been subtly exposed to the concept of *guanxi* (Brunner and Taoka, 1977; Yang, M.M., 1994; Grainger, 2005).

Having good *guanxi* with a partner implies having a successful history of working together, providing favours, and building up trust between one another over time. An important characteristic of *guanxi* is familiarity and for any two individuals to develop good *guanxi*, they must know a good deal about each other and share a good deal with each other (Bian and Ang, 1997). For *guanxi* to grow and last, both parties in the relationship also need to maintain contact and keep regular tabs on the state of their relationship (Ambler, 1995a).

The guanxi *base*

For two people to be able to develop *guanxi* the first thing needed is a *guanxi* base. The base may be geographical, teacher–student, kinship, co-worker, workplace supervisor–subordinate, political, classmate, friendship or sworn brotherhood relationship (Jacobs, 1979; Brunner *et al.*, 1989). The base is the point of commonality from which a relationship can begin and also remains a tie that binds those with *guanxi* together. The *guanxi* base, however, does not automatically ensure two people a level of emotional connection in their relationship. For instance, the *guanxi* base for two people may have arisen purely because both are alumni of the same university. But if one had already graduated before the other entered the university, the *guanxi* between the two would be weak or very distant. To strengthen the *guanxi*, both would have to invest time to cultivate an emotional bond. *Guanxi* tends to be built on the basis of shared kinships, work units, alma maters and birth places rather than on demographic or personal similarities (Jacobs, 1982; Tsui and Farh, 1997; Yang, D.T., 1997).

Depending on the basis of *guanxi,* an interpersonal relationship can vary in the degree of closeness or strength (Hwang, 1987; Kipnis, 1997). For example, a person's *guanxi* relationship with a co-worker who was also a college classmate would be stronger than with one who had not been a classmate and the strength of the *guanxi* relationship determines the weight of demands that can be sought and requested.

Chinese people perceive that one's existence in society is largely influenced by relationships with others through a strong orderly hierarchy (Brunner *et al.*, 1989; Luo, 1997a, p. 45; Park and

Luo, 2001). These Confucian relationships are a core component that contributes to the strong presence of *guanxi* in Chinese society (King, 1991; Yeung and Tung, 1996).

Core principles of building and maintaining guanxi *in 2013*

Yeung and Tung (1996, p. 62) identified four essential strategies for developing and maintaining *guanxi* relationships: (1) tendering favours; (2) nurturing long-term mutual benefits; (3) cultivating personal relationships; and (4) cultivating trust. McDonald's error in Beijing was their failure to keep in touch with the Beijing authorities and to cultivate and nurture their relationship after their contract was signed. They needed to maintain their contact to develop *guanxi* with the authorities as the long-term viability of *guanxi* depends on each member's commitment to one another and the amount of action taken to maintain the quality of their relationship. In the Chinese context, activities that promote good *guanxi* include social interactions after hours; invitations for meals together; sending gifts for special occasions; sharing of problems, needs and feelings and standing by partners during conflict (Law *et al.*, 2011).

Guanxi is reciprocal in nature and a person is viewed as being untrustworthy if they refuse to return a favour or follow the rules of reciprocity (Alston, 1989). This reciprocity is the critical essence of *guanxi*. If one denies their reciprocity obligations, such a person may pay the price by losing connections (Bian and Ang, 1997) or have their future requests ignored when they seek help. Those with effective *guanxi* with another are tied together through an invisible and unwritten code of reciprocity. While they enjoy the benefits of *guanxi*, they also incur the burdens of obligations which must be taken care of in the future (Chen, M., 2004). When one disregards this reciprocal obligation, he/she loses face, hurts the related party's feelings, and eventually jeopardizes their *guanxi* network (Luo, 1997a; Park and Luo, 2001).

Guanxi can also be transferable between parties (e.g. A and C) if they have a common connection (i.e. B); a characteristic exemplified in the case of Ms. Zhou, the train conductor. The extent of such *guanxi* transferability is dependent on the strength of the ties between A and B and B and C (Yeung and Tung, 1996; Park and Luo, 2001). To transfer *guanxi* successfully, a trusted intermediary is necessary because such a connecting person must help facilitate the familiarity, trust and obligation needed to help tie the *guanxi* seeker and the potential helper (Bian and Ang, 1997). In Ms. Zhou's case, the relationships the Director of the Labour Bureau and Ms. Zhou enjoyed with her uncle (the intermediary) were of critical importance. The higher social status of the parties involved creates greater commitment and face for the intermediary, which in turn leads to greater social obligations for the parties to develop and maintain their *guanxi* (Li and Wright, 2000). Intermediaries are not expected to gain anything for playing this role and if they act in their own interests, they may lose their 'credit' and the respect of the parties involved. This transferability of *guanxi* is always problematic, however, and involves the development of a new field of trust. Trust remains a core component of *guanxi* (Bian and Ang, 1997; Bell, 2000).

'Face' or *mianzi* is another key component in the dynamics of *guanxi* (Redding and Ng, 1982; Yeung and Tung, 1996). The quality of face a person holds is associated with appropriate personal behaviour, achieved status or a reputation for success (Chen, M., 2004). A person's *mianzi* often determines their position, credibility, honesty, reputation, power, income or network. Without *mianzi*, one is limited in the social resources at one's disposal to use in cultivating and developing one's *guanxi* network (Redding and Ng, 1982). Care must be taken in the acquisition and maintenance of face (Yeung and Tung, 1996) and a loss of face in Confucian society brings shame and embarrassment not only to the individuals but also to related family members (Bell, 2000) and makes it difficult to produce *guanxi*.

Guanxi exchange is distinctive in that it usually links people across different ranks. Often a weaker party who is seeking help or a special favour does not have the resources to provide a favour of equal value in return. As in the case of Ms. Zhou, she was the weaker member and the Director had much greater powers. The power of the Director in contrast to the poor single mother is a classic example of *guanxi* linking two persons of unequal rank or social status and the weaker side seeking more help than he or she could possibly reciprocate (Alston, 1989).

Gifts are an important supplement when building *guanxi* and are sometimes associated with seeking favour (Brunner and Koh, 1988; Hofstede and Bond, 1988). In building the correct environment to request a favour, these gifts are usually offered well in advance of the request and presented discreetly in private and not given in the presence of others in order to avoid embarrassment for the receiver (Yang, M.M., 1986; Brunner *et al.*, 1989; Kipnis, 1997). Chinese officials do not usually like to accept gifts due to the possible links to corruption, however, the right gift at the right time can always be accepted if done discreetly.

Guanxi as a necessity for doing business in China

In the business context, if a person has established *guanxi* with their partners, then deals become easier. In contrast, the outsider can find it difficult, time-consuming and sometimes impossible to make progress (Brunner and Taoka, 1977; Marcoux, 2002). Business advantages for insiders include access to capital and resources (Zhang *et al.*, 2012) through to smoothing transport difficulties or the collection of payments (Leung *et al.*, 1996; Seligman, 1999) and *guanxi* relationships with government officials are often regarded as a defining factor for securing government investments in venture capital funds (Bruton and Ahlstrom, 2003). *Guanxi* promotes interpersonal trust (Farh *et al.*, 1998), facilitates job mobility (Bian, 1994), and enhances firm performance (Peng and Luo, 2000), however, one must remember that *guanxi* does not necessarily ensure success and one must know how to effectively use *guanxi* in order to take advantage (Tsang, 1998; Peng and Lou, 2000; Fan, 2002; Chen, X-P. and Chen, C.C., 2004; Vanhonacker, 2004). Yeung and Tung (1996) drew the analogy between *guanxi* and a piece of wood thrown to a drowning swimmer. The wood does not have inherent magical properties that will automatically rescue the swimmer, but the swimmer can save themself if they know how to utilize the wood effectively. The *guanxi* network is a necessity but it is not sufficient on its own to guarantee the good performance of an individual or related firm.

Under China's sometimes questionable legal infrastructure (in particular, poorly developed or enforced contract law), the trust associated with strong *guanxi* replaces the variable support from this flexible rule of law (Xu, 1996; Wong and Chan, 1999; Yi and Ellis, 2000: Grainger, 2005). Even though China's legal and regulatory environment is developing and the uncertainty in China's transition economy is decreasing, in some cases the likelihood of fair legal outcomes in business has only improved marginally. The non-uniformity of the quality of evolution of better legal processes in different parts and industries across China has increased the debate over whether or not *guanxi* remains critical to managers and organizations in facilitating business success (Alston, 1989; Guthrie, 1998; Park and Luo, 2001; Yang, M.M., 2002). Firms may be more eager to use *guanxi* as an efficient mechanism to overcome or minimize the effect of administrative interventions and new legal interpretations by the Chinese government (Park and Luo, 2001) and to serve as a risk-mitigating device in venture capital investments (Bruton and Ahlstrom, 2003). Some argue that the higher level of uncertainty in the transition economy further induces market-oriented firms to seek *guanxi* to deal with competitive forces in the environment and with government officials. In many cases *guanxi* is the only insurance that transactions will go through (Tsui *et al.*, 2004) and without *guanxi* there is often uncertainty regarding business outcomes. Partners who have strong *guanxi* ties remain less likely to legalize all the terms and conditions of investments in formal contracts. They prefer to keep details of *guanxi* deals confidential (Lin, 2001) and resolve potential issues and problems through tacit understandings and actions. Contracts are regarded as backward- rather than forward-looking; the creditworthiness of counterparties is difficult to ascertain and the judicial system rarely grants relief to outsiders.

With China's patchwork of business modernization, the characteristics and utility of *guanxi* are being affected in different ways in differing parts of China. In central and western China, the changes in business characteristics due to the introduction of the market economy are progressing more slowly as are the changes to *guanxi* practice in comparison to what is occurring in coastal regions and in China's former Special Economic Zones (Guthrie, 1998; Grainger, 2003, 2012).

Debate continues as to whether China's rule of law and legal interpretation will ever strengthen to a level of consistency that will replace the insurance currently provided by reliable, quality *guanxi*. Alternatively, will business men and women still need to utilize *guanxi* to some degree to create a competitive advantage, manage organizational interdependence and to mitigate institutional disadvantage, structural weaknesses and other environmental threats? Questions remain as to whether or not the advent of the socialist market economy in China is resulting in the decay in the importance and usage of *guanxi* in business (Guthrie, 1998: Fan, 2002). Even though parts of China are changing at differing speeds to others, it remains true that modern Chinese business still operates within the realms of countless social and *guanxi* networks and it currently remains critical for businesses in China to understand and properly utilize *guanxi*.

Organizational *guanxi*

Guanxi at the organizational level

The utility of the *guanxi* network of a general manager or chief executive officer does have important implications for the success of their organization (Luo, 1997b; Farh *et al.*, 1998). Despite the enactment of new legislation in China, business laws at times remain vague and business people may have to operate in the unstable regulatory environment. In this context, guidelines, directives and policies are open to interpretation by those who occupy positions of power (Yeung and Tung, 1996: 59) and *guanxi* still provides some level of insurance and confidence in operations for Chinese companies.

For a Chinese company to facilitate *guanxi* relationships with an international firm, Li and Wright (2000) proposed a five-stage process between individuals representing each company. In Stage 1 an individual in management makes initial contact with an individual from a potential international partner company. Once contact is made, the parties need to proceed through a trust-building phase in Stage 2 to reach Stage 3 that will usually involve one of the individuals seeking some kind of small favour for their organization. In Stage 4 the *guanxi* relationship will be tested, and if the reciprocity of favours occurs successfully, then Stage 5 can commence with the consolidation of the relationship. From this point forward, maintenance of the relationship must be ongoing for the two organizations to begin to enjoy the utility of *guanxi*. This involves reciprocal favours and the inclusion of a *guanxi* partner in important events, e.g. the banquet involving the head of the firm's presidents or the grand opening of a new office. The *guanxi* will only be productive as long as the two individuals initially involved remain in their positions in each organization, however, broadening the *guanxi* base can be achieved with the careful introduction of a number of new individuals into the relationship between the companies over time (Grainger, 2005). In the long term, information concerning the *guanxi* relationship of managers within an organization needs to be passed on so senior staff know with whom *guanxi* has been established, how and why the relationship exists and how to respond to requests. Otherwise valuable relationships can be lost through ignorance or short-term expediency (Li and Wright, 2000).

Guanxi at the organizational level can serve as compensation for the lack of a formal institutional or legal framework (Zhang and Zhang, 2006). An example was seen when a manager of a South China company signed a one-year contract to lend money to a real estate developer. A year later he had difficulty getting his money back, in spite of the contract—a not uncommon occurrence in modern China. One day he happened to be having lunch with a banker from a state bank, with whom his company had developed strong *guanxi*. When he described his dilemma, the banker suddenly realized that his bank was considering giving a loan to the same developer under question. The firm manager after hearing this, asked the banker to delay approving the loan. The banker agreed and notified the company seeking the loan that without meeting the requirements to repay the loan to the member of his *guanxiwang*[1] (the manager of the company affected), the developer and his organization would not get the loan from his bank. A few days later the developer paid back the outstanding money in full (Li and Wright, 2000).

As the Chinese market economy evolves, *guanxi* can still bring strategic implications to the firm, including providing the means to limit transaction costs and as a means to access scarce resources (Zhang *et al.*, 2012). Firms should also be wary of forms of *guanxi* that violate emerging Chinese business norms within the market economy and that significantly disadvantage ordinary Chinese. No longer can outside investors just simply unethically accept *guanxi* as a Chinese cultural practice. Managers using their position or company resources for their own self-interest or the interest of those with whom they have *guanxi* or who benefit from such at the expense of the organization as a whole (Dunfee and Warren, 2001) now run a serious risk of exposure and prosecution.

Manager and subordinate guanxi

The new generation of Chinese managers and employees who have a stronger work ethic and reverence for the value of work are likely to have a less positive attitude towards *guanxi*. Zhang *et al.* (2012) suggest that potential employees who are performance-oriented are more suitable to deal with technology, budgeting, accounting and management while, in contrast, those with a high *guanxi* orientation may be better suited to liaison, negotiator or spokesperson type of roles. Fang (2003) found individuals who rely heavily on *guanxi* may have lower work performance. These findings create complexities for employee selection especially in the field of international joint ventures. Foreign companies need to monitor employee selection carefully and examine whether it is acceptable for their Chinese managers to make administrative decisions such as bonus allocation and promotions in their company (Law *et al.*, 2011).When a subordinate has good *guanxi* with their Chinese supervisor, the superior will have a higher tendency to allocate bonuses to them and recommend them for promotion (ibid.). These relationships need to be monitored closely to make sure they do not result in corrupt behaviour.

Chen and Chen (2004) found resentment of *guanxi* alliances between supervisors and subordinates when they resulted in some subordinates being treated better than others and especially when they unfairly influenced managers' reward decisions (Bozionelos and Wang, 2007). To discourage or eliminate this type of *guanxi*-based corruption, the mechanisms being used have included threats of dismissal, close monitoring of sales activities, the establishment of secure e-mail systems for suppliers to report on any requests for bribes from purchasing staff, purchasing staff and management jobs being rotated, team rather than individuals assessing potential suppliers; the person negotiating the contract not being the person signing the contract, and the prices of components and materials being systematically checked against other potential suppliers. In spite of all these measures, there is still a long way to go before this problem is brought under control (Wilkinson *et al.*, 2005).

The positive facet of *guanxi* in the workplace is enhanced by meaningful and ethical exchanges between the supervisor and their subordinate and through them showing concern, care, support, recognition, justice and the establishment of an outside work relationship (Wong *et al.*, 2003; Cheng *et al.*, 2004; Chen and Tjosvold, 2006; Law *et al.*, 2011). *Guanxi* does create reciprocal obligations between a manager and a subordinate and is a significant predictor of trust between both parties (Han *et al.*, 2012). Employees would like to build their relationships with supervisors who demonstrate attributes such as integrity, dependability and ability. Supervisors do value reciprocal exchanges with employees whom they view as being committed, trusted and capable (Han and Altman, 2009).

How is the market economy affecting nepotism?

Before the emergence of China's market economy, the *danwei* physically separated the Chinese state-owned enterprises (SOE) from the rest of society by brick walls (Yeh, 1997) and 'insiders' enjoyed the privileges available only to regular workers while outsiders (e.g. temporary labourers or others) were usually denied access to quality housing, food and the other provisions (Walder, 1986). This insider–outsider foundation of the *danwei* also offered opportunities for nepotism to take place. As insiders became aware of the jobs becoming available through their *guanxi* with those making the recruitment decisions, they were able to gain advantages for their family and friends who were looking for a job. This access to employment information provided a nepotistic advantage to insiders and was a core characteristic of organizational *guanxi,* especially in SOEs (Grainger, 2005).

Since Deng initiated the market economy in China, the evolution of nepotism in Chinese companies appears to be following a four-stage process. In Stage 1, prior to the introduction of the market economy, most jobs in Chinese SOEs were awarded through *guanxi* between officials and family members, trusted friends or well-connected third parties. In this stage, educational qualifications were irrelevant and the strongest *guanxi* connection could be appointed to senior positions despite at times having no qualifications or experience. In Stage 2, as the market economy and better education systems began to evolve, qualified and experienced personnel without any *guanxi* received opportunities to be interviewed for positions. However, candidates with strong *guanxi* connections still received the appointment despite the quality of the other candidates. In Stage 3, as the market economy continued to evolve and the pressure began to grow on employees to perform and for managers to generate a profit, the candidates with the strong *guanxi* connections still gained an invitation to the interview process. If they had the required qualifications and experience, then they would be likely to get the appointment regardless of the quality of the other candidates. However, if they did not have the qualifications or experience, then it was possible that the person with the *guanxi* would not get the position and it would be awarded to the most qualified and experienced candidate. In Stage 4, the stage that is currently evolving and gaining momentum in China (especially in professional positions (Zhang *et al.*, 2012), only the best applicants in terms of qualifications and experience will be selected for interview. Those with powerful *guanxi* may still get to the interview stage however, if they do not have the quality of qualifications and experience required for the position, they are not able to compete with the other candidates being considered who have better experience and qualifications. In Stage 4, the candidate chosen for the position would be based primarily on the quality of their experience and qualifications. If, by chance, the final two remaining candidates being considered both had strong qualifications and experience, one with *guanxi* and one without, then it is likely the *guanxi* candidate would only then have an advantage. Otherwise the most talented, qualified and proven candidate would get the position. The stage of the process for any organization seeking new recruits depends on a number of factors. As the requirements of the advertised position become more skilled and professional and the company becomes more exposed to international and competitive conditions, it is likely that their job selection criteria would tend towards Stage 4. As the level of professionalism and competitiveness of the industry declined, so would the characteristics of recruitment being undertaken. For example, an accountant position in a five-star hotel is likely to be selected using Stage 4 criteria while a housekeeping employee in a two-star domestic hotel would more likely be assessed under the Stage 2 criteria of the model.

In the past, managers who have been nepotistic have given the *guanxi* concept a dubious reputation in Western eyes (Foster, 1997; Snell, 1999) and this remains a concern for international managers operating in China today as sometimes these types of favours imply unfair or even fraudulent practices. In the past, nepotism has been linked closely to *guanxi* (Xin and Pearce, 1996; Pearce and Robinson, 2000; Grainger, 2004, 2005) though with the evolution of China's market economy, the signs have begun to emerge that *guanxi*-based nepotism may be decreasing. As early as 1996, Ding *et al.* (1997) found FIEs in Shenzen (one of China's first coastal Special Economic Zones) were beginning to move away from centrally planned job allocation, lifetime employment and egalitarian pay systems towards open job markets at all levels. Contractual employment based on an individual's skills, training and job demands were beginning, along with the first signs of the evolution of employee performance compensation plans.

Further inland in Yunnan Province in 1999, the recruitment process in the hotel sector was still primarily nepotistic and *guanxi*-driven (Grainger, 2004, 2005). Hotel regulations stated that 'staff relatives are not permitted to work in the same hotel' yet at one SOE in Kunming, 32 families were working in the same hotel, with up to 13 people from one family working in the same department. Some had no work skills, but because they had the right relationships, they could still get a good job. Family members had tight bonds, and family *guanxi* was an important tool in finding employment (Fried, 1953; Yau *et al.*, 2000; Grainger, 2008).

In this inland location at the turn of the century, job appointments were made under Stage 1 conditions and *guanxi* relationships were still more important than a university qualification and experience when applicants were trying to find a job. New graduates were frustrated to find that their educational qualifications drew only limited respect from the older generation of managers. Appointing and promoting those with *guanxi*, rather than proven experience and ability, often resulted in poor management, unnecessary waste, low productivity and further nepotism. Young employees, especially in SOEs, resented *guanxi* favours and, because of this, some had lost their motivation to work hard. Talented, educated and experienced employees were moving to other hotels or organizations with more modern management and recruitment methods because they could see only limited opportunities for promotion within the old-style hotels (Grainger, 2005). This supported Seligman's (1999) finding that in the past jobs in China have often gone to the best connected rather to the best qualified or experienced

As pressure from the market economy grows on employees to perform rather than to rely on *guanxi*, managers increasingly find themselves pressured by market forces and improving legal infrastructure to distance themselves from the 'crooked' ways of *guanxi* practice (Yi and Ellis, 2000). In the early part of this century, Cooke (2004) found a mixture of Chinese-style employment measures (e.g. paternalism, social welfare), Western management techniques (e.g. team working, employee involvement) and 'opportunistic' labour management behaviour (e.g. non-compliance with labour regulations—nepotism) in an American-owned toy manufacturing company in China, reflecting Stages 2 and 3 of the model. As the decade progressed, private-sector managers began to reduce their number of nepotistic appointments unless the individuals recruited with *guanxi* were talented enough to do well in the position or generate attractive returns as compensation.

In the Yunnan hotel sector, appointments changed from being almost 100 per cent nepotistic *guanxi*-based in 1999 to almost 100 per cent based on educational, qualification, experience and ability in 2012 (Grainger, 2012), evolving longitudinally through Stages 1–4 of the model. In the Chinese Agricultural Bank and Bank of China in 2012, instances were recorded of bankers quietly head-hunting for executives for new positions rather than openly advertising positions so as to eliminate the possibility of *guanxi*-based requests from senior government officials for jobs for their offspring or 'princelings'. As the new century evolves, multinational corporations (MNCs) have began using systematic and formal techniques of employee recruitment and selection, though in some cases nepotistic and familial hiring strategies are proving difficult to eradicate (Walsh and Zhu, 2007).

There is some hope that human resources practices in China appear to be converging toward a more Western norm (Warner, 1997; Ngo *et al.*, 2008). In 2013, those with *guanxi* are still able to gain an interview for a position but are now often no longer guaranteed the position. Managers under increased pressure to perform ethically are now feeling it is difficult but possible to refuse nepotistic requests as the pressure on them to be efficient and effective continues to grow. In family companies and some government departments, *guanxi* favouritism is still restricting the rate at which China's most talented graduates and potential managers reach decision-making positions (Grainger, 2008, 2012).

Conclusion

As the market economy develops, employees have begun to view management as being less trustworthy when their HRM decisions are made based on *guanxi* (Chen *et al.*, 2004). One major reason for the negative reaction lies in the belief that all employees should be treated with equality and the new concept of fairness in the twenty-first century. As the Chinese workforce becomes increasingly educated, global and diverse, Chinese managers are becoming more cognizant of the benefits and costs of *guanxi* in a more rule-oriented China. Looking forward this may reduce the negative repercussions of *guanxi* practices and channel personal *guanxi* in ways that benefit not just *guanxi* connections but other organizational members and the organization as a whole.

In conclusion, the importance of *guanxi* in doing business in China still remains a significant factor and the sometimes unreliable rule of law will insure this importance and significance remain at least in the short to medium term. From a nepotistic perspective, the growing pressure on managers to perform and generate profits under increasingly competitive conditions is having a much more significant impact on the practice of nepotism and its resultant decline at the beginning of the twenty-first century appears destined to continue.

Note

1 Ambler (1995b) defined the whole *guanxi* network as being a *guanxiwang* or a chain of interconnected persons.

Bibliography

Alston, J.P. (1989) '*Wa, Guanxi* and *Inhwa*: managerial principles in Japan, China and Korea', *Business Horizons,* 32: 26–31.

Ambler, T. (1995a) 'Reflections in China: re-orienting images of marketing', *Marketing Management,* 4(1): 22–30.

Ambler, T. (1995b) 'The derivation of *Guanxi*', *Marketing Management,* 4(1): 27.
Bell, D. (2000) '*Guanxi*: a nesting of groups', *Current Anthropology,* 41: 132–138.
Bian, Y. (1994) *Work and Inequality in Urban China,* Albany, NY: SUNY Press.
Bian, Y. and Ang, S. (1997) '*Guanxi* networks and job mobility in China and Singapore', *Social Forces,* 75(3): 981–1006.
Blackman, C. (1997) *Negotiating China: Case Studies and Strategies,* Sydney: Allen and Unwin.
Bozionelos, N. and Wang, L. (2007) 'An investigation on the attitudes of Chinese workers towards individually based performance related reward systems', *International Journal of Human Resource Management,* 17(1): 1530–1545.
Brunner, J.A. and Koh, A.C. (1988) 'Negotiations in the People's Republic of China: an empirical study of American and Chinese negotiators' perceptions and practices', *Journal of Global Marketing,* 2(1): 33–65.
Brunner, J.A. and Taoka, G.M. (1977) 'Marketing and negotiating in the People's Republic of China: perceptions of American businessmen who attended the 1975 Canton Trade Fair', *Journal of International Business Studies,* 8(2): 69–82.
Brunner, J.A., Chen, J., Sun, C. and Zhou, N. (1989) 'The role of *Guanxi* in negotiations in the Pacific Basin', *Journal of Global Marketing,* 3(2): 7–23.
Bruton, G. and Ahlstrom, D. (2003) 'An institutional view of China's venture capital industry', *Journal of Business Venturing,* 18(2): 233–259.
Butterfield, F. (1983) *China: Alive in a Bitter Sea,* New York: Coronet Books.
Chen, C.C., Chen, Y-R. and Xin, K. (2004) '*Guanxi* practices and trust in management: a procedural justice perspective', *Organisational Science,* 15(2): 200–209.
Chen, M. (2004) *Asian Management Systems: Chinese, Japanese and Korean Styles of Business,* 2nd edn, London: Thomson Business Press.
Chen, X-P. and Chen, C.C. (2004) 'On the intricacies of Chinese *Guanxi*', *Asia Pacific Journal of Management,* 21(2): 305–324.
Chen, Y.F. and Tjosvold, D. (2006) 'Participative leadership by western managers in China: the role of relationships', *Journal of Management Studies,* 43(8): 1727–1752.
Cheng, B.S., Chow, L.F., Wu, T.Y., Huang, M.P. and Farh, J.L. (2004) 'Paternalistic leadership and subordinate responses: establishing a leadership model in Chinese organisations', *Asian Journal of Social Psychology,* 7(3): 89–117.
Cooke, F.L. (2004) 'Foreign firms in China: modelling HRM in a toy manufacturing corporation', *Human Resource Management Journal,* 14(2): 31–52.
Davies, H., Leung, T., Sherriff, L. and Wong, Y. (1995) 'The benefits of "*Guanxi*"', *Industrial Marketing Management,* 24: 207–214.
Ding, D., Fields, D. and Akhtar, S. (1997) 'An empirical study of human resource management policies and practices in foreign-invested enterprises in China: the case of Shenzen Special Economic Zone', *International Journal of Human Resource Management,* 8(5): 595–613.
Dunfee, T.W. and Warren, D.E. (2001) 'Is *guanxi* ethical? A normative analysis of doing business in China', *Journal of Business Ethics,* 32(3): 191–204, Pt 1.
Fan, Y. (2002) 'Questioning *Guanxi:* definition, classification and implications', *International Business Review,* 11(5): 5543–5561.
Fang, T. (2003) 'A critique of Hofstede's fifth national culture dimension', *International Journal of Cross Cultural Management,* 3: 347–368.
Farh, J.L., Tsui, A.S., Xin, K. and Cheng, B.S. (1998) 'The influence of relational demography and *Guanxi:* the Chinese case', *Organisational Science,* 9(4): 471–489.
Foster, M. (1997) 'South China: are the rewards worth the risk?' *Long Range Planning,* 20(4): 585–593.
Fried, M.H. (1953) *The Fabric of Chinese Society: A Study of Life of a Chinese Country Seat,* New York: Praeger.
Grainger, S. (2003) 'Organisational *Guanxi* in China's hotel sector', in I. Alon (ed.) *Chinese Culture, Organisational Behavior, and International Business Management,* Westport, CT: Praeger, pp. 57–71.
Grainger, S. (2004) 'Differentiating between intra-organizational and inter-organizational *Guanxi*', in Proceedings of the 16th Annual Conference of the Association for Chinese Economics Studies, Australia (ACESA), Brisbane, Queensland, 19–20 July.
Grainger, S. (2005) 'Organisational *guanxi* and state-owned enterprises in South-west China', thesis, available at: http://repository.uwa.edu.au:80/R/?func=dbinjumpfull&object_id=7319&silo_library=GEN01.
Grainger, S. (2008) 'Roaring Dragon Hotel', *Harvard Business Review,* available at: http://hbr.org/product/roaring-dragon-hotel/an/908M04-PDF-ENG, Prod. #: 908M04-PDF-ENG.

Grainger, S. (2012) 'Roaring Dragon Hotel: a second attempt at modernization', *Harvard Business Review,* available at: http://hbr.org/product/roaring-dragon-hotel-a-second-attempt-at-modernization/an/W12392-PDF-ENG. Prod. #: W12392-PDF-ENG.

Guthrie, D. (1998) 'The declining significance of *guanxi* in China's economic transition', *The China Quarterly,* June: 254281.

Han, Y. and Altman, Y. (2009) 'Supervisor and subordinate *guanxi:* a grounded investigation in the People's Republic of China', *Journal of Business Ethics,* 88: 91–104.

Han, Y., Peng, Z. and Zhu, Y. (2012) 'Subordinate *guanxi* and trust in supervisor: a quality inquiry in the People's Republic of China', *Journal of Business Ethics,* 108: 313–324.

Hofstede, G. and Bond, M.H. (1988) 'The Confucian connection: from cultural roots to economic growth', *Organisational Dynamics,* 16(4): 5–21.

Hwang, K.K. (1987) 'Face and favor: the Chinese power game', *American Journal of Sociology,* 92: 944–974.

Jacobs, J.B. (1979) 'A preliminary model of particularistic ties in Chinese political alliance: *kan-ching* and *kuan-hsi* in a rural Chinese township', *China Quarterly,* 78: 237–273.

Jacobs, J.B. (1982) *The Concept of Guanxi and Local Politics in a Rural Chinese Social Interaction in Chinese Society,* New York: Praeger.

Kao, J. (1993) 'The worldwide web of Chinese business', *Harvard Business Review,* 71(2): 24–33.

King Y.A. (1991) '*Kuan-hsi* and network building: a sociological interpretation', *Daedalus,* 120(2): 63–85.

Kipnis, A.B. (1997) *Producing Guanxi: Sentiment, Self, and Subculture in a North China Village,* Durham, NC: Duke University Press.

Law, K.S., Wong C-S., Wang, D. and Wang, L. (2011) 'Effect of supervisor-subordinate *guanxi* on supervisory decisions in China: an empirical investigation', *The International Journal of Human Resource Management,* 11(4): 751–765.

Leung T.K.P. and Wong Y.H. (2001) 'The ethics and positioning of *guanxi* in China', *Marketing Intelligence and Planning,* 19: 55–64.

Leung, T., Wong, Y. and Wong, S. (1996) 'A study of Hong Kong businessman's perceptions of the role of "*Guanxi*" in the People's Republic of China', *Journal of Business Ethics,* 15(7): 749–759.

Li, J. and Wright P.C. (2000) '*Guanxi* and the realities of career development: a Chinese perspective', *Career Development International,* 5(7): 369–378.

Lin, N. (2001) '*Guanxi:* a conceptual analysis', in A. So, N. Lin, and D. Poston (eds) *The Chinese Triangle of Mainland China, Taiwan, and Hong Kong: Comparative Institutional Analysis,* London: Greenwood Press, pp. 153–166.

Lovett, S., Simmons, L. and Kali, R. (1999) '*Guanxi* versus the market: ethics and efficiency', *Journal of International Business Studies,* 30(2): 231–247.

Luo, Y. (1997a) '*Guanxi:* principles, philosophies, and implications', *Human Systems Management,* 16: 43–51.

Luo, Y. (1997b) '*Guanxi* and performance of foreign-invested enterprises in China: an empirical inquiry', *Management International Review,* 37(1): 51–70.

Luo, Y. and Chen, M. (1996) 'Managerial implications of *Guanxi* based business strategies', *Journal of International Management,* 2:193–216.

Luo, Y. and Chen, M. (1997) 'Does *guanxi* influence firm performance?' *Asia Pacific Journal of Management,* 14(1): 1–16.

Marcoux, M. (2002) 'Rulebook of red leadership: close personal connections offer key model for business success in China', *Business Weekly,* June 11, 7: 20.

Ngo, H-Y., Lau, C-M., and Foley, S. (2008) 'Strategic human resource management, firm performance and employees' relations climate in China', *Human Resource Management,* 47(1): 73–90.

Park, S.H. and Luo, Y. (2001) '*Guanxi* and organisational dynamics: organisational networking in Chinese firms', *Strategic Management Journal,* 22: 455–477.

Pearce, J. and Robinson, R. (2000) 'Cultivating *guanxi* as a foreign investor strategy', *Business Horizons,* 43(1): 31–39.

Peng, M.W. and Lou, Y. (2000) 'Managerial ties and firm performance in a transition economy: the nature of a micro-macro link', *Academy of Management Journal,* 43(3): 486–501.

Polin, T.H.W. (2000) 'Master of *guanxi*; how Li wins people and deals', *Asiaweek,* November 3, cover story.

Pye, L.W. (1992) *Chinese Negotiating Style,* Westport, CT: Quorum Books.

Redding, S.G. and Ng, M. (1982) 'The role of face in the organisational perceptions of Chinese managers', *Organisational Studies,* 3: 204–209.

Seligman, S. (1999) '*Guanxi:* grease for the wheels of China', *China Business Review,* 26(5): 34–40.

Snell, R. (1999) 'Obedience to authority and ethical dilemmas in Hong Kong companies', *Business Ethics Quarterly,* 9(3): 507–526.

Standifird, S. and Marshall, R. (2000) 'The transaction cost advantage of *guanxi*-based business practices', *Journal of World Business,* 35(1): 21–42.

Tsang, E.W.K. (1998) 'Can *Guanxi* be a source of sustained competitive advantage for doing business in China?' *Academy of Management Executive,* 12(2): 64–73.

Tsui, A. and Farh, J. (1997) 'Where *Guanxi* matters: relational demography and *Guanxi* in the Chinese context', *Work and Occupations,* 24(1): 56–80.

Tsui, A.S., Schoonhoven, C.B., Meyer, M.W., Lau, C.M. and Milkovich, G.T. (2004) 'Organization and management in the midst of societal transformation: the People's Republic of China', *Organization Science,* 15(2): 133–144.

Vanhonacker, W.R. (2004) '*Guanxi* networks in China', *The China Review,* 31(3): 48–53.

Walder, A.G. (1986) *Communist Neo-Traditionalism: Work and Authority in Chinese Industry,* Berkeley, CA: University of California Press.

Walsh, J. and Zhu, Y. (2007) 'Local complexities and global uncertainties: a study of foreign ownership and human resource management in China', *International Journal of Human Resource Management,* 18(2): 249–267.

Warner, M. (1997) 'China's HRM in transition: towards relative convergence?' *Asia Pacific Review,* 3(4): 19–34.

Wilkinson, B., Eberhardt, M., McLaren, J. and Millington, A. (2005) 'Human resource barriers to partnership sourcing in China', *International Journal of Human Resource Management,* 16(10): 1886–1900.

Wong, Y.H. and Chan, R.Y. (1999) 'Relationship marketing in China: *guanxi,* favouritism and adaptation', *Journal of Business Ethics,* 22(2): 107–118.

Wong, Y.T., Ngo, H. and Wong, J.M. (2003) 'Antecedents and outcomes of employees' trust in Chinese joint ventures', *Asia Pacific Journal of Management,* 20: 481–499.

Xin, K. and Pearce, J. (1996) '*Guanxi:* connections as substitutes for formal institutional support', *Academy of Management Journal,* 36(6): 1641–1659.

Xu, K. (1996) '*Guanxi,* the first step in any China venture', *Business Review Weekly,* 18(21): 62–63.

Yang, D.T. (1997) 'The effects of institutions on worker mobility and labor market efficiency', in G.J. Wen and D. Xu (eds) *The Reformability of China's State Sector,* London: World Scientific, pp. 347–364.

Yang, M.M. (1986) *The Art of Social Relationships and Exchange in China,* Berkeley, CA: University of California.

Yang, M.M. (1994) *Gifts, Favours and Banquets: The Art of Social Relationships in China,* Ithaca, NY: Cornell University Press.

Yang, M.M. (2002) 'The resilience of *Guanxi* and its new deployments: a critique of some new *Guanxi* scholarship', *The China Quarterly,* 170: 459–476.

Yau, O.H.M., Lee, J.S.Y., Chow, R.P.M., Sin, L.Y.M. and Tse. A.C.B. (2000) 'Relationship marketing the Chinese way', *Business Horizons,* 43: 16–24.

Yeh, W. (1997) 'Republican origins of the *Danwei:* the case of Shanghai's Bank of China', in X. Lu and E.J. Perry (eds) *Danwei: The Changing Chinese Workplace in Historical and Comparative Perspective,* New York: M.E. Sharpe, Inc., pp. 60–90.

Yeung, I.Y.M. and Tung. R.L. (1996) 'Achieving business success in Confucian societies: the importance of *Guanxi* (connections)', *Organisational Dynamics,* 25(2): 54–65.

Yi, L. and Ellis, P. (2000) 'Insider-outsider perspectives of *Guanxi*', *Business Horizons,* 43(1): 25–31.

Zhang, S., Liu, W. and Liu, X. (2012) 'Investigating the relationship between Protestant work ethic and Confucian dynamism: an empirical test in Mainland China', *Journal of Business Ethics,* 106: 243–252.

Zhang, Y. and Zhang, Z. (2006) '*Guanxi* and organisational dynamics in China: a link between individual and organisational levels', *Journal of Business Ethics,* 67: 375–392.

8

The bamboo network in China

An emerging phenomenon unlike the overseas Chinese

Bing Ren, Kevin Au and Na Shen

Introduction

The overseas ethnic Chinese normally create influential family business conglomerates in South-east Asia. Weidenbaum and Hughes (1996) coined the term "bamboo network" for this phenomenon. Since then this topic has attracted the interest of scholars and practitioners from both the East and the West. Questions have been asked about the valuable lessons Western and Eastern businesses can learn from these families who dominate and drive the economies of South-east Asia and other parts of the world.

Some revealing answers to this question have been suggested in a number of research studies in the 1990s (e.g., Chen, 1995; Redding, 1995; Hamilton, 1996; Whitley, 1992, 1999). It was argued that overseas Chinese have a cultural heritage of close-knit family and kinship ties, work diligently, and are highly entrepreneurial (Redding, 1995; Weidenbaum, 1996). They are flexible enough to stretch the business boundary from restricted regions to diversified geography (Rauch and Trindade, 2002), and thus they can develop their business from being small firms, through the bamboo network, to become large conglomerates (Peng, 2000; Weidenbaum, 1998; Yeung, 1997, 1999). Scholars observed that the bamboo characters are down-to-earth, flexible, and stretching the network-based boundary, have enabled the overseas Chinese to perform brilliantly, in South-east Asian and other overseas economies.

A recent article in *The Economist* (2011) argues that "China's vigor owes much to what has been happening from the bottom up, to a multitude of vigorous, (very) private entrepreneurs: a fast-growing thicket of bamboo capitalism." This remark sounds very much like a description of the overseas Chinese family conglomerates. Yet so far, there have not been any systematic investigations and dialogue undertaken in the management literature. Meanwhile, a great number of studies in fact have examined a similar phenomenon in alternative research streams. For example, the literature on China's institutional transitions, *guanxi* and network capitalism (e.g., Davis *et al.*, 1995; Boisot and Child, 1996; Peng and Heath, 1996; Xin and Pearce, 1996; Yeung and Tung, 1996; Peng, 1997; Guthrie, 1998; Park and Luo, 2001; Peng, 2003; Guo and Miller, 2010; Luo *et al.*, 2011) focused on the private business sector rather than on the peculiar "family business enterprises." Studies on Chinese family business enterprises are huge (e.g., Au *et al.*, 2011), but they did not discuss the bamboo network tradition that has developed as in South-east Asia.[1]

The current research landscape creates a challenge for us in drawing the attention of researchers to the phenomenon of the bamboo networks in China. We asked three questions in trying to integrate the diverse streams of literature: (1) what is the Chinese bamboo network?; (2) how do they grow?; and (3) in what way is the Chinese bamboo network different or similar to the South-east Asian case? Continuous research efforts and dialogue can benefit both the bamboo network research and the research on Chinese management in the context of Mainland China.

The Chinese bamboo economy and the Chinese bamboo network

The Chinese bamboo economy

The players

Entrepreneurs who start and develop their business in Mainland China can be classified into the following categories: the poorest individuals with harsh life experiences; former government officials with a stable and good life; the returnees and overseas Chinese who went abroad to study or to make a living and subsequently return to China for business. It is argued that these different groups of entrepreneurs have unique mindsets, respective resource endowments and constraints in creating and developing their businesses (Li *et al.*, 2012; Wang and Lu, 2012). The organizational forms thus created are diverse, ranging from the township and village enterprise that is a hybrid form under the joint efforts of rural entrepreneurs and local government,[2] the simple small business or partnership firms started by rural or urban entrepreneurs, and the private business type formed by former government officials or returnees (Redding, 2002; Li *et al.*, 2012; Wang and Lu, 2012). Some of these enterprises may be joint ventures with foreign investors and overseas capital (Wang, 2008).

The stages

Each of the aforementioned organizational forms corresponds to the respective development stage of the bamboo economy. The first stage is during the late 1970s and the 1980s when the rural and urban entrepreneurship activities and the township and village enterprises were active. This is an important historical period for the Chinese economy because it was the first time that the Chinese state had allowed private businesses to be formed outside of the state-owned system. As they say: private enterprises emerged and have grown like bamboo shoots all over the country since 1978. The township and village enterprises as hybrid forms and private businesses produced what had been ignored by the state-owned sectors, or just simply established trades to fill the gap in the market. During this period, some firms began to participate in the global value chain, and become important component suppliers of large international businesses operating around the world.[3]

The second stage is the mid-1980s to the late 1990s. During this period, the Chinese government decided to downsize the state-owned enterprises by keeping control of the large ones and releasing the small ones.[4] This created opportunities for management buyouts and for the transfer of government ownerships via mergers and acquisitions. Ownership transfer was common particularly from poorly performing state-owned enterprises (SOEs) to capable private business enterprises. With the aid of local governments, SOE managers or private business owners took advantage of the opportunity by acquiring the SOEs' assets as a good bargain and have turned around the poor business into prosperity. During the process, there were lots of accusations of corruption and exploitation in pricing and other issues; these complaints and suspicions led to some private entrepreneurs being put in prison.[5] Nevertheless, these former SOE managers and new private business owners helped reactivate the Chinese market economy and move the economy one step further.

The third stage is during the late 1990s and in the 2000s. Many returnees moved back to China and established their own private businesses (Zhang *et al.*, 2011). Most of these entrepreneurs are highly educated, and pay more attention to brand name and marketing (Wang and Lu, 2012). These generations were more aware of the potential risks of business–government connections and thus maintained loose business–government ties. They brought advanced technologies to China and helped local governments to develop new industrial areas. For example, they employed the dot.com ideas to set up Internet services such as search engines[6] or they used the Internet to develop information and transaction platforms in e-commerce.[7] During this period, China also became a member of the World Trade Organization (WTO). The cross-boundary exchange and flow of business opportunities, resources, people and information surged. Later on, China initiated the Eleventh Five-Year Plan promoting "The Go West Campaign" and development of new pillar industries in many different regions.[8] Private business entrepreneurs quickly responded to the new institutional and business environments, cultivated unique business models in global value chains, and developed their businesses to become world-level players.[9]

The Chinese bamboo network defined

The bamboo network originally referred to overseas ethnic Chinese family business enterprises. Weidenbaum gives a vivid definition of this phenomenon:

> One of the most important economic developments since the end of the Cold War is occurring with little notice in Southeast Asia. In Thailand, Malaysia, Indonesia, Taiwan, Singapore, Vietnam, the Philippines and the Coastal Zone of China, a remarkable economic change is taking place led by overseas Chinese business families, or what could be called the bamboo network.
>
> *(1998, p. 1)*

According to Weidenbaum, the bamboo network was founded by the Chinese who had emigrated during the period of civil unrest in the late 1940s. They fled their disrupted homeland and worked hard in their new homes, saving most of what they earned and then started their own businesses (Weidenbaum, 1996, p. 1). Many of those small family companies have grown into enormous conglomerates today. They became key economic players in the region, and their business spread throughout South-east Asia and beyond. Because of their unique abilities to deal with government regulations and restrictions, they are able to move money, people and resources from one country to another (Weidenbaum, 1998). This geographical stretch is significant and unique, because the networks of cooperation permeated across nations, regardless of the radically different political systems in the countries of Asia (Redding, 1995, p. 62).

In a historical view, Chinese private and family businesses just started to develop after 1978. Although China historically was known for the *Jin* and *Hui* merchant groups, who might be the earliest family business conglomerates, these traditional forms of businesses went out of style and disappeared when the Communist Party established the People's Republic of China under the leadership of Chairman Mao (Weidenbaum and Hughes, 1996; Wu, 2007).[10] In the late 1980s, private business development was allowed again and this grew under the market reform led by the Chinese leader, Deng Xiaoping. Accompanying this significant reform, Chinese private businesses began to grow rapidly "just like bamboo shootings after the rain." These private businesses took various forms, such as family-based, partnership-based, collective-owned, and township and village enterprises, etc. (Redding, 2002). With three decades' development, some of them have become large and influential family business enterprises operating all over the world (see Appendixes I and II).[11] The bamboo network has blossomed in Mainland China far beyond the optimistic scenario that Weidenbaum (1998) speculated on.

Table 8.1 shows the basic figures on family enterprises and the respective distribution of each category within the whole system, based on the data of the public-listed firms. As Table 8.1 suggests, the proportion of privately controlled enterprises within the whole public-listed economy is increasing with time, growing from 37 percent in 2011 to 56 percent in 2012 and 58 percent in 2013. The proportion of family-based enterprises has grown from 15 percent in 2011 to 20 percent in 2012, and to 28 percent in 2013. Two significant trends are suggested by the data: first, the proportion of privately controlled enterprises (56 percent) is larger than the state-controlled sector for the first time in 2011, suggesting that the private economy in China is gaining ground and is likely to be equal in force to the state-owned economy. Second, the proportion of family-based listed firms is close to half (49 percent) in the private-controlled sector, suggesting that family-based enterprises are becoming important private economic organizations in China.

Table 8.1 Family enterprises in China

	*2010**	*2011***	*2012****
A-share public-listed companies ALL			
State-controlled	2063	2272	2422
Private-controlled	1301	1004	1028
Family-controlled	762 (37% out of all) 305 (15% of all, 40% of private)	1268 (56% out of all) 460 (20% of all, 36% of private)	1394 (58% out of all) 684 (28% of all, 49% of private)
Industry distribution****	**Top 3**: Manufacturing, 71%; IT, 8.2%; Real estate, 6.8% **Among those non-listed**: 42% manufacturing; 14.9% Trade, wholesale and retail	**Top 3**: Manufacturing (Traditional chemical industry; Iron manufacturing; Machinery and equipment manufacturing)	**Top 3**: Manufacturing (Machinery and equipment manufacturing, electrical equipment, chemical products and specified equipment); Real estate; Computers **Among those listed in Hong Kong:** Raw materials; Durable consumer goods and clothing; Real estate
Region distribution****	**Top 3**, Guangdong, 69; Zhejiang, 60; Jiangsu, 32	Guangdong, Zhejiang, Jiangsu	Guangdong, Zhejiang, Jiangsu, together count for 82.5% of the total

Notes: Data are based on Forbes China. * Data is up to end of June 2010. ** Data is up to September 30, 2011. *** Data is up to July 15, 2012. **** Data refers only to family controlled companies.

The rapid development of private firms in the past few decades means that the experiences of overseas Chinese entrepreneurs and their vibrant forms of family, kinship and business networks have appeared again in Mainland China. Only this time, the network that has facilitated firm survival and growth turns out to be much broader due to the diversity of the business participants. The complexity of the institutional environment also shapes the formation of the Chinese bamboo networks in new directions. For example, apart from the family and kinship ties, there are other salient types of ties in the bamboo network economy, such as the business–government ties and the peculiar township and village enterprises. The bamboo network forms also change dramatically as environments change. In the next section, we will present a more detailed analysis of the Chinese bamboo network.

Analysis of the Chinese bamboo network

The Chinese bamboo entrepreneurs use family and kinship as their network core (see Figure 8.1). As well as emotional support and provision of essential resources such as capital, the family members also found and manage businesses together. Beyond the family, there are three types of personal network ties: (1) the ties with masters (mentors); (2) the ties with fellow townsfolk; (3) and the ties with close friends. The master inspires and coaches the entrepreneur in business and spiritual aspects, and some also supply resources and give support to the new ventures. Friends and fellow townsfolk provide important social capital to business entrepreneurs, as do middle-school classmates. These are life-long connections helping private entrepreneurs acquire critical resources and reliable information. To some extent, they also provide critical support when the focal business is suffering a crisis (Ren and Zhang, 2011).

Two other types of networks outside the core are important for private business enterprises:

1 the business–government connection;
2 the business–business connection.

Private entrepreneurs build alliances with governments (either at the central or the local level) in charge of the policy scheme and resource allocation. This type of bamboo network matters for both early stage venture creation and its subsequent expansion. Business–government connections range from entrepreneurs' political connection to governments' ownership participation in private businesses. Business–government ties will evolve with the life-stage of the private business. And it is more dynamic due to the rapid changes in both the firm and environmental aspects. In the early stage, it is likely that the private business will depend more on the

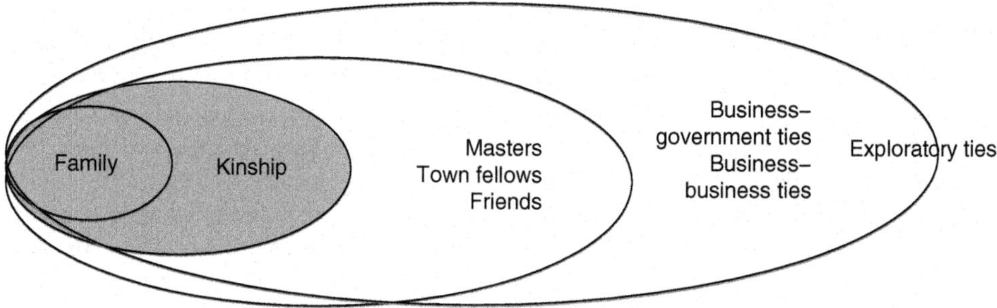

Figure 8.1 Chinese bamboo networks

government; however, the table turns in the later stage, and the government then depends more on the business. When companies grow big with huge capital under their control, both the local and non-local governments may come to the private enterprise asking for its contribution to the local economy. Mature entrepreneurs do not easily start a new relationship unless an important long-term connection will provide a guarantee for the new relationship.[12]

Entrepreneurs develop both long-term and short-term business connections. Long-term business connections are those created with trusted and helpful collaborators focusing on long-term returns. Short-term business ties are those created with unfamiliar and less trusted businesses, which can be transformed into long-term one depending on how cultivatable that relationship can be. Maintaining a certain proportion of short-term ties enhances the flexibility of the private business in pursuing new business opportunities. With flexibility, companies are able to adapt to environmental changes and reduce potential risks.

Exploratory ties are developed to pursue new business opportunities and generate better growth. For smaller firms in the bamboo network, this could be done by business founders simply through their personal networks and prioritizing new relationship possibilities based on their intuition. In large mature firms, this could be operationalized through a formal planning system such as through interlocking directorates (Ren *et al.*, 2009). Business executives first of all assign people who are going to participate in a search programme, set up a schedule, and clarify the roles of the participants in the search. The aim of opportunity-oriented searching is to look for new product opportunity, market trends and technological breakthroughs, etc. Mission-oriented searching can just be investigating the general management and organizational culture of the peer group firms for the purpose of exchange and mutual learning.[13]

How the Chinese bamboo network works

The above *guanxi* and network forms are beneficial to firm performance (Farh *et al.*, 1998; Bian, 2006; Luo *et al.*, 2011), if the proper governance mechanisms are in place (Zhang and Keh, 2009). One such governance mechanism is trust. The mechanisms of trust (the creation and maintenance of trust) in family and business connections are different (Song *et al.*, 2012). In family ties, trust originates in the blood relationship to fulfill emotional needs. In business ties, trust is based on transactional relationships, which fulfill efficiency needs (Farh *et al.*, 1998; Luo *et al.*, 2011). For friendship and long-term business ties, trust is pursued by fulfilling both emotional and transactional needs (Luo, 2005).

The bamboo network functions through important organizational processes as well. The first is the acquisition and allocation of resources, and the second is information processing. Business networks possess important resources and information that bamboo business players can acquire, coopt and leverage to enhance the firm's operation. It is known that strong ties bring in resources, and weak ties bring in non-redundant information (Granovetter, 1973, 1985; Burt, 1992). However, in the context of China, strong ties are found to matter to both resources and information and are more likely to enhance business performance (Bian, 2006; Xiao and Tsui, 2007). Chinese culture tends positively towards a close-knit network structure, so those who rely on weak ties or leverage bridge positions are less likely to be trusted as reliable partners (Xiao and Tsui, 2007; Chai and Rhee, 2009).[14]

Hite and Hesterly (2001) discussed the evolution of firm networks from emergence to early growth of the firm, and suggested that network forms are contingent on firm growth stage. Thus, the underlying resources and process development and constraints that drive certain bamboo networks function more effectively. When globalization starts to exert more influence on firms, it is argued that the renewal of business networks is necessary under the new business environment (Carney, 2005). The bamboo business network forms and functions thus evolve with environmental changes. When relating the business network formation to formal institutional development, Peng and Zhou (2005) suggest that firm network strategies would co-evolve with institutional transitions in Asia. A number of studies further suggest that the role of *guanxi* and social network forms will decline as the formal market institutions become more mature (Guthrie, 1998; Peng, 2003; Sun *et al.*, 2009).

The behavioral characteristics of the Chinese bamboo network

The behavioral characteristics of the network forms, however, are less addressed in the literature. They are not simply family- or kinship-based, and they are not the trust or efficiency-oriented business, government and exploratory ties. Chinese economic growth based on network forms has many significant characteristics due to the ambiguity and complexity of the reform environments. In this section, we attempt to characterize the Chinese bamboo network, and relate their characteristics to answer the question why the Chinese bamboo network matters:

- *Opportunity-driven.* Opportunity-driven means that as long as there exist opportunities with potential profit, entrepreneurs will pursue that opportunity with the aim of generating profitable returns. While entrepreneurs focus on discovering and exploiting opportunity (Shane and Venkataraman, 2009), being opportunity-driven, as a characteristic, reflects how Chinese entrepreneurs exploit and explore business opportunities by not focusing too much on long-term planning.

  A business entrepreneur we interviewed provides vivid evidence of the opportunity-driven side of Chinese bamboo players:

  > People like us lack professional knowledge, are opportunistic, are not fighting where we want to, but forming a goal where we can fight. During the process, it is hard to involve ourselves in certain kinds of core business, as we are opportunistic. This is indeed a very silent growth mode of many Chinese private enterprises
  >
  > *(private entrepreneur in Southern China)*

  Most Chinese bamboo entrepreneurs set the goal of reaping profits swiftly by exploiting different sets of opportunities that emerge in different time periods. Once the opportunities have been identified and exploited successfully, the profitable return is fast and big. Entrepreneurs thus do not care about long-term core competence, but focus more on the monetization of "playing new tricky games." During the transitional stage, it seems nothing will last for a long time, everything changes. Private enterprises just adapt to this and do whatever is profitable. A direct outcome of being opportunity-driven and the so-called "one possible version" growth mode is the lack of core competence in competing with global market players. It is those who have successfully walked out (survived) and specialized in a particular niche market and used their strong points who finally get a chance to grow.[15] The fellow in the case we just mentioned is indeed a survivor. However, being opportunity-driven was the most salient behavioral feature of the Chinese bamboo entrepreneur. It is the primary element behind the entrepreneurs' success or failure.
- *Flexibility.* Chinese bamboo networks maintain flexibility in order to cope with complex realities. For a business policy, there is no standard interpretation. Seeing that one way is not effective, people quickly try another way. The lack of institutional coherence pushes people to avoid being rigid and encourages flexibility (Storz *et al.*, 2013). Cultural drivers

include the limited codification and intimacy concern in diffusion (Boisot and Child, 1996). It also includes tolerance towards ambiguity and embrace of informal governance (Witt and Redding, 2013), all of which creates a demand for impromptu ways of thinking and doing. Impromptu management and adaptation are thus common. Organizational factors matter as well. Because most bamboo business enterprises are small[16] and lack formal structures and routines, their business operations rely more on flexible and informal codes of conduct.

Debates occur on how large these ambiguous and flexible firms are able to grow (Carney, 1998; Ahlstrom *et al.*, 2004). Conventional wisdom says that it is the codified knowledge, skills and organizational processes that enable organizational learning and economies of scale (March and Simon, 1958; Boisot and Child, 1996; March, 2010). We believe in alternative arguments. First, flexibility helps Chinese bamboo firms grow faster. Second, the influence of flexibility on firm size depends on the levels of analysis. Bamboo firms rely on networks to grow. In a network economy, individual firm size may be small, but when it is well connected, it is huge. Finally, choices of flexibility adopted by Chinese bamboo networks largely transcend the simple exploitation of dyadic *guanxi* or relationship behaviors. The more flexible, the more capable are entrepreneurs to stretch boundaries. And it is such boundary stretching in a complex network system that is followed by growth (Peng and Heath, 1996; Witt and Redding, 2013).

- *Cooperativeness.* The third characteristic of the Chinese bamboo network is cooperativeness. We adopt this idea from Redding (1995, p. 62):

> The cooperativeness is an important issue, as it is this feature which converts an otherwise disparate group of entrepreneurs into a significant economy, whose power is normally hidden from view due to the simple fact that it cannot be represented in any national statistics.

Modern China as seen today would not exist if we ignore the "cooperativeness" nature of any of the bamboo network relationships. Cooperativeness between private enterprise and the central and local governments is particularly important in the Chinese economy. People tend to see tension in the firm–government relationship, and suggest a power structure with the balance firmly skewed to the government side. We suggest that it is the dimension of cooperativeness in the firm–government relationship that drives Chinese bamboo networks' growth. Cooperativeness facilitates the growth of both the private businesses and the local economies. The entrepreneurs know that the growth of local government's GDP is important. The government knows that if regional economy has to grow, there must be micro-level firm growth. Thus, the two parties form alliances, draw up agreements, act practically and proactively to pursue each other's goals.[17] This is a scenario favorable to all parties.

Cooperativeness happens between the firm (or the entrepreneur) and the government subtly. Each side bears in mind what could be leveraged from the other parties, what is the baseline for the other. And they leverage each other's complementarities to develop their respective goals. While the cooperativeness between the firm and the government may influence policy-driven business sectors, the cooperativeness between business and business can determine wider market scope.[18,19] In general, we predict that it is such cooperativeness that propels regional economic growth and individual firms' success.[20]

The Chinese bamboo network and beyond

Employing Whitley's framework, Redding (2002) discussed the Chinese business system and suggested that China and the West differ in many fundamental ways, and it is those fundamental differences that shape a different Chinese business system. For example, he discussed "cause as connectedness," "science of relationship," and "passion for the concrete fact," etc., as the unique cultural dimensions that shape Chinese ways of thinking and doing. Subsequently, he also discussed the similarities and differences between the business groups located in different countries (Witt and Redding, 2013).

There are some commonalities between the Mainland and the overseas ethnic Chinese bamboo networks. The first commonality lies in the dominant role of *guanxi* and network forms in shaping the bamboo network economy. Second, it was the fact that *guanxi* and networks took the place of formal institutions that partly facilitated the growth of both markets. Third, business–government relationships played important roles in both places. Fourth, the ability of private businesses to cultivate and stretch relationship boundaries was essentially important for both economies. Finally, the importance of the business networks and boundary stretching to the growth of these economies lay in all three aspects: resource support, information sharing, and uncertainty avoidance.

Despite the similarities, significant differences exist between Chinese bamboo networks on the mainland and those outside China. The differences lie in the nature and extent of the role played by various network forms on the creation of economic mechanisms and process, and the levels of uncertainty and the development of bamboo networks in both societies. In the Chinese bamboo network economy, *guanxi* and social ties can be cultivated in more varieties of forms (as shown in Figure 8.1). Located outside the core, they play a more important functional role rather than an embedded role (Sun, 1996).[21] Yet, in South-east Asia, family and kinship ties are more important, shaping the economy to be more family-based. Although a small number of Chinese private businesses have grown into family-based conglomerates, the inter-firm relations and governance were not as mature as their South-east Asian counterparts (Witt and Redding, 2013). The well-documented phenomenon of "connection through marriage" (Weidenbaum and Hughes, 1996; Fan, 2012) was not common in China, partly because the second generation of Chinese family businesses were still young. A more fundamental role for family and kinship ties and stronger integration between different Chinese family business enterprises has yet to happen.

As for the role played by government network ties, the Chinese government has had a stronger influence in recent years and there was no evidence that China has had a chance to evolve into a mature market economy in the past. Consequently, the opportunity for private entrepreneurs to exploit openings, be flexible and cooperative has largely centered on the relationship building with the government. Yet for the overseas ethnic Chinese bamboo network, business has relied less on political-economic alliances, and the effects of the market and other forms such as professionalization and social organization have become stronger (Yeung, 2006). Consequently, the opportunity-driven and flexible cooperativeness in the market-oriented relationship contexts were more prevalent (ibid.).

Will the Chinese bamboo economy have a chance to move to where the South-east Asian countries had developed? As Chinese bamboo network researchers, we pay close attention to what has been going on in the broader category of private business, and we clearly saw that the prosperity of China had largely relied on both similar and different trajectories to South-east Asia. The recent attention to "Asian capitalism and bringing Asia into the comparative capitalism perspective" had shed some light on this issue (Storz *et al.*, 2013). We expect to see more studies being conducted in this direction to help enrich Chinese management studies in both Mainland China and in South-east Asian countries.

Conclusion

A brief review of the research and an analysis of the private economy in China reveals that bamboo networks are emerging on the Mainland. It is obvious that Chinese private firms widely use network forms for control and co-ordination, and they can expand through networks into large companies and international conglomerates. However, due to the marked differences in historical paths and institutional environments in China, these bamboo networks will present significant differences from the better-known South-east Asian bamboo network economy. Given the rigor and rapid changes in China, the bamboo network economy on the Mainland deserves more in-depth analysis in terms of its unique functional structures embedded within the broader political and institutional context.

Acknowledgements

The first author Bing Ren thanks Yajun Yu for excellent research assistance, and the financial support of the Humanity and Social Science Research Fund Project (Fund code: 12YJA630096) of the Ministry of Education, China.

Notes

1 Two important family research centers in China are: the Center for Chinese Family Business under the leadership of Prof. Xinchun, Li in Guangdong Sun Yat-sen University, and the Research Center of Entrepreneurship and Family Business under the leadership of Prof. Chen, Ling in Zhejiang University, that just started to report Chinese family business development in 2011.

2 Most of the township and village enterprises were owned by the local government in their start-up stage, however, as time went on, many of them were transformed to private-owned enterprises.

3 One successful example is the Zhejiang Xiao Shan Universal Joints Company founded by Lu, Guanqiu in the late 1970s which produced universal joints for automobiles.

4 This period was also accompanied by the layoff of the SOE workforce under Premier Zhu, Rongji's policies. And many workers who were made unemployed were forced to start their small businesses for survival.

5 An example is the company founder of Greencool, Gu Chujun who acquired Kelon in 2001 and was investigated in 2005 by China Securities Regulatory Commission (CSRC) and put into prison for the crime of exploitation of state-owned assets.

6 Two respective cases are the returnee Li, Yanhong who founded Baidu, and Zhang, Chaoyang who founded Sohu.

7 For example, Jack Ma established "China Yellow" after a visit abroad and further founded Alibaba, the largest B2B and B2C online business platform in China.

8 Detailed information can be obtained from XinhuaNet at http://news.xinhuanet.com/ziliao/2006–01/16/content_4057926.htm.

9 The most famous case is Shi, Zhengrong, a scientist and returnee who responded to the government policy and established Wuxi Suntech in 2000 to produce solar energy. The company was listed on the New York stock exchange in 2005, and Shi became the wealthiest person in China. However, the company filed for bankruptcy on 20 March 2013.

10 For example, a big family business enterprise led by the Rong business family during the late Qing Dynasty and the early Republican period in Wuxi controlled over half the Chinese textile industry. After 1949, the Rong business family supported the Communist Party to restructure its textile factory at Guangdong under the state-private cooperation plan released in 1953, aiming at reforming the capitalist economy into a socialist economy. Although the third generation leader, Rong, Yiren was appointed the Deputy Mayor of Shanghai in 1957, and became the vice-chairman of the CCPPCC in 1978, the family business assets in Mainland China were confiscated.

11 According to the Forbes' investigation of the top 10 Chinese family businesses around the world, two Chinese family business enterprises are on list: (1) the IT company Baidu, led by Li, Yanhong, ranked No. 5 with total net assets of US$9.4 billion; and (2) the manufacturing company Suny Group led by Liang, Wengen, ranked No. 7 with total net assets of US$8 billion in 2011. In 2013, these two companies dropped out of the top 10 list due to the stock market downturn while another Chinese family business enterprise Wahaha, led by Zong, Qinghou entered the list with a rank of No. 9 and the total net assets of US$11.6 billion.

12 We experienced such an occasion where a third-tier city mayor in China came to visit a private enterprise and ask the entrepreneur to invest in their region with beneficiary land and other infrastructure policies. The entrepreneur and one female top executive joined the welcome dinner for the mayor. The entrepreneur's description of the dinner meeting to us emphasized that if the mayor has important common connections with the private entrepreneur, things will be easier.

13 We experienced two real cases like this including the UFIDA and the Dawu Business Group where the UFIDA has a formal search system targeting new business opportunities, and Dawu has a search system targeting corporate culture, governance and succession.

14 An example is the Chinese business entrepreneur Mou, Qizhong, famous for taking advantage of the institutional niches, but his structural niche position in the trade network, however, has gained an infamous reputation in China.

15 One example is the Vanke Company, which transformed itself from a diversified multi-industry firm to a more focused real estate firm.

16 According to the Chinese family business report 2011, most Chinese family business enterprises are small and medium-sized. Some 1738 (63 percent) of all the sampled 2777 family business enterprises have a total equity below 5 million RMB.

17 For example, a little known private business entrepreneur in Tianjin expected that central government might have a big plan to develop the electronic commerce industry in Tianjin. He thus established an electronic commerce industrial park several years before the policy was really released. With his cooperative attitude, the entrepreneur obtained the government's attention and support. Later on, his proactive behavior regarding the local government leaders and policies gave him much more credit and development room. Through this process, the private entrepreneur also helped the government leaders to put forward the reform in that particular area.

18 More importantly, the two types of cooperativeness may jointly influence economic outcomes. For example, a local government may sign a big contract with a local private business to help build a bridge. That local private business may further find subcontractors to finish the project. And such a network phenomenon widely exists.

19 One story we heard is about a business entrepreneur who runs construction businesses in Tianjin. One of his friends is the leader in Liaoning Province in charge of the construction of municipal works. What the business entrepreneur commonly did was: he got phone calls from Liaoning inviting him to participate in certain municipal works, he then called other local partners and invited them to join in those projects.

20 In the dinner meeting case mentioned above, we see the pattern that local governments proactively come to successful private businesses to ask for collaboration. This observation supports such speculations that today's China has reached a stage where private capitalists and the government jointly play the game. But what the rules of the game are depends largely on the cooperativeness and bargaining process.

21 Sun (1996) offers a very good discussion of how the *guanxi* practice evolved in nature in Chinese society and suggested that after 1949 Chinese *guanxi* is more likely to be developed for functional purposes.

Bibliography

Ahlstrom, D., Young, M., Chan, E.S. and Bruton, G.D. (2004) "Facing constraints to growth? Overseas Chinese entrepreneurs and traditional business practices in East Asia," *Asia Pacific Journal of Management*, 21(3): 263–285.

Aoki, M. (2013) "Historical sources of institutional trajectories in economic development: China, Japan and Korea compared," *Socio-Economic Review*, 11(2): 233–264.

Au, K., Craig, J. and Ramachandran, K. (eds) (2011) *Family Enterprising in Asia: Exploring Transgenerational Entrepreneurship in Family Firms*, Cheltenham: Edward Elgar.

Bian, Y.J. (2006) "Social capital of the firm and its impact on performance: a social network perspective and analysis," in C.M. Lau, and A.S. Tsui (eds) *The Management of Enterprises in the People's Republic of China*, New York: Kluwer Academic Publishers, pp. 275–298.

Boisot, M. and Child, J. (1996) "From fiefs to clans and network capitalism: explaining China's emerging economic order," *Administrative Science Quarterly,* 41(4): 600–628.

Burt, R. (1992) *Structural Holes: The Social Structure of Competition,* Cambridge, MA: Harvard University Press.

Carney, M. (1998) "A management capacity constraint? Obstacles to the development of the overseas Chinese family business," *Asia Pacific Journal of Management,* 15: 137–162.

Carney, M. (2005) "Globalization and the renewal of Asian business networks," *Asia Pacific Journal of Management,* 22(4): 337–354.

Chai, S.C. and Rhee, M. (2009) "Confucian capitalism and the paradox of closure and structural holes in East Asian firms," *Management and Organization Review,* 6(1): 5–29.

Chen, M. (1995) *Asian Management Systems: Chinese, Japanese and Korean Styles of Business,* London: Routledge.

Davies, H., Leung, T.K.P., Lukc, S.T.K.L. and Wong, Y. (1995) "The benefits of *guanxi:* the value of relationships in developing the Chinese market," *Industrial Marketing Management,* 24(3): 207–214.

Family Business Research Group, China Private Economy Research Association. (2011) *Chinese Family Business Report 2011,* Beijing: CITIC Press (in Chinese).

Fan, J. (2012) *Key Generation: Out of the Puzzle on Succession in Chinese Family Enterprises,* Beijing: The Oriental Press (in Chinese).

Farh, J.L., Tsui, A.S., Xin, K. and Cheng, B.S. (1998) "The influence of relational demography and *guanxi:* the Chinese case," *Organization Science,* 9(4): 471–488.

Gold, T. and Guthrie, D. (2002) *Social Connections in China: Institutions, Culture, and the Changing Nature of Guanxi,* Cambridge: Cambridge University Press.

Granovetter, M. (1973) "The strength of weak ties," *American Journal of Sociology,* 78: 1360–1380.

Granovetter, M. (1985) "Economic action and social structure: the problem of embeddedness," *American Journal of Sociology,* 91: 481–510.

Guo, C. and Miller, J.K. (2010) "*Guanxi* dynamics and entrepreneurial firm creation and development in China," *Management and Organization Review,* 6(2): 267–291.

Guthrie, D. (1998) "The declining significance of *guanxi* in China's economic transition," *The China Quarterly,* 154: 254–282.

Hamilton, G.G. (ed.) (1996) *Asian Business Networks,* Berlin: de Gruyter.

Hite, J.M. and Hesterly, W.S. (2001) "The evolution of firm networks: from emergence to early growth of the firm," *Strategic Management Journal,* 22(3): 275–286.

Li, H.Y., Zhang, Y., Li, Y., Zhou, L.A. and Zhang, W.Y. (2012) "Returnees versus locals: who performs better in China's technology entrepreneurship?," *Strategic Entrepreneurship Journal,* 6: 257–272.

Luo, J.-D. (2005) "Particularistic trust and general trust: a network analysis in Chinese organizations," *Management and Organization Review,* 1(3): 437–458.

Luo, Y.D., Huang, Y. and Wang, S.L. (2011) "*Guanxi* and organizational performance: a meta-analysis," *Management and Organization Review,* 8(1): 139–172.

March, J.G. (2010) *The Ambiguities of Experience,* Ithaca, NY: Cornell University Press.

March, J. and Simon, H. (1958) *Organizations,* New York: John Wiley and Sons, Inc.

Park, S.H. and Luo, Y.D. (2001) "*Guanxi* and organizational dynamics: organizational networking in Chinese firms," *Strategic Management Journal,* 22(5): 455–477.

Peng, D.J. (2000) "Ethnic Chinese business networks and the Asia-Pacific economic integration," *Journal of Asian and African Studies,* 35(2): 229–250.

Peng, M.W. (1997) "Firm growth in transitional economies: three longitudinal cases from China, 1989–96," *Organization Studies,* 18(3): 385–413.

Peng, M.W. (2003) "Institutional transitions and strategic choices," *Academy of Management Review,* 28(2): 275–296.

Peng, M.W. and Heath, P.S. (1996) "The growth of the firm in planned economies in transition: institutions, organizations, and strategic choice," *Academy of Management Review,* 21(2): 492–528.

Peng, M.W. and Zhou, J.Q. (2005) "How network strategies and institutional transitions evolve in Asia," *Asia Pacific Journal of Management,* 22: 321–336.

Rauch, J.E. and Trindade, V. (2002) "Ethnic Chinese networks in international trade," *Review of Economics and Statistics,* 84(1): 116–130.

Redding, G. (1990) *The Spirit of Chinese Capitalism,* New York: Walter de Gruyter.

Redding, G. (1995) "Overseas Chinese networks: understanding enigma," *Long Range Planning,* 28(1): 61–69.

Redding, G. (2002) "The capitalist business system of China and its rationale," *Asia Pacific Journal of Management,* 19(2–3): 221–249.

Ren, B. and Zhang, J.T. (2011) "Entrepreneurial orientation, family resource pools and institutional influence in Chinese business enterprises: the case of Dawu business group," *China Management Studies [Zhongda Guanli Yanjiu]*, 6(1): 21–56 (in Chinese).

Ren, B., Au, K. and Birtch, T. (2009) "China's business network structure during institutional transitions," *Asia Pacific Journal of Management,* 26: 219–240.

Shane, S. and Venkataraman, S. (2000) "The promise of entrepreneurship as a field of research," *Academy of Management Review,* 25(1): 217–226.

Song, F., Cadsby, C.B. and Bi, Y.Y. (2012) "Trust, reciprocity, and *Guanxi* in China: an experimental investigation," *Management and Organization Review,* 8(2): 397–421.

Storz, C. Amable, B., Casper, S. and Lechevalier, S. (2013) "Bringing Asia into the comparative capitalism perspective," *Socio-Economic Review,* 11: 217–232.

Sun, L.P. (1996) "'Guanxi,' social relationship and social structure," *Sociological Studies,* 5: 20–30 (in Chinese).

Sun, P., Wright, M. and Mellahi, K. (2009) "Is entrepreneur-politician alliance sustainable during transitions? The case of management buyouts in China," *Management and Organization Review,* 6(1): 101–121.

The Economist (2011) "Bamboo capitalism," March 10.

Wang, H.Y and Lu, J.Y. (2012) *Researches on Collaboration and Comparison between Chinese Returnee Enterprises and Local Enterprises,* Beijing: Beijing University Press.

Wang, Y. (2008) *Contractual Joint Ventures in China: Formation, Evolution and Operation,* New York: Nova Science Publishers.

Weidenbaum, M. (1996) "The Chinese family business enterprise," *California Management Review,* 38(4): 141–156.

Weidenbaum, M. (1998) *The Bamboo Network: Asia's Family-Run Conglomerates.* Available at: www.strategy-business.com/article/9702?gko=4a3c6.

Weidenbaum, M. and Hughes, S. (1996) *The Bamboo Network: How Expatriate Chinese Entrepreneurs Are Creating a New Economic Superpower in Asia,* New York: The Free Press.

Whitley, R.D. (1992) *Business System in East Asia: Firms, Markets and Societies,* London: Sage.

Whitley, R.D. (1999) *Divergent Capitalisms: The Social Structuring and Change of Business Systems,* Oxford: Oxford University Press.

Witt, M.A. and Redding, G. (2013) "Asian business systems: institutional comparison, clusters and implications for varieties of capitalism and business systems theory," *Socio-Economic Review,* 11(2): 265–300.

Wu, X.B. (2007) *Surging Three Decades: Chinese Enterprises 1978–2008,* Beijing: CITIC Press (in Chinese).

Xiao, Z.X. and Tsui, A. (2007) "When brokers may not work: the cultural contingency of social capital in Chinese high-tech firms," *Administrative Science Quarterly,* 52: 1–31.

Xin, K.K. and Pearce, J.L. (1996) "*Guanxi:* connections as substitutes for formal institutional support," *Academy of Management Journal,* 39(6): 1641–1658.

Yeung, H.W. (1997) "Business networks and transnational corporations: a study of Hong Kong firms in the Asian region," *Economic Geography,* 73(1): 1–25.

Yeung, H.W. (1999) *The Internationalization of Ethnic Chinese Business Firms from Southeast Asia: Strategies, Process and Competitive Advantage*, Oxford: Blackwell Publishers.

Yeung, H.W. (2006) "Change and continuity in Southeast Asian ethnic Chinese business," *Asia Pacific Journal of Management,* 23(3): 229–254.

Yeung, I.Y.M. and Tung, R.L. (1996) "Achieving business success in Confucian societies: the importance of *Guanxi* (connections)," *Organizational Dynamics,* 25(2): 54–65.

Zhang, J.J. and Keh, H.T. (2009) "Interorganizational exchanges in China: organizational forms and governance mechanisms," *Management and Organization Review,* 6(1): 123–147.

Zhang, W.X., Wang, H.Y. and Alon, I. (2011) *Entrepreneurial and Business Elites of China: The Chinese Returnees Who Have Shaped Modern China,* London: Emerald Group Publishing Limited.

Table 8.A.1 Ethnic Chinese billionaires, Top 10 list, 2012

Year	*Total number of ethnic Chinese billionaires*	*Total number of Mainland ethnic Chinese billionaires*	*Proportion of ethnic Chinese billionaires of all billionaires in the world (%)*	*Proportion of Mainland Chinese billionaires of all billionaires in the world (%)*	*Proportion of Mainland Chinese billionaires of all ethnic Chinese billionaires*	*Total number of billionaires in the world*
2013	245	122	17.2	8.6	49.8	1426
2012	198	95	16.2	7.7	48.0	1226
2011	211	115	17.4	9.5	54.5	1210

Source: Forbes China at: www.forbeschina.com/review/201304/0025067.shtml, April 15, 2013.

Table 8.A.2 Mainland Chinese billionaires in the Top 10 list of ethnic Chinese billionaires around the world, 2011–2013

Family name	*Rank among Chinese*	*Global rank*	*Year*	*Net asset (billion US$)*	*Industry*
Zong Qing Hou	9	86	2013	11.6	Food and beverage
Li Yan Hong	5/6	95/86	2011/2012	9.4/2.1	IT
Liang Wen Gen	7/7	114/113	2011/2012	8/1.3	Manufacturing

Note: Based on data adopted from Forbes China at: www.forbeschina.com/review/201304/0025067.shtml, April 15, 2013.

9

Paternalism in Chinese business systems

Antony Drew, Anton Kriz and Gordon Redding

> The model society in traditional East Asia is harmonious; the ruler looks after the people, the people respect the ruler, and at each level such an unequal but reciprocal system of exchange serves to maintain order. The model society in the west is a civil society, where competing interests strive against one another under the rule of law which administers justice in a way as to keep the struggle within boundaries. The virtues of self-cultivation and work are central to the former system, just as the values of freedom and equality are central to the latter.
>
> *(Liu and Liu, 2003, p. 48)*

Introduction

This chapter discusses the origins, nature, role and continuing prominence of paternalism in Chinese business systems. It commences with a discussion of the western perception of paternalism and explains how and why the construct of paternalism has evolved differently in western and Chinese societies. It then examines paternalism in Chinese business systems in order to determine to what extent and under what conditions (where and when), paternalism and paternalistic leadership are applied. The chapter concludes with a discussion of implications for both Chinese and western business people and policy-makers.

The western concept of paternalism

Paternalism is a controversial construct in western literature in disciplines including management, law, philosophy, economics and political theory (New, 1999), not least because of its ideological and moral overtones (Aycan, 2006). Western perceptions of paternalism have been strongly influenced by philosopher, political economist and politician John Stuart Mill and in particular by his essay *On Liberty* ([1880] 2006). Mill decries the intrusion of the state or another agent on individuals, arguing that the state or another agent should only intervene in individual decision-making if such intervention prevents harm being done to others. Mill suggests that paternalism violates individual autonomy and that individuals generally have a better understanding of what is best for them than others. Therefore, individuals should have the liberty to determine their own thoughts and actions.

Dworkin (1971, p. 123) defines paternalism as 'the interference with a person's liberty of action justified by reasons referring exclusively to the welfare, good, happiness, needs, interests or values of the person being coerced'. In a similar vein, New (1999, p. 65), synthesises literature from a range of disciplines to establish three inclusive conditions an act must satisfy in order to be termed paternalistic:

- there is interference in the self-regarding decision-making autonomy of one person by another person or by the state;
- the interference is made in order to further the paternalised person's interests or welfare;
- the interference is made without the 'past, present or immediately forthcoming consent' of the individual concerned.

As these definitions suggest, paternalism is often perceived as an affront to individualism, a core value held strongly in societies underpinned by the Protestant Ethic (Weber, 1930). In societies such as the United States and Great Britain there is a preference for a loose-knit social framework with individuals expected to take care of themselves and their immediate families (Hofstede *et al.*, 2010). Individuals in such countries also place importance on the value of egalitarianism and are driven to seek an equal distribution of power and demand justification for inequalities in power (ibid.).

Meta-traditions, social axioms, values and institutions

In the context of this discussion we refer to values as the collectively shared assumptions, traditions and beliefs of a given society about factors such as religio-social philosophy; the state; family; the economy and; person–society relationships (Redding, 2008). Such values in turn are based on deep-seated meta-traditions that have evolved over millennia (Drew and Kriz, 2012), such as Judaism, Christianity and the Ten Commandments in the west and Confucianism and filial piety in Chinese societies (Redding, 2008). Meta-traditions in turn inform social axioms within a society, such as reward for application in the west, and paternalistic control in China (ibid.).

Over time, meta-traditions, social axioms and values (all components of a society's culture) become inculcated in what are termed institutions, or relatively stable 'established and embedded social rules that structure social interaction' (Hodgson, 2006, p. 18). Institutions are the collectively agreed 'rules of the game' (North, 2005, p. 3) on how one ought to behave in given reoccurring circumstances. As societies evolve, institutions tend to develop from being informal, generally agreed principles, to more formal codified rules of behaviour. Meta-traditions, social axioms, values and institutions within a given society are sticky and evolve over time in a path-dependent manner (North, 2005; Redding, 2008; Drew and Kriz, 2012). In general terms, 'path dependence means where we go next depends not only on where we are now, but also upon where we have been. History matters' (Liebowitz and Margolis, 2000, p. 985). Path dependency theory suggests that a given culture and its underpinning meta-traditions evolve in a manner in which what has gone before underpins and informs what evolves in the future. Previous and ongoing research (Drew, 2011; Drew and Kriz, 2012) drawing on national value orientations indicate societies vary from each other considerably. Why value orientations in China are so different to the west raises an important question. Addressing this historical and interdisciplinary question before examining paternalism in Chinese business systems has merit.

Evolution and the natural environment

Dependent on environmental resource abundance or scarcity, humans and other higher-level primates have a natural predisposition to engage in one of two different types of ordered social relationships and behaviours—hedonic and agonic (Chance, 1988). Hedonic relationships and behaviours evolve over time in conditions where resources are relatively scarce and give rise to group values that are individualistic, nurturing, egalitarian, future-oriented and indulgent. Agonic behaviours evolve over time in conditions where resources are relatively abundant and give rise to group values that are collectivist, hierarchical, masculine, past-oriented and restrained (Drew and Kriz, 2012). This section discusses the co-evolution of agriculture and society in China and the west in order to explain how our natural tendency towards hedonic and agonic modes have resulted in two divergent sets of meta-traditions, social axioms, value orientations and institutions over time.

Climatic and archaeological evidence suggests agriculture and the formation of community and then society commenced from around the end of the last Ice Age, some 12,000 years ago. Humans predominantly lived in small bands of hunter–gatherers (Aiello and Dunbar, 1993) and did not settle for long in one place until this time, as low levels of rainfall, climate variability and low levels of atmospheric CO_2 limited vegetation growth (Diamond, 1998; Richerson *et al.*, 2001). From the end of the last Ice Age onwards, however, humans began to experiment with agriculture and animal husbandry in regions where there were edible and farmable seed crops, fruit and nut trees and where there were animals suited to domestication (Drew and Kriz, 2012). Western agriculture commenced around 8500 BCE in the Fertile Crescent region, an area extending from Israel to western Iran and Turkey, whereas Chinese agriculture commenced by around 8000 BCE independently in both the Yangtze and Yellow River valleys in China (ibid.). In the process the early agriculturalists needed to establish semi-permanent and then permanent locations, along with collaborative workforces of often unrelated humans, to maximise their agricultural returns. Over time, such non-kin collaboration resulted in the development of shared meta-traditions, social axioms, values and informal institutions.

Critical to this discussion is the notion that resource endowments and ongoing climatic changes in the east and the west were quite different and that such differences would have impacted on the evolving meta-traditions. The Fertile Crescent region was endowed with wheat, barley, peas, lentils, olives, cattle, sheep and goats. Sheep and goats require substantial pastures on which to graze and prolonged periods of shepherding. Further, wild wheat and barley which had fewer grains per head than their modern varieties would have required extensive areas of cultivation in order to produce meaningful quantities. Evidenced by archaeological findings (Cavalli-Sforza *et al.*, 1996), it is likely that men would have had to travel widely in order to shepherd their flocks and gather grain, while the women would have remained in their villages looking after the children, the elderly and tending pulse crops (Drew and Kriz, 2012). Further, this region experienced ongoing desertification from almost the beginning of the agricultural period resulting in ongoing migrations out, and the consequent spread of agricultural practices. Under such conditions it might be expected that the evolving meta-traditions (e.g. the Ten Commandments) and social axioms (e.g. reward for application) would give rise to nurturing, egalitarian, future-oriented, indulgent and individualistic group values in order to manage social cohesion and cooperation.

Conversely, China has experienced relatively stable climatic conditions from the end of the last Ice Age. China was endowed with abundant soy beans, mung beans, pigs, cattle, poultry, fish, silkworms, fruit trees and wet rice in the south and foxtail millet in the north. The management of such resources requires intensive collective and collaborative cultivation with community members living close to the resources in order to maximise returns (Drew and Kriz, 2012). Under such conditions it might be expected that a meta-tradition such as filial piety and a social axiom such as paternalistic control would over time give rise to collectivist, hierarchical, masculine, past-oriented and restrained group values.

The previous discussion provides a theoretic explanation for what underpins differences in meta-traditions, social axioms, values and institutions in China and the west. It further explains why such differences came into being. The following section examines the development of indigenous Chinese meta-traditions and how they underpin a different understanding of paternalism in the Chinese context.

Chinese meta-traditions

China's meta-traditions, social axioms, values and institutions have evolved over thousands of years in a path-dependent manner and are illustrated and reinforced through Confucian, Legalist, Tao, Mohist and Buddhist philosophies and teachings. Confucian philosophy and the values, institutions and social behaviours that developed from that philosophy are an attempt by the Chinese to find a form of order that is in accordance with their perception of the natural world (Redding, 1993). These values, institutions and social behaviours tend towards agonic and are primarily concerned 'with the practical question of advancing the well-being of the individuals and the harmony of society and the state' (Cheng, 1972, cited in Leung, 2004).

Confucius (K'ung Fu-Tzu) was born in 551 BCE, when injustice, poverty and chaos provided a favourable environment for his teachings (Wu, 2012). During his career, Confucius was first a teacher, then a minister of justice and then spent 13 years as a travelling philosopher/teacher. It is allegedly during this period that he developed his philosophy of living (Wong *et al.*, 1998). This, however, does not mean that the essence of Confucianism did not exist prior to this time. Strong evidence suggests that what are deemed today to be Confucian values actually predate Confucius and are reflected in the *Chinese Book of Odes* and arguably in the *Canon of Yao* in the classic *Book of Documents* (Wong *et al.*, 1998). Further, Keightley (1988, p. 212) argues that what we deem to be Confucian social structure and social order was already in place by the late Shang dynasty (1750 BCE–1120 BCE).

Confucianism is a humanistic philosophy for moral living (Wong *et al.*, 1998) that evolved in an agrarian state in which the majority of the population were living at subsistence levels (Redding, 1993) and one in which family was the basic social unit (Redding, 1993; Wong *et al.*, 1998). Virtue, sincerity, respect and filial piety rose to prominence out of Confucian philosophy (Wong *et al.*, 1998) and the idea of the nuclear, extended and 'super family' of the Chinese people and 'morally binding relationships' uniting all Chinese developed (Redding, 1993, p. 44). Virtuosity entailed that a person would have the traits of 'humanity, righteousness, propriety and wisdom' (Wong *et al.*, 1998, p. 15). Sincerity required the individual to be completely truthful and not pretend to be something they were not (ibid.). Filial piety is based on the Five Cardinal Relationships of the Confucian *wulun* and reinforces 'the importance of family relationships with its particular emphasis on the role of father to son, husband to wife and elder brother to younger brother' (Kriz, 2009, p. 54). While filial piety lies at the heart of family design, it also establishes the foundations for larger social structures and the basic design of the total state (Redding, 1993). For 2000 years, the *Xiaojing* (*Book of Filial Piety*) was a key text in Chinese schools. It discusses a person's duty to a role and that 'the total system can be sustained, only if those in it remain faithful to the demands their role places on them' (ibid., p. 128).

In discussing Confucianism and the development of the Chinese state, Redding argues that jurisdiction had not traditionally been used to maintain order. Rather, due to China's size and the fact that the limited ruling elite were unable to directly govern social behaviour, it was imperative to embed the responsibility for the maintenance of order through a combination of prescribed social roles and the application of swift and severe punishment against transgressors. In other words, Confucian society is primarily a role-based society in which the male head of the household fulfils the role of the family law enforcer and mediator. This is quite different to western rule-based societies, in which the responsibility for judicial interpretation and enforcement is largely the domain of the state and civil authorities (ibid.). This is not to say that China did not have laws. On the contrary, laws in China were strict, following in the Chinese Legalist tradition. However, as Winston (2005) argues, in China's case there was an emphasis of *rule by law*, meted out in a particularist manner from above, rather than the western-style *rule of law*, applied to the members of society universally.

Legalism or legalist philosophy is attributed to Han Fei (280 BCE–233 BCE), a prince at the end of the Warring States period in Chinese history. However, there is evidence that the basic principles embodied in legalism were practised as far back as the Three Dynasties Era—around 1700 BCE—as a tool by which a single clan could exert authority over rival clans (Winston, 2005). Legalist philosophy comprises 55 treatises embodied in the *Book of Han Feizi* and proposes measures for effective government (Chan, 1969; Watson, 2003). The principal objective of legalism is the concentration of power in the ruler. It is divided into three categories, the first emphasises the concept of the law itself; the second emphasises statecraft as the art of conducting affairs and handling people; and the third emphasises the use of power (Hansen, 1994). While the specific Legalist philosophy of Han Fei was largely supplanted by the Confucian value system during the Han dynasty (206 BCE–220 CE), its essence is still reflected in the *Xiaojing*, *wulun*, filial piety and paternalism.

Taoism is more esoteric and concerned with duality and finding harmony and balance within and between all things. It is probable that Taoism has the most ancient roots of the five major Chinese philosophies. Keightley (1988, p. 387) suggests that the proto yin–yang metaphysics of Taoism may have already been developing and in place 'as the Shang [dynasty] emerged from the Neolithic' stage around 1750 BCE. Based on 'the principle of *wu-wei*, or active not-doing' (Redding, 1993, p. 50), Taoism seeks to understand the natural underlying order of things and their interrelationships. Taoism suggests that it is 'the way of nature, not the way of man' that is 'the standard to which all must conform' (Wong *et al.*, 1998, p. 15).

Mohism is attributed to the renowned military engineer Mo Zi (468 BCE–376 BCE). It is a philosophy that favours the masses in that it argues that leaders should be thrifty in their own needs and instead love and serve the people. It also resonates with some aspects of Confucianism, though, as with Taoism, it contained a number of more spiritual and metaphysical elements. Mohism 'advocates centralisation and authoritarianism such that common people need to be submissive to the talents and sages' (Cheung and Chan, 2005, p. 50) but also suggests that authority is only deemed legitimate when leaders are productive and altruistic. During the Han dynasty, the more pragmatic aspects of Mohism were subsumed into Confucianism while the more spiritual and metaphysical aspects were largely abandoned.

Buddhism was arguably first introduced to China around the beginning of the first century BCE, but was not influential until around three hundred years later (Redding, 1993). As with Taoism, Buddhism 'is about man's place in nature' (ibid., p. 50), however, it differs from Taoism in that it focuses on humans overcoming human weakness and achieving enlightenment by following prescribed steps in order to redefine their reality (Redding, 1993; Wong *et al.*, 1998).

Up until the tenth century CE, Confucianism, Taoism and Buddhism jostled with each other for dominance in China. From that time on, however, Confucianism in the guise of Neo-Confucianism, a value and belief system that rejects the more esoteric aspects of both Taoism and Buddhism, was the principal ethical and philosophical model. Neo-Confucianism was only usurped by Maoist thought during the Cultural Revolution (Wong *et al.*, 1998). The usurpation, however, appears to have been short-lived. A recent article in the *China Daily* (Mu, 2008) indicates that Neo-Confucian values are once again perceived as being of great importance to many Chinese. The stability and re-emergence of core Confucian values have also been addressed by Redding (2008, p. 280) who suggests that while China appears to be integrating rationality, professionalism and local participation in government-derived order into their ideational mix, 'China appears to be returning to its cultural roots—family, personalistic trust, hierarchy [and] government-derived order' and one in which 'paternalism lies at the centre' (ibid., p. 282).

Previous research (Drew, 2011; Drew and Kriz, 2012) suggests societal level values can and do change over time and their evolution may be influenced by factors including, but not limited to, changes in resource availability, acculturation, political activity and technology. However, we would argue that in the case of China, any deep-level change is unlikely in the short to medium term for the following reason. China's agonic heritage and the evolution of its meta-traditions reinforce high power distance, restraint, masculinity and past orientation—values that are resistant to change. From a pragmatic perspective, this raises important who, where and when questions in relationship to paternalism in Chinese business systems. Specifically, who is most likely to adopt a paternalistic leadership and management style and who is most likely to follow? Where is paternalism most likely to manifest in Chinese business systems and when is a paternalistic style most likely to be used by Chinese business people from Mainland and overseas Chinese communities?

Paternalism and paternalistic leadership

The latter half of the twentieth century saw an explosion of entrepreneurship among overseas Chinese throughout Eastern and South-east Asia (Chen and Fahr, 2010). Since the late 1960s scholars have engaged in both theoretical and empirical studies in order to better understand the leadership behaviour and management philosophies of owners and managers of overseas and, more recently, Mainland Chinese firms. Such studies have focused on exploring manager–subordinate relationships and the extent to which such relationships may be underpinned and informed by Chinese cultural values, in turn rooted in various combinations of Confucian, Legalist, Taoist, Mohist and Buddhist meta-traditions. In more recent decades, focus has also been centred on whether and to what extent manager–subordinate relationships might be changing. The most systematically researched, well-developed and clearly indigenous Chinese leadership theory is the paternalistic leadership (PL) model (Fahr and Cheng, 2000; Cheng *et al.*, 2004; Fahr *et al.*, 2008; Chen and Fahr, 2010). This model in turn has been built on seminal works on paternalism in the Chinese context by Silin (1976), Redding (1993) and Cheng (1995).

Paternalistic leadership has been defined as a style of leadership comprising strong discipline and authoritarian leadership with fatherly benevolence and moral virtue, contained within a personalistic atmosphere (Farh and Cheng, 2000; Cheng *et al.*, 2004). Cheng *et al.* (2004) suggest that in the Chinese context, paternalistic leaders assert total authority and control over subordinates and require uncompromising obedience. They also suggest paternalistic leaders act as role models and demonstrate self-discipline, superior personal virtues and unselfishness. In order to test the veracity of the three components of the definition, Cheng *et al.* (2004) conducted empirical research into the perceptions of 543 subordinates across a range of local Taiwanese firms in relation to western transformational leadership and paternalistic leadership. Transformational leadership has strong similarities with PL on three fronts: it is leader-centric; it unites subordinates towards a vision; and it provides for individualised consideration. However, it differs from PL in that it does not mirror the ongoing self-cultivation of the leader in terms of self-discipline, superior personal virtues and unselfishness (Chen and Fahr, 2010).

The original findings of Cheng *et al.*'s (2004) analysis suggest that while the authoritarian aspect of paternal leadership may be losing its influence in the Taiwanese context, the benevolent and influential aspects may be becoming more important. Based on their 2004 findings, they recommend that Chinese business leaders should adopt a style combining benevolence and morality and only adopt an authoritarian orientation for subordinates who personally display a high authority orientation. More recently, however, Chen and Fahr (2010) suggest the negative perception of the authoritarian aspect of PL held by subordinates may actually be related to the fact that the dimension of *authoritarian leadership* and its negative connotations was originally developed by western scholars. They suggest that the dimension should be re-contextualised from an indigenous Chinese perspective as *authoritative leadership*, so that the negative connotations are removed and then conduct further empirical research to see if the results vary. Such refinements and further research are likely to provide greater insights into the nature of paternalism in Chinese business systems and may explain Liu, Li and Yue's (2010, p. 589) finding that while authoritarianism has weakened in Taiwan over the past 20 years, benevolent authority is still alive and well with 'substantial segments of Taiwan's public still manifest[ing] fear of disorder and [showing] preference for communal harmony over individual freedom'.

On-going theory-building and empirical research by Larry Fahr and colleagues over nearly 20 years suggest that PL flourishes in the context of a range of specific facilitative social/cultural and organisational factors. 'The key social/cultural factors consist of a strong emphasis on familism and the Confucian values of respect for authority, personalism/particularism, the norm of reciprocity (*bao*), interpersonal harmony and leadership by virtuous example' (Chen and Fahr, 2010, p. 603). They suggest PL is likely to be more pronounced under the following organisational conditions: family ownership; unity of ownership and management; an entrepreneurial structure; a simple task environment; stable technology; and when subordinates are resource-dependent. Further, subordinates are more likely to respond to PL if they identify with traditional Chinese cultural values.

Empirical research undertaken in 2002 into the leadership styles of five Hong Kong Chinese CEOs (Cheung and Chan, 2005) provides interesting insights into the influence of Chinese meta-traditions on their respective leadership styles, attitudes and behaviours. Also salient to this discussion is that the CEOs came from five different industry sectors: banking; insurance; trading (supply chain management); engineering (infrastructure); and information technology. This latter point is important as it allows for the comparison of their leadership styles across industries.

The most prominent value independently espoused by the CEOs was that of the principle of benevolence. This principle was articulated through themes including paternalism, sympathy, forgiveness, friendliness (including the importance of reciprocal interpersonal relationships or *guanxi*), trust and fulfilling the needs of others. The next most common cluster of themes related to the principle of learning. Learning is critical to Confucian philosophy as it is deemed to be the most effective path through which people might grow and achieve a virtuous position in society (Redding, 1993). This principle was articulated through themes including learning from others, life-long learning, teaching others and how acquiring new knowledge helps the business. The third most common principle articulated was harmony. This principle was articulated through themes including solidarity, partnerships, networking, loyalty and the absence of factionalism. Other key principles articulated by the CEOs and underpinned by Chinese meta-traditions included humility, righteousness, flexibility, reversion, interest in the masses, thrift, independence, self-control and innovation (Cheung and Chan, 2005). In all five cases and regardless of their industry field, all CEOs expressed similar paternal behaviours, attitudes and beliefs towards their subordinates and demonstrated a strong interest in the social welfare and interests of their people.

The presence of indigenous Chinese value orientations, underpinned by Chinese meta-traditions, is also evident in both Mainland entrepreneurial ventures and state-owned enterprises. One of the most outstanding examples is Zhang Ruimin, entrepreneur, founder and CEO of the Chinese major appliance brand Haier. According to Haier corporate information, 'in management practice, Zhang integrates the essence of China's traditional culture with western modern management concepts, insisting on taking in everything, growing innovatively and having one's own style' (Haier, 2013). According to the corporate information, 'Zhang's management thinking smashes the shackles of conventional western management' (ibid.) and advocates win–win strategies. Zhang also places great importance on public welfare issues including education, charitable contributions to society and sustainable development. Zhang's profile clearly exhibits the indigenous Chinese values of benevolence, harmony, the importance of maintaining relationships, working with the masses, and identifying and developing talent.

Chery Automobile Company Limited, founded in 1997, is a Chinese state-owned enterprise and one of the largest motor vehicle manufacturers in China (Chery, 2013). Chery is an interesting organisation to examine as one might expect the management style and philosophy of a state-owned enterprise to be quite different to that of an entrepreneurial firm such as Haier. However, a review of Chery's corporate Human Resource Management philosophy reflects similar indigenous Chinese values and perhaps with an even deeper paternalistic theme.

> Always sticking to people-oriented principle through the following acts: keeping the employees by treating them with sincere feelings, attracting the employees by offering a splendid career, training the employees with challenging tasks, cultivating the employees through effective learning and encouraging the employees with reasonable systems.
>
> *(Chery-Culture, 2013)*

Chinalco is a major state-owned poly-metallic enterprise. It is the world's second largest alumina producer and the world's third largest primary aluminium producer (Chinalco, 2013). Chinalco's management philosophy clearly reflects Legalist and Confucian values with a strong agonic and collectivist underpinning. Chinalco's corporate information states that its management philosophy is 'Strict, Meticulous, Pragmatic, Innovative, Persistent and United', with the term united reflecting collectivist solidarity.

In this section we have provided a brief review of both empirical research studies and current corporate information. In each case we find that paternalism and underpinning Chinese values and meta-traditions are strong, active and openly promoted across industry sectors and organisational forms. We therefore concur with Cheung and Chan who suggest:

> [L]eaders of Chinese people need to understand the practices of paternalism, benevolence, forgiveness, flexibility, forbearance, self-control, working with the masses, and identifying and developing talents. These practices are helpful because they fit Chinese culture held by and prescribed for Chinese society. Leaders who deviate from the practices would contravene righteousness, which is a virtue for the good of society, and would thereby suffer from societal sanctions.
>
> *(Cheung and Chan, 2005, p. 60)*

Conclusion and policy and business implications

Based on the previous discussion, we define paternalism in the Chinese context as a state and familial patriarchal system of coercion and obligation around implicit or explicit moral responsibility, benevolence and consequent accepted norms and methods of behaviour. The dual importance of state and family is related to what in China is known as one country but two systems. There is a communist polity with strong top-down directives and planning but an economic system of increasingly private and family-based firms with an increasing market orientation. The modern state has inherited a paternal obligation from more feudal times of supporting meritocracy and serving the majority. Rulers have traditionally had a reciprocal psychological contract to be benevolent. The population equally has a responsibility to the leadership. No harm should come to the population without sufficient cause but sometimes this also means the whole is greater than the sum of the parts. Familial paternalism has similar beliefs and is implied now in commercial settings.

We agree with Fahr and colleagues that paternalism and PL are likely to be more pronounced under organisational conditions of family ownership, unity of ownership and management, an entrepreneurial structure, a simple task environment, stable technology and resource dependence by subordinates. However, our analysis suggests paternalism and PL in Chinese business systems are not likely to wane in the short to medium term. Indeed, if Confucian values continue to gain momentum in China as they have done over the past two decades, paternalism and PL are likely to be the rule, rather than the exception.

China has risen to economic prominence in an unprecedented short period of time. Shifting 500 million plus Chinese out of poverty within 30 years defies politico-economic logic. PL and the acceptance of top-down power have been recognised as the catalyst for China's economic miracle. Mao delivered the crisis that Deng harnessed to invigorate enterprise and opportunism back into the Chinese system. A series of Five-Year Plans, largely executed, has ensured that PL has delivered astonishing results. China has definitely used the power of a visible hand to make its radical economic change.

Taking a normative approach, the west could argue that the enforced coercion of China's PL has been quite brutal at times. Equally, however, the Chinese polity might argue that helping the society as a whole is more important than worrying about individuals, groups, towns and/or regions. J.S. Mill was right to suggest individual freedom is important, but as business increasingly understands, strong leadership is also essential. Consensus is a great thing but if it is not managed carefully, it can also be counter-productive. The rules of both political and business games are still not fully understood. Democratic governments are flagging as media and lobby groups intervene in policy debates and economic prescriptions. Singapore with its hybrid PL, a strong rule of law and democratic values, offers an interesting exception. Management theory still has a long way to go and advocating western values for others seems premature. PL has pros and cons but so do democracy and liberalism. This chapter demonstrates that our destiny has rich traditions and that our institutions are sticky and path-dependent. Two thousand plus years of Chinese paternalism and PL are not easily supplanted. For those like Mill, simply advocating control of one's own destiny—it may pay to be careful what you wish for.

References

Aiello, L.C. and Dunbar, R.I.M. (1993) 'Neocortex size, group size, and the evolution of language', *Current Anthropology,* 34: 184–193.

Aycan, Z. (2006) 'Paternalism: towards conceptual refinement and operationalization', in K.S. Yang, K. Hwang and U. Kim (eds) *Scientific Advances in Indigenous Psychologies: Empirical, Philosophical, and Cultural Contributions,* Cambridge: Cambridge University Press.

Cavalli-Sforza, L., Menozzi, P. and Piazza, A. (1996) *The History and Geography of Human Genes,* Princeton, NJ: Princeton University Press.

Chan, W.T. (1969) *A Source Book in Chinese Philosophy,* Princeton, NJ: Princeton University Press.

Chance, M.R.A. (1988) 'Introduction', in M.R.A. Chance (ed.), *Social Fabrics of the Mind,* Hove: Lawrence Erlbaum Associates, Ltd.

Chen, C.C. and Farh, J.L. (2010) 'Developments in understanding Chinese leadership: paternalism and its elaborations, moderations and alternatives', in M. Bond (ed.) *Oxford Handbook of Chinese Psychology,* Oxford: Oxford University Press.

Cheng, B.S. (1995) 'Paternalistic authority and leadership: a case study of a Taiwanese CEO', *Bulletin of the Institute of Ethnology Academic Sinica,* 79: 119–173.

Cheng, B.S., Chou, L.F., Huang, M.P., Wu, T.Y. and Farh, J.L. (2004) 'Paternalistic leadership and subordinate responses: establishing a leadership model in Chinese organizations', *Asian Journal of Social Psychology,* 7: 89–117.

Chery (2013) Available at: www.cheryinternational.com/company/ (accessed 15 May 2013).

Chery-Culture (2013) Available at: www.cheryinternational.com/company/chery-culture.html (accessed 15 May 2013).

Cheung, C.K. and Chan, A.C.F. (2005) 'Philosophical foundations of eminent Hong Kong Chinese CEOs' leadership', *Journal of Business Ethics,* 60: 47–62.

Chinalco (2013) Available at: www.chalco.com.cn/zl/web/chinalco_en_show.jsp?ColumnID=122 (accessed 15 May 2013).

Diamond, J. (1998) *Guns, Germs and Steel,* London: Vintage.

Drew, A.J. (2011) 'Chinese perceptions of *guanxi* in mainland and overseas Chinese business communities', unpublished thesis, University of Newcastle, Australia.

Drew, A.J. and Kriz, A. P. (2012) 'Towards a theoretical framework for examining societal-level institutional change', in L. Tihanyi, T.M. Devinney and T. Pedersen (eds) *Institutional Theory in International Business and Management: Advances in International Management,* vol. 25, London: Emerald Group Publishing Limited.

Dworkin, G. (1971) 'Paternalism', in R.A. Wasserstrom (ed.) *Morality and the Law,* Belmont, CA: Wadsworth.

Farh, J.L. and Cheng, B.S. (2000) 'A cultural analysis of paternalistic leadership in Chinese organizations', in J.Y. Li, A.S. Tsui and E. Weldon (eds), *Management and Organizations in the Chinese Context,* London: Macmillan.

Farh, J.L., Liang, J., Chou, L.F. and Cheng, B.S. (2008) 'Paternalistic leadership in Chinese organizations: research progress and future research direction', in C.C. Chen and Y.T. Lee (eds) *Leadership and Management in China: Philosophies, Theories and Practices,* Cambridge: Cambridge University Press.

Hansen, C. (1994) '*Fa* (Standards: Laws) and meaning changes in Chinese philosophy', *Philosophy East and West,* 44: 435–488.

Haier (2013) Available at: www.haier.net/en/about_haier/ceo/introduction/ (accessed 15 May 2013).

Hodgson, G.M. (2006) 'What are institutions?' *Journal of Economic Issues,* 40: 1–25.

Hofstede, G.H., Hofstede, G.J. and Minkov, M. (2010) *Cultures and Organisations: Software of the Mind,* New York: McGraw-Hill.

Keightley, D.N. (1988) 'Shang divination and metaphysics', *Philosophy East and West,* 38: 367–397.

Kriz, A.P. (2009) *Secrets to Building Personal Trust in China: An In-depth Investigation of the Chinese Business Landscape,* Saarbrucken: Lambert Academic Publishing.

Leung, T.K.P. (2004) 'A Chinese–United States joint venture business ethics model and its implications for multinational firms', *International Journal of Management,* 21: 58–66.

Liebowitz, S. and Margolis, S. (2000) 'Path dependence', in B. Boudewijn and G. De Geest (eds) *Encyclopedia of Law and Economics,* vol. 1, *The History and Methodology of Law and Economics,* Cheltenham: Edward Elgar.

Liu, J., Li, M.C. and Yue, X.D. (2010) 'Chinese intergroup relations and social identity', in M. Bond (ed.) *Oxford Handbook of Chinese Psychology,* Oxford: Oxford University Press.

Liu, J.H. and Liu, S.H. (2003) 'The role of the social psychologist in the "Benevolent Authority" and "Plurality of Powers" systems of historical affordance for authority', in K.S. Yang, K.K. Huang, P.B. Pedersen and I. Diabo (eds) *Progress in Asian Social Psychology: Conceptual and Empirical Contributions,* vol. 3. New York: Plenum Press.

Mill, J.S. ([1880] 2006) *On Liberty,* London: Elibron Classics.

Mu, Q. (2008) 'The Confucius craze', *China Daily,* 27 February, p. 18.

New, B. (1999) 'Paternalism and public policy', *Economics and Philosophy,* 15: 63–83.

North, D.C. (2005) *Understanding the Process of Economic Change,* Princeton, NJ: Princeton University Press.
Redding, S.G. (1993) *The Spirit of Chinese Capitalism,* Berlin: Walter de Gruyter.
Redding, S.G. (2008) 'Separating culture from institutions: the use of semantic spaces as a conceptual domain, and the case of China', *Management and Organization Review,* 4: 257–289.
Richerson, P.J., Boyd, R. and Bettinger, R.L. (2001) 'Was agriculture impossible during the Pleistocene but mandatory during the Holocene? A climate change hypothesis', *American Antiquity,* 66: 387–411.
Silin, R.H. (1976) *Leadership and Value: The Organization of Large-Scale Taiwanese Enterprises,* Cambridge, MA: Harvard University Press.
Watson, B. (2003) *Han Feizi Basic Writing,* New York: Columbia University Press.
Weber, M. (1930) *The Protestant Ethic and the Spirit of Capitalism,* trans. T. Parsons and R.H. Tawney, London: George Allen and Unwin, Ltd.
Winston, K. (2005) 'The internal morality of Chinese legalism', *Singapore Journal of Legal Studies,* 2: 313–347.
Wong, Y.Y., Maher, T.E., Evans, N.A. and Nicholson, J.D. (1998) 'Neo-Confucianism: the bane of foreign firms in China', *Management Research News,* 21: 13–22.
Wu, M. (2012) 'Moral leadership and work performance: testing the mediating and interaction effects in China', *Chinese Management Studies,* 6: 284–299.

10

The internationalization of ethnic Chinese family firms

Michael Carney, Ramzi Fathallah, Eric R. Gedajlovic and Daniel Shapiro

Introduction

What factors can explain the international scope of ethnic Chinese family firms (ECFFs)? Scholars are divided on whether firms owned and controlled by Chinese business families have any particular advantage in developing and sustaining superior international capabilities. In this chapter we identify four perspectives on the question. The first provides an economic account drawing upon the eclectic theory of the multinational firm (Erdener and Shapiro, 2005), a model that was originally developed to explain the more hierarchical form of the Western multinational enterprise (Dunning, 1979). The second is a sociological explanation that identifies a co-evolutionary unfolding of institutional development and Chinese firms' adaptations to their environment (Carney and Gedajlovic, 2002a). Third is a body of literature emphasizing the organizational constraints of family-owned and family-managed firms on the development of geographically dispersed organizational structure (Redding, 1990; Tsui-Auch, 2004). Fourth, we consider the literature emphasizing the network qualities of ethnic Chinese multinational enterprises (Mathews, 2006; Tsang, 2002). The economic and network perspectives suggest Chinese family owner-managers' skill in cultivating relationships is entirely consistent with the modern networked form of the multinational enterprise. In contrast, sociological and family business perspectives propose that strong family bonds combined with norms of partible inheritance among male successors fragment the firm at an early stage of development and thwart the establishment of long-lived and geographically dispersed international organization.

Despite the emergence of several plausible theoretical accounts, the empirical literature on the question is sparse and based largely on anecdotes and case studies. Few empirical studies employ a control group of non-Chinese firms or employ owner-manager ethnicity as an independent variable in studies of internationalization performance. For this reason, the literature is well developed but contains significant empirical gaps. Consequently, the international scope of the ECFF is subject to conflicting interpretations.

Academic literature on the internationalization of firms owned and controlled by ethnic Chinese entrepreneurs located in non-Chinese societies began developing in the early 1980s following a series of studies that identified Asian-based "third-world multinationals" (Lall, 1983; Lecraw, 1983; Wells, 1983). A surge of interest in the subject followed the publication of a World

Bank study that announced the existence of an Asian economic miracle (World Bank, 1993). The popular press heaped praise upon prominent Chinese entrepreneurs, describing them as the "world's most dynamic capitalists" (Kraar, 1994), "lords of the rim" (Seagrave, 1995), and "new Asian emperors" (Haley *et al.*, 1998). The unorthodox management style of these entrepreneurs was cast as an international bamboo network (Weidenbaum, 1996) and a "world wide web" that is "not based in any one country or continent . . . this [Chinese] commonwealth is primarily a network of entrepreneurial relationships" (Kao, 1993: 24).

Following the Asian financial crisis, the academic literature became more critical and divided. Scholars emphasizing the appearance of Chinese entrepreneurship during a phase of state-led economic development focused on their dependence upon relationships with prominent politicians (e.g. McVey, 1992; Mackie, 1992). In one view the relational style of Chinese entrepreneurship was described as ersatz (Yoshihara, 1988) or crony capitalism (Dieleman and Sachs, 2008). Other perspectives read the ethnic Chinese relational style of business as pioneering a new form of international business alliance (Dunning, 1995) that prefigured a less hierarchical networked form of multinational enterprise and one that was at once more attuned to a period of rapid globalization and fitting with Asian cultural norms.

Defining ethnic Chinese family firms

The early literature identifies a historically and geographically specific organizational form described as the "overseas Chinese family firm" (Limligan, 1986; Redding, 1995; Ahlstrom *et al.*, 2004). A diaspora of migrant Chinese into South-east Asia (i.e. Burma, Indonesia, Malaysia, the Philippines, Singapore, Thailand, and Vietnam) occurred during the colonial era. They took up intermediary occupations such as retailing, trading and other related commercial roles related to a resource-based colonial economy (McVey, 1992). With hitherto little entrepreneurial experience, ethnic Chinese attained the status of a cohesive and entrepreneurial commercial community. They were able to exert significant economic power though they represented only a small minority in each country. For instance, ethnic Chinese in the Philippines constitute less than 1 percent of the population but estimates suggest that ethnic Chinese families control 60 percent of the country's wealth. The majority Chinese populations of Hong Kong, Macau, and Taiwan are also considered by the People's Republic of China to be "overseas Chinese" and by the Mainland government as people living in Chinese territories temporarily outside of Mainland control.

Some scholars find the term "overseas Chinese" highly contentious because it implies a community of partially assimilated citizens who are legal citizens of their adopted countries but who maintain strong links with their homeland (Yeung, 2006). This ambiguous identity has engendered suspicion and collective mistrust in several South-east Asian states. In the postcolonial nationalist atmosphere Chinese communities have sometimes been scapegoated and subject to legal discrimination, political hostility, asset confiscation, and periodic violence (McVey, 1992). The visible minority status has subjected the population to a "relentless restriction" on their business activities (Wu and Wu, 1980, p. 89) and for this reason the identification of a visible minority population of "overseas Chinese," many of whom are very wealthy, is loaded with political and social significance (Chua, 2003). Yeung (2006) is uncomfortable with the term and suggests that it is no longer acceptable in English. Accordingly, in this chapter we adopt Yeung's preferred term "ethnic Chinese" to refer to communities located in South Asia and Hong Kong, Macau and Taiwan and refer to ECFFs as firms owned and controlled by Chinese entrepreneurs in the region. However, we exclude from our analysis the international activities of family firms located in Mainland China. The literature on this type of organization is very much in its infancy

(Lu *et al.*, 2011) and the study of internationalization of Mainland Chinese firms has primarily focused upon large state-owned groups (Yiu, 2011).

There is much greater consensus regarding the ECFF's archetypal characteristics. It is typically described as a small-scale firm with a simple organizational structure, a paternalistic culture, centralized decision-making in the hands of a patriarch, and with strategies characterized by the efficient use of assets and difficulties attaining economies of scale due to early fragmentation of business. However, some ECFFs defy these characteristics and have transcended the archetype to attain large size. Shapiro, Gedajlovic and Erdener (2003) distinguish between the traditional small-scale, domestically oriented Chinese family firm and the Chinese family enterprise, the larger, internationally active, family-owned and diversified enterprise that developed from the traditional Chinese family firm outside China. These organizations appear in the Chinese management literature as Chinese conglomerates (Yeung, 2000). A growing body of research on diversified business groups identify these firms as Chinese family business groups (FBGs) (Carney and Gedajlovic, 2003) to describe the conglomerate form of the ECFF. Despite their broad scope and large size, these firms are readily identified as family businesses due to ownership concentration and direct participation in management by the owner and family members. This holds true even in the largest firms employing professional managers, since strategic and even operating decisions are made by the family (Tsui-Auch, 2004).

The growth and international development of the ECFF

The population of ECFFs in Asia is now quite heterogeneous due to the differentiation and growth of a small number of firms who responded to the opportunities provided by the region's rapid economic growth during the twentieth century. In this section we identify some of the major contextual changes occurring in East and South-east Asia and their impact upon the ECFF's international activities. Table 10.1 identifies four distinct periods of activity and development. The pre-1945 colonial era provided opportunities for ECFFs to leverage their diaspora networks to develop a trading role within the colonial political economy. European companies found ethnic Chinese to be highly cosmopolitan, linguistically adept and able to interact at all levels in society, and so employed them as "comprador capitalists" (Hao, 1970). Such communities afford access not only to local resources but also to the diaspora extending across Asia and into China. Backman describes a cosmopolitan diaspora:

> They didn't so much as pour into any one location, but fanned out across Asia. One clansman from a particular village in China would migrate to, say, Bangkok, and another would settle in Singapore. The way the Chinese settled across Asia ensured that they had a ready-made international network of connections within which they could trade and raise capital.
> *(1999, p. 195)*

In this period many wealthy Chinese entrepreneurs diversified into industries such as agriculture, retail and distribution, rice milling, shipping and mining (Mackie, 1996). At the close of the colonial era, ECFFs increasingly occupied commercial roles that were previously the exclusive domain of the colonial elite. In the following years, ECFFs possessed a decisive entrepreneurial advantage over indigenous entrepreneurs due to their prior commercial experience, accumulated capital, and access to international networks.

Nationalist governments took power following the departure of colonial government in most countries of the region. Their main priority was national security due to a looming Communist threat, but they also needed to restart their lagging, post-World War II economies. They turned

Table 10.1 Major stages of the internationalization of ethnic Chinese family businesses

Period	*Context*	*International activities*
Colonial era, pre-1945	Chinese migrants occupy commercial positions between colonial elites and indigenous populations Founders of family firm are immigrants embedded in a migrant community and dependent upon it for financial and managerial support	Diaspora, middlemen minority in South-east Asia colonial states
Nationalist state-led economic development, 1955–1970	Wealthy visible minorities ethnic Chinese entrepreneurs are pariah capitalists Discriminatory measures against Chinese minorities	Import substitution International joint ventures with Japanese manufacturers Export-oriented development Capital flight
Economic miracle, 1971–1996	Absence of market-supporting institutions, ethnic Chinese entrepreneurs are paragon capitalists	Diversification, network internationalization
Post Asian financial crisis, 1997–2013	Economic crisis Diffusion of neoliberalism Transparency in corporate governance movement Rise of China	Foreign direct investment in business groups structures

to the ethnic Chinese as a community of "essential outsiders" (Chirot and Reid, 1997) who were indispensable for economic development, seeing as the indigenous populations appeared unable to produce an authentic capitalist class. Despite turning to them for assistance, in the eyes of nationalist governments, ethnic Chinese entrepreneurs were "pariah" capitalists (McVey, 1992) and thus legitimate subjects for discrimination and expropriation by politicians and bureaucrats. To mitigate these expropriation risks, ethnic Chinese cultivated relationships with powerful political patrons that became variously described as cronyism, patrimonialism, or clientelism (MacIntyre, 1994; Gomez, 2000). The international financial community viewed these relationships as indicative of corruption and inefficiency and have consistently pressured South-east Asian states to adopt international standards of political and corporate governance (Haggard *et al.*, 2008).

In the 1960s and 1970s, South-east Asian states adopted export-oriented development strategies. Spurred by the growth of outsourcing and offshoring of manufacturing by North American and European firms, ECFFs seized opportunities to develop export-based manufacturing businesses. In this period some ECFFs transformed their simple trading and manufacturing firms into widely diversified business groups under unified family control (Carney and Gedajlovic, 2002a). These diversified manufacturing, trading and commercial groups no longer resembled the small-scale archetype. Some began to resemble the giant business groups that are so prevalent in East Asia, such as the Korean *chaebol*. However, large ECFFs did not develop a technological capability or produce a cadre of professional managers comparable to their Korean counterparts. Nor did ECFFs engage in comparable levels of foreign direct investment in marketing, distribution and manufacturing assets. Rather, the international activities of ECFFs were focused upon participation in international global commodity chains related to the offshore manufacturing stage of the value chain. During this stage of rapid economic growth, perceptions changed and the leaders of ECFFs were now seen as entrepreneurial paragons (McVey, 1992). Their pioneering achievements in facilitating export-oriented development obscured the fact that exporting requires relatively few firm-specific organizational capabilities beyond efficient manufacturing (Hobday, 1995). Successful exporting through global commodity chains depends primarily upon the existence of country-specific factors such as the availability of low-cost and compliant labor combined with an efficient physical infrastructure. As labor and infrastructure costs have increased in newly industrialized economies, FBGs transferred production to other low-cost countries to access ever lower country-specific assets. In so doing, FBGs have become more international but, far from upgrading their firm-specific capabilities in research and development and marketing, they continue to rely on country-specific assets (Rugman, 2010).

In the 1980s, neoliberal economic policies were adopted in the region, leading to the extensive liberalization of capital markets and foreign direct investment policies. The short-term impact led many family firms to over-leverage their capital structure with foreign-denominated debt, which eventually triggered the 1997 Asian financial crisis. However, the longer-term effects of liberalized capital markets and foreign direct-investment rules offered Asia's BGs the opportunity to expand the scope of their international activities by investing directly in other countries (Carney, 2012). Nowhere were opportunities greater than in Mainland China, whose economic growth accelerated in the 1980s. ECFFs invested heavily in the manufacturing sectors in Guangzhou and Fujian. By the end of twentieth-century, Chinese entrepreneurs had remade their international networks and were linking large segments of the Chinese manufacturing sector to global markets (McNaughton, 1997). However, in retaining their family control, network organization, and focus on facilitating flows of capital and professional commodities, they have not evolved towards a Western model of the vertically integrated, managerially controlled multinational organization with a focus on proprietary technological and organizational competences.

Economic perspectives

The earliest attempts to describe the emergence of multinationals from Asia adopted the eclectic model often referred to as the Ownership, Localization, Internalization (OLI) framework. The eclectic model, first advanced in the 1970s (Dunning, 1977) to account for patterns of international business activity suggests the MNE can be understood by combining three existing economic theories pertaining to internalization of transactions, monopoly ownership advantages, and international trade theory. In a book of essays honoring Dunning, Lecraw (1992) seeks to explain the internationalization of Third World multinationals from Indonesia that seemingly lacked both ownership and location advantages. Lecraw (1993) prefigures much of the contemporary literature on emerging market multinationals in his suggestion that the mainly Chinese-owned Indonesian firms engaged in outward direct investment not to exploit their advantages but to acquire new ownership advantages from foreign markets and import these advantages back to the home market. In particular, Lecraw (1993) emphasizes the importance of internationalization to acquire managerial expertise, which was in short supply domestically. Lecraw also noted that the group structure adopted by these firms facilitated international diversification and allowed them to internationalize much faster than existing theories predicted (Johanson and Vahlne, 1977).

In an explicit application of the eclectic framework, Shapiro *et al.* (2003) identify important differences between ECFF and Western multinational enterprises (MNEs) and suggest that the eclectic model needed to be adapted for the Asian context and the particular preferences of ECFFs. Erdener and Shapiro (2005) propose that the key OLI advantage of the ECFF is its ability to deploy relational contracting among its networks and personal contacts to make deals that create value often in highly uncertain environments. Competitive advantage arises out of the ability to generate and rapidly deploy relational skills not only among networks of family, suppliers, distributors and bureaucratic institutions but to do so in a way that enables the firms to mobilize flexible and effective responses to fleeting entrepreneurial opportunities. Because relational advantages are intangible and sticky to the owner-entrepreneur, they cannot be easily transferred via market contracts, such as licensing or franchising, so they must be internalized to be exploited. As indicated in the eclectic model, Chinese family firms will seek to match their location choices with their ownership advantages. Because ECFFs rely on their ability to do business in relational contexts, they will tend to internationalize to countries with comparable cultures and institutional frameworks. In this respect, China stands out as an ideal target country for these firms (Shapiro *et al.*, 2003).

In their application of the eclectic model to the ECFF, Erdener and Shapiro (2005) raise the predominantly descriptive studies to a theoretical level, linking prevailing descriptions of the prominent organizational form in the literature to mainstream concepts in the field of international business. They further suggest that like the Western MNE, the ECFF is an effective organizational mechanism for capitalizing on particular configurations of competitive and locational advantages.

Interestingly, the rise of Asia in the 1970s and 1980s encouraged Dunning (1995) to reappraise the eclectic model to incorporate what he described as alliance capitalism to account for the prevailing networked form of organization favored by Asian firms. In the reappraised model Dunning suggested that ownership advantages should be widened to take explicit account of the costs and benefits of inter-firm relationships. He further suggested that, in assessing locational factors, firms will give more weight to territorial embeddedness and the spatial integration of complex economic activities, and, third, incorporate into internalization factors the dynamic capabilities that explicitly take into account the trade-off between control and the de facto use of intangible assets through the networks.

Contextual perspectives

Sociological accounts of Asian business networks repudiated purely economic explanations of Asian organizing models on the grounds that they represent a Western theoretical ethnocentrism stemming from a neoclassical economics view of proper organization and functioning (Biggart and Hamilton, 1992). In contrast, sociological accounts emphasized the deeply rooted institutional foundations of Asian markets that consisted of state- and family-centered conceptions of patrimonial authority (Hamilton and Biggart, 1988). These perspectives predict a continuing divergence of Asian and Western organizational models (Whitley, 1999). Focusing upon the origins and development of large-scale Chinese family-owned business groups, Carney and Gedajlovic (2002a) identified common institutional conditions among the Association of Southeast Asian (ASEAN) group of countries that kindled the emergence and path-dependent growth of Chinese family-controlled business groups (FBGs). In a co-evolutionary cause-and-effect cycle, the initial conditions of state-led industrialization in the region prompted economically functional organizational adaptations among Chinese entrepreneurs, who were the dominant entrepreneurial class in the region. The aggregate effects of their adaptations fostered a feedback loop to influence subsequent institutional development. For example, state-led industrialization became dependent for its success upon state allocation of scarce capital resources and the suppression of liquid equity markets. Capital market voids provided Chinese family business groups with an advantage since they could mobilize capital from their own networks and affiliated firms. In later stages of development, Chinese family firms did not seek capital on equity markets since they had developed their own sources, and equity markets stagnated. Similarly, ECFF preferences for relational contracting and opaque systems of corporate governance were given momentum by the politically hostile conditions of the nationalist era in the region. Subsequently, the major ECFFs were relatively indifferent to the development of legal institutions that would foster the development of arm's-length contracting and transparent corporate governance. Unsurprisingly perhaps, without the explicit support of a country's largest and most powerful entrepreneurs, contractual and corporate governance reforms failed to fully take root.

The significance of firm-institution co-evolutionary dynamics suggests Chinese family business groups may have developed an administrative heritage that does not necessarily favor competence-based international diversification. The concept of administrative heritage suggests that the firms' international capabilities are formed in the early stages of their growth and subsequently cast a long shadow over their capacity for profitable international expansion (Bartlett and Ghoshal, 1987). In their rapid growth phase, family business groups in the ASEAN were heavily focused upon developing their domestic market position due to the opportunities afforded by import substitution and export-oriented economic development. BGs' domestic orientation was reinforced following the liberalization of foreign investment rules because leading business groups were targeted by Western multinational enterprises seeking to enter ASEAN markets. New foreign entrants established alliances and partnerships with well-connected local entrepreneurs as a means of establishing their manufacturing operations. Protected from vigorous competition, family patriarchs were able to entrench themselves in their enterprises and, satiated by the lucrative opportunities provided to them by their foreign strategic alliance partners, family firms have grown complacent and possess little incentive to engage in foreign direct investment (Carney and Gedajlovic, 2003). For the most part Chinese-controlled business groups did not invest heavily in marketing and R&D activities nor develop firm-specific assets or the kinds of organizational structure that would support capability-based internationalization strategies (ibid.).

The outward foreign direct investment of Chinese FBGs located in ASEAN regions was often motivated by the desire to diversify risk and protect family wealth. The substantial fortunes of the largest business groups were frequently based on connections with prominent politicians and so the status of this wealth became precarious when democratic revolutions led to the demise of strongman politicians (Carney and Dieleman, 2011). For instance, after the overthrow of Indonesia's President Suharto in the wake of the Asian financial crisis, a reformist government sought reparations from the collapse of the Bank of Central Asia, an early victim of the financial crisis. The bank was the major financial affiliate of the Salim Group, which at that time was Indonesia's largest Chinese FBG and whose founder was a long-established Suharto crony (Dieleman and Sachs, 2006). The targeted amount for reparations was set at some US$6 billion, a figure equal to Salim's estimated market value at the time. Chinese entrepreneurs were fully aware of the contingent nature of their social capital with prominent politicians and had prepared the ground for the eventual downfall of their benefactors (Gomez, 2000). Much of their capital had been exported to safe havens in Hong Kong and Singapore by offshore holding companies they had established to manage their assets. For example, the Salim Group had established First Pacific Enterprises in Hong Kong, which became the main asset-holding company for Salim's diverse South-east Asian interests outside Indonesia. Whether outward foreign direct investment motivated by fear of expropriation is a sound basis for a multinational enterprise remains to be determined.

Family business perspectives

While sociological perspectives focus upon the external constraints on the ECFFs, the internationalization of family business literature identifies internal factors that reduce the incentives for family firms to engage in foreign direct investment. This literature has established that family firms are typically less internationally diversified than non-family firms (Fernández and Nieto, 2005; Gómez-Mejía *et al.*, 2010). The central issue constraining internationalization concerns the locus of managerial control of the family firm. Successful internationalization generally calls for the use of external resources such as professional managers and risk capital. However, the use of external resources reduces family control (Gómez-Mejía *et al.*, 2010) and firms will tend to use these resources sparingly.

A number of studies have found that ECFFs are especially reluctant to delegate control to non-family members (Redding, 1990; Carney and Gedajlovic, 2002b; Ahlstrom *et al.*, 2004; Tsui-Auch, 2004). Consequently, ECFFs will lack the ability to manage large-scale businesses for economies of scale and scope and to monitor geographically dispersed units, a phenomenon that Carney (1998) describes as a managerial capacity constraint. On the other hand, concentrating family wealth in a single jurisdiction exposes families to country-specific risk, which they can and do reduce by international diversification. A management capacity constraint that limits the scope of international activity combined with a need to diversify risks suggests that ECFFs are likely to invest in foreign assets that require little managerial oversight, such as investment in property and joint ventures in which the counterpart supplies managerial expertise.

Network perspectives

The most positive accounts of ECFF internationalization are found in perspectives that emphasize network relationships and their capacity for inter-organizational learning and asset sharing (Tsui-Auch, 2001; Tsang, 2002; Hitt *et al.*, 2002). These accounts point to ECFFs' ability to establish inter-ethnic networks that are transnational in character. The functional purpose is to access technological and managerial skills that are unavailable locally. Hobday (1995) documents the formation of strategic partnerships with Western firms in the gradual accumulation of skills, information and technologies that enabled Asian firms to climb up the value chain in the electronics industry.

Perhaps the best-known of these accounts is Mathews' (2006) accelerated internationalization thesis that advances a linking, leveraging, and learning (LLL) framework to account for latecomer internationalization. The multinational expansion of Western enterprises was based on capabilities that were honed and perfected over many years prior to their international expansion. In contrast, "Dragon" multinationals followed a path of accelerated internationalization by linking up with foreign firms with the goal of learning and subsequently leveraging their newly acquired knowledge to climb the value chain. Whereas Western multinationals have been cautious in their alliance choices as a means of protecting their proprietary advantages, Asian firms developed a far greater external orientation and network-based learning, and sought to maximize the number of linkages with partners across a wide range of activities. This process put them in contact with multiple opportunities and resources in both advanced and less developed economies.

Tsang (2002) describes the internationalization behavior of Chinese family businesses through the lens of organization learning. Tsang compares Chinese family businesses with non-family businesses from Singapore who invest in China. While both types of firm share similar motives in entering the Chinese market—to take advantage of China's large market, gain a strategic competitive position, and use the low labor costs—the learning processes and outcomes differ between family and non-family firms. In transferring their own know-how to Chinese subsidiaries, ECFFs adopt an informal and unstructured approach, involving family members in negotiations and as active participants in the mainland management team of the subsidiary in China. Once firms acquire experience in China, it is shared only with close family members. In contrast, non-family businesses shared and institutionalized their international experience broadly within the firm. Tsang (2002) concludes that constraints on ECFF learning from international experience in China resulted in concrete obstacles to continued internationalization, a conclusion that is similar to the management capacity constraint view.

In a contrary argument, Yeung (2000) suggests managerial learning in ECFFs' internationalization efforts is a strategy to overcome the limits of managerial capacity constraints because internationalization increases their exposure to professional management, an argument that echoes Lecraw's (1993) findings. Yeung identifies several mechanisms through which this occurs. The first entails the careful socialization of outsiders into the family who are subsequently placed in overseas operations. Second, placement in a foreign subsidiary is used as a mechanism to train and test a future family successor. Third, Chinese family firms expand mainly through capitalizing on their networks of personal and business relationships in international markets. In this view, international expansion is the means of loosening local constraints and the limited "cocoon" of their operations in South-east Asia.

Conclusion

The diverging perspectives on the ECFFs' preferred modes of internationalization suggests that this organizational form has both advantages and disadvantages. The advantages derive from a preferred network mode of operating an international organization while the disadvantages arise out of contextual and inherently related constraints in operating geographically dispersed organizational forms. Given the evident complexity of the subject, multi-theoretical perspectives such as the LLL and OLI are required to fully account for the observed patterns of behavior. It is evident that the ECFF approach to internationalization differs from other Asian approaches such as those of the Korean *chaebol* and Japanese *keiretsu* forms of the MNE as well as from traditional Western MNEs. In this regard, we expect the absence of substantive hierarchical and internal organization will limit the ECFFs' range of industries where we should expect them to gain a competitive advantage.

Future research might examine the extent to which ECFF international strategies differ from those of other family firms with ethnicities. For example, outward foreign direct investment from India has increased rapidly in recent decades and it is frequently observed that the majority of Indian firms are also family-owned and family-controlled, but there is no comparable literature on ethnic Indian family firms. Some scholars see the broad scholarly interest in the Chinese family firm as resonating with long-established stereotypes held by Westerners about Chinese culture and call for a "de-recentralization" of the discourse on the Chinese family firm (Greenhalgh, 1994). Asia is undergoing rapid social and economic growth and development, and the emergence of a prosperous population of firms owned and controlled by Chinese entrepreneurs defies ethnic stereotypes (Whyte, 1996). The evolving structure of the form questions the underlying cultural assumptions implicit in the concept of the ECFF (Singh, 2007). The search for the essence of a unique and enduring Chinese family firm may well confuse rather than clarify what are changing and heterogeneous characteristics of an adaptive and dynamic organizational form.

Bibliography

Ahlstrom, D., Young, M., Chan, E.S. and Bruton, G.D. (2004) "Facing constraints to growth? Overseas Chinese entrepreneurs and traditional business practice in East Asia," *Asia Pacific Journal of Management,* 21: 263–285.

Backman, M. (1999) *Asian Eclipse: Exposing the Dark Side of Business in Asia,* Singapore: Wiley.

Bartlett, C.A. and Ghoshal, S. (1987) "Managing across borders: new organizational responses," *Sloan Management Review,* 29(1): 43–53.

Biggart, N.W. and Hamilton, G.G. (1992) "On the limits of a firm-based theory to explain business networks: the Western bias of neoclassical economics," in N. Nohria, and R.G. Eccles (eds) *Networks and Organizations: Structure, Form and Action,* Boston: Harvard Business School Press, pp. 471–490.

Carney, M. (1998) "A management capacity constraint? Obstacles to the development of the Chinese family business," *Asia Pacific Journal of Management,* 15: 1–25.

Carney, M. (2012) "What is driving the internationalization of Asia's business groups?" in M. Beeson and R. Stubbs (eds) *The Handbook of Asian Regionalism,* London: Routledge, pp. 100–118.

Carney, M. and Dieleman, M. (2011) "Indonesia's missing multinationals: business groups and outward direct investment," *Bulletin of Indonesian Economic Studies,* 47(1): 105–126.

Carney, M. and Gedajlovic, E. (2002a) "The co-evolution of institutional environments and organizational strategies: the rise of family business groups in the ASEAN region," *Organization Studies,* 23(1): 1–31.

Carney, M. and Gedajlovic, E. (2002b) "Coupled ownership and control and the allocation of financial resources: evidence from Hong Kong," *Journal of Management Studies,* 39(1): 123–146.

Carney, M. and Gedajlovic, E. (2003) "Strategic innovation and the administrative heritage of East Asian Chinese family business groups," *Asia Pacific Journal of Management,* 20: 5–26.

Chirot, D. and Reid, A. (1997) *Essential Outsiders: Chinese and Jews in the Modern Transformation of Southeast Asia and Central Europe,* Seattle: University of Washington Press.

Chua, A. (2003) *World on Fire: How Exporting Free Market Democracy Breeds Ethnic Hatred and Global Instability,* New York: Doubleday.

Dieleman, M. and Sachs, W. (2006) "Oscillating between a relationship-based and a market-based model: the Salim Group," *Asia Pacific Journal of Management,* 23(4): 521–536.

Dieleman, M. and Sachs, W.M. (2008) "Coevolution of institutions and corporations in emerging economies: how the Salim Group morphed into an institution of Suharto's crony regime," *Journal of Management Studies,* 45(7): 1274–1300.

Dunning, J.H. (1977) "Trade, location of economic activity and the MNE: a search for an eclectic approach," in B. Ohlin, P. Hesselborn, and P.M. Wijkman (eds) *The International Allocation of Economic Activity,* London: The Macmillan Press Ltd, pp. 395–431.

Dunning, J.H. (1979) "Explaining changing patterns of international production: in defence of the eclectic theory," *Oxford Bulletin of Economics and Statistics,* 41(4): 269–295.

Dunning, J.H. (1988) "The eclectic paradigm of international production: a restatement and some posssible replications," *Journal of International Business Studies,* 19(1): 1–31.

Dunning, J.H. (1995) "Reappraising the eclectic paradigm in the age of alliance capitalism," *Journal of International Business Studies,* 26, 461–491.

Erdener, C. and Shapiro, D. (2005) "The internationalization of Chinese family enterprises and Dunning's eclectic MNE paradigm," *Management and Organization Review,* 1(3): 411–436.

Fernández, Z. and Nieto, M.J. (2005) "Internationalization strategy of small and medium-sized family businesses: some influential factors," *Family Business Review,* 18(1): 77–89.

Gomez, E.T. (2000) "In search of patrons: Chinese business networking and Malay political patronage in Malaysia," in *Chinese Business Networks: State, Economy and Culture,* Nordic Institute of Asian Studies, Copenhagen: Prentice Hall, pp. 207–223.

Gómez-Mejía, L.R., Makri, M. and Larraza-Kintana, M. (2010) "Diversification decisions in family-controlled firms," *Journal of Management Studies,* 47(2): 223–252.

Greenhalgh, S. (1994) "De-orientalizing the Chinese family firm," *American Ethnologist,* 21(4): 746–775.

Haggard, S., MacIntyre, A. and Tiede, L. (2008) "The rule of law and economic development," *Annual Review of Political Science,* 11(1): 205–234.

Haley, G., Tan, C.T. and Haley, U. (1998) *New Asian Emperors: The Overseas Chinese, Their Strategies and Competitive Advantages,* Oxford: Butterworth-Heinemann.

Hamilton, G.G. and Biggart, N.W. (1988) "Market, culture and authority: a comparative analysis of management in the Far East," *American Journal of Sociology,* 94: S52–S94.

Hao, Y.-P. (1970) "A 'new class' in China's treaty ports: the rise of the comprador-merchants," *Business History Review,* 44(4): 446–460.

Hitt, M.A., Lee, H.-U. and Yucel, E. (2002) "The importance of social capital to the management of multinational enterprises: relational networks among Asian and Western firms," *Asia Pacific Journal of Management,* 19(2–3): 353–372.

Hobday, M. (1995) "East Asian latecomer firms: learning the technology of electronics," *World Development,* 23: 1171–1193.

Johanson, J. and Vahlne, J.E. (1977) "The internationalization process of the firm: a model of knowledge development and increasing foreign market commitments," *Journal of International Business Studies,* 8: 23–32.

Kao, J. (1993) "The worldwide web of Chinese business," *Harvard Business Review,* 71(2): 24–36.

Kraar, L. (1994) "The overseas Chinese: lessons from the world's most dynamic capitalists," *Fortune* (October): 91–101.

Lall, S. (1983) *The New Multinationals: The Spread of Third World Enterprises,* New York: Wiley.

Lecraw, D.J. (1983) "Performance of transnational corporations in less developed countries," *Journal of International Business Studies,* 14(1): 15–33.

Lecraw, D.J. (1992) "Third world MNEs once again: the case of Indonesia", in P.J. Buckley and M. Casson (eds) *Multinational Enterprises in the World Economy,* Aldershot: Edward Elgar, pp. 115–133.

Lecraw, D.J. (1993) "Outward investment by Indonesian firms: motivation and effects," *Journal of International Business Studies,* 24: 589–600.

Limligan, V.S. (1986) *The Overseas Chinese in ASEAN: Business Strategies and Management Practices,* Manila: Vita Development Corp.

Lu, J., Liu, X. and Wang, H. (2011) "Motives for outward FDI of Chinese private firms: firm resources, industry dynamics, and government policies," *Management and Organization Review,* 7(2): 223–248.

MacIntyre, A. (1994) *Business and Government in Industrializing Asia,* Ithaca, NY: Cornell University Press.

Mackie, J. (1992) "Changing patterns of big business in Southeast Asia," in R. McVey (ed.) *Southeast Asian Capitalism,* Ithaca, NY: Cornell University Southeast Asia Program, pp. 161–190.

Mackie, J. (1996) "Introduction", in A. Reid (ed.) *Sojourners and Settlers: Histories of Southeast Asia and the Chinese,* Honolulu: University of Hawaii Press, pp. xii–xxx.

McNaughton, B. (1997) *The China Circle: Economics and Electronics in the PRC, Taiwan, and Hong Kong,* Washington, DC: Brookings Institution.

McVey, R. (1992) "The materialisation of the Southeast Asian entrepreneur," in R. McVey (ed.) *Southeast Asian Capitalism,* Ithaca, NY: Cornell University Southeast Asia Program, pp. 7–34.

Mathews, J.A. (2006) "Dragon multinationals: new players in 21st century globalization," *Asia Pacific Journal of Management,* 23(1): 5–27.

Redding, G. (1990) *The Spirit of Chinese Capitalism,* New York: De Gruyter.

Redding, G. (1995) "Overseas Chinese networks: understanding the enigma," *Long Range Planning,* 28(1): 61–69.

Rugman, A.M. (2010) "Reconciling internalization theory and the eclectic paradigm," *Multinational Business Review,* 18(2):1–12.

Seagrave, S. (1995) *Lords of the Rim: The Invisible Empire of the Overseas Chinese,* London: Bantam.

Shapiro, D.M., Gedajlovic, E. and Erdener, C. (2003) "The Chinese family firm as a multinational enterprise," *International Journal of Organizational Analysis,* 11(2): 105–122.

Singh, K. (2007) "The limited relevance of culture to strategy," *Asia Pacific Journal of Management,* 24(4): 421–428.

Tsang, E. (2002) "Learning from overseas venturing experience: the case of Chinese family businesses," *Journal of Business Venturing,* 17(1): 21.

Tsui-Auch, L.S. (2001) "Learning in global and local networks: experience of Chinese firms in Hong Kong, Singapore, and Taiwan," *Handbook of Organizational Learning and Knowledge,* Oxford: Oxford University Press, pp. 716–732.

Tsui-Auch, L.S. (2004) "The professionally managed family-ruled enterprise: ethnic Chinese business in Singapore," *Journal of Management Studies,* 41(4): 693–723.

Weidenbaum, M. (1996) *The Bamboo Network: How Expatriate Chinese Entrepreneurs Are Creating a New Economic Superpower in Asia,* New York: Free Press.

Wells, L.T. (1983) *Third World Multinationals: The Rise of Foreign Investment from Developing Countries,* Cambridge, MA: The MIT Press.

Whitley, R. (ed.) (1999) *Divergent Capitalisms: The Social Structuring and Change of Business Systems,* Oxford: Oxford University Press.

Whyte, M.K. (1996) "The Chinese family and economic development: obstacle or engine?" *Economic Development and Cultural Change,* 45(1): 1–30.

World Bank (1993) *The East Asian Miracle: Economic Growth and Public Policy,* Oxford: Oxford University Press.

Wu, Y.L. and Wu, C.H. (1980) *Economic Development in Southeast Asia: The Chinese Dimension,* Stanford, CA: Hoover Institution Press.

Yeung, H.W. (2000) *Entrepreneurship and the Internationalization of Asian Firms,* Cheltenham: Edward Elgar.

Yeung, H.W. (2006) "Change and continuity in Southeast Asia ethnic Chinese business," *Asia Pacific Journal of Management,* 23(3): 229–254.

Yiu, D.W. (2011) "Multinational advantages of Chinese business groups: a theoretical exploration," *Management and Organization Review,* 7(2): 249–277.

Yoshihara, K. (1988) *The Rise of Ersatz Capitalism in South-East Asia.* Oxford: Oxford University Press.

Incubation and types of entrepreneurship

11

Japan's new business incubation revolution

Kathryn Ibata-Arens

Introduction

The Japanese economy contracted in the 1990s, leading to unprecedented layoffs at big companies, and high levels of business bankruptcies in the small and medium-sized enterprise (SME) sector. Previously, it was assumed (at least by outsiders) that entrepreneurial businesses were the beneficiaries of big business (the *keiretsu* group) who controlled vertically integrated production arrangements within which SMEs prospered through supposedly trust-based subcontractor relations (Dore, 1986). By the end of the 1990s, the first of Japan's "lost decades" of economic malaise and stagnant growth, the historically big business-oriented national government policies and business practices (e.g. vertically integrated production) would be revealed as ill-suited to stimulate high growth entrepreneurship (Ibata-Arens, 2005).

Rising public discontent with the bureaucratic status quo led to a number of changes in Japan's industrial governance. Government ministries reformed and reorganized in the late 1990s. Another outcome of the so-called lost decade was recognition at the highest levels of government that the Japanese economy needed to become more entrepreneurial.

Japan has since undergone a revolution in new business incubation. Between 2000 and 2010, Japan invested many billions of yen in national capacity to support new venture businesses. A significant amount of funds have been put into encouraging university start-ups. A major part of the government investment has built new business incubators (facilities where new firms pay a nominal rent in exchange for a variety of hard and soft supports, outlined below). By 2006, about 1,300 firms had graduated (left incubators while remaining in business) from the 177 incubators in existence at that time. A study in 2006 found that 91 percent of incubator tenants in Japan remain in the regions in which they are incubated (compared to about 75 percent in the United States) (JANBO, 2006). By 2010, there were 336 new business incubators, up from a mere 30 in 1999, a stunning 900 percent growth.

This chapter analyzes the policy and incubation management practice behind Japan's revolution in new business incubation. The findings are based on a two-year study conducted in 2009 and 2010, followed by subsequent fieldwork in 2011 and 2012. Data compiled include an original database outlining key features of all incubators in Japan, interviews and site visits with 30 incubation managers and incubators in nine cities from Hokkaido in the north, to Okinawa in the south (Kawasaki, Kobe, Kyoto, Naha, Osaka, Otsu, Sapporo, Tokyo, and Yokohama). A hybrid incubation management model is identified as a potential best practice model for the Japanese economy. Model incubators tend to be non-governmental university-related hybrids that cultivate a "bamboo network root system" of entrepreneurial supports, as will be discussed below.

This chapter has four sections. First, the incubation revolution in Japan is situated in the origins of new business incubation worldwide. The second section outlines different incubator types around the world and proposes an incubation management typology to understand the different approaches to incubation. It argues that the most effective incubation management cultivates a bamboo network cultivation model to connect tenant firms to strategic supports. The variety and density of supports available to tenants' firms through incubation manager (IM) networks function like a bamboo grove around firms (discussed in detail below). Section three reviews the key policy history behind new business incubation in Japan and some of the challenges inherent in civil servant-led entrepreneurship. Section four discusses best practice in incubation management, highlighting three incubators in Japan: Kyoto Mikuruma, Shiga Collabo 21, and Venture Generation. The chapter will conclude with a review of the findings and discussion of policy lessons.

Origins and international context

Incubators take their name from the first such facility, in Batavia, New York, established in 1959 (Anselmo, 2009). Most incubators around the world are not-for-profit, and are often run by local, regional or national government institutions. There are three main types of business incubators: (1) *general/mixed use;* (2) *economic development* (promoting job creation, industrial restructuring, assisting under-developed communities); and (3) *technology* (development of technology-based firms, often university technology transfer and diffusion) (OECD, 1997).

As a tool of regional economic development and innovation policy, successful incubators produce high growth graduates that (1) contribute to local employment; and (2) produce products that contribute to the economic well-being of supporting sectors (ibid.). Since high technology start-ups are the most likely to be the high growth (employment, sales) firms that countries seek, national governments have targeted policy accordingly.

The following is a brief review of scholarly work on incubation/incubators. According to Hackett and Dilts (2004), initial studies emerged in the 1980s and focused on providing definitions, taxonomies and conceptual frameworks to understand incubation. By the 1990s, the study of business incubation had developed such that outcomes and measures of success went beyond just counting the "graduation" of firms, and addressed the economic impact on local communities, job creation and innovation.

Al-Mubaraki and Wong (2012) found that the length of incubator existence explains much of the variance in outcomes (successful graduated firms), previously noted in the 2004 findings of Hackett and Dilts. This reflects in part the development in incubation management expertise over time. In the United States, university-affiliated incubators (on university campuses or nearby with close collaboration with universities) produce the most start-ups that survive in the long term, and further, remain in the communities that nurture them, producing a return on investment for stakeholders.[1]

Etzkowitz (2002) reviews incubator models, including the evolving role of universities in supporting new business-based economic development. Comparing university incubation development in Albany, New York, to Rio de Janeiro, Brazil, Etzkowitz found that networking (with area firms, state and other research labs in Albany, with other local incubators in Rio) played a critical role in the rapid growth of incubators in these regions. Research has also called into question the over-emphasis on technology-type incubators worldwide and cites the related policy failures in promoting entrepreneurship and economic development (Tamasy, 2007). In short, too many regions have attempted to emulate places like Silicon Valley without taking into account the sources of its success: *historical* (military), *institutional* (proximity to Stanford University and the Bay Area) and *policy* (legal framework in the USA allows IMs to take an equity stake in start-ups).

Others, including Aernoudt (2004) and Bergek and Norrman (2008) suggest best practice models of incubation management. These models include the critical role of connections between incubators and local angel investment networks (Aernoudt, 2004). Bergek and Norrman argue that measurement of incubator outcomes should track the type of incubation management model of a particular incubator. Bergek and Norrman introduce an important aspect of understanding the incubation process: outcomes (number of graduates, firm growth) often correspond to a continuum of management types (e.g. the "pickier" incubators are about selecting tenants, the higher the success ratio in firm-level outcomes). They observe (in Sweden) differences across incubators in terms of the approach to *selection* ("survival of fittest" to "picking-the-winners") of tenant firms, and *mediation* ("laissez-faire" to "strong intervention") of firm activities. An attenuated model, comparing incubation management in terms of a matrix of selection versus development is proposed below.

Worldwide, it is estimated that there are more than 4,000 new business incubators, an increase from 3,000 in the year 2000. Since 2000, the world has experienced a steady growth in the number of incubators, while Asia has experienced the greatest increase. Table 11.1 outlines the number of incubators in countries worldwide as of 2010, compared to 2000.

National governments have recognized the role of new business incubators in supporting successful start-ups and have followed suit by investing in national incubation capacity. The number of incubators in China and Korea has grown significantly since 2000, with China leading Asian economies in the number of graduates. On a per capita basis, Korea is the leader in establishing incubation facilities, followed by Japan. India is increasing the number of incubators, but has yet to match the growth in other Asian countries. Further, India has focused on building capacity in large research parks (housing MNC anchor tenants and mid-stage start-ups) particularly in high technology fields, including biotechnology, rather than new start-ups *per se* (Bergek and Norrman, 2008; Sharma *et al.*, 2010). These practices can be understood in terms of a selection versus development typology, which compares the impact of incubation management styles on tenant firms.

Incubation model types and the bamboo network cultivation approach

While most Japanese incubators are government-run (100 percent of Chinese incubators are government-run), a few public-private hybrids have emerged. These hybrids appear to be

Table 11.1 Incubators by country

Country	*# of incubators in 2000*	*# of incubators after 2000*
US	721 (1999)	1,000+ (2010)
Brazil	10 (1990)	237 (2004)
India	25	100 (2010)
China	131	548 (2006)
Korea	144 (2006)	269 (2008)
Japan	30	336 (2010)

Sources: Etzkowitz *et al.* (2005) (Brazil); Sun (2004), Zhang and Sonobe (2011) (China); Sharma *et al.* (2010) (India); Kim and Ames (2006), Cho and Son (2009) (Korea).

developing successful incubation management models. One measure of success for business incubators is generating start-ups that survive and grow, thus contributing to local employment and economic development.

Further, developing the *leadership skills* of the incubation managers is critical. According to the Entrepreneurship Summit Summary (Kauffman Foundation and the International Economic Development Council, 2008), leaders must have management skills including "[the] savvy to influence people over which they have no authority or control." This is proving to be a challenge in Japanese incubators which are top-heavy with bureaucracy, where it is not unheard of to have as many incubation managers (mostly civil servants on secondment or retired bureaucrats) as tenant firms. In the USA, incubators are usually run by one or two people.

Figure 11.1 outlines the four types of incubator management styles. The y axis indicates how choosy incubators are about whom they allow to become tenants. For example, if an incubator is high on selection, it will have a competitive application process where potential tenants must submit detailed business plans to demonstrate the viability of the idea/technology, as well as the market potential and entrepreneurial skills of its executive team (Aerts *et al.*, 2007).

Incubators with low selection criteria are more like standard office buildings, in which tenants are admitted as long as they are able to pay the rent. In the lower left quadrant, firms have easy entry, but receive little support once they enter. Incubation facilities run by real estate developers tend to be of this type (facilities management).

On the right-hand side, corresponding to the x axis of development, tenant firms receive a number of soft supports as outlined above, the difference being whether or not the firms have gone through a competitive selection process. In the lower right quadrant, it is akin to a lottery system or random placement in intramural sports/Little League teams. The coach is assigned a roster of players, some who might have natural talent, but many who do not. The coach's role is to coax players to train to reach the best of their ability. Likewise, in coaching-style incubators, incubator managers (IMs) provide a menu of services such as a call center, usually on a pay-per-use basis.

In the upper right quadrant, the cultivation or hybrid model ("hybrid" because it combines government and private sector approaches), high growth potential firms are selected from a larger pool of applicants, and in addition to benefiting from being around other "best of the best" entrepreneurs (facilitating peer mentoring), they also obtain a variety of soft supports. Of these supports, helping entrepreneurs to develop strategic support networks is most critical, and the incubator managers who are able to do this effectively draw from their own deeply connected

INCUBATOR MANAGEMENT

Selection	Low Development	High Development
High	Picking winners	Bamboo network Cultivation (Hybrids)
Low	Facilities (Landlords)	Coaching (Private)

Figure 11.1 Incubator management styles

private sector networks. Honig and Karlsson (2010) find that IMs are instrumental for their tenants in this regard, as well as in connecting other new firms in their communities to resources that they need. This has also proven a challenge for Japan's incubators, since more than a third of them are run by retired bureaucrats and civil servants, whose personal networks are mostly with other public sector employees. This is in contrast to the United States, where IMs are more likely to be serial entrepreneurs or others with hands-on business experience.

On the whole, Japan has moved from the upper left of the selection vs. development typology matrix (picking winners, but offering little support, such as the former Ministry of International Trade and Industry (MITI) did in the 1950s to 1970s) to coaching (lower right quadrant), with a few incubators of a hybrid type. The hybrid type in Japan has three features, reflecting its governance structure, ties with universities and incubation management style. It is estimated that less than 10 percent of Japanese incubators are of this type.

First, hybrid-type incubators may access government funds, but avoid employing IMs from government agencies. Instead, these incubators hire IMs who have had some degree of private sector experience with the concomitant social networks. Rather than be a subordinate partner to the national government, hybrid incubators have some institutional balance, for example, having a joint venture between the prefectural government and local banking community in Shiga's Collabo 21 incubator, and with the Kyoto Venture Forum (a group of successful serial entrepreneurs) as in the Mikuruma incubator, discussed below.

Second, in terms of their incubation management style, hybrid incubators focus primarily on developing the strategic resource networks of entrepreneurs, and secondarily on training entrepreneurs in effective business management. These practices cultivate an extensive network of private sector supports for tenant firms. These interlocked networks around firms—their ecosystem—can be likened to a bamboo grove. Bamboo are tubers, and underneath a group of bamboo trees is a dense, lattice structure root system that connects the trees, seedlings and shoots together. A shock to one part of the root system does not destroy the grove, and new shoots pop up elsewhere in the network.

Cultivating a bamboo stakeholder network root system type of network for start-up firms helps firms to withstand external shocks (e.g. drying up of a given capital source) by assisting firms in avoiding being dependent on any single support source. Effective incubation managers prioritize this network cultivation, and further, they have dense private sector networks themselves, usually a result of years of experience in private industry. While effective IMs develop networks for their tenants, they also assist firms in connecting those that can provide training in the art of managing a business. This observation in Japan is consistent with findings in prior studies on the importance of incubator networks in incubation success discussed above.

The third feature of the emerging hybrid incubation management model is the ties with universities. That is, the close socio-spatial location of incubators to universities has positive effects on the incubation process. Start-ups are like bamboo shoots (akin to seedlings), nurtured by IMs, who to the extent they are able, draw from government resources (while keeping management in the hands of private sector individuals), and connect firms with technology resources at local universities.

The evolution of the bamboo network cultivation model is the result of decades of (both effective and ineffective) policy stimuli, led by Japan's economic and education ministries.

Policy history: from technopolis to incubator[2]

In Japan, the Ministry of Economy, Trade and Industry (METI) has been the main source of the funds to build and manage new business incubators, while the Ministry of Education, Science, Sports and Culture (MEXT) has been responsible for policies encouraging university start-ups (new businesses established by faculty/students and/or based on university-generated science and technology). METI, in conjunction with MEXT, has taken a three-tiered approach to stimulating new business start-ups: first, targeting university ventures (135.5 billion yen), second, building incubation facilities (175 billion yen), and third, creating regional economy-level networks (researcher and industry) (66.5 billion yen). The aim is to create an incentive and institutional system conducive to new firm start-ups, what can be called an "entrepreneurial ecosystem." Of the three types of capacity investment, the largest has been in building incubation facilities. Having visited 30 of the government-sponsored new business incubators built since 2000, this author observed stylish building façades, marble and crystal fixtures in restroom facilities, and high tech (bio-sensor) entryways, as well as state-of-the art clean rooms and wet lab space. Japan has clearly excelled at building the physical capacity to support (high tech) start-ups.

In 2000, METI and MEXT began to offer financial incentives to university faculty who started businesses, encouraging technology start-ups especially. Consequently, the overall number of university start-ups has increased dramatically since 2000, from a few hundred to more than 1,800 by the year 2008. However, most university start-ups under these programs have yet to introduce new products to market.

Japanese incubators are nurturing thousands of new business start-ups in a variety of sectors, including information technology, environmental technology, and services. Considering that before 2000 there was little institutional support (sponsored by the government in particular) for new firm start-ups, the past ten years have truly represented a revolution in new business incubation. Further, the entire country of Japan (of 130 million people) is only about the physical size of the State of California (population 36.9 million) in the United States (US Census Bureau, 2009). Having more than three hundred incubators built in this space in less than a decade (in addition to being a boon to the Japanese construction sector) is a testament to the hard work of Japanese civil servants behind these policy initiatives.

The highest concentrations of incubators are found in the metropolitan area of Tokyo (23 districts), followed by Osaka City, Kyoto City and Kita Kyushu City. Japan's focus on incubators that began in 2000 is rooted in decades of prior national attempts to stimulate firm-level capacity. Japan's national policy aimed at creating an entrepreneurial economy is divided into five historical periods: (1) top-down (late 1980s); (2) decentralization (early 1990s); (3) privatization (late 1990s); (4) university–private sector alliances and facilities building (early 2000s); and (5) strategic management (late 2000s). Each period is outlined briefly below.

Period I: top down (late 1980s) technopolis policies

Still riding on the euphoria of the high growth, cash-rich period (1950s–1970s), METI (then MITI) embarked on an ambitious series of projects intended to build major capacity in "technopolis"-scale mega-research parks, and other facilities. Widely acknowledged to be a wasted investment, the "build it and they will come" approach of this period failed to generate significant new technology innovations or start-ups.

Period II: decentralization (early 1990s)

In the early 1990s, after the collapse of the asset bubble in 1989, local governments began to establish quasi-public organizations and facilities to support new business start-ups and existing small businesses. While some high tech (e.g. testing) equipment was put in place, local firms often complained that the machinery was of little use to them without the technical expertise necessary to use them effectively.

Period III: privatization (late 1990s)

In the late 1990s, of the handful of incubators existing at that time, some were established and run by private firms, while local and regional governments continued to build small-scale incubation facilities. In 1999, METI promoted projects to build additional incubation facilities as part of "regional platform"-based national policy. This was outlined in the 1999 Venture Business Creation Law. This year marked a turning point in the activities sponsored by the national government to support entrepreneurial development.

Period IV: university–private sector alliances and facilities building (2000–2008)

As outlined above, most incubation facilities in Japan were established after 2000, when METI and MEXT began to make substantial investments in capacity upgrading. For the first time, Japan targeted universities as a potential center for entrepreneurship development, through policies encouraging university ventures. Included in initiatives were the establishment of a number of university-affiliated technology licensing organizations (TLOs) and also university-housed incubation facilities. Historically, business has been the purview of METI, while MEXT has managed education, including universities. Sharing turf for the first time, some activities have been more competitive than collaborative. Witness the two incubators on the Katsura Campus of Kyoto University, built across a parking lot from each other, one by METI and the other by MEXT. Interviews with incubator managers (IMs) in each incubator as recently as 2009 indicated that little communication occurs between the two neighbors.

Period V: strategic management (late 2000s)

Seasoned IMs in the United States say that it takes at least a decade to begin seeing a return on investment in incubation facilities (interview with Mellitz, 2005). Japan is nearing this stage, and successful incubators have emerged, while failing incubators have begun to exit. The national government is doing its part to raise incubator performance, for example, by focusing on improving the skills of IMs via government training programs, discussed below. One initiative that fell victim to the budgetary crisis beginning in 2008 is the Japan Association of New Business Incubation Organizations (JANBO) program that began in 1999.

JANBO, JBIA and InnoNet

JANBO was established in 1999 as a quasi-governmental organization with ties to METI to act as a clearinghouse of information and to coordinate the expected increase in facilities and programs nationwide to support new business creation. JANBO's activities were divided into research and training. The organization conducted a number of surveys of IMs and tenant firms, as well as put together public databases of incubators and tenants. JANBO also established an IM training program to improve the ability of IMs to support new start-ups. Incubation managers trained through JANBO continue to coordinate various soft supports for start-up tenants.

In 2008, JANBO lost all its funding and closed in June 2009, with an unintended yet serendipitous consequence. A group of IMs (those with private sector experience) established JBIA, the Japan Business Incubator Association, modeled on the National Business Incubator Association (NBIA) in the United States, while the civil servant members of JANBO went to Innovation Network (InnoNet), a new organization that would focus on training IMs. JBIA is an individual membership organization comprised of IMs, while InnoNet is a conglomeration of mostly government and quasi-government business support organizations. In sum, one half of JANBO went private, while the other remained public.

One of the main criticisms of InnoNet by outsiders is that it has too many bureaucrats (an estimated 80 percent of its members are civil servants). As a consequence, the training provided by the organization for incubation managers is focused on codified (book learning) rather than practical or tacit (such that experiential learning provides). A number of informants referred to their training as "*tsukue no ue no kenshu*," literally "training on the top of a desk," meaning something that lacks practical applications or is unproven in reality.

On 18 March 2010, Masao Horiba, honorary chairman of InnoNet, which was modeled after his own KVF (Kyoto Venture Forum), affiliated with the Mikuruma Incubator in Kyoto, discussed below), opened the second annual Regional Forum on a dour note: "Looking around this room, I cannot say that this past year has been a success." The previous year (2009), prior to the split off between InnoNet and JBIA, private sector people made up about half the audience in the first annual Regional Forum (this author attended both events). In 2010, it was virtually all civil servants. An official of InnoNet confirmed that there is little collaboration between the two organizations, though a few IMs are members of both. Despite these challenges, Japan's bureaucratic model of industrial governance has been slowly transforming, intentionally and sometimes unintentionally, into a more private sector-driven model.

The Organization for Small and Medium Enterprises and Regional Innovation, Japan (SMRJ), established in 2004, has taken the primary role in the building and management of the newest incubators in Japan. The SMRJ is a quasi-governmental organization affiliated with METI. The organization seeks to provide a variety of hard and soft supports to small and medium-sized businesses as well as venture businesses. Its historical expertise has been in the brick and mortar (e.g. building and facilities) aspects of supporting business enterprise.[3] If an incubator is built using SMRJ funds, it usually hires IMs from the SMRJ, either through secondment or post-retirement (via *amakudari*).[4] The majority of government-funded Japanese incubators follow this bureaucratic management model.

The majority (71 percent) of Japanese incubators (241 out of 336, excluding NPOs) are run by governmental or quasi-governmental organizations such as the SMRJ. Further, many of the university incubators have received significant SMRJ funding, and also staff.

Most Japanese incubators began accepting tenants in the mid-2000s, and since the incubation process lasts between three to five years, data on incubator graduates is just becoming available. A survey by the Japan Industrial Location Center (JILC) and the Japan Innovation Network (InnoNet) shows that start-ups housed in incubators are more than twice as likely to remain in business (85 percent v. 35.9 percent survival rate) (JILC, 2009). The same survey reported that among incubated firms, those in electronics and electrical machinery experienced the most sales growth, followed by environmental (e.g. green technology) and recycling start-ups. Graduated start-ups (i.e. those leaving incubators after three to five years) employed an average of 13 people.

Like most business investments into new business start-ups, the majority of existing Japanese incubators will likely struggle, many going under or being converted to other uses. The budgetary crisis that began in 2008, and struggles "learning the ropes" in incubator management have been the two main challenges so far, not to mention the dearth of venture capital investment in Japan. Nevertheless, the odds are that a few of these incubators will survive and be successful in growing firms from birth to independence.

A survey conducted by JANBO in 2006 confirmed that government IMs themselves were frustrated with the limits of their predominantly public sector networks in connecting tenant firms to the resources that they need (JANBO, 2006). As a result, SMRJ has made an effort to hire IMs who have had private sector experience. While they have been less successful in luring successful serial entrepreneurs to the helm of incubators, they have had better luck identifying willing and available semi-retired bank executives, thanks in part to the contraction of the financial markets since the 1990s. The following case studies illustrate the aforementioned challenges.

Incubator case studies

Kyoto Mikuruma and Kyoto Venture Forum: network model

The Kyoto Mikuruma incubator was built in 2005, refurbishing an unused 2,500 sqm Kyoto University building after receiving funds from the SMRJ in 2003 and 2004. The building is located near the Kyoto University campus. The incubator features wet and dry lab space and caters especially to biotech start-ups (Kyoto Mikuruma Incubator, 2010). Mikuruma began accepting firms in 2006. The majority of tenants have research collaborations with local universities. Currently, 35 percent of its tenants have R&D ties to either Kyoto University or the Kyoto Prefectural University (interview with Sawamura, 2009). Kyoto is home to more than 40 higher education institutions, including universities, colleges and technical schools, making the region a hub of intellectual capacity in Japan. The incubator takes its name from the ancient name of the street where it is located. "Mikuruma michi dori" was named thus due to its role as route to the Imperial Palace in Kyoto ("Gosho").

The selection process to enter the Mikuruma incubator is arduous, and preference is given to firms that receive "A Rank" status from the Kyoto Venture Forum (KVF). The KVF was formed in the mid-1990s by a group of successful local entrepreneurs, who had taken their companies global, including Masao Horiba of Horiba Manufacturing and Osamu Tsuji of Samco International. The group functions like a loose network of pro bono management consultants, who in an annual nation-wide business plan competition, select a small subset for A Rank status, i.e. those demonstrating the most potential for growth. These A Rank firms receive a number of soft supports from KVF members, including advice on product development, finance and marketing. Further, if a firm is KVF A Rank, it receives about a 50 percent discount on Mikuruma rent for up to three years. KVF members also assist firms in making connections to other strategic supports, in Kyoto and also internationally. A research study on life science entrepreneurs identified KVF as a major network hub for start-ups in Kyoto (Ibata-Arens, 2009).

Four of the five Mikuruma IMs have private sector experience. As of August 2010, the incubator was full, hosting 19 start-ups, more than a third of which had grown into multiple spaces. Eight firms had graduated. As early as 2008, ten firms were selling finished products, and five were already profitable.

Shiga Collabo 21 and finance networks: training model

Across Lake Biwa (*biwako*) to the East of Kyoto, is Shiga Prefecture, which though it lacks the critical mass of intellectual capacity of Kyoto, is a manufacturing center for the Japanese electronics industry. Shiga Collabo 21 in Otsu City has less of the R&D network strength of Mikuruma, as there are no university campuses nearby. Instead, Collabo 21 nurtures its start-ups via a boot camp-style training approach.

The Collabo 21 incubator, a 3,000 sqm facility in Otsu City, Shiga Prefecture, shares space with government industrial promotion offices (Collabo Shiga 21, 2010). The Collabo 21 incubator was opened in 2004, the brainchild of the governor of Shiga and Takayuki Nishioka, a retired bank executive. About half of the tenants work in technological fields, while others are in small manufactures and digital media. In August 2010, 11 of the 13 rooms were occupied (interview with Nishioka, 2009).

Nishioka runs a tight ship at Collabo 21, putting potential tenants through a grueling application process. Once selected, firms begin a brief probationary period, where they can use a tiny cubicle-sized room: enough space for a chair, a laptop and a small desk (these are called "booths" in Japanese). If they show progress after a month or two, they might be upgraded to a larger space. Firms not showing progress and long-term viability after 6 months are asked to leave.

At the same time, he encourages trial-and-error with his incubatees. He meets with his tenants one-on-one each week to work on their business planning, particularly finance and marketing strategies. Once a month, for a 500-yen boxed lunch (*o bento*) fee, he brings together tenants and a guest speaker from industry, banking, or venture capital and has tenant firms give a 3-minute (maximum) presentation, after which the floor is open to intense discussion and debate. Under Nishioka's mentorship, firms spend the first year in Collabo 21 in an intense "learning by doing" training program. At the same time, Nishioka thinks that the biggest challenge for start-ups is accessing the international market, which means putting together an entrepreneurial team that includes people with international experience.

Nishioka also works with graduates to place them in local office buildings, offering introduction and advice on how to be on their own after graduation, cultivating Collabo 21's bamboo network root system for future start-ups. Graduates are encouraged to maintain their ties with the incubator. One of his graduate firms is working on its initial public offering (IPO) (interview with Nishioka, 2010).

Venture Generation: mentorship and international network cultivation

Venture Generation's founder Jeffrey Char built a career in Silicon Valley as an attorney for Morrison and Foerster (its employees refer to the firm as "MoFo"). After leaving MoFo, he established J-Seed Ventures, a venture capital firm in Tokyo. J-Seed has had 17 exits, including Mixi (Japan's version of Groupon). Venture Generation (VG) began operating in March 2012, near the Yaesu side of Tokyo Station. By April 1, 2012, a number of the first tenants had moved in, setting up their (mostly internet and software) businesses in the shared space.

VG has built an enviable mentoring and network new business incubation model. VG has an international network of 70 advisors with marketing, technology, IP law and finance, particularly in the software development and IT space, functioning like an extended bamboo network for incubatees. Like Collabo 21 and Mikuruma, applicants must go through a rigorous screening process, to ensure that those placed in the incubator will benefit from an environment of competitive advantage (interviews with J. Char, 2011, 2012).

According to Allen Miner, founder of Global Venture Habitat (GVH), which has three Japanese entrepreneur-focused incubators (in Osaka, Tokyo, and Silicon Valley), the Japanese government-led investment scheme "baramaki" is absent in these incubators. "Baramaki" is a pejorative term used to refer to the government's tendency to spread Japanese taxpayer money out "fairly" or "evenly" across many projects and especially regions. As a consequence, opportunities for strategic, focused investments are missed (interview with Miner, 2012). The unique feature of the bamboo network cultivation model in VG and GVH is that these incubators provide opportunities for Japanese start-ups that develop international (particularly US West Coast Silicon Valley) networks for firms. Consistent with the emerging hybrid bamboo network cultivation incubation model in other Japanese incubators, VG and GVH provide ample opportunities for tenant firms to develop their strategic networks.

Conclusion

Challenges remaining for Japan in establishing bamboo network-type incubation manager practices on a national scale include hiring incubation managers with extensive private sector experience (e.g. in business or banking) and concomitant networks, or at the very least, privatizing the networks of incubation managers.

Japan has in the past decade placed an unprecedented emphasis on new business incubation policy as the national government tries to craft an entrepreneurial economy, i.e. one that creates a supportive ecosystem for entrepreneurial firms. An initial public sector top-down push has resulted in privatization (JANBO to JBIA is one example). This affords an opportunity to observe and compare public and private sector initiatives targeting incubation management (e.g. InnoNet and JBIA).

Second, these activities are occurring in a national context of a breakdown of socio-political hierarchies, whereby the lobbying power of large corporate conglomerates has been tempered by the rise to national prominence of entrepreneurial ventures.

Third, bamboo-like strategic resource network cultivation and effective incubation managers appear to be improving the state of entrepreneurial ecosystems around new start-ups. Consistent with the international research findings discussed above, hybrid incubators that maintain some kind of socio-spatial tie with universities may be best positioned to nurture high growth start-ups and thus should be the focus of further research and policy.

If Japan manages to successfully incubate a new generation of entrepreneurial start-ups into high growth firms that help to transform the Japanese economy from one characterized by a bureaucratic-industrial complex to an entrepreneurial ecosystem, the national policy push of the last decade will have been a success, even if the majority of Japanese incubators cease to exist.

Acknowledgements

The author is grateful for funding from the Fulbright New Century Scholars Program, 2009–2010, University as Innovation Driver. An earlier version of this chapter was published as a Stanford University Business School, Stanford Project on Japanese Entrepreneurship (STAJE) Working Paper, November 2011.

Notes

1 Association of University Technology Managers (AUTM) and National Business Incubation Association (NBIA) reports, various years.
2 In the United States, in the 1980s, the SBA played an early role in the establishment of new business incubators, sponsoring facilities upgrading and building new incubators.
3 SMRJ is a consolidation of the Japan Small and Medium Enterprise Corporation (JASMEC), the Japan Regional Development Corporation (JRDC) (established 1962), and the Industrial Structure Improvement Fund (ISIF) (established 1986).
4 SMRJ representatives have explained that it has been difficult to attract private sector IMs, given the low salaries and legal prohibition of IMs to have other incentives such as equity in tenant firms.

Bibliography

Aernoudt, R. (2004) "Incubators: tool for entrepreneurship?" *Small Business Economics,* 23: 127–135.

Aerts, K., Matthyssens, P. and Vandenbempt, K. (2007) "Critical role and screening practices of European business incubators," *Technovation,* 27: 254–267.

Al-Mubaraki, H.M. and Wong, S.F. (2012) "A preliminary view of the relationship between incubator performance and their length of establishment," in H.H. Lean and S. Mohd (eds) *Proceedings of USM-AUT*

International Conference 2012 Sustainable Economic Development: Policies and Strategies, Universiti Sains Malaysia, Penang, Malaysia, 17–18 November 2012, pp. 221–227.

Anselmo, P. (2009) "Batavia's business incubator celebrates 50th anniversary," *The Batavian,* January 19. Available at: www.thebatavian.com/blogs/philipanselmo/batavias-business-incubator-celebrates-50th-anniversary/4077 (accessed 18 August 2010).

Bergek, A. and Norrman, C. (2008) "Incubator best practice: a framework," *Technovation,* 28: 20–28.

Cho, B.J. and Son, E. (2009) "The role dynamics of the IKED, government agencies, supporting institutions and incubation centers in Korea," *Asia Pacific Journal of Innovation and Entrepreneurship,* 3.

Collabo Shiga 21 Incubator (2010) Available at: www.collaboshiga21.jp/ (accessed 19 August 2010).

Dore, R. (1986) *Flexible Rigidities: Industrial Policy and Structural Adjustment in the Japanese Economy, 1970–1980,* Stanford, CA: Stanford University Press.

Etzkowitz, H. (2002) "Incubation of incubators: innovation as a triple helix of university–industry–government networks," *Science and Public Policy,* 29(2): 115–128.

Etzkowitz, H., de Mello, J.M.C. and Almeida, M. (2005) "Meta-innovation in Brazil: the evolution of the incubator and the emergence of a triple helix," *Research Policy,* 34: 411–424.

Hackett, S. and Dilts, D. (2004) "A systematic review of business incubation research," *Journal of Technology Transfer,* 29: 55–82.

Honig, B. and Karlsson, T. (2010) "Social capital and the modern incubator: a comparison of in-group and out-group social networks," *Journal of Small Business and Entrepreneurship,* special issue, pp. 719–731.

Ibata-Arens, K. (2005) *Innovation and Entrepreneurship in Japan: Politics, Organizations and High Technology Firms,* Cambridge: Cambridge University Press.

Ibata-Arens, K. (2009) "Kyoto cluster culture: social and spatial variations in Japan and the United States," *Journal of Asian Business and Management,* 8: 395–428.

JANBO (2006) "Graduate firms," in *Report of Basic Investigation on Business Incubators, Japan Association of New Business Incubation Association (JANBO),* Kyoto: Japan Industrial Location Center (JILC).

JILC (2009) *Results of Firm Supports, According to Incubation Managers (IMs),* Kyoto: Japan Industrial Location Center (JILC).

Kauffman Foundation and the International Economic Development Council (2008) Entrepreneurship Summit Executive Summary, September.

Kim, H. and Ames, M. (2006) "Business incubators as economic development tools: rethinking models based on the Korea experience," *International Journal of Technology Management,* 33, 1–4.

Kyoto Mikuruma Incubator (2010) Available at: www.smrj.go.jp/incubation/cckm/ (accessed 25 October 2010).

Ministry of Finance (MOF) Budget, Ministry of Economy Trade and Industry (METI) Budget, Ministry of Education, Culture, Science and Technology, Preliminary Budgets 2009, 2010 (MEXT) (n.d.). Available at: www.mof.go.jp/ (accessed 18 August 2010).

NBIA (National Business Incubation Association) (n.d.) FAQ "What is a virtual incubator?" Available at: www.nbia.org/resource_library/faq/#13a (accessed 25 October 2011).

OECD (1997) *Typology of Incubators, Technology Incubators: Nurturing Small Firms.* Paris: Organisation for Economic Cooperation and Development. Available at: www.oecd.org/dataoecd/35/11/2101121.pdf (accessed 25 October 2011).

Sharma, P., Nookala, S. and Sharma, A. (2010) "Innovation capacity in India: challenges, barriers and opportunities," paper presented at Technology Transfer Society (T2S) Conference, Washington, DC.

Sun, D. (2004) *Technology Business Incubator in China,* Xiaman: Research Center of Business Incubator, Xiamen University, China. Available at: www.aspa.or.kr/files/Webzinevol 8_050810/050810 ASPA%20paper10_eg.htm (accessed 15 April 2011).

Tamasy, C. (2007) "Rethinking technology-oriented business incubators: developing a robust policy instrument for entrepreneurship, innovation and regional development?" *Growth and Change,* 38: 460–473.

US Census Bureau (2009) *California Quick Facts.* Available at: http://quickfacts.census.gov/qfd/states/06000.html (accessed 18 August 2010).

Zhang, H. and Sonobe, T. (2011) "Business incubators in China: an inquiry into the variables associated with incubatee success," *Economics: The Open-Access, Open-Assessment E-Journal,* 5:7.

12

Chaebols as South Korean entrepreneurship

Sung Wook Joh

Introduction

Over the past 50 years, South Korea has transformed itself from a poor country with per capita GDP of $87 in 1962 to a member of the OECD and a G20 member with $22,451 per capita GDP in 2011. While many companies in North America and Europe suffered from the 2008 global financial crisis, the Korean corporate sector continued growing. Far from suffering from huge losses or bankruptcies, large business groups (*chaebols*), such as Samsung or Hyundai, became some of the most innovative and successful firms in the world. For example, Samsung Electronics has become one of top makers of mobile phones, memory chips, LCD panels and smart TVs. Meanwhile, Hyundai Motors has increased its market shares in many developed countries, and Hyundai Heavy Industries became the largest shipbuilder in the world. On the other hand, GM, one of the oldest car makers in the US, relied on the US government's bailout policy for its own survival. The spectacular economic performance of Korea and Korean business groups has attracted the attention of scholars, policy-makers and business people around the world.

Economists have debated the sources of Korea's magnificent economic growth along different dimensions: (1) productivity increase vs. accumulation of production inputs such as labor and capital (Young, 1995; Hsieh, 1999); (2) government policy to promote exports and substitute imports vs. more general and extensive government interventions (Frank *et al.*, 1975; Krueger, 1979; Amsden, 1989; Haggard, 1990); (3) and other factors such as foreign direct investment (Hong, 1998), legal and institutional development (Garcia-Blanch, 2001) and so on. In addition, the *chaebols*' successful entrepreneurship has accounted for a large portion of Korea's GDP, GDP growth, and exports and imports. Furthermore, Korea's economic development has created massive business opportunities that benefit the *chaebols*. The *chaebols*' growth mirrors Korea's economic growth from a poor agricultural economy to a high technology-oriented economy. Agriculture's share of Korea's GDP fell from 37 percent in 1962 to 3 percent in 2011. In manufacturing sectors, the portion of light industry which required little capital fell from 71 percent in 1962 to 14.5 percent in 2011.

During Korea's economic growth, business groups implemented government growth plans to exploit new investment opportunities. They entered new industries by starting new firms, building new factories, and hiring workers and adopting new technology through licensing and imitation. Due to the country's small domestic market, Korean firms eventually competed in global markets through exports. As these young firms had inferior technology, they usually adopted (licensed or imitated) foreign companies' technology, rather than investing capital in costly and risky R&D projects. Rather than investing heavily in one industry, they diversified into many industries and gradually entered new industries as the Korean government created investment opportunities for them to exploit. Meanwhile, *chaebols* kept their old businesses, creating a very diversified business portfolio.

Chaebols' internal capital markets (ICMs) facilitate their diversification strategy through channeling resources from one affiliated firm to another. A typical business organizational structure consists of several dozens of vertically and horizontally diversified subsidiaries and firms operating in many different industries. While the *chaebols* have widely expanded their business and increased their subsidiaries using their ICMs, founding families have maintained their control over these firms.

Due to their size and interconnection with other economic entities, the financial distress of large *chaebols* can devastate the Korean economy, as shown during the 1997 financial crisis. *Chaebols* have shared resources and reduced their risk through equity investment, cross-debt payment guarantees and intra-group trading – all of which could improve efficiency. However, this is not the full picture before 1997. When some subsidiaries went bankrupt, these financial links among affiliated firms triggered the cascading failures of affiliates. The bankruptcies of large *chaebols* in turn bankrupted their suppliers, subcontractors, and business partners. This chain reaction of bankruptcies led to the collapse of creditor-financial institutions including large banks, sparking a financial crisis. To reduce the systemic risk from distressed *chaebols*, Korean corporate reform after the 1997 crisis tried to revive the shaken corporate sector by strengthening the *chaebols'* governance system, improving their capital structure, and limiting their ICM operations (Joh, 2004). Partially due to corporate restructuring and reform, surviving *chaebol* firms became stronger with a healthier capital structure and showed better performance.

This chapter examines how macro-economic growth and government policy have affected the rise and growth of diversified *chaebols* which expanded their operation by entering new industries. Furthermore, it describes the organizational conditions and strategies that the *chaebols* have adopted, and reviews their weaknesses that caused the failure of several large business groups. Note that this study focuses on finance-related attributes and governance issues. Due to space limitations, it does not address important issues such as human resource management or innovations that have also contributed to the *chaebols'* growth and success.[1]

By analyzing the conditions of these business groups before and during the crisis, the chapter tries to identify factors affecting their successes and failures. Analyzing the interactions and experiences between business groups and different macro-economic environments (i.e., high growth, crisis and post-crisis) can provide insights for policy-makers. This study can provide meaningful implications not only for entrepreneurs and policy-makers in emerging markets but also in advanced countries as well.

The birth and rise of the *chaebols*

Many *chaebols* have been competing in global markets. These *chaebols* have shown their prowess in high tech industries through innovative products with new designs and functions. During the 1997 economic crisis, few would have predicted the *chaebols'* successful economic performance two decades later, especially considering their origins as small venders, small producers of substitutes for imported goods, or original equipment manufacturing (OEM) firms.

The first firms in some *chaebols* started in the 1930s during the Japanese colonial period, but many large firms in large *chaebols* were founded later, producing new innovative designs and functions. For example, Samsung, currently the largest *chaebol*, established its original firm in 1938 and many of their main subsidiaries in the electronics and chemical industries appeared in the 1960s and 1970s. *Chaebols* have diversified into different industries both to reduce their overall risk and to capitalize on investment opportunities, especially those supported by the Korean government. The composition of the *chaebols'* sales reflected the development of the Korean economy. For instance, Samsung's 1965 sales of 26 billion won consisted of 48 percent food (including sugar and flour), 40 percent textiles, and 12 percent insurance (Figure 12.1), in part because earlier *chaebol* firms had little capital and used their abundant, unskilled, cheap labor. These early *chaebols* did not engage in research and development to create technologically advanced innovations. Note differences in some venture firms during the dot com bubbles in the late 1990s or new start-up firms in the 2000s. Recently established venture firms are concentrated in information and communication industries and have large R&D expenditures, and hold patents.

In the 1970s, the Korean government supported investment in heavy chemical industries (HCI), so the *chaebols* entered petroleum, petrochemical, chemical, shipbuilding, electronics and construction. The Korean government designed economic development plans and implemented them by channeling resources through government-controlled financial institutions to complying firms. As these industries require many years to mature, their sales increased gradually. Samsung's sales were nearly 25 times larger in 1976 (640 billion won) than in 1965 (26 billion won). Its 1976 sales consisted of 28 percent textiles, 25 percent food, 24 percent home appliances and electronics, 18 percent insurance, 3 percent paper, and 1 percent construction.

In the 1980s, two oil shocks triggered a recession and deflation, so highly-leveraged firms with overcapacity faced bankruptcy. The Korean government rescued these distressed firms and restructured them, reinforcing a belief in the implicit government guarantee to help large, poorly performing firms. Afterwards, the Korean corporate sector showed very low profitability below prevailing bank loan interest rates, implying a very low efficiency of its investment. See the section on evaluation on p. 163 for more discussion.

After surviving the recessions in the early 1980s, the *chaebols* increased their overall sales and further diversified their business portfolios. Samsung's total sales in 1987 were 26 times larger (16.7 trillion won) than in 1976 (0.6 trillion won). Its 1987 sales consisted of 35 percent wholesale and retail, 30 percent finance and insurance, 18 percent home appliances, 4 percent food and leisure, 4 percent textiles, 3 percent vehicles (e.g., cars), 2 percent construction and less than 2 percent in semiconductors, telecommunications, papers and other services.

After the financial crisis in 1998, Samsung's largest sales components remained the same, but other components changed. Its sales consisted of 35 percent wholesale and retail trade, 24 percent finance and insurance, 20 percent home appliances, 6 percent vehicles, 6 percent semiconductors, 5 percent textiles, food and leisure, and the rest was non-metallic minerals, machinery, iron and steel, paper, and other services. Note that sales from textiles and food fell from 88 percent in 1965 to less than 5 percent in 1998, showing how business portfolios have changed and how new businesses contribute to the *chaebols'* growth.

In 2009, Samsung's sales from semi-conductor-related business and mobile phone business skyrocketed to nearly 60 percent of its total sales when including home appliances. Meanwhile, its finance and insurance fell to 14 percent and wholesale and retail trade fell to 9 percent of its total sales. Other industries with significant sales include chemical industries, machineries and construction. These changes in Samsung's sales mirror changes in the Korean economy and its transformation of industrial structures.

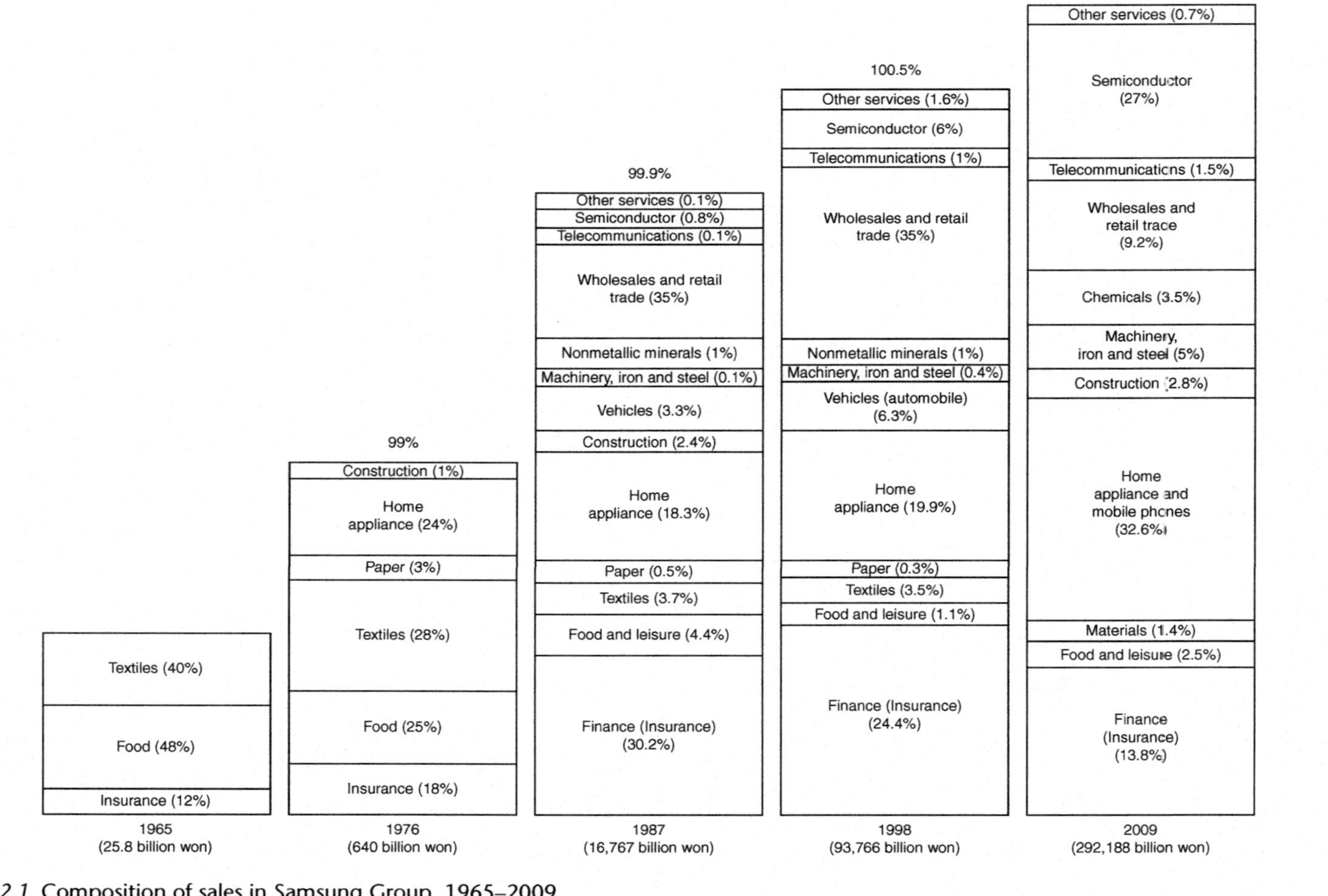

Figure 12.1 Composition of sales in Samsung Group, 1965–2009

Note: The figure shows composition of sales in Samsung Group, 1965, 1976, 1987, 1988, and 2009.

Source: Kim (1998) for 1965 and 1976 data. Chang (2003) for 1987 and 1998 data. 2009 data are compiled from corporate financial reports submitted to Korea Stock Exchange.

Currently, the *chaebols* are conglomerates operating in many related and unrelated industries. For example, the top five *chaebols* had an average of 42 subsidiaries operating in 30 industries in 1993. Not including financial firms, the top four *chaebols* had an average of 68 subsidiaries operating in 26 non-financial industries in 2010.[2] (Daewoo, one of the top five *chaebols* before the 1997 crisis, collapsed in 1999.) In 2010, Samsung, the largest *chaebol,* had 65 subsidiaries, and 10 financial companies.[3] The proportion of *chaebol* sales from foods, textiles, or other manufacturing sectors with relatively simple technology has shrunk dramatically while the proportion of products from high tech industries has skyrocketed. Jang, Ha and Lee (2011) used a diversification index to find that subsidiaries within a *chaebol* are not closely related.

After the financial crisis in 1997, most surviving *chaebols* have large exports and thus face large international competitors with proven technology and access to financing, unlike their domestic competitors. To survive and prosper, they need to improve their production and operations to prepare for price competition. As they compete on the frontline of their own industries, they have to change their focus on innovation and establish their own brands.

Factors in the growth of the *chaebols*

What has contributed to the growth and organization of Korean *chaebols?* Government-directed investment and rapid economic growth (over 10 percent per year) opened enormous growth opportunities for the *chaebols* in new industries and prepared them for export-oriented growth. Under government-driven economic development plans in the 1960s and 1970s, the *chaebols* had greater access to capital, human resources and management skills, and thus outperformed smaller, independent firms.

Macro-economic environments and government policies

Macro-economists and development economists argue that favorable initial conditions such as geography (far from the tropics) (Sachs, 2000), a high literacy rate, a young nation and high population density (Bloom *et al.*, 1999) drove Korea's economic growth. Furthermore, Amsden (1989) and Haggard (1990) argued that government policies also played an important role.

Macro-economic environments and government policies provided the *chaebols* with new investment and growth opportunities. During the early high growth stages, the Korean government initiated economic development plans and adopted an outward-looking strategy. With few natural resources and a tiny domestic market, Korean governments promoted labor-intensive manufactured exports in the 1960s, then HCI in the 1970s. Promoting HCI yielded large spillover effects into the manufacturing sector as firms in these industries were connected to many suppliers and subcontractors. During the second five-year economic development plan (1967–1971), the government enacted several laws that helped provide financial and tax incentives to targeted industries. The laws included the Machinery Industry Promotion Act (1967), the Shipbuilding Industry Promotion Act (1967), the Textile Industry Modernization Act (1967), the Steel Industry Promotion Act (1969), the Electronics Industry Promotion Act (1969), the Petrochemical Industry Promotion Act (1970), and the Nonferrous Metal Producing Business Act (1971).

After a military coup in 1961, the government repossessed the bank ownership from large stockholders and founded a series of special banks (Lim, 1998). In the early 1960s, the government liberalized interest rates, raising bank lending rates from 15 percent to 30 percent to mobilize scarce capital. In addition, government-controlled banks brought in foreign capital, which had lower interest rates than domestic market interest rates. The government used nationalized-banks as a vehicle to mobilize and allocate scarce capital to targeted firms. Based on its assessment of their contribution to the nation's industrialization and modernization plan, the government supported light exporting firms in the 1960s and HCI firms in the 1970s (Lee, 1992). For instance, exporting firms borrowed capital from the national investment fund, or from government-controlled commercial banks at lower interest rates than time-deposit interest rates until 1981 (Cho and Kim, 1997). Partially due to such government support, some *chaebol* firms acquired valuable technology and R&D experience. For example, Hyundai Motors (founded in 1967) successfully produced its first unique car, the Pony, in 1976. Hyundai Motors became the world's 16th car maker with its own model. That indispensable experience helped Hyundai Motors become a global player with its own brands and products beyond being an OEM producer. In 1976, Hyundai Motors began exporting its cars.

In addition to providing inexpensive financing to firms, the government also bailed out distressed firms in the early 1970s. The government issued a presidential decree for economic stability that nullified underground borrowings, changed short-term loans to long-term loans, reduced interest rates, created a credit guarantee system, and established an industrial rationalization fund in 1972.[4]

The government also bailed out poorly performing HCI firms. Taking advantage of government policy, large corporations entered HCI in the 1970s and expanded rapidly, creating over-capacity problems. The government used financial institutions to rescue them, by providing capital at a lower interest rate. Financial institutions were used as a vehicle to implement industrial policy even in the 1980s, serving as an implicit guarantor for distressed large firms.[5] Joh and Ko (2009) criticized this bailout policy as a harmful precedent of government control in the financial markets and for creating the belief of guaranteed government intervention for large distressed firms.

Along with the 1987 political liberalization that brought profound changes in the social and political structure, the government increased its regulation of large business groups which dominated the economy. As the *chaebols* had inflated their asset size through equity holdings of affiliated firms, the government limited *chaebol* firm investment in affiliated firms to 40 percent of its net equity. Specifically, firms belonging to business groups with 400 billion won of assets cannot invest more than 40 percent of their assets after subtracting their debt (see Joh and Kim, 2010).

In short, government initiatives were the midwife to industrialization with foreign capital to targeted firms, supplementing its shortage of capital. Although the government initially favored firms with successful past performance, it also rescued distressed firms.

Diversified chaebols *and their internal capital markets (ICMs)*

Chaebols found new business opportunities in large part due to the government's industrial policies. *Chaebols* entered new businesses while keeping their old businesses going. *Chaebols*' business organization as a conglomerate is an outcome of their growth strategy over time. Instead of specializing in one industry through increasing its capacity, and building up reputation over time in the global market, the *chaebols* started new businesses, built new plants and recruited new employees while raising capital through their ICMs which facilitated borrowing money from government-controlled financial institutions.

While the *chaebols*' overall sales and assets increased quickly, their sales distribution across industries dramatically changed over time. Adapting to industrial policies offering new investment opportunities, the *chaebols* entered new industries. In a developed economy, firms diversify to capitalize on economies of scale and scope to utilize idle capacity (Chandler, 1962). Related diversification yields more values than unrelated diversification, as it enables firms to share resources and transfer resources among related business units (Porter, 1986; Prahalad and

Hamel, 1990). In a less developed economy, firms diversify in pursuit of growth and risk aversion (especially by insiders such as CEOs or controlling shareholders). While these factors might not contribute much in a developed economy, they can drive diversification in small, fast-growing economies (such as Korea in the 1970s and 1980s).

When the *chaebols* entered new industries, they needed financing. While internal financing is more prevalent in large mature firms, fast-growing young firms typically lack adequate internal funds. However, financial companies in most *chaebols* helped channel external resources to affiliated firms. Buttressed further by government-supported financing, the *chaebol* firms relied heavily on external financing, especially loans, resulting in high debt-equity ratios (396 percent for manufacturing firms) beyond those of firms in other countries (154 percent in the USA and 193 percent in Japan) in 1997.[6] Furthermore, the *chaebol* firms had higher debt ratios for long periods, even after accounting for other factors (Borensztein and Lee, 2002).

External financing is very costly in underdeveloped financial markets with information asymmetry problems. Korea was no exception, especially during the high growth periods in the 1960s and 1970s. Opaque accounting standards and lack of management transparency prevented banks and investors from receiving accurate corporate financial information to judge the potential borrowers' creditworthiness. As a result, banks required borrowers to provide collateral or debt payment guarantees, even for firms with subsidized loans from government-controlled banks. By requiring loan guarantees from affiliated firms, banks reduced their potential loss when borrowing firms go bankrupt. When each firm's risk is small, debt payment guarantees can reduce information asymmetry problems between borrowing firms and creditors.

ICMs can increase access to scarce capital and reduce the *chaebol* firms' financing costs. When capital is scarce, firms with greater access to capital can outcompete other firms. Low cost financing is especially critical for firms with long-term projects, or with high debt-equity ratios. In *chaebols*, young or less profitable firms tend to be financially constrained. But they can tap the external financing sources of successful and reputable affiliated firms (which act as a *de facto* holding company) through the *chaebols'* ICM. Large, profitable firms tend to guarantee the debt payments of other affiliated firms. As debt payment guarantees lower potential bankruptcy risk, firms can reduce their funding costs and constraints.

ICMs also allow the *chaebol* firms to invest in affiliated firms' equity.[7] By creating additional affiliated firms rather than divisions within existing firms, *chaebols* create opportunities to invest in affiliated firms' equity. Controlling shareholders of the *chaebols* use these equity investments in affiliated firms to strengthen their control over all the subsidiaries and to inflate the *chaebols'* asset size. Since financial institutions' lending decisions are partially based on the size of assets that can be pledged as collateral, firms with greater equity investments can use their inflated asset size to borrow more from creditors, which further increases their size and their likelihood of a government bailout if needed.

In some situations, ICMs can increase the value of efficient firms. Capitalizing on their economy of scale, efficient *chaebols* can move resources from less profitable firms to more profitable ones, thereby reducing information asymmetry (especially of small, young firms) and financing costs to improve performance. However, firms with substantial agency problems can allocate resources inefficiently and lower the firm value.

Evaluations of *chaebol* performance and growth strategy

From the perspective of surviving *chaebols*, their organizational structure and growth strategy have been successful. As Joh and Ko (2009) show, total employment in the 30 largest *chaebols* is less than 5 percent, but these *chaebols* account for 14 percent of GDP, 46 percent of gross output, and 47 percent of total assets. Furthermore, the top five *chaebols* accounted for nearly 55 percent of total market capitalization in 2013.[8]

However, organizing a country's economic growth around *chaebol*-like business groups and ICMs is risky. First, about half of the top 30 *chaebols* had high debts, had low profits and went bankrupt during the 1997 economic crisis. Second, diversification and investment in affiliated firms in even surviving *chaebols* often yield negative stock market responses, suggesting that agency problems result in inefficient ICM resource allocations. Third, poor external and internal corporate governance systems yielded inadequate monitoring and discipline for *chaebols* to improve firm value rather than wasting corporate resources.

Vulnerability and poor performance

Due to the "leverage effects," firms with high debt-equity ratios are expected to yield high profitability. But, Korean firms with high debt-equity ratios had low corporate profitability for many years. Specifically, the *chaebols*' average rate of return on equity in 1989–1997 was generally lower than the prevailing interest rates for loans (which serve as the opportunity cost of capital, see Figure 12.2), suggesting that capital was often wasted on unprofitable projects (Joh, 2003). Joh also showed that profitability deteriorated over time, even controlling for firm-specific factors, industry-specific factors, and macro-economic conditions. Furthermore, the profitability of the 30 largest *chaebols* was substantially lower than those of stand-alone independent firms before the 1997 financial crisis. Krueger and Yoo (2002) also showed that the rate of return on assets (ROA) of the Korean manufacturing sector were lower than those of Japan, Germany, the USA, and Taiwan. Thus, these findings reject the claim that ICMs and resource sharing within *chaebols* are an unqualified boon to a country's economy.

Chaebols' persistent, low profitability resulted in the bankruptcies of six of the 30 largest business groups before the currency crisis in 1997, starting with a surprise default by Hanbo in January, followed by Sammi in March, Jinro in April, KIA in July, Haitai and New Core in November. A series of large *chaebols*' defaults increased non-performing loans at banks, raised suspicion about

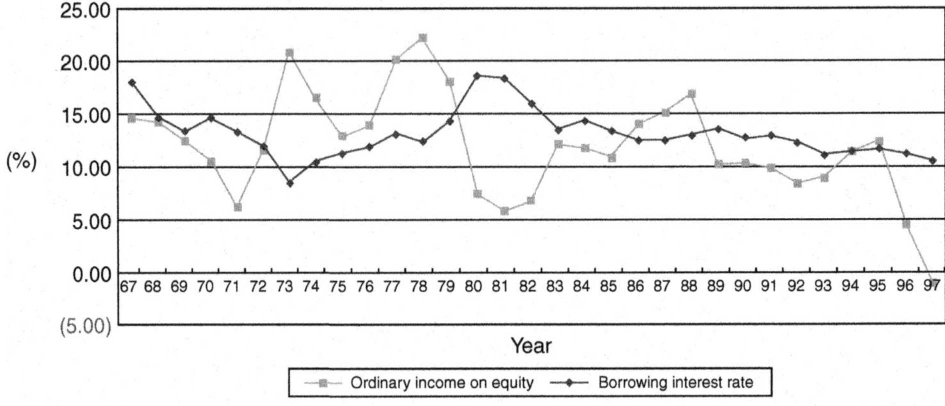

Figure 12.2 Profitability of Korean firms from 1967 to 1997

Note: The figure shows average ordinary income on equity and average borrowing interest rate of firms covered by the Bank of Korea's annual survey. The survey covers all large firms and uses a stratified random sampling for small firms.

Source: Joh (2003).

the fundamental soundness of the corporate and financial sectors, triggered a flight of foreign investors from the Korean market and eventually led to a financial crisis.

Inefficiency in resource allocation through ICM

Despite the potential ICM benefits discussed earlier, *chaebols* can also use their ICMs to tunnel firm resources for the private benefits of the controlling shareholders. As Joh and Kim (2013) showed, *chaebols* can waste corporate resources through investment in firms in unrelated industries or cross-subsidization in poorly performing firms with lower growth opportunities. When poorly performing firms face difficulties in raising capital through newly issued equities, relatively healthy affiliated firms invest in the shares of poorly performing affiliates, exposing themselves to recipient firms' performance and default risk. Although diversifying investment in unrelated industries lowers the firm value, it also inflates the *chaebol* assets and can benefit insiders' private interests.

While ICMs can reduce overall risk in some cases, they can increase risk in others. When affiliated firms have imperfectly correlated cash flows, diversification can reduce the probability of insufficient debt service and, hence, overall firm risk (Lewellen, 1971). However, the firms providing the debt-payment guarantees are exposed to both their own corporate risks and those of the guaranteed firm; if the latter cannot pay its debt, the guarantor firm must pay the debt. As the 30 largest *chaebol* firms had huge loan guarantee over equity capital ratios (470 percent in 1994), distressed guaranteed firms can pull guarantor firms into bankruptcy together. In short, inefficient ICMs can erode diversification benefits and increase *chaebols*' risks to negative shocks.

Poor corporate governance

External and internal corporate governance systems failed to provide sufficient monitoring and proper discipline for *chaebol* firms to improve firm value. The control and ownership structure of the *chaebols* hindered their internal corporate governance system. The families of the *chaebol* founders control many of its affiliated firms. For example, Samsung and Hyundai are each controlled by the families of their respective founders (Lee Byung-Chull and Chung Ju-Yung). While the family members of the founders directly own relatively few shares in the publicly traded firms, they are nevertheless the largest shareholders and they use interlocking ownership of affiliated firms to secure their control. In general, the *chaebols* show a very high disparity between control rights (a controlling family's total voting rights) and cash flow rights (ownership that entitles cash flows such as dividends). For example, Lee family members' aggregate ownership in Samsung electronics was less than 5 percent in 2012, but the ownership of affiliated firms in Samsung electronics was 13 percent, yielding 18 percent control rights. *Chaebols*' ownership structure is a typical example of controlling minority ownership structure (Bebchuk *et al.*, 1999).

Founding families use their disproportionate control rights in *chaebol* firms for their private interests. As many studies have documented, under poor corporate governance, a large disparity between control rights and cash flow rights is linked to lower profits in *chaebols*. Without an effective internal governance system, insiders are not monitored and the interests of minority shareholders are not protected. For example, controlling shareholders nominated most of the directors on the board including outside directors.[9] Consequently, outside directors rarely opposed the agenda items even in meetings discussing major transactions with controlling shareholders.[10]

The external governance system also performed poorly for several reasons. While external exit threats can overcome a poor internal governance system (Jensen and Ruback, 1983), large firms in Korea faced few, if any, exit threats unlike small firms. The government had rescued large, distressed *chaebol*-affiliated firms, creating a belief that "*chaebols* are too big to fail." Also, the Korean laws prohibiting both hostile and foreign M&As protected incumbents, entrenching controlling shareholders. A mandatory tender offer legally required any investor acquiring 25 percent of a firm's shares to buy at least 50 percent of the shares at the same or higher price, which effectively prevented takeovers. These legal environments created a gap in which neither the government nor market analysts could monitor the *chaebols*' investment activities during the transition from the Korean government's central economic planning to its economic liberalization in the 1980s (Chang, 2003).

Challenges for future success

The success of the *chaebols* mirrors the fast growth of the Korean economy for the past 50 years. In the past, the *chaebols*' ICMs inflated their assets, allowing them greater access to capital markets and more financing compared to independent firms. However, the Korean economy has changed. For example, the private sector has dramatically accumulated capital. Also, the capital market has become more open, while government intervention in the economy has dwindled. At the same time, the Korean population is aging, and wages have risen, reducing firms' reliance on cheap labor. Along with these changes, large *chaebols* have grown beyond the domestic Korean economy into a global market. Increasingly, Korea's future growth depends on the success of *chaebols*.

Some surviving *chaebols* have performed very well in a global market. Still they face new challenges for future success and for the long-run viability. To compete with global players outside their home markets, the *chaebo*ls must adapt to new growth strategies and improve their efficiency. Many *chaebols* must become innovators rather than followers in their industries. The most successful *chaebol*, Samsung, also faced these challenges. Khanna, Song and Lee (2011) argue that Samsung reinvented itself as it reached a global market. Samsung moved away from its once successful strategy of old Japanese style management to its hybrid-management style that embraces some of western-style management, including embracing diverse young talents from different cultural backgrounds. To become a viable global innovator, the *chaebols* will have to focus on fewer core businesses instead of maintaining several unrelated businesses. Recent studies show that diversification increases the firm's value only when external capital markets are inefficient or when the various firms of a diversified group would be financially constrained as stand-alone firms or due to business cycles (Dimitrov and Tice, 2006; Yan *et al.*, 2010; Hovakimian, 2011). Otherwise, diversification lowers resource allocation efficiency as the group allocates resources to inefficient firms.

Chaebols need to improve their corporate governance system in addition to enhancing human capital management to facilitate innovation. After the crisis in 1997, many governance reform measures were introduced to the corporate sector. See Joh (2007) for changes in the Korean corporate governance system after the crisis. In addition, foreign investors have substantially increased in many *chaebol* firms. So, *chaebol*-affiliated firms are exposed to outside pressure to improve their governance. *Chaebols* also need to improve their governance system to improve their efficiency. As discussed earlier, *chaebols* performed worse than independent firms until early 2000, bankrupting several *chaebols*. Part of their inefficiency results from the distortion of their governance structure which was designed in pursuit of the private interest of the founding families. In short, the *chaebols* have yet to resolve the problem of inefficiency in business structure or the problem of ICM related to the ownership and control issues.

Notes

1 For detailed discussions of these issues, see Lee *et al.* (2012) and Chang and Hong (2000).
2 As the industrial classifications have changed since 1993, this comparison must be interpreted cautiously.
3 KFTC, large business groups, 2010.
4 For more discussion on this, see Cho and Kim (1997), Lim (1998) and Joh (2004).
5 For further details, see Cho and Kim (1997), Lim (1998) and Joh (2004).
6 Source: Bank of Korea's Financial Statement Analysis for 1997.
7 See Joh and Kim (2010, 2013) for the causes and effects of equity investment in affiliated firms and detailed discussion of internal capital markets in Korea.
8 YTN, "Total market cap of top 10 business group almost reaching 60%," 7 July 2012. "Top five group reaches 54.8%, historically high," 9 April 2013.
9 See Joh and Kim (2010).
10 Despite the introduction of new rules regarding directors after the economic crisis, outside directors routinely approved agenda items (over 99 percent, Joh, 2001)

Bibliography

Amsden, A.H. (1989) *Asia's Next Giant: South Korea and Late Industrialization,* New York: Oxford University Press.

Bank of Korea (1997) *Financial Statement Analysis 1997,* Seoul, Bank of Korea.

Bebchuk, L., Kraakman, R. and Trinatis, G. (1999) "Stock pyramids, cross-ownership, and dual class equity: the creation and agency costs of separating control from cash flow rights," NBER Working Paper 6951, Washington, DC: NBER.

Bloom, D.E., Canning, D. and Malaney, P.N. (1999) "Demographic change and economic growth in Asia," Harvard University Center for International Development, Working Paper no. 15, Cambridge, MA.

Borensztein, E. and Lee, J-W. (2002) "Financial crisis and credit crunch in Korea: evidence from firm-level data," *Journal of Monetary Economics,* 49: 853–875.

Chandler, A. (1962) *Strategy and Structure,* Cambridge, MA: MIT Press.

Chang, S-J. (2003) *Financial Crisis and Transformation of Korean Business Groups: The Rise and Fall of* Chaebols, Cambridge: Cambridge University Press.

Chang, S-J. and Hong, J-B. (2000) "Economic performance of group-affiliated companies in Korea: intragroup resource sharing and internal business transactions," *Academy of Management Journal,* 43: 429–448.

Cho, Y.J. and Kim, J-K. (1997) *Credit Policies and the Industrialization of Korea,* Seoul: Korea Development Institute.

Dimitrov, V. and Tice, S. (2006) "Corporate diversification and credit constraints: real effects across the business cycle," *Review of Financial Studies,* 19(4): 1465–1498.

Frank, C., Kim, K.S. and Westphal, L. (1975) *Foreign Trade Regimes and Economic Development: South Korea,* New York: Columbia University Press.

Garcia-Blanch, F. (2001) "An empirical inquiry into the nature of South Korean economic growth," CID Working Paper No. 74.

Haggard, S. (1990) *Pathways from the Periphery: The Politics of Growth in Newly Industrializing Countries,* Ithaca, NY: Cornell University Press.

Hong, W. (1998) "Financing export-oriented catching-up in Korea: credit-rationing, sustained high growth and financial chaos," *International Economic Journal,* 12(1): 141–153.

Hovakimian, G. (2011) "Financial constraints and investment efficiency: internal capital allocation across the business cycle," *Journal of Financial Intermediation,* 20(2): 264–283.

Hsieh, C-T. (1999) "Factor prices and productivity growth in East Asia," *American Economic Review* (Papers and Proceedings), 89(2): 133–138.

Jang, J., Ha, J. and Lee, G.K. (2011) *Trends and Determinants of Diversification in Large Business Groups,* Research Monograph 2011–621, Seoul: Korea Institute for Industrial Economics and Trade.

Jensen, M. and Ruback, R. (1983) "The market for corporate control: the scientific evidence," *Journal of Financial Economics,* 11: 5–50.

Joh, Sung Wook (2001) *Empirical Analysis on Post-Crisis Chaebol Reform,* Seoul: Korea Development Institute.

Joh, S.W. (2003) "Corporate governance and firm profitability: evidence from Korea before the economic crisis," *Journal of Financial Economics,* 68(2): 287–322.

Joh, S.W. (2004) "Corporate restructuring," in D. K. Chung and B. Eichengreen (eds) *The Korean Economy Beyond the Crisis,* Cheltenham: Edward Elgar, pp. 194–217.
Joh, S.W. (2007) "The Korean corporate governance system: before and after the crisis," in M. Woo (ed.), *Neoliberalism and Institutional Reform in East Asia: A Comparative Study,* Basingstoke: Palgrave-Macmillan and UNRISD.
Joh, S.W. and Kim, M.A. (2010) "Financial and economic analysis of the regulation of equity investment in large business groups," *Journal of Korean Economic Analysis,* 16(3): 73–110.
Joh, S.W. and Kim, M.A. (2013) "The drivers and stock market's assessment of internal capital markets: evidence from business groups in Korea," *Asia Pacific Journal of Financial Studies,* 42(2): 287–313.
Joh, S.W. and Ko, Y. (2009) "Examination of success and failure of corporate reform," Working Paper, KDI.
Khanna, T., Song, J. and Lee, K. (2011) "The paradox of Samsung's rise," *Harvard Business Review,* July–August: 142–147.
Kim, In-Young (1998) *The Economic Growth of Korea: Government Initiative vs. Corporate Initiative,* Seoul: Center for Free Enterprise.
Krueger, A.O. (1979) *The Developmental Role of the Foreign Sector and Aid,* vol. 87, Cambridge, MA: Harvard University Press.
Krueger, A.O. (1985) "The experience and lessons of Asia's super exporters," in V. Corbo *et al.* (eds) *Export Oriented Development Strategies: The Success of Five Newly Industrializing Countries,* Boulder, CO: Westview Press.
Krueger, A.O. and Yoo, J. (2002) "Chaebol capitalism and the currency-financial crisis in Korea," in *Preventing Currency Crises in Emerging Markets,* Chicago: University of Chicago Press, pp. 601–662.
Lee, C.H. (1992) "The government, financial system, and large private enterprise in the economic development of South Korea," *World Development,* 20: 187–197.
Lee, C.H. (1999) "Preparing Korea for global competition in the 21st century: an agenda for institutional reform," *Seoul Journal of Economics,* 12(2) 105–125.
Lee, J-W., Seong, J.Y. and Lee, J.H. (2012) "A new perspective on human resource management research: an organizational systematics approach," *Business and Management Research,* 1(1).
Lewellen, W.G. (1971) "A pure financial rationale for the conglomerate merger," *Journal of Finance,* 26(2): 521–537.
Lim, H. (1998) *Korea's Growth and Industrial Transformation,* New York: St. Martin's Press.
Porter, M.E. (ed.) (1986) *Competition in Global Industries,* Cambridge, MA: Harvard Business Press.
Prahalad, C.K., and Hamel, G. (1990) "The core competence of corporations," *Harvard Business Review,* 461: 79–91.
Sachs, J. (2000) "Tropical underdevelopment," Harvard University Center for International Development, mimeographed.
Yan, A., Yang, Z. and Jiao, J. (2010) "Conglomerate investment under various capital market conditions," *Journal of Banking and Finance,* 34(1): 103–115.
Young, A. (1995) "The tyranny of numbers: confronting the statistical realities of the East Asian growth experience," *The Quarterly Journal of Economics,* 110(3): 641–680.
YTN (2012) "Total market cap of top 10 business group almost reaching 60%," YTN, May 7.
YTN (2013) "Top five group reaches 54.8%, historically high," YTN, April 9.

13

Entrepreneurship of SMEs in South Korea

Hun Joo Park

Introduction

Korea's newly-elected President Park Geun Hye had proclaimed she wanted to become "*chungsokiop taet'ongryong*" or president for small business[1] at the Korean Federation of Small Business (KFSB) on the morning of December 26, 2012, the choice of her very first public visit as the President Elect. In fact, strengthening small and medium-sized enterprises (SMEs) constitutes a key to crafting a "creative economy" or what her administration has identified as the number one national policy objective. The imperative has long been clear. Especially since the 1980s, Korea's economic environment has significantly changed. The rapid rise in wages weakened the country's price competitiveness vis-à-vis that of other developing countries such as China, particularly for the light industries that had served as the export growth engines for decades. Meanwhile, increased pressure for the liberalization of Korea's domestic market has resulted in Korean companies competing with multinationals at home. As a result, the Korean economy's growth has slowed down, and its potential growth rate has fallen below 4 percent and keeps falling with declining savings rate and quality job creation. Productivity gaps are widening between manufacturing and service sectors, between export-oriented and domestic market-oriented industries, and between *chaebol* or family-controlled big business conglomerates and SMEs. And accordingly, income disparity has widened, undermining not only social cohesion but also the potential for economic efficiency and productivity. The Gini coefficient, for instance, jumped to 0.32 by 2008 and stayed at 0.31 as of 2011, from 0.26 in 1992 (Statistics Korea).

Clearly, the country's undemocratic *dirigisme* or collusive system of state-led development—with a highly *chaebol*-oriented economy and a very weak small business sector—has outlived its usefulness, and the nation's long-term socio-economic health requires not only the development of new growth engines in more advanced technology sectors, parts and materials sectors, and more knowledge-based service industries, but also doing so especially by enhancing the competitiveness of SMEs. As of 2010, Korea's SMEs represented 3.1 million or 99.9 percent of the total number of firms, and 12.3 million or 86.8 percent of the total number of employees (KFSB, *Korean SME Statistics*, 2012). In manufacturing, the SMEs in the same year made up 99.5 percent of the total or 112,897 firms, and 77.1 percent or 2.3 million of the total employees. However, the share of the value-added of the nation's manufacturing SMEs recorded only 47.4 percent of the total or 216 trillion won, and their per capita productivity a mere 26.8 percent of that of the large firms (ibid.).

Nonetheless, Korean SMEs have proved more important than hitherto recognized or credited as sources of economic expansion and industrial power. The rather abrupt shift in the early 1980s of Korea's highly *chaebol*-biased economic development strategy did start to result in a less discriminatory flow of industrial credits to SMEs (Park, 2001). Changes in the top-down government policy in favor of SMEs, however, turned out to be less than full-fledged, and in the absence of strong or organized small business interests, the persistent *dirigiste* institutions and practices have continued to fetter the development of the SME sector (Park, 2007). Despite the traditionally harsh and unsupportive policies and business environments, however, both the first and second generation small entrepreneurs have strived to make something of themselves as viable business enterprise operators, contributing to the country's rapid economic growth and industrial expansion. From the perspective of small business entrepreneurs, therefore, this chapter offers a more balanced and nuanced picture of the past and present state of Korean SMEs, which would provide a tentative basis for considering alternative, more genuinely small business-based approaches to a creative economy.

Revisiting the place of SMEs in the Korean economy and society[2]

The academic and popular literature has conventionally portrayed Korean SMEs as a weak, backward, and far from modern part of a dual economic structure.[3] In molding such an image, the Korean state's unbalanced modernization strategy, its accompanying industrial and financial policies and historical-institutional ramifications had a major effect, to which we now turn for a brief examination. First, the credit rationing system arguably represented the state's most powerful industrial policy tool especially during the rapid development decades of the 1960s and 1970s, and having access to the heavily subsidized export or National Investment Fund (NIF) loans constituted an immense source of wealth and an extraordinary opportunity from which politically well-connected *chaebol* firms benefited the most. Such a pronounced bias in credit flows resulted in an abundance of petty firms and a dearth of healthy medium-sized corporations. Petty or micro SMEs with less than ten regular employees still made up 87.9 percent of all SMEs in 2010, while medium-sized firms with 50–299 employees constituted only 3.8 percent or 119,999 companies in the same year (KCCI, 2013). The existence of huge pockets of petty enterprises fed the prevalent public perception of the plight of the nation's SMEs.

The government did at times try to provide special help and support for those small firms. The official definition of small business itself was revised in 1982 to distinguish petty firms from larger ones with more than 20 employees. However, without influential connections or competent personnel in a country where information rarely flowed freely, many of these petty and poorly equipped SMEs benefited little from the official promotional programs. Many programs designed to support SMEs never really trickled down to the very bottom rung of the Korean political economy, where numerous firms struggled for survival.

The late President Park Chung Hee himself had been concerned with nurturing SMEs, but the government's support and subsidies for them did not seem to produce sufficiently quick and visible growth. The inability of SME programs to shore up the legitimacy of the military authoritarian regime placed the political leadership in a dilemma. Small businesses just seemed too numerous, too widespread geographically, and too diverse in needs for the government to engineer easy and glorious policy success. As the late President Park confronted the pressing task of generating immediate growth in an underdeveloped economy, pursuing a balanced, SME-based modernization strategy looked neither politically desirable nor strategically compelling

(Oh, 1995: 51–52). The dilemma was reflected in the adoption of the 1966 Small Business Basic Law, which could not have been enacted without the late president's personal interest in SMEs. Yet the political imperative of executing unbalanced modernization turned the law and accompanying policy measures for SMEs into more or less empty words—advisory in nature and hence lacking enforcement teeth (ibid.: 178–179).

A second source of chronic SME trouble came from the historical pattern of their interactions with financial institutions, which included such practices as demanding full collateral for loans or redeposit of a certain portion of credit as "compensating balances" in the same financial institution that originated the credit. A third source stemmed from the institutionalized patterns of small firms' interaction with big ones. Up until the 1990s, in fact, 70 percent of the country's small manufacturers relied in varying degrees upon big firms' purchasing power and oligopolistic market control to sell their parts, components, or semi-finished products, and 80 percent of them depended on a single big firm for more than 80 percent of their sales (KFSB, *General Statistics on the State of SMEs*). Although the dependency ratio has been in decline since 2002 (KCCI, 2013: 42–44), such dependence by small subcontracting firms proved costly and hazardous, as they had to face adverse terms of payment, big firms "passing the buck" in hard times, and big firms gobbling them up even in industries where statutory restrictions remained in effect.

In short, the rapid development decades left SMEs out in the cold. Devoid of strong membership, SME organizations suffered from lack of resources, representation, and political clout. The number of SME associations stagnated in the 1970s after a gradual increase in the 1960s. After renewed encouragement and support from the early 1980s, the number grew quite impressively.[4] To this day, however, the organizational strength and cohesion of SME associations remain weak, and the KFSB has yet to become an effective focal agency for interest aggregation, articulation and representation. The weak and fragmented SME sector, in effect, explained at least in part the limit to the depth of SME policy change in the early 1980s and the impact of its implementation. A case in point was the so-called *Yumang Chungsokiop* (Promising SMEs) Program, the centerpiece of the Chun Doo Hwan government's small business promotion policy in the early 1980s.

In September 1980, immediately after Chun became president, he issued a presidential decree concerning the *yumang chungsokiop* program.[5] According to my interviews, Kim Jae Ik, then presidential economic advisor, and Suh Suk Joon, then MTI minister, were the two principal architects and driving forces of the program. The initial goal was to find and nurture 1,000 "promising" SMEs over the first three-year period. The selection was made from small manufacturing (or manufacturing-related service sector) firms with fewer than 150 regular employees. The criteria included: possession of high technologies, patents, or technology-intensive products; specialty in products that the government's subcontracting promotion policy designated exclusively for SMEs; and commitment to quality and product innovation as well as plant automation. The government ensured that the selected SMEs were properly funded through privileged access to low-cost policy loans.[6]

Ostensibly, the reason why the government resorted to a presidential decree to institute the SME program was because it took less time and energy than enacting a new bill, which also could potentially have conflicted with existing laws. Presidential decrees carried an extra-legal authority and thus could override other laws and statutes.[7] However, such top-down policy changes hindered bottom-up voluntarism, frustrated more flexible mid- and local-level initiatives, and caused the body politic to degenerate (Park and Kim, 1992). The effectiveness of government officials in policy implementation, in particular, frequently depended on pressure from the top. Once the impetus from above weakened, in fact, no policy or program could be thoroughly implemented. Such was the fate that befell the program for developing promising SMEs. After

October 1983 when Kim Jae Ik and Suh Suk Joon died in a terrorist attack in Rangoon, the SMEs selected under the program ceased enjoying all-out government support. The program continued, but only in a watered-down version without much of its initial dynamism.

Nevertheless, Korea's relatively marginalized small entrepreneurs coped with adversities and demonstrated their tenacity, adaptability and resilience. The industries and areas of business they engaged in were often inefficient pockets of the economy, but they took root in these pockets, increasing efficiency and creating value-added, even if on a small scale. They were willing to work long and hard hours for even a modicum of return and carry themselves like viable entrepreneurs to prove their self-worth. Given the vivid memory in their minds that even the top *chaebol* had started from scratch less than a generation ago, the sentiment that "anybody can do just about anything" still prevailed.

And from the early 1980s, the fabric of small business also began to change. For instance, those with college and white-collar backgrounds replaced those with less educated, blue-collar backgrounds as more prominent SME founders. As a vestige of the traditional Confucian social structure, the best and the brightest had flocked to the civil service, legal profession, or academia. When Korea's successful modernization broke that spell, top college graduates entered business, but they preferred the prestigious career of progressing up a *chaebol* ladder. However, some changes were discernible by the 1990s, with more and more technological and managerial talent opting to establish independent, niche market-oriented enterprises, if not venture start-ups, rather than becoming the "organizational man" of a large firm. In more traditional industrial sectors as well, old small livelihoods evolved into new enterprises, or faced elimination by more modern, innovative, and lightweight players.

We can illustrate this evolution by examining the development of one of Korea's oldest traditional markets—called Dongdaemun or East Gate. The origin of Dongdaemun Market can be traced back to 1905, when it started as a "modern" market called Kwangjang, specializing in textiles.[8] After the devastation of the Korean War, the street peddlers returned and converted military uniforms and blankets into clothes in the now renamed Peace Market. Dongdaemun Peace Market became a thriving national hub of clothes manufacturers and wholesalers through the 1960s and 1970s, as a myriad of small sewing companies clustered around it to produce low-priced, relatively fashionable clothes. By the late 1990s, more than 27,000 little shops in Dongdaemun Market, which owned or had ties with over 20,000 factories around the area, successfully transformed the place into one of the nation's hottest shopping and tourist attractions. Daily business transactions exceeded ten billion won, and informal exports alone made by domestic and foreign suitcase traders amounted to $1 billion per year.[9]

Their successes stemmed from clustering, or sectoral and geographical concentration of enterprises.[10] As the critical problem of umpteen SMEs was not necessarily their size but isolation, as Sengenberger and Pyke (1991) point out, clustering facilitated key developments: specialization and division of labor; provision of customized machinery and spare parts and just-in-time delivery of raw materials; the pooling of skilled workers and availability of speedy services in finances and fashion design; plus a mixture of intense competition and cooperation especially vis-à-vis other contending markets. In the crucible of cluster, only those merchants and clothes makers who successfully competed for customers and orders survived. Given the close proximity and collaboration among raw materials suppliers, clothes designers, producers and subcontractors, in fact, it took only a couple of days to produce, say, a modified version of an outfit once the idea for it from any of the world's top fashion shows was accessed.[11] Dongdaemun falls short of leading global fashion, but it stays hot on the trail.[12] With modern shopping malls, formally educated fashion designers, younger entrepreneurs, and former *chaebol* employees partaking of the cluster, whether Dongdaemun Market will further evolve into a world-class pioneer in quality, design, and name brands is a test case of just how far the SMEs will continue on their growth trajectory as the economy further opens space for them.

For Korea's clothes manufacturing and distribution industry, in any event, the Dongdaemun cluster certainly became a pioneer and benchmark. However, the concept of industrial districts was not new to other industries, as the origins of some of them could be traced as far back as the export-led industrialization drive of the 1960s. By 1996, there existed 28 national industrial districts, 150 provincial industrial districts, and 19 other industrial districts. They remained far from all being equally successful or highly innovative, but their combined total employment and production amounted to 925,070 persons and 171 trillion won, or over one-third of the nation's manufacturing employment and almost one-half of manufacturing production, respectively.[13]

The rise of the second generation SMEs

Also from the 1980s, a new generation of small entrepreneurs capitalizing on technology-driven niche market strategies began to spring up, and by the 1990s, SMEs which focused on R&D and technology-driven quality, niche market specialization, productivity and profit rose to new heights. Since the secrets to their performances may offer a key to Korea's ongoing efforts at revitalization or transition to a more knowledge-based, creative economy, it is worthwhile taking a detailed look at some of the more successful SMEs in order to garner what lessons or policy implications can be gleaned, in the hope of helping to improve and expand such successes.

First, the new small business entrepreneurs solidified their product competitiveness and technological lead in specialized niche markets. As of the late 1990s, for example, Jinwoong controlled 65 percent of the US market and 35 percent of the global market for tents, with annual sales of $400 million. Hongjin Crown, an unknown name in Korea, captured 40 percent of the motorcycle helmet market in the United States. Daesung Metal, a rather obscure maker of nail clippers in Korea, had a 40 percent share of the global market. Medison, a leading medical equipment company, was the world's top manufacturer of low and medium-priced ultrasound systems. Daeryung Precision made satellite video receivers (SVRs) and had a 25 percent share of the global market (Shin and Kim, 1999).

Second, leading medium-sized companies acquired their fame not only for the scarce foreign exchange their exports generated especially during the 1997 crisis, but also for the rather novel way they made big money: through stocks or foreign direct investment (FDI). One of the exemplary cases was Locus, a telecommunications equipment manufacturer. Founded in 1990 with only 10 million won by Kim Hyung-Soon, a former doctoral student in Columbia's business school, Locus became Korea's top maker of computer telephony integration (CTI) systems in 1996 and sold a 38 percent share to Jardine Fleming Electra for $16 million in 1999.[14] Once Locus was listed in Kosdaq in November 1999, the company's market value reached 260 billion won. Even a traditionally labor-intensive manufacturer like Jinwoong, which never had equity or direct financing, made $50 million by offering a 90 percent share to Warburg Pincus in 1999.[15]

The new SMEs, however, were not born overnight in mid-crisis. Many of the leading ones got their start in the early 1980s, and these second-generation small business owners were better educated, usually with college degrees. By 1983, in fact, almost half of SME owners had a college education or beyond (KFSB, *Survey Report on the State of SMEs*).[16] And their business plans were based on technology-based innovation and niche market-driven specialization, and more often than not, they anticipated eventually raising funds or making a good deal of money in the stock market, at a time when listing in the market seemed a long shot for small firms.

Representative of this new cohort of SMEs was Daeryung Precision's founder Lee Hoon.[17] Lee, a son of a small business owner, had majored in applied physics at Seoul National University and obtained an MBA from Columbia University. In 1982, at the age of 34, Lee established an export, technology, and niche market-oriented SVRs manufacturing company. Of the seven founding members, five were engineers engaged in research and development. Having started out as a small original equipment manufacturer for various North American companies, the company had its ups and downs. Lee, however, believed that a technology-based niche market strategy would be particularly rewarding with the growth of the capital market in the future. Hence, he distributed 30 percent of shares to his six employees, sealing the bond among the founding members. The company was successfully listed in the stock market in June 1989, and by 1998, it had 223 employees and earned 217 billion won in sales and 1.7 billion in profits. It enjoyed a 50 percent market share in North America, 25 percent in Europe, and 20 percent in the rest of the SVRs market.

The new generation of innovative SMEs rose not only in high tech sectors, but in more traditional ones as well. Jinwoong represented such a case in point.[18] Lee Yun-Jae, a Yonsei University graduate, had created the company in 1979 to make higher quality, higher value-added tents. The challenge came in the 1990s when Korea's labor-intensive industries lost price competitiveness to Chinese and South-east Asian manufacturers. Exploiting the trend of increasing globalization, however, Jinwoong adopted a two-pronged strategy: while attracting FDI and perfecting state-of-the-art technology and high value-added production at home, it shifted low-end production to less developed countries. By 1998, at its peak, Jinwoong had 81 employees in Korea and 84 employees abroad.

However, Lock & Lock remains a better example of attaining business success by way of global market exploitation.[19] Its founder, Kim Jun-il, first established the company in 1978 as a trading firm called Kukjin. It started manufacturing products of its own in 1985, and in 1998 it produced the world's first double-locking, airtight plastic containers with four-winged flaps, the so-called Lock & Lock products, and the company then renamed itself after these products. When the domestic market response turned out to be cold, it turned to the global market opportunities by participating in international homeware expositions or shows, and taking up a Canadian buyer's suggestion, it began to tap in on foreign TV home shopping channels with a more pro-active marketing approach. The big success came in the USA in 2001, when the QVC TV home shopping introduced the Lock & Lock products on the air. It then re-entered the domestic market, and by 2011, it controlled 60 percent of the market, with its 2010 sales recording 388 billion won. Lock & Lock continues to invest 5 percent of its total profit into R&D, keeps growing exponentially, currently operates in 112 countries, and already enjoys the biggest market share of its kind in such countries as China, Vietnam and Taiwan.

Originally established in 1981 as a motorcycle parts company with 16 employees in Chinju, South Kyongsang Province, Bumwoo constitutes yet another SME which has flexibly adapted to the changing environment in a traditional industrial sector: By 1994, it had developed into a respectable auto parts company with 70 employees.[20] Annually, it showed over 30 percent growth in sales because of founder Lee Chun-Bum's determination to accumulate capital and technology, by doggedly specializing in certain engine and transmission parts like shafts and gears, and by making constant innovations in products and production processes. Since 1990, as a result of more rigorous quality control, ambitious investments in precision equipment, factory automation, and its own R&D lab producing domestic substitutes for various imported parts, the per capita value-added jumped from 16.1 million to 34.5 million won, and the defective product ratio dropped from 1.8 to 0.2 percent.

Some SMEs joined the new wave by diversifying or transforming themselves into sunrise industries from declining traditional sectors, thereby creating new domestic markets and stimulating structural changes in the economy. A case in point is Youngbo Chemical, founded in December 1979 in Taejon, South Chungchong Province by Lee Bong-Joo, who had been operating a coal mining company since the early 1970s.[21] Sensing the centrality of petroleum and the inadequate supply of petrochemical products such as plastic gourds and vessels in Korea, Lee traveled through Germany and Japan to visit companies in related industries. Believing in the growth potential of polyolefin foam products in automobile and boxcar interiors as well as the construction materials market, Lee concluded licensing agreements with various Japanese firms, including Furukawa Denzo, Hitachi, Toray, and Sekisui. Lee's flexibility in introducing new technologies and products from Japan, practicing customer-oriented marketing and management, and devoting an increasing share of sales to R&D (3.35 percent by 1998) paid off over time. By 1998, Youngbo with 238 employees enjoyed 75 percent of the domestic polyfoam market, exported 38 percent of its output, and competed head-on with Japanese products. It recorded three billion won in profit out of 37 billion won in sales in 1998, about one-third less than what it made the previous year, but still a very decent performance in the wake of the nation's financial crisis.

Established in 1980 in Pusan with 30 employees, Namyang Industry represented yet another small enterprise that successfully ventured into new territory (Moon, 1994). Park Yun-So's small business had been in construction materials production, but it could not thrive in the highly competitive, cyclical industry dominated by well-capitalized and powerful firms. His search for a new, small niche market hit on sea-borne fire-safety equipment. He had luckily learned that Korea imported all its sea-borne fire-safety equipment, as manufacturing them required high technological standards and rigorous quality specifications. By sheer will and perseverance, Namyang bore all privations and acquired stamps of approval from SOLAS (Safe of Life at Sea) and USDOT (US Department of Transportation) as well as the KS (Korean Standard). With less than 100 employees it obtained a 30 percent global market share by 1993, earning 20 billion won in domestic sales and $20 million in exports.

Empowering the second generation SMEs

The new generation of Korean SMEs caught up with those in Japan and the USA in terms of R&D spending by the mid-1990s.[22] The nation's leading medium-sized companies at the forefront of the new wave of creative, innovative and technology-oriented SMEs invested at least 3 percent of their sales (Shin and Kim, 1999). Accordingly, the number of independent in-house research centers operated by small firms jumped to 2,278 by 1997, up from 708 in 1991 (KFSB, *Korean SME Statistics*, 1998: 144). The 3 percent of sales spent on R&D often went a long way for SMEs, as they tended to engage in a narrow range of businesses, exploited economies of scope, and focused R&D effort on specifically applicable technologies or concrete product innovation. The new small entrepreneurs also sensed a bigger chance of realizing their dreams through the burgeoning capital market as an alternative source of funding and profit. Even with little capital, if they gained competitiveness in a niche market, the capital market could bring a tremendous boon to them. Such promises of future profits and employee stock options provided a strong incentive structure for the SMEs to invest in technology-based product innovation and market creation. By the 1990s, venture businesses had become a buzzword and a focal point in both public policy and private circles,[23] and thanks in part to the government's increased financial support, tax breaks, and relaxed listing requirements, Korea's Kosdaq stock market for small and venture firms recorded a phenomenal expansion, with its market valuation as of the end of 1999 reaching almost the 100 trillion won mark, nearly one-third of the Korea Stock Exchange that was dominated by big business. Kosdaq has had its own ups and downs since then, while undergoing an adjustment and stabilization process especially in the wake of the dot.com bubble burst in the early 2000s, but its market valuation remains at about 10 percent of the Korea Stock Exchange.[24] Although it is still a long shot for Korean venture firms to become truly like those in the Silicon Valley or the Massachusetts Route 128, they, along with leading medium-sized companies, have become as important and indispensable as big business to Korea's industrial structure and competitiveness.

However, to transform Korea's small or venture firms into Silicon Valley-style high-tech companies would require changes in the government's fundamental policy approach or changes in the framework from a top-down *dirigiste* to a more empowering one. When nearly one-third of Korea's 2.7 million big business employees were laid off in the aftermath of the 1997 financial crisis (Woo, 2005: 37), for instance, the government doubled the outstanding balance of its credit guarantee funds to SMEs from 17 trillion won or 3.6 percent of GDP in 1997 to 33 trillion won or 6.8 percent of GDP in 1998—only to increase it again to 47 trillion won or 7.6 percent of GDP in the wake of the 2001 venture business bubble burst (MOFE, FSC, and SMBA, 2006: 2; Yun, 2009: 280–281; Kang, 2009: 231–232).[25] As Yun points out, however, such a policy largely failed to enhance the small firms' market competitiveness or capacity to create good jobs. It was so because the Korea Credit Guarantee Fund (KCGF) and the Korea Technology Credit Guarantee Fund (KOTEC), the two public credit guarantee funds entrusted with the operation of the governmental funds, tended to base their decisions on needs rather than merits or qualifications of the applying firms. As a result, for instance, the allocation of over 60 percent of the KCGF and KOTEC funds went to small firms with no R&D activities or technological qualifications (MOFE, FSC, and SMBA, 2006: 33).

The Korean government's radical expansion of SME credit guarantee funds was consistent with its *dirigiste*-style policy-making and implementation. The Korean developmental state continued to use its financial policy tools aggressively to promote its industrial policy objectives, and particularly after the country became a democratic polity and a richer economy, it was rather natural for the state to spend far greater sums of money on supporting SMEs. However, given the problematic way the credit guarantee decisions were made and monitored, such an aggressive financial policy was becoming increasingly dysfunctional, threatening to crowd out private investment or create moral hazard. The utility or effectiveness of mechanically increasing the quantitative inputs into or resources given to various SME promotion measures had reached its limits.

Especially in the wake of the 1997 crisis, the government did emphasize promoting both technology development and business innovation in SMEs. In 1997, for instance, it enacted the "Special Law for Promoting Venture Companies" to channel resources to create small venture companies, and as a result, the number of government-certified venture companies increased from 4,934 in 1999 to 24,645 in 2010. The number of patents per venture company, an index for innovation, rose from 0.9 in 1999 to 2.9 in 2010 (SMBA, n.d.). Although the government initially focused on expanding funding or increasing the number of beneficiaries, more recently, it has introduced a more holistic or integrated support type of policy. Once the government has selected a limited number of promising start-ups based on feasibility studies of their technological potential, for instance, it provides them with consistent support through technology development, commercialization and marketing phases by way of a more streamlined review process. However, the authorities have a long journey to systematically coordinating the overall support system, which still falls far short of becoming an efficient and effective innovation eco-system. Meanwhile the system involves more than 20 public agencies operating 149 programs in areas such as tax credits, subsidies, financing, recruiting and training, technological support, licensing support and procurement.[26]

Conclusion

While the story of Korean economic development has been dominated by big business, the role of both old and new small and medium-sized entrepreneurs has become more crucial over time.

Even though Korea's undemocratic *dirigisme* had largely slighted SMEs, both the first and second generation small entrepreneurs poured themselves into making something of their enterprises, working endlessly and incrementally increasing efficiency and productivity gains. The level of big business success itself may well have been unattainable without the successes of many old and new SMEs, which not only supplied cheaper labor-based parts and components but also generated domestic demand for the raw materials and products that big businesses produced. Had the nation's political leadership embraced more inclusive and democratic state–society relations, a far more vibrant, independent and balanced private sector could have been formed. The dearth of democratic governance, a thriving and globally competitive SME sector, and an autonomous, healthy civil society under Korean *dirigisme* as a new basis for equitable and sustainable development proved particularly painful in the wake of the 1997 crisis.

Yet, since the crisis the Korean economy and society have been undergoing a structural change, which entails a bigger gap or deeper level of polarization between global market-oriented big exporting firms and domestic market-oriented small companies. Hence, the need to duly address the structural problem has become far more compelling. The need really lies in transforming the nation's political economic structure and practice into a more enabling kind that is not only more efficient and competitive, but also more equitable and just. The government's full commitment to providing a more level playing field in favor of promoting small businesses would surely be a good way to help ordinary citizens not only to partake of a fairer share of the country's economic growth, but also to identify themselves as contributing and respected members of the society. With respect to what sort of policy and how to support SMEs in an increasingly globalizing economy, helping to empower more organically-linked clusters, autonomous and enabled industrial districts, and collaborative horizontal networks—if not a full-fledged innovation ecosystem—rather than merely increasing top-down subsidies for individual firms, would offer a more plausible and promising path, as the successes of the Dongdaemun market and the new generation of SMEs illustrate.

Acknowledgments

The author wishes to thank the KDI School of Public Policy and Management for faculty research support.

Notes

1 The terms small businesses or small and medium enterprises (SMEs) used interchangeably in this chapter denote manufacturing enterprises with no more than 300 employees in Korea, albeit with some exceptions allowed since 1992 for labor-intensive industries. In the service sector, SMEs are those with less than 200 employees. While the official definitions of small business in other countries even in the same North-east Asian region are not exactly the same as Korea's, most of their statistical publications on SMEs are actually based on the number of a firm's regular employees, which make international comparison possible.

2 The sections that follow heavily draw on Park (2007).

3 The dual industrial structure argument and its traditional image of exploited small business came most forcefully from Japan's Marxist political economists. Following in their footsteps, Lee Kyung-Eui became the biggest proponent of such a perspective on small business in Korea. For more details on the perspective and literature, see his 1991 book.

4 As of 1987, small manufacturing firms that joined SME associations numbered 24,809 or less than 15 percent of the total (KFSB, 1992: 330–331).

5 The following account draws heavily on my interviews with Kim Eun Sang, the President of KOTRA, on July 8, 1996, and Lee Won Gul, the Director of the Aerospace Industry Division, Basic Industry Bureau at the Ministry of Trade, Industry, and Energy (MTI) on July 10, 1996. Kim Eun Sang was Director

General of the Small Business Bureau at MTI from 1980–1983, and Lee Won Gul was his assistant at the time. See also my interviews with officials at the SME Promotion Corporation on June 25, 1996.

6 Many SMEs which graduated from the program became respectable medium-sized firms, which included Samhwa Printing, Co., Samcholli Bicycle, Co., Samick Musical Instrument, Kwangdong Pharmaceutical Co., Tongwon Industry, Donga Trading Co., Heungchang Mulsan, Susan Heavy Industry, and Kyungin Industry.

7 Interestingly, the democratically elected Kim Young Sam government of the 1990s similarly issued a presidential decree to institute the Structural Adjustment Fund, a key piece of its own SME policy designed to promote small firms' factory automation, modernization, and technological innovation. By pooling fiscal and bank funds, it provided 1.4 trillion won in 1993, 500 billion won in 1994, 1 trillion won in 1995, and 1.5 trillion won in 1996 for the structural adjustment fund. My interviews with officials at the SME Promotion Corporation, June 25, 1996.

8 The following section on Dongdaemun Peace Market draws on Kim and Koo (1999) and my interviews.

9 Dongdaemun Market, together with Namdaemun (South Gate) market, handled 30 percent of the nation's wholesale transactions in clothing.

10 On the vitality of small business clusters or industrial districts, see Piore and Sabel (1984), Friedman (1988), Whittaker (1997), Sengenberger and Pyke (1991), Schmitz (1995), and Humphrey and Schmitz (1996).

11 It took several months for large, upscale department stores to design and produce a new line of clothing.

12 Today, Dongdaemun Market supplies the great bulk of clothes that the nation's rapidly expanding online shopping malls sell.

13 See http://kicox.or.kr:9000 (KFSB, *Korean SME Statistics,* 1998).

14 See their website: www.locus.co.kr; *Maeil Kyongje,* January 27, 1999; *Chosun Ilbo,* Sept. 3, 1999.

15 See *Far Eastern Economic Review (FEER),* July 29, 1999, pp. 36–37. It should be noted, however, that Jinwoong's subsequent efforts at diversifying into new, unrelated industries through M&As have utterly failed.

16 Although no systematic data on the earlier period are available, educational attainment had improved remarkably by the 1980s over previous decades. As of 1944, for instance, the nation's college graduates totaled 29,438 persons, or 0.1 percent of the population. The proportion of those with tertiary education impressively rose to 5 percent by 1955, 6.9 percent by 1965, 9.5 percent by 1975, 16 percent by 1980, 35.6 percent by 1985, and 54.6 percent by 1995 (*Maeil Kyongje,* December 27, 1999; McGinn *et al.*, 1980; KEDI, 1996).

17 My discussion of Daeryung Precision draws on Financial Supervisory Commission's (FSC) corporate data; various media reports including *Hankook Kyongje,* August 1, 1997 and June 26, 1999; and my interview on October 25, 1999.

18 This section draws on FSC corporate data; various media reports including *Maeil Kyongje,* July 21, 1999 and *FEER,* July 29, 1999, pp. 36–37.

19 See http://us.locknlock.com/; KCCI, 2013, pp. 76–78.

20 This section draws on Moon (1994).

21 The discussion on Youngbo draws on FSC's corporate data; *Maeil Kyongje,* December 22, 1997; and interview with Lee Bong-Joo on October 3, 1999.

22 Korea's R&D spending as a percentage of GDP rose to almost 3 percent by the mid-1990s.

23 The number of officially recognized venture companies increased to nearly 25,000 by the end of 2010, from 2,042 in 1998. See, for instance, *Kukmin Ilbo,* November 12, 2012.

24 See, for instance, *Seoul Kyongje,* March 12, 2013.

25 This section draws on Park (2010).

26 The new government under Park Geun Hye has proposed to nurture 3,000 small giant firms or what H. Simon has called "hidden champions" by providing them with customized supports by 2017, each of which would export more than $10 million worth of high-tech, niche-market products per year. See *Hankyoreh,* May 10, 2013 and Simon (2009).

Bibliography

Friedman, D. (1988) *The Misunderstood Miracle,* Ithaca, NY: Cornell University Press.

Humphrey, J. and Schmitz, H. (1996) "The triple C approach to local industrial policy," *World Development,* 24(12).

Kang, D. (2009) "SMEs in distress: the role of Korea's credit guarantee scheme in restructuring," in J.H. Kim and S.-H. Lee (eds) *Restructuring Small and Medium-Sized Enterprises in the Age of Globalization,* Seoul: KDI.

Kim, Y. and Koo, B. (1999) *Chaerae Euiryusijangeui Puhwalkwa Sisajom [The resurrection of traditional clothing market and its implications]*, Samsung Economic Research Institute (October).
KCCI (Korea Chamber of Commerce and Industry) (2013) *Chungsokiop Songjangch'okjineul wihan Chongch'aekkwaje [The Policy Task of SME Growth Promotion]*, Seoul: KCCI.
KEDI (Korea Educational Development Institute (KEDI) (1996) *Educational Indicators in Korea,* Seoul: KEDI.
KFSB (Korean Federation of Small Business) (various years) *Chungsokiop Hyonhwang [Korean SME Statistics]*, Seoul: KFSB.
KFSB (various years) *Chungsokiop Silt'ae Chosa Pogoso [Survey Report on the State of SMEs]*, Seoul: KFSB.
KFSB (various years) *Chungsokiop Silt'ae Chonghap Tongkyejib [General Statistics on the State of SMEs]*, Seoul: KFSB.
KFSB (1992) *Kihyop Samsipnyonsa [The Thirty-Year History of KFSB]*, Seoul: KFSB.
Lee, K. (1991) *Hankuk Chungsokiopeui Kujo [The Structure of Korean Small Business]*, Seoul: P'ulbit.
McGinn, N., Snodgrass, D., Kim, Y., Kim, S. and Kim, Q. (1980) *Education and Development in Korea,* Cambridge, MA: Harvard University Press.
MOFE (Ministry of Finance and Economy), Financial Supervisory Commission (FSC) and Small and Medium Business Administration (SMBA) (2006) "Chungsokiop Keumyungjiwon Ch'ekye Kaep'yon" [On Improving the Financial Support System for SMEs], Seoul. June.
Moon, W. (1994) *Case Studies of Innovative SME Management,* Seoul: KDI (in Korean).
OECD (1999) *OECD Science, Technology and Industry Scoreboard 1999,* Paris: OECD.
Oh, W.C. (1995) *Hankukhyong Kyongje Konsol [Economic Engineering Korean Style]*, Seoul: Kia Economic Research Institute.
Park, C. and Kim, B. (1992) "Hankuk Kukka Kwanryoeui Euisik" [The Korean State Officials' Mindset]. *Hankuk Haengjonghakpo [The Korean Journal of Public Administration]*, 25(4).
Park, H.J. (2001) "Small business in Korea, Japan, and Taiwan: *dirigiste* coalition politics and financial policies compared," *Asian Survey,* 41(5).
Park, H.J. (2007) "Small business' place in the South Korean state-society relations," *Asian Journal of Political Science,* 15(2).
Park, H.J. (2010) "Faulted dirigisme: the limits to top-down statist labor market reform in post-1997 Korea," in Y. Lim (ed.) *Making Reform Happen: Lessons from Korea since the 1987 Democratization,* Seoul: KDI.
Piore, M. and Sabel, C. (1984) *The Second Industrial Divide,* New York: Basic Books.
Schmitz, H. (1995) "Collective efficiency: growth path for small-scale industry," *The Journal of Development Studies,* 31(4): 529–566.
Sengenberger, W. and Pyke, F. (1991) "Small firm industrial districts and local economic regeneration," *Labour and Society,* 16(1): 1–24.
Shin, H. and Kim, J. (1999) "Kanghan Chungsokiopeso Paeunun Chihye" [Gaining Wisdom from Strong Small Business], *CEO Information,* Samsung Economic Research Institute (February).
Simon, H. (2009) *Hidden Champions of the 21st Century,* London: Springer.
SMBA (Small and Medium Business Administration). Available at: www.smba.go.kr. and www.smba.go.kr/eng/smes/statistics.
Statistics Korea. Available at: http://kostat.go.kr.
Whittaker, D.H. (1997) *Small Firms in the Japanese Economy,* Cambridge: Cambridge University Press.
Woo, C.S. (2005) *Kyongjekujopyonhwawa Yangkeukhwa [The Change of Economic Structure and Polarization]*. Seoul: KDI (Classified Report to the Blue House).
Yun, J. (2009). "Labor market polarization in South Korea," *Asian Survey,* 49(2).

14

Technology entrepreneurship in China

Charles E. Eesley and Jian Bai Li

Introduction

From a Western perspective, technology entrepreneurship in China is at once familiar and foreign. Technology entrepreneurship in China is familiar because it is spearheaded by individuals with largely grassroots origins, as it is in many Western economies. Indeed, the prototype of the Silicon Valley entrepreneur, i.e. the individual who starts an innovative tech venture out of his or her college dorm room, mirrors the experience of many Chinese tech entrepreneurs. At the same time, technology entrepreneurship in China is foreign because it originated from policy directives within a command economy and continues to be influenced by this same command economy (Li, 2010). Over the past 30 years, the increasing market-based reform (often known as marketization) of the Chinese economy has fostered technology entrepreneurship and contributed to the creation of successful high-tech firms like Baidu, Sohu, and Alibaba. Yet, China still lacks the regulatory and judiciary institutions that are needed to support a true market economy, and many sectors of the Chinese economy still operate in a patrimonial fashion. Technology entrepreneurship is at once a representation of China's attempt to become a modern economy and a reflection of the nation's struggle to do so thus far.

To survive and succeed in China's dual market-patrimonial economy, technology ventures must transform themselves into a unique breed of organizations. At their core, they must have the human capital, technological capabilities, and the strategic acumen necessary to transform raw supplies into competitive products. At the same time, they must build personal relationships with the economic elites of China, i.e. powerful bureaucrats and influential managers in state-owned enterprises, in order to protect their core operations and defend against opportunistic behavior. The nature of China's economic order makes the ability to operate ambidextrously in both market-like and patrimonial fashions a prerequisite for high performance. This ambidexterity is difficult to achieve and maintain. As such, the top-down, patrimonial economic order of China's economy is simultaneously the force that first enabled technology entrepreneurship to flourish and the barrier that prevents technology entrepreneurship in China from reaching its true potential.

The history of technology entrepreneurship in China

A discussion of technology entrepreneurship in China necessarily starts with an overview of its history. Many of the observations we make regarding Chinese high-tech firms are closely linked to how technology entrepreneurship in China began and developed. As the development of technology entrepreneurship in China happened in concert with the development of China's economy over the past 30 years, we begin our discussion of technology entrepreneurship in China with a short overview of China's economic reform.

China's economic reform

Formally, China's economic reform began during the Third Plenary Session of the Eleventh Central Committee of the Communist Party of China in 1978 (Li, 2010). Reform-minded policy-makers under the leadership of Deng Xiaoping consolidated their hold on the national government during this session and implemented a series of economic reforms. In aggregate, these reforms are known as China's "Reform and Opening Up."

"Reform and Opening Up" has three major themes. Each of these themes can be thought of in general as intending to spread resource allocation and investment decisions out from the top to a broader range of the population. The first is *decentralization*, which refers to the central government's efforts to stimulate local and regional economic development by delegating economic obligations to provincial and local governments (Boisot and Child, 1996). This delegation was typically done by having the provincial and local governments assume fiscal responsibility over their jurisdiction and was often coupled with a loosening of oversight from the central government (Li, 2010). Overall, this central-to-regional redistribution of responsibility and power successfully incentivized provincial and local governments to pursue economic development within their jurisdiction. The result was strong incentives for local government officials to make investments for local economic growth, with the trade-off of investment-led, rather than consumer-led, growth. To summarize, one of the consequences of "Reform and Opening Up" was that government bureaucrats at the regional and local levels gained power over the regulation of economic behavior and the execution of economic policies within their jurisdiction.

The second theme of "Reform and Opening Up" is *marketization*, which we define as the central government's efforts to stimulate economic development by making state-owned enterprises responsible for their own decisions and performance. One of the ways that the central government marketized state-owned enterprises is via privatization, where ownership of state-owned enterprises was transferred to private entities and individuals. The government may still hold a significant ownership stake post-privatization, but controlling shares are often held by private entities, many of which are composed of former managers of these state-owned enterprises (Walder, 2009). In privatizing state-owned enterprises, the central government forced the private owners of these enterprises to become responsible for the survival and performance of the enterprises. The process of marketization also occurred in state-owned enterprises that were not privatized. Since 1979, the managers of many state-owned enterprises in China were given discretion over production, inputs, outputs, organizational policies, and personnel decisions (Child, 1994). From 1981 onwards, many state-owned enterprises were also made to assume full financial responsibility (Li, 2010). Similar to what decentralization did for bureaucrats at the provincial and local level, privatization reflects a policy prerogative on the part of the central government to transfer decision-making power and economic responsibility to the private entities that control or manage state-owned enterprises.

The third theme of "Reform and Opening Up" is *modernization*, which refers to the central government's attempt to stimulate economic development by increasing the scientific and technological capabilities of Chinese firms. The development of technology entrepreneurship in China—which we discuss in the following section—is one significant dimension of the modernization of the Chinese economy. Yet, modernization—as both an economic trend and as a policy prerogative—was not limited just to technology entrepreneurship in the private sector. The government invested very significant financial and human resources into modernizing the state-owned sector, mostly via technology transfer from foreign sources in the form of equipment import, intellectual property licensing, and technology consulting (Wang, 2011). From 1979 to 1991, the majority of technology transfer took place in the energy sector (28 percent), the manufacturing and telecommunications sector (24 percent), the petroleum and chemicals sector (20 percent), and the metallurgy sector (18 percent), all of which are dominated by large state-owned enterprises (Chen, 1997). This trend did not change after China joined the World Trade Organization (WTO) in 2005 (Wang, 2011). Thus, while technology entrepreneurship has contributed significantly to the overall modernization of China's economy, the Chinese government invested far more resources in modernizing state-owned enterprises.

As significant as the three trends just mentioned is the fact that China's economic "Reform and Opening Up" was not accompanied by political and legal reforms. Despite the Chinese government's attempts to establish a capitalist market economy, the government has not established the necessary institutions that regulate firm behavior in a capitalist market (Boisot and Child, 1996). In many other cases, the laws do exist, but their implementation and enforcement are limited and under the influence of decisions by government officials. For example, although the central government adopted a patent law as early as 1984, the institutions necessary for the implementation of the law are still rudimentary (Baark, 2001). This has hampered the government's ability to adjudicate cases involving patent infringement and intellectual property disputes (Fawlk, 1996). Similarly, China lacks well-developed contract laws and judiciary institutions, which inhibits the courts' ability to adjudicate disputes arising from market transactions (Peng and Heath, 1996; Xin and Pearce, 1996). Overall, while policies since "Reform and Opening Up" have attempted to stimulate economic development by influencing firms to behave in a market-like manner, the Chinese government has either not established or not systematically implemented the formal institutions necessary to support a mature market economy.

As a result, "Reform and Opening Up," rather than spreading economic decisions broadly across society, instead caused a large amount of economic and political power to fall into the hands of a select group of individuals. When the central government transferred decision-making power to lower-level bureaucrats and managers of state-owned enterprises without establishing institutions capable of regulating how these individuals used their new power, the central government effectively increased the degree to which these individuals at lower levels can act unilaterally within their jurisdiction. Unsurprisingly, these individuals often used their new and often unchecked power to transform their jurisdiction—be it a geographical region, a government bureau, or an enterprise—into patrimonial estates that they controlled with near absolute power and often exploited for personal benefit (Nee, 1992; Walder, 1995; Boisot and Child, 1996). This is not to say that these effectively patrimonial regions, bureaus, or enterprises are necessarily inefficient. Rather, what we do observe is that economic reform coupled with the lack of political and legal institutions has given a select group of individuals in China the power to make decisions pertaining to matters within their jurisdiction in accordance with their personal objectives.

Development of technology entrepreneurship in China

As a part of China's economic modernization effort, technology entrepreneurship in China began with policy initiatives from the central government (Baark, 2001). The political legitimation of technology entrepreneurship was quickly followed by explicit policy support, of which there are three types.

The first type of policy initiative aimed to increase the quantity and quality of scientific and technological research being done in research institutions and stimulate the transfer of knowledge from these institutions to entrepreneurial ventures. One example of such a policy initiative is the Torch Program. Launched in 1988, the Torch Program aimed to increase the diffusion of technology from research institutions to entrepreneurial ventures (Baark, 2001). A second example is Project 973, which the government launched in 1997 in order to support scientific research in areas that are critical to China's economic modernization (Ministry of Science and Technology of the People's Republic of China, 2008). Overall, the first type of government policy initiative attempted to increase the quality and size of the body of knowledge from which entrepreneurs can draw on to create profitable innovations.

The second type of policy initiative aimed to improve the quality of individuals who could potentially become entrepreneurs or contribute to entrepreneurial ventures. Some policies of this type were direct attempts at influencing high-quality individuals to start new ventures. For example, China recently introduced a new policy that graduates from the top 100 universities must all take a class in entrepreneurship before graduating (Ministry of Education of the People's Republic of China, 2012). Other policies were broader initiatives that aimed to increase the quality of individuals who may not become entrepreneurs themselves but can nevertheless contribute to the growth of technology entrepreneurship in China. One such policy initiative is Project 985, which implemented a range of reforms to top universities in China so that these universities can educate the scientists, innovators, entrepreneurs, and financial investors who are necessary to support the ecosystem surrounding technology ventures (Eesley *et al.*, 2013). Another example is the Outstanding Young Scientist Fund of the National Natural Science Foundation of China, which the central government established in 1994 in order to attract Chinese expatriate scientists from foreign institutions back to China (Ministry of Science and Technology, 2008). The government established this fund because, though these scientists may not themselves become entrepreneurs, their research and their experience of working in overseas institutions and firms are nevertheless valuable for the growth and success of technology entrepreneurship in China. Overall, the second type of policy initiative aimed to increase the quality of individuals that the entire ecosystem surrounding technology entrepreneurship in China relies on for support, innovation, and growth.

The third type of policy initiative attempted to establish fields within which high-tech entrepreneurial ventures can survive and grow. These policy initiatives include measures that directly established science parks specifically designed to aid the founding and growth of new technology ventures. One example of such a science park is Beijing's Zhongguancun Science Park, which was established in 1988 (Eesley and Yang, 2013). We differentiate science parks from other funding programs or reform policies because science parks—such as the Zhongguancun Science Park—provided far more than simple financial support or policy aid. The true function of the science park institution was to give new technology ventures both a physical space and a figurative playing field with conditions that are more favorable to their growth than those in the wider economy. As such, by establishing science parks, the Chinese government essentially provided a series of "cocoon institutions" within which entrepreneurs with little social and financial capital could still establish successful ventures (Eesley and Yang, 2013). In addition to establishing "cocoons" with conditions favorable to technology ventures, the Chinese government also pursued policy initiatives that increased the favorability of existing industries or fields to technology entrepreneurship. For instance, Eesley (2012) showed that the Chinese government had successfully encouraged entrepreneurs to enter into industries that were traditionally dominated by state-owned enterprises by implementing policies that lowered the barriers to growth for these industries. Overall, the third type of policy initiative aimed to foster technology entrepreneurship by making conditions more favorable to technology ventures in particular fields within the Chinese economy.

Interestingly, as technology ventures in China began to flourish, they became less patrimonial and more market-like than firms in other sectors of the Chinese economy. While bureaucrats and top managers often dominate industries such as metallurgy or petroleum in a patrimonial fashion, entrepreneurial ventures in sectors such as the internet industry often compete and innovate in ways that resemble their counterparts in mature Western economies (Eesley and Yang, 2013). This is not to say that technology ventures in China do not need to build *guanxi* or engage in particularistic behavior the way that other firms in China do. In fact, one of the major conclusions from the research on technology entrepreneurship in China is precisely that firms that engage in network building with powerful bureaucrats and top managers in state-owned enterprises generally perform better (Li and Zhang, 2007). What we do claim is that technology ventures in China are more similar to firms in mature market economies than other firms in China, and we attribute this similarity to three sources.

First, the grassroots origin of many Chinese technology entrepreneurs may have inhibited high-tech ventures from exerting patrimonial dominance over their industries, forcing them instead to rely on innovation and strategy in ways that are similar to the competitive behavior of technology ventures in Western economies. The bureaucrats and top managers who came to dominate the Chinese economy after "Reform and Opening Up" were generally already a part of China's social and economic elite prior to the reforms. As such, these individuals already possessed significant human and social capital during the initial stages of the economic reforms, and they quickly took advantage of their resource superiority to dominate their respective sectors. In contrast, upstart high-tech sectors such as the internet industry did not exist before the economic reforms and consequentially did not contain "royalty" who could use their historical resource advantages to rise to the top of the Chinese economic order. Instead, entrepreneurs who entered China's high-tech sectors were generally individuals from grassroots origins with little or no connections to China's economic elite (Walder, 2009). To survive and grow, these technology entrepreneurs often had to rely on novel innovation and savvy competitive strategy to outmaneuver their competitors—just like their counterparts in Western economies. Thus, the grassroots origins of China's technology entrepreneurs may have forced these entrepreneurs to operate and compete in "market-like" ways.

Second, the presence of Chinese expatriates in many technology ventures may have influenced these ventures to behave in ways that are similar to their counterparts in Western economies. These expatriates are often individuals who have received education from Western universities and have worked for an extended period of time in Western research institutions or corporations. Having studied and worked in Western society, the Chinese expatriates may have become accustomed to how technology ventures innovate, grow, and compete in the Western economy. When these expatriates return to Chinese research institutions or ventures at the calling of government programs, they are likely to bring with them Western managerial concepts of how technology firms should operate and compete. Given that a significant number of Chinese expatriates are present in the ecosystem surrounding technology ventures as researchers, entrepreneurs, and financiers, these expatriates may influence Chinese technology ventures to become more similar to their Western counterparts.

Third, certain features of high-tech fields influence these fields to become similar to mature market economies, which then causes the ventures that operate in these fields to behave in market-like ways. In some cases, the Chinese government intentionally incorporated particular features into certain high-tech fields with the intention of causing these fields to become more market-like. In the case of Beijing's Zhongguancun Science Park, the government granted all employees of technology firms within the park Beijing residency and reduced taxes on technology transfers, R&D expenditures, services, and consulting activities (Eesley and Yang, 2013). The government implemented these measures to lower the barrier to entry for the Zhongguangcun Park and attract grassroots entrepreneurs so that the Zhongguancun Park could become a field in which technology ventures can compete in a market-like fashion. In other cases, certain attributes of the technology that form the basis of high-tech fields influence these fields—and the ventures within these fields—to become more market-like. An example of this is the internet industry. Firms operating in the petroleum or mining industries need financial resources to purchase the necessary equipment, access to the raw materials, and approval from government bureaus for their products and processes in order to even begin operation. As a result, elite individuals who have ties with equipment manufacturers, raw materials producers, and bureaucrats in the relevant regulatory agencies have a significant advantage over grassroots entrepreneurs—an advantage that these elites then leverage to out-compete rivals and dominate their industries. In contrast, firms operating in the internet industry face much lower entry barriers: they need only a computer with internet access and knowledge of how to build a website to create an internet start-up. As a result, large internet firms cannot squeeze out new internet start-ups the way state-owned corporations squeeze out private petroleum processing plants or steel mills in China. To summarize, technology ventures in China may be similar to their counterparts in the West because the fields they operate in are similar to those in mature market economies.

Technology entrepreneurship in China is a curious fusion of patrimonial control and market economy. As with many other sectors of the Chinese economy, the high-tech sector was created because of top-down government policy initiatives. Powerful bureaucrats within government agencies still hold significant power over technology ventures in China and may still engage with these ventures in the same patrimonial manner as the way they engage with firms in most other sectors of the Chinese economy (Peng, 2004; Walder, 2009). At the same time, the grassroots origins of China's technology entrepreneurs, the influence of expatriates returning from Western economies, and the characteristics of high-tech fields all influence technology ventures to innovate and compete in ways that are not dissimilar from their counterparts in the West.

How technology entrepreneurs succeed in China

Chinese technology entrepreneurs who possess network ties with powerful bureaucrats and influential managers of state enterprises gain significant competitive advantages. In the context of Chinese society, these network ties are usually personal relationships embedded in norms of reciprocity, trust, and long-term commitments (Granovetter, 2007). Given that a select order of bureaucrats and top managers at large enterprises dominate the Chinese economy, technology entrepreneurs who are tied to these economic elites and could gain favors from them would most certainly enjoy competitive advantages over rivals. As such, technology entrepreneurs who possess ties to the economic elite generally perform better than entrepreneurs who do not (Li and Zhang, 2007). More specifically, the technology entrepreneur who possesses ties to the economic elites of China gains three kinds of competitive advantages.

First, network ties with economic elites may act as a defense mechanism against patrimonial expropriation. Chinese economic elites often abuse their power and status to expropriate organizations within their jurisdiction (Nee, 1992). By forming a personal relationship with select economic elites, the entrepreneur can utilize the norms of reciprocity and trust to deter expropriation. The existence of a personal relationship also enables the entrepreneur to lure the economic elites into incurring social debt with gifts and special services (Granovetter, 2007). Bonded by the norms of personal relationships and obligated to repay the social debt, the economic elites refrain from expropriating the entrepreneurs they are personally tied to (Park and Luo, 2001). The well-connected technology entrepreneur thus gains competitive advantage over his rivals by being more "immune" to the harmful effects of patrimonial expropriation.

Second, network ties with economic elites enable entrepreneurs to defend themselves against illegal competition from rival firms. The lack of well-developed regulatory and judiciary institutions in China increases the latitude for firms to behave opportunistically and engage in illegal competition (Peng and Heath, 1996; Xin and Pearce, 1996; Li and Atuahene-Gima, 2001). As a result, firms in China regularly break contracts, ignore patents, violate copyrights, and engage in other forms of unlawful behavior in order to gain competitive advantage (Li and Zhang, 2007). The economic elites of China, by the power they possess, do have the power to regulate economic activity (Nee, 1992; Walder, 1992). Technology entrepreneurs who are connected with the economic elites can thus utilize the power of these elites to ensure that their own contracts are protected, that their own patents are upheld, and that rivals who attempt to compete in an unlawful way are punished. The well-connected technology entrepreneurs thus gain competitive advantages because their ties to China's economic elite makes them more immune to the harmful effects of rivals' illegal competitive behavior.

Third, the possession of network ties with economic elites enables technology entrepreneurs to access the resources and information controlled by these elites. Economic elites in China possess the power to allocate resources and provide insider information in accordance with their personal preferences (Nee, 1992; Walder, 1995). Entrepreneurs who possess ties with these economic elites could use these ties to access government funding, acquire contracts from government agencies and state enterprises, and gain insider news on upcoming policy changes (Park and Luo, 2001; Acquaah, 2007). This is particularly true if the elites have incurred social debt towards the entrepreneurs, in which case the entrepreneurs could use this debt as social leverage to acquire resources and information from the elites. Given the transitional and turbulent nature of China's economy, technology entrepreneurs who could gain preferential access to resources and anticipate upcoming policy changes would gain significant competitive advantages over less privileged rivals.

Although ties with economic elites may be a complement to high human capital, novel innovation, and savvy strategy, it is not a substitute. Technology entrepreneurs in China remain dependent on human capital, novel innovations, lucrative alliances, and sound competitive strategy for success. For instance, Li and Zhang (2007) find that the relevant functional experience of managers in entrepreneurial ventures is positively related to venture performance. Similarly, Eesley (2012) finds that entrepreneurs who possessed higher quality human capital are more likely to found high-performing ventures. Together, these findings suggest that the quality of human capital within Chinese tech ventures may be as critical for performance as ties with economic elites. Li and Atuahene-Gima (2002) find that technology ventures that possessed agency business relationships with foreign firms benefited from the foreign partner's status and financial resources and were consequentially higher performing. This suggests that sound alliance partner selection and management are also critical to the success of technology ventures in China. Li and Atuahene-Gima (2001) find that pursuing a product innovation strategy is more likely to result in increases in firm performance in turbulent environments. Given the transitional and often unstable nature of China's economy, this finding suggests that investing in innovation—especially in nascent industries and ambiguous markets—may be a rewarding strategy for technology ventures in China. Finally, Eesley and Yang (2013) find that entrepreneurs who pursued strategies consistent with their institutional environments were more likely to achieve high performance. This finding suggests that firms operating in more market-like fields, e.g. science parks or high-tech industries, may actually perform better if they lessened the amount of resources devoted to networking and instead invested more resources in innovation, alliances, and human capital. Overall, research on technology entrepreneurship in China suggests that innovation, alliances, and human capital are just as critical to the success of technology ventures in China—and in some cases more so—as networking with economic elites.

Furthermore, the outcomes of networking with economic elites may not be entirely rosy. Building and maintaining relationships with members of the economic elite may be both time-consuming and costly, as entrepreneurs must repeatedly utilize a complex array of gift-giving gestures in order to curry favor with the elites and maintain relationships (Granovetter, 2007). If the benefits the entrepreneur gains from his ties with elites does not equal the time and money he expends to build and maintain these ties, then the possession of ties with elites may actually harm the venture's performance. Indeed, Park and Luo (2001) find that the utilization of political ties positively affects firm sales growth but has no significant effect on net profit growth, which suggests that the resources expended to build and maintain ties with elites may often offset any extra profit gained from these ties. Far from being a panacea, networking with economic elites is a strategy with its fair share of downsides.

Overall, the conclusion that emerges from our overview of the strategies of technology ventures in China is this: high-performing technology ventures in China are often ambidextrous organizations that are capable of profitably engaging with the patrimonial side of the Chinese economy while simultaneously implementing the strategies necessary to achieve high performance in the more market-like high-tech sectors. The patrimonial aspects of China's larger economic environment and the market-like characteristics of China's high-tech industries and science parks put two different and often conflicting sets of institutional pressures on China's technology entrepreneurs. The successful technology entrepreneurs in China are often the individuals who are able to navigate the patrimonial-market duality of China's economy and pull competitive advantages from both sides of this duality. Unfortunately, organizational ambidexterity is difficult to master, and many technology entrepreneurs place too much faith on the profit potential of their innovations while neglecting to engage the patrimonial side of the Chinese economy (Eesley *et al.*, 2013). As a result, while China has produced a select number of successes in the high-tech sector (e.g. Baidu, Alibaba), many of the highly-innovative technology ventures in China today are nevertheless likely to fail.

Technology entrepreneurship in China: directions for future research

Patrimonial-market duality and organizational ambidexterity

That technology ventures need to simultaneously engage with the patrimonial and market-like dimensions of the Chinese economy is evident from our discussion above. Yet, entrepreneurship and management scholars have not looked at how entrepreneurial ventures in China successfully respond to the institutional pressures from both the patrimonial and market-like dimensions of the Chinese economy. Successfully engaging both the patrimonial economy and the market-like sectors is difficult because the "rules of the game" of these two dimensions of China's economy are often conflicting. Transactions in a market economy are generally conducted in a hands-off and universalistic manner. Building close, personal ties with one's business partners is generally considered unprofessional, while giving favorable deals selectively to one's friends or kin is seen as corrupt and illegal. In contrast, transactions in a patrimonial economy are generally conducted using personal relationships as a catalyst. Building close, personal ties with one's business partners is often a prerequisite for closing a deal, and giving favorable deals selectively to one's friends or kin is merely a normal part of business. In fact, under traditional Chinese norms of reciprocity and social justice (*yi*), *not* giving favorable deals selectively to one's friend or kin is considered to be a sign of weak moral character. Given that technology entrepreneurs must nevertheless engage both dimensions of China's economy in order to succeed, they must build organizational routines and structures that are capable of simultaneously engaging with the environment in a contradictory manner. Clearly, this is difficult.

The presence of successful technology ventures in China suggests that technology entrepreneurs *can* construct organizational routines and structures that are capable of engaging with contradictory institutional pressures from the environment. Prior research suggests that modularity may be one way that this is done: that is, technology ventures institute separate departments for engaging the market-like sector and for building particularistic networks with economic elites. Equally likely, however, is the possibility that technology firms utilize organizational structures or routines that do not exist in Western economies in order to meet this challenge. Overall, an understanding of how technology ventures in China successfully respond to institutional pressures from both the patrimonial and the market-like dimensions of the Chinese economy is likely to both advance scholarly understanding of entrepreneurship and organizations and contribute significantly to the performance of technology ventures in China and similar emerging economies.

Regional differences within China

A fruitful area of research would be to compare and contrast the development of technology entrepreneurship across different regions within China. So far, the majority of research on technology entrepreneurship in China has treated China as a single institutional and cultural bloc. Yet, different regions within China exhibit significant institutional and cultural differences. Overall, an examination of ventures in different regions of China is needed to gain a more granular understanding of technology entrepreneurship in the country.

Interestingly, cross-regional analysis of technology entrepreneurship in China may provide a way for researchers to separate the effects of institutions and culture. Given all regions of China are governed by the Chinese Communist Party and are subject to the same centralized governance, institutions may not vary much across regions within China. This may provide researchers the opportunity to examine technology entrepreneurship across institutionally similar but culturally different regions, with the aim of understanding how cultural norms, values, and ways-of-life affect the organizational behavior of technology ventures in China.

Entrepreneurship and institutional flexibility

An additional avenue for understanding how technology ventures in China survive and succeed is to examine how institutional flexibility impacts entrepreneurial firms. Yang and colleagues (2013) define flexible institutions as institutions that outline goals or objectives but do not specify how they are to be met. In the same paper, Yang and colleagues find that flexible institutions foster innovation and entrepreneurship by allowing greater freedom of choice and lessening the constraints to exploratory activities. Yet, while Yang and colleagues examined how flexible institutions impact firm founding rates, how flexible institutions influence entrepreneurial performance remains under-studied.

Flexible institutions may give individual firms the freedom to operate either in a patrimonial fashion or in a market-like manner, so long as these firms ultimately meet the objectives that the institutions set. Firms could choose to operate in a way that best suits their technology, their culture, and their industry norms. Overall, the concept of flexible institutions provides a novel avenue for examining how high-tech entrepreneurial ventures survive and succeed in China.

Conclusion

Technology entrepreneurship in China has come a long way since the "Reform and Opening Up" policy was first announced. Taking a longer historical view, China was a world leader in new technologies in ancient times (and had the world's largest economy in 1800). Yet, only in recent history has it begun to make significant strides towards developing the institutions and expertise in commercializing those technological innovations via technology entrepreneurship. While great strides have been taken and a first generation of successful technology entrepreneurs are now investing in and mentoring the younger generation of entrepreneurs, more reforms and progress on institutional development are needed. Technology entrepreneurship in China is still hindered by a number of factors related to the lack of political and legal reforms relative to progress in economic reforms. Regulations and effective enforcement of existing regulations on intellectual property, the legal system for contract enforcement, entrepreneurial finance and fundraising, as well as bankruptcy and public financial market reforms need to occur for technology entrepreneurship in China to reach its full potential. In addition, the industrial policy balance between private entrepreneurs, state-owned enterprises, and foreign-invested firms needs to be balanced towards giving entrepreneurs a level playing field to compete on. China has made progress in its plans to transition to a science- and technology-driven economy, yet the challenges of moving up the value chain from a manufacturing and export-driven economy are significant. As wages continue to rise, the opportunity for greater domestic consumption-led growth must be balanced with the movement of more economic activity to the less-developed interior provinces. Further reforms along these lines alongside additional investment in developing the western, interior provinces should enable China to take advantage of prior groundwork of reforms. Whatever the future holds, these challenges will continue to provide organizational theorists and entrepreneurship scholars with plenty of research opportunities to further our understanding and to contribute to the development of technology entrepreneurship in China and beyond.

References

Acquaah, M. (2007) "Managerial social capital, strategic orientation, and organizational performance in an emerging economy," *Strategic Management Journal,* 28: 1235–1255.

Baark, E. (2001) "Technology and entrepreneurship in China: commercialization reforms in the science and technology sector," *Policy Studies Review,* 18(1): 112–129.

Boisot, M. and Child, J. (1996) "From fiefs to clans and network capitalism: explaining China's emerging economic order," Administrative Science Quarterly, 41: 600–628.

Chen, H. (1997) *Research on Technology Transfer and Technological Process.* Beijing: Economy and Management Publishing House.

Child, J. (1994) *Management in China During the Age of Reform.* Cambridge: Cambridge University Press.

Eesley, C.E. (2012) "Who has 'the right stuff'? Human capital, entrepreneurship, and institutional change in China," Working Paper, Stanford University, CA.

Eesley, C.E. and Yang, Y. (2013) "Changing entrepreneurial strategies to developing capitalist institutions: a look at Chinese technology ventures," Working Paper, under review, Stanford University, CA.

Eesley, C.E., Li, J. and Yang, D. (2013) "Does public funding of university R&D influence high-tech entrepreneurship?: Evidence from China's Project 985," Working Paper, Stanford University, CA.

Fawlk, M. (ed.) (1996) *Intellectual Property Protection in China*. Hong Kong: Asia Law & Practice Ltd.

Granovetter, M. (2007) "The social construction of corruption," in V. Nee and R. Swedberg (eds) *On Capitalism*. Stanford, CA: Stanford University Press, pp. 152–172.

Li, H. and Atuahene-Gima, K. (2001) "Product innovation strategy and the performance of new technology ventures in China," The Academy of Management Journal, 44: 1123–1134.

Li, H. and Atuahene-Gima, K. (2002) "The adoption of agency business activity, product innovation, and performance in Chinese technology ventures," Strategic Management Journal, 23: 469–490.

Li, H.Y. and Zhang, Y. (2007) "The role of managers' political networking and functional experience in new venture performance; evidence from China's transition economy," Strategic Management Journal, 28: 791–804.

Li, J. (2010) *China's Economy into the 21st Century*. Beijing: Economy and Management Publishing House.

Ministry of Education of the People's Republic of China (2012) "Basic requirements for undergraduate entrepreneurship education." Available at: www.moe.gov.cn/publicfiles/business/htmlfiles/moe/s5672/201208/xxgk_140455.html/.

Ministry of Science and Technology of the People's Republic of China (2008) Available at: www.most.gov.cn/kjbgz/200807/t20080719_63130.htm.

Nee, V. (1992) "Organizational dynamics of market transition: hybrid forms, property rights, and mixed economy in China," Administrative Science Quarterly, 37: 1–27.

Park, S.H. and Luo, Y. (2001) "Guanxi and organizational dynamics: organizational networking in Chinese firms," Strategic Management Journal, 22: 455–477.

Peng, M.W. (2004) "Outside directors and firm performance during institutional transitions," Strategic Management Journal, 25: 453–471.

Peng, M.W. and Heath, P.S. (1996) "The growth of the firm in planned economies in transition: institutions, organizations, and strategic choice," The Academy of Management Review, 21: 492–528.

Walder, A. (1992) "Property rights and stratification in socialist redistributive economies," American Sociological Review, 57: 524–539.

Walder, A. (1995) "Local governments as industrial firms: an organizational analysis of China's transitional economy," American Journal of Sociology, 101: 1060–1073.

Walder, A. (2009) "From control to ownership: China's managerial revolution," Management and Organization Review, 7(1): 19–38.

Wang, X. (2011) *Research on the Innovation Strategy of Chinese Enterprises*. Beijing: Economy and Management Publishing House.

Xin, K.R. and Pearce, J.L. (1996) "Guanxi: connections as substitutes for formal institutional support," The Academy of Mangement Journal, 39: 1641–1658.

Yang, D., Eesley, C.E., Tian, X. and Roberts, E.B. (2013) "Institutional flexibility and training for entrepreneurship?: Evidence from China," Working Paper, Stanford University, CA.

15

Female entrepreneurship in East Asia

Nerys Fuller-Love

Introduction

This chapter looks at female entrepreneurship in East Asia and at some of the issues and challenges that women starting a business in these countries face. Following the increasing participation of women in the workforce and in entrepreneurial activities, attitudes are changing all over the world. Women are becoming more positive about the opportunities to start a business and more confident in their abilities. There is recognition that female entrepreneurs are a catalyst for economic growth and job creation. However, there is also an understanding that female entrepreneurs may face additional barriers in starting a business. The effect of these barriers on GDP and job creation may be considerable and this has led to an increasing interest by academics and policy-makers.

The rationale for looking at female entrepreneurship is mainly the contribution to economic growth in terms of job generation. However, there is also the general assumption that women underperform compared to male entrepreneurs (Ahl, 2006). Much of the literature on female entrepreneurship has focused on why there are fewer women starting businesses than men, and why their businesses are smaller, less profitable and employ fewer people. The reasons can be divided into internal factors, i.e. the character and motivations of the entrepreneur, and, second, environmental and cultural factors such as infrastructure, attitudes and support for women to start a business and help for them to overcome barriers such as lack of self-confidence, skills and finance.

The Global Entrepreneurship Monitor 2010 Women's Report (Kelley *et al.*, 2011) found that 104 million women in the countries surveyed had started and managed a new business. These women made up between 1.5 per cent and 45.4 per cent of the adult female population in these countries, illustrating that there is a wide variation in the start-up rates of businesses started by female entrepreneurs. In addition, a further 83 million were running established businesses which had been in existence for more than three and a half years. In the countries surveyed, there was only one country, Ghana, where more women started a business than men. Minniti (2010) looked at the Global Entrepreneurship Monitor (GEM) data collected in 34 countries in 2004, including Hong Kong, Japan and Singapore. Hong Kong and Singapore were categorised as middle-income countries and Japan as high-income based on Gross Domestic Product (GDP) per head. In the middle-income countries men were 75 per cent more likely than women to be active entrepreneurs, and 33 per cent more likely in the high-income group.

From the 1980s onwards there has been considerable interest in female entrepreneurship. One of the factors has been the increasing participation of women in the workforce. This has led to women participating in education and training with a view to career advancement. Despite the existence of the 'glass ceiling', women are achieving top managerial positions, though they are still a minority.

East Asia

East Asia includes the high-income 'Asian Tiger' countries such as Hong Kong, Singapore and China, as well as less developed countries. They also vary in population size, political environments and culture. According to Ellis *et al.* (2010), East Asia is a region of dynamic economic growth. The increase in economic growth can partly be attributed to the increasing participation of women in the workforce. The ease of doing business is an important contributory factor in the number of female entrepreneurs. However, despite the increasing participation of women in entrepreneurial activities, they are still under-represented in East Asia compared to men.

Women in countries such as China have endured thousands of years of discrimination (Deng *et al.*, 2011). After the People's Republic of China (PRC) was founded in 1949, the Chinese government introduced gender equality legislation which has contributed to China's economic growth. Another factor which has facilitated female entrepreneurship is education. In China, policies to support female entrepreneurship include training, loan guarantees, favourable taxation and infrastructure. In the past 30–40 years, women are increasingly playing a role in the workforce and in entrepreneurship.

Gender and entrepreneurship

The literature on female entrepreneurship can be divided into three groups (Harding, 1989). The first group is the liberal feminist theory which sees men as similar and equal. The second group sees men and women as different and that female traits should be used constructively. The third group is the socially constructed approach which looks at what is regarded as masculine and feminine, regardless of biological sex, and states it is largely dependent on upbringing and social interaction. The gender approach to entrepreneurship examines whether people behave in a masculine or feminine way (Bruni *et al.*, 2004). Research on female entrepreneurship can be categorised into those that see gender as describing biological sex, i.e. the physical characteristics of males and females and those who see gender as 'socially constructed' attributes of femininity or masculinity irrespective of sex (Ahl, 2006, p. 596). According to Ahl (ibid.), entrepreneurship is a male gendered concept and has had masculine connotations and the entrepreneur is a masculine concept and it is not gender-neutral.

Lewis (2006) also found that women could be divided into those who thought that gender was an issue and those who did not. Some women participating in an online business forum objected to one female entrepreneur asking for advice about her forthcoming wedding. These women were clearly concerned that discussing stereotypical issues would undermine their recognition as entrepreneurs, and they tried to deny the impact of gender on their business. However, by playing down the importance of gender, they are actually acknowledging that it is an integral part of entrepreneurship.

Gender stereotypes can often be used to describe the activities of men and women and their roles in society. The characteristics suitable for business are often considered to be masculine. This is reflected in their roles in the work environment. As the number of women in senior positions increases, it may lead to attitudes changing, especially in the perception of the characteristics required to be a senior manager as they become more aligned with feminine values. This process is likely to affect entrepreneurship, which has, traditionally, been aligned with male characteristics. Gupta *et al.* (2009), in a survey of business school students in three countries, found that there was a relationship between those people who saw themselves as having masculine characteristics, whether male or female, they were more likely to have entrepreneurial characteristics. However, the success of some female entrepreneurs is likely to reinforce the value of feminine aspects such as having a more caring attitude and a focus on looking after others.

Female entrepreneurship

According to Ahl (2006, p. 603), the reasons why women underperform men in business can be attributed to the following:

1 Women are less entrepreneurial than men.
2 They do not have sufficient relevant education and experience.
3 They have less motivation to start a business.
4 They are risk-averse.
5 They do not network optimally.
6 They behave in an irrational or 'feminine' way.
7 They perceive other women as less entrepreneurial.
8 They fail to raise finance.
9 They attribute problems to gender rather than to a poor business concept.

One of the consequences of women's greater participation in the workforce was the realisation that female entrepreneurship was still much lower than that of men. This led to an increasing interest in why there were fewer women starting a business and, if they did, why their businesses were smaller and employed fewer people. One of the reasons was the type of businesses that were started by women, which have low barriers to entry. Women may also be constrained by family and domestic responsibilities which may limit the amount of time they can devote to their business. On the other hand, some female entrepreneurs start a business because the flexibility enables them to spend more time looking after their family.

According to Bruni *et al.* (2004, p. 262), the typologies of female entrepreneurs involve the following characteristics:

- the women who set up a business as an alternative to employment;
- the women who chose entrepreneurship as a long-term career strategy;
- the women who hit the glass ceiling and see entrepreneurship as giving them the opportunity for top management;
- the women who start a business because of the flexibility so that they can look after family responsibilities;
- the women who start a business after another career;
- the women who run the family business;
- the women who start a business in order to change the way they are viewed in society.

These typologies are very gender-oriented. For example, there is not one that describes women as having what are considered the typical entrepreneurial approach of spotting an opportunity, being innovative or taking a risk. In addition, there are women who start a business because they need the income. The inclusion of family responsibilities, according to Bruni *et al.* (2004), reinforces the stereotypical approach.

The Global Entrepreneurship Monitor (GEM) survey

The GEM survey divides countries into three types of economic development levels: factor-driven, efficiency-driven and innovation-driven. These are based on the World Economic Forum's Global Competitiveness Report which is based on GDP per capita and the share of exports of primary goods. The geographic groups were: Sub-Saharan Africa, the Middle East and North Africa, Latin America and the Caribbean, Eastern Europe, Asia Pacific and the United States and Western Europe. The Asia Pacific countries in in the GEM 2010 Women's report included Malaysia, China, Taiwan, Japan, the Republic of Korea, Vanuatu and Australia (Table 15.1).

Women in factor-driven economies are more likely to identify opportunities and be confident of their abilities to be an entrepreneur. They are also more likely to know someone who is an entrepreneur, and have a lower fear of failure than those in developed countries. Generally, men are more likely to perceive opportunities and are less worried about failure than women, especially in innovation-driven economies.

The total early stage entrepreneurial activity varies from 19.9 per cent in the factor-driven economies, 9.7 per cent in the efficiency-driven economies and 3.9 per cent in the innovation-driven economies (Kelley *et al.*, 2011). In the Asia Pacific countries, Korea and Japan have relatively few women entrepreneurs, whereas Malaysia has a relatively high proportion of female entrepreneurs and China and Taiwan have moderate levels. In China, however, over the period 2002–2010, the rate of female entrepreneurship did not keep up with the male entrepreneurial rates and a gender gap opened up.

In the factor-driven economies, women are more likely to be driven by necessity to start a business. Generally, women are more likely to be driven by necessity than men. However, there is an increase in the number of women identifying opportunities especially in efficiency-driven and innovation-driven economies. With regard to sector, women were more likely to work in the services sector than men. In Malaysia, women are more opportunity-driven than necessity-driven to start a business whereas in Japan women were likely to be motivated by necessity. In Korea there were the lowest proportion of female entrepreneurs in the innovation-driven economies and they were motivated by opportunity, whereas male entrepreneurs were motivated by necessity.

Women entrepreneurs tend to be older on average than men, with 35–44 and the 45–54 age group in the innovation-driven economies. Education levels are important for early stage entrepreneurial activity, with women entrepreneurs more likely to have a higher educational qualification than non-entrepreneurial women. In the Asia Pacific region, female entrepreneurs in Taiwan, Malaysia and China had lower perceptions of opportunities and capabilities than other factor-driven economies, and in Korea and Japan they had the lowest. Chinese women showed a lower than average fear of failure whereas female entrepreneurs in Taiwan, Malaysia and Japan had a much higher level. The status of entrepreneurship as a career was low in Japan but high in Malaysia, though women did not rate it highly as a career choice. With regard to growth expectations, male entrepreneurs in China were three times more likely than women to have growth

Table 15.1 Asia Pacific countries in the GEM 2010 Women's Report and economic level

Economic level	*Country*
Factor-driven	Vanuatu
Efficiency-driven	Malaysia, China, Taiwan
Innovation-driven	Japan, Republic of Korea, Australia

Source: Kelley *et al.* (2011).

expectations of employing more than 20 people in the next five years (Kelley *et al.*, 2011). These growth expectations were affected by the global economic downturn in the period 2009–2010 and women were generally more pessimistic than men.

Barriers

The barriers that are seen as having a negative effect on women's ability to start a business include family responsibilities and access to networks which can provide a valuable source of knowledge and information, such as sources of capital, etc. Access to networks may be limited as women form close networks with family and friends rather than wider contacts that can provide links to other networks in order to obtain the resources required to start a business (Dawson *et al.*, 2011). Women may find it more difficult to raise finance to start a business for a number of other reasons. They may face assumptions based on gender stereotypes. However, it is possible that there is no discrimination, but that the business proposals themselves are less economically viable. Women may also find it more difficult raise finance because of a lack of financial skills or collateral.

Women in the Far East may face additional barriers to starting a business because of access to assets, business regulations, governance and conditions for economic growth (Ellis *et al.*, 2010). Access to assets including land and capital on an equal basis to men is a critical factor in exploiting entrepreneurship opportunities. If women cannot gain access to assets such as property, this makes it more difficult for them to raise finance. In some countries in East Asia, the laws regarding property favour men. However, despite gender equality in laws on property, such as in Cambodia, Hong Kong, China, the Philippines and Singapore (Ellis *et al.*, 2010), there are cultural factors which discriminate against women. In China, for example, although there are equal property rights, the custom in rural areas is for the wife to move to her husband's village. In Cambodia, there are also equal property rights, but the man is considered to be the head of the household. If property is only registered in the husband's name, then the wife will find it difficult to use it as collateral to raise money. In Vietnam, the World Bank worked with the government to ensure that family assets were registered in both the husband's and wife's names. In Cambodia, both men and women have equal property rights but women may be unaware of their rights because of low levels of literacy (ibid.).

Women may be at a disadvantage with regard to the bureaucratic and other requirements to start a business. Women have less access to networks which can provide them with information and therefore they may need more support. In some countries in the Far East, such as Cambodia and Vietnam, there are particularly difficult entry conditions (ibid.). There is also a financial cost to starting a business which may deter women with poor access to assets though some countries such as Singapore have no minimum capital requirements.

Motivations

Entrepreneurs start a business because they have to, i.e. economic necessity or because they spot an opportunity. Some women start a business because they need an income and do not have any other employment options. The reasons for starting a business can be categorised into pull and push factors. Pull factors are when an entrepreneur spots an opportunity, identifies the need for independence, financial success and status in the community. Push factors are when an entrepreneur starts a business because of the need to generate an income, possibly because of redundancy or failure to get employment elsewhere. There are many countries and regions in the world where women and men are forced into self-employment in order to feed themselves and their family.

Chu (2000) noted that the number of female entrepreneurs in Hong Kong increased by 44 per cent between 1991 and 1996 and found that the reasons for starting a business for women included carrying on the family business, helping the husband in the business, personal achievement and necessity. In Hong Kong, the 'Chinese female entrepreneurs view their family as a unit and their husbands as head of the unit' (ibid.). They see supporting their husbands and fulfilling the wishes of their parents as the key reasons for becoming entrepreneurs. However, the majority of the female entrepreneurs cited personal fulfilment as the main reasons for becoming entrepreneurs. The glass ceiling was also cited as a reason. The male entrepreneurs, on the other hand, cited making money as a reason for starting a business and did not state helping their wives run a business as a reason for becoming entrepreneurs.

Characteristics

Many entrepreneurs start their businesses in the sector where they have experience and knowledge. However, women often lack the technical expertise and background required in manufacturing and high technology sectors (Bruni *et al.*, 2004). Female entrepreneurs may often find it difficult to obtain the resources required such as finance which limits them to sectors where there is only a requirement for low investment. These sectors have low barriers to entry and they are susceptible to competition which can also limit their growth.

Female entrepreneurs are usually older and better-educated than male entrepreneurs and Lee (1997) found that this was the case in Singapore. The female entrepreneurs were more likely to have a parent who was self-employed. They were also more likely to be married with children than women in employment. Therefore, flexibility to be able to look after children and other family responsibilities and duties may be important.

Debroux (2010) found that the need for self-achievement and self-esteem was the main motivation for female entrepreneurs to start a business in South Korea, Malaysia, Vietnam and Japan. Higher earnings were also important, though this was a lower priority in Japan than the other three countries. The female entrepreneurs were also motivated by job satisfaction, the need for new challenges and wanting to be one's own boss.

Access to finance

There may be two different constraints for female entrepreneurs to access finance to start and grow their businesses. First, women may not have sufficient information as to what is available as their networks may be focused on family and friends. Networks provide access to resources, including finance that they would not otherwise be able to afford (Fuller-Love and Thomas, 2004). Entrepreneurs will start with friends and family and, in order to grow their business, they have to widen their networks. However, there is evidence to suggest that women rely more on family and friends whereas men will have wider networks (Dawson *et al.*, 2011). Women may face problems in accessing male networks and they may prefer female-only networks. However, this may have an adverse effect on business growth as it is the wider networks that will open up new opportunities and access to resources such as finance.

Second, there may be differences in the way that proposals from women are considered by bankers and financiers. Although it is possible that both men and women are adversely affected when trying to raise finance, there are some countries where it is more difficult for female entrepreneurs. In China, for example, women may find it more difficult to raise finance except where microcredit institutions have specifically targeted women. When women in China do obtain a loan, they are more likely to repay the loans and have success in business. They may still, however, have to show their husband's identity when applying for a loan. In Korea, women have to have a longer track record and more credit or assets compared to men (Ellis *et al.*, 2010).

One of the biggest constraints to raising finance by women is the type of business they own or want to start. Women's businesses are often smaller and employ fewer people. Women also focus on particular sectors where there are fewer growth opportunities. Smaller businesses are disadvantaged when it comes to raising finance, first, because of the size of the business. Second, if an entrepreneur is unable to raise money, then this can act as a constraint on growth. Banks may also set conditions that smaller businesses cannot fulfil. In some countries in East Asia such as Vietnam, women are far more likely to use sources of informal credit which can provide an alternative to the banks and formal financial institutions. Female entrepreneurs may find the bureaucratic process of raising finance more difficult, especially if they do not have the relevant skills to prepare the information required.

Education and management skills

Education plays an important role in creating employment opportunities for women, which, in turn, can give them the management experience to run their own business. Countries in East Asia perform well on female education, but there is evidence that women do not have relevant business education (Ellis *et al.*, 2010). Women in East Asia are less likely to study vocational or technical subjects. The lower retirement age in some countries may also have a negative effect on career opportunities and access to training and promotion opportunities. The top management positions and decision-making are dominated by men in many sectors.

Gadar and Yunus (2009) found that education and experience had a positive effect on female entrepreneurs' income levels in Malaysia. The majority of the women in the survey were married with children. Almost half of the women in the survey had inherited a family business. More than half the women were over 40 and had three children or more, and 70 per cent had secondary education qualifications. Job dissatisfaction and retrenchment and social networking were also important influences. Technology and information play an important role in influencing female entrepreneurs in Malaysia.

Women's management skills may also be adversely affected by the type of job. Women are more likely to have low-paid jobs such as cleaning, child care and community services where they may not be able to develop the skills needed to start and run a business.

Culture

Cultural factors can influence the behaviour of entrepreneurs. In China, for example, hard work and good financial management are important values as well as respect for others. Female entrepreneurs in China are more risk-averse towards borrowing more money and are more 'low key' in their approach to business than male entrepreneurs (Deng *et al.*, 2011). Chinese culture, for example, is considered to be collective rather than individualistic.

There are social and cultural factors that also affect the role of men and women. In some countries such as Malaysia and Thailand, men are more likely to be favoured for jobs, especially when there are few positions available. Creating a favourable culture for female entrepreneurship involves less regulations and supplying facilities such as childcare. In East Asia, though the laws are generally equal for men and women, there are still cultural factors which make it more difficult to start a business.

Family responsibilities can affect the time that women have available to start a new business. In China, Vietnam and Cambodia, women shoulder both domestic and family responsibilities.

A survey of access to childcare showed that Hong Kong, China and Singapore had good access to childcare, Japan had modest access and Malaysia had the lowest score.

Time constraints and cultural factors may also make it more difficult for women to develop new business opportunities. Attendance at trade fairs and exhibitions and other networking opportunities may be difficult for women in some countries. Women may also be excluded from male-dominated social situations where 'deals' are often agreed.

Institutional factors

Governments recognise the importance of female entrepreneurship to the economy and the need to provide additional support for under-represented groups. The Chinese government, for example, has a programme to support female entrepreneurs, including training and loan guarantees. Female entrepreneurs can also take out bank loans without having to use their personal assets as security after gaining an entrepreneurial training certificate.

There are different levels of entrepreneurial activity in different countries for both men and women. The levels of both male and female entrepreneurial activity in various countries can make a significant contribution to both GDP and job creation. However, because the levels of female entrepreneurial activity has been identified as significantly lower than for men, despite the increased participation of women in the workforce, this has led to considerable interest in supporting women to start a business both by academics and governments.

Baughn *et al.* (2006) looked at the data from 41 countries in the period 2000–2003 and found that, of the countries in the Far East, Thailand had the highest levels of overall entrepreneurial activity and Hong Kong and Japan were amongst the lowest. However, Thailand had the highest proportion of female entrepreneurship and Japan the lowest. Generally, the level of female entrepreneurship was highest in less wealthy countries, gender equality was not a significant factor, though general entrepreneurial norms and support for female entrepreneurship were significant. These results suggest that female entrepreneurs respond well to support and initiatives to help them start a business.

Socio-cultural factors influence the gender roles in shaping stereotypes of male and female behaviour. Many societies define women's roles through domestic and family responsibilities and women have to balance these with work and business commitments. The role of the entrepreneur has also traditionally been associated with masculine rather than feminine characteristics and this may adversely discourage women from starting a business. Women may still encounter additional problems in starting a business based on stereotypical perceptions. Some gender inequalities may also be present in pay differences, inheritance of property through the male line, customs which dictate women moving to where the husbands live, etc. Social expectations may also affect education and career choices. Women can also be segregated from men in society or in occupations and rank. Women, for example, may find a glass ceiling for promotion in the work environment or be excluded from social and networking activities by norms and traditions.

The levels of self-employment may also be an important factor in a country. High levels of self-employment may be found in countries with low levels of economic development. However, as economies become more prosperous, levels of self-employment decrease only to increase again in the most prosperous countries. This trend may also apply to female entrepreneurship (Minniti *et al.*, 2005).

Self-employment may provide an alternative in situations where women are excluded or fail to achieve top positions. Entrepreneurship provides women with the opportunity for social and cultural mobility, especially if the business is successful. It can also provide women with the flexibility for childcare and family commitments. However, gender inequality can also act as a barrier in that parents in some societies may invest more in the sons' rather the daughters' education, and women may have fewer assets because of inheritance laws and have lower earnings which prevent them from accumulating the capital required to start a business. Women may also have less managerial experience and access to networks. Gender equality in a society, therefore, is expected to lead not only to increased female entrepreneurship but to an improvement in the prospects for women-owned businesses. Support for women to start a business is also considered to be a contributory factor.

Siong-Choy and Teoh (2007) found that there was a steady increase in the number of female entrepreneurs in Malaysia. Government support for female entrepreneurs provides infrastructure, business advice and soft loans. Networks for female entrepreneurs have been established though there are concerns that women may not be able to participate due to family and other commitments.

Conclusion

Although great strides have been made in the past 20–30 years to increase our understanding of female entrepreneurship, there is still a lot more than can be done. Female entrepreneurs make an important contribution to the economy but they do face additional barriers. There are still traditional norms and cultural factors which can make it more difficult for women to start a business. These barriers are often institutional, based on gender stereotypes. Social and cultural factors play an important part in shaping attitudes towards women. Many female entrepreneurs choose industries with low barriers to entry and this makes it difficult for them to develop and grow the business. In countries in the Far East such as China, the transformation of society and the economy has provided opportunities for female entrepreneurship. Governments have also provided support for female entrepreneurs. However, as women in these countries become better educated, this is likely to have a positive effect, not only on their confidence and ability to become entrepreneurs, but also on the general well-being of society.

Bibliography

Ahl, H. (2006) 'Why research on women entrepreneurs needs new directions', *Entrepreneurship Theory and Practice,* 30(5): 595–621.

Baughn, C.C., Chua, B.L. and Neupert, K.E. (2006) 'The normative context for women's participation in entrepreneurship: a multicountry study', *Entrepreneurship Theory and Practice,* 30(5): 687–708.

Bruni, A., Gherardi, S. and Poggio, B. (2004) 'Entrepreneur-mentality, gender and the study of women entrepreneurs', *Journal of Organizational Change Management,* 17(3): 256–268.

Chu, P. (2000) 'The characteristics of Chinese female entrepreneurs: motivations and personality', *Journal of Enterprising Culture,* 8(1): 67–84.

Dawson, C., Fuller-Love, N., Sinnott, E. and O'Gorman, B. (2011) 'Entrepreneurs' perceptions of business networks: does gender matter?' *The International Journal of Entrepreneurship and Innovation,* 12(4): 271–281.

Debroux, P. (2010) *Female Entrepreneurship in East and South-East Asia: Opportunities and Challenges,* Oxford: Chandos Publishing.

Deng, S., Wang, X. and Alon, I. (2011) 'Framework for female entrepreneurship in China', *International Journal of Business and Emerging Markets,* 3(1): 3–20.

Ellis, A., Kirkwood, D. and Malhotra, D. (2010) *Economic Opportunities for Women in the East Asia and Pacific Region,* Washington, DC: The World Bank.

Fuller-Love, N. and Thomas, E. (2004) 'Networks in small manufacturing firms', *Journal of Small Business and Enterprise Development,* 11(2): 244–253.

Gadar, K. and Yunus, N.K.Y. (2009) 'The influence of personality and socio-economic factors on female entrepreneurship motivations in Malaysia', *International Review of Business Research Papers,* 5(1): 149–162.

Gupta, V.K., Turban, D.B., Wasti, S.A. and Sikdar, A. (2009) 'The role of gender stereotypes in perceptions of entrepreneurs and intentions to become an entrepreneur', *Entrepreneurship Theory and Practice,* 33(2): 397–417.

Harding, S. (1989) 'Is there a feminist method?' *Feminism and Science,* 42: 18–32.
Hu, P. (2000) 'The characteristics of Chinese female entrepreneurs: motivation and personality', *Journal of Enterprising Culture,* 8(01): 67–84.
Jamali, D., Sidani, Y. and Safieddine, A. (2005) 'Constraints facing working women in Lebanon: an insider view', *Women in Management Review,* 20(8): 581–594.
Kelley, D.J., Brush, C.G., Greene, P.G. and Litovsky, Y. (2011) *2010 Report: Women Entrepreneurs Worldwide,* Global Entrepreneurship Monitor, Babson Park, MA: Center for Women's Business Research.
Lee, J. (1997) 'The motivation of women entrepreneurs in Singapore', *International Journal of Entrepreneurial Behaviour and Research,* 3(2): 93–110.
Lewis, P. (2006) 'The quest for invisibility: female entrepreneurs and the masculine norm of entrepreneurship', *Gender, Work and Organization,* 13(5): 453–469.
Minniti, M. (2010) 'Female entrepreneurship and economic activity', *European Journal of Development Research,* 22(3): 294–312.
Minniti, M., Arenius, P. and Langowitz, N. (2005) *Global Entrepreneurship Monitor: 2005 Report on Women and Entrepreneurship,* Babson Park, MA: The Center for Women's Leadership, Babson College.
Siong-Choy, C. and Teoh, W.M. (2007) 'Theorising a framework of factors influencing performance of women entrepreneurs in Malaysia', *Journal of Asia Entrepreneurship and Sustainability,* 3(2).

Part II

East Asia cases

Entrepreneurial firms and their founders

Japan

16

Toyota and Kiichiro Toyoda

Building a company and a production system based on values[1]

Jeffrey K. Liker

Introduction

The genesis of Kiichiro Toyoda's entrepreneurial contribution to society, Toyota Motor Company, and its impactful production system, began with the philosophy and accomplishments of his father, Sakichi Toyoda. We cannot understand the son without knowing about his father's huge influence.

Sakichi Toyoda is famous in Japan as the "King of Inventors" and the father of the Japanese industrial revolution. His passion in life was to develop new kinds of looms, at first to help the women in his family and the community who were "working their fingers to the bone." His vision gradually expanded to helping Japan industrialize and then he contributed to the world a fully automated loom. The culmination of decades of *kaizen*—continuous improvement—was the G-Type fully automated loom and he immediately retired and passed onto his son, Kiichiro, the responsibility to do something great for society.

The Toyoda Precepts, reflecting Sakichi Toyoda's teachings, were assembled in the 1930s by those close to him and still influence Toyota today:

1 Be contributive to the development and welfare of the country by working together, regardless of position, in faithfully fulfilling your duties.
2 Be ahead of the times through endless creativity, inquisitiveness and pursuit of improvement.
3 Be practical and avoid frivolity.
4 Be kind and generous; strive to create a warm, homelike atmosphere.
5 Be reverent, and show gratitude for things great and small in thought and deed.

Sakichi Toyoda believed his mission was to contribute to the community, Japan, and society at large. He did this by constantly innovating new loom technologies until he created the G-Type, fully automatic loom. He expected no less from his son.

Kiichiro Toyoda, born on June 11, 1894, is not nearly as well known as his father. Many of his contributions were behind the scenes. In fact, he resigned from the car company he had created after near bankruptcy, and pressure from debtors, led to laying off employees, thus violating a promise he had made to the union.

Known at a young age as a "sickly boy," Kiichiro Toyoda in today's analytic terms would be classified as an introvert. He had a modest social life and intensely dedicated himself to his studies—whether in school or studying practical issues like the making of looms.

Kiichiro's lack of recognition is symbolized at his death on March 28, 1952 (Wada and Yui, 2002):

> The newspapers carried a short obituary. He was still young: 57 years of age. The only title given . . . was "former president of Toyota Motor Co . . ." In the days that followed, none of the nationally distributed newspapers devoted any space to a prominent article on the passing of Kiichiro.

Despite this relative anonymity, behind Sakichi's crowning achievement, the fully automated G-Type loom, was Kiichiro slaving away to make his father's dream a reality. He set the foundation for Toyota Motor Company. And behind the famed Toyota Production System were the seminal ideas of Kiichiro Toyoda.

A bronze bust of Kiichiro Toyoda in front of the main administration building of Toyota Motor Company was erected in 1954 and reflected the deep love felt for Kiichiro by management, labor, and union alike. The inscription reads:

> Cherishing the spiritual legacy of the late Kiichiro Toyoda, who, in pioneering Japan's automobile manufacturing industry, built our company here in Koromogaoka and devoted his precious life to the most arduous task of building a solid foundation for the automobile industry, we the employees erect a bronze bust of the deceased on this site hallowed by his memories, in order that we may always remember that countenance that was so full of placid gentleness.

Many of the principles of the "Toyota Way" that are broadly taught and adopted by organizations throughout the world in every sector (banking, energy, healthcare, government, mining, aerospace, and more) can be traced to the teachings of Kiichiro Toyota. I will illustrate several of these principles as they were learned and then taught by Kiichiro. But first I will start with some general background on his life.

Background on Kiichiro Toyoda

There is not a great deal to say about Kiichiro Toyoda's early years. As mentioned, he was regarded as a sickly child and not particularly athletic. He was a good, not great student, but an extremely hard worker. He was an introvert and had a few good friends.

He grew up in a poor farming village, in a straw-thatched farmhouse. His father was slaving away on inventing the automatic loom and in his early years spent little time with him. In fact, when Kiichiro was born, Sakichi was working out of town in Toyohashi. He came home for the birth, but then immediately returned to Toyohashi. His mother then left to live in her parents' home and Kiichiro was raised by his grandparents. His father in 1897 remarried and returned to raise Kiichiro when he was 3, but his father was constantly working at home or traveling. Sakichi's second wife, Asako, made an effort to be sure Kiichiro had a good life and, as the eldest son and successor to the family business, had good training. She in reality raised Kiichiro and was perhaps the greatest influence on him when he was growing up (Wada and Yui, 2002).

As Sakichi Toyoda's inventions, reputation, and success grew, Kiichiro grew up in more wealthy surroundings. Yet he never thought or acted like a spoiled rich kid.

Toyoda Loom Co. was founded in 1907, with Sakichi as managing director and a major, but not majority shareholder. Sakichi's passion was invention, not mass production. In fact, perhaps as a result of this passion, the business suffered and he resigned his position in 1910, continuing as a shareholder and major influence for several years.

Sakichi then went overseas to the United States, where among other things he was amazed by the abundance of automobiles compared to Japan. There he met Jokichi Takamine, a Japanese medicine pioneer who inspired him. He learned that an inventor should never put his invention into the hands of a capitalist until it was developed as a practical product with useful social results. This inspired Sakichi to continue his research and ultimately form a new company in 1911, on his own, without partners. The company weaved cloth using Toyoda looms. In 1913, he chose a buyout option from the Toyoda Loom company which funded the Toyoda Automatic Weaving factory, later becoming Toyoda Spinning and Weaving Co., or Toyoda Boshoku.

Kiichiro Toyoda, despite being both introverted and prone to sickness, finished high school and enrolled in Tokyo Imperial University, studying engineering. By the time he finished schooling in 1920, he was knowledgeable, confident, and ambitious.

Perhaps because he was not a naturally gifted student, he developed exceptional discipline and the practice of obsessive note taking and he included in his notes elaborate sketches. His favorite subject was drafting. This ability to sketch and document would become an important skill as Kiichiro matured and began intensive study of the weaving and loom business.

In 1921, he joined Toyoda Boshuku as an employee in the spinning business making cloth. But he quickly realized there was a limit to what he could learn there and later that year, at the age of 27, headed off to the USA for one year and then to England to work for the Platt Brothers' loom company. He was encouraged by his father to see the world, who in a famous quote said: "Open the blinds and look out! There's a wide world out there!"

In the USA it is often thought he learned about automobile making, but he actually was looking at the production of automatic looms. Yet, it is probably the time in England that had the greatest impact on Kiichiro where he actually worked for the Platt Brothers, a global leader in loom making. This is where his meticulous note taking and sketching became a major asset as he recorded in great detail the technical characteristics of the looms and the process of making them.

Kiichiro was asked by his father to stay away from R&D in the looms. He should focus on the spinning business and making money for the company. Fortunately Kiichiro had too much natural inquisitiveness, and had studied every aspect of loom technology and production when working for the Platt Brothers. At first, he would sneak into the laboratory at night to do his own research on the looms. Later his father recognized his contributions and permitted him to formally engage in the loom research.

The last technical challenge to making a fully automatic loom was to develop a functioning automatic shuttle changer—changing the shuttles of thread. Kiichiro had some different ideas from his father about how to do this, but eventually built on his father's idea. In March 1938, Kiichiro got a commendation from the Imperial Institute of Invention for his patent for the automatic shuttle changer, the final piece of the puzzle for the G-Type loom.

On September 11, 1929, Toyoda Automatic Loom Works and the Platt Brothers agreed on the transfer of patent rights to the Platt Brothers. On December 21 of that year an official contract was signed for the rich sum at the time of £100,000. This was later reduced by £16,500. But this money helped finance the early beginnings of the auto business.

It is not entirely clear how Kiichiro decided to enter the automotive business. Wada and Yui (2002) note that he had doubts about the viability of the spinning and weaving business and on his second overseas trip in 1929, purportedly to investigate machine tools for the loom business, he was also trying to make a decision about whether to switch industries. He returned to Nagoya in April 1930 with the conviction to switch industries for the sake of the future and felt there was no time to waste. He had not decided on autos yet, but was in a search mode for the next business. One month after his return, he set up an automotive research room at Toyoda Automatic Loom Works. By 1933, movement into the automotive industry began fast and furiously and an automotive department was set up in the Loom Works.

As we have seen, Kiichiro played a key role in his father's automatic loom business, but is most credited for creating what is now Toyota Motor Company. Unfortunately, with technical difficulties, business challenges, and bad timing, namely World War II, the company struggled and the primary owners of the business (non-family members) accepted Kiichiro's resignation from the company he had bravely formed. Yet, his legacy, and that of Sakichi Toyoda, live on in the core values still operating in Toyota today.

Toyota Way principles in action in the forming of the companies

Just-in-time

In 1938, in an article in the industry magazine *Motor*, Kiichiro wrote some truly golden words (Toyota Way, 2001):

> I plan to cut down on the slack time within work processes and in the shipping of parts. As the basic principle in realizing this plan, I will uphold the "*Just in time*" approach. The guiding rule is not to have goods shipped too early or too late.

It was interesting that in a Japanese language text, the words "Just in time" (JIT) are written in English, as if he got the idea from his journeys abroad. But of course JIT would not be part of the common vocabulary of the business world for decades. So where did this come from?

From the book by Wada and Yui (2002), we get some clues. JIT they see as coming from his experience several times of missing trains in England and realizing that arriving one second early is waste and one second late means he will miss the train. In fact, he missed the train on his first meeting at the Platt Brothers. He had just started writing a diary and in his first entry he wrote (ibid., p. 85):

> I was supposed to leave at 11, but it dragged on till 11.30. I ran to the station, but I didn't make it on time for the train leaving Central Station at 12.20. There was nothing I could do except catch the train leaving the station at 1:15.

Wada and Yui speculate this was linked to his use of JIT in the automotive industry. They quote Jiro Iwaoka, former chairman of Aisin Seiki, a major automotive supplier in the Toyota Group, who explained:

> This happened the first time he talked when he started up in automobiles. He stuck the words "JUST IN TIME" on the wall, you see, and he said people talk about missing a train by one minute, but if you're late by a minute, or even just by a second, you won't be able to get the train. But the words "just in time" don't mean only being on time, they also mean it doesn't help to have things be on time that don't need to be.

Eyes for waste

The phrase "eyes for waste" has become common in today's lean parlance. Managers go on "waste walks" to learn to see waste. Kiichiro Toyoda developed a deep understanding of waste when he intensively studied the Platt Brothers' automatic loom making, perhaps leading to his conviction to "cut down the slack time in our work processes" in the new automotive company.

In his intensive and detailed observations, he first noted a discrepancy between the official production numbers published and the reality he saw in the shop (Wada and Yui, 2002, p. 92):

> They claim they assemble 6 or 7 machines every week in this shop, but it seems they cannot really make that figure. Workmen do some work for a short time and then soon they're idle. Certain workmen carry the frames and the other small items, but they take their time going to get them.

Kiichiro was particularly interested in the assembly of complex machines in one of the world's leading equipment makers, so observed this intensively at Platt Brothers. The company was set up with the machine in place and skilled workmen coming to the machine in turns, like Ford's original craft production of automobiles before the moving assembly line. He noted that this operation depends on each workman finishing his task within the allotted time. He also noted that very often various workmen, who at the time do not have a specific task to do on the machine, have nothing to do.

He carefully watched the production process to check the actual times for each step and totaled the hours for one machine. Based on this he calculated what they could build in a week, a month, a year. This data showed the Platt Brothers could not be making their claimed production numbers unless there were various points where the process was speeded up—like a last-minute spurt just before a delivery date.

Kiichiro was critical of the attitude and work ethic of the workmen, noting, for example (ibid., p. 93): "The workmen act as if they're half playing around; it takes them a long time to do something. It seemed to me they're only working about 3 out of 8 hours."

He also noticed waste due to poor layout. For example, the biggest part of the workman's job was fitting parts together that did not fit properly at assembly, which was in the center of the shop. But the fitting required a vise and other tools located around the walls of the assembly shop. They had to walk over with the part to file it down to adjust the fitting and go back and forth to assembly until it fit.

He did admire the quality of the finished product, but that came as a result of a lot of waste. Workmen had to meticulously file down parts to get them to fit together. We now call this waste repaired-in quality rather than the preferred built-in quality.

In these operations we get a glimpse of Kiichiro's acute eye at spotting "waste," a core concept of the Toyota Production System. He was observing the waste of waiting, excess motion, and rework. The way he wrote down his observations showed obvious distaste for any waste which he wanted to drive out of his auto shop to allow for JIT production.

Eventually Toyoda looms were made on moving assembly lines. In this case, like Henry Ford's Model T, the work is brought to the worker instead of the worker going to where the work is done. The assembly line also paces the operation so the workers either keep up with the pace or it will be obvious if they fall behind. To ensure they can do the work in the time they have before the machine moves to the next person requires standardized work—taking craft knowledge and making it explicit teachable knowledge. The right materials and tools must be at the worksite so the worker does not have to leave the line and go hunting for them, which would surely cause a halt in production that would be very visible.

In short, we see in Kiichiro Toyoda's deep observation at the Platt Brothers and his proclamation that his auto factory would follow the JIT principle and eliminate all "slack time in our work processes," the foundation of the Toyota Production System.

Leading from the gemba, learning by doing

Kiichiro seemed to be a natural at studying in detail products and production processes. He naturally dove in and observed people at work at the *gemba* (where the work is done) as we saw in the Platt Brothers' case.

His skills in doing hands-on work actually helped his father finish the "perfect automatic loom." The final challenge was automatic shuttle changing and Sakichi was struggling. Kiichiro played a major role in that and in fact the first patent he acquired was for the "automatic cop changer" in 1925. In fact, he had sketched this solution in 1922 when he was secretly conducting his own research in the evenings. Sakichi Toyoda believed in a different approach, the "shuttle change method."

Kiichiro led the effort to test his father's idea. As he described (Wada and Yui, 2002, p. 126):

> We hauled out the automatic loom Father had made years ago, and we made three more exactly like it. Next we spent two years making sure we could get thirty looms operating. During that time the original loom underwent a lot of modification. Then we built the thirty looms to the point where they were all working perfectly. When father came back from Shanghai and saw them, he was very happy.

They next decided to make two hundred looms to test, but had difficulties as Toyoda Boshuku was not equipped to manufacture them. So Kiichiro approached Toyoda Loom Co. (which his father still had some bad feelings about after being pushed out) and asked them to produce the 200 looms. They absolutely refused and claimed they in fact owned the patents the loom was based on. Kiichiro knew that in the process of making the loom they had made many changes and calmly wrote (ibid., p. 127):

> In this situation we did not panic. The reason was, in the course of our experimental manufacture of the thirty looms, various ideas came up and we tried different things, as a result of which we realized that the single-stage method of changing the shuttle that resulted from our new ideas was better than the two-stage shuttle changer of the old patent.

Thus, Kiichiro himself applied for and got the patent for the single-stage method which was the final touch to perfecting the fully automatic loom. The building and testing of the 200 looms led to continual improvement, which really opened up Kiichiro's eyes to the power of trying before going live with mass production. Kiichiro described this as follows (ibid., p. 126):

> Something happened that impressed me very much. During the testing of the 200 looms I came up with various suggestions, and [Father] tried every single one of them. Humans come up with a surprising number of useless ideas; when you actually try them out, the ones you thought were good ideas sometimes prove to be unexpectedly useless, and the ones you thought were bad ideas sometimes turn out to be unexpectedly good. This is the principle that practice is number one.

I learned of a great *gemba* story when interviewing Akio Toyoda for *Toyota Under Fire* (Liker and Ogden, 2011) about the recall crisis in the United States. We met at an internal Toyota museum commemorating Sakichi and Kiichiro Toyoda. One exhibit is a small model under glass of a scene in which there is a Toyota truck on the side of the road broken down. A Toyota car is stopped nearby and there is someone from that car with the truck owner examining the truck. The figure of that same person, Kiichiro Toyoda, is then in a Toyota building—a second time in the scene.

The story is that Kiichiro Toyoda, on seeing the broken-down truck, stopped and examined it with the driver. Seeing that the problem involved a defective part, Kiichiro drove to the R&D lab to request that they redesign the part so it would not break in that way. He then followed up to make sure that was completed and that the re-engineered part had gone into production and he followed it up in production. He then got the part delivered to the truck owner. This was *gemba* leadership at its best and showed Kiichiro's deep concern for the customer.

"Customer first" is a Toyota mantra. Ironically I was being told this story during an interview about the recall crisis. In reality, Akio Toyoda and Toyota engineers knew that claims being made about electronic causes of sudden unintended acceleration had no basis in facts—it was pure speculation and incorrect. There also was no objective evidence of an increase in quality or safety problems in Toyota vehicles. Yet, Toyota as a company always must learn from any problem and the public relations nightmare and associated costs were a huge problem. The lesson extracted was that Toyota needs to respond more quickly to customer concerns and here was Kiichiro Toyoda's example of the ideal way to respond.

Of course Toyota is now a huge global organization and it is not just a matter of driving down the road to fix a problem. But the broader implication in the current environment was that there is still a need to act quickly like a small company, despite being a globally distributed very large company. Many countermeasures were put in place including strengthening of regional autonomy so local leaders who were at the *gemba*, e.g., in the United States, could make decisions quickly without the level of central control in Japan at that time.

Standardizing processes and labor harmony

Kiichiro had noticed at Platt Brothers the problem of craft knowledge staying in the heads of workers who then controlled the work processes. Standardization was slow to come to the spinning industry. In 1912, one company, Kanebo, adopted a "scientific method" of documenting and standardizing operations and when he saw what they were doing, Kiichiro wanted to follow suit.

Workers intentionally kept their methods secret from management to maintain control and this was the current state at Toyoda Boshoku when Kiichiro first joined in 1921. Kiichiro observed that (Wada and Yui, 2002, p. 116): "the standard methods the spinning technicians were keeping to themselves were something akin to professional secrets."

At first Kiichiro had to learn these "secrets on his own" from his work with westerners spending a whole year studying the jobs. He also learned from Toyoda Boshoku's sister company, Kikui Boshoku, which had been started with the philosophy of labor–management harmony, giving shares of the company to employees.

Later Kiichiro would work hard to turn poor labor–management relations into positive ones. Standardized work in Toyota is considered essential for continuous improvement. And continuous improvement depends on all workers sharing what they learn—both successes and failures. To this day, harmonious relations form the basis for continuous improvement of processes, even when those improvements aim to eliminate processes, which eliminate the need for employees.

This requires a remarkably high level of trust that is constantly worked on by Toyota leaders, for example, by avoiding ever letting go of team members because of productivity improvements.

Self-reliance

What set Sakichi Toyoda and his early automated looms on the path to success was the quality of the cotton cloth that was clearly superior to hand-woven cloth. It therefore must have been extremely disturbing to Sakichi when a comparative assessment was conducted just before Toyota Loom Co. started operations. Compared to the automatic looms of four of the main producers, Platt Brothers came out on top in performance while the Toyoda loom did not perform well, suffering "teething problems" (Wada and Yui, 2002).

This loom was a prototype so it should not be judged too harshly, but part of the problem was the relatively low quality of the yarn. Other parts of the loom purchased from outside, such as the metal parts, were also weak points. Sakichi Toyoda used the results as motivation to make significant improvements to the loom and to reduce reliance on outside firms. For example, he studied metal parts so they could be made in-house. To solve the problem of low quality yarn, in the Spring of 1913, Sakichi added another building that would spin enough of his own thread so he could be self-sufficient.

We continue to see the strong drive for self-reliance in Toyota Motor Company today. For example, when Toyota was developing the first version of the Prius, they attempted to develop all the core technologies for this car for the future in-house, even building their own plant to make electronic circuits (Liker, 2004: Chapter 6).

An even more dramatic lesson that led to Toyota's strong tendency toward self-reliance, still talked about within Toyota today, was the resignation of Kiichiro Toyoda from his own auto company.

In 1937, Kiichiro engineered the separation of the automotive department from the labs of Toyoda Automatic Loom Works and established Toyota Motor Company. In 1941, he was named its first president. Starting a car company was even more challenging than building an automatic loom. There were thousands of parts, and so many complex components to understand, like the engine, the transmission, the braking system, and more. Kiichiro and his engineers patiently decided to learn each core technology on their own and committed to developing their own cars. Early versions were low quality and unsuccessful, but they showed the relentless spirit that has always driven Toyota when facing a challenge. They did develop a successful model, though the huge economic and business disruption of World War II and its aftermath was too much for the company and the company was struggling financially. Another critical weakness was that their cars simply were uncompetitive with those of established foreign companies like Ford and Dodge.

As a desperation measure the company proposed a cut in all wages by 10 percent and a cut in retirement payments in half. After intense negotiations the union agreed to the reductions and in exchange Kiichiro promised that the company would not dismiss any workers. Tragically he could not keep that promise. Through the tensions of trying to keep the car company going, and the tensions of these negotiations, Kiichiro's health, after years of suffering chronic high blood pressure, took a turn for the worse, and others on the management team took over decision-making. At the time the large majority of the company was owned by the original Toyoda loom and spinning businesses. The financial situation of the company continued to deteriorate and in April of 1950 they decided to eliminate 1600 jobs.

The Toyota workers went on strike. Relations between management and the union became strained—the opposite of the harmony Kiichiro strived for. Even worse, Kiichiro's personal commitment to no layoffs was violated. The union leaders actually went to Kiichiro's home to plead for his support, to which he replied (Wada and Yui, 2002, p. 305):

> I said once before that I would not dismiss anyone, but then I could not avoid dismissing some people. If now I make another promise not to dismiss anyone, it would be like lying twice. This would be very wrong of me, so forgive me, but I cannot do that.

Kiichiro Toyoda resigned as president in June, ending the labor dispute. The union and its members were shocked at his resignation as to them he was the company and they so deeply respected him. We saw evidence of this in the erection of the bronze statue after his untimely death.

As a result of the personal sacrifice and dishonor of Kiichiro, the leaders who took over the company made some critical vows. Taizo Ishida became the second president. A joint commitment was made by the union and management to work together to make the company grow so that all layoffs could be avoided in the future.

Self-reliance is still the foundation of the Toyota Motor Company today. It is said in Toyota that "we protect our own castle." In order to do this, the company must:

- continually develop and build products that consumers will trust and value;
- operate with no debt so outsiders cannot force the company to violate its values;
- continuously reduce cost to stay competitive and make enough profit to reinvest in the future of the company.

Kiichiro Toyoda and the Toyota Way

Continuous improvement and respect for people are the two pillars of *The Toyota Way*, presented in 2001 internally to Toyota as their core beliefs and principles. The foundation is the spirit of *challenge*, relentless *kaizen*, going and seeing first hand (*genchi genbutsu*), *teamwork*, and *respect.* These values were at the core of Kiichiro Toyoda's being.

The auto company eventually grew and thrived, but only by facing setback after setback with a positive outlook and the belief that through teamwork and *kaizen*—continuous improvement—every part of the company could always be improved. In fact, the core belief in these values has led to the confidence that Toyota has a huge competitive advantage—their people.

Kiichiro Toyoda is quoted in *The Toyota Way* (2001) as saying, after design plans for a loom were stolen from his father's firm:

> The thieves may be able to follow the design plans and produce a loom. But we are modifying and improving our looms every day. They do not have the expertise gained from the failures it took to produce the original. We need not be concerned. We need only continue as always.

As the Toyota Motor Company faced four years of one crisis after another: the Great Recession, the United States recall crisis, the Great East Japan Earthquake, and record flooding in Thailand, this same positive spirit was evident. Under the leadership of Kiichiro's grandson, Akio Toyoda, the company worked to solve problem after problem, finding ways to turn crisis into opportunity, and emerged with remarkable resilience, an even stronger company. It was another example of continuous improvement and respect for people—values modeled by Kiichiro Toyoda.

Note

1 There is not a great deal of documentation of the life of Kiichiro Toyoda. One exception is *Courage and Change: The Life of Kiichiro Toyoda*, by Kazuo Wada and Tsunehiko Yui, published by the Toyota Motor Corporation in English in 2002. This book is not widely available, therefore I have used it as a primary source. I do not cite every piece of information I learned from this book, but rather direct quotes.

References

Liker, J. (2004) *The Toyota Way,* New York: McGraw-Hill.

Liker, J. and Ogden, T. (2011) *Toyota Under Fire: Lessons for Turning Crisis into Opportunity,* New York: McGraw-Hill.

The Toyota Way (2001) internal Toyota Motor Company document.

Wada, K. and Yui, T. (2002) *Courage and Change: The Life of Kiichiro Toyoda,* Tokyo: Toyota Motor Company.

17

Leadership transition during intense industry change

Japan's Takara Toys

Peter St. Onge

Introduction

Entrepreneurship usually refers to opportunity discovery and firm creation (Kirzner, 1973; Gartner, 1988). Discovery and creation are no guarantee of survival, however, as firms may prove unable to sustain their competitive advantage. Research bridging corporate entrepreneurship and strategic management is a growing literature (Stevenson and Jarillo, 1990; Covin and Miles, 1999; Ireland *et al.*, 2009) that can profitably be augmented by the role of tacit knowledge (Hayek, 1945; Kirzner, 1973; Jacobson, 1992). An especially interesting challenge to the survival of the firm is that of firm succession (Shen and Cannella, 2002; George, 2007) particularly when constrained by the requirements of a family succession. This chapter examines the downfall of one of the world's largest toy firms, when faced with simultaneous leadership and industry transitions. This chapter demonstrates one dark side of entrepreneurial success; the challenge of sustaining the firm as the founder passes the baton.

Takara Toy Company was, before its merger with Tomy in 2006, Japan's second-largest and the world's fourth-largest toy company. The firm's demise is an excellent example of failed entrepreneurial venturing in an innovative Asian company with strong market share in a large but declining industry. Takara's overly-ambitious approach to needed horizontal diversification, coupled with its failure to navigate a family CEO transition, forced the firm to seek rescue in the arms of rival Tomy.

The leadership transition period (1955–2003)

The founder period

Takara was founded in 1955 by Yasuta Satoh as Satoh Vinyl Industries. Their first "hit" toy product was Dakko-chan, a vinyl doll about the size of a small dog. In 1967, the firm introduced the Licca line of dolls, similar in look to Barbie dolls, still using vinyl processing technology (Takara-Tomy, 2013). In the 1970s, Takara branched away from vinyl dolls, introducing the Microman series of action figures in 1974 and then the Penny Racers line of wind-up cars in 1980. We can clearly see production synergies at work as all these products followed the general concept of mold-focused product with increasingly complex add-on parts such as axels and wind-up engines on Penny Racers.

Takara's break-out onto the international stage came in the early 1980s with the Car-Robots series of toys that could be "transformed" into cars or robots. Rebranded as Transformers, the line became a major hit and was licensed to Hasbro for the US market. With a series of hits under their belt—Transformers, Penny Racers and Microman—on top of their bread-and-butter doll lines, Takara listed on the Second Section of the Tokyo Stock Exchange in 1986 (TakaraTomy, 2013). Toy production was still based in Japan, which maintained low labor costs; as late as 1984, labor costs in Japan were only 70 percent of the US level (FRED, 2011).

By 1988, with rising production costs squeezing margins, Takara began to branch out from its core toy business. It introduced "lifestyle" products under the Hearty Series banner, which licensed popular TV characters for products not aimed exclusively at children. Meanwhile, Takara entered the emerging industry of video games where, like other toy companies that pursued the same move, it found only modest success with games such as Fatal Fury and Samurai Showdown. Despite these modest results in videogames, with its core toy business enjoying top-line growth and with the positive market reception of the Hearty Series, the firm listed on the First Section of the Tokyo Stock Exchange (TakaraTomy, 2013).

Leadership transition to first son, Hirohisa

In 1994, after nearly 40 years at the helm, Yasuta Satoh announced his retirement, passing the reins to his first son, Hirohisa Satoh. The elder Satoh remained on the board but focused his energies on other projects such as enrolling in a PhD program despite his advanced years.

Hirohisa felt that Takara's systems for vetting new products was too informal, too intuitive, and so he introduced a five-stage review process whereby every proposed product would have to pass a series of approvals across the firm. The approvals process reduced the number of new products and Takara did not see a major hit until the 1999 Beyblade series of fighting spinning-tops. New product introductions were limited to line extensions, a category conservative enough to pass Hirohisa's strict approvals process.

Takara, like the toy industry in general, depends on hits. Demand for older products fades relatively quickly and a firm that chokes off its stream of hits will see its results rapidly erode. Hirohisa's failure to produce enough "hits" led Takara's board of directors, strongly influenced by his father Yasuta, to offer the CEO job to Yasuta's second son, Keita.

Leadership transition to second son, Keita

Keita's personality strongly contrasted with his relatively conservative brother. Keita described himself as the "black sheep" in the family and his management style was in sharp contrast to the more formal and logical model of his elder brother. In an interview contrasting his marketing style with that of his brother, he said, "My brother will go to his grave thinking he did everything he was supposed to, which for him is the most important thing" (Raskin, 2003).

Upon taking up the reins, Keita held a meeting with the R&D team and asked them "What do you really—really—want to do?" (ibid.). Takara's R&D department reacted enthusiastically, dusting off projects mothballed under Hirohisa. The first hit product under Keita came in the 2000s with the e-Kara hand-held karaoke system, followed quickly by a Japanese version of the Game of Life, Robot jellyfish, life-size Penny Racers and vintage electric cars.

One product manager in particular, Masahiko Kajita, heeded the call for lifestyle products. Kajita noticed growing demand for cell-phone accessories and felt that the market lacked fun external handsets. He prototyped several—one shaped like a mackerel, another like a high-heeled shoe, one shaped like a banana. (*CNN*, 2003). To gauge customer demand, Kajita walked about the streets of Tokyo taking calls with the prototypes and noting reactions from passers-by.

Meanwhile, Keita's promiscuous product development was concerning Takara's main bank, an influential financial partner in Japan. They were particularly concerned about his investing 100 million yen in a new dog translator styled the "Bow-Lingual." In an interview, Keita dismissed the concerns, saying: "They're bankers, so they're afraid of the risks I'm taking." He doubled-down on his high-risk style, saying,

> When my people are at the plate, I don't want them to swing for base hits. I don't even want them going for regular home runs. I want us to hit it out of the stadium and splash it in the water like [Barry Bonds].
>
> (*ibid.*)

Keita's projects became more and more ambitious. No longer content with banana-shaped head-pieces, he was investing company resources into increasingly expensive products. Aside from the Bow-Lingual dog translator, Keita announced a series of street-legal life-size Penny Racer electric cars, the Q-Car. The cars retailed for $7,490 and initial sales targets were 1,000 units per year. In his introduction, Keita noted that cars were a product that "some users even spend all they earn on" and that Takara "could contribute to this field by adding a spice of fun to electric cars through our position as a toymaker" (Nikkei BP, 2002). Given that street-legal electric cars in 2002 were a risky proposition for even non-toy manufacturers, Keita displayed a striking confidence in his ability to sense consumer demand. Indeed, he doubled-down on his aggressive marketing, announcing that Takara would launch stores called "Q-Square" to sell the $7,490 novelties and would promote charging stations shaped like vending machines (*Asahi Shimbun*, 2002). For a toy company with no automotive experience, this was quite ambitious.

In the meantime, Takara's Bow-Lingual dog translator had experienced surprising success, selling 50,000 units in Japan. Keita decided to sell the product overseas beginning with the US. The firm announced variously that 50,000 to 100,000 units would be produced for the US market and the current author was hired as marketing manager for the product, with a marketing budget approximately one hundred times higher than the previous year's. I remained in that role until 2004 when, like the elder Yasuta, I resigned from Takara to pursue my PhD.

Upon joining Takara, one of my first actions was to estimate US demand for the Bow-Lingual. I created a basket of somewhat comparable products, compared Japan-to-US sales ratios, and concluded that current sales estimates were overstated by a factor of five or more. When I raised my concerns, I was told that I should be a team-player and not be seen as pessimistic. My sense at the time was that many inside the firm felt that the US sales targets were absurd but nobody wanted to be blamed for sabotaging the team-spirit. Meanwhile, the original estimates had come merely from Keita's personal insight that, because Americans keep their dogs inside the house (not in the yard as Japanese do) implying they value their dogs more highly, then Americans would buy a lot of dog translators.

As it turned out, Bow-Lingual sales did fall dramatically short of forecasts and Takara was left with tens of thousands of units of unsold inventory. Inventory that initially retailed for $120 was ultimately cleared out, often at $5 per unit retail. Keita had gone double-or-nothing and he had lost.

Takara's failure

Merger with Tomy

Undeterred by the Bow-Lingual fiasco, Keita continued to aggressively push into new product categories requiring expensive R&D. His lead developer Kajita was not helping; in reaction to the Q-Car roll-out, Kajita said his first thought was "the next thing should be a jet," an idea he actually explored until deterred by the 80-billion yen ($650 million) development costs and the unfortunate fact that few potential customers possess pilot licenses (*Taipei Times*, 2003). Continuing his risky ventures, in 2004, Keita bought game software firm Broccoli and invested in partnerships with popular designers including "Superflat" artist Takashi Murakami. Headline-grabbing products continued, including the Dream Machine, a device to control one's dreams while sleeping, the inevitable Meow-Lingual, and a baby-cry translator (internally called the "Baby-Lingual"). The single "hit" among traditional toys over this four-year period was the Walkie Bits line of small dancing turtles—too minor to cover the ambitious investment demands of Keita's many projects.

Takara's losses mounted as its focus drifted. In January 2005, Keita was finally pushed out to a largely ceremonial role, replaced by Takara veteran Nobuyuki Okude, internally credited as the creator of the Transformers. Okude acted quickly to stem the red ink; he announced a refocus on Takara's traditional toys, terminating projects such as the electric Q-Car (*Taipei Times,* 2003). But the damage from Keita's "home runs" had been done; the company announced write-downs on April 21, 2005, for "poor sales abroad and restructuring costs" (Gibson, 2005) and within days video-game maker and long-time strategic partner Konami announced it was cutting ties, selling its Takara holdings to relatively obscure Index, a mobile content distributor. Within a year, Takara would enter into merger talks with long-time rival Tomy, seen in the industry as a rescue. Keita joined the new firm as Chief Marketing Officer, responsible for the toy business at the combined firm.

The role of demand estimation in Takara's failure

What went wrong at Takara? The critical factors revolve around Takara's failure to sustain its demand-estimation capabilities, and to extend them into new markets. This failure proved disastrous for two reasons. First, the firm was operating in an innovation-rich environment, where demand-estimation deficiencies would have a rapid and magnified impact relative to a firm less dependent on innovation. Second, the firm had a consensus among its board of directors as well as industry peers that it must exit its current industry and enter new ones. Insofar as industry migration, like new product development, involves estimating demands that can be satisfied by a firm's resources, this meant that Takara's demand-estimation failings were magnified in their performance impact. Essentially, the firm had a crippled demand-estimation capability at the very moment it needed it most.

As discussed above, the elder Yasuta had successfully extended his firm's demand-estimation capabilities to navigate Takara's early existential threat from rising costs in Japan. He had done this by shifting to higher-margin products: first with toys and then non-toy "lifestyle" goods. His efforts were not all successful; as mentioned, Yasuta's results in video-games were particularly weak. Nonetheless, Takara's evolution from knock-off vinyl dolls to Transformers displays an impressive development of demand-estimation capabilities. Takara learned what customers wanted.

The environment was very different during the leadership transition to the two sons. The Japanese toy industry in the 1990s was under twin assault: On the one hand, toy demand was shrinking as the numbers of Japanese children shrank. Indeed, Japan experienced one of history's largest peacetime reductions in its child population. At the same time, thanks to Japan's "Bubble Economy" in the 1980s, Japanese production costs had risen dramatically, even surpassing those in the USA. This eroded the long-standing competitive cost advantage of Japan's toy industry, as Japanese joined foreign competitors in simply outsourcing production to China.

Meanwhile, Japan's own relatively stagnant economy contributed. Flat incomes curtailed consumer demand for higher-end toys aimed at adult collectors, an important source of toy profits. The weak economy further restrained demand in the very sectors Keita was targeting—high-end non-toy lifestyle products. Finally, new product development from overseas firms continued. Chinese firms were absorbing lower-margin toy production, while competitors, especially in the USA, continued introducing new products, now with access to cost parity via Chinese production.

Takara was perhaps unlucky in going through a leadership transition during this period. While leadership transitions are common in firms, Takara's transition was particularly challenging for two reasons: first, the firm was transitioning from a dominant founder who had run the firm for 40 years. Second, leadership was being transferred to a very small candidate population—in practice, only two possible candidates: Yasuta's two sons. We may expect a leadership transition to be traumatic and risky after a 40-year reign of a founder, but constrained to only two candidates, we might be surprised if things did go well at all.

Keita's influence on Takara's demand-estimation capabilities

Keita Satoh, it turns out, over-emphasized his ability to intuitively estimate demand. Whether this was a conscious or unconscious reaction against his elder brother's overly-analytical approach, the results were a never-ending escalation of new product gambles, each more ambitious than the last. Like a gambler compelled to double-down every play, once Keita had started on this path, it was only a matter of time before his bets would blow up.

As if Keita needed more encouragement in his gambles, the Takara turnaround story became a media favorite and Keita was lionized by the media. A fawning best-selling book, *Takara no Yama* (a pun meaning both "Takara's Challenge" and "Mountain of Treasure") was even published about his turnaround. Copies of the book were handed to employees, one senses more for vanity than training. Keita was warming to his media image, which did not help to restrain his increasingly grandiose projects. Worse, his media-image was increasingly painting him in a corner, strategically. That is, once the firm emerged into the limelight, reporters begin to track its narrative more closely. A CEO who trumpets a shift into new headline-grabbing categories may find it hard to reverse the strategic shift without reporters coming to the conclusion that the firm is "floundering" strategically. To avoid this problem, Keita could have represented his "lifestyle" products as evolutions of Takara's core business, giving the media a narrative that can be reversed in the future. Instead, he framed his new products as a break with Takara's core business, a frame that is difficult to undo.

Finally, Keita was given too much freedom by his board. His father remained influential, personally and through substantial minority holdings. This lack of constraint was initially positive, as Keita allowed his R&D staff, not spreadsheets, to make product decisions in an industry where demand-estimation is fundamentally subjective. However, drunk with early success and enjoying the media limelight, this lack of constraint led Keita to take progressively bigger risks until he ultimately over-played his hand. Had Keita's demand-estimation been sound, this lack of constraint might have allowed him to build the firm to great success. In reality, because Keita's demand-estimation was not sound, because his gambles were not particularly wise, lack of constraint instead led the firm to failure.

Lessons from Takara's failure

Constrained leadership transitions

Family leadership transitions are generally bad for firms. Bennedsen *et al.* (2006) find "a large negative causal impact on firm performance" with operating profitability on assets falling by "at least four percentage points" around family CEO transitions. Reflecting these difficulties, Handler and Kram (1988) find that "only 30 percent of the family firms in the United States survive the transition to the second generation, and only 10 percent make it to the third generation." Notably for Takara, the Bennedsen *et al.* (2006) study finds that "family-CEO underperformance is particularly large in fast-growing industries, industries with highly skilled labor force, and relatively large firms." Takara checks most of these boxes: it was in a fast-innovating industry, had a highly-skilled labor force (with actual production off-shored) and was one of the largest firms in the industry.

Why such difficulties in family transitions? I propose an explanation that does not rely on psychological themes (Handler and Kram, 1988) but rather draws on an approach used in Daron Acemoglu's (2008) work on oligarchies. This begins with the trivial statistical observation that drawing from a smaller sample size reduces the likelihood of outliers. This implies that a CEO hunt constrained to a few people is unlikely to discover a particularly qualified candidate. In Acemoglu's work, the constrained population of an oligarchy tends to lower expected competence. Oligarchies' comparative advantage in entrepreneurship deteriorates over time, raising the costs of barriers to entry. So, too, limiting transition to family reduces expected competency by sample size alone, while the second and third generations should, logically, have a smaller expected competence boost from selection effects. Handler and Kram's (1988) results above suggest such deterioration occurs at the firm level, as each generation becomes less likely to enjoy comparative advantage in entrepreneurship, thus the costs of excluding outsiders rise, evidenced by an approximately linear decline in survival rates by generation.

Logically, we would expect weaker versions of this oligarchic penalty to occur any time leadership choice is constrained, for example, by nationality, gender, or social relationship. Logically, the constraint would have a greater effect, the more it actually restricts sample size. The problem, of course, is that with such a small pool of potential leaders, the probability of choosing an inappropriate leader approaches certainty.

To counter this problem requires a clear-headed recognition that the pool-restriction itself statistically lowers the expected competence of the new CEO. This would recommend measures to initially limit the discretion of the CEO, allowing them to "grow into" their new responsibilities. Executive functions can be devolved to a lower level, remaining in the hands of experienced managers until the CEO has proven their competence in the area. Like Acemoglu's democracy, this distributes power to people more likely to wield it competently. The approach would resemble incentive trusts used in inheritance, where money is doled out as performance targets are met. In this case it would be decision-making power that is being doled out as performance targets are met. Indeed, Takara's second-generation CEOs may well have grown into their positions had they not been given so much responsibility at once.

In contrast to the standard apprenticeship model, where a favorite candidate is groomed for the role via training, this conditional escalation of power model allows the CEO to be gradually tested in the job, winning powers commensurate with their competency. This escalation of responsibility mechanism is particularly important when a constrained-pool CEO will be responsible for demand-estimation. MIT's Clay Christensen has claimed that up to 95 percent of all new consumer products fail (Nobel, 2011). In an industry with slow-moving product cycles, an untested CEO may indeed have time to learn on the job. On the other hand, in an industry where new product introductions are frequent, as in toys, the difficulties of developing and managing demand-estimation may prove fatal to the company before the CEO ever has a chance to find their footing.

If a firm is destined to fall in the hands of an untested leader, gradual escalation of responsibilities would allow a feedback mechanism that could limit damage to the organization. A truly incompetent CEO nevertheless handed the firm for family reasons would then, at worst, be a figurehead CEO with executive power resting one layer below.

Sustaining dynamic demand-estimating capabilities

A second strategic area informed by Takara's experience is in the dynamic nature of demand-estimation capabilities. Forecasting is an inherently difficult task, with a very high failure rate, as noted above. Interestingly, Takara's success rate in new product introduction was not random; the firm enjoyed long periods of success, followed by long periods of failure. As discussed above, both the founder, Yasuta, and his second son, Keita, enjoyed strings of successes, and strings of failures.

How to account for apparent changes in a firm's ability to estimate which products will enjoy customer valuations above production costs? Why do firms apparently fluctuate in their ability to process external information?

A possible solution exists in the Hayekian concept of "tacit" knowledge (Hayek, 1945, 1978). For Hayek, knowledge could be divided into two categories: that which is observable and that which is unobservable (Jacobson, 1992). This second is "tacit" knowledge. Hayek writes: "the knowledge of the circumstances of which we must make use never exists in concentrated or integrated form but solely as the dispersed bits of incomplete and frequently contradictory knowledge which all the separate individuals possess" (Hayek, 1945). Kirzner contrasts this view of tacit knowledge with what he terms "orthodox price theory" based on "perfect knowledge . . . with resource owners aware of all selling possibilities, and with firms aware of all possible cost and revenue conditions" (Kirzner, 1973).

Hayekian tacit knowledge implies that new-product introduction involves, not just risk, but Knightian uncertainty (Knight, [1921] 2009) whereby the degree of risk cannot even be measured, a concept sometimes called "radical uncertainty" and a useful analytical tool that drives, for examples, Nassim Taleb's recent critique of financial markets (Taleb, 2007).

In the Hayekian framework, then, competition is a "discovery process" (Hayek, 1978) with unknown parameters. This process relies on knowledge that is distributed, is often unknowable concretely ("unobservable") and as such tacitly resides in the head, as it were, of individuals. Further, thanks to Knightian uncertainty, that discovery process aims at an unknown target (indeed, unknown with unknown probability) that must therefore be tacitly sensed by the strategist. Variation in new product success rates in firms may consist, then, of differences in availability or use of tacit knowledge, as often occurs with shifts in decision-making influences. We would expect these shifts to occur with both personnel changes and organizational restructuring, explicit or implicit.

A nice illustration of this process can be seen in Takara, where various regimes radically changed new product decision-making dynamics and subsequently enjoyed strings of successes and failures. Taking Takara's tacit new product regimes in turn, forecasting of sales was done implicitly under founder Yasuta, relying on his sense of what customers want rather than formal modeling. The first son tried to rationalize this process, while maintaining a top-down approach. In contrast, the second son imitated the founder's intuitive style but without, it turns out, the same good demand-estimation intuition. On paper, Keita ruled as Yasuta, but in reality his own demand-estimation intuitions subtracted from, rather than added to, the firm's ability to accurately estimate demand.

The results of these three regimes were that, under Yasuta the company went from imitator (Licca) to innovator (Transformers) an impressive display of demand-estimation sense. First son Hirohisa seemed to understand his own demand-estimation limitations, relying on restrictive rational standards. But what he may have seen as abdicating in favor of rationality actually, in practice, became just as top-down as his father but now with spreadsheets as the glove on his hand that could not estimate demand. In contrast, Keita seemed to have a reasonable ability to sense value in toys (e-Kara, Walkie Bits) but unfortunately gave maniacal reign to his demand-estimation ability, trying his weak hand at demand-sensing in lifestyle and as far as the automotive industry.

A consistent theme in Takara's family leadership transitions, indeed Takara's entire history, has thus been a centrally-focused demand-estimation process centered on the CEO. Both new product decisions and actual forecasts of units sold were influenced "top-down." While this structure appears to have worked for the founder, who apparently had a very good intuition of consumer demand, his sons struggled with the enormous power the structure invested in the executive role.

This analysis would recommend a conscious effort by firms to discover where their tacit demand-estimation knowledge resides; who holds it, and what are the internal dynamics governing how it is used or valued. They must understand what unobservable tacit knowledge has created or sustained their success. Second, make a conscious effort to sustain and extend the use of valuable tacit knowledge that survives changes in personnel and organizational structures. A CEO transition would, logically, be a particularly threatening moment for a well-functioning tacit knowledge capability, a moment well-illustrated by Takara's fall.

Exit from a declining industry

A third strategic challenge informed by the Takara experience is defensive industry migration—shifting out of one's core business into an area with brighter prospects. While much of the literature on exit considers it a form of "regress" (Ghemawat and Nalebuff, 1990) or groups it together with "failure" (Jensen, 1993) we can re-use much of the analysis of the preceding section on innovation. That is, exit can be seen economically as simply a re-allocation of resources. Just as new product development involves re-allocating resources to new lines, so too an industry migration involves re-allocating resources to a new set of products. Therefore, just as new product innovation depends on tacit knowledge, so too industry migration should be successful to the degree it takes account of tacit knowledge about both consumer preferences and resources available.

Using the resource-based view (Wernerfelt, 1984; Langlois and Foss, 1999) we can consider both new product introduction and exit as operating on the same principles, whereby firms have at their disposal certain resources or capabilities, and must use their knowledge, observable as well as tacit, to estimate the best use of those resources in future. The future is always unknowable (von Mises, 1996) so tacit knowledge becomes an increasingly important component of a firm's strategic choice as that choice impacts a longer time horizon. On this logic, tacit knowledge should be even more important in industry migration than new product development: to the extent that a change of industry may impact a longer future horizon than a mere product introduction, tacit knowledge may properly play a dominant role in migration strategies.

In the case of Takara, as discussed above, the Japanese toy industry in the 1990s was casting about for new industries to enter, in response to falling margins in the toy business. Japanese toy production was migrating to China-based contract manufacturers, reducing the importance of production synergies available to the toy firms. Paradoxically, outsourcing of production left Takara less guidance in industry migration. Like the rest of its industry, Takara's contribution to production was increasingly limited to R&D; it was shifting from a manufacturer to a designer.

With production outsourced, the industry in practice turned to marketing synergies. Logically, marketing synergies leverage two valuable assets: brand equity among a particular customer segment, and demand-estimation capabilities for a particular segment. Takara's diversification efforts almost exclusively focused on this second synergy, a sense of what consumers want—in practice, they embraced the designer role and sought to expand the range of what they designed. While Takara did enjoy modest success at transferring this capability from toys into lifestyle products and video-games, in practice, Hirohisa and Keita's dominance of the demand-estimation function appears to have crowded out what may otherwise have been a competent transfer of demand-estimation capability.

Lessons for other firms

Takara faced two common key challenges of demand-estimation at the same time without a clear idea of exactly why its demand-estimation had been successful in the past. It simultaneously pursued the industry-wide consensus need to shift to a new industry just as it was navigating a family-based CEO change. Each challenge should have been approached with a careful tending of the firm's tacit demand-sensing capabilities, which the firm failed to manage.

What lessons does Takara hold for other firms to respond to the demand-estimation shocks of leadership transitions and industry migration? First, a firm needs to concretely identify why its demand-sensing works well. If it doesn't work well, go back to the period when it did work and ask what has changed. Any significant firm will have had a period of successful demand-estimation (a trivial statistical observation based on survivorship) which is exactly how the firm became significant in the first place. So the first task in protecting and promoting the demand-estimation process is to explicitly understand how it works when it works.

Second, a new CEO should tread carefully in changing demand-estimation. Product introduction is a radically uncertain process, with a high rate of failure, and demand-estimation involves tacit knowledge that includes a blend of rational and intuitive sense. A new CEO should treat their own personal demand-estimation abilities as "on probation" until they have been validated.

If the firm's demand-estimation capabilities, and the forecasts it creates, are not at least understood, then it may be very easy for a new leader to "blunder" in and upset a process that had heretofore worked very well. In the case of Takara, because the existing demand-estimation capability was not recognized, it became very easy for the new CEOs to replace it with spreadsheets in the one case and with personal whims in the second.

Conclusion

The fall of Takara Toys as an independent company is a fascinating case study into the optimal degree of innovation, expansion, and the unique challenges posed to both areas in a leadership transition. Takara faced a number of simultaneous transitions that it was ultimately unable to successfully navigate. In this chapter I have argued that Takara's failures can be summarized as a failure to sustain and extend its tacit demand-estimation capabilities. Takara's experience may serve as a cautionary tale, helping firms refine and make explicit their tacit knowledge as it relates to product and industry strategies, and to curate this knowledge so that it can survive changes in personnel and organizational structure.

References

Acemoglu, D. (2008) "Oligarchic versus democratic societies," *Journal of the European Economic Association,* 6(1): 1–44.

Asahi Shimbun (2002) "Toymaker Takara to market real cars," January 24. Available at: www.electrifying times.com/takara.html (accessed 10 April 2013).

Bennedsen, M., Nielsen, K.M., Pérez-González, F. and Wolfenzon, D. (2006) "Inside the family firm: the role of families in succession decisions and performance," Working Paper. National Bureau of Economic Research, July.

CNN (2003) "Dog translation device coming to U.S.," March 24. Available at: http://edition.cnn.com/2003/TECH/biztech/03/24/tech.dogs.language.reut/ (accessed 10 April 2013).

Covin, J.G. and Miles, M.P. (1999) "Corporate entrepreneurship and the pursuit of competitive advantage," *Entrepreneurship Theory and Practice,* 23(3): 47–64.

FRED (2011) *Unit Labor Costs in Manufacturing, U.S. Dollar Basis, in Japan (JPNULCM)* Federal Reserve Economic Data, Federal Reserve Bank of St. Louis. Available at: http://research.stlouisfed.org/fred2/series/JPNULCM (accessed 10 April 2013).

Gartner, W.B. (1988) " 'Who is an entrepreneur?' is the wrong question," *American Journal of Small Business,* 12(4): 11–32.

George, B. (2007) "An embarrassment of succession fiascoes," *Business Week,* Nov. 29.

Ghemawat, P. and Nalebuff, B. (1990) "The devolution of declining industries," *The Quarterly Journal of Economics,* 105(1): 167.

Gibson, E. (2005) "Konami cuts ties with Takara," April 25, *Games Industry International.* Available at: www.gamesindustry.biz/articles/konami-cuts-ties-with-takara (accessed 10 April 2013).

Handler, W.C. and Kram, K.E. (1988) "Succession in family firms: the problem of resistance," *Family Business Review,* 1(4): 361–381.

Hayek, F.A. (1945) "The use of knowledge in society," *American Economic Review,* 35(September): 519–530.

Hayek, F.A. (1978) *New Studies in Philosophy, Politics and Economics,* Chicago: University of Chicago Press.

Ireland, R.D., Covin, J.G. and Kuratko, D.F. (2009) "Conceptualizing corporate entrepreneurship strategy," *Entrepreneurship Theory and Practice,* January: 19–46.

Jacobson, R. (1992) "The 'Austrian' School of strategy," *The Academy of Management Review,* 17(4): 782.

Jensen, M.C. (1993) "The modern industrial revolution, exit, and the failure of internal control systems," *The Journal of Finance,* 48(3): 831–880.

Kirzner, I.M. (1973) *Competition and Entrepreneurship,* Chicago: University of Chicago Press.

Knight, F.H. ([1921] 2009) *Risk, Uncertainty, and Profit,* Kissimmee, FL: Signalman Publishing, 2009.

Langlois, R.N. and Foss, N.J. (1999) "Capabilities and governance: the rebirth of production in the theory of economic organization," *Kyklos,* 52(2): 201–218.

Nikkei, B.P. (2002) "Takara unveils electric vehicles," January 22. Available at: www.electrifyingtimes.com/takara.html (accessed 10 April 2013).

Nobel, C. (2011) 'Clay Christensen's milkshake marketing," *Harvard Business School Working Knowledge, item #6496.* Available at: http://hbswk.hbs.edu/item/6496.html (accessed 10 April 2013).

Raskin, A. (2003) "How a banana saved a company," March 1, *Business 2.0 Magazine.* Available at: http://money.cnn.com/magazines/business2/business2_archive/2003/03/01/338109/ (accessed 10 April 2013).

Shen, W. and Cannella, A.A. Jr. (2002) "Revisiting the performance consequences of CEO succession: the impacts of successor type, post-succession senior executive turnover, and departing CEO tenure," *Academy of Management Journal,* 45: 717–733.

Stevenson, H.H. and Jarillo, J.C. (1990) "A paradigm of entrepreneurship: entrepreneurial management," *Strategic Management Journal,* 11: 17–27.

Taipei Times (2003) "Takara reinvents playing around," April 7. Available at: http://taipeitimes.com/News/worldbiz/archives/2003/04/07/201208 (accessed 10 April 2013).

TakaraTomy (2013) "Corporate history." Available at: www.takaratomy.co.jp/english/company/company/history.html (accessed 10 April 2013).

Taleb, N. (2010) *The Black Swan: The Impact of the Highly Improbable,* New York: Random House.

von Mises, L. (1996) *Human Action: A Treatise on Economics,* Irvington-on-Hudson, NY: Foundation for Economic Education.

Wernerfelt, B. (1984) "A resource-based view of the firm," *Strategic Management Journal,* 5(2): 171–180.

18

The Sony Corporation

Market leadership, innovation failure and the challenges of business reinvention

Richard A. Gershon

Introduction

The Sony Corporation is a leading transnational media corporation in the production and sale of consumer electronics, music, film entertainment and videogame technology. Throughout its 60-plus-year history, the Sony name has been synonymous with great innovation. During that time, Sony introduced a number of firsts in the development of new communication products. Words like Walkman, compact disc, and PlayStation have become part of the global lexicon of terms to describe consumer electronics (Beamish, 1999). Such products were truly revolutionary from a planning and design standpoint. They have contributed to a profound change in consumer lifestyle.

Innovation failure

In 1942, Joseph Schumpeter introduced the principle of *creative destruction* as a way to describe the disruptive process that accompanies the work of the entrepreneur and the consequences of innovation. In time, companies that once revolutionized and dominated select markets give way to rivals who are able to introduce improved product designs, offer substitute products and services and/or lower manufacturing costs. The resulting outcome of creative destruction can be significant including the failure to preserve market leadership, the dissolution of a once highly successful product line or business failure itself. Starting in 2002, Sony saw the beginning of a decade-long decline in major product development. In June 2012, Sony's stock price fell below the 1,000 yen barrier (£8.30) for the first time since 1980, representing a 75 percent decline in the company's stock value (Hartung, 2012). The following case study analysis presents a unique opportunity to look at a modern media company and the problems associated with preserving market leadership. Specifically, this chapter will address the following question; why do good companies fail to remain innovative over time? Special attention is given to five contributory reasons that have led to Sony's current decline. They include: (1) the tyranny of success; (2) executive leadership failures; (3) the challenges of a disruptive technology; (4) a risk-averse culture; and (5) lengthy development times and poor coordination. Today's Sony Corporation now finds itself in the fight of its life for business survival.

Historical overview

The Sony Corporation was founded by Masaru Ibuka in the months following Japan's defeat in World War II. In September 1945, Ibuka left the countryside, where he had sought refuge from the bombings, and returned to the war-torn capital of Tokyo to begin a new business. Shortly thereafter, Ibuka established the Tokyo Tsushin Kenkyujo (Tokyo Telecommunications Research Institute). In the beginning, the new start-up company was nothing more than a few individuals who occupied a small space on the third floor of the Shirokiya Department Store in Nihonbashi. It became the workshop for Ibuka and his newly founded group (Sony, 1988, p. 22).

During its initial start-up, Ibuka's shop was primarily in the business of radio repair. Ibuka and his small group of engineers made shortwave adapters that could convert medium-wave radio receivers into superheterodyne (or all-wave) receivers. The shortwave adapters caught the attention of the public and a feature article appeared in the *Asahi Shimbun* newspaper (Kaiji, 1945). One such reader of the *Asahi Shimbum* article was Akio Morita who had returned home to Kosugaya in Aichi Prefecture. Morita knew Ibuka from their past association on Japan's Wartime Research Committee. The article prompted Morita to write to Ibuka who replied at once. He urged Morita to come to Tokyo and join him in the start-up of this new business venture (Gershon and Kanayama, 2002).

Ibuka and Morita officially incorporated the new company as the Tokyo Tsushin Kokyo (Totsuken) or the Tokyo Telecommunications Engineering Corporation on May 7, 1946. The new start-up company had a capital investment of ¥190,000 (or $500). The founding of the company spoke directly to the challenges of post-war Japan and the need to rebuild. At the time, Ibuka was 38 and Morita was 25. Both were knowledgeable and enthusiastic engineers. And both understood the importance of what new technology meant to the future of Japan and their company in particular.

From the outset, Totsuken's most immediate problem was financing. In order to meet the payroll bills, Totsuken manufactured both communication and non-related devices, including electric rice cookers and heat cushions. One of Totsuken's first important contracts was issued by Japan's NHK television service which had an urgent need to restore its national broadcasting network. This included the repair of its many studios and transmitters. It would mark the beginning of a long-standing business relationship between the future Sony Corporation and NHK. Throughout the late 1940s, the engineers at Totsuken concentrated on the development of consumer electronic goods, including Japan's first ever tape recorder (Sony, 1986, p. 3).

Establishing the Sony name

During the early 1950s, Japanese products suffered from a public perception of poor quality. The description "made in Japan" evoked an impression of inferior product quality in design and manufacturing. At the time, Morita reasoned that if Sony was going to start the manufacture and sales of electronic equipment, it was necessary to establish a market presence in the USA (Morita *et al.*, 1986). In 1952, Morita made the first of two trips to America to examine how US companies manufacture and market tape recorders. He also wanted to examine potential market opportunities for future Totsuken exports. During Morita's second trip in 1953, he acquired the licensing rights to the transistor patent which was invented at AT&T's Bell Labs. Due to Morita's effort, Totsuken was the first company in East Asia that was licensed by AT&T to manufacture and use the transistor in new product designs. In 1955, Totsuken developed the TR-55 transistor radio in Japan and introduced it to the US market that same year (Sony, 1988). A year later,

Totsuken was able to successfully improve on the transistor radio and produced the TR-63: the world's smallest pocket radio. The newly developed radio had the name "Sony" (derived from the Latin word *sonus* for sound) affixed to it. The name Sony soon became more familiar in the world of international electronics than the parent company. At the time, Morita believed that Totsuken was not a name that would be easily understood overseas. Thus, despite much internal disagreement, the company's name was officially changed to Sony in January 1958.

Sony's entry into world markets

Most companies do not set out with an established plan to become a major international company. Rather, as a company's exports steadily increase, it establishes a foreign office to handle the sales and services of its products (Robock and Simmonds, 1989; Gershon, 2007).

Early on in his tenure, Akio Morita developed the kind of business skills that allowed him to successfully enter foreign markets. He did not initially have a global strategy in mind. Morita tended to operate in those markets that he believed were important and where Sony's products would be readily accepted. The USA represented the first step in realizing that objective. The first phase of Sony's international expansion plans was the creation of the Sony Corporation of America in 1960. The company established its first showroom in New York City. During the next few years, Sony established locations in Switzerland, the UK, Germany and France.

The Trinitron television set

Throughout the 1960s, the Sony Corporation achieved a number of firsts in product design and innovation, including the portable videotape recorder, the transistor condenser microphone and the integrated radio circuit. One of the more notable discoveries came in 1968 when Sony engineers unveiled a new approach to color television technology. The Trinitron TV set was the culmination of a ten-year attempt to find a better way to produce a color television set (Sony, 1988). It was the most successful display monitor of its kind, outperforming its rivals both in terms of sales and the versatility of applications. The Trinitron TV set proved to be a real turning point in the history of the company. Says Ibuka, "We bet the company on that basic technology" (Schlender, 1992, p. 82).

The Sony Walkman

The creation of Sony's highly popular Walkman portable music player was serendipitous in its origins. From 1966 onward, Sony and other Japanese manufacturers began the mass production of cassette tapes and recorders in response to a growing demand. At first, cassette tape recorders could not match the sound quality of reel-to-reel recorders and were mainly used as study aids and for general purpose recording. By the late 1970s, audio quality had steadily improved and the stereo tape cassette machine had become a standard fixture in many homes and automobiles.

It so happened that Masaru Ibuka (who was then honorary Chairman of Sony) was planning a trip to the USA. Despite the heavy weight of the machine, Ibuka would often take a TC-D5 reel-to-reel tape machine when he traveled. This time, however, he asked Norio Ohga for a simple, stereo playback version. Ohga contacted Kozo Ohsone, general manager of the tape recorder business division. Ohsone had his staff alter a Pressman stereo cassette by removing the recording function and had them convert it into a portable stereo playback device. When Ibuka returned from his US trip he was quite pleased with the unit, even if it had large headphones and no recording capability (Nathan, 1999, pp. 150–155).

Ibuka soon went to Morita (then Chairman) and said, "Try this. Don't you think a stereo cassette player that you can listen to while walking around is a good idea?" (Sony, 1996, p. 207). Morita took it home and tried it out over the weekend. He immediately saw the possibilities. In February 1979, Morita called a meeting of staff that included a number of the company's electrical and mechanical design engineers. He instructed the group that this product would enable someone to listen to music anytime, anywhere. It was understood that the target market was to be students and young people and that it should be introduced just prior to the summer vacation of that year. As Nathan (1999, p.152) writes: "The Walkman project was founded on Morita's certainty and determination; there was no conventional development process, and no market testing. From the outset, Morita insisted that the product must be affordable to teenagers."

Akio Morita was the quintessential marketer. He understood how to translate new and interesting technologies into usable products. After rejecting several names, the publicity department came up with the name "Walkman." The product name was partially inspired by the movie *Superman* and Sony's existing Pressman portable tape cassette machine (Sony, 1996). The Walkman created an altogether new market for portable music systems and unleashed an important change in consumer lifestyle.

The Sony/Philips compact disc

In the early 1960s, the general junction laser was developed at MIT's Lincoln Labs and later improved at Bell Research Labs. But it was Sony and the Philips Corporation that would refine the idea into the modern compact disc (CD). In 1975, the optical and audio teams at Sony and Philips began work on the digital recording of information on to laser discs. Sony President Norio Ohga, a former student of music, was enamored with the possibilities of digital recording. He designated a small group of Sony engineers to give the laser disc top priority.

In the meantime, Philips' audio division lab in Eindhoeven, Holland, was busy at work on their own version of the optical laser disc. A decision was eventually made to create a joint partnership between the two companies. From 1979–1982, both teams of engineers worked together to refine the CD player (Gershon and Kanayama, 2002). Demonstrations of the CD were made worldwide in preparation for the planned launch of the CD in October 1982. Norio Ohga was convinced that the compact disc would eventually replace records, given the technology's superior sound quality. At the same time, Ohga recognized that the development of the CD would meet with fierce resistance from many in the recording industry who felt threatened by CD technology. To many observers, the CD format was an unproven technology made by hardware people who knew nothing about the software side of the business. Worse still, the conversion to a CD format would require enormous sums of money while potentially destabilizing the entire music industry.

In 1968, Sony entered into a joint partnership with CBS Records to form CBS/Sony Records. That partnership would prove vital in promoting the cause of CD technology. On August 31, 1982, an announcement was made in Tokyo that four companies: Sony, CBS, Philips and Polygram had jointly developed the world's first CD system. In time, the Sony/Philips CD became the de facto standard throughout the industry. By 1986, sales of CDs had topped 45 million titles annually, overtaking records to become the principal recording format. CD technology would ultimately redefine the field of recording technology and spawn a whole host of new inventions, including the portable CD music stereo, the digital video disc (DVD) and the CD-based videogame console (Gershon and Kanayama, 2002).

The Sony PlayStation

The Sony PlayStation was the brainchild of an engineer named Ken Kutaragi, who was fascinated with designing an entertainment device that could combine the power of a computer workstation with high resolution graphics. For two years, Kutaragi operated without a sponsor until his friend, Teruo "Terry" Tokunaka, a senior executive at Sony, interceded on his behalf. Tokunaka took Kutaragi to see Norio Ohga in order to discuss his idea. Ohga was so impressed that he authorized Kutaragi to begin building a working prototype of his videogame console (Asakura, 2000). Not everyone at Sony was enamored with the idea of videogame technology. For some Sony executives, videogame technology was seen as a toy. Worse still, companies like Nintendo and Sega were the established leaders in videogame technology and software. Nevertheless, Sony's Executive Planning Committee approved $50 million in start-up costs in order to allow Kutaragi and his design team to develop the basic computer chip necessary for a future videogame console.

Sony was now faced with the task of having to convince the major software developers to create innovative games to support the new platform system. Sony's future success would depend on high quality software games. In November 1993, Sony Computer Entertainment (SCE) was created for the purpose of marketing and licensing videogame consoles and titles. The new company was compiled from various parts of Sony (Asakura, 2000). One of the most critical elements to the new Sony videogame platform was the use of CD technology instead of the existing 16-Bit cartridge. It was recognized that the CD possessed greater storage capacity than a videogame cartridge and was much cheaper to produce (Gershon and Kanayama, 2002).

On December 3, 1994, the Sony PlayStation was launched in Japan with eight game titles. The PlayStation was launched a year later in the USA and achieved immediate success. By 2004 (some ten years later), Sony had sold an estimated 100 million units worldwide. Today, PlayStation includes an online service with over 70 million users worldwide. It comprises an online virtual market, the PlayStation Store, which allows the purchase and downloading of games, a subscription-based online service known as PlayStation Plus and a social gaming networking service called PlayStation Home.

Music and film entertainment

The Sony Corporatio's entry into music and film entertainment was a direct response to a triggering event. By the late 1970s, the videocassette recorder (VCR) for home use was beginning to take off. In the USA, there was no industry standard for home VCR use. As early as 1975, Sony had already begun promoting its own proprietary standard with the introduction of its half-inch Betamax VCR. In the meantime, several of Japan's other major consumer electronics companies, most notably Panasonic and Japan Victor, rallied around a different standard called VHS. After several years of competition, VHS became the de facto standard largely due to cost and widespread availability.

In retrospect, Sony made two critical errors in planning. The first was the lack of film and television programming that was exclusively available on the Betamax format. The second mistake was to propose Betamax as an industry standard, while insisting that every Betamax VCR set carry the Sony name. JVC, by contrast, promoted an open VHS standard and let others manufacture its system under license. As the VHS format became more commonly accepted, several of Hollywood's premiere film studios would no longer release films using the Betamax format (Compaine and Gomery, 2000). By 1984, VHS had acquired 90 percent of the world market. The resulting failure cost the Sony Corporation billions of dollars in lost revenue and time (Muneshige, 1991).

The lessons of the Betamax experience, however, proved very instructive. In future, Sony would make a firm commitment to software development as part of an enhanced strategy for selling its technical equipment. To that end, Sony entered the world of music and film entertainment with the $2 billion purchase of CBS Records Inc. in 1988 and $3.4 billion acquisition of Columbia Pictures in 1989. The Columbia purchase included two film studios, a television unit and the Loews theater chain ("Media Colossus," 1991). In doing so, Sony firmly believed that ownership of music and film entertainment would provide a critical leverage in promoting its technical business. The company was renamed Sony Pictures Entertainment on August 7, 1991.

During the 1980s, Sony adhered to Morita's philosophy of global/localization. In principle, the foreign manager is selected based on a presumed knowledge of local business conditions. The idea, while correct in principle, was difficult to implement in practice. A telling example of what can go wrong in terms of managing a foreign subsidiary can be seen with the Columbia Pictures acquisition. Throughout the early 1990s, Sony sustained repeated losses. Wall Street was highly critical of Sony's performance. In 1994, Sony was forced to take corrective action, but not before writing off an estimated $3.2 billion in losses through its foreign investment in Columbia Pictures. The Columbia Pictures débâcle was the result of poor performance at the box office combined with excessive spending on the part of then Columbia Pictures CEO, Peter Guber, and his associate partner, Jon Peters. In the end, it came down to poor management oversight between Sony's Tokyo headquarters and its Hollywood subsidiary (Gershon, 1997). According to then SCA President, Howard Stringer, the Sony culture was scarred from the Columbia Pictures disaster (Gunther, 2001).

Organizational structure

On March 27, 2012, Sony announced the establishment of a new management structure led by President and CEO Kazuo Hirai. The proposed organizational changes are intended to drive revitalization and growth across Sony's six primary business areas: (1) Electronics; (2) Game; (3) Music; (4) Pictures; (5) Mobile Products and Communications; and (6) Financial Services (see Table 18.1).

Table 18.1 The SONY Corporation: organizational structure and primary business areas

Division	*Primary business areas*
1 Consumer Products and Services	Home Entertainment and Sound The HE&S segment includes the Televisions and Audio and Video categories. Televisions includes LCD/LED televisions; Audio and Video includes home audio, Blu-ray DiscTM players and recorders, and memory-based portable audio devices. Games Sony Computer Entertainment (SCE) is best known for producing the popular line of PlayStation videogame consoles. Imaging Products and Solutions The IP&S segment includes the Digital Imaging Products and Professional Solutions categories. Digital Imaging Products includes compact digital cameras, video cameras and interchangeable single-lens cameras; Professional Solutions includes broadcast- and professional-use products.

(Continued)

Table 18.1 (Continued)

Division	*Primary business areas*
2 Professional Devices and Solutions	The Devices segment includes the Semiconductors and Components categories. Semiconductors includes image sensors; Components includes batteries, recording media and data recording systems.
3 Music	SME is the second-largest music recording company in the world and is controlled by Sony Corporation of America. The company owns full or partial rights to the catalogues of Michael Jackson, the Beatles, Usher, Eminem, Adele, Beyoncè and others.
4 Pictures	SPE is the television and film production/distribution unit of Sony. With 12.5% box office market share in 2011, the company was ranked third among movie studios.
5 Mobile Products and Communications	On February 15, 2012, Sony acquired Ericsson's 50% equity interest in Sony Ericsson, and changed its name to Sony Mobile Communications having become a wholly owned subsidiary of Sony.
6 Financial Services	Sony Financial Services oversees the operation of Sony Life (Japan and the Philippines), Sony Assurance, Sony Bank, and Sony Bank Securities. Sony Financial accounts for 15% of Sony's global earnings.

Sources: Sony Corporation Annual Reports (2011, 2012).

Financial performance

Between 2008 and 2011, Sony experienced four straight years of revenue decline. During that same period, the company absorbed a 25 percent drop in overall revenues. In 2012, Sony achieved revenues of ¥6,493 billion in 2012 as compared to the year before where the company realized revenues of ¥7,181billion. This represents a 9.6 percent decline in revenue performance. A review of Sony's financial performance for the years 2008–2012 can be seen in Table 18.2.

On May 31, 2013, Sony posted its first annual profit in five years. Sales and operating revenue were up 4.7 percent. The company earned ¥6.8 trillion ($72.3 billion) which can be attributed to the aggressive selling of assets, the favorable impact of foreign exchange rates, and a significant increase in financial services revenue in the financial services segment. The company's profitability was partially offset by a decline in unit sales of key electronics products. One important change in 2012 was the decision to acquire a controlling interest in mobile telephone communication from its one-time international partner, Sweden-based, Ericsson Corporation.

Table 18.2 Consolidated financial performance, 2008–2012 (yen in billions)

	2008	*2009*	*2010*	*2011*	*2012*
Sales and operating revenue	8,871.4	7,730.0	7,214.0	7,181.0	6,493.2
Operating income	374.5	(227.8)	31.8	199.8	(67.3)
Net income	369.4	(98.9)	(40.8)	(259.6)	(456.7)

Sources: Sony Corporation Annual Reports (2011, 2012).

Innovation and business failure

We begin by asking the question; what is business failure? At first glance, business failure is typically associated with bankruptcy or poor financial performance. But at a deeper level, business failure is also about the proverbial "fall from grace." On one level, the fall from grace is best illustrated by the dramatic downturn in Sony's stock value. At a second level, Sony's decline has to do with public perception. The name Sony still resonates in the minds of people who appreciate great communication technology. Sony products like the Trinitron TV set, the Sony Walkman, the compact disc and PlayStation were absolute game changers in their time. Very few companies can boast that kind of technology pedigree. Yet for a company once known for its innovative prowess, the twenty-first-century Sony appears to have run out of ideas. Sony is no longer the same company that it once was. The company is faced with a public perception that it has lost all relevancy in an otherwise highly competitive business and technology environment. The consequences are very real both financially and symbolically.

In this next section, we now consider several contributing reasons that help to explain why Sony has experienced the business failure that it has. They include:

- the tyranny of success;
- executive leadership failures;
- the challenges of a disruptive technology;
- a risk-averse culture;
- lengthy development times and poor coordination.

The tyranny of success

Past success can sometimes make an organization very complacent; that is, they lose the sense of urgency to create new opportunities (Tushman and O'Reilly, 1997). Companies, like people, can become easily satisfied with organizational routines. They become preoccupied with fine-tuning and making slight adjustments to an existing product line rather than preparing for the future. They are engaged in what MIT's Negroponte (1995) describes as the problem of "incrementalism." Says Negroponte, "Incrementalism is innovation's worst enemy" (p. 188). The history of business is filled with examples of past companies where senior management failed to plan for the future. Such examples include: Eastman Kodak and Blockbuster Video, to name only a few. Such companies did not anticipate a time when a substitute product or changing market conditions might come along and dramatically alter the playing field.

The rise and fall of a once great company

Sony's decade-long decline was the result of a number of self-inflicted wounds. What went wrong is a story of missed business opportunities, repeated failures to take necessary risks, and disastrous corporate in-fighting. It is also the tale of a once proud company that traded on its name and reputation rather than face the realities of a highly competitive global marketplace. Today, Sony is being challenged on a number of technology fronts by a host of international rivals that include Korea-based Samsung and LG as well as US-based Apple and Microsoft, to name only a few. Sony, like other Japanese companies, has also suffered under the yoke of a strong Japanese yen. It has made the company's competitive position very difficult when it comes to foreign exports. This, in combination with a failure to advance timely, innovative products, has made Sony's day-to-day business environment punishingly difficult (Kotaku, 2012).

Executive leadership failures

Leadership is a process that involves influence and the art of directing people within an organization to achieve a clearly defined set of goals and outcomes. Successful leaders know what they want to accomplish in terms of organizational outcomes. In his classic work, *Leading Change* John Kotter (1996) suggests that a leader's strategic vision should convey a picture of what the future will look like as well as appealing to the long-term interests of organizational members, customers and others who have a stake in the enterprise. At issue, is the fact that senior leaders can sometimes make strategic errors in decision-making that can have a variety of intended and unintended consequences on the organization as a whole.

Sony: the challenges of executive leadership

Some of Sony's current business challenges can be traced back to the leadership of Nobukei Idei who introduced an altogether new management philosophy. Under Idei's tenure, Sony underwent a corporate reorganization that was built on what the company called its five pillars of operation. This included: (1) Electronics; (2) Entertainment; (3) Financial Services; (4) Game; and (5) Internet Services. The objective was to transfer day-to-day management responsibility from Sony's Tokyo headquarters to the company's foreign operations. To that end, Sony's Tokyo headquarters was reorganized into two areas called the Global Hub (GH) and the Electronics Headquarters. The purpose of the GH was to develop corporate-wide strategy and to promote strategic intra-group alliances among the five pillars of business operations. The Electronics HQ was expected to serve as the strategic center for Sony's electronics business and focus on strategy development as well as strengthening ties with the company's other business areas (Gershon and Kanayama, 2002). The organizational model was described as "integrated/decentralized management."

At the time, Sony officials believed that in order to be more globally competitive, the company had to promote greater responsibility and autonomy in the field. The Sony manager was

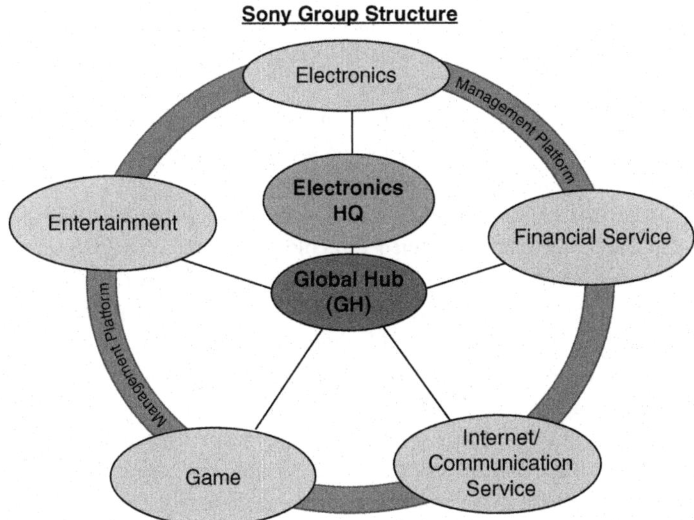

Figure 18.1 The SONY Corporation: integrated/decentralized management
Source: Sony Corporation Annual Report (2001).

expected to rely less on corporate headquarters and display more individual initiative. In time, the integrated/decentralized management approach would set into motion a variety of unintended consequences. One such consequence was that individual companies increased their investment and dependency on dependable products that could be tapped for quick, reliable profits. Instead of planning for the next generation in product design, there was a strong tendency toward legacy products (i.e., products with a proven track record).

The integrated/decentralized management approach made it difficult for CEO Idei and his senior administrative staff to interfere with individual company decisions, especially when they were making money. As an example, Sony's audio and video divisions were highly profitable during the early years of the twenty-first century. Both divisions felt no pressing need to develop digital technology. Even if Idei had urged them to respond to this challenge, they would have ignored him (Chang, 2008, p. 117). The TV business began responding only after it began suffering huge losses in 2003. Suddenly, the company found itself in catch-up mode rather than being the industry leader that it should have been.

Nobuyuki Idei also made the controversial decision to streamline the company and do a massive restructuring. A number of Sony executives and engineers were given early retirement options. There was a substantial brain drain of veteran and middle-aged engineers and technicians. Several were responsible for having contributed to Sony's past success. They left behind a younger group of engineers and technicians who were less willing to experiment, preferring instead to work with proven technology rather than build from the ground up. Several of those same retired engineers sought work elsewhere. Sony's proprietary technology became steadily diffused. As one observer wryly noted:

> During this period, Korea and Taiwan immediately welcomed the exiting Sony techies with open arms. It was better than industrial espionage—Samsung could openly buy the technology that Sony had developed simply by rehiring their best and brightest.

One story is very apocryphal of the problem. When an investor pointed out that Sony's operating profits on electronic products were roughly 2–4 percent and that Samsung was making similar products at a 30 percent profit margin, Idei hushed him up by reportedly saying: "They make the parts for our products. We put them together. It's the difference between a steel maker and an automobile maker. We make the automobiles."

The investor apparently countered, "Well, I've got news for you: the people you laid off from the car plant are now working at the steel mill, and soon the steel mills will be building cars with your technology" ("How Sony is Turning into a Ghost," 2012).

The loss of intellectual capital combined with low cost foreign production has taken a financial toll. In April 2005, the aforementioned difficulties prompted Sony to select Welsh-born, Howard Stringer, then President of Sony Corporation of America, to the position of Chairman and CEO. It was a first for Sony, given the fact that Stringer was not Japanese-born or spoke the language for that matter. As head of Sony Corporation of America, Stringer had a reputation for being a change agent. At his first news conference, Stringer made it known that he would "accelerate cross-company collaboration, thereby revitalizing the company and promoting creativity" (Gunther, 2001). Despite his best effort, Stringer was unable to tear down many of the existing business fiefdoms at Sony. In February 2012, Stringer was replaced by Kazuo Hirai, Head of Consumer Products. Hirai's most immediate task is the need for better cooperation between the company's various operating divisions for the purpose of harnessing natural synergies and creating a more unified information/entertainment experience for the user.

The challenges of a disruptive technology

A disruptive technology represents an altogether different approach to an existing product design and process. Authors Collins and Porras (1994) make the argument that highly successful companies are those that are willing to experiment and not rest on their past success. In time, tastes, consumer preference and technology change. Researcher Clayton Christensen (1997) suggests that even the best-managed companies are susceptible to innovation failure. In fact, past success can sometimes become the root cause of innovation failure going forward. Ironically, the decisions that lead to failure are made by executives who work for companies widely regarded as the best in their field.

The innovator's dilemma

Christensen (1997) posits what he calls the innovator's dilemma; namely, that a company's very strengths (i.e., realizing consistent profits and being responsive to customer needs) now become barriers to change and the agents of a company's potential decline. Successful companies are highly committed to serving their existing customers and are often unable (or unwilling) to take apart a thriving business in favor of advancing unfamiliar and unproven new technology. In contrast, advancing new technologies and services requires expensive retooling and their ultimate success is hard to predict. Such companies lose because they fail to invest in new product development and/or because they fail to notice small niche players who enter the market and are prepared to offer customers alternative solutions at better value. The anticipated profit margins in developing a future market niche can be hard to justify given the high cost of entry, not to mention the possible destabilization of an otherwise highly successful business. Therein, lies the innovator's dilemma.

Sony and the challenges of a disruptive technology

A disruptive technology is the quintessential game changer. Consider, for example, the impact that the Apple iPod had on the Sony Walkman portable music player. As illegal music downloads exploded in popularity in the late 1990s, Sony, like the rest of the music industry was unable or unwilling to adapt to the changing technology environment. With its catalog of music and foundation in electronics, Sony had the tools to create a version of the iPod long before Apple introduced it in 2001. Yet Sony was not prepared to move quickly enough and adjust strategy in order to preserve market leadership in the area of portable music. Instead, Sony's audio division was fully committed to its own proprietary (now defunct) mini-disc technology (Gershon, 2013b). Even when the threat of MP3 design was clear and obvious, Sony responded with an improved version of MD players that ultimately failed in the end.

The Apple iPod in combination with the iTunes music store in 2004 transformed the music industry by creating the first sustainable music downloading business model of its kind. By the time Sony's music and hardware divisions were forced to cooperate, that effort proved too little, too late. Sony's *Connect* online store, (the company's answer to the Apple iTune music store), was discontinued after three years. During the next five years, Sony lost an estimated 65 percent of the portable music market. The more important lesson was that Sony missed the MP3 revolution.

A risk-averse culture

Organizational culture (or corporate culture) refers to the collection of beliefs, values and expectations shared by an organization's members and transmitted from one generation of employees to another (Schein, 1983). Organizations (even large ones) are human constructions. They are made and transformed by individuals. But what happens when organizational culture stands in the way of innovation? What happens when being tied to the past (and past practices) interferes with a company's ability to move forward? The combination of past success coupled with an unbending adherence to management orthodoxy can seriously undermine a company's ability to step out of itself and plan for the future. Suddenly, creative thinking and the ability to float new ideas get tangled up in a stifling web of bureaucracy. Sometimes what passes for management wisdom and experience is inflexibility masquerading as absolute truth (Hamel, 2006).

Successful businesses with an established customer base find it hard to change. There is a clear pattern of success that translates into customer clients and predictable revenue that makes such companies risk-averse. The adage "why mess with a winning formula?" slowly becomes the corporate norm. The difficulty, of course, is that playing it safe presents its own unique hazards. Even well-managed companies can suddenly find themselves outflanked by changing market conditions and advancing new technologies (Gershon, 2013b).

Television set design

Sony's approach to the design and manufacture of high-definition television sets is highly illustrative of this point. Rather than advancing new and original research in the area of digital television set design, the company chose instead to extend the life of its analog-based Trinitron CRT (and later WEGA TV). Sony's senior leadership team did not want to give up the immediate profits that WEGA generated because it contributed to the company's overall profitability. That kind of short-term thinking would cause them irreparable damage.

By 2002, Sony began to feel the full effects of international competition from a variety of Asian rivals located in South Korea, China and Taiwan. That year, Korea-based Samsung Corporation surpassed Sony in terms of market capitalization. Such challenges were particularly noticeable in the area of television set design. Despite having been a pioneer in television set design (including early prototype work in high-definition television), the world's population was now buying LCD plasma TVs from Samsung and LG. They proved to be less expensive, well designed, and the difference in quality was not significant. Samsung, for its part, has mastered the process of fast and efficient low cost television manufacturing (Chang, 2008). A related problem has to do with the fact that Sony makes almost 30 different television models which tends to confuse consumers as well as undermine brand recognition. In sum, the company's catalog of products has become bloated and confusing to the consumer. This stands in marked contrast to companies like Apple that emphasize a few distinct brands and can rightfully say, this is our best product (Kotaku, 2012).

Sony's missed Internet strategy

Sony's Internet strategy was problematic from the start. Sony failed to recognize the shift toward software development and the importance of the Internet. One by one, every major product category where Sony competes—from portable music players (i.e., the Sony Walkman) to music recording devices (the compact disc) to videogame systems (the Sony PlayStation)—has felt the punishing effects of disruptive changing technology as well as unrelenting competitive challengers. First and foremost, Sony was slow to develop an integrated common platform to deliver music, movies and games. Given the company's multiple business silos, there was a lot of resistance from various divisions in terms of surrendering control over their individual operations.

Lengthy development times and poor coordination

The combination of changing technology and shifting consumer demands makes speed-to-market paramount today. Yet companies often cannot organize themselves to move faster. Too often, companies that are highly compartmentalized can become immobilized when it comes to fast turnaround times, given the entrenchment of existing departments and area silos. This, in turn, results in a lack of coordination that can seriously impair product innovation and development times. There is preoccupation with process rather than end results. Lengthy development times and poor coordination are closely tied to the execution of strategy (Gershon, 2013b).

Research project and collaboration

As noted earlier, one of Sony's long-standing problems is the fact that management (both past and present) have trouble wielding authority over the company's many subsidiaries and divisions. Executives complain privately of recalcitrant managers who refuse to share information or work with other divisions. Sony's top management, both publicly and privately, acknowledge that Sony remains dominated by proud, territorial engineers who often shun cooperation. The Japanese refer to it as "*tatewari.*" For many such engineers, ceding intellectual territory and cost-cutting are the enemy of creativity.

As an example, Sony marketed its PlayStation 3 console as an integrated entertainment system that would serve as a hub in the living room, connecting the Internet and television. A delay in developing the console's Blu-ray DVD player marred that strategy and forced Sony to push back its release date. Sales suffered because the PlayStation 3 cost much more than its rival models from Nintendo and Microsoft. Sony was also slow to move into the world of online games, giving Microsoft a significant head-start as well. The problem, in short, was the direct result of executive leadership failures to properly address territorial disputes between divisions and departments (Chang, 2008).

Conclusion

Throughout it history, the Sony name has been synonymous with great innovation. From the Sony Trinitron TV set to the PlayStation videogame system, Sony had an astonishing ability to meet the next technical challenge: a brighter TV set with increased resolution, a more versatile CD player with better sound capability, an integrated camcorder, and the list goes on. Sony could do it better, faster than any of its nearest competitors. Sony was one company that stirred the consumer's imagination.

All this changed with the successful emergence of Samsung and Apple at the start of the twenty-first century. Suddenly, Sony found itself being challenged by a set of rivals in two very different ways. Samsung proved to be the organizational master in fast and efficient (almost military-like) production. Samsung focused on becoming a superior manufacturer. The company learned how to manage and work through the highly volatile world of commoditized products (Chang, 2008). In contrast, Sony's organization steadily became more bureaucratic over time and its business units tended to operate as independent silos which made strategic planning and resource allocation very inefficient. Sony's current challenges are the result of past organizational failures to make everyone accountable to the larger Sony mission.

Sony's other major rival has been the Apple Corporation. Apple has focused public attention on the issue of the user experience. Technology is not enough. Apple products like the iPhone and iPad provide users with the capability of experiencing information and entertainment on multiple levels, including one or more combinations of text, audio and video. This is the very essence of convergence. Moreover, such devices allow the user to customize their media experience (Isaacson, 2012). Sony, for its part, missed the MP3 revolution. Sony failed to grasp the importance of the user experience in terms of being able to customize one's music and video playlist. By leveraging the power of the Internet and digital distribution, Apple let music lovers browse and download a song or album in a fraction of the time it had previously taken to record music onto a Sony Walkman tape or CD (Gershon, 2013a). Moreover, Apple took a page out of Sony's playbook by redefining the principle of portability in a whole new way by allowing music owners to place an entire music collection onto a simple device that could fit into one's coat pocket. Sony was caught flat-footed. It was adhering to an old industrial model where the emphasis was on stand-alone products sold in great volume (Hartung, 2012).

In looking to the future, Sony can no longer be in all areas of consumer electronics and media entertainment. Instead, Sony will need to sharpen its focus by exiting some product lines and focusing on being excellent at a few things. The company will have to cultivate a new management approach, whereby all departments (and senior executives) are answerable to the larger corporate mission. CEO Kazuo Hiraihas wants to rationalize the electronic divisions and unify the company under his "One Sony" plan. Accordingly, Hiraihas has indicated that the company will focus on three major businesses areas: (1) mobile devices (including smart-phones and tablets); (2) television (television/film program entertainment, television monitors, studio cameras and camcorders); and (3) videogame systems. The one thread that ties all of it together is television itself. Despite previous losses, Sony remains fully committed to the future of television. As CEO Hirai notes, "The television is at the center of every home. It is part of Sony's DNA."

All companies like to talk a good game about being innovative. But in practical terms, highly successful companies are not comfortable with change. They are uncomfortable with mavericks (or individualists) who stand apart from the rest of the group. Even Ken Kutaragi, when developing the Sony PlayStation, had to overcome a lot of resistance at the top by convincing his superiors that the PlayStation was a lot more than a toy. The smart, innovative company learns how to recognize and use such individuals and allows them the freedom to create great ideas on behalf of the organization. Even if it sometimes means product failure. If indeed television is part of Sony's DNA, the company needs to go back to the start-up mentality that it once possessed in the Shirokiya Department Store in Nihonbashi and recreate the entrepreneurial spirit that made Sony the great company that it once was.

Acknowledgments

The author would like to thank Dr. Tsutomu "Tom" Kanayama (Ritsumeikan University) for his contributions to an earlier article that provides some of the historical foundation for this chapter.

References

Asakura, R. (2000) *Revolutionaries at Sony: The Making of the Sony PlayStation and the Visionaries who Conquered the World of Video Games,* New York: McGraw-Hill.

Beamish, P. (1999) "Yoshide Nakamura on structure and decision-making," *Academy of Management Executive,* 13(4): 12–16.

Chang, S.J. (2008) *Sony vs. Samsung: The Inside Story of the Electronics Giants' Battle for Global Supremacy,* Singapore: John Wiley and Sons.

Christensen, C. (1997) *The Innovator's Dilemma,* Boston, MA: Harvard Business School Press.

Collins, J. and Porras, J. (1994) *Built to Last,* New York: HarperCollins.

Compaine, B. and Gomery, D. (2000) *Who Owns the Media?* Mahwah, NJ: Lawrence Erlbaum Associates.

Gershon, R.A. (1997) "The transnational media corporation: cultural trespass and challenges to national sovereignty," in J. Jaksa and M. Pritchard (eds) *Ethical Communication in Risk Technologies*, Cresskill, NJ: Hampton Press, pp. 285–303.

Gershon, R.A. (2007) "The transnational media corporation and the economics of global competition," in Y.R. Kamalipour (ed.) *Global Communication,* 2nd edn, Belmont, CA: Wadsworth, pp. 55–78.

Gershon, R.A. (2013a) "Digital media innovation and the Apple iPad: three perspectives on the future of computer tablets and news delivery," *Journal of Media Business Studies,* 10(1): 41–61.

Gershon, R.A. (2013b) "Innovation failure: a case study analysis of Eastman Kodak and Blockbuster Video," in A. Albarran (ed.) *Media Management and Economics: Research in a Transmedia Environment,* New York: Routledge, pp. 46–68.

Gershon, R.A. and Kanayama, T. (2002) "The Sony Corporation: a case study in transnational media management," *The International Journal on Media Management,* 4(2), 44–56.

Gunther, M. (2001) "Sony's boogie knight Sir Howard Stringer is on a quest," *Fortune,* 19 March. Available at: http://money.cnn.com/magazines/fortune/fortune_archive/2001/03/19/299185/.

Hamel, G. (2006) "The what, why and how of management innovation," *Harvard Business Review,* February: 72–87.

Hartung, A. (2012) "Sayonara Sony: how industrial, MBA-style leadership killed a once great company," *Forbes,* 4 April. Available at: www.forbes.com/sites/adamhartung/2012/04/20/sayonara-sony-how-industrial-mba-style-leadership-killed-once-great-company/2.

How Sony is turning into a ghost in Japan and around the world, (2012, 14 November) *Kotaku.* Available at: http://kotaku.com/5960411/how-sony-is-turning-into-a-ghost-in-japan-and-around-the-world.

Isaacson, W. (2012) *Steve Jobs,* New York: Simon & Schuster.

Kaiji, R. (1945) "Blue pencil," *Asahi Shimbun,* Editorial, 6 October.

Kotter, J. (1996) *Leading Change,* Boston, MA: Harvard Press.

Media Colossus. (1991, 15 March) *Business Week,* pp. 64–65.

Morita, A., Shimomura, M. and Reingold, E. (1986) *Made in Japan,* New York: E.P. Dutton.

Muneshige, H. (1991) *Sony Morita Akio no keiei tetsugaku,* Tokyo: Kodansha.

Nathan, J. (1999) *Sony: The Private Life,* New York: Houghton-Mifflin.

Negroponte, N. (1995) "The balance of trade of ideas," *Wired,* April, 188.

Robock, S. and Simmonds, K. (1989) *International Business and Multinational Enterprises,* Homewood, IL: Irwin.

Schein, E. (1983) "The role of the founder in creating organizational culture," *Organizational Dynamics,* 11: 13–28.

Schlender, B. (1992) "How Sony keeps the magic going," *Fortune,* 22 February, pp. 77–84.

Schumpeter, J. (1942) *Capitalism, Socialism and Democracy,* New York: Harper and Row.

Sony Corporation, Inc. (1986) *The Spirit Toward a New Excellence,* vol. 5 in Sony's Innovation in Management Series, Tokyo: Sony Inc.

Sony Corporation, Inc. (1988) *Genryu: Sony Challenges 1946–1968,* Tokyo: Sony Inc.

Sony Corporation, Inc. (1996) *Genryu,* 2nd edn, Tokyo: Sony Inc.

Sony Corporation, Inc. (2001) *Annual Report,* Tokyo: Sony Inc.

Sony Corporation, Inc. (2011) *Annual Report,* Tokyo: Sony Inc.

Sony Corporation, Inc. (2012) *Annual Report,* Tokyo: Sony Inc.

Tushman, M. and O'Reilly, C. (1997) *Winning through Innovation,* Boston, MA: Harvard Business School Press.

19

UNIQLO and Tadashi Yanai

Eugene K. Choi

Introduction

This chapter introduces a unique nonconformist in usually one of the most conservative, introverted, and "defensive" industrial sectors in the Japanese economy, apparel retailing. Tadashi Yanai, now the richest man in Japan, is surely worth our attention in both scholarly and business terms of how a striking innovation could be actualised in the most mature economy in East Asia. Rather than an efficient adaptor of the emerging new market trend, Yanai and his company have been creating a new one instead. Yanai was the initiator of a new style of mass apparel production, distribution, and consumption in East Asia today.

Not a professional marketer with a Western education, Yanai instead was a studious merchant who understood which products would jolt the incumbent marketing categories and encourage new patterns of apparel consumption. Not an engineer, instead Yanai was a rational coordinator who appreciated well which Japanese technologies would provide his brand with new sources of competitive differentiation. Not a fashion designer, instead Yanai was a talented visionary who intuitively grasped the optimal product display for better sales. Not a big fan of politics, instead Yanai was an attention-grabbing sensationalist who shocked Japanese business society by realising unprecedented corporate schemes. Last but not least, Yanai has been one of the most-experienced Japanese businessmen in the field of international apparel production and retailing in Asia.

This UNIQLO case will provide an interesting study for readers from the following three research perspectives. First, it is always remarkable to see how a local merchant transforms herself or himself into the owner of a multinational corporation, namely, the context and process of the evolution of a domestic venture business into a multinational corporation (Buckley and Casson, 1976, 2007; Jones, 2000; Casson and Casson, 2013; Mason and Harvey, 2013). This questions the essential nature of entrepreneurship. Second, this chapter reveals the disciplinary significance of business history in today's management studies (Jones *et al.*, 2012, pp. 225–235). Business history investigates every entrepreneurial contingency of how opportunities were sensed and seized upon to drive corporate development, and this supplies a vast knowledge reservoir with the potential to theorise (Sarasvathy, 2001; Popp and Holt, 2013). The final point revisits the further growing promise of entrepreneurship as a key field of research (Venkataraman, 1997; Shane and

Venkataraman, 2000; Jones *et al.*, 2012, pp. 226, 233); since East Asia has risen as the hub of the global economy, certainly, the attempt of this book will be appreciated more from now on.

Tadashi Yanai and the rise of UNIQLO

The apparel industry and fashion market in Japan: an overview

Has Japan influenced the global fashion market? Although a group of top-notch Japanese fashion designers, especially in the 1970s and the 1980s, produced a series of sensations in global fashion, their innovation has been framed within the exotic luxury segments (Fukai, 2001, pp. 15, 18–21, 101; Tomizawa, 2003, pp. 129–130). Paris, Milan, London, and New York have never lost their position as the shiny beacons of global vogue, and the Japanese talents in fashion creativity have to be well "assimilated" into Western values to be recognised globally. In East Asia, a considerable number of occult costumes for the fan communities of Harajuku fashion or inspired by Manga (Japanese animation) have emerged since the 1980s; nevertheless, they have never formed a major force in global fashion.

Although it is low-tech, fashion apparel has constituted the frontline of new business model creation and marketing innovation. It has also been a lucrative business field due to its cyclical trends, fast global diffusion, and low-cost manufacturing. Despite the size of market in their territories, East Asia has never spearheaded the global trend of modern fashion apparel. The West has led; the East has followed by mass consumption. The world in the 1980s witnessed the rise of China as a new powerhouse of manufacturing. Unsurprisingly, the Japanese apparel industry accelerated its offshore production from the end of the 1980s in tandem with the rapid loss of cost competitiveness (Itami, 2001, pp. 44–48; Yano Keizai Kenkyuusho, 2012). As a consequence, Japanese apparel production rapidly internationalised.

In both the industrialisation of the late nineteenth century and the post-WWII recovery, Japan depended heavily upon textiles. The first Japanese global competitiveness as an industrialised nation was achieved in textile production and export during the 1920s, but the accomplishment remained in commodity production (Abe, 2004, pp. 461–493). The burgeoning of the modern fashion industry, partly due to the devastating war, was postponed until the second half of the 1950s. Yet, even throughout the 1960s, the yarn manufacturers drove the domestic clothing trade, and the fashion apparel sector was still immature. It was the 1970s when Japanese consumers could experience fashion retailers' chic advertising that fashion apparel started to be important. Fashion represented a modern lifestyle and the cultural values of the West, and virtually every fashion trend was one-way traffic: from Western Europe and the USA to Japan.

In his detailed investigation of the salient dynamics between demand and supply of high fashion in the late Tokugawa period (1603–1868) as well as the early Meiji period (1868–1912), Tamura highlighted the remarkably high level of public fashion consciousness (Tamura, 2004). Immediacy in the application of new textile technology, either domestic or foreign, was striking. The public obsession with chasing the fashion vogue was strong enough for the late Tokugawa regime to hysterically pronounce the virtue of frugal clothing. In the following eras of Meiji, Taisho (1912–1926), and even very early Showa (1926–1989), the significance of wearing fashionable and quality clothes was an important part of public values. Then, the consequent military "dark age" in the 1930s and the 1940s destroyed Japanese social values. During the decade after World War II, the Japanese apparel production did not require sophisticated branding; anything produced could be sold. From the late 1950s, a few apparel companies took off by developing their original brands; Onward Kashiyama, Renown, Sanyo Shokai, Itokin, and World ("*Wa-rudo*" in Japanese) were the emerging leaders.

Kinoshita's investigation of the driving forces of industrial growth from this period to the 1970s pinpointed two categories of essential perspectives: the external and the corporate (Kinoshita, 2011, pp. 35–59). As external conditions, the first was the marketing activities of textile material suppliers and spinning companies; the next was the growth of department stores that accelerated the diffusion of new fashion trends; and last but not least, the state regulation such as JIS (Japanese Industrial Standards) provided an institutional foundation for mass production and sales. As regards the corporate factors, first, the leading companies became technically independent through active learning from collaborations with foreign firms. Second, the domestic system of mass manufacturing was created, and, third, their marketing channels grew during the 1960s. Finally, in the same period, as soon as Onward Kashiyama enlarged its brand portfolio, the rest also rushed to increase their sub-brands (Kinoshita, 2011: Chapters 2–6).

Along with the surge in income, the Japanese consumers in the 1970s began to pursue more variety in fashion products. Even the following series of oil shock panics little affected this trend, and until the middle of the 1980s, the industry achieved constant growth. The re-evaluation of the yen in 1985 introduced the era of the "Showa Bubble" economy, then foreign luxury clothing from France and Italy flooded in; the Japanese fashion market became unprecedentedly international (Yamazaki, 2007; Senken Shimbunsha, 2009). Simultaneously, the domestic apparel producers' cost competitiveness disappeared.

During the post-bubble economy in the 1990s, the fashion market still sustained its pace of growth. The public taste changed noticeably, however, as clothing lost its priority in public consumption. Price competitiveness became the crux in marketing. This has been tendency until today; the 2000s were dominated by fast fashion companies such as H&M and Zara, i.e. the domestic brands lost considerable shares of their turfs (Yano Keizai, 2001–2011).

The Japanese apparel industry had been neither outward-looking nor pioneering in leading the global consumption of fashion: it has been one of the most inward-looking sectors in the Japanese economy. The domestic firms were very efficient at chasing the global trend, but the Japanese have competed merely domestically. In a global perspective, their presence has been virtually invisible.

Tadashi Yanai, a nonconformist

The global media has announced the world rankings of the rich, and Yanai has been introduced as the richest man in Japan. *Forbes* of America on 4 April 2013 ranked Yanai as the matchless top in Japan as well as 66th in the world from his estimated assets of US$15.5 billion. As already noted, the Japanese apparel industry was a typical case of "the introvert" dealing with the limited domestic shares; and it is surprising why on earth an owner-CEO in that "lukewarm" business has occupied the top position for the past five years.

Bond with his entrepreneurial father

Tadashi Yanai was born in February 1949, in Ube, a rural city located in Yamaguchi Prefecture of West Japan. His father, Hitoshi Yanai, was the owner of a tailor's shop, *Men's Shop Ogori Shoji*, in the central shopping district of the city. Remarkably, this business was started in 1949, in the same year of Tadashi Yanai's birth. The son saw his father as an energetic "macho" entrepreneur, engaging several new areas such as local civil engineering and constructions, tearooms, and even a cinema, once the original business of the tailor's shop took off. After his education at Waseda University in Tokyo, his father wanted his son to learn the nature of business practice in a large retailer. Tadashi Yanai stayed only for 9 months at the offered workplace, and returned to his hometown. Despite the considerably brief period of his apprenticeship in the large retail firm, Yanai noted that he had absorbed a comprehensive knowledge of an advanced retailing system of the time (Yanai, 2003, p. 26).

Ogori Shoji's key business was in retailing men's formal couture, and the young university graduate, Tadashi Yanai, began his apprenticeship on the floor in earnest. Soon his attempt to change the existing system of sales and maintenance resulted in arguments, and finally, he found only himself and a floor assistant working in his father's shop. Instead of firing him, Hitoshi Yanai transferred the shop management to his son, and from that moment in 1972, Tadashi Yanai started his career as an independent and "multifunctional" manager, involved with every daily practice of apparel retailing (Yanai, 2003, pp. 25–28). Since then, for over a decade, Yanai's frantic learning-by-doing on a daily basis continued until the launch of Unique Clothing Warehouse in 1984.

Learning and the evolution of a business idea

Together with the original business of men's couture sales, some ranges of casual wear were included in his business portfolio. However, the location of Ube city provided no advantage in the fashion business. Yanai tried to overcome the inescapable disadvantage in accessing the most updated sources by grasping every possible opportunity. Both domestic and overseas information was rigorously collected; on an annual basis, he made research trips to the USA and the UK and invested in new brands, especially in the segments of casual wear with high sales turnovers.

Sales of men's couture and formal wear necessitate close assistance and courtesy. Despite the high profit ratio per sale, considerably low turnover had to be compromised. So Yanai's interest shifted to trendy casual wear retailing. Moreover, the following couple of characteristics attracted Yanai's attention: first, casual wear attracts a much wider category of consumers, and, second, most of them did not require committed assistance on the sales floors, i.e. the customers would serve themselves without assistance. Yanai's understanding of this latter point was acquired interestingly enough from his field study at university coops in the USA (ibid., pp. 29–30).

Yanai paid close attention to the new retailing models in the USA of the early 1980s, e.g. Limited, Esprit, and Gap. At that same time, Japanese consumers began to purchase so-called "DC (Designer & Character) apparel", which meant new modes of highly personalised fashion brands (Yamazaki, 2007, pp. 49–52). Since certain premiums were given to these newly branded products, their prices were noticeably high. Despite the striking attraction for these products from the young people, the price factor deterred the further growth in that area. Yanai looked at this specific cul-de-sac, and considered how to bust the high price. He noted that a long train of thought during this period introduced a few conceptual prototypes of UNIQLO: how could he sell these fast-moving DC apparels much cheaper? How would the price range that even fashion-conscious teenagers could purchase with their pocket money be realised? (Yanai, 2003, pp. 30–31).

Through nearly a decade of trial and error since 1972, and with both domestic and overseas field experience in different apparel segments, Yanai foresaw the upcoming Japanese era of mass casual wear in the early 1980s. Gradually, the proportion of men's couture was reduced in his business portfolio. Sales turnover was concerned mostly with how to attract more customers more often. Price was still a vital measure. But even more significantly, the secret of sales was to seize the best mix of functionally different products in the shop display: some products attract people's attention, some induce additional purchases, and some should provide his company with certain profits (author's interview with Mr Tadashi Yanai, 24 July 2009a). In Yanai's view, the managerial essence was found in continuously creating the most optimal combination of "functionally and reciprocally co-specialised" fashion goods.

In the 1970s and the early 1980s, Yanai sold ready-made clothing. In the category of "attracting attention," he offered quality clothes and accessories from overseas, and mostly, Yanai himself had purchased those goods when he went on his business trips to London, Hong Kong, and New York. Then, the product segments of "additional purchases" as well as "profit builders" were filled with domestic supplies, especially from Osaka, Gifu, and Nagoya. However, as the number of his shops increased in the vicinity of Ube, the technical difficulty in sustaining quantity, quality, and variety became obvious. Besides, it was difficult to meet the critical mass. In consequence, Yanai had to move to somewhere urban; from Ube, from where he stood, the big cities were either Hiroshima or Fukuoka (Yanai, 2003, p. 31).

Considering the essential worry with the size of the demand pool, Yanai saw another critical bottleneck in his upcoming apparel retailing: smart branding for differentiation. This would become even more severe in urban markets, filled with a vast number of retailers, positioning themselves in rich fashion categories. Since most of their stock came from the same domestic producers as Yanai's, price competition became unavoidable. So the more desperate in price competitiveness he became, inevitably the worse the operational profit per sale was. As a chronically low profit ratio continued, no growth could be accomplished. This could turn finally into an inescapable vicious circle.

Yanai and the genesis of UNIQLO

Critical insights from business operation

His idea matured for a decade, and then Yanai's daring venture kicked off. To target the mass volume zone quickly, first, Yanai's ultimate choice was the casual wear segment, which was undifferentiated in age and gender. The second element was to provide the light-hearted and relaxed shoppers with easier access to every shop floor; the American-style self-service approach was applied to create a new shopping ambience (Yanai, 2003, pp. 30–31). This approach also saved on staffing costs. The shop interior was minimised and simplified as Yanai's idea of minimalism was applied. In the eyes of the visiting customers, this made a striking impression of the store being an industrial "depot" rather than an art-inspired fashion boutique. The opening time created another sensation: Yanai's new shop opened at 0600 hours. The aim of breaking with custom and having longer business hours was to attract more customers and increase the daily sales turnover.

At 6 a.m. on 2 June in 1984, Yanai, at the shop entrance, welcomed a crowd of waiting customers to his new venture business; it was the first Unique Clothing Warehouse open in the city centre of Hiroshima. From the architectural perspective, the ceiling was much higher, and the aisles of the shopping areas were designed to be much wider. The provision of more space (and air) was an attempt to let shoppers "feel free, stay longer, look around more, try more and buy more." The floor staff behaved differently too: Yanai's staff focused on keeping the zones clean and neat, refolding and rearranging the products on the shelves, and left the shoppers alone. Only when asked for assistance, did they respond and serve. Unique Clothing Warehouse introduced a set of new retailing techniques, and it was an initial indication of Yanai's innovations in the Japanese fashion apparel industry.

Once the first shop had proved successful after operating for a year, Yanai began to consider a couple of business models: one was identical to the first shop in Hiroshima, namely, an urban model; the other was a suburban type. In June 1985, the second shop opened in Shimonoseki, and this was followed by the third (urban type) and the fourth (suburban model) at the end of the same year (Yanai, 2003, p. 35). Within a couple of years, Yanai was already grasping most of the fundamentals behind the UNIQLO model. Remarkably, the suburban type provided him with much richer insights, Yanai noted.

His insights were threefold. First, the customers in the suburban model were well motivated to make a trip and visit the remote location because their intention was to shop. The adoption of the motor car in Japan was further accelerated in the early 1980s, especially among the young people. Young couples, whether married or single, owned cars not only for work but also for recreation. If sufficiently well informed, those young people loved to drive and shop in the suburbs. The bottom line to this first insight was thus smart marketing that would effectively stimulate people's "craving for shopping". The second involved the importance of the undifferentiated unisex casual wear segment. This was derived from Yanai's continuous comparison of sales turnovers among different apparel markets. Last but not least, another vital finding was the constancy as well as universality in the public demand for basic and quality clothing. Yanai thus saw a new potential in the most basic clothing, which did not require a high brand premium (author's interview with Mr Tadashi Yanai, 24 July 2009a).

In the pursuit of new identity: inspiration from Hong Kong

"To be remembered" is an essence of branding (Aaker, 1991, 1999, 2011). Yanai targeted undifferentiated consumers, and without an original and bold identity that well delivered his voice, a few Unique Clothing Warehouses in Hiroshima and Okayama could have been as short-lived as the mediocre discount shops nearby. Yanai's lasting concern since the take-off of his venture in 1985 was the name of his shops. Soon, to make it more memorable, Unique Clothing Warehouse was renamed as Uni·Clo, then soon as UNICLO. In his memoirs, Yanai mentioned an interesting episode: due to an unexpected typo during the registration paperwork of UNICLO Trading Co. in Hong Kong in March 1988, the C was replaced by a Q. This "mistake" then resulted in the entire change of brand identity in Japan as well. The reason was simple: Yanai found that UNIQLO looked "cooler" than UNICLO (Yanai, 2003, p. 33).

From the beginning in Hiroshima and Okayama, Yanai well reckoned that a model of merely retailing "somebody else's tags" would soon stagnate in growth. Sustaining high sales turnover was the basic rule of thumb in his model; a chronic race of severe price discounts was inevitable to get rid of piling inventories. The risk of outsourcing wholesale products got higher as the complexity of the product portfolio soared. So from his perspective of competitive branding, the ideal model was to control the entire process of apparel business, all stages, from planning and design to production, then from distribution to final retailing under one recognisable brand (ibid., pp. 37–38). If his company could position itself as the headquarters of managing the entire value chain in apparel production as well as retailing, Yanai thought that the typical risk in the traditional retailing scheme could be managed (author's interview with Mr Tadashi Yanai, 24 July 2009a; Yanai, 2009b, pp. 86–89).

When considering building this new system, Hong Kong was, again, a significant hotspot for Yanai's business inspiration. After nearly a decade of casual wear retailing, UNIQLO could at last establish its own international system of planning, designing, and manufacturing original products from 1993. Hong Kong was the gateway to the apparel factories in South China, and, at the same time, a reliable conduit for seizing the global trend. Yanai clearly noted that Jimmy Lai, the founder of Giordano, was a great role model for apparel business (Yanai, 2003, p. 39; Yanai, 2012, pp. 38–39).

In 1986, Yanai discovered Giordano polo shirts during his research trip to Hong Kong: in his eyes, the premium products were uniformly and boldly branded as Giordano, but the prices were surprisingly reasonable. "Ko-Re-Da!" (This is it!), a flash of inspiration instantly hit Yanai, and made him send an immediate request to meet Jimmy Lai (Yanai, 2003, pp. 38–39). Soon Yanai foresaw the following: first, no national boundaries in production will be required to pursue the best price competitiveness in international trade; and, second, production and retailing should not be separated, namely, the two operations must be combined to brand most effectively. Remarkably enough, 1986 was the year when GAP in the USA identified its new business as "Specialty Store Retailer of Private Label Apparel".

The second half of the 1980s was the period when Yanai was conceptually enlightened regarding his new business model from a global perspective. Then the following first half of the 1990s turned into a vital phase of corporate renewal. Yanai's goal was to transform himself from a local "casual wear merchant" to a professional manager of a global fashion apparel company (ibid., pp. 48–59; Jones, 2000). The change became noticeable in 1990, when he began to hire professional accountants, auditors, and consultants for corporate finance; also, at the same time, his international team of product designers, manufacturing engineers, merchandisers, marketers, and lawyers was formed.

This series of determined transformations were intended to rebrand his firm from being a domestic retailer of casual wear to being an international "SPA" (Yamazaki, 2007, pp. 88–90) (i.e. a new term, produced in Japanese from Specialty Store Retailer of Private Label Apparel) with the flagship brand UNIQLO. Furthermore, Yanai renamed his company, changing from the Ogori Shoji Corp. to the Fast Retailing Corporation in September 1991 (Yanai, 2003, pp. 49–50). As the name itself indicates, Yanai's business philosophy is immediacy in every managerial engagement.

The Fast Retailing way, the fast road to innovation

Paradigm shift and conceptual breakthrough

As one of the most basic concepts in modern capitalism, price is the ultimate index that indicates the value of a commercial product. Price should be correlated positively to quality. Yanai's first conceptual challenge was to break down this common sense correlation (author's interview with Mr Tadashi Yanai, 24 July 2009a). He considered that destruction of this traditional rule of price mechanism would open a new window of business opportunities. Yanai's ambition was to prove that top quality could come at a reasonable price.

The following three technical necessities had to be met to realise his aim. The first was to control the entire value chain in the apparel industry. Partly, this was due to the minimisation of transaction costs, including information and negotiation costs; but most significantly, the quality must be constantly monitored, assessed, and sustained by headquarters. The second derived from the first: a considerable level of technology and knowledge transfer was required to fulfil the "UNIQLO standard". Since every level of both technical and managerial skills in offshore factories was different, the headquarters dispatched teams of technicians, e.g. well-experienced Japanese textile engineers and liaison managers, according to their respective position, to different regions. This supportive system of providing "technical experts" was called, "*Takumi Seido*" (*Takumi* in Japanese means craftsman or *Meister* in German). Once these two necessities were fulfilled, then the third could be accomplished: searching for and obtaining the apparel factories with the required cost competitiveness in a global perspective. In considering the average labour cost in Japan, offshore production was an absolute essential. The globalisation of every business operation became compulsory.

In the early days of UNIQLO, the second half of the 1980s, Yanai's concept of casual wear was virtually identical to the traditional categorisation of apparel products, since his business model was based on a local retailer. However, once his company transformed into a model of SPA in the first half of the 1990s, it could begin to plan, design, manufacture, and retail its original products:

Fast Retailing could involve managers in every stage in the entire value chain of the apparel industry. So UNIQLO then needed its original marketing segment, strategically differentiated from others, massive and stable enough to guarantee high sales turnover. Yanai and his management team agreed that it would be more sensible to re-jig the traditional concept of categorising apparel market segments and "re-define" them using an unprecedented taxonomical framework (author's interview with Mr Tadashi Yanai, 24 July 2009a).

First of all, Yanai introduced a big twist to the traditional custom. Rather than emphasising the art and fashion factors in the value of apparel goods, Yanai stated that fashion apparel is (merely) an industrial product. Creating an ungraspable fantasy of *art nouveau* would harm UNIQLO's key value; instead, the pursuit of perfection in functional quality and reasonable pricing would result in new value creation (Yanai, 2003, pp. 33–34). To do this, industrial technology should be fully appreciated and applied for innovation. Based upon this path-destructive viewpoint, another conceptual definition was supplied: the tradition of total fashion was defied (Choi, 2011, pp. 93–95).

By considering fashion apparel as an industrial product, Yanai introduced the modularisation of apparel goods. Clothing can be modularised, and every piece of clothing can be designed as a module. Each product, sold in the UNIQLO shops, could be seen as a part (or piece) that would contribute to the completion of individual fashion. It is utterly an individual customer's own fashion sense and own decision to choose each of UNIQLO's offerings in a wide variety of casual wear goods, and Fast Retailing's obligation should be to continuously deliver the best quality and the most reasonable price to the mass customers (Choi, 2011, pp. 95–101).

Because of Yanai's key philosophy for the apparel business, UNIQLO would be different from the deepest conceptual echelon of product development; or to rephrase this differently, UNIQLO would succeed in positioning itself uniquely in global brand competition. From the beginning of the 2000s, Fast Retailing brought its novel fashion taxonomy to create new demands and capture the increasing users en masse, both domestically and globally. The framework was derived from their high expectation of the potential of Japanese advanced textile technologies.

The fleece sensation, UNIQLO take-off in fashion functionalism

UNIQLO was a completely infant brand, compared to all the well-established domestic ones with long corporate histories. As Yanai noted frequently, he experienced severe operational difficulties at the launch stage, particularly in East Japan, the surrounding regions of Greater Tokyo. Along with the inevitably low profile, if the company name was known already, the original bias of UNIQLO as "a rural discount warehouse from far west" was so much more deeply-rooted than expected. Until 1998, virtually nothing made Fast Retailing and its flagship brand, UNIQLO, outstanding in the Japanese fashion market.

Far from his home city, Yanai felt and witnessed this harsh reality better than anybody else, since he attended every opening ceremony of a new shop (Yanai, 2003, pp. 65–66; author's interview with Mr Tadashi Yanai, 24 July 2009a). So when Fast Retailing decided to open a new Tokyo flagship store in 1998, Yanai was determined to make a daring decision: UNIQLO should ring the bell of the Japanese fashion avant-garde, Harajuku in Tokyo. Until that moment, Fast Retailing could not establish a clear inroad into "Japan fashion".

The inauguration of the Harajuku shop was realised with the following three critical implications. First, the opening itself was turned into Yanai's signal that UNIQLO was making a strategic shift in its key format of a shop belonging to a group of regional roadside apparel warehouses to a become a dynamic cluster of fashion retailers, deployed in urban cores. The second concerned the shift in Yanai's branding strategy of uniting the entire offering under one brand name,

UNIQLO. Namely, it was also a public declaration of Fast Retailing's position as an SPA in the fashion industry.

Harajuku has always been the most chic and showy centre of high fashion, and certainly the competition in the milieu was always cut-throat; the ever gorgeous street has never allowed any store to stay in business unless it proved it was "worth" being in the heart of fashion. Deploying every resource, all his experience accumulated for nearly 15 years since his 6 a.m. opening of the Hiroshima shop in 1984, Yanai bet on his Harajuku debut. Then, last but not least, the third innovation came from Fast Retailing's surprising choice of fleece as the opener. As this was not one of the normal Harajuku fashion categories, placing what was considered an outdoor product in the frontline was the rational choice for Fast Retailing in pursuit of high turnover from undifferentiated mass consumers.

Fleece, an outdoor product, known as high-tech-driven and special (i.e. costly) but relatively fashion-free (i.e. function-oriented), was offered uniformly with UNIQLO tags at the surprisingly affordable price of 1,900 yen, in a fancy variation of 51 vivid colours. The strategic management of colour turned into an innovative essence (Blaszczyk, 2012). At the Harajuku shop, nothing else but the fleece was displayed to maximise the visual impact. This approach was a smart combination of Yanai's ideology of apparel retailing as well as his firm's technical competence in product development up to 1998 (Prahalad and Hamel, 1990).

The unique value of the UNIQLO fleece appealed to the fashion chasers in Harajuku, first, then sensible shoppers in every high street in Tokyo. In considering the choice and the following success of the UNIQLO fleece, the production management team deserves our close attention: including the manager, Mr Kotani, the team consisted of apparel design experts from sports and outdoor wear (Yanai, 2003, p. 40). This is an important clue that, from the early phase of corporate development, Fast Retailing was involved with particular apparel requiring the combination of design and function. This did not happen out of blue in this way; UNIQLO was already good at it, and they knew what to do.

It was a historic sensation in the history of the Japanese apparel industry: the UNIQLO fleece fever of 1999–2001. The unprecedented sales figures of 35 million pieces (the sales of fleece only) convinced the management of Fast Retailing of the massive potential found in the innovative combination of apparel function and fashion. Fleece was the first blockbuster that formed the foundation of corporate-level strategy afterwards. The lesson thus introduced a new business paradigm, namely, fashion functionalism. Furthermore, this new concept introduced the "UNIQLO Shift" (Choi, 2011, pp. 92–95), which was a whole re-categorisation of fashion clothing within a new frame of functional performance, such as preserving comfort in use (Yunikuro, 2008, pp. 35–57).

The essential breakthrough of the UNIQLO Shift had the following two-fold consequences. First, the new perspective of categorising the mass consumers into functions broke down all the traditional fashion marketing divisions, based upon age groups, gender, regional and geographical elements, cultural factors, or purchasing-power-related factors, etc. This became the first step to realising Yanai's ideology of offering quality goods to undifferentiated mass customers. Then, the second result was to facilitate new types of collaboration between fashion apparel retailing and textile and material manufacturing. The fashion functionalism concept requires solid technological foundations to actualise both uniqueness and sustainability within apparel functions.

Since the early twentieth century, Japan has been blessed by the innovations and growth of world-class textile producers, and their corporate progress was one of the most critical sources of both pre-war economic growth and post-war recovery (Itami, 2001, pp. 48–55; Senken Shimbunsha, 2009, pp. 24–37). The global powerhouses such as TORAY, TEIJIN, KURARAY, UNITIKA, and so on, have shaped the frontier of advanced textiles and materials. Fashion functionalism became a new conceptual platform where Fast Retailing and those Japanese textile giants could explore emerging business opportunities in more efficient collaboration. Yanai's manifesto of fashion functionalism has enabled the two industrial sides to map out win-win strategies.

"LifeWear, Made for All": Yanai's vision

UNIQLO's catchphrase between 2011 and 2012 was "Made for All". This clarified Tadashi Yanai's tenet of new apparel business since 1984: providing the undifferentiated mass consumers with quality products as well as at the most reasonable prices. The significant gist in this expression should be Yanai's vision, or to put it more precisely, his aim of what should be accomplished through UNIQLO henceforth. The indispensable business policy for the UNIQLO model has been unchanged; first, high sales turnover per shop must be maintained, and the widest segment of basic and daily casual wear should be the principal marketing target.

"Made for All" was the ultimate expression of both the business tenet and the branding philosophy. At the same time, his definition of "All" implies everybody in an international perspective. Regardless of its Japanese origin, Yanai's aim has always been to make Fast Retailing a multinational enterprise, covering every market region in the world. To get more market shares and higher sales turnover, going global should not be optional. Rather, it should be a vital lifeline for UNIQLO's survival and further growth.

In 2013, UNIQLO began to use a new keyword "LifeWear" in every advertisement. This is another piece of remarkably understandable jargon: it is a powerful appeal that UNIQLO would provide "fundamental" (more than casual) apparel goods for everybody's daily life. With certain confidence in overall quality, basic functions, price competitiveness, and universality in designs, Fast Retailing is showing its approach to shaping the undifferentiated mass consumers' life styles. This is synchronised very well with the corporate motto, changing the conventional wisdom and the world through apparel innovation.

"LifeWear, Made for All" is the most decisive consequence of Yanai's every entrepreneurial management act for the past three decades. From the perspective of the most original Schumpeterian theme of entrepreneurship and innovation, Yanai's first daring venture in the Unique Clothing Warehouse in Hiroshima was surely the result of his new combination as well as the use of his attained business resources. His business concept was derived from the integration of a rich variety of technical ideas, field experience, knowledge of foreign models, and most of all, unremitting learning-by-doing on a daily basis. Behind his positive implementation of this Schumpeterian characteristic for innovators, there was another thing worth our attention. As the title of his first publication, full of memoirs and records, *Issho Kyuu Hai* "One Win, Nine Losses" in English) shows, the most distinctive element in Yanai's entrepreneurial approach has been his steely determination when facing countless trial and error.

However, Yanai has never claimed that errors should be repeated; once a trial has proved a failure, the speed of full retreat must be "relentlessly prioritised" to save business resources for the next attempt. The quintessence of his risk management resides not in single-minded avoidance but in rigorous assessment before and after, and minimisation of loss through the quickest withdrawal. Remarkably enough, Yanai has practised what Richard Cantillon argued in his classic concept of entrepreneurship in the eighteenth century (Murphy, 1987, pp. 246–281; Brewer, 1992; Higgs, 2012); it is a merchant's valour to calculate and bear every risk in commercial transactions. The core nature of entrepreneurship has not changed in this way.

This chapter has used the term, "nonconformist", to depict the evolutionary path of Yanai's leadership in the industry. From the product and marketing concept to corporate policy, Yanai has not limited himself to the customs taken for granted in his industry. Instead, he has pursued a considerable level of industrial irregularity to unshackle his business from the incumbents' common sense in management (Yonekura 1998; Choi, 2009). English was established as an official language in Fast Retailing Corporation from 2012 (Yanai, 2012, pp. 67–69), and this was one of the earliest corporate-level attempts in Japan.

In May 2013, Yanai clarified his new plan of equalising Fast Retailing's wage scheme globally (or resetting the entire scheme under a single scale of currency) regardless of different regional living costs and standards in the world (WEB RONZA, *Asahi Shimbun*, 31 May 2013). This announcement reflected his understanding of globalisation as the direct concept of getting rid of every traditional border, both geographical and institutional. Beyond the current industrial borders, Yanai's entrepreneurial leadership is attracting public attention and facilitating debates by other industrial leaders on Japan's next innovation strategy in globalisation. The manifesto of "Made for All" is now being applied not only to the level of apparel production and retailing but also to the stage of providing the themes of Japanese public opinion in global perspective. Most of these schemes for change certainly came from Tadashi Yanai's subjectivity in deviating from the socio-economic customs from the past.

Bibliography

Aaker, D.A. (1991) *Managing Brand Equity: Capitalizing on the Value of a Brand Name,* New York: The Free Press.

Aaker, D.A. (1999) *Harvard Business Review on Brand Management,* Boston: Harvard Business School Press.

Aaker, D.A. (2011) *Brand Relevance: Making Competitors Irrelevant,* San Francisco, CA: Jossey-Bass.

Abe, T. (2004) "Organizational changes in the Japanese cotton industry during the inter-war period: from inter-firm-based organization to cross-sector-based organization", in D.A. Farnie and D.J. Jeremy (eds) *The Fibre that Changed the World: The Cotton Industry in International Perspective, 1600–1990s,* Oxford: Oxford University Press, pp. 461–493.

Aoshima, Y. and Kato, T. (2003) *Kyoso Senryaku Ron* [A Theory of Competitive Strategy], Tokyo: Toyo Keizai Shimpo Sha.

Blaszczyk, R.L. (2012) *The Color Revolution,* Cambridge, MA: The MIT Press.

Brewer, T. (1992) *Richard Cantillon: Pioneer of Economic Theory,* New York: Routledge.

Buckley, P. and Casson, M. (1976) *The Future of the Multinational Enterprise,* London: Macmillan.

Buckley, P. and Casson, M. (2007) *The Multinational Enterprise Revisited,* Basingstoke: Palgrave.

Casson, M. and Casson, C. (2013) *The Entrepreneur in History: From Medieval Merchant to Modern Business Leader,* Basingstoke: Palgrave Pivot.

Choi, E.K. (2009) "Entrepreneurial leadership of Meiji cotton spinners in the early conceptualisation of global competition", *Business History,* 51(3) (November): 298–328.

Choi, E.K. (2011) "The rise of UNIQLO: leading paradigm change in fashion business and distribution in Japan", *Entreprises et Histoire,* Paris, France: Editions ESKA, No. 64 (September): 85–101.

Fukai, A. (2001) *Fassion Burando Besuto 101* [The 101 Best Fashion Brands in the World], Tokyo: Shinshokan.

Higgs, H. and Cantillon, R. (2012) *Essai sur le Commerce,* reprinted for Harvard University, Ulan Press.

Itami, H. (ed.) (2001) *Nippon No Sen'i Sangyo: Naze, Korehodo Yowaku Natte Simattanoka* [The Textile Industry of Japan: Analyses of the Industrial Decline], Tokyo: NTT Shuppan.

Itami, H. and Numagami, T. (1992) "Dynamic interaction between strategy and technology", *Strategic Management Journal,* 13: 119–135.

Jones, G. (2000) *Merchants to Multinationals: British Trading Companies in the Nineteenth and Twentieth Centuries,* Oxford: Oxford University Press.

Jones, G., van Leeuwen, M.H.D. and Broadberry, S. (2012) "The future of economic, business, and social history", *Scandinavian Economic History Review,* 60(3) (November): 225–253.

Kinoshita, A. (2011) *Apareru Sangyo No Ma-Ke-Tin-Gu-Shi* [Marketing History of the Japanese Apparel Industry], Tokyo: Dobunkan.

Mason, C. and Harvey, C. (2013) "Entrepreneurship: contexts, opportunities and processes", *Business History,* 55(1) (January): 1–8.

Murphy, A.E. (1987) *Richard Cantillon: Entrepreneur and Economist,* Oxford: Oxford University Press.

Popp, A. and Holt, R. (2013) 'The presence of entrepreneurial opportunity', *Business History,* 55(1) (January): 9–28.

Prahalad, C.K. and Hamel, G. (1990) "The core competence of the corporation", *Harvard Business Review,* 68(3): 79–91.

Sarasvathy, S.D. (2001) "Causation and effectuation: toward a theoretical shift from economic inevitability to entrepreneurial contingency", *Academy of Management Review,* 26: 243–263.

Senken Shimbunsha (1999) *Nippon Ryuu SPA No Chousen: Fassion Bijinesu Seichou No Jyouken* [The Challenge of Japanese-Style SPA Business: The Prerequisites for Fashion Business' Growth], Tokyo: Senken Shimbunsha.

Senken Shimbunsha (2009) *Sen'i Fassion Bijinesu No Rokujyuu Nen* [The 60 Years of the Japanese Textile and Fashion Business], Tokyo: Senken Shimbunsha.

Shane, S. and Venkataraman, S. (2000) "The promise of entrepreneurship as a field of research", *Academy of Management Review,* 25: 217–226.

Tamura, H. (2004) *Fassion No Shakai-Keizaishi: Zairai Orimonogyo No Gijyutsu Kakushin To Ryuukou Sijyou* [The Socio-Economic History of Fashion: Technological Innovation of the Traditional Weaving Sector and the Fashion Market], Tokyo: Nippon Keizai Hyouronsha.

Tomizawa, O. (2003) *Fassion Sangyo Ron: Ifuku Fassion No Shouhi Bunka To Sangyo Sisutemu* [A Theory of the Fashion Industry: The Culture of Fashion Apparel Consumption and the Industrial System], Tokyo: Soufuusha.

Venkataraman, S. (1997) "The distinctive domain of entrepreneurship research: an editor's perspective", in J.A. Katz and R. Brockhaus (eds) *Advances in Entrepreneurship, Firm Emergence and Growth,* vol. 3, Greenwich, CT: JAI Press, pp. 119–138.

WEB RONZA, *Asahi Shimbun* (2013) "UNIQLO no Sekai Douitsu Chin'gin Shock" [UNIQLO's shocking announcement of equalising the global wage scheme], 31 May. Available at: http://astand.asahi.com/magazine/wrbusiness/2013052400001.html.

Yamazaki, M. (2007) *Gendai Apareru Sangyou No Tenkai – Chousen, Zasetsu, Saisei No Rekishi Wo Yomi Toku* [The Evolution of the Modern Apparel Industry: An Analysis of the Industrial History of Challenge, Failure, Recovery], Tokyo: Senken Shimbunsha.

Yanai, T. (2003) *Issho Kyuu Hai* [One Win, Nine Losses: "winning the competition once beside nine defeats"], Tokyo: Shincho-Sha.

Yanai, T. (2009a) *Seikou Ha Ichinichi De Sute Sare* [Just Forget About Your Success in a Day], Tokyo: Shincho-Sha.

Yanai, T. (ed.) (2009b) *UNIQLO Sikoujyutsu* [The UNIQLO-Style Thinking Techniques], Tokyo: Shincho-Sha.

Yanai, T. (2012) *Genjitsu wo Miyo* [Just Look at the Reality Squarely], Tokyo: PHP.

Yano Keizai Kenkyuusho (2010) *Sen'i Hakusho* [White Paper on the Textile Industry, the Years from 1975 to 2009], Tokyo: Yano Keizai Kenkyuusho.

Yano Keizai Kenkyuusho (2012) *Sen'i Hakusho* [White Paper on the Textile Industry, the Years from 2009 to 2011], Tokyo: Yano Keizai Kenkyuusho.

Yonekura, S. (1998) "Kei'ei shigaku no ho-ho-ron: Itsudatsu, Hu-kisokusei, Shukansei" [Research Methodology of Business History: Deviation, Irregularity, and Subjectivity], *Hitotsubashi Ronso* [The Hitotsubashi Review], 120(4): 78–92.

Yunikuro (UNIQLO) (2008) *Yunikuro No Dezain* [UNIQLO's Design and Advertisements, 1999–2007].

20
The Seven & i Group

Nobuo Kawabe

Introduction

The Seven & i Group's financial results for the year ending 28 February, 2013 show that the company had 4,991.6 billion yen in revenue from operations, 295.6 billion yen in ordinary income, a net profit of 138 billion yen, and 134,689 employees, situating the company in a heated battle with the Aeon Group for supremacy in the Japanese retail industry (Seven & i Holdings, 2013a). Both companies trace their roots back to "superstore" beginnings—but that is where their paths diverge. By leveraging numerous partial M&A initiatives and M&A-oriented financial strategies toward growth, the Aeon Group has aligned itself with the more "American" mode of company management.

The Seven & i Group, meanwhile, fused business formats from abroad with unique, independent management systems to drive development. When the Southland Corporation—the company that operated and essentially served as the parent company for 7-Eleven in the United States—went bankrupt, the Seven & i Group made the Southland Group part of its subsidiary structure, applied 7-Eleven Japan's very own "Japanese-style convenience store" concept, and set the Southland Corporation back on its feet (Kawabe, 2003).

Group founder Masatoshi Itō was so thoroughly deliberate and careful in his approach to management that he would often find himself ridiculed by his contemporaries, some of whom said he adhered to a "better safer than safe" strategy. While other founders embodied a showier, brasher style, Itō remained consistently restrained and methodical; this approach, however, did not undermine his business acumen. In the 1960s, when Itō's company (Ito-Yokado) was still just a single local chain, one observer lauded the company for adopting a "solid management structure that gives the company what it takes to make any initiative it pursues a successful one" (Hayashi and Shibata, 2008, p. 94).

Based on Seven & i Holdings, the Seven & i Group currently has seven main business areas (see Figure 20.1): convenience stores (7-Eleven), general merchandise stores (Ito-Yokado), department stores (Sogo/Seibu), supermarkets (York Benimaru, etc.), food service (Denny's, etc.), financial services (Seven Bank), and IT and related services (Seven Net Shopping and 7dream.com, etc.). Without question, the engine propelling this varied mix of business initiatives forward is the commercial spirit of Itō, who constructed the group through his efforts to establish general

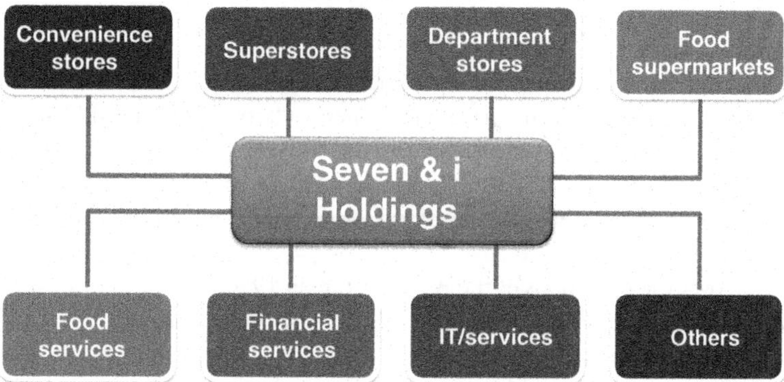

Figure 20.1 Group companies

merchandise stores, and Toshifumi Suzuki, who engineered the development of the company's convenience store operations.

This chapter explores the business activities and defining characteristics of Masatoshi Itō and Toshifumi Suzuki, two of the most influential figures in the history of the Seven & i Group.

From a clothing shop to a general merchandise store

A merchant pedigree

The direct origins of the modern-day Seven & i Group can be traced back to 1958, when Masatoshi Itō founded Ito-Yokado Co., Ltd. Itō came from a complicated family background. His mother, Yuki, was the daughter of Kumakichi Yoshikawa, the proprietor of a large dried food wholesaler located in Kanda, Tokyo. The family's next child was Toshio, a boy. Just as the store began to enjoy sustained success, Kumakichi succumbed to an illness at the young age of 29. With their immediate family life in disarray, Yuki and Toshio went to live with their grandmother, Nobu. Years later, Toshio left home to become an apprentice at the Myōgaya Tabi-Socks establishment in Tokyo's Asakusa district (Itō, 2003).

Yuki married Tadaharu Itō, a reporter for the *Osaka Mainichi Shimbun* (now the *Mainichi Shimbun*) and bore a son named Yuzuru. After the death of her first husband, Yuki married Senzō Kaneko, the son of a landowner in Yoshino-mura (now Kawagoe-shi), Saitama-ken, and opened up a small cooked beans shop in Musashi-Koyama in Meguro-ku, Tokyo. Although the cooked beans shop folded, Yuki took advantage of her business knack to convert the store into a grocer and even open branch locations in Jiyūgaoka and Ōokayama. Musashi-Koyama is where Yuki and Senzō had their first child, Masatoshi, in April 1924 (in 1952, at the age of 28, Masatoshi married Nobuko Nakamura, whose father ran the "Kikuya" clothing shop in Kūenji, Tokyo; by that time, however, he had already adopted the name of his mother's deceased first husband).

For Yuki and Senzō, their business fared much better than their marriage. When Masatoshi was a sophomore in high school, Yuki took him to Asakusa to live with Yuzuru, his half-brother. Yuzuru worked at Myōgaya, which his uncle Toshio had inherited in 1920 (and later renamed "Yokado" in 1928). By that time, the company had expanded the scope of its business from tabi-socks alone to other forms of men's accessories and apparel, including shirt collars, hats, ties, suspenders, socks, and underwear. From Asakusa, Masatoshi commuted to the Tokyo City Shiba Commercial School (now Tokyo Metropolitan Shiba Commercial School) and later the

Yokohama City College of Commerce (now Yokohama City University), with Yuzuru covering all his tuition fees.

At the time, clothes were stocked in sets of 12; retailers would price the items so that they would gain profits equivalent to the price of two items ("a two-piece profit") for a margin of 16.6 percent. Commercial concepts of label pricing, low-margin, high-volume sales, and customer service skills passed from Toshio to Yuzuru and Yuki; with these ideas so deeply ingrained in the family fabric, Masatoshi would esteem Yuki as a "model merchant" and revere Yuzuru as "master merchant."

Yuzuru took over the operations of the Asakusa store in 1940 under a *noren-wake* arrangement (in which a master sets up business for an apprentice). Masatoshi, having graduated early from the city college, joined Mitsubishi Mining in 1944 and took up a post at the Ozawa Mine in Akita-ken. The Great Tokyo Air Raids of March 1945 destroyed the family's Asakusa store, leading Yuki and Yuzuru to open a tiny, 6.6 sqm supply store in Senju, Adachi-ku, Tokyo, in 1946.

That same year, Masatoshi decided to quit his job at Mitsubishi Mining and move back to Tokyo from Akita-ken. Before leaving, however, he went to the company library and came across a book called *Ichishōnin to shite* [Being a Merchant] by Aizō Soma, the owner of the famous Nakamuraya in Shinjuku, Tokyo. Soma's compelling merchant philosophy and commitment to self-sustenance not only spurred Masatoshi to leave his position at Mitsubishi Mining but also sculpted his perspective on commerce.

Post-war development

Yuki and her sons, Yuzuru and Masatoshi, may not have had a very spacious store after their relocation, but it still managed to thrive. The Yokado *gōshi-kaisha* (a Japanese limited partnership) was established in August 1948, with Yuzuru serving as its senior partner. By 1949, the company had hired two male employees and seven or eight females. The company maintained the "two-piece profit" business model and hung a sign in the store proclaiming "A Modest Outlook on Life + A Rational Business Approach = The Low-Margin, High-Volume Way" in large block letters.

Masatoshi was in charge of purchasing. Due to the shortage of goods available at the time, wholesalers wielded a considerable influence that made purchasing a rather challenging task. For Masatoshi, work mostly consisted of inspecting the items that wholesalers would bring in, and negotiating with customers. When it came to doing the product purchasing, Masatoshi benefited immensely from the help of Hiroyoshi Sekiguchi. The president of the popular Umeya department store in Hiratsuka-shi, Kanagawa-ken, Sekiguchi would give Masatoshi valuable purchasing information, show him around various key locations, and even offer a wealth of advice on management in general; to Masatoshi, Sekiguchi became a mentor in both business and life.

Yuki put the register in the middle of the store and kept an eye on customers and employees from that central station. Her approach to educating her employees focused on two core tenets: first, she emphasized the importance of being "always grateful and appreciative"; and second, she encouraged workers to "learn from customers." Overall, her management style was extremely family business-oriented.

In July 1956, with the store posting yearly sales of 100 million yen and anticipating even better results moving forward, Yuzuru had an asthma attack and died suddenly at the age of 44. Masatoshi took over from his half-brother and assumed leadership of the company. One of his first actions as president was to reorganize the enterprise into a joint-stock corporation in April 1958. That same year, the company renovated and expanded the store to cover 256 sqm. A subsequent renovation in 1963 brought the store's footprint to a walloping 1,826 sqm.

The company's Senjū location also operated self-service operations at its second-floor food corner in 1960. Incidentally, the pioneer of the self-service approach in Japan was the Kinokuniya grocery store in Aoyama, Tokyo, which launched self-service in 1953 (Itō, 2003).

Observing the United States and developing a chain

The 1956 "Economic White Paper" declared that the post-war era was over. The Japanese economy began to overcome the chaos of the aftermath of World War II and make a steady resurgence. The Japanese people, likewise, started to pick themselves back up. Although the availability of housing was spotty, food and clothing—the other two basic necessities—grew more and more abundant. "Westernization" and "electrification" dominated civilian life. With the Japanese economy reviving up into a period of high-speed growth, "consumption is a virtue" became a popular catchphrase.

As Japan hurtled into prosperity in the late 1950s, the chief issue for the national economy became modernizing and streamlining its distribution sector. The distribution sector at the time was the "dark continent" of the Japanese economy, where an "overabundance of undersized players" in the retail sphere pitted countless small-scale stores against one another. Companies in the sector responded in two ways: by firming up distribution control through manufacturing grouping and implementing the "chain store" strategy (JCI, 1967).

Japanese modern stores based their operations on the supermarket format popular in the United States, which preceded Japan in becoming an arena for mass consumption. The supermarket concept took off on the widespread appeal of affordability, a goal that companies pursued by stocking in bulk, selling in bulk, implementing self-service operations, and maximizing the effects of economies of scale in other ways (Kawabe,1993).

In the spring of 1961, Masatoshi Itō traveled throughout Europe and the United States as a delegate for the "Third Modern Merchandising Method Seminar" organized by National Cash Register Japan. What Itō noticed in the United States were the country's high-mass consumption society, the ongoing decay of the department store, and the pronounced countervailing power that Sears, Roebuck and Co. and A&P had compared to manufacturers. At the time, Sears, Roebuck and Co. was the world's biggest retailer. For Masatoshi, seeing the company's chain system and robust management structure was an eye-opening experience.

Itō decided to adopt the chain store development approach on his very first overseas observation tour. Upon returning to Japan, he immediately expanded the product selection at the Senjū location to include items like processed foods, household goods, cosmetics, and pharmaceuticals and also decided to open up a store in Akabane, Kita-ku, which represented the first link in the company chain.

The company opened its Akabane location, its first superstore (with a sales floor area of 566 sqm), in October 1961. It then proceeded to open a location in Kita-Urawa (its third overall; 371 sqm) in December 1962, a store in Koiwa (Edogawa-ku, Tokyo; 990 sqm) in May 1963, and a store in Tateishi (Katsushika-ku, Tokyo; 1,190 sqm) in June 1963. The following year saw more expansion, with the company launching operations in Kamata (Ota-ku, Tokyo; 1,830 sqm) in April and quadrupling the size of its Akabane location in December (Itō, 2003).

Establishing the Japanese-style superstore

Efforts to create a new "Self-Service Discount Department Store" (SSDDS) business format began in Japan in the early 1960s as chain stores continued to expand. Applying the "self-service" sales method, low-price strategies, and a comprehensive product line-up approach, the format traced its origins back to 1948, when American businessman Eugene Ferkauf founded the E.J. Korvette discount department store. In the United States, however, the discount store set-up did not include groceries in its scope of operations, while supermarkets did not deal in anything but groceries. The Japanese SSDDS format (SSDDS came to be called "General Merchandise Store" (GMS) or "Superstore" later), which encompassed groceries, clothing, and supplies alike, got its official start when Isao Nakauchi launched the Daiei's first SSDDS in Kōbe in July 1963, thus producing the "superstore" wave that swept across the chain store landscape (Nakauchi, 2000).

In July 1964, the Ito-Yokado store in Oyama became the company's first SSDDS location. The store had three floors that offered certain product categories: men's clothing, underwear, bedding, bags, and shoes were on the first floor; women's clothing, children's shoes, cosmetics, and accessories were on the second; and food, daily commodities, household goods, and electrical equipment were on the third. Ito-Yokado also established full-fledged food sections, complete with perishables, at all new locations beginning with the opening of its Hikifune store in 1967.

Many department stores and new superstores in the 1960s relied heavily on existing wholesale dealers for supplies of products, making purchasing a common task at each store location. However, Ito-Yokado created a merchandise division in October 1961 to effectively centralize the purchasing process—and thereby became the first company to do all of its purchasing from the head office. The move helped not only standardize quality and pricing but also reduced purchasing prices by allowing for larger purchasing quantities. These various initiatives eventually coalesced into "total merchandising," a framework through which buyers would use the information they had gathered and input from experts to create their own product plans and ask manufacturers to commercialize their conceptions.

Ito-Yokado had high hopes of becoming a national chain, but the company actually opened stores at a slower pace than its competitors did, never achieving more than 10 new locations in a year. In Masatoshi Itō's eyes:

> The competition to open new stores doesn't end in a year or two—it's a drawn-out battle. If you take a broader perspective, you'll see that companies with strong internal structures and good business practices tend to come out on top in the struggle for "new store" supremacy.

To earn the "trust of the customer," the most crucial asset for any retailer, Itō believed that a company needed to enhance the quality of each and every store through a sound deployment policy.

Given how difficult it would be to maintain management quality while simultaneously working to boost earning capacity, avoid all debt, and on top of that forge mergers and partnerships with companies that operate under different corporate cultures and organizational climates, Ito-Yokado has remained firm in its stance against all merger strategies.

Developing convenience store business

Toshifumi Suzuki, the professional manager

In November 1973, roughly 10 years after the birth of the Japanese-style general merchandise store, Ito-Yokado established York-Seven as an area franchisee for 7-Eleven (later renamed Seven-Eleven Japan in January 1978), a convenience store run by the Southland Corporation (a US-based company). The new company opened its first 7-Eleven franchise location in Toyosu, Kōtō-ku, Tokyo, in May 1974 (Kawabe, 2003).

Selling approximately 2,800 different items from stores of around 100 sqm in size, Ito-Yokado's convenience store business initially put more of an emphasis on the "convenience" idea than on affordability. 7-Eleven was a success right out of the gate; in 2001, 30 years after its inception, Seven-Eleven Japan surpassed general merchandise giant Daiei in terms of sales and carved out a foothold as Japan's leading retailer—a position that, as a single retail entity, the company has yet to relinquish.

Ito-Yokado's venture into the convenience store market began with its 1973 organizational reshuffling, which created a business development office charged with cultivating new business opportunities. The efforts of this new organization spurred the development of Denny's, a family restaurant, the 7-Eleven convenience store, and more. Ito-Yokado pushed ahead with measures designed to bolster its group structure, such as bringing York-Benimaru, an existing company, under its corporate umbrella. Behind many of these business development initiatives was Toshifumi Suzuki, an Ito-Yokado company director formerly in charge of personnel matters and publicity.

Born into a prominent family that had produced several mayors of Sakaki-machi, Hanishina-gun, Nagano-ken, Suzuki grew up in the lap of luxury. As a child, he was apparently shy and withdrawn. After graduating from the Chuo University Faculty of Economics in 1956, he took a position at Tokyo Shuppan Hanbai (now TOHAN). Working on public relations magazines, he attracted a public following for his interviews with popular contemporary writers, brought statistical and psychological viewpoints to research efforts, and developed a scientific, intellectual way of looking at things. Suzuki's experiences at TOHAN would later prove instrumental in molding his managerial style. He eventually left the company and joined Ito-Yokado mid-career in 1963. He spent all his time in the personnel and administration departments, never once working on the sales floor (Suzuki, 2008).

Unlike superstores and their focus on bargain prices, convenience stores in Japan started out under the banner of convenience. Originally open from 7 a.m. to 11 p.m. (and later 24 hours a day), convenience stores adopted a slogan of "I'm glad it's open" and fueled the spread of the convenience store concept on the appeal of the convenience idea. By the mid-1970s, the effects of high-speed economic growth in the country had infused everyday life with a new dimension of diversity that ordinary Japanese citizens had never enjoyed and shifted the consumer market away from the purchasing domain of housewives and more toward the young, rapidly changing personal market. Whereas general merchandise stores were a place for housewives to buy groceries and products for their families, convenience stores presented an outlet for individuals to make purchases for their own consumption.

Small-scale convenience stores attract an average of around 1,000 customers a day but lack the sufficient space for inventory, which makes product shortages a common issue. If a customer visits a store and cannot find what he wants, the store fails in its mission to provide the customer with the convenience he expects. However, attempting to provide products to multiple stores on a frequent basis would entail prohibitive distribution costs.

The convenience store format needed to create a thorough, scrupulous system. Although they could have used the bulk purchasing, bulk distribution, and bulk sales approach favored by conventional general merchandise stores to keep prices down, such a strategy would have forced convenience stores to sacrifice a considerable degree of product diversity. Instead, convenience stores had to find some way to cut costs with high-frequency, small-lot distribution and meet the multifarious needs of the personal market. This hole in the framework was a perfect fit for Suzuki, whose logical approach to satisfying customer demands centered on persistent efforts to improve business efficiency. The business management system that Seven-Eleven devised also went into practice at Ito-Yokado Group companies via various implementation channels, including weekly meetings of the restructuring committee. As a result of his efforts, Suzuki became the chief executive officer of not only Seven-Eleven but the entire Ito-Yokado Group as well.

For Ito-Yokado and the other superstores of the 1970s, every effort to open a new store was met with fierce opposition from local merchants. This discord led to the repeal of the existing Department Store Law and the 1973 creation of the "Act for the Adjustment of Retail Business Operations in Large-Scale Retail Stores," which aimed to regulate how department stores, general merchandise stores, and other large-scale retailers opened new locations. Given these circumstances, Ito-Yokado had to develop its business activities in a way that would enable cooperation with local stores if it wanted to continue thriving (Seven-Eleven, Japan, 1991).

Establishing the Japanese-style convenience store

Suzuki was tipped to head up the effort to implement the convenience store set-up, a small-store model that could promote co-prosperity with local merchants through the franchise system and help modernize independent retailing. In founding Seven-Eleven, Suzuki assembled a team of people with no experience whatsoever in retail, devoted his attention to building a system that could control the flow of each and every product under the *tanpin kanri* (item-by-item management) concept, and outsourced the capital and particulars (Kawabe, 1995).

First, the store side converted the liquor stores and other existing merchants that owned the land and store locations to the convenience store format via the franchise system. To define store operations, the company assigned the parties clear franchiser and franchisee rules. By basing store operations around order placement and taking extensive measures to ensure proper hypothesis/verification processes, the company worked hard to fully embrace the *genba shugi* (hands-on, bottom-up) approach and eliminate both opportunity loss and inventory loss.

On the supply side, the company established consolidated and joint transport systems that linked competing companies to make sure that stores had the necessary products at the necessary times and in the necessary quantities. Under this arrangement, the manufacturers and vendors established distribution centers, but Seven-Eleven itself did not. Product development followed a similar pattern: the company shared sales information with manufacturers and vendors in a "team merchandising" set-up.

In addition, Seven-Eleven Japan created a management information system for integrating the sales and supply sides. It also constructed a system for managing the flow of products with POS and other tools. Suzuki urged colleagues to recognize the vital importance of solid data management; for him, data was the key to correcting many problems. The company enjoyed strong improvements in sales after opening its first location, but inventory problems held profits back. At the time, the store purchased items by the lot; while popular items flew off the shelves quickly, less popular sizes and products piled up in inventory. Seeing this, Suzuki introduced a "*tanpin kanri*" system, designed to track the sales and inventory volumes of each individual item, in hopes of doing away with poorly performing items and stocking up on hot sellers.

From the time that the company originally fleshed out its *tanpin kanri* initiative with a POS system in 1982 to the implementation of its Sixth Generation Total Information System in 2006, Seven-Eleven Japan worked to build a robust management information system and collect massive amounts of data on what times certain products sold well and how many products customers bought during various periods. Using these resources, the company created a far-reaching database that helped analysts form hypotheses on how best to order products based on weather conditions, temperature, and upcoming events in different areas. The company then verified the results of these hypotheses to minimize inventory loss and keep business opportunities from getting away (Figure 20.2).

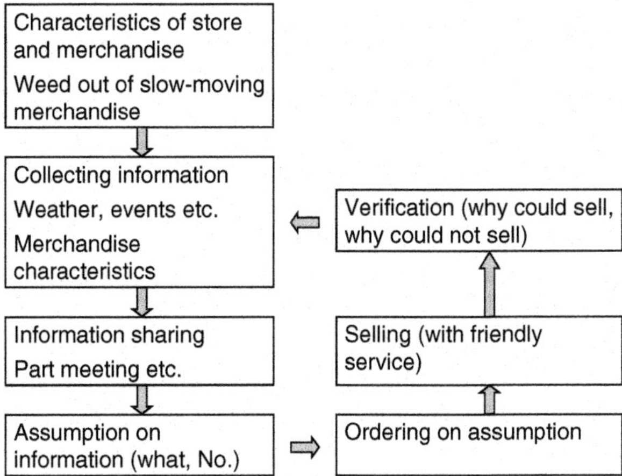

Figure 20.2 Process of item-by-item management

Real and virtual integration

From distribution to service

In the late 1990s, the retail business climate witnessed the beginnings of a sea change. Not only had the once booming convenience store industry hit the murky waters of high saturation, but competitive heat from supermarkets and other businesses that kept their doors open for extended hours had started to flare up. Perhaps even more concerning for retailers were the mounting tides of Japan's dwindling birth rate and aging population. The population of citizens aged 65 and older rose from just 12 percent of the total population in 1990 to 17.2 percent in 2000 and 22 percent in 2010. Ever-accelerating advances in information technology, too, had opened the expansive realm of the Internet to commercial activity in the mid-1990s and fueled the rapid development of e-commerce thereafter.

Given the circumstances, the Seven & i Group had to formulate a new strategy. First, its convenience store business at the time focused on the sale of goods and relegated services to a merely supportive role. From very early on, Seven-Eleven convenience stores have provided services like copying and DPE in an effort to save customers time and also enhance overall service convenience. The range of services gradually began to diversify in myriad directions, but one of the biggest service-related transitions came in 1986, when stores started allowing customers to pay bills to the Tokyo Electric Power Company and other utility providers. With this change, people no longer had to go to the bank to pay their bills—they could just head to a convenience store whenever they pleased. This enhanced service convenience moved convenience stores further into the public spotlight and prompted the addition of a wide variety of other services, including package tours and event tickets, to the line-up of service offerings available at convenience store locations (Seven-Eleven, 2003).

As the business format continued to evolve, the company established a pure holding company called Seven & i Holdings in September 2005 to help streamline the management of a large group comprising various retailers and service companies. At the time, the Japanese business world was humming with speculative M&A activity. There was a need to protect high-performing, cash- and asset-rich companies, such as Seven-Eleven Japan. In December 2012, the company announced a capital tie-up and management integration with Sogo (which was busy rebuilding) and Millennium Retailing, the holding company for Seibu Department Stores.

Development in the IT/service sphere

The development of the service industry also triggered the start of e-commerce. The global collapse of the "IT bubble" around the turn of the century temporarily tripped up the IT industry, but e-commerce kept right on going and growing. Seven-Eleven joined forces with seven existing companies—NEC, Nomura Research Institute, JTB, Sony, and Mitsui & Co., among them—to form 7dream.com in February 2000, marking the company's official entry into the e-commerce market (Kawabe, 2003, pp. 344–378).

The American-type "virtual" model of e-commerce is one in which customers order products on their computers, pay for the items by credit card, and have the products delivered to their doors. 7dream.com expanded on this format by allowing customers to order products on their computers, their mobile phones, and convenience store terminals, pay for them at convenience stores, and even pick them up at convenience stores. This "Japanese-style" model of e-commerce made the convenience store itself into a platform. As shown in Figure 20.3, it builds e-commerce, finance, meals, and service businesses on top of existing store systems (shown by the thick lines) as a way of fusing real store locations with the virtual world of information technology.

The e-commerce concept became in important piece of business operations at Ito-Yokado, Sogo, Seibu, and other group companies. Ito-Yokado launched its "Internet supermarket" initiative in March 2001, coming on the heels of Seiyu, which opened Japan's first Internet supermarket in May 2000. However, Ito-Yokado outstripped its competitors in the field. When the customer places an order online, employees take the ordered products off the shelves at that store and deliver them to the customer. Essentially, buying from the Ito-Yokado Internet supermarket is the same as going to the store and checking products out at the register.

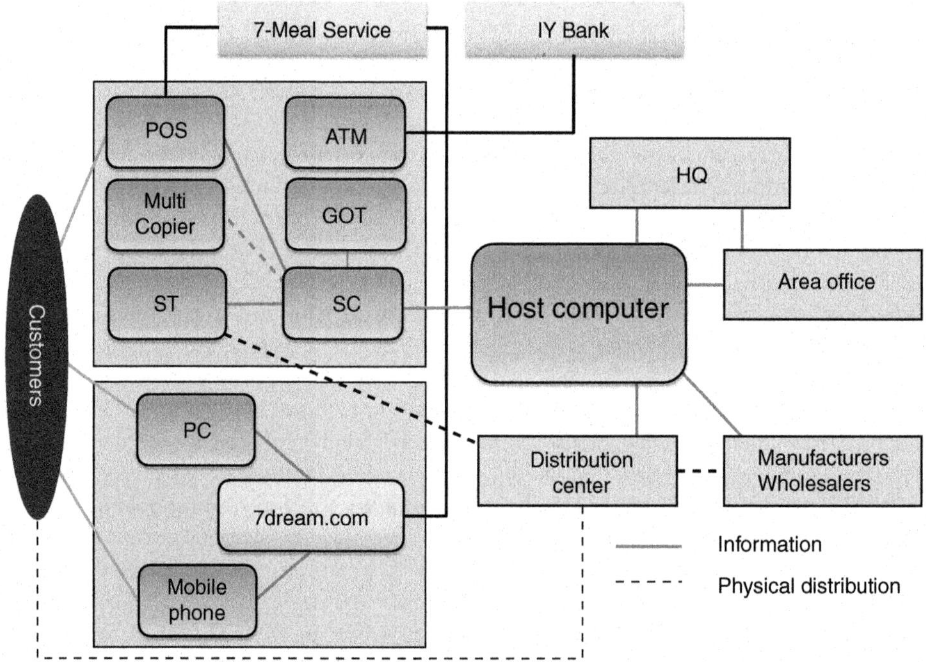

Figure 20.3 Japanese business model for e-commerce

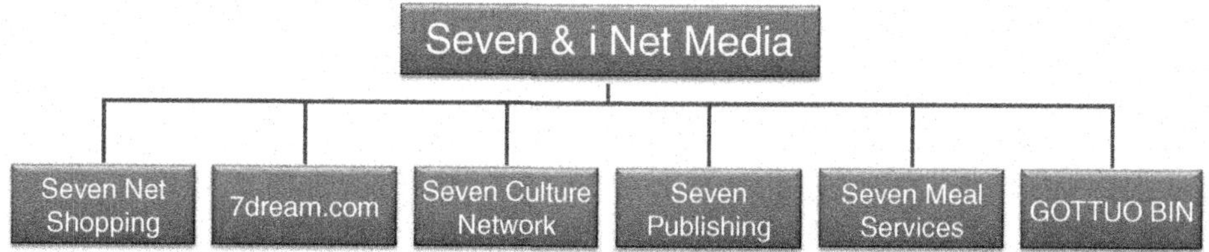

Figure 20.4 The Seven & i Group's IT/service businesses

Seven & i Holdings also created Seven & i Net Media in July 2008 to oversee the group's Internet-based business and launched full-scale operations at the new venture the following year. Seeing 2009 as the "first year of Net Services," Suzuki worked to push the company's IT and service businesses to an even higher level. Seven & i Net Media is not an operating company; rather, it affiliated itself with subsidiaries like Seven Net Shopping—a subsidiary formed via a joint venture with Softbank—and 7dream.com to function as an intermediary holding company in charge of group Internet business (see Figure 20.4).

Improving financial services

The Seven & i Group has also been active in the financial business sphere. When restrictions on bank locations eased in September 1997, banks could install ATMs, set their operating hours, and create branches—even in-store branches—as they pleased. Seven-Eleven Japan joined with its parent company (Ito-Yokado) and financial institutions to propose a banking plan based around personal transactions. However, the plan quickly hit a roadblock due to disagreements over how to handle the service fees that users would pay the bank upon making ATM transactions. To remedy the situation, the parties decided to scrap the shared ATM idea in favor of establishing their own bank. In hopes of exercising its leadership in the financial field, Ito-Yokado submitted a prospectus to the Financial Supervisory Agency in November 1999 to obtain preliminary licensing for the IY Bank, a settlement-only bank. In April 2001, the Financial Supervisory Agency granted the IY Bank a preliminary license, and IY Bank was established (Kawabe, 2003, pp. 379–397).

Ito-Yokado Group companies installed in-store ATMs at 7–11 locations and other stores. In addition to partnering with other banks to provide transaction services, the company has also forged links with security companies and insurance companies to make a variety of financial products available to customers.

The IY Bank launched online banking services for Internet and mobile phone users in December 2001, a step that allowed users without ATM access to open accounts, submit applications, and send funds at any time of day via an Internet connection.

Seven & i Holdings made its second major venture into the financial arena in the spring of 2007 with the creation of "nanaco," an original form of pre-paid e-money that customers can use at Seven-Eleven and Ito-Yokado stores. In the fall of 2007, the company began accepting other forms of e-money, including Suica and Edy.

Meal services

After its foray into the financial arena, Seven-Eleven Japan proceeded to create a new company, Seven-Meal Service, with Nichii Gakkan, Mitsui & Co., and NEC. Using its parent company's network of over 8,000 stores and sophisticated information distribution infrastructure, the company has delivered meals and conducted long-term care-related business since September 2000 (Kawabe, 2003, pp. 399–401).

The new company not only enrolls members and accepts/delivers daily meals at Seven-Eleven locations but also delivers meals from distribution centers to users' residences. Responsible for making the meals are the dedicated plants that manufacture the boxed lunches and side dishes on the food shelves at Seven-Eleven stores.

Members receive two types of monthly menus: a selection of meals and side dishes that you can warm up in the microwave and eat right away and a line-up of easy-to-cook fresh materials that are essentially pre-made except for the final cooking step. Meals feature one main dish, two side dishes, and one dessert for the price of around 900 to 1,000 yen. Users can choose to pay either at Seven-Eleven stores or via automatic payments from their bank accounts. The service boasted approximately 250,000 customers in October 2011, the majority of whom were users aged 60 or older.

Conclusion

Japan's high-mass consumption society took shape in the country's period of high-speed economic growth that began in the late 1950s and ended with the first "oil shock" in 1973. As a result, people started moving away from the conventional, traditional way of life and toward a new lifestyle brimming with prosperity and affluence. The general merchandise store format developed to meet these needs, with numerous traditional merchants and department stores transforming and aligning themselves with the new model. Ito-Yokado, created by Masatoshi Itō, is one of the most prominent superstores. Like his fellow executives at other companies, Itō traveled to Europe and the United States to observe business operations, held study sessions with his business friends, and adapted the American chain store system to the Japanese environment in the form of the superstore.

Itō was flanked by Toshifumi Suzuki, who joined Ito-Yokado partway through his career and has maintained his position as a ranking corporate employee ever since. Suzuki was the one primarily responsible for launching and building the Seven-Eleven Japan convenience store brand. Suzuki had loads of great ideas—but no matter how perfect his plans were, the initiative could never get off the ground without the consent of Itō, a cautious owner who some said operated on the idea that the company was "better safer than safe." In the end, the relationship between Itō, the decision-making owner, and Suzuki, the dedicated executive with an eye for novel ideas, helped the company find an effective balance in furthering its aims.

Itō and Suzuki—the company's two main entrepreneurs and managers—worked to meet the needs of their respective times in unique ways; Itō drove the development of the general merchandise store, while Suzuki introduced the new convenience store format. Both helped revolutionize the distribution arena and played significant roles in making life in Japan more convenient than ever before.

However, these two distribution revolutionaries have appeared to demonstrate fundamentally different personalities and abilities. Having grown up in a merchant household, Itō valued the traditional Japanese merchant spirit and placed a considerable amount of importance on interpersonal relationships. Suzuki, meanwhile, harnessed the advertising and statistics abilities he had honed at TOHAN into an active, rational approach as a professional executive.

The ability to create a company and the ability to organize a new company do not normally go hand in hand; executives with both abilities are few and far between. Neither Itō nor Suzuki actually conceived the ideas behind the general merchandise store or the convenience store—rather, what they did was to understand the fundamental essence of retail, think about the business formats from a broad perspective, and build new systems to streamline the business formats and ultimately satisfy customer needs.

Two of the pair's most important contributions to the convenience store field were the *tanpin kanri* system, which discarded the bulk purchasing/selling of the second industrial revolution for a format more attuned to the personal market of the third industrial revolution, and a joint transport system that had never been seen before in the retail industry. These systems were so compelling that they even took hold at general merchandise stores from the second industrial revolution. Clearly, Itō and Suzuki were blessed with two often exclusive traits: first, an entrepreneurial spirit that spawned altogether new business formats and systems, and second, a managerial knack for adapting to changing business conditions and sustaining growth (Kawabe, 2012).

Itō and Suzuki, the company's two phenomenal entrepreneurs, have molded the Seven & i Group into what it is today. Based on its existing store systems, the entire group is currently hard at work on a "new total consumer industry" that aims to leverage IT technology, shape new service business, and bring the "real" and "virtual" into fuller harmony. However, the two cannot go on heading the company forever; Itō is already 89, while Suzuki is 80. After the retirement of these two business luminaries, particularly standing CEO Suzuki, their successors will have massive shoes to fill and a sprawling business empire to nourish (Kawabe, 2011).

Bibliography and further reading

Hayashi, S. and Shōei Shibata (2008) *Sangyo seisaku ritsuansha no taikenteki kiroku* [The Record of Industrial Policies by Their Planners], Tokyo: Kokusai Shōgyo Shuppan.

Itō, M. (2003) *Itō Masatoshi no akinai no kokoro* [Merchant Spirit of Masatoshi Itō], Tokyo: Nihon Keizai Shinbunsha.

Ito-Yokado Co., Ltd (2007) *Henka taiō: Akinaki sōzō e no chōsen, 1920–2000* [Responding to Changes: Challenge to Endless Creation, 1920–2000], Tokyo: Ito-Yokado.

Japan Consulting Institution for the Betterment of Retail-Business (JCI) (1967) *Nihon kourigyō keieishi* [Business History of the Japanese Retail Industry], Tokyo: JCI.

Kawabe, N. (1993) "The development of the retailing industry in Japan," *Entreprises et Histoire,* 4(November): 15–25.

Kawabe, N. (1995) "A new business system and Japan–U.S. cooperation: the case of Seven-Eleven Stores," *Waseda Journal of Commerce,* 365(October): 1–35.

Kawabe, N. (2003) *Shinpan 7-Eleven no Keieishi: Nihongata Jōhō Kigyō e no chōsen* [Business History of 7-Eleven: Challenge to Japanese Style of Information Company], new edition, Tokyo: Yuhikaku.

Kawabe, N. (2011) "Net Super no Seisei to Hatten: Virtual Business to Real Business no Togo" [The historical development of internet supermarkets in Japan: integration of virtual and real businesses], *Waseda Commercial Review,* 429(September): 23–78.

Kawabe, N. (2012) "Social infrastructure for daily life: the development of convenience stores in Japan," in P. Fridenson and T. Yui (eds) *Beyond Mass Distribution—Distribution, Market and Consumers: Proceedings of Japanese and French Business History Conference,* Tokyo: Japan Business History Institute, pp. 85–99.

Nakauchi, I. (2000), *Ryutsu kakumei wa owaranai: Watashi no rirekisho* [Never-Ending Distribution Revolution: My Personal History]: Tokyo, Nihon Keizai Sinbunsha.

Seven & i Holdings (2013a) *2013 Annual Report.* Available at: www.7andi.com/group.

Seven & i Holdings (2013b) "Group companies." Available at: www.7andi.com/group/index.html (accessed 30 June 2013).

Seven-Eleven Japan (1991) *Seven-Eleven Japan: Owarinaki innovation 1973–1991* [Endless Innovation, 1973–1991], Tokyo: Seven-Eleven Japan.

Seven-Eleven Japan (2003) *Seven-Eleven Japan: Owarinaki innovation 1991–2003* [Endless Innovation, 1991–2003], Tokyo: Seven-Eleven Japan.

Suzuki, T. (2008) *Chōsen, waga roman: Watashi no rirekisho* [Challenge, My Ambition: My Personal History], Tokyo: Nihon Keizai Shinbun.

Taiwan

21

Absorptive capacity and the growth of an electronic firm

The case of ASUSTek Computer Inc.

Chyong Ling Judy Chen

Introduction

Taiwan's economic success today is rooted in the IT industry. Because Taiwan has come to play such an important role in the global IT industry, it is well known as the "Silicon Island."

Taiwan is a small business-dominated economy, small businesses accounting for about 97 percent of all firms. The average life of Taiwanese small businesses is 13.3 years. The advantage of a small business is its flexibility in weathering adversity such as the Asian financial crisis in 1997; but it has the disadvantage of limited growth due to financial and technological constraints. ASUSTek Computer Inc. (ASUS) has demonstrated entrepreneurial success globally in a relatively short period of time. Established in 1990 with four owner-employees and NT$30 million (US$1 million) start-up capital, with revenue of less than NT$1 billion (US$31.7 million) in its first year of operation, ASUS has grown to be a global company with market capitalization of NT$49 billion (US$1.5 billion), and revenue of over NT$755 billion (US$24 billion), the historical high, in 2007. ASUS has been in the top three for name brand value in Taiwan since 2003 with a value of US$1.66 billion in 2012 ("Top Taiwan Global Brands," 2013). This phenomenal success in only 13 years makes ASUS an interesting case study to investigate the entrepreneurial activities leading to its continuing success.

The growth of an entrepreneurial firm depends upon whether it can create competitive advantages (Porter, 1985). Since the economy is complex and dynamic, competitive advantages change constantly and the creation of competitive advantages depends upon the absorptive capacities of the entrepreneurial firm (Cohen and Levinthal, 1989). As argued by Alvarez and Barney (2007), effective entrepreneurial action usually includes opportunity discovery and involves leadership, strategic planning, and competitive advantage creation. The success of entrepreneurial activities is closely related to the absorptive capacities of the firm.

This chapter will discuss the entrepreneurial activities of ASUS by focusing on the leadership and organizational culture, in-house R&D and apprenticeship-style on-the-job training, as well as a favorable government policy, and how these have provided the foundation and environment for great absorptive capacity to develop and adapt technology, enabling it to become a "Giant Lion" in the global computer industry.

The second section briefly presents key research linking absorptive capacity to business success; the third section links the success of ASUS to its tremendous absorptive capacity, identifying the factors which provide the foundation for it; finally the conclusion.

Absorptive capacity

Cohen and Levinthal (1989) first introduced the term "absorptive capacity" (hereinafter AC) to the business literature and their definition of it is still the most widely cited as "the firm's ability to identify, assimilate and exploit knowledge from the environment." In their subsequent paper (Cohen and Levinthal, 1990), they suggested that a firm's AC is "an ability to recognize the value of new information, assimilate it, and apply it to commercial ends." Mowery and Oxley (1995) later defined AC as a broad set of skills needed to deal with the tacit component of transferred knowledge and the need to modify this imported knowledge, while Kim (1998) defined AC as the capacity to learn and solve problems.

Zahra and George (2002) re-conceptualized AC as a dynamic capability pertaining to knowledge creation and utilization that enhances a firm's ability to gain and sustain a competitive advantage. They added two major stages to the process of converting knowledge into action: potential AC, which includes acquisition and assimilation capability; and realized AC, which includes transformation and exploitation capability. Potential AC captures a firm's capability to value, acquire, and extend knowledge but does not guarantee the exploitation of this knowledge. Realized AC reflects the firm's capability to utilize the knowledge that has been absorbed. They asserted that potential AC is more important than realized AC because firms with well-developed potential AC are more likely to sustain a competitive advantage. They believe that potential AC is an antecedent while realized AC is the outcome.

Zahra and George (2002) also redefined AC as a set of organizational routines and processes by which firms acquire, assimilate, transform, and exploit knowledge to produce a dynamic organizational capability. These four capabilities represent four dimensions of AC and play different but complementary roles in explaining how AC can influence the organizational outcome.

Lewin, Massini, and Peeters (2011) decomposed the construct of AC into internal and external capabilities. They postulated the importance of balancing the internal knowledge-creating processes with the identification, acquisition, and assimilation of new knowledge that originates in the external environment. Lee and Wu (2010) suggested that the AC should be comprised of employees' ability and motivation. Both of the components can facilitate knowledge transfer.

The factors that have been identified in the AC literature which are important in explaining the success of ASUS are: (1) management leadership style, which fosters an organizational culture that emphasizes learning and innovation; (2) a robust R&D department, which provides the foundation for innovation and the development of new technology; and (3) an apprenticeship-style on-the-job training program, which emphasizes learning and innovation. In addition, this chapter identifies government policies, which encourage and support the development of new technology and products in the private sector, as another significant factor that enhances the AC of a company, particularly in the manufacturing sector.

The absorptive capacity in the success of ASUS

Brief history of ASUS and the development of its absorptive capacity

ASUS was founded on April 2, 1990, by four engineers from Acer Inc,.[1]—T.H. Tung, S.C. Ted Hsu, M.T. Liao, and W.C. Wayne Hsieh[2]—with capital of NT$30 million. It was initially a professional design company for motherboards without a manufacturing division. After seeing the potential in the clone market, the decision was made to integrate design, production and marketing activities, to provide non-original equipment manufacturer (OEM) services to small computer and clone companies.

In the beginning, motherboards were ASUS' only business. In 1990, during ASUS' first year of operation, the Intel 486 processor was released as engineering samples. ASUS decided to design its own 486 motherboard, using only the technical details published by Intel and the experience gained while making 386 compatible motherboards. The result was that ASUS' prototype functioned perfectly while Intel's, which had been produced by IBM, had design flaws. Intel was stunned by ASUS' technology and contracted ASUS as their "direct customer," which qualified ASUS to obtain specifications for Intel's new products (Wu, 2007). ASUS was Intel's first Taiwanese direct customer, which not only helped ASUS to market its products 3–6 months earlier than its competitors, but it also gained advanced technology from Intel. Since the life cycle of motherboards is short, ASUS took advantage of this technology protection to reduce time to market and time to volume to gain profit and market shares. ASUS was able to achieve this goal because of its excellent R&D department.

By obtaining new CPU specifications as Intel's direct customer, ASUS was able to keep its focus on what they knew best: designing high quality motherboards. In the clone market, profits are higher than for OEM/ODM; however, the quantity of each order is small and specifications are varied. ASUS moved toward simplification by designing a few prototypes from which buyers could choose. Due to excellent quality, advanced design capability, no minimum order requirement, and excellent after-sales technological support, ASUS gained a good reputation and became a leading manufacturer in a short time. It can be said that ASUS is able to sell its products via technology, rather than marketing.

ASUS became the global leader in motherboards, gaining them the nickname, "golden board," due to their outstanding quality. Visiting Taiwan in 1996, Andy Grove, ex-CEO of Intel, said, "I never thought that motherboards could become an important industry on their own" (Chang, 2005). Taking advantage of the technology in motherboards as a niche, ASUS diversified its business to other PC-related products.

With confidence in their technology, ASUS gradually moved its focus to high-end motherboards, giving their competitors an opportunity to take over the low-end market, ASUS' profits dropped by US$6 billion in 2002, a phenomenon Christensen (1997) called "the innovator's dilemma"—losing business because of excellent technology, not because of lagging in developing new technology. ASUS fell into the trap of focusing only on the high-end market with the best technology, ignoring the low-end market, which is a much bigger market. This crisis taught Jonney Shih (the CEO of ASUS) a big lesson. After a period of deep reflection, he developed a strategy referred to in Taiwan as the "Giant Lion" strategy.

ASUS always operated as an original equipment manufacturer/original design manufacturer (OEM/ODM) and original brand manufacturer (OBM) simultaneously for motherboards and notebooks, but after 2002, they focused more on being OEM/ODM in order to get more customers and a bigger market share. Rather than continuing on their path of focusing on the high-end market, ASUS made use of its OEM/ODM experience to increase production capacity and economy of scale, learn new technology, and gain marketing experience. All of these advantages were applied to support its name brand business, both in PCs and notebook computers.

Founders rooted in R&D provided significant absorptive capacity

The founders of ASUS had all worked in the R&D department at Acer Inc., as professional engineers, so they remained focused on the importance of R&D to build on their knowledge and skills and to increase the AC of the company. ASUS spent over 60 percent of its total operating expenses on R&D during its early stage. ASUS' R&D employees are highly educated, 99 percent of whom have at least a college diploma. As Cockburn and Henderson (1998) have pointed out, in-house research is necessary for firms to be able to effectively assimilate external knowledge and technology.

According to Lane, Koka, and Pathak (2002), AC helps the speed, frequency, and magnitude of innovation, and that innovation produces knowledge which becomes part of the firm's AC. They also found that AC has a significant effect on profitability and that this impact is moderated by the pace of technological change: the greater the pace of change, the greater the impact. Mei and Nie (2008) found that the role of AC in a company's innovation is more important than knowledge sharing with customers and suppliers during a firm's early stages.

Sometimes, however, it is cheaper to acquire external knowledge and technology, as was the case when ASUS acquired ASKEY(the biggest modem manufacturer in Taiwan) and ASUS' association with Intel and Microsoft. In the case of ASKEY, ASUS was able to acquire the company cheaply, 7.1 ASKEY shares for one ASUS share, far below their market value. ASKEY, however, accepted the deal because they realized that ASUS was capable of making its own modems; and since ASKEY's sole product was modems, ASKEY could have found itself out of business. Lane, Koka, and Pathak (2002) reported that well-developed absorptive capability lowers the transaction costs of contracting or purchasing for knowledge-intensive technology, products or services.

Jonney Shih's leadership and absorptive capacity

The management leadership style can set the organizational culture of a firm, which can contribute or detract from its AC. In 1993, Jonney left his position as Senior VP of the Engineering Division of Acer where he had been employed since 1979, to join ASUS as its CEO. He was well known and respected by ASUS' four founding members who had been subordinates of Jonney at Acer. Having earned a B.S. degree in Electrical Engineering at the National Taiwan University and an MBA degree from the National Chiao Tung University, Mr. Shih was well qualified to engage in R&D in the high tech industry. Like the four founders, Jonney believes that technology and product quality are the core factors necessary for success in business and that R&D as well as employee training provide the foundation not only to generate innovation but to enable the company to counter challenges. It is the shared background, interests, and vision of the founders and Jonney, which continue to provide the bedrock for ASUS.

In 1994, Jonney thought that the post-PC era would be a 3C era, so that 3C integration and branding would be the next critical shift in the high tech computer market. ASUS then started designing and manufacturing notebook computers in 1998 and later servers and other related PC products.

Although ASUS adopted a diversification strategy, building vertical integration to maintain a competitive advantage, however, ASUS did not develop products outside their area of expertise or merge with companies carrying out unrelated business, focusing instead on their own technological advantages.

This constancy of focus has enabled ASUS to become a truly "great" company with a financial performance several times better than the market average over a sustained period of time. Collins (2001) identified the main factor necessary for achieving the transition from a small company to a great company to be narrowly focused on the company's resources in their field of competence.

The netbook and the creation of a new market

In 2006, Jonney saw a golden opportunity for a technological breakthrough and untapped markets: the development of small, inexpensive, high quality, easy-to-use notebook computers for children, the elderly, and others who either had little access to computers or people who would use the small one as their second computer. He estimated that this potential market was 0.2 billion world-wide.

Although the non-profit One Laptop Per Child (OLPC) and the Intel's Classmate PC global programs initiated the idea of the netbook, ASUS was the first to develop such a small computer, which was named the Eee PC,[3] "easy to learn, easy to work, easy to play." In fact, Jonney first approached Intel for cooperation. Intel gave ASUS a challenge by saying that they wanted to see the prototype in one month, to frighten ASUS off since they had already joined the Classmate PC program. More than 20 designers and engineers at ASUS worked intensively day and night on this monumental task and completed the prototype in just one month. This remarkable achievement in November 2007, the same month that OLPC started production of its XO-1, proved the innovation power of ASUS, based on its incredible AC centered in the R&D department.

Growing market share and financial success

At the end of 2007, ASUS' total revenue reached NT$755 billion, the historical high, making it the number two private enterprise in Taiwan, with a market capitalization of NT$49 billion and NT$43.6 billion cash in hand (*ASUSTek Computer Inc., 2008 Annual Report*, 2009). This all-time high for ASUS is due largely to sales of ASUS' branded products, which the company expects will continue to increase (Anon, "What's in a Name?", 2007).

In 2012, ASUS was still the number one motherboard manufacturer in the world (*ASUSTek Computer Inc., 2011 Annual Report*, 2012). ASUS' name brand notebooks were ranked number ten in global sales in 2007, but ASUS set a goal to be number five by 2010 and number three by 2013 (*ASUSTek Computer Inc., 2007 Annual Report*, 2008). They became number three in 2012, a year earlier than their targeted date.

The market share of ASUS' brand notebooks reached 4.1 percent in 2006, which is slightly higher than Apple's but 0.1 percent lower than Sony's, yet ASUS is the major notebook manufacturer for both companies. They were not happy with the situation and withdrew their orders from ASUS. Thus, ASUS, faced with a conflict of interest, was forced to restructure its business.

Separation of the name brand and manufacturing department

Therefore, in July 2008, ASUS announced that it would split into three distinct operational units: (1) ASUSTek Computer Inc.; (2) Pegatron Technology Corporation; and (3) Unihan Technology Corporation. The actual spin-off was completed in May, 2010. This includes independent financial statements, separate stock codes, and stock prices.

Pegatron, the largest of the three companies, is a design manufacturing service which produces motherboards, desktop PCs, notebooks, servers, and other components. Unihan Technology focuses on non-PC manufacturing. Unihan remains under the control of Pegatron. Pegatron stock went public and was listed on the Taiwan Stock Exchange on June 24, 2010, the same day as the new ASUS.[4]

ASUS' brand is used solely for ASUSTek Computer Inc. Jonney still remains the Chairman of ASUS; T.H. Tung, one of the founders and former Vice-Chairman of ASUS, was named the new Chairman of both Pegatron and Unihan.

ASUS' stock went public in Taiwan stock market in 1996. Its stock return has remained higher than average for the electronic category index before 2000 and less volatile after 2000 (Chen and Belcher, 2010). After the split, ASUS' revenue, profits, and EPS have increased every year,

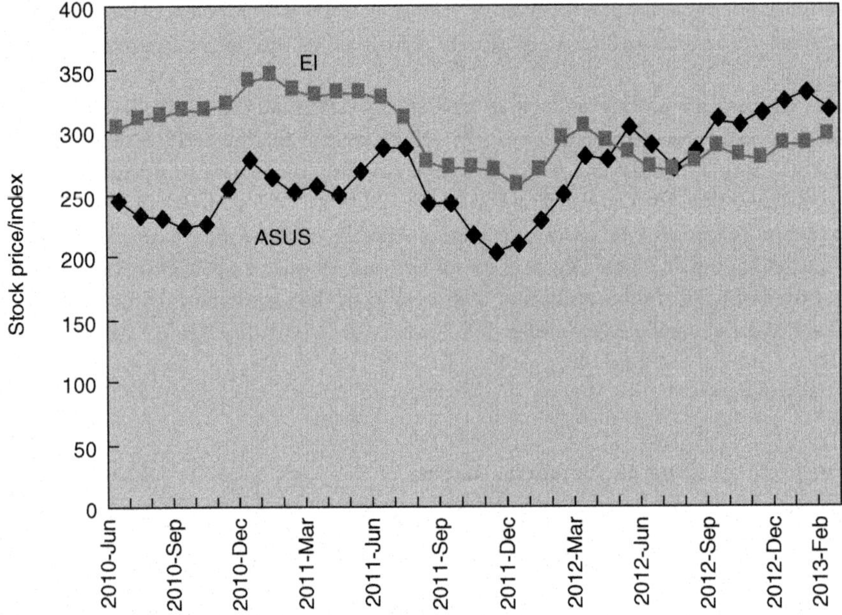

Figure 21.1 ASUS stock price (ASUS) and Electronic Index (EI), June 2010–February 2013

Source: Taiwan Stock Exchange, http://newmops.tse.com.tw.

reaching NT$448.7 billion, $22.5 billion, and $29.79 respectively in 2012. ASUS' stock price also performed better than the electronic index (EI)[5] (Figure 21.1) and hit its highest at $377 per share on March 5, 2013.

Jonney Shih's leadership style and organizational culture in building ASUS' absorptive capacity

Although Jonny knew that his former colleagues wanted him to join them at ASUS, his departure from Acer was delayed until after Acer recovered from a critical financial situation because of his loyalty and deep respect for Stan Shih, its founder. As a result, he has never recruited employees from Acer. This tells us much about the integrity of his character.

He grew up in a family that lived a rural, simple life. Mr. Shih has remained humble, gentle, and scholarly. Not talking much, but leading by action, not by words. For example, he participated in Lean Six Sigma (LSS)[6] training courses for an entire week and then personally trained employees at ASUS. His personality and character have formed an industrious and upright atmosphere within the company.

Jonney is eager to learn and studies a wide range of material from fields as diverse as philosophy, new technology, management, and the arts. As a professional engineer, it is not surprising that he is particularly crazy about technology. ASUS does business not only by socialization but by building customer trust. He took GE and Toyota as role models and strove to catch up with them. Thus, Jonney strives to incorporate external knowledge and technology, as well as to innovate on internally-developed knowledge and expertise, to increase the company's AC.

Jonney blends Western practices with Chinese philosophy and has promoted the PDCA[7] processes used in the TQM (Total Quality Management) system within the company for many years. In 2005, Jonney earnestly devoted time and resources to personally take and then initiate the LSS program at ASUS, in the hope of sustaining the spirit of innovation and improvement necessary to become a first class enterprise. He has, however, modified the program to better suit the company. He also looks to the example of the Chang-shan snake in Sun Tzu's *Art of War*: when attacked at one end, the serpent counterattacks with the other. "We need that kind of fast reaction," said Jonney (Einhorn *et al.*, 2005).

T.H. Tung, one of the original founders of ASUS, as well as Jonney Shih's subordinate at Acer, said that: "Jonney is like a high priest. He does not talk much but he thinks a lot. He takes action only when he thinks everything through. He is far-sighted, deeply analytic, and extremely accurate" (Shu, 2007; Wu, 2007). This "thinking and following through" characteristic has formed the basis of ASUS' business culture and its core spirit of "focusing on fundamentals and results." Jonney thinks technology and quality are core factors for success in business. Thus, ASUS continues to invest a sizeable amount of its money on R&D and training programs, to maintain a solid foundation for innovation and quality control.

This "thinking and following through" characteristic can also be seen when ASUS spun off the OEM/ODM division. Jonney sensed the conflict of interest with his customers and the different value streams of OBM and OEM. Jonney decided to spin off the OEM businesses. On January 3, 2008, the company announced the split of ASUS into branded and manufacturing companies; yet it was only carried out in operations. ASUS confused its customers and, as a result, lost a significant amount of its OEM business. Total sales dropped from NT$755 billion in 2007 to NT$664 billion in 2008 and decreased further to NT$610 billion in 2009.

The difficulty in this financial spin-off was due to the huge capital of Pegatron, over NT$90 billion in 2009. Issuing new stock for an OEM with such a huge amount of capital and during the subprime mortgage crisis is almost impossible. Jonney decided to take the risky step of restructuring ASUS' capital by deducting 85 percent and forcing investors with 1,000 shares of ASUS stock to hold 150 and 404 shares of new stock for ASUS and Pegatron, respectively. After the announcement of the capital restructuring on December 11, 2009, ASUS' stock price dropped to the trading floor two days in a row and lost over NT$30 billion of market value. Meanwhile, investors worried about the liquidity problem of Pegatron's stock since it could only be listed 2–3 months behind new ASUS' stock. Jonney worked hard with investors and the Security Exchange Committee (SEC). Finally, the SEC revised its regulation by allowing Pegatron's stock to be listed on the same day as new ASUS' stock to solve ASUS' dilemma, to soothe the investors and keep them from selling off ASUS' stock. Jonney turned the impossible around and ended up creating a new giant in the IT industry, called Pegatron.

R&D and apprentice-style on-the-job training in building ASUS' absorptive capacity

Robust R&D

ASUS' "Giant Lion" strategy was developed in 2002 to revive the company from a serious drop in business. Its goal was for ASUS to become the frontrunner in the industry and far outpace its competitors. This would require a significant investment in R&D and intensive on-the-job apprenticeship-style employee training programs, to achieve the innovative technology and superior quality necessary to realize ASUS' slogan of being "Rock Solid."[8]

"Rock Solid" means being superior in quality and technology. Superior quality requires having superior technology, whether it is purchased or developed in-house. In order to develop superior technology, a company needs a robust R&D department, one that has sufficient resources and talented personnel to meet the challenge.

Lokshin, Belderbos, and Carree (2008) found that internal R&D enhances AC and the effective utilization of external knowledge. With solid internal R&D, it becomes easy for ASUS to adapt new outsourcing technology, either from joint R&D with ITRI (see next section) or purchasing from other firms which, as mentioned earlier, may be cheaper than developing it in-house.

ASUS' R&D expenses on average were between 60–70 percent of its total operating expenses in its early stages. This percentage has dropped to 25–30 percent while promotional expenses increased from 20–30 percent to 60–65 percent, after 2002 when ASUS engaged in its branding strategy, leaving 10 percent for management and general expenses. This results-driven management style has encouraged innovation, enabling ASUS to ride out global downturns and avoid mergers. Unlike Acer who kept most marketing personnel but fewer R&D personnel after it spun off the OEM division, ASUS kept more than half of the R&D personnel. Although this caused a heavy financial burden, it proved to be the right decision. Today, ASUS' stock price is more than 10 times that of Acer.

After partnering with HTC, Samsung, and Motorola to develop its tablet and failing, Google turned to ASUS. The Nexus 7, developed by ASUS, became successful and won an award as the "Best Tablet" at the Mobile World Congress (MWC), in Spain in 2013, beating the iPad mini and the Samsung Note 10.1 ("Samsung best smartphone . . .," 2013). Usually it takes one half to one year to develop a new model of tablet; yet, it took ASUS only four months to develop the Nexus 7. ASUS' R&D capacity surprised Google's top management (Huang, 2013). ASUS also took advantage of this joint venture to increase its production scale and purchasing power for components.

In an interview with Jerry Shen, the CEO of new ASUS, he said, "Asus has launched into the market with a slew of new innovative tablets (Transformer), ultrabooks (Zenbook), hybrid notebook (Taichi), and 3-in-1 padphones (PadFone); all pushing the boundary in performance and usability." Jerry also said that even when the market got tough and the global PC growth became stagnant, ASUS has grown every quarter in 2012 due to its focus on innovation. ASUS already had a very strong engineering background, but today it employs more than 4,000 engineers in its R&D centers in Taipei and China, who are constantly working on new innovations and new designs, to keep one step ahead of the market (Mahanta, 2012).

ASUS was founded on a strong R&D footing. In 2004, it was awarded the G-Mark of Japan, the only winner from Taiwan. In 2005, it received the iF gold award, the Oscar of industrial design in Germany, making it the first Chinese brand winner of this award in the past 50 years (*ASUSTek Computer Inc., 2007 Annual Report*, 2008). In 2011, ASUS earned 3886 awards domestically and world-wide, and 2647 awards in 2012 (www.asus.com/tw/award). The mounting abundance of international awards reaffirms ASUS' commitment to combine the best of the East and West, in design and aesthetics, as well as to boost ASUS' drive toward propelling a strong Taiwanese brand presence worldwide.

"Do things right the first time" is Jonney's principle. He believes that marketing does not start from sales but from design. Products have to be designed to be beautiful, reliable, unique, and durable.

Recruitment and apprenticeship-style on-the-job training

The quality of R&D depends not only on sufficient financial resources, but on its human capital. In order to find the right person for the right job, Jonney recruits his people personally. Engineers and other key personnel earned their university degrees from the top national universities in Taiwan. Despite their elite education, new entrants do not work independently for the first 6–12 months. They spend this time reviewing the knowledge they learned in school. Then, senior engineers will train them one-on-one where they will learn by doing. Junior engineers are hired in proportion to the pool of senior engineers as ASUS believes that this master–apprentice system is the best way to transfer tacit knowledge. The engineers are trained to think through a problem and follow through. They need to know "why" as well as "how." They are expected to think "outside the box" and constantly strive to develop new and better technology. Employees are trained in three basic ways: (1) being apprenticed to a senior engineer; (2) working on a project as a junior member of the team; and (3) rotating from station to station to learn how things are done throughout the department.

ASUS also provides all kinds of on-the-job and off-the-job trainings. In 2011, over 2,000 employees participated in their "Learning and Growth Plan" (*ASUSTek Computer Inc., 2011 Annual Report*, 2012).

The Taiwan government's pro-business policies

Science and industrial parks and ITRI

Taiwan is a small island with few natural resources. Since the 1960s, small-scale entrepreneurial activity and international trade, particularly in the IT industry, have been the engines of modernization and growth. The most important technology trade show is the Computex which has been held annually in Taipei for the past 30 years. One of the primary goals of the government has been to encourage and support this IT sector. Government policies have focused on the development of new technology in government-backed research institutes and it gives tax incentives to private companies.

The Industrial Technology Research Institute (ITRI) was established in Hsin-chu in 1973 to train engineers, import technology, and invest in research and development. It created new product prototypes which were then handed over to private companies to further develop and market. ITRI continued to have alliances with scientists and engineers at US institutions such as MIT, UC Berkeley, and Carnegie Mellon University (ITRI, 2010).

ITRI has been a major anchor in the establishment of the Hsin-chu Science-based Industrial Park. It has acted as a magnet for individuals and companies to participate in research and development in the IT industry. Currently there are over 400 high-tech companies in this park, creating a cluster effect.[9] This maximizes communication, productivity, and transportation.

In addition, the government has established certain export processing zones to facilitate the success of Taiwanese companies. ITRI not only develops product prototypes, but also focuses on intellectual property, services, and design, filing on average five patent applications per day and licensing them mostly to local firms (*The Economist*, 2010).

Although ASUS has never located to an industrial park, it is only 30 minutes from the Ne-hu Science Park in Taipei and has undoubtedly benefitted from the spill-over effect created by the research at this and other science and industrial parks in Taiwan.

Credit programs and tax incentives

The government of Taiwan has many programs to help finance start-ups and provide credit to companies, such as the Small and Medium Business Credit Guarantee Fund which provides credit guarantees to small and medium-sized enterprises (SMEs), and the Development Fund of the Executive Yuan (Parliament) which sets aside funding in cooperation with banks to provide low interest loans to companies (MOEA, 2010).

Since enacting the Statute for Upgrading Industries (SUI) on January 1, 1991, Taiwan has established tax incentives for the promotion of the IT industry. Tax credits of up to 30 percent are allowed for investments made in new machinery or equipment, and for expenses on research and development as well as personnel training (Lien, 2009).[10]

Data shows that ASUS has benefitted from the SUI since its start-up. Between 1990 and 2004, ASUS' tax rate was less than 8 percent, even less than 1 percent in 1994. ASUS saved a huge amount of income tax in its first 14 years of operation, providing timely funding for its R&D and personnel training expenses.

Conclusion

ASUSTek Computer Inc. is a global company, known as the "Giant Lion" of Taiwan. With its effective entrepreneurial activities directed in the past 20 years by its Chairman, Jonney Shih, ASUS has built up its solid AC which led to its continuing success. However, ASUS still faces many challenges due to the rapid technological advancements and intense competition from China.

Among the many factors discussed in this chapter that have allowed ASUS to amass AC to allow the company to innovate and become a forerunner in the IT industry, entrepreneurial leadership and its established organizational culture are considered the most critical.

Jonney has confidence in ASUS' future. He has indicated that the numerous patents in 3C and 4C that the company owns will be their best weapons. Jerry Shen, the CEO, is also optimistic that the company will remain a dominant force in the market. He believes that companies will need to have expertise in the areas of tablets, notebooks and smartphones in order to succeed in the future global marketplace. "After spending two years to perfect our 3-in-1 padfone, we think we are ready to go to the mainstream market. We are betting on this platform," says Shen (Mahanta, 2012).

Intel's John Antone compares Taiwan to long-distance runners who are being challenged but continue to be in the lead. "As long as they are committed to run very aggressively, I don't see anyone catching them" ('Why Taiwan Matters . . .," 2005). ASUS should be able to meet every challenge to maintain its global position as a leader in the IT industry, as long as they remain under the same leadership and continue to enhance their AC.

Acknowledgments

An earlier version of this chapter by Chen and Belcher under the title "The Importance of Absorptive Capacity in the Road to Becoming a 'Giant Lion' –ASUSTek Computer Inc.," was published in 2010, in *Global Economic Review*, 39(3): 291–315.

Notes

1 Stan Shih founded Acer in 1976 with his wife and five others (originally named Multitech, but the name was changed to Acer in 1987). Shih chaired Acer until his retirement in 2004 when, at the age of 60, he realized that a company must be driven by fresh blood with new and powerful ideas (http://en.wikipedia.org/wiki/Stan_Shih). Under Stan's leadership, Acer became a significant brand-named PC company in Taiwan and the world. From 1994 to 1995, Acer advanced from 14th place to 9th among the world's largest computer manufacturers for OBM/OEM business. In 2000, due to a conflict of interest, Shih spun off its contract business, renaming it Wistron Corporation. In 2003, Acer became the fifth largest PC maker in the world. In 2007, Acer bought Gateway (USA) and Packard Bell (Europe), becoming the number 3 world provider of computers and number 2 for notebooks (http://en.wikipedia.org/wiki/Acer_Inc.).

2 M.S. Liao retired in 1997 and W.C. Hsieh left ASUS in 2003.

3 Eee PC became the most popular Christmas gift on Amazon.com in 2007. Yet, ASUS overestimated the number of Eee PCs that they would sell and did not expect so much competition within six months from other companies, so they overstocked components and ended up encountering a loss in 2008

("ASUS reported . . .," 2009; "Jonney Shih talks . . .," 2009). In January 2013, ASUS officially ended production of their Eee PC series due to declining sales as a result of consumers favoring tablets and Ultrabooks over netbooks (ASUS, 2013).

4 After the spin-off from ASUS, Pegatron gradually gained trust from big customers, such as Apple due to their solid foundation in technology that has attributed to high absorptive capacity embedded in the top management. Pegatron's revenue reached NT$884.9 billion in 2012, a 50 percent increase from the previous year, with NT$2.71 earnings per share.

5 On June 24, 2010, the day when the new stocks of ASUS and Pegatron were listed on the market after capital restructure, the EI index was 358.06 and ASUS' stock price per share was $225.1. On March 5, 2013, those numbers are 387.17 (+8 percent) and $377 (+67 percent) respectively (http://newmops.tse.com.tw).

6 Six Sigma is a commercial program for "improving measurable results for any organization" ("Six Sigma," 2008). In order for an organization to get Six Sigma Certification, it must complete an actual Six Sigma project. There are live and on-line Six Sigma programs. In addition, there is a Lean Six Sigma program which advocates concepts that complement Six Sigma. Lean Six Sigma trains people "to identify and eliminate sources of waste and activities that do not add value, in order to create flow with maximum productivity, capacity, throughout the organization".

7 The PDSA cycle, or Deming cycle, is a quality improvement model consisting of a spiral circular path of four steps for continuous improvement and learning: (1) Plan (plan ahead for change.); (2) Do (execute the plan); (3) Study or Check (study the results); and (4) Act (take action to standardize or improve the process). See www.valuebased management.net/methods_demingcycle.html.

8 The slogan was changed to "Inspiring Innovation, Persistent Perfection" after the spin-off of ASUS.

9 Taiwan is ranked by the WEF (World Economic Forum) 1st out of 144 economies around the world in terms of the "state of cluster development" (World Economic Forum, 2013).

10 The SUI was replaced by the Statute for Industrial Innovation (SII) at the beginning of 2010.

Bibliography

Alvarez, S.A. and Barney, J.B. (2007) "Discovery and creation: alternative theories of entrepreneurial action," *Strategic Entrepreneurship Journal,* 1(1–2): 11–26.

ASUS (2009) "ASUS reported USD82.24 million net losses in Q4 2008"(2009) February 16. Available at: www.chinatechnews.com/2009/02/16/8825-asus-reported-usd8224-million-net-losses-in-q4–2008 (accessed 12 August 2009).

"ASUS" (2013) Available at: http://en.wikipedia.org/wiki/Asus (accessed 10 March 2013).

ASUSTek Computer Inc., 2007 Annual Report (2008) Taipei, April 25. Available at: www.corpasia.net/taiwan/2357/annual/2007/EN/Asus_ar_07_e.pdf (accessed 12 August 2009).

ASUSTek Computer Inc., 2008 Annual Report (2009) Taipei, April 23. Available at: www.mzcan.com/taiwan/2357/annual/2008/CH/asus_annual%20report(20090612-Final).pdf (accessed 12 August 2009).

ASUSTek Computer Inc., 2011 Annual Report (2012) Taipei, April 27. Available at: www.mzcan.com/taiwan/2357/annual/2011/CH/2011%20annual%20report_nbMj3tFfNATe.pdf (accessed 7 January 2013).

Chang, D.W. (2005) "20 rules, discover Intel's management," *Business Next,* April 14 (in Chinese).

Chen, C.L.J. and Belcher, S. (2010) "The importance of absorptive capacity in the road to becoming a 'Giant Lion'–ASUSTek Computer Inc.," *Global Economic Review,* 39(3): 291–315.

Christensen, C.M. (1997) *The Innovator's Dilemma: When New Technologies Cause Great Firms to Fail,* Cambridge, MA: Harvard Business School Press.

Cockburn, I.M. and Henderson, R.M. (1998) "Absorptive capacity, co-authoring behavior, and the organization of research in drug discovery," *Journal of Industrial Economics,* 46(2): 27–41.

Cohen, W.M. and Levinthal, D.A. (1989) "Innovation and learning: the two faces of R&D," *The Economic Journal,* 99: 569–596.

Cohen, W. M. and Levinthal, D. A. (1990) "Absorptive capacity: a new perspective on learning and innovation," *Administrative Science Quarterly,* 35: 128–152.

Collins, J.C. (2001) *Good to Great: Why Some Companies Make the Leap . . . and Others Don't,* New York: HarperCollins Publishers.

Einhorn, B., Kovac, M., Engardio, P., Roberts, D., Balfour F. and Edwards, C. (2005) "Why Taiwan matters. The global economy couldn't function without it. But can it really find peace with China?" International cover story, *Business Week,* May 16. Available at: www.businessweek.com/magazine/content/05_20/b3933011.htm.

Huang, Y.Y. (2013) "Why did Google choose ASUS?', Cover story, *Common Wealth Magazine,* 514, January 16 (in Chinese).

ITRI (Industrial Technology Research Institute) (2010) Available at: www.itri.org.tw/eng/ (accessed 10 July 2010).

"Jonney Shih talks about ASUS: Giant lion enters tunnel" (2009) October 16. Available at: http://finance-news.sina.com/it/2009–10–17/03093514856.shtml (in Chinese) (accessed 20 January 2010).

Kim, L. (1998) "Crisis construction and organizational learning: capability building in catching-up at Hyundai Motor," *Organization Science,* 9: 506–521.

Lane, P.J., Koka, B. and Pathak, S. (2002) "A thematic analysis and critical assessment of absorptive capacity research," *Academy of Management Proceedings,* BPS, M1-M6. Available at: http://helios.univ-reims.fr/Labos/EUROP/Karama/7516527.pdf (accessed 12 May 2009).

Lee, C.Y. and Wu, F.C. (2010) "Affecting knowledge transfer and absorptive capacity in multinational corporations," *Journal of International Management Studies,* 5(2): 118–126.

Lewin, A.Y., Massini, S. and Peeters, C. (2011) "Microfoundations of internal and external absorptive capacity routines," *Organization Science,* 22(1): 81–98.

Lien, Y.P.V. (2009) "Tax incentives of the statute for upgrading industries and the statute for industrial innovation," Industrial Development Bureau (IDB), Ministry of Economic Affairs, June 26. Available at: www.amcham.com.tw/component/option,com_docman/task,doc_download/gid,326/Itemid,378/ (accessed July 10, 2010).

Lokshin, B., Belderbos, R. and Carree, M. (2008) "The productivity effects of internal and external R&D: evidence from a dynamic panel data model," *Oxford Bulletin of Economics and Statistics,* 70(3): 399–416.

Mahanta, V. (2012) "How Asus is challenging established PC firms and what India can learn from it," *ET Bureau,* November 16. Available at: http://articles.economictimes.indiatimes.com/2012–11–16/news/35155056_1_asus-eee-pc-jerry-shen-pc-firms/3 (accessed January 20, 2009).

Mei, S.E. and Nie, M. (2008) "An empirical investigation into the impact of firm's capabilities on competitiveness and performance," *International Journal of Management and Enterprise Development,* 5(5): 574–589.

MOEA (2010) "ROC Ministry of Economic Affairs, Taipei." Available at: www.moea.gov.tw/Mns/english/home/English.aspx (accessed July 10, 2009).

Mowery, D.C. and Oxley, J.E. (1995) "Inward technology transfer and competiveness: the role of national innovation systems," *Cambridge Journal of Economics,* 19(1): 67–93.

Porter, M.E. (1985) *Competitive Advantage,* New York: Free Press.

"Samsung best smartphone, ASUS best tablet in MWC" (2013) *Apple Daily,* February 28.

Shu, Z.C. (2007) "A report about ASUS' turnover," *Global View,* May 23 (in Chinese).

"Six Sigma" (2008) Available at: www.6sigma.us/ (accessed 15 January 2010).

The Economist (2010) "IT in Taiwan and China: Taiwan's tech firms are conquering the world—and turning Chinese," May 27.

"Top Taiwan global brands" (2013) Available at: https://zh.wikipedia.org/wiki/%E5%8F%B0%E7%81%A3%E5%9C%8B%E9%9A%9B%E5%93%81%E7%89%8C (accessed 20 April 2013).

"What's in a name? Fatter profits. Largely unknown Taiwan contract manufacturers are trying to reposition themselves as consumer brands" (2007) *Business Week,* November 12. Available at: www.businessweek.com/magazine/content/07_46/b4058072.htm (accessed 20 January 2010).

World Economic Forum (2013) *Global Competitive Report, 2012–2013.* Available at: www3.weforum.org/docs/WEF_GlobalCompetitivenessReport_2012–13.pdf (accessed 3 August 2013).

Wu, J.C. (2007) *Jonney Shih's Ambition and Strategies,* Taipei: Wu Nan Publishing Co. (in Chinese).

Zahra, S.A. and George, G. (2002) "Absorptive capability: a review, reconceptualization, and extension," *The Academy of Management Review,* 27(2): 185–203.

22

The development of Taiwan's machine tool cluster and key entrepreneurs

Liang-Chih Chen

Introduction

Although not as well known as its electronics industry, Taiwan had become the world's fourth largest exporter and sixth largest producer of machine tools by 2012 (Gardner Publications, 2012). Unlike other current major machine tool manufacturing countries such as Japan, Germany, the United States, and Italy, all of whom have more than a hundred years of history in machine building, machine tool industry in Taiwan did not begin until the late 1940s when Taiwan was still predominantly an agricultural society with weak industrial capabilities. In 1969, the total production of machine tools in Taiwan was merely US$9 million (Liu and Brookfield, 2000). By 2012, however, that figure amounted to US$5.4 billion, about a 600-fold increase (Gardner Publications, 2012). The phenomenal success of Taiwan's machine tool industry has therefore attracted many researchers to study why this industry in Taiwan has been able to advance to its current global competitive position in the context of late industrialization. In addition to the earlier literature that asserts the influences of the market and government policy (Amsden, 1977, 1985; Fransman, 1986), recent studies particularly emphasize the presence of a spatially concentrated and networked industrial system in the central Taiwan region, including Taichung, Nantou and Changhwa (see Figure 22.1), that allows clustered actors to enjoy the external economies in terms of production and technological learning, contributing to the competitive advantages of Taiwan's machine tool industry (Liu, 1999; Sonobe *et al.*, 2003; Yeh and Chang, 2003; Brookfield, 2008; Chen, 2011a; Chen and Lin, 2014).

Recognizing the significance of industrial clustering to the competitiveness of Taiwan's machine tool industry raises questions regarding how this industry has agglomerated geographically. According to Gau (1999), the concentration of machine tool firms in central Taiwan did not become apparent until the 1970s, before which machinery firms were actually geographically dispersed along the west coast of the island. Nevertheless, it is suggested that because the climate in central Taiwan is less humid than in northern Taiwan and cooler than in southern Taiwan, thus reducing the potential for rust and expansion in manufacturing processes, machinery makers gradually moved to central Taiwan in a bid to improve the quality of their products (Hwang, 2001).

While the favorable climate might explain the prerequisite conditions attracting Taiwanese machine tool makers to the central Taiwan region, such a geographical characteristic does not

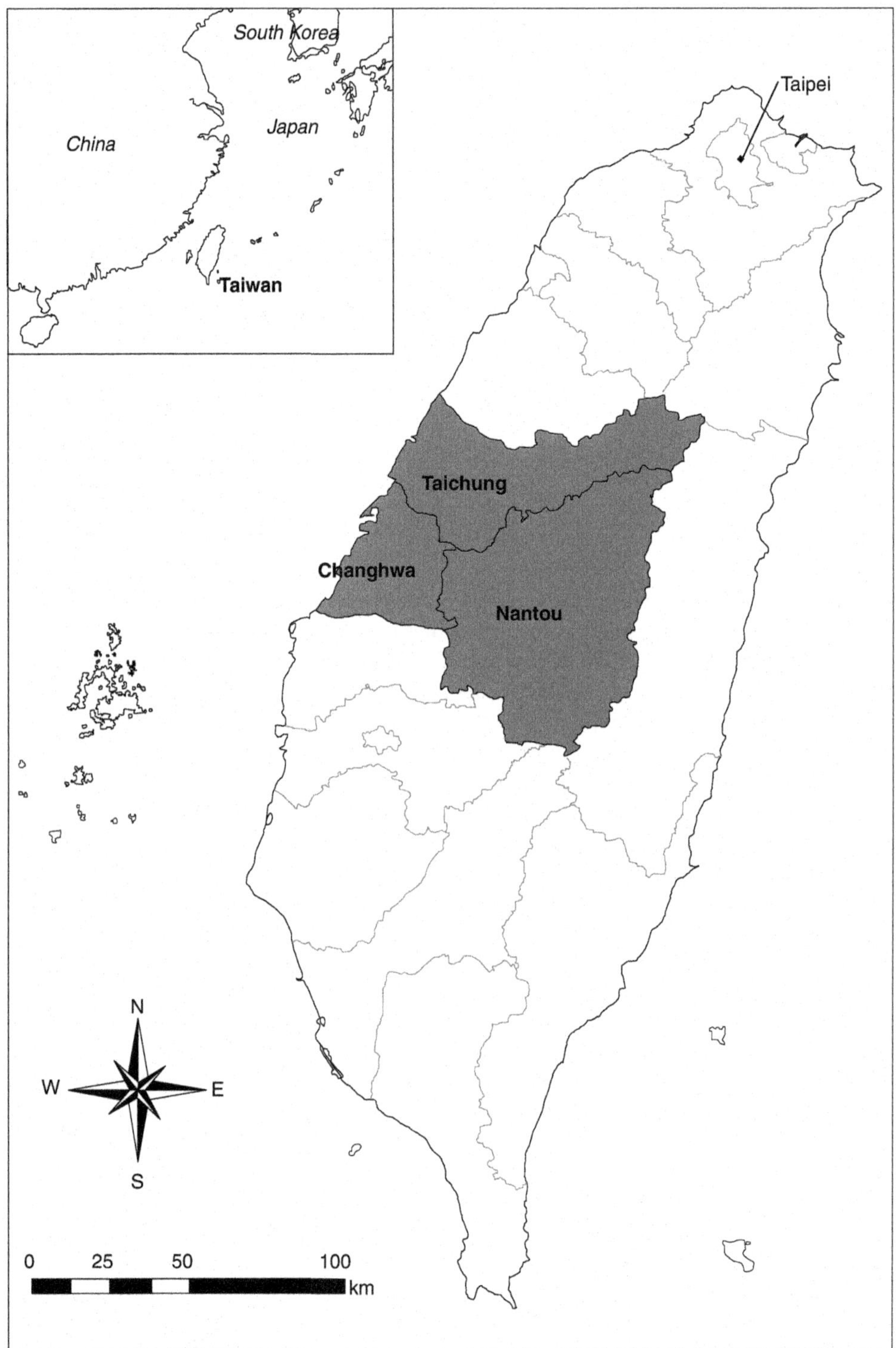

Figure 22.1 Taiwan's machine tool cluster

adequately account for the dynamic processes which gave rise to this industrial cluster. Some scholars have already pointed out that the emergence and development of clusters might also be the result of historical accidents and be influenced by shifts in the dominant techno-economic paradigm (Krugman, 1991; Kenney and von Burg, 1999; Marsili, 2002; Chen, 2011b). In the specific case of Taiwan's machine tool cluster, it is argued that the development of this cluster has been affected by some contextual factors, such as the market and technological opportunities, government policies, social-economic and institutional environments and the networking efforts of actors within the industry (Amsden, 1977, 1985; Fransman, 1986; Yeh and Chang, 2003; Brookfield, 2008; Chen, 2011a, 2012; Chen and Lin, 2014). However, these macro- and meso-level accounts are found to ignore the micro-level analysis, especially the role of local entrepreneurs as economic-changing agents in spurring the evolution of the cluster in which they situated.

Scholars of entrepreneurship have studied how entrepreneurs stimulate the development of a cluster and its distinct production organizations (Baark, 1994; Kenney and von Burg, 1999; Feldman and Francis, 2006; Klepper, 2007; Garavaglia and Breschi, 2009). Varaldo and Ferrucci (1996), for instance, argue that cluster firms are based on an organizational model centered on entrepreneurship. In a more comprehensive account, Feldman and Francis (2006, p. 116) suggest that it is the entrepreneurs whose entrepreneurial activities, including active learning and experimentation, reinvesting profits and expertise, extending relationships with universities and government labs, building local institutions such as industrial associations and the subsequent pulling of a new group of actors to the region, spark the formation of a cluster. On the one hand, entrepreneurs may act collectively to shape their local environments by building institutions that further the interests of their emerging industry, thus forming innovative industrial clusters. On the other hand, the cluster and its characteristics emerge over time from the individual activities of various entrepreneurs and from the organizations and institutions that evolve to support them (Feldman and Francis, 2006; Garavaglia and Breschi, 2009).

By adopting the above perspective of entrepreneurship, this chapter considers the formation of Taiwan's machine tool cluster to be the result of entrepreneurial activities, and would like to study the contributions of entrepreneurs to the subsequent development of Taiwan's machine tool industry, and the industrial cluster in particular. Before presenting the research results, the next section first provides a brief introduction to Taiwan's machine tool industry.

Taiwan's machine tool industry and its clustering advantages

Despite being a latecomer in the production of machine tools, Taiwan has rapidly developed to become one of the major global players in this industry. According to the latest statistics, Taiwan's machine tool industry accounted for 6 percent of the global production in 2012 (Gardner Publications, 2012). While domestic consumption takes only about one-fifth of the total output, nearly 80 percent of Taiwan-made machine tool products was shipped to the overseas markets like China (35.3 percent), the United States (12.6 percent), Thailand (6.3 percent), Turkey (4.8 percent) and Germany (3.1 percent), etc. (TAMI, 2012). On the market front, Taiwanese firms are most competitive in the low- and medium-end segments of the machine tool products,[1] and compete with their counterparts from both industrialized and industrializing countries. In the low-end machine tools segment, Taiwanese machine tool firms have striven to maintain their competitive advantages against rivals from other newly industrialized countries including South Korea and China by offering higher quality and faster delivery at competitive prices. They have also upgraded to compete with European, Japanese and Korean firms in the middle-end machine tool market. Although they might not be able to compete on specifications or quality, Taiwan's middle-end machine tools have been promoted by higher price/performance ratio. For instance, in the global market, Taiwanese machine tool makers claim that their products are capable of delivering comparable performance of those Japan-made products but at only half of their prices (Wang, 2012).

In the literature, it is emphasized that the main element behind the strength of Taiwan's machine tool industry has been the existence of a well-articulated production system composed of numerous small and medium-sized machine tool manufacturers and suppliers agglomerated in the central Taiwan region (Liu, 1999; Brookfield, 2008), which is estimated to host more than 60 percent of Taiwanese machine tool firms and their suppliers (MOEA, 2007). In this cluster, machine tool makers can literally outsource each step of the production process to capable local subcontractors, allowing these firms to minimize overheads while maximizing flexibility for both internal and external operations. In the meantime, they are able to take advantage of their suppliers' respective specializations to improve manufacturing quality and efficiency (Chen, 2009, 2011a). The institutional environment of Taiwan's machine tool cluster also supports the creation of new ventures, either as machine tool manufacturers or suppliers (Brookfield, 2000; Chen, 2014), which has helped develop various specialized competencies in each phase of machine tool production and has injected innovative ideas and vitality into the industry. Furthermore, industrial clustering has enabled local manufacturers to respond to changing competitive conditions by experimenting with various forms of production organization (Liu and Brookfield, 2000; Chen, 2011a).

While existing studies have mainly related the clustering advantages of Taiwan's machine tool industry to its networked-type industrial system, one should note that such a system did not appear in the cluster naturally, and, moreover, has experienced various changes throughout the cluster's development processes. To understand the dynamics behind the development of this cluster we might therefore be required to examine critical issues regarding how the localization of machine tools production emerged, how the production networks were formed, and how the relevant industrial structure within the cluster evolved. The following section will address these issues with a specific focus on the strategic role of entrepreneurs.

Key entrepreneurs and their contributions to the evolution of Taiwan's machine tool cluster

This section provides examples to demonstrate how the development of Taiwan's machine tool cluster could be due to the activity of certain entrepreneurs. While it is not possible to investigate all the entrepreneurial ventures within the cluster, here we particularly discuss four key Taiwanese entrepreneurs and perform historical analyses of their respective entrepreneurial behaviors that have had a significant influence on the emergence and transformation of the Taiwan's machine tool cluster and its industrial organizations.

Ru-Ming Yang and the emergence of Taiwan's machine tool firms in central Taiwan

The development of Taiwan's machine tool industry can be traced back to the 1940s when Taiwanese mechanics, having learned metalworking skills from working in sugar mills, military plants or local machinery firms during the Japanese colonial period, started establishing metalworking shops to capitalize on the emerging local demand from civilian industries, such as woodworking, textiles and agriculture (Amsden, 1977). While their business activities mainly involved the provision of repair services, spare parts or small and simple machines to domestic industries, a handful of local mechanics also started producing machine tools (TAMI, 2005).[2] However, the most notable among these ventures was the founding of Yang Iron, Taiwan's then largest machine tool firm from 1970–1990, by Ru-Ming Yang.

Son of a sugar mill mechanic, Yang was born in central Taiwan and established Yang Iron in Taichung in 1943. By providing repair services for broken machinery, he accumulated knowledge and experience related to the repair and manufacture of machinery and in the early 1960s expanded his business to the manufacture of machine tools. Being encouraged by his trader, Yang began to produce simple light-weight lathes exported to Vietnam for the production of bullets, and undertook the development of machine tools afterward. After visiting a Japanese machine tool firm, Yang purchased a Japanese high-speed lathe as the target to be imitated and introduced his first lathe to the market in 1964. Although the function and performance of Yang's newly-developed machines were hardly comparable to those he imitated, these products perfectly met the demands of machinery firms in Taiwan and some South-east Asian countries which were not able to afford the expensive imported products but were in urgent need of simple machine tools for their manufacturing activities. As a result, Yang's venture achieved great success in the domestic and foreign markets, allowing his firm's capitalization to grow from NT$2.9 million (US$72,500) in 1967 to NT$72 million (US$19 million) in 1974 (Hwang, 2001, p. 122). As the first Taiwanese machine tool entrepreneur who had successfully promoted his products to overseas clients, Yang's endeavor later inspired other local counterparts to follow suit (TAMI, 2005). From that time, Yang Iron was not only the seedbed for domestic machine tool machinists, but also became prominent as the pioneer of Taiwan's machine tool manufacturing, as it introduced Taiwan's first high-speed lathe in 1967 and the first NC lathe in 1974.

During this period, some other native central Taiwan entrepreneurial mechanics also began to establish specialized machine tool companies in central Taiwan, including Victor (founded in 1954, specializing in planers and lathes), Yeong Chin (founded in 1954, specializing in milling machines), Chin Fong (founded in 1948, specializing in press machines) and Supertech (founded in 1954, specializing in grinders). Sharing a similar evolutionary trajectory to Yang, these entrepreneurs capitalized on their accumulated technical knowledge and experience in the repair and manufacture of industrial machinery to produce simplified yet serviceable versions of imported machine tools. With the strong growth of domestic and foreign demand and the influx of a fairly large number of would-be machine tool builders, the production of machine tools in Taiwan grew from NT$3.3 million (US$82,500) in 1954 to NT$424 million (US$10.6 million) in 1970 (Amsden, 1985; Wu, 1993). Moreover, many of the new ventures were located in central Taiwan, forming the roots of a regional concentration (TAMI, 2005).

Chien-Chun Chang and the formation of a spatialized subcontracting production system

The expansion of Taiwan's machine tools industry was fueled by growth in demand from South-east Asia in the early 1970s, followed by the United States in the late 1970s (Amsden, 1985; Sonobe *et al.*, 2003). At the time when the production of machine tools in Taiwan was still predominantly integrated,[3] a group of new entrepreneurs sought to adopt subcontracting practices through the supplier networks nurtured by Taiwan's sewing machine industry which, beginning in the 1960s, had helped cultivate a number of domestic metalworking shops in central Taiwan that were capable of taking subcontracting orders for machine parts manufacturing or processing from other machinery-related industries, including the machine tool industry.[4] In this context, for machine tool entrepreneurs who did not intend to or could not afford to invest in manufacturing equipment in their plants as their predecessors had done, subcontracting became a feasible and economic option.

Another crucial factor that influenced the emergence of a spatialized subcontracting production system in Taiwan's machine tool industry was the development of CNC (computer numerically controlled) technology. With technical assistance from Japanese CNC controller suppliers, some Taiwanese machine tool firms started introducing commercialized CNC machine tools (Fransman, 1986; Tsai, 1992). And the successful production and sales of these higher value-added products allowed local leading machine tool firms like Yang Iron, Victor, and Yeong Chin to hit annual sales of over NT$1 billion (US$30 million) by the second half of the 1980s.[5] In the meantime, the benefits from developing CNC machine tools spread beyond those leading integrated machine tool firms. Thanks to the introduction of CNC technology, it was possible to subcontract higher-end machine tool manufacturing without necessarily compromising the quality of final products.[6] As a result, local machine tool builders who relied on subcontracting were able to market CNC machine tools with a quality comparable to that of the leading firms.

However, the potential and advantages of subcontracting production for CNC machine tools were not fully recognized and exploited until Chien-Chun Chang founded Leadwell. Graduating from one of Taiwan's prominent universities with a degree in mechanical engineering, Chang had spent the 1970s as general manager of two major Taiwanese machine tool firms, Lien Fong and Yang Iron. To start his own business venture, Chang established Leadwell in 1980 with capital of only NT$8million (US$220,000) (Leadwell, 2001). As a small start-up aiming to engage in the production of CNC machine tools, Chang devised a mass production system for standardized NC machines, especially machining centers. By recruiting experienced machinists and workers to oversee subcontracting and be in charge of machine tool design and assembly, Chang's start-up sourced most of their supplies externally (Liu, 1999). Through leveraging the manufacturing capacity of local subcontractors, Leadwell quickly achieved competitiveness in speed-to-market and speed-to-volume. Coupled with the world's sharp-rising demands for machining centers, Chang's ingenuity paid off with huge business success. In less than 10 years, Leadwell had outpaced the then domestic leaders to become Taiwan's largest machine tool firm with annual turnover of NT$2 billion (US$76 million) in 1989 (Leadwell, 2001). Later, not only did the smaller Taiwanese machine tool builders mushroom in Leadwell's wake, but existing integrated firms were also inspired to adopt subcontracting arrangements for greater production flexibility. The quest of local machine tool makers for CNC products resulted in a remarkable increase in the production value of Taiwan's machine tools, amounting to NT$26.1 billion (US$1.04 billion) in 1992 (MIRL, 1999). The total number of machine tool firms in Taiwan further grew to more than 1150 in 1990 (MIRL, 1995: 3–102). Owing to Chang's proactive entrepreneurial activities and the subsequent endeavors of other new and incumbent local machine tool firms in cultivating and exploiting local subcontractors, a specialized subcontracting network for the manufacture of machine tools gradually developed in central Taiwan, leading to the clustering of machine tool firms and suppliers in this region.

Yung-Tsai Chuo and the advancement of domestic supply capacity

Despite the continued success of Taiwan-made CNC machine tools in the world market in the 1990s, profitability was limited by local firms' heavy reliance on imported bought-in components, such as CNC controllers, ballscrews, etc. The manufacture of these components is more capital- and technology-intensive, and has been dominated by a handful of advanced firms in countries like Japan and Germany. Yet these high technological and marketing thresholds have not stopped entrepreneurs in Taiwan's machine tool industry from trying to develop domestic competencies in this field. Of all these entrepreneurs, Yung-Tsai Chuo has been the most successful. By establishing Hiwin to explore domestic and foreign market opportunities, Chuo helped advance the supply capacity and international sales of Taiwan-made machine tool components, particularly linear-motion components.

Taiwan began producing ballscrews in the early 1980s. In 1981, Finest Ballscrew was established as a public–private joint venture between Lien Fong and two domestic public banks: the Bank of Communication and the China Development Trust. After licensing the required technology from the UK, Finest launched its ballscrew products in 1983. Unfortunately, a combination of financial problems at Lien Fong and the dumping of Japanese ballscrews put Finest out of business in 1989. Chuo, a former high-level manager at the Bank of Communications specializing in international trade and business, acquired this bankrupt firm and renamed it Hiwin.

After identifying and solving internal production and management issues in the newly acquired firm, Chuo attempted to sell Hiwin's ballscrews to local machine tool firms. However, due to the low acceptance of its products in domestic market, largely attributed to the severe competition from Japanese firms, as well as local users' doubts about the quality of its ballscrews, Hiwin was forced to promote its products to foreign machine tool makers in countries like India and the United States where no single ballscrew manufacturer had established a commanding lead.[7] In the meantime, Chuo conducted one critical overseas investment in 1993 as he bought a 40-year-old German ballscrew maker, Holzer. At the time when Hiwin's development was suppressed by Japanese ballscrew makers who blocked Hiwin's access to critical technological and manufacturing supplies, Chuo had to seek alternative technology sources for the survival of his venture. Learning through his global information network that the bankrupting Holzer had technologies that might help Hiwin to break through Japan's obstruction, Chuo made a great deal of effort to acquire this firm.[8] As a result of this investment, Hiwin obtained knowledge transferred from Holzer that helped the former to fill its technological gap in the manufacturing and development of ballscrews. This acquisition further advanced Hiwin competence in the development of linear guideways, a critical and more advanced mobile component in machine tools, now accounting for roughly 50 percent of Hiwin's annual sales (Hiwin, 2011).

To enhance Hiwin's marketing capacity in foreign markets, Chuo also undertook outward investments in countries including the United States and Japan. The company's international success gradually convinced Taiwanese clients to adopt Hiwin's products. With the promotion of domestically-made ballscrews from Hiwin and other entrepreneurial entrants like PMI and ABBA,[9] by 2001, more than 75 percent of the ballscrews installed in Taiwan's machine tool products were provided by local suppliers, led by Hiwin (IEK, 2002). Being able to source such critical components locally rather than from distant foreign suppliers greatly improved the production efficiency of the Taiwanese machine tool makers. Furthermore, through mobilizing its technological and production competences within and outside the cluster, Hiwin has now become the world's leading manufacturer of linear-motion components for machine tools, reaching an annual turnover of NT$82 billion (US$259 million) in 2010 (Hiwin, 2011). In addition, with his business achievements and the demonstration of his leadership, Chuo has increased his influence on Taiwan's machine tool industry, as he was elected by domestic machine tool makers and suppliers to be the current chair of the TMBA (Taiwan Machine Tool and Accessory Builders' Association), the industry's key association, positioning him to play a more important role in directing this industry's future development.

Chih-Yang Chu and the founding of machine tool business group

Its small scale and specialization have been recognized as the main competitive strengths of Taiwanese machine tool firms. Such characteristics, however, also come with some disadvantages. For instance, unlike the large, leading global firms, the small and medium-sized Taiwanese machine tool manufacturers will encounter greater difficulty negotiating better import deals for components and accessories or better sales terms with their foreign marketing partners. Specialization in certain machine tool product segments has also limited these machine tool makers' capacity to satisfy larger customers that might prefer to purchase various types of machine tools from a single manufacturer. In addition, they have been endowed with restricted resources to undertake critical but costly activities such as marketing and R&D. Thus, promoting the development of a few larger firms equipped with greater internal technological and operational capacity could be one strategy for Taiwan's machine tool industry to improve its competitive position in the global market. In recent years, some major Taiwanese machine tool makers have actively sought to create business groups consolidating suitable local firms with complementary resources. In the machine tool cluster, one such project is being actively pursued by Chih-Yang Chu's Fair Friend.

In 1979, Chu, an importer of Japanese machinery, established Fair Friend that specialized in selling construction machinery. When Taiwan's construction industry suffered a serious recession in 1982, Chu broadened his business to the production of conventional machine tools, such as cutting and grinding machines, through the acquisition of two machinery firms in central Taiwan, Lien Fong and Yuan Chow. After spotting the business opportunities of CNC machine tools in the world market, in 1985, Chu further decided to engage in the manufacture of CNC machine tools by utilizing the local emerging subcontracting networks. By whole-heartededly embracing the possibilities of outsourcing and an emphasis on minimizing in-house manufacturing investments, Chu managed to compete against his local rivals on the price advantages of Fair Friend's products.[10] Moreover, with his marketing expertise and rich business networks, Chu was able to access more up-to-date market information, giving his ventures an advantage over other local machinist-run firms.

In addition to his business strategies, Chu has a unique characteristic which differentiates him from other domestic machine tool entrepreneurs: his greater eagerness in undertaking mergers and acquisitions (M&A) to expand his businesses. In 1989, Taiwan's major business magazine, *Business Weekly*, called Chu the "King of Taiwan's M&A" as he aggressively bought out bankrupt local electronic and machinery firms. In the case of machine tools, it was through purchasing two local firms that Chu was able to enter this industry. Having little personal background in machine tool making, Chu retained the managerial and technological staff so as to ensure the manufacturing capability of his new ventures, and concentrated on improving the firm's financing and marketing, which were seen as the main reasons for the original bankruptcies.[11] Consequently, Chu's efforts paid off as Fair Friend successfully became one of Taiwan's top 10 machine tool makers from 1990 (MIRL, 1999).

In the early 2000s, Chu had another opportunity to further expand his machine tool business through buying out local firms. The East Asian financial crisis in the late 1990s and the downturn in global demand in the early 2000s had made some Taiwanese machine tool firms, including Leadwell, one of Taiwan's machine tool leaders, suffer a business crisis. Equipped with healthier financial and managerial resources, Chu took over Leadwell in 2001, and subsequently acquired other local struggling machine tool makers specializing in machine tools complementary to Fair Friend's existing product line. The resulting economies of scale and scope from the newly-consolidated business group allowed Fair Friend to quickly become Taiwan's largest machine tool maker. Moreover, Chu also replicated his strategies in acquiring foreign machine tool firms in countries like the United States, Germany, Italy, Japan and South Korea. Currently his machine tool business group encompasses nine Taiwanese and nine foreign firms, making the Fair Friend group one of the largest global machine tool makers with an annual turnover of over NT$35 billion (US$1.2 billion) in 2012 (Hsiung, 2013).

Conclusion

Taiwan is widely considered an entrepreneurial island, featuring a complex network of social relationships that provides a fertile ground for new start-ups and small and medium-sized enterprises (Shieh, 1992; Hayashida, 1994; Hamilton, 1997; Luo, 1997; Numazaki, 1997; Ding and Abetti, 2003; Wu and Huang, 2003). Based on such an understanding of Taiwan's strong entrepreneurship, this chapter uses Taiwan's machine tool industry as an example to discuss the influence of entrepreneurs on the development of an industrial cluster. It further argues that the entrepreneurs and their firms have played a key role in constructing or restructuring the economic activities and organizations within the cluster as they sought to exploit greater business opportunities or to sustain their competitiveness in a volatile business environment, consequently shaping the specific characteristics of the cluster's industrial system and affecting the trajectory of the cluster's transformation.

In the discussion, examples are presented of four key Taiwanese entrepreneurs who have made significant contributions to the emergence and evolution of Taiwan's machine tool cluster. Ru-Ming Yang was one of Taiwan's machine tool pioneers whose successful venture inspired the influx of Taiwanese mechanics to explore and exploit the domestic and foreign markets for machine tool production, triggering the early development of this industry in Taiwan, specifically in central Taiwan. In the case of Chien-Chun Chang, he was regarded as the originator of Taiwan's subcontracting production arrangements of CNC machine tools and helped cultivate local supply capacity, thus stimulating the formation of specialized production systems and promoting the further geographical concentration of Taiwan's machine tool industry. Later developments are exemplified by Yung-Tsai Chuo and Chih-Yang Chu. Unlike their predecessors, these two entrepreneurs lacked a background in mechanical engineering. However, with their entrepreneurship and expertise in business and financial management, both of them have created leading global firms out of Taiwan's machine tool cluster which are not only larger, but also have progressed to become critical figures in the world's machine tool industry. Being endowed with greater resources and international access, Chuo's and Chu's firms are seen to play a crucial role in driving the continuing evolution of this relatively mature industrial cluster in Taiwan.

There is a great body of literature discussing why entrepreneurship is crucial in influencing the economic growth of a territory (Garavaglia and Breschi, 2009, p. 96). In the case of industrial clusters, through the analytical lens of entrepreneurship we are able to examine the dynamics within and outcomes of the development of such a spatialized industrial system. While our empirical study has illustrated how entrepreneurs and their entrepreneurial ventures facilitated the construction or restructuring of economic activities as well as organizations within an industrial cluster, the study's entrepreneur-focused approach that places greater emphases on the dominant roles of entrepreneurs, however, neglects an analysis of the interaction between entrepreneurial activities and local supporting institutions. More specifically, it is suggested that the characteristics of the cluster emerge not only from the individual activities of entrepreneurs, but also the organizations and institutions that co-evolve to support them (Feldman and Francis, 2006). In this regard, to better understand the dynamic relationships between entrepreneurship and cluster development, further studies are required regarding the evolution of local institutions that might affect the actions of entrepreneurs.

Notes

1 Based on technological capability and machine quality, the world machine tool industry can be divided into three categories: (1) high-end machine tools, utilized for precision engineering, are the specialty of German, Swiss, Japanese, and US manufacturers. For instance, the USA specializes in high productive

and performance machines for the aerospace industry, while Switzerland specializes in high precision machine tools for the watch industry, Germany in high precision special purpose machine tools, and Japan in mass-produced high productive CNC machines; (2) middle-end machine tools, the major equipment for the automotive industry, are the market in which Japan is predominant, along with others like Germany, Italy, South Korea and Taiwan; and (3) low-end machine tools, general purposes machines used mainly by small metalworking job-shops, are produced mostly in China, South Korea, Taiwan, and the United States.

2 San Yuan, for instance, was one of the pioneers in the production of machine tools in Taiwan. Founded in 1936 in Taipei by Yi-Yuan Chuo, a former engineer in a Japanese aircraft factory, San Yuan started by manufacturing machine parts for local machinery firms and introduced a planing machine in 1957 through copying Japanese products, and a lathe a few years later. Given the stagnant domestic demands, these early local machine tool entrepreneurs' endeavors, however, were not properly capitalized.

3 In the 1970s, Taiwan's leading machine tool firms produced roughly 90 percent of their parts themselves (Amsden, 1977).

4 From the 1960s to the 1990s, central Taiwan was the major production site of sewing machines, where manufacturing plants of leading foreign sewing machine firms, such as Singer from the USA, and their suppliers were agglomerated. Since the manufacture of sewing machines was based on excessive subcontracting, i.e., where sewing machine firms focused on assembly and subcontracted all their production to specialized suppliers, these manufacturers helped cultivate and train a great deal of the metalworking labor force in central Taiwan, which was later utilized by nearby machine tool firms as subcontractors.

5 The value added by CNC can be exemplified by comparing the prices of CNC machine tools with conventional ones. For instance, the average export price of a Taiwan-made CNC lathe during this period was about US$30,000–50,000, while a conventional lathe cost less than US$6,000 (Jacobsson, 1986).

6 In the manufacture of CNC machine tools, machine part quality requirements are not as strict as for conventional machine tools. Even if some of the installed parts sourced from external suppliers are poorer in quality, the performance and precision of CNC machine tools might not be affected, since the issues resulting from inferior parts might, to some extent, be solved through adjusting the programs of the CNC controllers (Arnold, 2001). Therefore, machine tool firms can manage to produce higher quality CNC machine tools through subcontracting.

7 Author's interview with Yung-Tsai Chuo, 9 November 2005.

8 According to Chuo, his appearance was actually not welcomed by the people of Holzer in the beginning, as they were skeptical that Chuo might be interested only in transferring technologies but not the firm's sustained operation. However, after paying three visits and persistent communication, Chuo successfully persuaded his German partners to accept his proposition of acquisition, and more importantly, at a reduced price. Chuo commented that it might be due to his personal social skills, which enabled him to get close easily to those German senior engineers, allowing his investment in Germany to be made possible and successful. For instance, bringing one or two bottles of Shao-Hsing wine, a famous Taiwan-made liquor, to hang out with German engineers at informal events is one of Chuo's strategies. Such social skills later also helped him to recruit local talent to enhance the technological competence of Hiwin's German branch. (Author's interview with Yung-Tsai Chuo, 9 November 2005.)

9 PMI was founded in 1991, while ABBA was established in 1999.

10 As opposed to other Taiwanese mechanical managers who were observed to have greater interest in undertaking investments in improving their firms' in-house technological capabilities, Chu, a business entrepreneur, seemed more conservative and calculating about the technological advancement-related investments of his firm, considering the fact that such investments often earn a low rate of return.

11 In the report by *Business Weekly*, Chu was considered not only as one of the forerunners in the field of M&A in Taiwan, but also as a gifted financial manager. Most of the owners of firms that were bought by Chu admitted that it is due to Chu's financial management expertise that they were willing to hand over their firms to him (Lee and Wu, 1989).

Bibliography

Amsden, A. (1977) "The division of labour is limited by the type of market: the case of the Taiwanese machine tool industry," *World Development,* 5(3): 217–233.

Amsden, A.(1985) "The division of labour is limited by the rate of growth of the market: the Taiwan machine tool industry in the 1970s," *Cambridge Journal of Economics,* 9(3): 271–284.

Arnold, H. (2001) "The recent history of the machine tool industry and the effects of technological change," LMU Working Paper 2001–14, Institute for Innovation Research and Technology Management, University of Munich.

Baark, E. (1994) "Technological entrepreneurship and commercialization of research results in the West and in China: comparative perspectives," *Technology Analysis & Strategic Management,* 6(2): 203–214.

Brookfield, J. (2000) "Localization, outsourcing, and supplier networks in Taiwan's machine tool industry," unpublished PhD thesis, University of Pennsylvania.

Brookfield, J. (2008) "Firm clustering and specialization: a study of Taiwan's machine tool industry," *Small Business Economics,* 30(4): 405–422.

Chen, L.-C. (2009) "Learning through informal local and global linkages: the case of Taiwan's machine tool industry," *Research Policy,* 38(3): 527–535.

Chen, L.-C. (2011a) "The governance and evolution of local production networks in a cluster: the case of Taiwan's machine tool industry," *GeoJournal,* 76(6): 605–622.

Chen, L.-C. (2011b) "Technological learning in the process of technological capability building in low and medium technology industries in newly industrializing countries: selected examples from Taiwan," in P.L. Robertson and D. Jacobson (eds) *Knowledge Transfer and Technology Diffusion,* Cheltenham: Edward Elgar.

Chen, L.-C. (2012) "The evolving roles of the state and public research institutes in the technological upgrading process of industries: the case of Taiwan's machine tool industry," *Journal of Social Sciences and Philosophy,* 24(1): 19–50 (in Chinese).

Chen, L.-C. (2014) "Entrepreneurship, technological changes, and the formation of a subcontracting production system: the case of Taiwan's machine tool industry," *International Journal of Economics and Business Research,* 7(2):198–219.

Chen, L.-C. and Lin, Z.-X. (2014) "Examining the role of geographical proximity in a cluster's transformation process: the case of Taiwan's machine tool industry," *European Planning Studies,* 22(1): 1–19.

Ding, H.-B. and Abetti, P. (2003) "The entrepreneurial success of Taiwan: synergy between technology, social capital and institutional support," *Advances in the Study of Entrepreneurship, Innovation, & Economic Growth,* 14: 91–123.

Feldman, M. and Francis, J.L. (2006) "Entrepreneurs as agents in the formation of industrial clusters," in B. Asheim, *et al.* (eds) *Clusters and Regional Development: Critical Reflections and Explorations,* New York: Routledge, pp. 115–136.

Fransman, M. (1986) "International competitiveness, technical change and the state: the machine tool industry in Taiwan and Japan," *World Development,* 14(12): 1375–1396.

Garavaglia, C. and Breschi, S. (2009) "The co-evolution of entrepreneurship and clusters," in U. Fratesi and L. Senn (eds) *Growth and Innovation of Competitive Regions: The Role of Internal and External Connections,* Heidelberg: Springer.

Gardner Publications (2012) *2012 World Machine Tool Output and Consumption Survey.* Available at: www.gardnerweb.com/articles/2013-world-machine-tool-output-and-consumption-survey (accessed 1 June 2013).

Gau, S.-C. (1999) "Production network and learning region: the production of machine tools in Taichung," unpublished PhD thesis, Tunghai University, Taiwan (in Chinese).

Hamilton, G. (1997) "Organization and market processes in Taiwan's capitalist economy," in M. Orru, *et al.* (eds) *The Economic Organization of East Asian Capitalism,* Thousand Oaks, CA: Sage Publications, pp. 237–293.

Hayashida, M. (1994) "Entrepreneurship in Taiwan and Korea: a comparison," *Asia-Pacific Review,* 1(1): 59–82.

Hiwin (2011) *Hiwin 2010 Annual Report,* Taipei: Hiwin (in Chinese).

Hsiung, Y.-H. (2013) "Taiwan's largest machine tool group: Fair Friend," *Common Wealth,* vol. 521 (in Chinese).

Hwang, Y.-J. (2001) *Revolution of Black-Hands: The Legendary Black Hawk,* Taipei: Linking.

IEK (2002) *The Study of Critical Components of Precision Machinery,* Hsinchu: Industrial Technology Research Institute (in Chinese).

Jacobsson, S. (1986) *Electronics and Industrial Policy: The Case of Computer Controlled Lathes,* Boston: Allen and Unwin.

Kenney, M. and von Burg, U. (1999) "Technology, entrepreneurship and path dependence: industrial clustering in Silicon Valley and Route 128," *Industrial and Corporate Change,* 8(1): 67–103.

Klepper, S. (2007) "Disagreements, spinoffs, and the evolution of Detroit as the capital of the US automobile industry," *Management Science,* 53(4): 616–631.

Krugman, P. (1991) *Geography and Trade,* Cambridge, MA: MIT Press.

Leadwell (2001) *Leadwell 2000 Annual Report*, Taipei: Leadwell (in Chinese).

Lee, H.-L. and Wu, S.-H. (1989) "King of Taiwan's merger and acquistion: Chih-Yang Chu," *Business Weekly,* 84 (in Chinese).

Liu, R.-J. (1999) *Networking Division of Labor: Examining the Competitiveness of Taiwan's Machine Tool Industry,* Taipei: Linking (in Chinese).

Liu, R.-J. and Brookfield, J. (2000) "Stars, rings and tiers: organisational networks and their dynamics in Taiwan's machine tool industry," *Long Range Planning,* 33(3): 322–348.

Luo, J.-D. (1997) "The significance of networks in the initiation of small businesses in Taiwan," *Sociological Forum,* 12(2): 297–317.

Marsili, O. (2002) "Technological regimes and sources of entrepreneurship," *Small Business Economics,* 19(3): 217–231.

MIRL (1995) *1995 Machine Tools Yearbook,* Hsinchu: MIRL (in Chinese).

MIRL (1999) *1999 Machine Tools Yearbook,* Hsinchu: MIRL (in Chinese).

MOEA (2007) *2007 Machinery Industry Yearbook,* Taipei: MOEA (in Chinese).

Numazaki, I. (1997) "The laoban-led development of business enterprises in Taiwan: an analysis of the Chinese entrepreneurship," *The Developing Economies,* 35(4): 440–457.

Shieh, K.-H. (1992) *"Boss" Island: The Subcontracting Network and Micro-entrepreneurship in Taiwan's Development,* New York: P. Lang.

Sonobe, T., Kawakami, M. and Otsuka, K. (2003) "Changing roles of innovation and imitation in industrial development: the case of the machine tool industry in Taiwan," *Economic Development and Cultural Change,* 52(1): 103–128.

TAMI (2005) *Sixty Years of Machinery Industry in Taiwan,* Taipei: TAMI (in Chinese).

TAMI (2012) *2010–2012 Directory of Taiwanese Machinery Firms in China,* Taipei: TAMI (in Chinese).

Tsai, S.D.H. (1992) "The development of Taiwan's machine tool industry," in A. Amsden and N.T. Wang (eds) *Taiwan's Enterprises in Global Perspective,* Armonk, NY: M.E. Sharpe, pp. 151–169.

Varaldo, R. and Ferrucci, L. (1996) "The evolutionary nature of the firm within industrial districts," *European Planning Studies*, 4(1): 27–34.

Wang, C.-C. (2012) "A brief introduction to the 2012 Japanese Machine Tool Exhibition," *Taiwan Machinery Monthly,* 670: 5–13.

Wu, R.-I. and Huang, C.-C. (2003) "Entrepreneurship in Taiwan: turning point to restart," in MCPA (ed.) *Entrepreneurship in Asia: Playbook for Prosperity,* Washington, DC: Mansfield Foundation.

Wu, S.-C. (1993) *The History of Mechanical Industry Research Laboratory,* Hsinchu: Industrial Technology Research Institute.

Yeh, C.-C. and Chang, P.-L. (2003) "The Taiwan system of innovation in the tool machine industry: a case study," *Journal of Engineering and Technology Management,* 20(4): 367–380.

23 Giant Bicycle and King Liu

Mei-Chih Hu and Ching-Yan Wu

Introduction

Since the 2000s, Taiwan has been transformed into the world's foremost bicycle producer while the average export price has increased more than four-fold, from US$100 in 1998 to US$417 in 2012. Taiwanese bicycle makers, such as Giant, have demonstrated the characteristics of entrepreneurship, starting from scratch to become international brands today. In this chapter we intend to show how Giant and its founder King Liu achieved this.

Entrepreneurship essentially emphasizes the discovery of opportunities, the exploitation of profit, and the development of a firm to fulfill an entrepreneur's vision (Kirzner, 1973; Gartner, 1988; Shane, 2004). Although entrepreneurial activities have been commonly defined in the context of the creation of new organizations, they are also to be found within existing organizations. In a dynamic economy, opportunities change constantly and entrepreneurial activities need to be created and applied appropriately. As Drucker (1985, p. 144) has argued, even large businesses need to acquire entrepreneurial competence to survive. Facing rapidly changing environments, firms need entrepreneurship strategies to rejuvenate their competitive advantages and innovate in the market (Lumpkin and Dess, 1996). For that reason, strategic management mainly deals with issues within established firms, focusing on creating resources that are costly to copy, so as to maintain the firms' competitive advantages (Porter, 1990; Barney, 1991; Alvarez and Busentiz, 2001). It is the synergy of entrepreneurship and strategic management that mostly explains the growth of a firm in a dynamic economy.

Kuratko and Audretsch (2009) argue that the effectiveness of firms depends on this combination of strategy and entrepreneurship, because opportunity alone cannot be effectively exploited without incorporating strategy into the blueprint. From another viewpoint, competitive niches may evolve, shift, and disappear rapidly in an ever-changing economy so that searching for new opportunities is essential for a growing firm (Ireland and Hitt, 1999). Accordingly, integrating entrepreneurship into strategic management can offer sustainable growth for a firm (Ireland *et al.*, 2003).

This chapter illustrates the characteristics of strategic entrepreneurship, manifested in Taiwan's bicycle industry as entrepreneurial alertness, discovery of opportunity, resource leverage and organization re-configuration, traced over four recent decades (from the 1970s to the 2000s). We begin by exploring the evolutionary history of the Taiwan bicycle industry from the 1970s to the 2000s, following the developmental trajectory of the Giant Bicycle Corporation, associated with the entrepreneurial behavior of its founder King Liu. He has not only raised Giant to be one of the top three players in world bicycle production, but has also led the transformation of Taiwan's bicycle industry from its crisis period in the 1990s (due to competitive pressure from lower-cost Chinese performers) to a historically high-profit stage during the 2000s. This chapter intends to show how King Liu has successfully led Giant, and more widely, Taiwan's bicycle industry, to navigate a variety of stages of upgrade, along with their particular crises, by adopting the promotion of technological specifications and branding activities, and later on by initiating an innovation platform (e.g. the A-Team formulation). At each stage, this approach has helped to build up numerous competitive advantages through strategies tailored differently for Giant and for Taiwan's bicycle industry as a whole.

The development of the Taiwan bicycle industry

Until the 1970s, the world bicycle industry was dominated by the developed countries such as the USA, Japan, Italy, France and the UK, together producing about 50 percent of the world's output. At that time, developing countries such as Taiwan, China, and South Korea accounted for only 13.7 percent of global production (Lee and Lin, 1991). However, beginning in the 1980s, the structure of the global bicycle industry underwent tremendous change, due to latecomers in developing countries such as Taiwan building their mass production capability. As a consequence, the major producers in advanced countries either dropped out of the market or merged with other companies, because the rise of the latecomers had overtaken their production positions in the global bicycle market. Although Taiwan enjoyed a 'Golden Age' era in bicycle exports during the 1980s and the first half of the 1990s, the good times did not last long when late arrivals, such as China and the South-east Asian countries (with the advantage of significantly lower costs) joined the market in the mid-1990s. To break through this bottleneck, Taiwan strategically transformed its bicycle industry from a lower cost base to high value-added production while building its own brands. By focusing on innovative processes, Taiwan has now become one of the leading countries in the high-end bicycle market (Hu and Wu, 2011). As indicated in Figure 23.1, bicycle export volumes gradually increased along with export value until the mid-1990s. However, while the volume of bicycle exports has showed a significant decline since the 2000s, the export value continuously rose to a historical peak, demonstrating the successful transformation of Taiwan's bicycle industry from low-end to high value-added products. This evolution is addressed below in terms of four developmental stages.

Initiating the export platform: the 1970s

Until 1971, Taiwan exported only 270,000 bicycles with a value of US$4.2 million. It was the first energy crisis in 1973 that stimulated demand for bicycles and provided the first opportunity for the rapid growth of the industry. A milestone for the Taiwanese bicycle industry in the international market was set when Tai Hsing Wang, the Taiwanese agent of Japan's Kyokuto Company, began selling Taiwanese bicycles to an American firm for the first time, a turning point in 1974 leading to rapid and successful growth in the US markets. Because of profitability, many underground bicycle assemblers emerged at that time, producing large numbers of bicycles of low quality with high levels of faults. This led to anti-dumping actions being brought by the USA and Canada against Taiwanese bicycle imports, with the consequence that Taiwan lost the

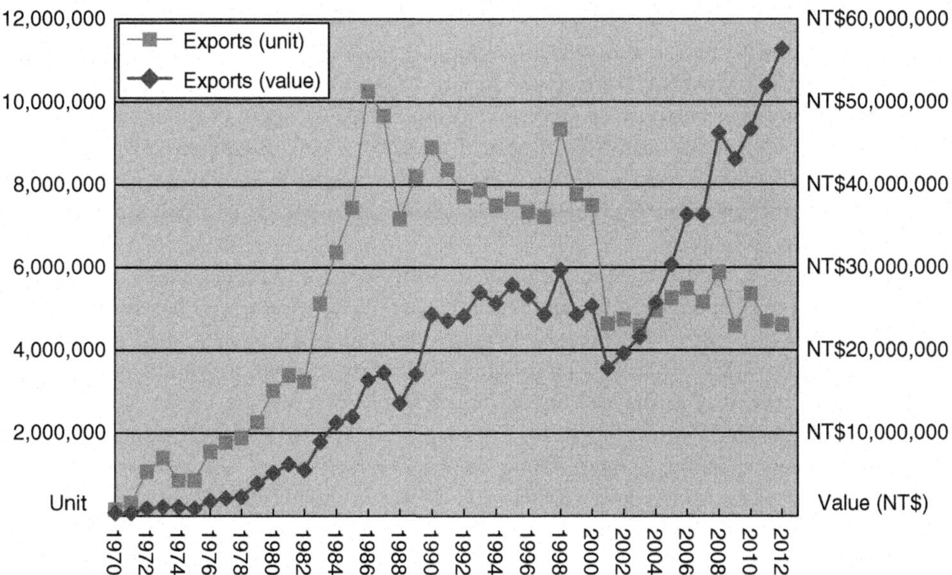

Figure 23.1 Export units and values of bicycles from Taiwan, 1970–2012
Source: Taiwan's Customs statistics, various years.

Canadian bicycle market, leading to a decline of the export volume to only 815,000 units in 1975. The CEO of one bicycle company recalls that Taiwan's poor manufacturing quality before 1974 led to signs being displayed in front of many US specialty bicycle stores, stating: "No sales or service for bicycles made in Taiwan."

What brought Taiwanese manufacturers back to life was the advent of types of bicycle designed for the new sport of Bicycle Motocross, now better known as BMX. Gaining access to such new designs and technology presented a crucial hurdle for the Taiwanese bicycle industry of that time. Eventually, a new production profile for the special welding technology required for BMX was successfully developed by the public research institute, Metal Industries R&D Center, and offered to many Taiwanese bicycle companies. This technology enabled the production of lighter bicycles and gave Taiwan an improved chance of competing with Japanese products in the US market. When the USA imposed bicycle tariffs on the basis of weight (lower than 36 pounds being levied at 5.5 percent, with others at 11 percent), as a type of protection policy, this gave the Taiwanese and Japanese with their lightweight products a chance to secure a significantly greater share of the US market. At that time, many American dealers tended to buy BMX bikes from Japan, but since the Japanese bicycle companies failed to see the marketing promise of these small unorthodox cycles, these orders were passed on to Taiwan, creating an extremely profitable future for Taiwan's bicycle industry. Since that time, original equipment manufacturer (OEM) contracts have flooded into Taiwan from the USA so that Taiwan's bicycle industry entered the Golden Age.

The 1980s: the Golden Age of the bicycle

In 1980, the Taiwanese bicycle industry overtook Japan to become the world's leading exporter in terms of units. The export volume grew more than 38-fold from 270,000 units in 1971 to 10 million in 1986. However, this rapid growth was accompanied during this period by stagnating average export prices. As a consequence, Taiwan's government and the bicycle companies started to be concerned with higher value-added production activities. The outcome was the launch, in 1984 and 1985, of two R&D projects to upgrade Taiwan's bicycle industry, focused on the application of advanced materials in bicycles. During the 1980s, high-, medium-, and low-end bicycle frames were typically made of carbon steel, Cr/Mo steel, and aluminum alloy, respectively. However, then, lightweight and sturdy bicycles were the popular models in the global market. Simultaneously, the dependence on imports of bicycle components started rising, along with the increasing quality of bicycles.

In 1984, the Industrial Development Bureau ran its first R&D project under the auspices of the Ministry of Economic Affairs, establishing an executive team referred to as the Center-Satellites System (the former Corporation Synergy Development Center), aimed at enhancing the development of higher value-added products while helping firms to handle their financial problems. The success of this project strengthened Taiwan's bicycle production networks and influenced the detailed division of labor in the industry. The second R&D project extended beyond Taiwanese manufacturing, focusing on the development of new materials, and was executed by the Materials Research Laboratories (MRL) in the Industry Technology Research Institute (ITRI). It consisted of a two-year R&D activity (1985–1987) applying carbon fiber materials to bicycle frames. This effort enabled the MRL to successfully develop carbon fiber components with alloy lugs, to create one-piece monocoque frames, composite forks, and composite three-spoked wheels. The subsequent diffusion of this carbon fiber technology has contributed to an increased volume of orders flowing into Taiwan for medium- and high-end bicycles.

The success of such higher value-added production activities has promoted Taiwan's bicycles in the global market. The orders placed with Taiwanese bicycle companies can easily be seen as different from those going to China and India in the 1980s, explaining how, despite the decline from 1983 to 1989 of 35 percent in the foreign exchange rate between US dollars and Taiwan dollars the average export price still rose 16.8 percent, with no drop in export volume. The diffusion of the technology by the public research institutions helped Taiwan's bicycle industry access advanced technologies, and by applying these to mountain bike (MTB) production, Taiwan was able to infiltrate the European market successfully. The effect of technology diffusion originating from the public research institutions (such as ITRI) is similarly associated with the success story of Taiwan's semiconductor industry.

The mature stage: the 1990s

The Taiwanese bicycle industry reached another milestone in the 1990s. Taiwan's bicycle export value recorded in 1991 reached US$1 billion for the first time, but since then, Taiwanese bicycle production has declined as it entered its mature stage. The marked decline in average export prices in this period was caused by cut-throat competition (mainly from China and India).

The success of the Taiwanese bicycle industry not only depended on its hard-working labor force and its advantages in lower production costs, but also on the significant support of the government and the public research institutions. The involvement of the public sector and its links with private companies have greatly helped Taiwan to overcome its latecomer disadvantages during the 1990s. In 1991, the Industrial Development Bureau of the Ministry of Economic Affairs committed the MRL to develop the composite carbon fiber frame. The results were successful and the technology has been transferred to the major companies such as Giant, Merida, Hodaka (Taiwan), and Ta-Ming in 1992. In the same year, the Taiwan Bicycle Industry R&D Center was established (with the support of IDB), specifically for the Taiwanese bicycle industry. This is a non-profit organization originally devoted to linking the support of the public sector with the needs of bicycle firms, aiming at promoting and upgrading Taiwan's bicycles in the international markets. Its main tasks have since been extended to the development of key bicycle components, including gearshift mechanisms, bicycle design, mechanical systems, and standardization of testing. Along with these efforts, the Ministry of Economic Affairs has set up strategies to attract foreign investment in developing key bicycle components such as gearshift mechanisms. Consequently, some top international gearshift suppliers, such as SRAM and SunTour, have established their production bases in Taiwan.

The innovation stage: the 2000s

The 1990s proved a golden era for the industry, with annual exports reaching 10 million units, but these have steadily declined in the face of stiff competition from China. By the 2000s, China's bicycle exports exceeded those of Taiwan. In 2003, Taiwan's bicycle export volume was down to 3,880,000 units and has remained at a similar level since.

Facing severe competition with lower labor costs from China since the 1990s, many Taiwanese bicycle suppliers were forced to move to China (Brookfield *et al.*, 2008), creating a significant crisis for the Taiwanese bicycle industry. Taiwan's two leading companies, Giant and Merida, had to decide whether to stay in Taiwan or transfer their production bases to China. The decision made by Giant and Merida, the two hubs of Taiwan's bicycle industry, would greatly influence the satellite companies along their respective supply chains. After several intense meetings, King Liu (the CEO of Giant) and Ike Tseng (the CEO of Merida) and top managers in the two companies decided to stay, but agreed they needed to do something to overcome this crisis. Eventually, they decided to devise an innovation team (called the A-Team) through close collaboration, aiming once again at upgrading the whole bicycle supply chain in Taiwan in order to differentiate Taiwan's high-quality products from the Chinese low- to medium-end bicycles.

The A-Team, comprising Taiwanese bicycle assemblers and suppliers, was established quickly after several rounds of meetings in 2002, with the aim of revitalizing Taiwan's prospects in the industry. It amounted to an integration of the whole supply chain, with members of the A-Team sharing knowledge and experience. The A-Team soon became the innovation platform for those involved in the supply chain, for diffusing knowledge, experience, and expertise in technology and management. These efforts have enabled the average export price of Taiwan's bicycles to increase from US$100 in 1998 to US$209 in 2006, and to double again in 2012 to US$417 (according to the data extracted from the Taiwan's Customs' Statistics in 2013).

The evolving stages of Giant and King Liu

The successes of Taiwan's bicycle industry in the 1980s and 1990s, and the achievements of the A-Team in the 2000s, can be significantly attributed to close linkage with the global production networks, government support, as well as other factors (Hu and Wu, 2011). Giant is the major turning hub of Taiwan's bicycle industry, with its developmental course over recent decades perfectly reflecting the trajectory of Taiwan's bicycle industry as a whole. To better understand the growth of Giant and how King Liu deftly implements strategic entrepreneurship, we need to look closer at Giant's development trajectory. The growth of Giant has evolved over the three characteristic growth phases that particularly apply to latecomers: starting with an imitative strategy; experiencing a technological upgrading stage; and then reaching the innovation stage. We detail these three stages as follows.

Initiating stage: 1970s–1980s

Giant's founder and spiritual leader, King Liu, was born when the island was a Japanese colony—a 50-year period that ended in 1943. It was in the year 1972 that Giant was established, a critical milestone for King Liu as well as for the entire bicycle industry of Taiwan. Before 1972, King Liu had a youthful creative spirit, which showed up in many different business operations, such as the production of screws and wooden boxes, as well as the eel-feeding business. His prior experiences and creative personality were the keys influencing King Liu's entrepreneurial alertness; though they did not bring big success then, they were later of great help to Giant's international business operations (Ardichvili and Cardozo, 2000).

The establishment of Giant emerged from a reunion of friends in 1972, resulting in a group of ten stockholders with a shared understanding of the future of bicycle development in Taiwan. Interestingly, none of the ten stockholders possessed bicycle-related knowledge. Giant spent decades of hard work and struggle to turn it from an unknown small firm into the leading world brand it is today. Giant was unprofitable during its first few years because of Taiwan's image of low quality in the US market. Liu's expertise is in metal forming, whereas the co-leader, Tony Lo, specialized in international trade and business negotiation. So Liu handled internal manufacturing operations and Lo took charge of external customer relationships. In the 1970s, the specifications of bicycle components were not regulated by the Taiwan authorities. It was King Liu who took the initiative of adopting the Japanese Industry Standard (JIS), and tried to persuade bicycle parts suppliers to unify the specifications of a range of components. It was an awkward step for an unknown small firm at that time, but King Liu persisted in his beliefs to improve quality. This prior insight into emphasis on quality had a profound influence on Giant's production operations and has since become part of Giant's culture.

The early years after Giant was established did not run smoothly. This hard-pressed situation was not relieved until Tony Lo finally took an opportunity to secure the first orders from one of America's biggest bicycle dealers, Schwinn, in 1976. Originally, Schwinn did not intend to place orders with Giant, but the finish quality of Giant's steel tubes changed their opinion. This order from Schwinn enabled Giant to become the largest bicycle manufacturer in Taiwan, because the quality of its bicycles was recognized by the global bicycle market. Giant and other Taiwanese bicycle makers had turned the island into the world's top bicycle exporter by the 1980s.

Schwinn brought Giant vitality, but also produced a crisis. In the 1980s, 75 percent of Giant's production was tied up in OEM orders with Schwinn. At that time, King Liu recognized that Giant was in difficulty, having very little control over technology, marketing information, and business negotiation assets. This sense of crisis became the stimulus for Giant to launch its own brand (also called Giant), so that it set up the Taiwan Giant Sales Company in 1981. Such own-branding activity spread like wildfire when Schwinn announced it would shift its OEM orders to the China Bicycle Company in 1985. In response, King Liu took the company into new directions through rapid expansion of its overseas branches around the world, so that in time it could compensate for the capacity loss due to the loss of Schwinn's orders. The overseas branches were all set up to promote their own-brand Giant bicycles. The first of these overseas branches was established in the Netherlands in 1986, followed by the US branch in 1987, a Japanese branch in 1989, Canadian and Australian branches in 1991, and a branch in China in 1992.

The business crisis for Giant in 1985 provoked by Schwinn turned out to be a driving force in innovation for Giant, prompting Giant and the Material Research Laboratories (MRL) in ITRI to embark on a joint advanced materials project on the development of carbon fiber bicycle frames. Within only one year, the outcome of this joint collaboration was successfully promoted to the global bicycle market in 1986. In the same year, Giant also collaborated in two more technology diffusion projects for aluminum welding technology with another public research institute, CSIST (Chinese Society for Imaging Science and Technology). In 1988, Giant started the mass production of its jointly developed carbon fiber bicycle frame, producing one million pieces per annum, while the revenues grew to over NT$1 billion. This success advanced Giant's brand name and has kept Giant at the forefront of bicycle industry. Up to now, Giant is the largest supplier of carbon fiber bicycles in the world. The carbon fiber composite bicycle gained an award as one of five runners-up in the 1993 showcase of excellence for products made in Taiwan.

Certainly, the salient feature of early internationalization is a sequence of entrepreneurial processes, comprising: (1) discovery of opportunities; (2) deployment of resources; and (3) engagement with international competitors (Mathews and Zander, 2007). The application of advanced materials like chromoly (chromium-molybdenum), aluminum and carbon fiber in mass production makes Giant an industrial leader in design and innovations. In the 1980s, while most bicycle frames were made of heavier steel tube, Giant was the first company to mass-produce bicycles using lighter chromoly in 1981 and its mass production capability reduced the price of chromoly bicycles to under US$300. In the meantime, King Liu enhanced the opportunity to develop Giant's R&D capability by taking advantage of governmental assistance from public research institutes, such as ITRI and CSIST. Cooperation and technology transfer from ITRI and CSIST in 1986 not only helped to supersede the heavy steel frame bicycles but also laid a firm foundation for Giant's high-end carbon fiber bicycle manufacturing capability.

However, a serious challenge came when Giant established a company in the USA, the most competitive market, in 1987. Because of its disadvantage as a foreign company, the model of own-branding strategy was not successful in the US market. In the beginning, King Liu persisted in using old methods to solve the new problems and was resistant to change, until he finally found that prevailing methods are not able to solve new problems (de Bono, 1992, p. 17). Previously unsuccessful activities made him need to revise his plans. Thus, as time went by, King Liu learned, by trial and error and experimentation, to adopt new methods, while the entrepreneur's novel ideas and new plans were exposed to market tests, based on the responses of market participants. These processes helped King Liu to learn the most appropriate choice of action. In 1999, Giant finally invited Skip Hess, an experienced local expert in the US bicycle industry, who had worked for Mongoose and Schwinn, to join Giant and re-deploy Giant's own-brand strategy in the US. Targeting the Independent Bicycle Dealers (IBD) market since 2000 has allowed Giant's bicycles at last to get a successful response in the US market.

Internalization and expansion: 1990s

Giant decided to accelerate the marketing of its own brand when Schwinn abruptly abandoned its long-term partner and switched its OEM orders to the China Bicycle Company in Shenzhen. Because of Schwinn, numerous Taiwanese bicycle firms had established factories in China since the beginning of the 1990s, whereas experience in the US market held back Giant's movement into China. Becoming more cautious, Giant started participating in business seminars in order to gather more information to build its knowledge stock about China, a highly uncertain market. Finally, Giant set up a wholly-owned subsidiary, Giant (China), in 1992 and cemented its position by entering a joint venture with Phoenix, one of the Mainland's largest bicycle makers. To increase the reputation and credibility of its own brand, Giant went public on the Taiwanese Stock Exchange in 1994. However, having started as an OEM, Giant had the disadvantage of being unfamiliar with international management and marketing. Indeed, the process of trial-and-error caused the US subsidiary to suffer losses for 13 years, and the China subsidiary grew slowly in the first two years because of inappropriate marketing strategies.

Despite the marketing setbacks in the USA and China, Giant is still aware of the potential applications of advanced materials, particularly on the bicycle frame, which would greatly increase the value of bicycles. So Giant formed a carbon composite innovation team (specializing in the application of advanced materials to bicycle frames) in Los Angeles and established a factory in the Netherlands in 1996 so as to be close to the immediate market and to technology information. The result was the adoption of MCR carbon composites, which enabled Giant to produce the world's first carbon-composite bicycle. The road bike of the MCR series won *Business Week*'s Best New Product in 1998, named along with Intel's Pentium II, Porsche's New Model and Nokia's PDA (Personal Digital Assistant). In addition, the Giant TCR Compact Road frame, a combination of unique product design and extremely lightweight aluminum construction, weighing only 1 kilo (2.2 pounds), is the lightest road frame available today.

Rather than directly competing for transmission systems with the technological leaders such as Shimano, Giant realized that developing bicycle frame materials could be its competitive advantage and strove not only to find the best applications of the various frame materials, but also to become involved in the manufacturing and design of its own materials, including drawing and butting of aluminum for bicycle frames, processes for which the Chuans in Metal Products (Kungshan, China) Company was set up in 1997. While Giant consolidated its innovative niche on frames and materials processes, other key components were also targeted and sought out internationally in order to create a consistent image for Giant bicycles. For example, these highly modularized bicycles were split into six technological subsystems (materials, frame system, transmission system, steering system, brake system, and wheel system) in pursuit of the best comfort and quality for the range of bicycle models, and the key components were selected from more than 100 component suppliers around the world (Hu and Wu, 2011).

In 1989, Giant set up a Japanese subsidiary. However, sales did not grow in that country due to high loyalty for domestic brands. It was not until Giant purchased a 30 percent stake in the Japanese firm Hodaka, in 1998, that Giant's market share in Japan started to increase, relying on Hodaka's mass-market distribution channels. Consequently, in 2000, all Giant's worldwide sales subsidiaries became profitable and grew steadily, including their formerly loss-making US subsidiary. Furthermore, Giant-Phoenix, the joint-venture brand of Giant and Phoenix in China, has become one of the top quality brands in the Chinese market.

Recognizing the importance of building its own brand, Giant not only concentrates on manufacturing but also spends roughly 5 percent of its annual turnover on worldwide marketing expenses and 2 percent of its annual revenues in its three R&D centers in Taiwan (its headquarters), the USA and Europe. The reduction in OEM business enabled Giant to minimize the sales loss when Schwinn went bankrupt in 2001, by which time the orders from Schwinn represented only 1.24 percent of Giant's annual revenue.

The successful "*Giant Experience*" and Giant Production System (which uses state-of-the-art machinery and computer-enhanced management) are widely admired by the rest of the industry. Today, 70 percent of Giant's sales are its own brands, with the other 30 percent from contract manufacturing. Giant is the biggest brand in both Taiwan and China, one of the three biggest players in Europe, and is listed as the second in the US IBD (Independent Bicycle Dealers) market. Giant is also one of the leading brands in Japan, Australia, Canada and the Netherlands.

The innovation-driven stage: the 2000s

As shown in Figure 23.2, both Giant's sales and net profits have recorded historical peaks and have been growing continuously until the last observation year in 2011, after a fluctuation during the late 1990s due to serious competition from China and India, and because of excess capacity

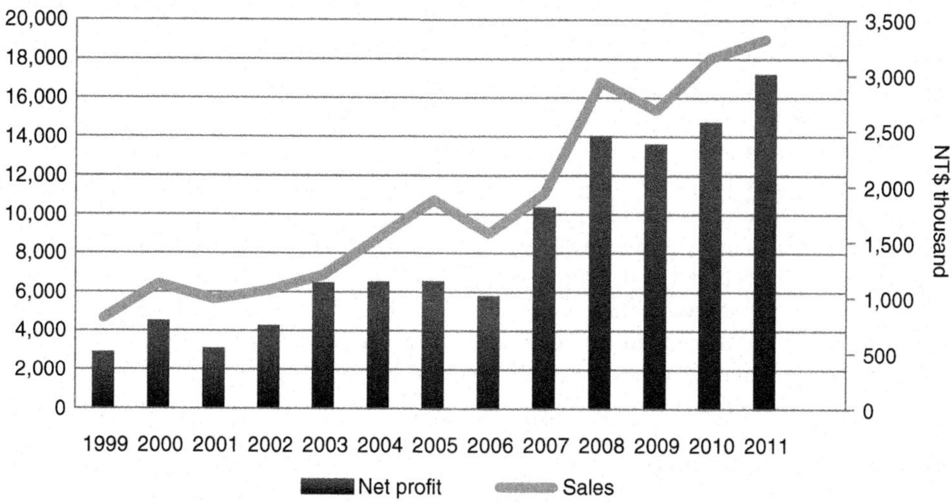

Figure 23.2 Giant's sales and net profits, 1999–2011
Source: Giant Annual Reports, various years.

in the global bicycle industry. In these circumstances, King Liu, based on his subjective stock of knowledge accumulated from his past experience, considered that Taiwan's bicycle manufacturing capability needed to be distinguished from those countries with cost advantages, such as China and India (Minniti and Bygrave, 2001).

Market differences in manufacturing costs have been recognized as "sources of opportunities" (Cohen and Winn, 2007, p. 30). Giant, therefore, proposed a system for high value-added bicycles, to be known as the 'A-Team', and called for network collaboration by key component suppliers and dealers. The A-Team was officially initiated in 2002 as a non-profit R&D consortium by Giant and Merida, the two major Taiwanese bike manufacturers, together with 11 of Taiwan's leading component makers involved in the six defined subsystems (including Alex, Dah Ken, Formula, KMC, SR Suntour, SRAM, Tektro, TienHsin, Velo, VP Components, and Wellgo). For highly modular products like bicycles, achieving substantial growth is largely reliant on new and critical products or applications and product innovation, while sustaining that growth requires greater emphasis on incremental innovations or process innovations (Romer, 1990; Nell, 1992). A-Team members are thus committed to striving for manufacturing and operational excellence and delivery of the highest quality products. Their agreement also extends to exclusive use of just-in-time inventory control systems. Members will endeavor to deliver more innovative designs in new products and bring products to market more rapidly, creating a new high value-added marketing strategy. The sweet taste of success attracted international leading companies, such as Shimano (Japan) and Specialized (the USA), and various bicycle distributors to join this consortium.

Conclusion

During the 1970s and 1980s, King Liu's entrepreneurial awareness led to him discovering the opportunity to capture competitive advantages for Giant (Yu and Hu, 2012). Liu took action to improve the manufacturing quality in order to overcome anti-dumping measures and win orders from Schwinn. Rather than employing a cost reduction strategy, Liu's insistence on high quality standards helped Giant survive the domestic and international price-cutting wars.

Based on prior experience, Liu realized that innovation is crucial to maintaining sustainability in the industry. To access new technologies or materials and production methods, Liu leveraged the resources from public research institutions, such as ITRI, supported by the national innovation system for product-data-management (PDM), toward the development of the carbon fiber frame. Apart from exploiting these external resources, Liu was also sourcing internally from the industry, initiating a collective partnership to form the A-Team, creating an innovation platform for Taiwan's bicycle industry as a whole. The A-Team innovation platform has successfully upgraded the whole bicycle industry through collective learning and made Taiwan a leading producer of high value-added bicycles. The developmental trajectory of Giant over the past four decades has clearly demonstrated the ways that entrepreneurial alertness, pursuit of opportunities, strategic resource leverage and organization re-configuration have helped to gain and maintain the company's continuous competitive advantages in the global bicycle industry.

The ways that entrepreneurs deal with crisis are what makes them different. While most people see the risks in opportunity, entrepreneurs see opportunity in the crisis. As summarized in Table 23.1, King Liu exerted his strategic entrepreneurship by recognizing and capturing opportunities during the successive crises and uncertainties that Giant encountered and by implementing competitive strategies in the global market (Knight, 1921). Accordingly, Liu initiated the framing of new visions for Giant (e.g. own-branding in 1980s–1990s) and for Taiwan's bicycle industry (i.e. targeting high-end products in the 2000s), then he put the vision into action to aggregate related partners and supporters while formulating a close network in the open system through mutually beneficial collaborations in the global supply chain. Liu's efforts enabled the industry to evolve from a traditional mode into a professional mode, while creating competitive advantages for both individual firms and the industry as a whole.

Taiwan has been one of the critical power-houses in the global bicycle industry over recent decades. While Taiwan had accumulated a great deal of resources and capabilities in manufacturing, engineering, and technological development, King Liu helped Giant not only to achieve the world's leading market position but also to upgrade Taiwan's bicycle industry as a whole. Giant overcame the crisis of losing OEM orders in the 1980s from its largest client, Schwinn. This crisis, in its turn, became an opportunity for Giant to deploy its own-branding strategy. Furthermore, Giant learnt from its experience of failure in the US market and found ways to adapt its strategy so that Giant US finally became profitable in 2000. The processes of Giant's three developmental stages led by Liu are closely linked with the OEM/ODM activities in Taiwan's bicycle industry in the 1970s, technology upgrading in the 1980s, OBM strategy (adopted by many bicycle component makers) in the 1990s, and building a technology platform (the A-Team) in the 2000s.

During these processes, Liu's strategic entrepreneurship further captured the opportunity for resource leverage and deployment. For example, with government support, the collaboration on developing advanced materials with ITRI became the essential competitive niche for Giant while

Table 23.1 Turning crisis to opportunities: King Liu's strategic entrepreneurship

Crisis/opportunity	*Strategic implementation*
Crisis 1: Taiwanese bicycles faced international charge of anti-dumping	Improving bicycle production quality
Crisis 2: Giant's major OEM client Schwinn shifted the orders to China and went bankrupt	Deployment of own-branding strategy
Crisis 3: Competition from low cost countries (China and India)	Formed A-Team to make high value bicycles and call for open innovation from the global supply chain to reinforce innovations

this, in turn, reinforced Giant's core competitive advantage in own-branding activity through the development of the world's first lightweight and sturdy one-piece carbon fiber bicycle. These demonstrated how resources leverage, allocation, and re-configuration have been developed and utilized to help Giant's growth in the 1980s and 1990s. The integration of resources, initiated in the early 2000s by Giant, calling for open innovation from the global supply chain, was further demonstrated in the A-Team. The synergy of the A-Team not only saved Taiwan's bicycle firms from moving to China but has also created a new wave for Taiwan's bicycle industry in the niche market through collective partnership and learning. Associated with the developmental trajectory of Taiwan's bicycle industry over the past decades, Liu's entrepreneurial behavior in Giant Bicycle enabled the industrial paradigm to be transformed from a regular traditional old regime into an innovative professional new regime in the global market.

References

Alvarez, S.A. and Busenitz, L.W. (2001) "The entrepreneurship of resource-based theory," *Journal of Management,* 27(6): 755–775.

Ardichvili, A. and Cardozo, R.N. (2000) "A model of entrepreneurial opportunity recognition process," *Journal of Enterprising Culture,* 8(2): 103–119.

Barney, J.B. (1991) "Firm resources and sustained competitive advantage," *Journal of Management,* 17: 99–120.

Brookfield, J., Liu, R.J. and MacDuffie, J.P. (2008) "Taiwan's bicycle industry A-team battles Chinese competition with innovation and cooperation," *Strategy & Leadership,* 36(1): 14–19.

Cohen, B. and Winn, M. (2007) "Market imperfections, opportunity, and sustainable entrepreneurship," *Journal of Business Venturing,* 22(1): 29–49.

de Bono, E. (1992) *Serious Creativity,* New York: Harper Business.

Gartner, W.B. (1988) "Who is an entrepreneur? is the wrong question," *Entrepreneurship Theory Practice,* 13(4): 47–68.

Hu, M.C. and Wu, C.Y. (2011) "Exploring technological innovation trajectories through latecomers: evidence from Taiwan's bicycle industry," *Technology Analysis & Strategic Management,* 23(4): 433–452.

Ireland, R.D. and Hitt, M.A. (1999) "Achieving and maintaining strategic competitiveness in the 21st century: the role of strategic leadership," *Academy of Management Executive,* 13: 43–57.

Ireland, R.D., Hitt, M.A. and Sirmon, D.G. (2003) "A model of strategic entrepreneurship: the construct and its dimensions," *Journal of Management,* 29(6): 963–989.

Kirzner, I.M. (1973) *Competition and Entrepreneurship,* Chicago: University of Chicago Press, pp. 212–219.

Knight, F.H. (1921) *Risk, Uncertainty, and Profit,* New York: August M. Kelley.

Kuratko, D.F. and Audretsch, D.B. (2009) "Strategic entrepreneurship: exploring different perspectives of an emerging concept," *Entrepreneurship Theory and Practice,* January, 1–17.

Lee, U. and Lin, S. (1991) *Upgrading the Bicycle Industry in Taiwan,* Division of Small and Medium Enterprises, the Ministry of Economic Affairs, Taiwan (Chinese version).

Lumpkin, G.T. and Dess, G.G. (1996) "Enriching the entrepreneurial orientation construct: a reply to entrepreneurial orientation or pioneer advantage," *Academy of Management Review,* 21(3): 605–607.

Mathews, J. and Zander, I. (2007) "The international entrepreneurial dynamics of accelerated internationalization," *Journal of International Business Studies,* 38(3): 387–403.

Minniti, M. and Bygrave, W. (2001) "A dynamic model of entrepreneurial learning," *Entrepreneurship: Theory and Practice,* 23(4): 41–52.

Nell, E. (ed.) (1992) "Transformational growth: from Say's Law to the multiplier," in *Transformational Growth and Effective Demand,* New York: New York University Press.

Porter, M.E. (1990) *The Competitive Advantage of Nations,* New York: Free Press.

Romer, P.M. (1990) "Endogenous technological change," *Journal of Political Economy* 98(5): S71–S102.

Shane, S. (2004) *A General Theory of Entrepreneurship: The Individual-Opportunity Nexus,* Cheltenham: Edward Elgar.

Yu, F.L. and Hu, M.C. (2012) "Giants: Taiwan's world brand bicycle," in F.L. Yu (ed.) *Entrepreneurship and Economic Development of Taiwan,* New York: Springer.

24

Terry Gou and Foxconn

Charlie Z.W. Chiang and Ho-Don Yan

Introduction

Foxconn was established in 1974 by its founder Terry Tai-Ming Gou as a single-product manufacturer of TV tuner knobs. Through his leadership, Foxconn has risen to become the world's largest electronics manufacturing services (EMS) provider, among the top 50 of Fortune Global 500 firms, and the largest company in terms of consolidated revenue in Taiwan. It has factories and branches dispersed across Asia, Europe, and North and South America, with over 1.3 million total employees around the world (Foxconn, 2012) (see Table 24.1). Its businesses have diversified into the fields of computer, communication, and consumer-electronics (3C), car electronics, digital content, health care, clean energy, and communication systems. How a small business, starting with capital of US$7,500, has grown into a vast enterprise with annual sales of more than US$130 billion in less four decades provides an interesting case for study.

Owing to the outsourcing trend from Western countries after the 1960s, particularly from the USA, many small and medium-sized enterprises (SMEs) in emerging countries, such as Hong Kong, South Korea, and Taiwan, took the opportunity to integrate into the world production network by conducting original equipment manufacturing (OEM). The OEM contracts spread not only across traditional manufacturing industries, but also in high-tech industries, including consumer electronics, information technology, communication peripheral devices, and electronic equipment's (Hobday, 2001). Due to their lower overhead costs and their ability to specialize in certain niches, and because smaller companies can often do some things more efficiently than larger ones, SMEs in Taiwan have succeeded in collaborating with multinational corporations (MNCs) to improve their productivity (Krywulak and Kukushkin, 2009).

The creation of Foxconn Group is associated with the emergence of the electronics manufacturing services (EMS) business model.[1] Table 24.2 shows EMS and other relevant types of business models, and some of these types of business models may simultaneously exist in the same firm. For instance, Foxconn is simultaneously an OEM, ODM, EMS, and eCMMS manufacturer. The growth of EMS firms is closely related to the global value chain, which takes advantage of the global division of labor and allows goods and services to be traded in fragmented and internationally dispersed production (UNCTAD, 2013). Zhai *et al.* (2007) argued that EMS firms usually start by selectively penetrating and positioning themselves along the supply chain. Their

Table 24.1 Profile of Foxconn

Growth path	Through OEM to upgrading OEM & cross-industry OEM
Year established	1974
Capital	Started up at US$7,500 and now US$4 billion
Founder	Terry Gou
Employees	Over 1.3 million
Products	Computers, communication, consumer electronics, car electronics, 3C Channel, content, clean energy, health care
Patent applications	Over 55,000
Annual revenue	Over US$130 billion
Stock went public	1991
Headquarters	Taipei, Taiwan
Branches	China, the USA, Czech Republic, Hungary, India, Finland, Mexico, Brazil, Vietnam
Business model	OEM, ODM, EMS, eCMMS
Customers	Atari, IBM, Intel, Dell, Nokia, Sony, Motorola, Apple, HP, UTStarcom, Compaq

Source: Compiled by the author from data from Foxconn (2012).

Table 24.2 Definition of different models of business

Type	*Definition and description*
OEM	Original equipment manufacturing: a firm that serves as a contractor for MNCs and stamps MNCs' brand names on the products
ODM	Original design manufacturing: a firm that designs and builds products using the brand name of its MNC customers; also called contract design manufacturing (CDM)
OBM	Own brand manufacturing: a firm that sells its own brand name through its own distribution channel
EMS	Electronics manufacturing service: a firm that offers electronics-related product manufacturing and relevant comprehensive services for OEM or OBM customers
CEM	Contract electronics manufacturing: one category of EMS firms that concentrates more on production
eCMMS	e-enabled components, modules, moves, and services: a term created by Foxconn to define a vertically integrated one-stop-shopping business model that covers solutions ranging from molding, tooling, mechanical parts, components, modules, system assembly, design, manufacturing, maintenance, logistics, etc.

Note: Data resources are from Zhai *et al.* (2007) and Foxconn (2012).

business growth takes place along three intertwined dimensions: production, the supply chain, and capability development (Zhai *et al.*, 2007). Krywulak and Kukushkin (2009) proposed that partnering with MNCs provides five advantages for SMEs: (1) increased sales and enhanced firm reputation; (2) access to new markets through the MNCs' established channels; (3) leveraging the MNCs' technical knowledge and other expertise; (4) improved quality and productivity to meet the MNCs' supplier standards; and (5) a stronger base for future growth. On the other hand, by outsourcing key parts of the supply-chain management to the EMS industry, MNCs can improve quality, reduce costs, and accelerate time to market, leading to higher customer satisfaction, higher profit margins, and larger market share gains.

From a TV knob maker to the world's dominant consumer electronics manufacturer, Terry Gou has helped steer Foxconn with rapid growth for nearly four decades. With Foxconn Group producing over 70 percent of the components, modules, and parts within the global PC industry, Terry Gou boasted "Intel inside and Foxconn outside!" (Chang, 2005). Since 2005, Foxconn has become the world's number one EMS company. The entrepreneurial adventure of Terry Gou is a fascinating story, and studies of Foxconn mostly focus on one or two aspects, such as financial operations, strategic management, or technological upgrading.[2] In this chapter we re-focus on the role of entrepreneurship in studying the case of Terry Gou and Foxconn.

Entrepreneurship is a complex activity involving the discovery, evaluation, and exploitation of opportunities to introduce new goods and services, ways of organizing, markets, processes, and raw materials by systematizing efforts that previously had not existed (Shane and Venkataraman, 2000). Alvarez and Barney (2007) argue that effective entrepreneurial action usually includes opportunity discovery and involves leadership, strategic planning, and competitive advantage creation. The growth pathway of Foxconn is unequivocally complicated and it is not easy to comprehend one aspect or another.

We illustrate the emergence of a big enterprise, such as Foxconn, by focusing on three stages: formation, growth and transformation. At the formation stage, entrepreneurship of opportunity discovery and firm creation are usually the focus. At the growth stage, strategic management becomes the main consideration. Finally, when the firm transforms to a global corporation, leadership is always the center of the discussion. The demarcation of these three stages and the related focus of the research fields are for illustration purposes. Without a doubt, the operation of a corporation at each stage involves whatever it needs. For instance, even in the early stage of firm formation, entrepreneurs not only need to deal with opportunity discovery in order to organize a firm, but it is necessary also to have the skill of strategic management, and leadership becomes important as well for a vision of future development.

In the rest of this chapter, we delineate how Terry Gou took the opportunity to set up Hon Hai Precision Industry Corporation Ltd (listed on the Hong Kong stock market as Foxconn in 2005), and through his connections with MNCs how he learned and invested in managerial skill to increase organizational efficiency. The third section explains how Foxconn has created its competitive advantages by scaling up and diversifying production and accumulated capabilities through continuous mergers and acquisitions (M&A). The next section focuses on how Terry Gou has led Foxconn through its transformation into a global giant, and the final section is the conclusion.

Opportunity discovery and new venture creation

Every new venture creation starts from discovering an opportunity. With a keen perception of market trends, Terry Gou sensed a profitable opportunity from a small part of a TV set. Being able to join the global value chain brings even wider opportunities. The business relationships with MNCs have enabled Foxconn to increase sales, to accumulate capabilities and capital, and to build a strong base for future growth. As a quick learner, Terry Gou has been able to expand his vision and explore new opportunities.

Opportunity discovery and the connection with MNCs

During Terry Gou's college education, he held part-time jobs in the factories around the neighborhood where he lived. After finishing compulsory military service, he started his career as a clerk in a shipping company. From the experiences of dealing with trading affairs in this company and his earlier part-time jobs in factories, Terry Gou realized that manufacturing is the underpinning of international trade. He started his own business by taking an order for TV tuner knobs and borrowed US$7,500 from his mother to establish Hon Hai Plastics Corporation (changed to Hon Hai Precision Corporation the next year) with his friend in Taipei in 1974 when he was 24 years old (Shu, 2008).

While seeking to improve the quality of TV knobs, Terry Gou found that the molding procedure, one of the important processes in a supplier's production, was inefficient and could be improved. Abandoning the traditional molding process, which was usually conducted through the tutor–apprentice model, in 1978 Terry Gou built his own molding factory with a standard operation procedure for molding (Shu, 2008). This transformation not only helped Foxconn establish great precision in molding and thus created high-end manufacturing ability in its fledging stage, but also cultivated a strong base for its future growth.

Two years later, Terry Gou discovered an opportunity to produce PC connectors. The process of manufacturing PC connectors is one of the important stages of manufacturing video games and PCs. Terry Gou noticed that Foxconn possessed at least 40–50 percent of similar molding technology and skill, and hence it should not be hard for Foxconn to manufacture PC connectors. After Foxconn started producing PC connectors, Terry Gou immediately realized that the quality of a small PC connector, which connects parts including the motherboard, memory chips, and hundreds of circuits, is pivotal for the regular operation of a PC (Chang, 2005). Terry Gou decided to purchase advanced equipment from Japan in order to upgrade Foxconn's subcontracting capability and to enable Foxconn to work with global IT firms such as Atari and IBM.

Foxconn started with 2,600 pieces of connector production in 1980 for Atari, a provider of video games. Terry Gou later launched his business expansion in the US, visiting 32 states within 11 months in the early 1980s. In Raleigh, NC, he booked himself into a motel close to an IBM facility. Being a small potato at that time and after hanging around for three days, Terry Gou finally got an appointment and acquired a PC connector order from IBM (Balfour and Culpan, 2010). Due to the high precision of its mold manufacturing, Foxconn had the competitive advantage to produce high-quality connectors for those IT companies and soon won their trust. The popularity of video games in 1981 and the first PC launched by IBM that same year helped Foxconn achieve rapid growth, accumulate capabilities, and gain a great deal of revenue through PC connector production.

Entrepreneurial learning and capability accumulation

Although Foxconn had started receiving large OEM orders, Terry Gou began to find that managerial capability is necessary for the firm to remain competitive. Taking advantage of doing business with global IT firms, Terry Gou learned from the top managers in the Taiwan branches of foreign firms, such as Texas Instruments, Dell, and Philips, about their business administration models and operation systems. Simultaneously, Terry Gou adopted the 5S management system and "Just in Time" (JIT) production model from the automobile industry in Japan and brought in CAD/CAM software systems from a US firm to enhance production efficiency and capacity.[3] The aim of 5S management is to maximize efficiency and effectiveness and to increase the quality of production (Gapp *et al.*, 2008). The JIT approach has significant effects in improving manufacturing performance (Gunasekaran and Lyu, 1997).

In 1995, in order to obtain orders for the chassis of desktop computers from Compaq, Terry Gou took the purchasing manager of Compaq to survey the farmland in Lunghwa of Shenzhen, where the campus of Foxconn in southern China would be located. He daringly showed the would-be production program to the Compaq manager, even though at that time Foxconn had experience of only PC connector production. Due to Terry Gou's aggressive attitude and Compaq's plan of looking for lower cost suppliers, he eventually acquired the orders for the PC chassis from Compaq. Terry Gou soon contracted with six Taiwanese firms to initially assimilate parts of the order. In the meantime, he copied, learned, and researched the production lines of a PC chassis made by these firms and then shrewdly refined the process to construct his own production lines in Lunghwa Park. With immediate coordination, Terry Gou expeditiously accomplished the construction of the chassis production lines after six months in 1996 and then started to produce the PC chassis to fill the rest of the order (*Common Wealth*, 2007). The successful working with Compaq not only allowed Foxconn to acquire the capability to produce PC chassis, but also emboldened Terry Gou to undertake new ventures.

To upgrade his employees' ability to keep up with the fast growth pace of Foxconn, Terry Gou first spent about US$274,000, or about 1.67 percent of his total sales, on a training budget to send employees to be trained abroad in 1987. Training is fundamental for the growth of the firm, Terry Gou said in an interview (Chang, 2005), and he encouraged his employees to practice learning-by-doing. His philosophy of success can be simplified through four stages: (1) imitation; (2) research; (3) creation; and (4) innovation (Chang, 2005). Taking advantage of imitation, one can step into a new business as an outsider. Through research based on existing technology, one can create new skills and knowledge incrementally. After inspiration from new knowledge and skills, a pioneering innovation will be born. Through imitation, learning, and in-house R&D to continuously upgrade its capabilities, Foxconn has gradually improved its competencies.

Competitive strategies, dynamic capabilities, and firm expansion

What helped Foxconn grow so fast in such a short period of time is its competitive strategies. The competitive strategies of Foxconn are diverse and remarkable and have become an excellent example worth carefully studying. Wang (2007), Shu and Chang (2008), and Chu (2009) emphasized that the patent management of Foxconn is an important factor in its success. Chen (2003a), Lin (2007), Wang (2007), Shu and Chang (2008), and Chu (2009) deemed that Foxconn's integration strategy, or merger and acquisition (M&A) strategy, has contributed to its rapid growth. Foxconn's R&D and patent management enables its technology portfolio strategy to initiate an M&A strategy. This section addresses how Foxconn has coordinated and integrated its resources to develop its capabilities by emphasizing the creation of cost advantages, strategic alliances, and patent management.

Economies of scale, global division of labor, and cost advantage

Most EMS companies leverage global deployment, which takes advantage of the global value chain to reap the benefits from segmented and geographical dispersed production. Many of their electronics products are complex and specialized, and thus EMS manufacturing usually needs to be relocated close to the end customer (Venture Outsource, 2007). For instance, in order to serve the US market, many EMS companies have facilities located in Mexico; for the Western European market, the EMS companies build manufacturing facilities in Eastern Europe or in the former Soviet bloc countries; whereas for the Asian market, China and India are their choices.

Roughly 90 percent of Foxconn's manufacturing capacity is located in low-cost countries, particularly in China (Venture Outsource, 2007). Since 1988, Terry Gou has established 20 industry parks there and hired about million employees in China for his mass production. He built a series of related synergy factories in the same parks in order to reduce transportation costs and time. The Shenzhen Lunghwa Park thus provided the capacity to perform time-to-market (TTM) and time-to-profit (TTP). Fast TTM and TTP are key to customer satisfaction and firm competitiveness in the EMS industry. Introducing a new product to the market requires reaching customers faster than the competitors and helps enable the firm to promptly capture the market share and profits (Folgo, 2008). Foxconn's complete and effective production system in the Lunghwa factories simplified computer assembly. Assembly starts with a coil of sheet metal at one end that is cut, formed, welded, and stamped to make the top and bottom of the chassis. The employees then assemble it, installing a floppy drive, power supply, and cables. Foxconn's customers only have to insert the motherboard, CPU, memory, and hard drive (Balfour and Culpan, 2010).

Aside from the efforts spent on production, Terry Gou also pays great attention to establishing local networks. To effectively establish and manage local relationships to enter the market, Terry Gou initially decided to invest in China in a wholly owned subsidiary (WOS), which makes it is easier to build local response capability under his control (Chen, 2005). To construct an electronic customs system that directly connects to the government's Shenzhen customs for rapid cargo delivery in Lunghwa Park, he built up relationships with local authorities. Time is money, and saving time is one way of cutting costs. Taking advantage of local institutions and networks, Foxconn has strengthened its speed of service response and accelerated its TTM capability.

Through adaptation with local business culture, aggregation with its production and in-house R&D capacities worldwide, and arbitrage through geographic cost discrepancy, Foxconn has successfully initiated economies of scale and global deployment, which allow it to price its products lower than its competitors (Ghemawat, 2007). By dint of continuous cost reduction efforts within manufacturing and in administration procedures, Terry Gou has earned the title of "Cost-down Terry."

M&A strategy and vertical integration

After accumulating sufficient capabilities and generating abundant capital through manufacturing PC connectors, Terry Gou commenced a strategy of M&A and making strategic alliances to expand the reach of Foxconn. M&A is one way to achieve technologies and is also helpful for vertical integration in the PC production. Unlike other Taiwanese firms, such as Giant and Acer, which transformed from OEM into OBM, Terry Gou's expansion plan has been through conducting cross-industry subcontracting.[4] In order to reinforce cost reduction to be more profitable and expedite the one-stop-shopping service for his customers, Foxconn initiated vertical integration to utilize in-house materials, components, and software in its PC assembly.

In 1996, Foxconn showed its intention to enter the PC business by establishing a PC business department. In 1998, Foxconn purchased GEM Top Component to take over the PC connector orders of the Elite Group, and in the same year it acquired Shamrock to enter LCD monitor manufacturing (this firm is now called Foxconn Technology Corporation, see Table 24.3). In 1999, it acquired Pan-International to expand into the fabrication of bare-bone PCs. Foxconn initiated its vertical integration within PC manufacturing step-by-step. Finally, Foxconn's M&A strategies turned its attention to MNCs. From 2003 to 2004, Foxconn conducted the following business actions: to take over Compaq's PC chassis orders, Foxconn purchased Omni; to obtain Cisco's Internet peripheral orders, Foxconn bought Ambit; and to acquire CD-Rom reader and driver orders from HP, Dell, Sony, and Microsoft, Foxconn acquired Thomson. Terry Gou eventually controlled most of the production orders by integrating the whole series of PC system assembly, such as desktop chassis, bare-bone computer, CD-Rom reader, driver, LCD monitor, Internet peripherals, etc. as shown in Table 24.3.

Table 24.3 Chronology of M&A by Foxconn

Year	*Firm*	*Key product*	*Main goal*
1998	GEM Top Component Inc.	Connector	Taking over the orders of Elite Group
1998	Shamrock Technology	LCD monitor	Vertical integration
1999	Pan-International	Connector, system assembly	Vertical integration
2003	Eimo Oyj	Handset shell	Acquiring orders from Nokia
2003	Motorola Chihuahua, Mexico Plant	Handset	Handset eCMMS vertical integration
2003	Omni Switch Inc.	PC chassis	Acquiring orders from Compaq
2004	Ambit Microsystem	Internet peripherals	Acquiring orders from Cisco
2004	Thomson	CD-Rom reader and driver	Acquiring orders from HP, Dell, Sony, and Microsoft
2005	Antec Electronics	Car electronics	Moving from 3C to 6C
2005	Chi Mei Communication	RF, Handset JDSM/JDVM	Becoming the world's largest handset manufacturing service provider
2006	Premier Image Technology Corp.	Digital Still Camera (DSC)	Mechanical–electrical–optical integration enforcement
2007	Jemitek Electronics	TFT-LCD	Vertical integration
2007	Alibaba.com (to be a holding company)	e-Commerce	To enter e-commerce market
2007	Diabell	Acrylic window, insert window, keypad, hinge	eCMMS enforcement
2008	Sanmina-SCI	Optical and RF Microwave, Interconnect server	Acquiring orders from IBM and Dell
2009	Bionet	Bio-technology	To enter bio-technology and to serve its own employees
2009	METRO Group	3C distribution	To provide a distribution channel service for IT customers
2009	TPO Displays	TFT-LCD	Vertical integration
2009	Chi Mei Optoelectronics	TFT-LCD	Vertical integration: to be the world's biggest display firm
2012	Sakai Display Product	LCD	Vertical integration: acquiring TV orders for above 60" panel

Note: Data resources are from Chang (2005), Shu and Chang (2008), and Foxconn (2012).

While Foxconn integrated vertically in the PC sector, it also launched its horizontal diversification into handset manufacturing simultaneously, counting on its adequate capabilities and plentiful resources. Aside from acquiring orders from MNCs, Foxconn launched its M&A strategies to obtain technologies. For example, Foxconn purchased Eimo Oyj in order to take over Nokia's handset shell casing orders and bought Motorola's Chihuahua Mexico plant to initiate handset eCMMS vertical integration. In 2005, Foxconn acquired Chi Mei Communication to become the world's largest handset manufacturer and to take the number one EMS spot globally from Flextronics with US$17.2 billion revenue. Foxconn also initiated its Mechanical-Electrical-Optical engineering integration and purchased Premier Image Technology to expand its business scope to digital cameras, bought Jemitek to get into the TFT-LCD business, and merged with Sanmina-SCI to acquire the interconnect server orders from IBM and Dell (see Table 24.3).

In the late 2000s, Foxconn further expanded its business into e-commerce, 3C distribution channel, and even the bio-technology industry. Through the synergy with economies of scale and economies of scope, Foxconn has gathered tremendous capabilities to meet its customers' demands. For example, through producing 3C products for its MNC customers and expanding into the 3C channel in China, Foxconn consolidated its customers' market share in China and at the same time reinforced Foxconn's competitive advantage.

Patent management and technology portfolio strategy

After Foxconn attained rapid growth through its PC connector manufacturing and obtained a large market share from the global IT firms, it began to squeeze the incumbents' market shares and made some enemies. In 1992, the US PC connector manufacturer AMP filed a lawsuit against Foxconn for patent infringement and asked the US government to cease the importation of Foxconn's connectors. During the lawsuit, Foxconn started analyzing the patent and attempted to change the design in the portion of the connector involved in the lawsuit. The new design was released and substituted for the original model into the market at a cheaper cost. The new connector model soon reached the position of the old model and acquired the market share again. Terry Gou then gave up defense of the lawsuit and settled out of court.

After the bitter lesson from AMP, Terry Gou learned the importance of the ingenuity of patent management, and employees at Foxconn realized as well that patents are one crucial part of market competition. Since then, Foxconn has developed 1,780 patents to take the number one spot in 2003 as the firm with the most patents in Taiwan (*Business Weekly*, 2008). By 2010, Foxconn's legal department had grown to 400 employees and held over 20,000 patent applications around the world. Moreover, Foxconn held over 55,000 patent applications around the world by 2012. "With the patent accumulation and management for two decades, Foxconn has played a decisive role in the Asian supply chain," said Jou Yen Pong, the first chief of Foxconn's legal department (*Global Views Monthly*, 2011).

Strong patent management not only helps avoid costly errors and reduces the failure of M&As, but also makes the firms realize the value from the technological assets they have acquired (Andrew *et al.*, 1998). Wang (2007) contended that the success of Foxconn's M&A strategy can be attributed to its excellent patent management. A constant flow of R&D and patent management has constituted Foxconn's technology portfolio strategy. This strategy enhances the competitive advantage of Foxconn among its competitors and reveals the pivotal position of Foxconn in the global value chain. Through its technology portfolio strategy, Foxconn has the ability to map out its vertical integration framework, and work from a successful vertical integration strategy, Foxconn has expanded its core business from connectors to related technology businesses such as system assembly, desktop chassis, and Internet peripherals (Lin, 2007; Wang, 2007). These accomplishments enabled Foxconn to expand simultaneously into high precision manufacturing and mass production.

Strategic leadership and firm transformation

For SMEs to transform themselves into large enterprises, radical changes are essential, and radical changes need leadership. Two types of leadership are referred to quite often: transactional leadership and transformational leadership (Burns, 1978). Transactional leaders principally provide stable, risk-averse leadership in exchange for their followers efforts and performance, and therefore they generate stable profits (Howell and Avolio, 1993). In contrast, transformational leaders exhibit charisma, provide inspirational motivation and intellectual stimulation for followers in the organization, and thus create a vision for the future that is meaningful and challenging (Bass, 1990, 1998; Avolio, 1999; Mariano *et al.*, 2011). Bass (1985) proposed that transformational leadership builds upon transactional leadership, and that successful leaders display both types of behavior. The characteristics of ideal leaders indicated by Bass (1985) are consistent with those of strategic leadership in the research field of strategic management champions.[5] The essences of strategic leadership are in accordance with those of effective leadership, which supplements transactional leadership with transformational leadership (Howell and Avolio, 1993; Judge and Piccolo, 2004). Strategic leaders not only make day-to-day decisions that enhance the organization's long-term viability, but at the same time also maintain the firm's short-term financial stability. Terry Gou is an archetypical strategic leader.

Transactional leadership: militarized administration

Terry Gou is a workaholic with great vigor and has worked nearly 16 hours a day for over three decades. His working attitude transmits a signal to his subordinates of never slacking off at work. "I shall be responsible for those stockholders; making money is my only responsibility," Terry Gou often proclaimed (*Business Weekly*, 2008). His morning meeting often starts at 8:00 a.m. and lasts until 11:00 a.m., and he takes charge of all the discussions, from information system integration to materials distribution. During his visits to factories in China, he always dines with employees, and often reminds assembly-line workers not to ignore the tiny details of their work. Terry Gou contends that "the devil is in the detail." He also reminds employees that "the precision of the product is in your mind, not attributed to its technology" (*Business Weekly*, 2008).

With a million employees dispersed around more than 20 factories in China, it is a staggering challenge to administer the entire Foxconn Group. Terry Gou carries out an autocratic leadership and "militarized administration," practicing militarized training with employees so as to constitute an obedient work culture. To maintain the strong morale and employees' discipline, there are many encouraging signs displayed on the walls of the Foxconn factory, similar to what is usually perceived in a military barracks. The headquarters even looks like a command module. The Lunghwa campus, drab but utilitarian, is a fully functioning city, with a food store, gym, and even a book store. By implementing a strict work schedule, having controlled rest times, frequent spiritual education, and requesting a demanding work performance of his employees, Foxconn has enabled its manufacturing centers in China to maintain stable production and attain rapid service response time to meet customers' demands from around the world.[6] With a steady stream of mass production lines, these manufacturing centers generate vast cash inflows to maintain Foxconn's financial stability.

As the leader of Foxconn, Terry Gou exhibits both severity and kindness. He may ask a manager to remain standing for more 10 minutes as a punishment in a meeting with 200 people if this manager's reply appears unsatisfactory. Terry Gou did not spare his family from his sternness for perfection, even his younger brother Tai-Chiang Gou, who was a division executive in Foxconn, was not exempt. Tai-Chiang Gou was once scolded by Terry Gou in front of Foxconn's customer for his unsatisfactory performance. On the other hand, Terry Gou also gives compelling bonuses out of his own pocket to reward his employees for good performance. At Foxconn's annual Chinese Lunar New Year party raffle, Terry Gou often offers a big prize to employees. For example, in 2008 the top prize was 300,000 shares of Foxconn, which would have been worth US$1 million one year later (Balfour and Culpan, 2010).

Inspirational motivation, intellectual stimulation, and transformational leadership

With a strong personality and a lot of executive ability, Terry Gou is the indispensable factor that has turned Foxconn into a huge and successful MNC. Terry Gou said in an interview, "When I watch the story of Genghis Khan in the video, it is as if I watched my own story" (*Business Weekly*, 2008). Terry Gou has often been in the vanguard of leading Foxconn to venture abroad into China, North America, Scotland, Ireland, the Czech Republic, and Germany. With an unremitting business expansion, the organization of Foxconn frequently goes through a transformation. For an organization constantly in expansion, how to motivate and inspire people are daunting challenges for its leaders. It is usually the mindset that lags behind.

Transformational leadership encourages individuals to think "outside of the box" and pursue a firm's exploratory innovation, which transforms and motivates followers through an entrepreneur's idealized influence, intellectual stimulation, and individual consideration (Burns, 1978; Bass, 1985). When Terry Gou bought the Czech factory "Tesla" in 2000, the Czech employees who originally worked for the Czech military arsenal were used to working at a slow life-style pace. To build an archetypical factory model overseas, Terry Gou gathered managers and directors from China, the USA, and Taiwan to help train the Czech employees in China's Lunghwa campus. They held meetings day and night to integrate their opinions from diverse backgrounds into a common consensus and discussed information systems, logistics, layout, and even employees' habits in order to build a European model. The design of the norms was drafted in accordance with employees' diversity, and significant rewards were set up to induce employees to exhibit a superior performance. Through intensive interactive communication and intellectual stimulation, the managers and employees of the Tesla factory have been amalgamated fully into the Foxconn Group's culture. This factory started production in August 2002 and hit a capacity of over one million computers for Compaq by March 2003. Compaq's Vice President Edward Pensel hailed, "Terry's efforts at building a standard factory in Czech have built an excellent paradigm of suppliers among Compaq's supply chain" (Chang, 2005).

Terry Gou imposes a division shift upon Foxconn's managers in order to abandon the way they used to do things when dealing with their businesses. "During my on-the-job-training at Lunghwa campus in China, I was shifted to four places within a month to tie into Foxconn's transformation. If this case occurred in Western countries, employees may get angry at the firm for being disrespected and go on strike. The flexibility of Foxconn left an enduring impression on my career," said Mark Buckley, manager of a European branch (Chang, 2005). To blend cultures and help the employees adapt, Terry Gou adopts three steps: gathering, integration, and amalgamation. Although employees of a department come from different nations with diverse culture backgrounds, he gathers them together at first and then arranges them to live, work, or meet together so as to integrate them with a common consensus, and eventually they are amalgamated into a work team.

Conclusion

Using the case study of Foxconn, this chapter has presented entrepreneurship as a key element and has drawn upon the research fields of strategic management and leadership to study firm formation, growth, and transformation. Through entrepreneurial discovery, Terry Gou has led Foxconn to climb to the top of the global value chain. After continuous entrepreneurial learning and using effective strategies to manage the competitive EMS market, Foxconn has generated abundant capital and accumulated capabilities to raise its core competence, enabling it to advance. Terry Gou is a keen creator of opportunities and a strategic leader who has been able to encourage his employees to balance short-term financial stability with a long-term viable vision during Foxconn's growth path.

While many theories about catch-up strategies for emerging markets have focused on how to transform a company from OEM into original brand manufacturing (OBM), the case of Foxconn demonstrates that this is not necessarily so. Foxconn has continued its growth path through OEM all the way, indicating that to grow into a global enterprise, moving from OEM to OBM is not the only way. Which growth model is better? It is up to the calculation and judgment of entrepreneurs, who are characterized as innovators and rule breakers. Hence, there is no definitive growth pattern for entrepreneurs.

There have been enormous discussions about the unprecedented expansion of a corporation like Foxconn. Perhaps the most intriguing part is the leadership style of Terry Gou. Some have argued that Terry Gou is like Genghis Khan, or even a tiger, which is known for being "fast," "accurate," and "fierce," when it tries to catch its prey. Some have described Terry Gou as a fox, which is shrewd and well-calculating (Chang, 2005). With the ongoing expansion in every corner of the world, Foxconn, under the leadership of Terry Gou, remains an interesting case worth further study.

Notes

1 EMS is used by firms that design, test, manufacture, distribute, and provide return/repair services for electronics components and assemblies for OEM subcontractors.

2 Aside from Lin (2003), who adopted empirical data analysis to explore Foxconn's financial operations in mainland China, most studies in the literature have conducted empirical case studies with Foxconn through theoretical discussions, such as some studies that focused on strategic management (Chen, 2003a, 2003b; Lin, 2007; Wang, 2007; Shu and Chang, 2008; Folgo, 2008; Chu, 2009; Lee, 2011), and some studies that emphasized the learning process of technological upgrading (Chen, 2003a; Chu, 2009; Lee, 2011). However, few studies have integrated more than one discipline and theory, and none of them have focused on the role of entrepreneurship to explain Foxconn.

3 The 5S system is based on five Japanese words translated into *Sort, Set* in order, *Shine, Standardize*, and *Sustain*. The system aims to eliminate unnecessary items from the workplace, improve order and tidiness (making sure everything has a home), and maintain a clean workplace, ensuring that a workable system is in place and that improvements are sustained.

4 Giant is a world famous Taiwanese firm that was established by its founder King Liu in 1972 (see Chapter 23 in this volume). The firm originally practiced OEM for its US customer, Schwinn, and later built its own brand since 1989 with more than 12,000 retail partners worldwide. Acer is a multinational corporation and the world's fourth largest PC maker, headquartered in Taipei, Taiwan in 1976. The firm was established by its founder Stan Shih who initially practiced OEM for MNCs and then launched OBM since 1987.

5 Rowe (2001) argued that there are three types of managerial leadership. First, visionary leadership is future-oriented and concerned with risk-taking. Visionary leaders, viewing the organization as an outsider, are not dependent on their organizations for the sense of who they are. Second, managerial leadership involves stability and order, as well as preserving the existing order. Managerial leaders are more comfortable handling day-to-day activities and are short-term-oriented. The third type is the ideal, strategic leadership, which contains capabilities in both effective managerial skill and visionary thinking.

6 However, such strict administration and high pressure have resulted in 11 employees committing suicide by jumping from buildings in Lunghwa Park in 2010. Terry Gou admitted that there was something wrong in Foxconn's administration. He swiftly went to Lunghwa Park to cope with the emergency. By raising the wage rate and shifting the production line of Lunghwa Park more inland in China, the suicide crisis of Foxconn calmed down.

Bibliography

Alvarez, S.A. and Barney, J.B. (2007) "Discovery and creation: alternative theories of entrepreneurial action," *Strategic Entrepreneurship Journal,* 1, 11–26.

Andrew, D.J. Luke, G. and Stanley, J. (1989) "Integrating Technology into Merger and Acquisition Decision Making," *Innovation,* 18(8/9): 563–591.

Avolio, B. (1999) *Full Leadership Development: Building the Vital Forces in Organization,* Thousand Oaks, CA: Sage Publications.

Balfour, F. and Culpan, T. (2010) "The man who makes your iPhone," *Bloomberg Businessweek,* Sept. 9.

Bass, B.M. (1985) *Leadership and Performance Beyond Expectations,* New York: Free Press.

Bass, B.M. (1990) "From transactional to transformational leadership: learning to share the vision," *Organizational Dynamics,* 13: 26–40.

Bass, B.M. (1998) *Transformational Leadership: Industry, Military, and Educational Impact,* Mahwah, NJ: Lawrence Erlbaum Associates.

Burns, J. (1978) *Leadership,* New York: Harper and Row.

Business Weekly (2008) "Terry Gou Review: The Legend of Hon Hai Empire," Taipei: Business Weekly Consultant Co. (in Chinese).

Chang, D.W. (2005) *Tiger and Fox: The Global Competitive Strategy of Terry Gou—Terry Gou and Foxconn,* Taipei: Common Wealth Magazine Co., Ltd (in Chinese).

Chen, P.T. (2003a) "The business strategy of Hon Hai Precision Industry Co., Taiwan," Master's thesis, Institute of Management of Technology of NCTU (in Chinese).

Chen, S.M (2003b) "The specialization, labor division, and integration strategy of high tech industry: the case studies of TSMC, Foxconn, and Quanta," Master's thesis, Management School of NCU (in Chinese)

Chen, T.J. (2005) "Liability of foreignness and entry mode choice: Taiwanese firms in Europe," *Journal of Business Research,* 59: 288–294.

Chu, W.W. (2009) "Can Taiwan's second movers upgrade via branding?" *Research Policy,* 38: 1054–1065.

Common Wealth (2007) "The secret base of Terry Gou," 364, Jan. (in Chinese).

Folgo, E.J. (2008) "Accelerating time-to-market in the global electronics industry," MBA and MSc thesis, Massachusetts Institute of Technology.

Foxconn (2012) Available at: www.foxconn.com.tw/GroupProfile/GroupProfile.html (accessed 27 October 2013).

Gapp, R., Fisher, R. and Kobayashi, K. (2008) "Implementing 5S within a Japanese context: an integrated management system," *Management Decision,* 46(4): 565–579.

Ghemawat, P. (2007) "How to choose your global strategy," *Notes on Globalization and Strategy,* 9, Sep.–Dec., Center for Globalization and Strategy, University of Navarra.

Global Views Monthly (2011) "Brazil, clouds, software, and robots: the future empire of Foxconn," *The Cover Story of Global Views Monthly,* Dec. No. 306 (in Chinese).

Gunasekaran A. and Lyu, J. (1997) "Implementation of just-in-time in a small company: a case study," *Production Planning and Control,* 8(4): 406–412.

Hobday, M. (2001) "The electronics industries of the Asia-Pacific: exploiting international production networks for economic development," *Asian-Pacific Economic Literature,* 15: 13–29.

Howell, J.M. and Avolio, B.J. (1993) "Transformational leadership, transactional leadership, locus of control, and support for innovation: key indicators of consolidated business-unit performance," *Journal of Applied Psychology,* 78: 891–902.

Judge, T.A. and Piccolo, R.F. (2004) "Transformational and transactional leadership: a meta-analytic test of their relative validity," *Journal of Applied Psychology,* 89(5): 755–768.

Krywulak, T and Kukushkin, V. (2009) "Big gains with small partners: what MNCs look for in their SME suppliers," The Report of Conference Board of Canada, BDC.

Lee, B.Y. (2011) "Trajectory of global resources distribution in Hon Hai Precision Corporation," Master's thesis, Institute of Technology Management of NTHU (in Chinese).

Lin, I.J. (2007) "The M&A strategy of Taiwan electronics industry: a case study of Foxconn Purchases Premier," Master's thesis, Accounting Department of Soochow University (in Chinese).

Lin, S.T. (2003) "The finance channel and loan model of Taiwanese firms in Mainland China: a case study of Foxconn," Master's thesis, Business Administration Department of NCU (in Chinese).

Mariano, J.A., Molero, F., Topa, G. and Mangin, J-P. (2011) "The influence of transformational leadership and organizational identification on intrapreneurship," *International Entrepreneurship and Management Journal.* Online First, 14, July.

Rowe, W.G. (2001) "Creating wealth in organizations: the role of strategic leadership," *Academy of Management Executive,* 15(1): 81–94.

Shane, S. and Venkataraman, S. (2000) "The promise of entrepreneurship as a field of research," *Academy of Management Review,* 25(1): 217–226.

Shu, M.T. (2008) *Terry Gou and Foxconn,* Taipei: Fullon Culture Publishers (in Chinese).

Shu, S.Q. and Chang, K.S. (2008) "The dilemma of subcontracting and the confusion of upgrading: the analysis of the false relationship from OEM to OBM," paper presented at the Doctorial Conference of Taiwan Industry and Finance Development in Tung Hai University.

UNCTAD (2013) *World Investment Report 2013: Global Value Chains: Investment and Trade for Development,* United Nations Conference on Trade and Development, New York: United Nations.

Venture Outsource (2007) "Reading tea leaves for top EMS providers." Available at: www.ventureoutsource.com/contract-manufacturing/trends-observations/2007 (accessed 20 October 2011).

Wang, G.S. (2007) "Patent analysis oriented research on technology portfolio strategy of business group: case study of Hon Hai (Foxconn) and BenQ Group," Master's thesis, Graduate Institute of Management of Technology of Feng Chia University (in Chinese).

Zhai, E., Shi, Y. and Gregory, M. (2007) "The growth and capability development of electronics manufacturing service (EMS) companies," *International Journal of Production Economics,* 107: 1–19.

South Korea

25

Chung Ju Yung and Hyundai

A retrospective of entrepreneurship in the global financial crisis

Myeong-Kee Chung

Introduction

During the past four decades, the Korean economy has seen a remarkable record of high and sustained economic growth. Since 1965, the Korean economy has grown faster than any other country in the world. In fact, from 1971 to 2011 the Korean economy grew at an average annual rate of nearly 6.8 percent in real terms. In the span of roughly one generation, Korea has achieved the kind of economic development that other countries can do nothing but envy. Korea currently is the eighth largest trading nation in the world. Korea's per capita income in 2012 surpassed the US$20,000 mark, which is a big leap from the meager US$87 mark back in 1962.

Today, the Korean economic scene is totally different. Since the global financial crisis of 2008, the advanced economies of the world have struggled while many nations have dipped into recession. Yet Korean companies during this period have still managed surprisingly strong performances. The recent success of Korean companies can be partially attributed to the painful lessons learned during the 1997 Asian currency crisis. How did Korean companies achieve such astounding growth within such a short period of time? To answer this question, we need to look at the growth of Korean companies over the past few decades. From this perspective, research which focuses on entrepreneurship is very important.

Entrepreneurship is the stepping stone at the heart of Korea's economic miracle. Korean companies have turned largely to technological innovation, constantly reinventing capital and consumer goods. Business innovation is one of the most important preconditions for economic growth. The economic recession caused by a worldwide financial crisis has continued to affect unemployment and reduced income in all regions of world. Unemployment and employment insecurity are widespread. There is an urgent need to revive the spirit that drove entrepreneurs to create new economic wealth. Without a doubt, the spread of entrepreneurship promises incremental recovery and growth over the long run.

This chapter presents a portrait of the role of entrepreneurship with regard to its contribution to economic development in Korea. It emphasizes the shape of historical development of the Hyundai Group which is one of largest conglomerates in Korea and a symbol of success in the Korean economy. It explores the role of entrepreneurship based on the management strategy, principles and enterprising spirit of the Hyundai Group. The first part of this chapter briefly describes the business environment of the past few decades which will provide the background to the creation and operation of Korean firms.

The second part tells the story of how the Hyundai Group achieved business success and the role that Chung Ju Yung's entrepreneurship played in that success. The story of Chung Ju Yung, the founder of the Hyundai Group, characterizes the growth of the Korean economy that the Korean people could identify as a common goal that needed to be accomplished.

A brief overview of the business environment: the growth of Korean firms

Korea was liberated from Japanese colonial rule at the end of World War II and faced extreme socio-economic disruption until the cease-fire agreement with North Korea was signed in 1953. After the Korean War, economic reconstruction began gradually to open up new business activities. The traditional landlord class failed to transform itself into industrial entrepreneurs due to the Korean War which did offer new opportunities to entrepreneurship.

In the first period of economic reconstruction, business opportunities were mostly based on the purchase of vested properties at cheaper prices, the preferential allocation of hard currency and the right of businesses to import. Under Japanese rule, the Japanese state had owned 94 percent of the total firms in Korea which the Korean government confiscated and then managed. Therefore, business activities in the 1950s had some common features. The import licenses with their allocation of hard currency by the government played an important role in accumulating capital. This business environment rapidly changed with the export-oriented industrialization policy of the 1960s and the heavy/chemical industry drive policy of the 1970s.

Since the 1960s, the state-led export drive policy and massive foreign capital inflows have provided opportunities for new business start-ups in Korea. This favorable business environment has substantially contributed to the expansion of Korean business activities. Since then, these entrepreneurial energies have been channeled into development activities. During the industrialization period, the number of entrepreneurs increased remarkably and their quality was also enhanced. No doubt, at that time entrepreneurs played an important role as the engine of economic growth in Korea. While the government promoted specific capital- and knowledge-intensive industries, Korean entrepreneurs could accumulate industrial capital and entrepreneurial skill through a variety of mechanisms. All welcomed technology transfers and foreign capital which proved to open up more opportunities and extended the new business boundaries.

Using various measures, export promotion became the first priority of the Korean economic policy in the 1970s. The most important policy instruments for export promotion were preferential credits for exports, tax subsidies and tariff exemptions for raw material that engaged export commodities. The government had to assume some responsibility for joint ventures with foreign companies with which the government had been involved in indirectly. Most of these measures contributed to expanded business start-ups. Learning by doing in the process of joint ventures was also a vital force to increase entrepreneurial skills.

The drive for heavy and chemical industrialization since the middle of the 1970s was deemed necessary to increase and diversify exports and to achieve a more advanced industrial structure. On the basis of this strategy, the Korean government planned to establish plants in the steel, petrochemical, industrial machinery, automobile, and electrical industries. During the heyday of the promotion of heavy and chemical industries, the most important decisions of the firms investing in priority industries (e.g., size of foreign loans, size and conditions of commercial loans, type and size of investment, and product prices) were allocated to the government (Cho, 1994, p. 42). In these circumstances, Korean entrepreneurs expanded their business activities in line with the government's industrial policy and took advantage of the new business activities. Obviously state support and political connections played an important role in their business activities.

This opportunity helped some firms accumulate capital and they began to grow quickly during this period. First and foremost, most of the existing big companies took advantage of finance resource allocation so they could rapidly grow into the representative industrial conglomerates, known as *chaebols*. These *chaebols* strongly resembled the pre-war Japanese *zaibatsu* in their degree of family ownership and control and in the way that they came to extend their influence throughout the economy through continuous aggressive expansion (Bridges, 2001, p. 7).

Since 1988, the Korean economy has met both the internal and external challenges of the business environment. The democratization of authoritative political systems and liberalization and market opening commencing with the 1985 Plaza Agreement had reduced government subsidies to the big firms, and monopoly profits in the domestic market were removed by the abolition of trade barriers. This inevitably required a new growth strategy for entrepreneurs, involving the development of a management system. Nevertheless *chaebol*-friendly policy continued, and the concentration of their economic power was exacerbated. Big firms pursued the dynamics and large-scale investment in key industries. They grew faster during this epoch based on the liberalized capital market. According to this new policy, a *chaebol* could borrow directly from overseas financial institutions, and, consequently, there was overlapping investment among the *chaebols* which resulted in over-investment, even though profitability was low and international competitiveness was also weak. This was one of the main reasons for the 1997 financial crisis.

The Asian financial crisis was accompanied by a great transformation of Korean firms. At that time, many inefficient firms were phased out by a structural adjustment policy in the corporate sector as well as in the banking sector. Nevertheless, Korean firms undertook decisive and drastic structural adjustment and management innovations, seeking the means for their survival during the relevant period. These efforts made the fostering of global competitive firms today possible. In particular, the newly emerging IT and traditional industries substantially contributed to the sustainment of higher growth in the Korean economy (Kim, 2010, p. 340). Additionally, the government provided several measures to promote venture start-ups and small and medium-sized enterprises in the field of cultural business, especially in the technology and media sectors. In 2001, the KOCCA (Korea Culture and Contents Agency) was established to develop and promote the culture industry. As a result, we now see that this policy brought about a large number of new business start-ups in Korea (Jung, 2002). Some young entrepreneurs opened firms in social media enterprises, such as SNS and cyber games. Furthermore, the government provided training programs for professionals working in the media industries, especially movies, television and music. It is obvious that this government action was the foundation of the Korean wave in entertainment. Korea firms also fundamentally changed their management paradigm as result of the financial crisis. They shifted their focus to innovation and profitability which increased their international competitiveness. This led to an improvement of their internal core competencies during the global financial crisis.

As noted above, the way to encourage entrepreneurs and entrepreneurship in Korea was to forge a close relationship with industrial policy. Even though Korean entrepreneurs are characterized by "creative destruction" as the drive to succeed, Korean economic policy has strongly supported this attitude and intention due to the government's desire to prevent firms from failing. This environment creates entrepreneurial challenges in many varieties; some are particularly suited for expansion; others are conducive to technological innovations. This does not mean that the Korean people are more entrepreneurial than any other people. South Koreas do work extremely hard; however, for a long time, Koreans had to work in conditions that were not conducive to entrepreneurship. I think that we should distinguish between entrepreneurship and hard work. It might be the case that most, if not all, entrepreneurs work hard, but it is not the case that all hard workers are entrepreneurs (Cheminant, 2010, p. 3). Entrepreneurs should not try to create and improve their competitive abilities by introducing new technology and organizational innovation that cannot survive.

Industrial entrepreneurship: the Hyundai Group and Chung Ju Yung

The growth process of Hyundai

The Hyundai Group is one of South Korea's biggest *chaebols* or industrial conglomerates. Since the mid-1970s, the Hyundai Group has earned its position as Korea's largest *chaebol*. The group has displayed spectacular growth since its founding in 1946 and its rapid expansion—to a point where its interests include car manufacturing, construction, shipbuilding, electronics, and financial services—reflected the achievements attained during South Korea's economic miracle. The Hyundai Group's sales for 2006 surpassed US$135 billion which accounted for 16 percent of Korean GNP. Overseas sales alone surpassed US$48 billion or about 13 percent of Korea's entire export for 2007 (Hyundai Research Institute, 2008, p. 1). This is remarkable considering that the company is approaching 70 years in existence. Despite the recent global financial crisis and increased global competition, Hyundai continues to prosper. The growth history of Hyundai which we have identified also looks at the life and times of its founder Chung Ju Yung. In 1946, Chung set up Hyundai Motors and offered a car repair service for US military personnel. In 1947, he founded Hyundai Construction. This was the start of the Hyundai myth. Over a period of 40 years, he built a conglomerate, which is now engaged in most comprehensive industrial fields.

After the Korean War, the beginning of the construction of the infrastructure was a prosperous business. Hyundai accumulated technical experience and capital through government orders for projects such as port facilities, road and bridge construction, and military camps. In 1957, Hyundai completed the Han River footbridge construction project with the introduction of high-tech construction techniques used by the US Army, and all these experiences during the construction projects paved the way to later enabling Hyundai to access the overseas construction market (Kim, 2010, p. 331). From 1965, Hyundai started to aggressively bid on overseas construction projects.

In the 1960s and 1970s, Hyundai's business activities expanded through the construction of the Gyeongbu Express Highway as well as the Seoul Subway, plus other key industrial facilities. Hyundai believed that social overhead capital facilities expansion was absolutely necessary for the economic development of Korea. In 1965, Hyundai won a bid to build the Thailand Expressway and in 1970 completed the 428 km Gyeongbu Expressway in 290 days. During the Vietnam War, Hyundai was also willing to take risks to get business opportunities as well as get the job done. They learned to execute construction work in terms of global standards in part by learning by doing. There is no doubt that these experiences later contributed to their penetration of the Middle East market in the 1970s. In 1976, Hyundai successfully completed the Jubil industrial port in Saudi Arabia, at that time the largest construction project of the twentieth century. Successfully accessing the Middle East construction boom provided the foundation for increased business activities. To run an expanded construction business, Hyundai needed related manufacturing businesses such as cement, ready-mixed concrete, steel and aluminum. Hyundai Elevator was created to supply elevators to apartments and commercial buildings that had been constructed by Hyundai Engineering & Construction.

Hyundai's next major venture was the shipbuilding business. Their experience of Middle East construction provided a positive impact on the shipbuilding business. As Mr. Chung saw it, if

Hyundai was going to construct harbors, ports, housing, and other facilities in overseas locations like Iran, Bahrain, Kuwait and Saudi Arabia, it might as well also make the ships that served those ports (Steers, 1999, p. 2). For the shipbuilding business, Hyundai wanted a negotiated transfer of capital and technology from the Japanese firm of Mitsubishi Heavy Industries. Mitsubishi did not want the birth of a potentially competing firm in the future so it suggested that Hyundai's shipyard capacity be limited to relatively small 50,000 dead weight ton (DWT) vessels. Mitsubishi also insisted that it retain sole management rights to oversee all projects. Eventually negotiations broke down so Hyundai had to search for a new source of technology and capital. Finally, Hyundai signed up the British engineering firms of Appledore and Scott Lithgow to provide engineering, administration, and marketing support for its new venture. Hyundai got credit of US$50 million from Barclays Bank, and Korea's Export-Import Bank had to insure the loan. At this point Hyundai contracted two 260,000 DWT oil tankers for US$31 million each with an initial US$2 million from a Greek shipping tycoon.

With no experience in shipbuilding and no facilities, Hyundai created the Ulsan shipyard which later became the largest shipyard in the world. What made this project remarkable was that Hyundai set out to build both the shipyard and vessels simultaneously. Generally these two different tasks are impossible to complete concurrently. Hyundai delivered its first vessel to its owner within three years rather than the expected five years. Hyundai started a furniture business to supply interior goods to shipyards and a paint manufacturing firm to produce painting materials for the ships it built through Hyundai Heavy Industries. As the group's trading volume increased, Hyundai founded a shipping company to handle export cargoes of its own goods.

This sector developed rapidly throughout the 1970s, but the group was hit by the first oil crisis and the consequent decline in demand for large tankers. Hyundai, however, quickly won four orders for large tankers from the Japanese, its main competitor, and concluded technical cooperation deals with Kawasaki Heavy Industries of Japan and Scott Lithgow of the United Kingdom. Before the market collapsed, 12 large tankers were built at the yards. This collapse forced Hyundai to turn to building medium-sized vessels. Hyundai also took steps to remain abreast of technological developments in the industry and to develop spin-offs. In 1975, Hyundai Shipbuilding and Heavy Industries created an industrial-plant and steel-fabrication division, and in the following year began to produce marine engines carrying famous names such as Sulzer and B&W. A further collaboration was clinched in 1977 with Siemens, of West Germany, which led to the creation of the electrical engineering division. In the following year the company changed its name to Hyundai Heavy Industries Company (HHI) to reflect its diverse operations. At the same time it incorporated its engine and electrical engineering divisions into Hyundai Engine and Machinery Company and Hyundai Electrical Engineering Company, respectively. Today, these companies, through business diversification and production of high value-added products such as LNG and LPG carriers, drill ships and submarines, have grown into some of the world's leading companies. Hyundai's shipyard, the largest in the world and the most profitable in Korea, also boasts huge profits. Since 2004, the success of shipbuilding has also helped Korea surpass Japan to become the world leader in volume of new shipbuilding orders.

During the heavy and chemical industrialization period of the 1980s, Hyundai ventured massively into new businesses such as automobiles, electrics and oil refinery, and then the business structure of Hyundai was quickly expanded through diversification into these new industries. Hyundai Motors was founded in 1967 as part of the Hyundai Group. Hyundai assembled knocked down (KD) vehicles (Ford Cortina and Taunus) with the technical assistance of Ford, though the output was extremely small. After seven years of KD and semi-knocked down (SKD) production, Hyundai succeeded in developing Korea's first independently designed and manufactured model, the Pony, in accordance with the government's long-term Automobile Promotion Plan of 1973.

For this project Hyundai engaged in technical cooperation with Mitsubishi, obtaining chassis components and other parts which were difficult to manufacture, such as gearboxes and engines, directly from Mitsubishi, while fabricating the cylinder head and blocks, housings, and transmission cases in-house. The Hyundai Pony was the first indigenous Korean model, and went into production in 1976. It was equipped with a four-cylinder, 1,238 cc Mitsubishi Saturn engine.

Afterwards Hyundai quickly developed its own production technology on the basis of embodied knowledge from the joint venture and began to pursue independent operations in production and R&D. Hyundai created and transformed itself from a licenser of technology to a designer and exporter of its own cars and engines in less than four decades. In 1986, Hyundai exported its first cars to the US market, and began to produce models with its own technology in 1988, beginning with the midsize model. In 1991, the company succeeded in developing its first proprietary gasoline engine, the four-cylinder Alpha, and also its own transmission, thus paving the way for technological independence.

Hyundai adopted a two-step approach to increasing their international competitiveness. The first step was the adoption of best practices concepts, and the second step was the adoption of a high technology approach to rationalize production and increase efficiency. These are preconditions for an independent survival strategy in a fierce global competitive market. Hyundai planned to increase production overseas. This was a critical task in gearing up to be a global player. In 1996, Hyundai completed their first overseas plant in an emerging market in India. Now Hyundai has invested in manufacturing plants in North America, the Czech Republic, the USA, Russia, Brazil, China and Turkey as well as R&D centers in Germany, the USA, and China. These plants are not without their problems even though they have managed to weather the global crisis relatively well. Hyundai sold 3.21 million vehicles for the third consecutive year, 2012, in the global market and has reached 5.3 percent of world market share (*Joongang Newspaper*, 19 Nov. 2012). Hyundai acquired Kia Motors in 1998, which was in bankruptcy at the time due to an over-ambitious expansion strategy and the Asian financial crisis. Since 2004, Hyundai Motors has been Korea's second largest company or *chaebol* behind only Samsung. In 2011, Hyundai sold 4.05 million cars worldwide and the Hyundai Motor Group was the world's fourth largest automaker behind GM, Volkswagen and Toyota. Hyundai vehicles are sold in 193 countries through some 5,000 dealerships.

Hyundai continued to explore new technologies during the 1980s and 1990s, incorporating semiconductors and magnetic levitation train technology into Hyundai automobiles. Following the creation of Hyundai Electronics in 1983, Hyundai stepped up its presence in the electronics field and produced semiconductors, telecommunication equipment, and industrial electronic systems. The company, which focused on industrial markets, sought to increase its presence in consumer electronics. With a huge investment, Hyundai completed a new 18M DRAM factory with a 4 million chip capacity in 1993 and then in 1994 moved on to a new project with a 64M DRAM plant. Together these two plants are capable of producing thin film transistor liquid crystal displays. As part of its globalization strategy, Hyundai already had invested in the construction of a semiconductor plant overseas. The initial investment was US$10 million in a Chinese semiconductor production facility in 1993. In May 1995, the company built a semiconductor plant in Oregon, USA. The plant was initially to employ up to 1,000 people and produce 64M DRAM. It was completed in 1997. Hyundai developed the world's first 1-gigabyte DRAM in 1997 and completed Korea's first complete HDTV broadcasting transmitter and receiver system in 1998.

The late 1990s brought with them economic turmoil for South Korea. In order to restore the nation's financial health, the new government launched a series of restructuring programs designed to reform the *chaebols*, many of which had become heavily debt-burdened. This structural adjustment policy in both the banking and corporate sectors included changing the ownership, business, and financial structures of the region's large conglomerates. By this time, the Hyundai Group was responsible for approximately 20 percent of Korea's GDP. The major goal of this policy was to reduce the affiliates of *chaebols* so that they could concentrate on core industrial sectors, based on reduced debt-equity ratios. As a result of government pressure, Hyundai and other Korean *chaebols*, including the Daewoo Group, set plans in motion to sell off many of their businesses in order to bring down debt and shore up profits. The number of Hyundai's subsidiaries decreased to 32 in 1999 from 63 in 1997. Hyundai's focus remained on autos, electronics, heavy industry, construction, and finance. The reconstruction and consolidation of this key industry through government policy led to a merger between Hyundai and LG semiconductors. At this time, LG semiconductors was renamed Hynix. Even as Hyundai struggled under its debt load, it strengthened its holdings with the purchase of Kia Motors Co. Ltd. Indeed, at the time many Hyundai affiliates, including Hyundai Engineering & Construction and Hyundai Electronics, were nearing bankruptcy as debt continued to spiral out of control.

Today, Hyundai is divided among the founder's sons. The auto unit is managed by Chung Ju Yung's eldest son, Mong-Ku; construction, shipping electronics and trading are managed by his fifth son Mong-Hun; heavy industries is managed by his sixth son Mong-Joon; and distribution is managed by Mong-Keun. This allows the sons to run their own smaller groups. While this marked an end to the Hyundai Group's history, it pointed to a fresh start for many companies bearing the Hyundai name. Today, all four Hyundai companies continue to grow.

Entrepreneurship of Chung Ju Yung

Not all start-up businessmen can be entrepreneurs, just as not all business owners engage in entrepreneurship. Entrepreneurs create value in the marketplace or in society (Shim, 2010, p. 33). Chung Ju Yung (1915–2001), founder of the Hyundai Group, is characterized as being one of the most remarkable entrepreneurs of the twentieth century. Mr. Chung was born in a small town, which now is part of North Korea. He ran away from home at the age of 19, his hometown was suffering from drought and famine, and began working for a rice retailer in Seoul. The myth of Hyundai was begun with the foundation of Hyundai Construction in 1947. As we have seen with the history of the Hyundai Group, Chung Ju Yung was a pioneer of entrepreneurship in Korea. His management philosophy called for endless business expansion. "If someone asks me, 'What are the engines to become an international company, as well as the driving force of economic growth?' I will answer, 'An enterprising and pioneering spirit' without hesitation" (Hyundai, 2010, p. 2). Naturally, this philosophy conceived of a breakthrough management strategy which consisted of seven principal objectives (Hyundai Research Institute, 2008).

First, Chung Ju Yung preached that entrepreneurs must create a new growth engine ahead of the era. During the reconstruction period after the Korean War, Chung founded a construction company. Later in the 1970s, he founded an automobile and a shipbuilding firm. He thought that Hyundai needed to build shipyards in order to expand overseas construction, and so he had them made. In the 1980s, he entered the semiconductor and financial sectors to respond to diversified customer demand and to foster high-tech industries to drive growth in the future. With a creative point of view and insight into the future, he established many "First Companies" in many different types of industries. Also, he strove to establish Hyundai as a leading company in the global market of the future. As a consequence, he tried to diversify his business activities so as to enable them to enjoy a synergic effect.

Second, Chung Ju Yung had a vision of markets and the ability to create new markets. He also had the drive to take the risks needed to follow his vision and create new markets. Chung hedged his bets, however, by realizing it would probably be necessary for domestic enterprise to grow further if they were to achieve success in the outward-looking market strategy that was required. He entered the Thailand market in 1965 and the Middle Eastern market in the mid-1970s due to his prediction that the domestic construction market would become saturated. Hyundai Motors was already exporting to South America in the 1970s. Hyundai felt required to expand its business overseas owing to the limitations of the domestic market.

Third, Chung Ju Yung had a strong sense of maximizing customer satisfaction by keeping his promises and respecting contractors even when he lost money because of unexpected costs. For example, in 1966, a deficit of US$100,000 was incurred due to the cost overruns of the Thailand Highway construction project through which valuable experience of project management was gained and global standards adopted. Subsequently he contracted seven more projects leading up to the mid-1970s (Hong, 2006, pp. 140–148). The Thailand project became the springboard to the penetration of the Middle East. With the successful completion of the Jubil industrial port in Saudi Arabia, he was able to build trust with his customers that eventually led to the promotion of further business expansion in the Middle East and Asia. This expansion has continued since the 1970s. And by reducing the delivery time in shipbuilding to as short as possible, he went ever further in trying to meet the interests of contractors. He believed that time was a very important factor and keeping promises to clients was of critical importance for the entire enterprise. He sought the substantial growth of the company based on building long-term customer trust rather than short-term profit.

Fourth, Chung Ju Yung emphasized the spirit of self-reliance. The enterprise must grow by pioneering new frontiers with creativity and leading-edge technology based on the principle of free market competition. He considered it dangerous to believe that any external power would help his own business succeed. He also stressed the importance of a continued effort to think positively. He always was interested in developing his own technology, even though technology which was either imported or licensed in the early stage was what initially started the company. For example, Hyundai Motors and Hyundai Heavy Industry quickly achieved technological independence through their own R&D activities and then later achieved international competitiveness.

Fifth, for a long time Chung Ju Yung considered human resources to be a critical issue as far as an enterprise's ability to expand was concerned so a great deal of effort went into encouraging the development of all employees. Human resource development was geared to shaping the Hyundai family, not only in the pursuit of on-the-job training (OJT). This would ensure the formation of Hyundai-style efficiency and loyalty among the employees. He used to refer to his company as "our Hyundai," emphasizing the community spirit of the Confucian family system. According to Mr. Chung:

> People can be changed depending upon how they are educated. If a person is born without great talents but is diligent, trustworthy, and good natured, he can learn to be a good executive. Hyundai encourages all employees to pursue self-development.

In 1980, Chung established the Hyundai Institute for Human Resource Development, which is responsible for providing a strategic direction for the group's human resource development (Steers, 1999, p. 214).

Sixth, Chung Ju Yung pursued the practice of leadership and positive thinking. He said: "I am 90 percent assured that 'a thing is possible,' and 10 percent assured that 'I can': There isn't the slightest doubt that 'something is impossible'" (Hyundai, 2010, p. 5). This leadership and positive thinking were reflected in the construction plan of the Gyeongbu Expressway. Construction plans were delayed because the cost was equal to the total Korean government's budget for two years. The government's calculations were that it would cost US$68 million. But Chung Ju Yung's estimation was that it would cost US$38 million. he final cost was US$33 million and the highway was completed in less than one year. A second example of this leadership is how Chung Ju Yung pioneered shipyard construction. He succeeded in the construction of a shipyard while acquiring funding, technology licenses and ship orders all at the same time. Hyundai is now the world's number one shipbuilding company.

Seventh, Chung Ju Yung actively implemented various corporate social responsibility (CSR) activities in Korean society. He has founded two universities, five middle schools and high schools and the Asan Foundation, which fundamentally supports the building of hospitals in rural areas. These significant legacies of Chung Ju Yung show that he has tried to improve public welfare. One might argue that all of his CSR activities were elaborately focused on the elimination of social poverty. This idea demonstrates that the success of the identified enterprise activities originated with the process of leaving poverty behind at both the personal and national level. As a consequence, his spirit gained its competitive advantage while the Korean society continued to prosper.

Chung Ju Yung has established a set of management principles that are formulated into corporate goals that guide the enterprise activities of business. Chung noted:

> Simply Hyundai is not just a business group, but a company which strives for the economic development of the country to play a pivotal role. I can confidently say that over the past 50 years of growth, Hyundai has had a leading role in the development of the national economy as well as its own development.
>
> *(Hyundai, 1997, p. 51)*

In conclusion, the entrepreneurship of Chung Ju Yung has several characteristics not unlike those of many other entrepreneurs in Western society. His style of managing has focused on enterprise-based patriotism and national interests offset these problems, and the realization of his Hyundai spirit became the basis of economic growth. Nowadays, his entrepreneurship has gained renewed attention in the context of the global financial crisis because of the need to create new job opportunities and the recreation of social wealth.

Conclusion

The world is converting to a single market economy in line with globalization and faces long-term depression which requires new entrepreneurial leadership. That enables the world to start up new and emerging firms that will lead to technological change and gain in productivity. Also, creativity and entrepreneurial spirit are the driving forces behind global economic growth. No doubt, entrepreneurship represents an essential mechanism in order to solve the problem of today's global economy. Even though the economic crisis in 1997 brought a paradigm shift in business activities, the entrepreneurship of Chung Ju Yung is still alive.

Chung Ju Yung built a *chaebol* conglomerate structure from out of the ashes of the Korean War. His significant contribution to the economic miracle of Korea is indisputable. His business initiatives and confidence often attracted international attention. With all the foregoing discussion, I would like to suggest a retrospection and evaluation of Chung's entrepreneurship in a new environment. In response to this new environment, Chung's entrepreneurship could solve depression-style unemployment through new business strategies and performance. Indeed, entrepreneurship has changed over time in association with a changing environment and the emergence of new entrepreneurs. The new paradigm will concentrate on sustainable and qualitative growth to reach advanced economic development, replacing the early-stage economic development strategies for fast and quantitative growth. Nevertheless, we learn from Chung's spirit that a person uses these crises as an opportunity to seek new business activities. In today's intense global competition, it requires pioneering entrepreneurship to create a new business ecosystem. To sustain the competitive advantage in the global market, we should learn how to make the optimal use of international resources by using Chung's management strategy. Obviously the source of wealth and development in the era of globalization is mainly heroic individual entrepreneurial efforts. The attempts to revive entrepreneurship in East Asia will be the driving force behind continued economic growth. Our prosperity and our future could well depend on it.

Bibliography

Bridges, B. (2001) *Korea after the Crash: The Politics of Economic Recovery,* London: Routledge.

Cheminant, W.L. (2010) "Korean politics and the spirit of entrepreneurship," in T. Youn-Ja Shim (ed.) *Korean Entrepreneurship,* New York: Palgrave Macmillan, pp. 1–16.

Cho, S. (1994) *The Dynamics of Korean Economic Development,* Washington, DC: Institute for International Economics.

Chung, M.K. (1998) "Hyundai tries two industrial models to penetrate global markets," in M. Freyssenet, A. Mair, K. Shimizu, and G. Volpato (eds) *One Best Way? Trajectories and Industrial Models of the World's Automobile Producers,* Oxford: Oxford University Press, pp. 154–176.

Chung, M.K (2009) "Hyundai: is it possible to realise the dream of becoming a top five global automaker by 2010?" in M. Freyssenet (ed.) *The Second Automobile Revolution: Trajectories of the World Carmakers in the 21st Century,* New York: Palgrave Macmillan, pp. 141–162.

Hong, H. S. (2006) *Management Spirit of Chung Ju Young,* Seoul: Bada Press (in Korean).

Hyundai (2010) "Asan's philosophy and HYUNDAI's DNA." Available at: www.ghrforum.org/abstract/down/pdf/B4_PPT_Bong-rak%20YOON.pdf (accessed 6 February 2013).

Hyundai Group (1997) *Fifty Years History of Hyundai,* Seoul: Hyundai Group (in Korean).

Hyundai Research Institute (2008) *Management Strategies of Chung Ju Young,* VIP Report (in Korean).

Hyundai Research Institute (2011) *Chung Ju Yung Talks to Management,* Seoul: HRI Books (in Korean).

Jung, K.H. (2002) "An upsurge of entrepreneurship in Korea and its possible reasons," paper presented at Expert Workshop on Entrepreneurship in Asia: Creating Competitive Advantage in the Global Economy, Hong Kong, 8–11 July.

Kim, D.H. (2010) "The expansion of Korea's private business and role of entrepreneurship," in K.J. Sung (ed.) *Development Experience of the Korean Economy,* Seoul: Kyung Hee University Press, pp. 327–348.

Kim, S.S. (2005) "A study of Ju-Yung Chung and the Hyundai Group regarding their contribution to the economic development of post-war Korea," *Journal of Business History,* 20(2): 83–107 (in Korean).

Shim, T.Y.J. (2010) "Korea Inc.: building pre-entrepreneurship in Korea," in T. Youn-Ja Shim (ed.) *Korea Entrepreneurship,* New York: Palgrave Macmillan, pp. 17–42.

Steers, R.M. (1999) *Made in Korea: Chung Ju Yung and the Rise of Hyundai,* London: Routledge.

26

The innovation of the four dragons in the Korean online game industry[1]

Jong Hyun Wi

Introduction

Online gaming has been taking the world by storm since the 1990s, and Korean developers have been among the leaders in this field. Korean games are being successfully exported to China, the Asian countries and highly developed nations such as the United States, Japan, and Europe. The spectacular growth of online gaming marks a new chapter in the history of game industry (Figure 26.1).

The first major online game, *Ultima Online*, was American in origin but was commercialized and marketed by Koreans. Online gaming is a field where Korea is no longer forced to compete on price, but instead on technology and service.

Korean games have created different business models from other online games. Games created by American companies (such as *Everquest* and *Ultima Online*) use what is called a "selective monthly payment" model, in which users pay a monthly subscription fee for access to the game. Korean games made a system of micro-transactions, where players have free access to the game but can purchase power-ups and aesthetic items for their characters. This micro-transactions system has been adapted by game companies around the world.

Japanese and American game companies had a very difficult time competing with Korean companies in developing games due to their massive development processes. They often spend many years and massive amounts of money on a title, only to see it reach a comparatively small market. A prime example is the Japanese game company, Square Enix's *Final Fantasy 11*, which cost around US$100 million to develop and host. Compare those costs to the US$5–$10 million that the average Korean 3D online game costs to produce, and the inadequacy of Japanese game development and server hosting techniques is clear.

This disparity in development quality and costs has led American and Japanese companies to become very interested in the Korean online game model. Many of these companies hope to learn from and emulate the success that Korean developers have found. Mark Berner, the senior technical director of America Online, says the following:

> I'm profoundly interested to see how casual online games have so spectacularly succeeded in Korea. And I believe that there's a good chance of importing those games to America, too.

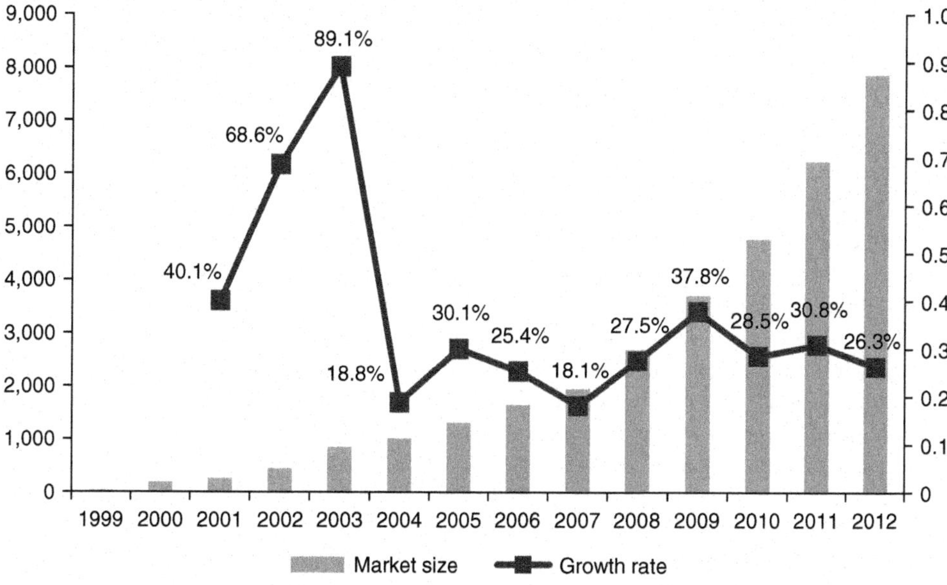

Figure 26.1 Development of the Korean online game industry
Source: White Paper of Game Industry, KOCCA.

> Of course, the cultural differences between the two worlds would have to be balanced first. But come to think of it, I see some positive prospects of such favorable Korean games being equally prosperous in American market as well.

The actual online gaming industry is far larger than just the games themselves. Businesses supporting mobile accounts for payment processing are completely independent from game developers, and such businesses are successful primarily due to online gaming. The vast majority of their transactions come from teenagers who are unable to obtain credit cards, and use these payment processing services to pay for their gaming.

Internet cafés also benefit greatly from the growth of online gaming. Internet cafés offer high-speed broadband access for optimal gaming, and internet cafés are springing up in other Asian countries to serve gamers who are unable to get high-speed access at home.

Furthermore, Korean online games have influenced SNG (Social Network Games) and smartphone-based games which became popular around the world. ZINGA, the largest SNG company adapted the item based payment model which was developed by Korean casual games.

This chapter introduces details of the Korean online game innovation model, the road to its success and four innovators who have contributed greatly to the online game industry.

Innovation in the game industry: online games versus offline games

While the world continues to witness an explosive expansion of online games with millions of players logging in from almost every country on the planet, and the entertainment industry and other businesses maneuver to position themselves so as to take advantage of this exciting growth, relatively few people understand that the rate of expansion could be even greater were it not for an inherent tension between offline games and online games. To understand how this is the case, we must look at the fundamental differences between offline and online games.

In the past, all video games were offline. Users played games on ROM cartridges or CD-ROMs via game consoles, PCs and TVs. For players, this meant either playing alone or with a few other people in the same real space using the same, single piece of equipment. In the offline game business, software makers developed the game and sold it, usually through traditional retail channels. This business model has been dominant in the offline game industry for over 20 years.

But starting in the mid-1990s, a new type of gaming emerged: online gaming. These online games involved users connecting to servers via game consoles, PCs and communication networks. Players no longer needed to be in the same physical space or use the same machine or console in order to play a game, and over time they were able to play with more and more people. Using their own machines and connecting from remote locations around the world, they were able to log in to the same game simultaneously. Today players interact with hundreds or even millions of other players within online game worlds.

It is crucial to understand that the creation of online games was induced by disruptive technology. Technology developed to make offline games more enjoyable for players by allowing them to play with others has led to the tension in gaming we see today. When a disruptive innovation so different from previous technology and existing business models is generated, even leading companies often fail to adapt to the newly created environment. When technology or the very structure of the product undergoes enormous changes in a short period of time, such as the changes involved in going from offline to online gaming, management resources accumulated by the corporation can turn into obstacles and hinder the organization's ability to adapt. Henderson and Clark (1990), Leonard-Barton (1992) and Christensen (1997) have described this phenomenon as the "innovator's dilemma" or "core rigidities."

To best appreciate the dilemma offline game-makers faced in the past and continue to face in the present vis-à-vis online games, as well as understand the challenges online games have had to contend with and continue to confront because of offline games, we can compare and contrast the two forms with respect to several key differences. The differences are as follows: (1) product attributes; (2) the product development process; (3) the revenue model; and (4) the distribution channel.

Product attributes

Offline and online games differ with respect to certain product attributes. Product attributes refer to endemic attributes that can be identified and evaluated by users. Before proceeding to discuss the product attributes of offline and online games and the major differences between them, we need to say more about what product attributes are and how they are important.

For example, a laptop PC has two critical product attributes. A laptop PC is typically evaluated according to: (1) how little it weighs; and (2) how efficiently it processes information. These two product attributes are important in laptop PCs, but their relationship is inversely proportional. The lighter the laptop becomes, the less efficient it will be. To shed weight, CPU efficiency has to be scaled down and generated heat has to be reduced, as does the hard disc capacity (Wi, 2004, 2006a, 2006b). Accordingly, laptop developers must choose between championing lightweight machines or information processing ability, or attempt to balance the two. Consumers manage their priorities with respect to machine weight and information processing ability, and they make their purchases accordingly.

Enormous differences in product attributes exist between offline and online games and the central tension mentioned at the start of this chapter arises from the fact that an online game is a type of modified offline game architecture with community added to the game play (Wi and Nojima, 2003). Game play is a general term referring to what users experience and evaluate with respect to graphics, sound, story structure, character design and other categories that fall under the rubric of what it is like to play the game. In other words, the aesthetic and functional satisfaction, or lack thereof, users obtain from the game is referred to as game play. On the flip side, community is a product attribute particular to online games that creates a sense of solidarity, camaraderie and satisfaction among users via communication, competition and other forms of interaction. Many user communities such as guilds, clans and alliances have been formed in online games. These communities facilitate the game play of new members, and strengthening a sense of unity for community members is critical to generating quality extended game play and thus retaining players over the long term.

Offline games usually involve one player vying against a pre-set program while online games feature a massive number of users engaged in mutual warfare or cooperation. Accordingly, offline and online game preferences vary. Hence, offline gamers usually engage in individual play while online gamers cooperate and compete with other users via communities.

Offline games strive to offer high-quality sound, graphics and plot, and those game play elements are often their main focus. One of the goals of the Japanese developer Square-Enix is to create outstanding graphics no matter how much the development cost entailed.

However, that is not the case with online games. Game play elements such as graphics and sound must be balanced with community. Unlike with offline games, community is critical in online games and so chat and other enabling functions are offered. The developer of an online game must therefore strike a balance between pursuing excellent graphics, sound, and plot with other needs such as supporting user communities. Online game developers support user communities in various ways by creating communication tools such as chat windows, building user events and web sites, and holding offline meetings.

As the number of user communities increases, the value of the game increases. This leads to more players, and again greater value. A set of more players can result in a larger monthly user fee, which in turn translates to greater corporate profits.

The product development process

Technology needs differ between offline and online games. Unlike with offline games, servers and network technology are essential for online games. Offline games do not require network technology as they involve an individual player vying against the game or multiple players waging battle against one another but playing on the same machine. Online games are composed of server and client programs which are installed on the user's PC and on the server, while offline games are composed of only the client program on the user's machine or on a disc.

With online games, many players engage in game play via the server. Hence, technology addressing how to accommodate players on a restricted server and how to deal with an inundation of players logging onto the server at once is essential. Consequently, server management, maintenance and repair costs are a formidable expense that only online game developers face. Jake Song, CEO of XLgames (former CTO of NEXON and NCsoft), recounts an early server programming learning process:

> I majored in computer science in college and picked up server technology by collecting text MUD open sources from the Internet and elsewhere. I obtained MUD sources and studied and improved them. I deemed myself an able programmer but it was my first time dabbling in network programming. By providing game services, I discovered many ways to increase

> server efficiency with repeated improvements. I took a network-programming course in college and it was a big help. Those who took graduate courses in server or network technology have an advantage.

This combination of server and network technologies required for online game development makes a smooth transition from creating offline to online games difficult for dominant offline game companies. For Japanese companies looking to expand beyond offline games, there are few engineers who have developed games based on server and network technology that they can hire. The lack of experienced developers to build server programs requires extensive trial and error, and consequently an enormous cost in online game development.

Another way we can appreciate the difference between offline and online games in terms of development is to consider the development of offline games as analogous to film production. Once a film reel leaves the editing room and is transported to the theater, no more revisions are possible. With offline games as well, once bugs are removed in the final stage and CD-ROM production is under way, no more revisions can be made. If a severely detrimental bug is detected after the offline game's release, the only remedy is to recall it. But it is a different story for online games. Even after an online game is released to the public, continuous content revision is possible.

Online games can be revised in various ways with respect to a number of post-release needs. For example, character ability balancing is critical in online games. If one type of character is especially strong, word spreads among users that this type of character is easy to do well with, that it has an advantage over other characters. Soon, players swarm to play that type of character. When something like this over-powered character class occurs, the GMs (Game Masters) who monitor the game report it to the developer, who can implement a patch to address character balance. The same applies to controlling the volume of virtual items and the game's economy. Players tend to concentrate at sites where it is easy to acquire specific items or in-game money. If it is determined that a game item being traded—a powerful sword, for instance—is too easily found or purchased, the developer lowers the acquisition rate. That way the supply decreases and prices increase, and not as many players are able to wield such a powerful sword. In online games users are constantly observed, enabling developers to address their needs via system modifications in real time.

Online games evolve through mutual interaction with users, and this interaction typically proceeds through stages. Figure 26.2 refers to online game development and the update process. After an offline game is developed and released, the development team is disbanded and development-related tasks are terminated. But online games go much further.

After the basic game has been built, a point at which an offline game would exit development, the online game enters a closed (private) alpha test phase. At this stage, the development team is not disbanded but supplemented with additional developers to prepare for revisions.

The second stage is the closed beta test. The beta is different from the alpha test phase in that the game has been further developed and more users are added to the test pool. For high-profile games that enter the beta test phase, participants are often selected from pools. Such selection processes are extremely critical marketing decisions, as many of the gamers participating in these beta test phases have the power to sway public opinion. As such, it is important to take very seriously the judgments of private test participants and possibly make revisions reflecting their preferences.

At the third step, the online game advances to the open beta test phase. Many more users are invited. This large pool of users actually tests the game under the same conditions as when it will be offered commercially. The final stage is commercialization. In the commercialization stage users are charged a fee to play the game.

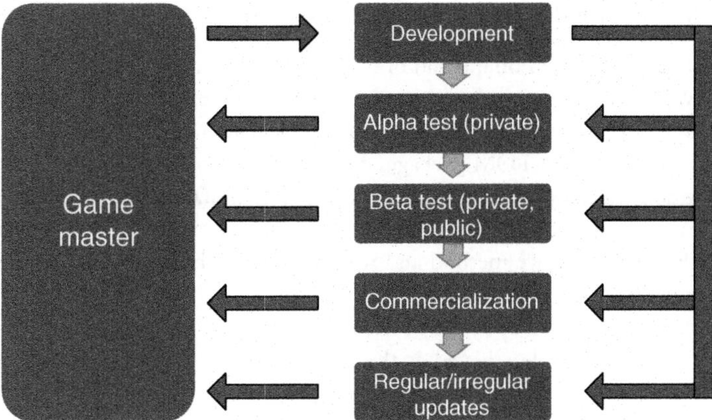

Figure 26.2 Online game development and update process
Source: Wi (2009, p. 17).

Throughout all phases, GMs (Game Masters) perform a vital function. GMs absorb user comments and requests and relay them to the development team in the form of feedback during the alpha, both beta, and commercial phases. Developers repair bugs and execute updates based on that feedback. Of course, the function of the Game Master is nonexistent in offline games.

The revenue model

The third difference between online and offline games involves the revenue model. With offline games, the developers' source of revenue is via the retail sales of their game. However, for online games the main source of revenue is the recurring fee users pay for connecting to the game server.

Offline game developers acquire revenue through software sales. Prospective players must purchase the console and the software in order to play the game. The profitability of offline games rests solely on how many game packages can be sold. For the majority of offline game software packages, sales peak with release and decline with time, adhering to a right-descending pattern. Seen as a whole, most of the total sales volume is concentrated in the extremely short period immediately following release, in what is known as a distinctly characteristic "early concentration" sales pattern (Shintaku, 1994). This makes the decision of how many game units to produce and release in the first week of sales critical.

But with online games, payment for rendering services instead of payment for software is the main source of revenue. Users of online games are required to pay a connection fee to access and play the game. These fees range between US$20 and US$30. With the partial pay model of item sales, users pay for their server connection through making in-game item purchases. If a server connection fee is not paid consistently on a monthly basis or in the form of item purchases, users of online games are typically unable to connect to the server or cannot play the game smoothly or to their full satisfaction. Of course, online games require the game to be installed, usually by downloading the client from the Internet. But this does not necessarily constitute a sale; it is merely a process of exchanging information. In online games, once users are secured, a continuous stream of revenue can be generated.

The distribution channel

The fourth difference between online and offline games is the manner of the distribution channel of games. With offline games, the game console manufacturer is routinely commissioned to manufacture CD-ROMs containing the game software, which are sold via retail and wholesale vendors to the consumer. CD-ROM packages containing the software for game consoles are sold via two distribution trajectories. For one, the package is manufactured by the software producer and sold via retail and wholesale outlets to the consumer. For the other, the package is manufactured according to the above method and reaches the user by way of the software developer directly, such as via website or catalog sales.

In cases like those discussed above, the software company typically develops a game autonomously with the game console selected as the foundation for development. As game consoles are stable for a set period without much changing with respect to their features, the developer can concentrate exclusively on software development. For offline games, software developers and manufacturers are disparate with respect to development and distribution. With such a clear division of labor and vested interests, game software developers need only focus on developing the software.

But in the distribution model for MMORPGs (Massively Multi-player Online Role Playing Games) the middleman disappears. Either the developer or the publisher possesses and operates game servers in-house. The servers are directly owned and operated by the developer, or the servers are placed on IDC and the management of the servers is contracted out. In offline games the distributor was a separate entity, but in online games the developers have personally taken on distribution tasks. Because of this, in countries where offline games are dominant, the resistance of retailers to online games exists. These middlemen are aware that the distribution model of online games has excluded them. To overcome this resistance, when NCsoft was distributing *Lineage 2* in the USA, they signed a contract precluding online downloads and sold the game via offline distribution channels only.

In the distribution model of online games, frequent content upgrades are essential to ward off user boredom, which could lead to subscription cancellation. In other words, to keep current users from growing bored as well as to draw in new users, performing incessant revisions that inject new, appealing content is imperative. NCsoft performs minor daily revisions and major updates every six months.

The four dragons

The history of the Korean online gaming industry began in the late 1980s. Though online games would not be widely regarded as a distinct industry by the government and other entities until the late 1990s, the foundations were laid in the previous decade. The Korean online game industry began to develop at KAIST (Korea Advanced Institute of Science and Technology) around 1990.[2] At the time, internet access in the country was limited to a few research facilities such as KAIST and Seoul National University. In the late 1980s some KAIST students were involved with a project to overhaul and revamp DIKU MUD, a game originally developed by students at the University of Copenhagen, with a public source code. Only a few students were involved with this project, though. Online gaming remained relatively unknown in Korea at this point.

Text MUDs (Multi-User Dungeons) were the forefathers of modern online gaming. MUDs, which are devoid of graphics and are played solely via reading and inputting text, first appeared in Korea with the launch of *Jurassic Park* in 1994. This was just over a decade after MUDs had originally been developed and released in the Western world. *Jurassic Park* was originally played via PC communication networks such as Hitel and Chollian. The success of *Jurassic Park* quickly led to other MUDs being marketed, such as *Land of Dangun* and *Ghost Fortress.*

Text-based MUDs were a technologically primitive form of online game that nevertheless attracted large numbers of Korean users. Having to take in all of the information from the game via text and input commands in English was inconvenient for users, though. In 1996, Nexon released *Kingdom of the Wind*, the first MUD to include graphic content (referred to as a MUG, or Multi-User Graphic). In 1998, NCsoft launched *Lineage*, a full-fledged graphical MMORPG, and the Korean online gaming industry took off on its path of explosive growth.

NEXON by two dragons, Jake Song and Jung Ju Kim

Nexon is one of the biggest global game companies born in Korea and was listed on the Japanese stock market in 2011. The aggregate value of listed stock is about US$5 billion and its revenue was US$1.7 billion in 2013. Jake Song and Jung Ju Kim are the founders of Nexon.

Jake Song had graduated from Seoul National University in 1990 and entered KAIST as a master's student. He caught a glimpse of Kit MUD while it was in development. Kim Jiho, a KAIST graduate and long-time MUD developer, was working on Kit MUD, an improved version of the University of Copenhagen's DIKU MUD. Song became enamored with Kit MUD and began working on it, learning different types of MUD source code as well as about the networking and server technology required to access a MUD online.

After completing his master's course Song enrolled in a PhD program at KAIST, but withdrew after a year and a half to take a job at Hansoft, which is a firm developing a Korean word processing program. Song aspired to develop games, but was repeatedly turned down by Hansoft, which had no interest in creating video games. Song continued to push online gaming to Hansoft and was finally allotted one month to work on online game development. He partnered with Lee See-hang (currently the Vice President at NCsoft) and with Jake Song on the server and Lee on the client, development of the game engine looked promising. They named their engine DOOMVAS (Distributed Object Oriented Multimedia Virtual Active System), and it was designed solely to create online games.

While developing DOOMVAS they met with IBM Korea and secured a venture capital investment. IBM Korea was excited by the prospect of the game they had in development in which large numbers of users could play simultaneously via the Internet. At the time IBM Korea had an affiliate program which provided for collaboration with start-up companies. IBM would provide the technology, funding, sales network and marketing and the start-up firm would develop the product and share the profits.

Song established Nexon in 1994 in cooperation with Jung Ju Kim, a Seoul National University graduate. Nexon's goal was to focus solely on online game development. Nexon's first game, as discussed previously, was *Kingdom of the Wind*. IBM Korea was still interested in Nexon's work, and they signed a joint-development agreement with Nexon. IBM invested over US$50,000, provided another US$90,000 worth of server equipment needed for online game development, and agreed to act as Nexon's global marketing agent. Development took longer than anticipated, however, and Nexon faced a cashflow crisis in 1995. In December of that year IBM Korea provided another US$45,000 in funding and gave Nexon the first Korean website, that of Hyundai Motors, as a project to provide some revenue to get by.

In October of 1995, two months before the additional round of investment from IBM Korea, Jake Song left Nexon due to differences with co-founder Jung Ju Kim. His terms of departure stipulated that "while giving up on 50% of Nexon shares he is free to develop new games employing *Kingdom of the Wind* source code, and after 1997 games developed in such a manner can be launched."

In spite of Song's departure, Jung Ju Kim had continued to develop the game and finally Nexon launched the beta version of *Kingdom of the Wind* via the ISP Chollian in December 1995. The full commercial version would follow in April 1996. Nexon was the first domestic game developer to implement graphics in a MUD.

Nexon were pioneers, but they faced many difficulties in bringing their games to market. Gaming was not yet viewed as a full-fledged industry, and thus gaming companies struggled to recruit able developers. Many developers also failed to grasp the concepts and principles behind the MUG, as the games were split between a server to run the game and connect users, and a client on the user's PC to connect to the server with and display the game's graphics.

Most game developers shied away from following Nexon into the realm of graphical online games. Industry forecasts for the success of MUGs were dismal, and most game developers did not have programmers on staff who had the skills to create this type of software. *Kingdom of the Wind*, the trailblazer of graphical online games, was not a commercial success in its early stages. When it was first released, the number of concurrent users stagnated in the low hundreds. Without a PvP (Player vs Player) or castle siege system, *Kingdom of the Wind* had no content to promote inter-guild strife or intra-guild cooperation. These elements were what drew players to MUDs and what kept them playing over the long term, and without them *Kingdom of the Wind* had trouble attracting and keeping players.

Despite its unprofitability, *Kingdom of the Wind* was important to the game industry as a whole, serving as a prototype of the first graphic-based game in a predominantly text-based industry. In the mid-1990s, the viability of a graphical online game had not yet been established, and *Kingdom of the Wind* provided proof of both the technological capacity to build such a game and the existence of prospective users. Unlike text-based MUDs, which were populated by hardcore gamers, *Kingdom of the Wind* succeeded in drawing in ordinary users with its graphical appeal.

Kingdom of the Wind was also the introduction of the real-time graphical role-playing game (RPG) system, in which players create and build up a character in a graphical online world. It was a pioneer in the Korean game market where the RPG was still a novel concept.

NCsoft: the third dragon, Taek Jin Kim

NCsoft is one of the most famous MMORPG development companies in the world. NCsoft had been established in 1997 by Taek Jin Kim. It was listed on the Korean stock market in 2000. The aggregate value of listed stock is about US$4 billion and its estimated revenue in 2013 is about US$800 million. Their famous MMORPGs are *Lineage*, *Lineage 2*, *Aion*, *Blade* and *Soul*.

After leaving Nexon, Jake Song took a position with an ISP named Inet and began development on *Lineage* in September 1996. He was given one year to create the full game. Before he could complete his project, the Asian financial crisis of 1997 struck, and difficulties caused Inet to scrap many of its projects, including *Lineage*. Discouraged by yet another failure in trying to create *Lineage*, Song left Inet and looked elsewhere.

While he was looking for another job, Taek Jin Kim, CEO of NCsoft, suggested that Song come on board. Jake Song began working at NCsoft in late 1997, continued working on *Lineage*, and the game finally launched in September 1998. One year and 10 months after launch, *Lineage* recorded 3 million registered users, leading the charge of the Korean online game market's amazing growth story.

Lineage by NCsoft is the game which would become the foundation of the Korean online game industry and which even today, 16 years after its launch, still boasts over 220,000 concurrent users. *Lineage* broke the 1,000 concurrent user mark four months after launch, 10,000 within one year, and would eventually set a world record two years after launch with 300,000 concurrent users at that time. Released at a time when Blizzard's *Starcraft* was dominating the Korean game market, NCsoft's *Lineage* triggered a massive influx of players to online games and solidified the online game business model.

Lineage used the basic RPG system of classes and character levels, but emphasized fast action to hold the players' interest. Users could choose from five character classes: monarch, knight, elf, mage, and dark elf. All classes distinguish between male and female characters, thus players actually have 10 different character types to choose from. *Lineage* presented the most sophisticated online world including complete inter-guild warfare and castle siege systems in a game.

One of the major factors contributing to *Lineage*'s success was that it was targeted towards ordinary users, not hardcore gamers. The game could be controlled solely with a mouse and the interface was simple and easy to understand. *Lineage* was a very approachable game for new players, which aided in its rapid expansion.

The defining characteristic of *Lineage* was that it behaved like an actual online society, not just a game. Instead of the developer hosting events and guiding the story of the game, the players are the ones who decide in which direction the game will go. In *Lineage* there exists a type of guild known as a "blood alliance," in which players swear fealty to a monarch and fight for a common cause. Blood alliances draw players together into tight-knit communities, and these alliances have contributed significantly to extending the shelf life of *Lineage* in the market.

Lineage's success brought many competitors. Game developers saw the huge profits NCsoft was earning and rushed to create their own graphical online games. Developer after developer announced that they were building a new MMORPG, and the number of MMORPGs released surged from 9 in 1999 to over 100 in 2000. It seems safe to conclude that most of these games were inspired by the success of *Lineage*.

Lineage also created a new revenue model for online games known as "item cash transactions," in which players purchase in-game items with real-life currency. This was a switch from the older model of paying a per-minute, per-hour, or per-month fee to connect to a game. *Lineage* currently boasts the largest number of item cash transactions of any MMORPG.

NHN (Han Game): the fourth dragon, Bum Su Kim

NHN is the largest portal in Korea. The aggregate value of its listed stock is about US$40 billion and its estimated revenue in 2013 is about US$4 billion. NHN was born through the combination of Naver and Han Game in 2001. Naver was an internet search company and Han Game was an internet casual game company.

With the introduction of Han Game in the late 1990s, another shift took place in the online gaming market, which up to this point had been dominated by MMORPGs. Han Game offered more traditional games such as Go-Stop (Korean card games), poker, and chess on the internet. While users of MMORPG like *Lineage* were generally limited to a particular demographic group (young males), Han Game's titles were accessible to anyone. Women and older adults, who tended to avoid games like *Lineage*, realized there was a game they could enjoy on the internet.

Han Game was founded in September 1998 and launched its online service in December 1999. Its site was an immediate success, with a registered membership of over 1 million users within 3 months and daily page views over 10 million. Han Game quickly became one of the leading online casual game sites in Korea.

Han Game was founded by Bum Su Kim, who had graduated from Seoul National University in 1990 and was a former employee of Unitel, Samsung's internet service provider. Well aware of the limitations of direct PC communication as well as the awesome potential of the internet, Han Game decided to build its site with an eye towards the future. He predicted that in the near future the prevalence of the internet would render connection to a communication network via modems unnecessary and that the direct-connection PC communication industry would become obsolete. The internet's prospective user base also consisted of every online user, rather than being limited to the registered users of a specific service provider. This gave the internet an almost infinite potential for growth.

In its early days, Han Game adhered to the typical internet business model of "internet as medium." Their model was to collect users via websites and generate revenue by selling advertising on those websites. One difference between Han Game and the plethora of other internet start-ups attempting to do the same thing is that Han Game formed a registered user base with its games. That distinction is precisely what made today's Han Game possible.

There was careful reasoning behind selecting games as the method with which to secure registered users for their sites. Han Game believed that games had a high possibility of successfully turning commercial, as opposed to other online content (such as news) which would likely always remain free. Selling advertising was the central source of revenue in their business model, but they believed that if they needed to, they could commercialize their games and also earn a profit in that way.

When the dotcom bubble burst in 2000, internet companies faced an almost total loss of advertising revenue. Most of them collapsed as they had no other source of income. Han Game faced the same loss of advertising revenue and realized it could not survive without going commercial. The executives at Han Game were concerned with the ramifications of going commercial, though, such as user protests and losing users altogether. Their answer to this was partial commercialization.

Han Game began their commercialization in March 2001 with a twofold approach. The first method was via item sales, selling items for games such as Tetris, Go-Stop, etc. at prices ranging from $0.10 to $0.60 per item. The second method was by charging a monthly usage fee of roughly $8.00 which allowed unlimited play of all Han Game's titles. The strategy behind this was to collect fees via item sales from heavy users who spent large amounts of time on the service while allowing light users to play for free. Despite some user protests, the commercialization of Han Game was a success.

The successful commercialization of Han Game is telling not only for the online game market, but for the internet as a whole. Very few advertising-driven sites were successful in their efforts to commercialize their user base following the dotcom implosion. At a time when users were opposed to the idea of paying for internet content, Han Game's success demonstrated a model that could be applied to other businesses, and indeed many other internet companies would follow in Han Game's footsteps in their commercialization plans.

Han Game's most significant achievement as applies to the online game industry as a whole was not its commercialization, however, but its widespread user appeal. Online games had previously been the domain of MMORPG players, and Han Game changed that and opened up online gaming to a much broader base of casual players. Their games were widely known, such as Go-Stop and billiards, and were thus very accessible to and popular with female and older adult users. Han Game's success introduced a large number of internet users to the concept of playing games online.

Conclusion

This chapter has analyzed an innovative industrial model and the innovators in Korean online games. The Korean online game industry shows the following characteristics.

First, the Korean online game industry has gained global competency through innovations, especially disruptive innovations. It combined old game products with new technology and new product attributes which were different from old ones such as PC and console games.

Second, the innovation of the Korean online game industry came not from a sole innovator but from multi-innovators who had interacted together. Four innovators such as Jake Song and Jung Ju Kim had led the industry and made innovations in heterogeneous game genres such as MMORPG, casual, board games, etc.

Third, four innovators accumulated their development knowledge for more than ten years. They tried and attempted to develop text MUD in 1980s and early 1990s. Although Korea was not a superpower in the MUD industry in 1980s, they absorbed MUD development knowledge step by step and finally succeeded in developing online games which were new and innovative.

The Korean online game industry presented an innovation model that changed from follower to innovator. Other Asian countries share the same industrial aim to become an innovator from an imitator. It is the perfect model to show the path for the countries who are trying to create a path as an innovator.

Notes

1 This chapter is a revision based on *Innovation and Strategy of Online Games*, published by Imperial College Press in 2009 (Wi, 2009).

2 The Korea Advanced Institute of Science and Technology is a renowned research and education facility in the sciences.

Bibliography

Christensen, C. M. (1997) *The Innovator's Dilemma,* Boston: Harvard Business Press.

Henderson, R.M. and Clark, K.B. (1990) "Architectural innovation: the reconfiguration of existing product technologies and the failure of established firms," *Administrative Science Quarterly,* 35: 9–30.

Leonard-Barton, D. (1992) "Core capabilities and core rigidities: a paradox in managing new product development," *Strategic Management Journal,* 13: 111–225.

Prahalad, C.K. and Hamel, G. (1990) "The core competence of the firm," *Harvard Business Review,* May–June: 79–91.

Shintaku, J. (1994) *Competitive Strategy of Japanese Firms,* Tokyo: Yuhigaku (in Japanese).

Wi, J.H. (2004) 'The industrial formation process of Korean online game: analysis of new industry formation through supplementary infrastructure," *2002 Game Industry Journal,* 74–95 (in Korean).

Wi, J.H. (2006a) "Organization design for new product architecture devlopment: comparative analysis of Sharp and Casio on PDA development," *Asian Journal of Technology Innovation.*

Wi, J.H. (2006b) "Organizational design for the development of new product architecture: comparative analysis of NEC and Toshiba," *Journal of Technology Innovation* (in Korean).

Wi, J.H. (2008) *Industrial Development Strategy of Online Games,* Beijing: Tsinghua University Press (in Chinese).

Wi, J.H. (2009) *Innovation and Strategy of Online Games,* London: Imperial College Press.

Wi, J.H. and Nojima, M. (2003) "The analysis of difference of attributes of user group by path dependence: a comparison of 'Lineage' users in Korea and Japan," *Akamon Management Review,* 1(1): 1–23 (in Japanese).

27

Samsung Electronics and its growth strategy

Seung-Joo Lee

Introduction

Samsung Electronics is a multinational electronics company from South Korea and a global leader in memory chips, smartphones, TVs and LCD panels. In 2012, the company achieved total revenues of US$187.8 billion, surpassing Apple, IBM and Hewlett Packard to become the world's largest electronics company measured by sales. Its net profit of US$21.7 billion in 2012 was higher than that of the top six Japanese electronics firms combined (Panasonic, Sony, Hitachi, Toshiba, NEC, and Sharp). The company generated 85 percent of its revenues outside of Korea and employed around 236,000 people in 79 countries.

Established in 1969 as a subsidiary of the Samsung Group, Samsung Electronics began producing black-and-white TVs and radios in collaboration with Sanyo and NEC. In the 1970s, it was producing color TVs and home appliances such as refrigerators, washing machines and microwave ovens. In the 1980s, it expanded into semiconductors, computers, LCDs and mobile phones. For years, Samsung Electronics was viewed as a low-end producer of imitative products and struggled with a poor quality image in the world market. Since 1992, however, the company has emerged as the world's leading producer of memory chips such as DRAM (Dynamic Random Access Memory) and flash memory. In 2006, Samsung Electronics surpassed its Japanese rival, Sony, to become the world's largest producer of TVs. In 2012, the company overtook Apple and Nokia to become the world's largest smartphone maker, capturing 30.4 percent of the global smartphone market, according to research firm Strategy Analytics. Its global brand image has improved significantly, moving to the ninth place in the Interbrand Best Global Brands survey, with an estimated brand value of US$32.9 billion in 2012.

Samsung Electronics has made a remarkable transformation from a low-end producer to become one of the world's most dynamic and innovative technology companies. What has made this transformation possible? What are the key drivers of success? Previous research on Samsung Electronics has analyzed its growth and transformation from the perspective of technological learning and latecomer strategies (Kim, 1997; Cho *et al.*, 1998; Mathews and Cho, 1999), organizational processes and leadership (Chang, 2008), corporate life-cycles (Michell, 2010), and hybrid management systems (Khanna *et al.*, 2011). This chapter provides additional insights by examining the growth and transformation of Samsung Electronics from the perspective of dynamic capabilities. The concept of dynamic capabilities was developed in the field of strategic management to analyze the drivers of firm performance in a dynamic business environment (Teece *et al.*, 1997; Eisenhardt and Martin, 2000; Wang and Ahmed, 2007; Danneels, 2010). Given the rapidly changing nature of the technology-intensive industries in which Samsung Electronics competes, the development and exercise of dynamic capabilities are considered to be critical determinants of its success.

The central message of this chapter is that the successful growth and transformation of Samsung Electronics can be attributed to its dynamic capabilities, in particular: (1) the entrepreneurial insights and bold investment by top management; (2) rapid technology catch-up through dynamic learning and resource leverage; and (3) relentless innovation in products and processes to achieve global market leadership. This chapter will examine those key elements of Samsung's dynamic capabilities through case studies of its semiconductor and mobile phone businesses.

Entrepreneurial insights and bold investment

Previous literature on dynamic capabilities has identified top management's ability to recognize and seize new business opportunities as a key dimension of dynamic capabilities (Teece, 2007; Wang and Ahmed, 2007; Harreld *et al.*, 2007). Samsung's decision to enter the semiconductor industry provides a good example of top management's opportunity recognition and entrepreneurial insights. In February 1983, Chairman Lee Byung-Chul (the founder of the Samsung Group) announced in Tokyo that Samsung would enter the semiconductor industry and become a DRAM producer. The announcement, known as the "Tokyo declaration" is regarded as a key milestone in the history of Samsung Electronics, as it transformed the company from a producer of low-end consumer appliances to a high-tech powerhouse. Chairman Lee viewed the semiconductor business as the "rice" of high-tech industries and a strategic platform for upgrading Samsung's business portfolio. Despite negative opinions and skepticism about its likely success, he made a bold decision by making large-scale investments in the highly uncertain DRAM business.

Chairman Lee's bold decision eventually paid off as the semiconductor business became the main growth engine and cash generator of Samsung Electronics since the mid-1990s. How did Chairman Lee recognize this business opportunity? Where did he get the insight? Analysis of historical data indicates that his decision was influenced by multiple factors, including government policy to promote the semiconductor industry, benchmarking of Japanese firms, strong advocacy by his son, and the results of two feasibility studies (Samsung Electronics, 1999; Electronics Industry 50-Year History Publishing Committee, 2009; Lee, 2011).

First, Chairman Lee's decision was influenced by the Korean government policy to promote the semiconductor industry. In 1981, a special committee was formed at the Presidential Office (the Blue House) to develop a vision and roadmap for Korea's electronics industry (Electronics Industry 50-Year History Publishing Committee, 2009). Due to rising wage rates and trade protectionism, Korea was losing its competitiveness in labor-intensive consumer electronics and needed to move up the ladder toward the higher value-added, technology-intensive sectors. After much debate and discussion, the committee identified semiconductors, computers and telecommunication equipments as the top three priority sectors for development, given their high level of import dependence, future growth potential and technological spillovers. Even though the committee did not specify the semiconductor products and technologies for intensive development, its policy direction provided a signal and guideline that influenced Chairman Lee's decision to pursue the semiconductor business.

Second, Chairman Lee gained more knowledge about the semiconductor business by benchmarking Japanese companies. Chairman Lee maintained an extensive network of contacts in

Japan and frequently visited the country to learn about new business opportunities with business partners and industry experts. He was quite impressed with Japan's recovery after the oil shock and its development of high-tech industries such as semiconductors, robotics, new materials, biotechnology and aerospace. After benchmarking Japanese firms' success in the global market and identifying the key success factors of the semiconductor business, he developed the conviction that Samsung could effectively compete in this business, leveraging its strengths in low-cost manufacturing and timely investment in production, R&D and human resources.

Third, Chairman Lee's son, Lee Kun-Hee (who is the current Chairman of the Samsung Group) was a strong advocate of the semiconductor business and played a critical role in persuading his father to invest in the business (Samsung Electronics, 2010). Lee Kun-Hee was a technology enthusiast with a strong interest in the latest gadgets and technology trends. While exploring new business opportunities for Samsung, he learned about semiconductors as the key technology drivers of the electronics industry and their future growth potential. He thought that the semiconductor business was well suited to Samsung's culture, given the high level of technical skills, precision and discipline needed for its successful operation. In 1974, he invested his own personal money to acquire the Korea Semiconductor Company, a small integrated circuit (IC) chip maker, to learn about the business. He organized benchmarking trips to US and Japanese firms and persuaded his father on numerous occasions to invest in the semiconductor business.

Fourth, before making the investment decision, Chairman Lee commissioned a task force to investigate the feasibility of entering the semiconductor industry. The task force collected industry and market data through Samsung's overseas networks and conducted interviews with Korean industry experts. However, there was a lack of sufficient knowledge and expertise in Korea, so a second task force was dispatched to Silicon Valley to develop a more detailed business plan. After much intelligence gathering and field interviews, the task force developed the following recommendations: (1) establish an R&D center in Silicon Valley to monitor technology trends, develop new products and recruit engineers with relevant experience; and (2) invest in VLSI (Very Large Scale Integrated Circuits) production facilities in Korea for mass production over the next five years. There was much debate about product portfolio and priority for investment, but Chairman Lee decided to focus on the Dynamic Random Access Memory (DRAM) market. Despite the high investment required and cyclical nature of the DRAM business, it was projected to be a large and rapidly growing market, driven by rising PC demand. The product and process technologies were relatively standardized and could be acquired through technology licensing from the USA or Japan. Samsung could leverage its skills in operational excellence and timely investment in production and R&D to rapidly catch up with the Japanese. Chairman Lee made a bold decision by investing more than US$500 million in state-of-the-art production equipment and R&D facilities, despite incurring heavy losses in the first four years of operations. Samsung's centralized coordination of resources at the group level enabled the company to rapidly mobilize the financial and human resources needed for large-scale investment in the semiconductor business (Samsung Electronics, 1999).

Despite the rising cost of developing the next-generation product and process technologies, Chairman Lee Kun-Hee continued to invest aggressively in the semiconductor business. Samsung made bold investments in economic recessions when other competitors were holding back, and gained considerable profits when the industry demand recovered. For example, in 1993, Samsung took the risk of investing more than US$1 billion in 8-inch diameter wafer processing technology, being the first in the industry to move from 6-inch to 8-inch mass production (Chang and Podolny, 2002). With a larger wafer size, productivity could be improved as more chips could be produced at the same time, but the feasibility of the technology was not yet proven. Despite the high risk involved, Chairman Lee decided to make the investment, which eventually paid off, resulting in significant profits and market share gain. Such aggressive investment in a high-risk situation was possible due to the leader's strong commitment and entrepreneurial insights based on deep knowledge of the business, and a corporate governance system which enabled a long-term investment horizon and rapid decision-making by top management.

Rapid technology catch-up and resource leverage

Despite its initial lack of technological capabilities in the semiconductor business, Samsung Electronics was able to rapidly catch up with the established competitors and become the world's leading producer of memory chips. How was Samsung able to acquire and develop its technological competence? Previous literature has found that the external acquisition of technologies through dynamic learning and resource leverage can be a key element of dynamic capabilities for latecomer firms (Kim, 1997; Cho *et al.*, 1998; Mathews, 2002). Complementary resources and capabilities can be acquired from external sources and combined with internal resources in a dynamic process of organizational learning (Mathews and Cho, 1999). Samsung was able to rapidly develop its technological capabilities through external acquisition and assimilation of technologies from multiple sources leveraging a variety of channels such as joint ventures, acquisitions, technology licensing, strategic alliances, equipment suppliers, part-time consultants as well as in-house R&D activities to rapidly internalize and improve on those technologies.

Samsung's initial experience in producing basic consumer electronics products and components provided the basic foundation for its entry into the semiconductor industry. In 1968, Samsung formed a joint venture with Sanyo to produce black-and-white TVs and radios. In 1970, another joint venture was formed with NEC to produce cathode ray tubes and components for TVs. Some 137 newly hired Samsung engineers were sent to Sanyo and NEC factories in Japan to learn basic production and operations skills (Samsung Electronics, 1999). Even though the technology learned was very basic, Samsung was able to gain operational knowledge and skills in the mass production of electronics goods and in implementing large-scale investment projects.

In 1974, Samsung acquired Korea Semiconductor Company, a high-tech venture that produced linear integrated circuit (IC) chips and transistors. The acquisition was a stepping stone for gaining experience in semiconductors and for securing its own captive supply of IC chips for its consumer electronics business. The founder of the company was a Korean-American scientist who had semiconductor design experience at Motorola and played an important role in transferring his tacit knowledge and experience to Samsung engineers. In 1978, the company was fully integrated into Samsung's operations and successfully developed IC chips for electronic watches and color TVs based on Large-Scale Integration (LSI) technology.

To produce DRAM chips, Samsung approached several US and Japanese companies for technology licensing, but no one was willing to license their technologies, as they feared Samsung as a potential competitor. In 1983, however, Samsung found Micron Technologies, then a small memory chip maker based in Boise, Idaho, who was willing to license its 64K DRAM design technology in return for a cash payment. Samsung sent a team of engineers to Micron Technologies to learn about the technology, and after much trial and error assimilating the design and production technologies, successfully developed Korea's first 64K DRAM chip in six months.

DRAM process technology was acquired through technology licensing from California-based Zytrex and Japan's Sharp. Samsung adopted Sharp's production system to minimize errors and expedite its process development (Kim, 1997). Given the rapid pace of change and intense competition among DRAM producers, speed of product development and timing of mass production were critical. In preparation for the mass production of 64K DRAM, Samsung established a stretch goal of six months for completing the construction of the fabrication line, a task that in the USA and Japan took three times longer. Working around-the-clock, the project team completed the construction in six months as planned, narrowing the gap with Japanese competitors to two years (Siegel and Chang, 2009). In the process, Samsung worked closely with equipment suppliers and moonlighted technical consultants and retired engineers from Japan for troubleshooting, consulting and training.

In 1983, Samsung opened an R&D center in Silicon Valley to keep track of technology trends and to recruit engineers for its semiconductor business. Samsung aggressively recruited Korean scientists and engineers with PhDs in electronics engineering from top-notch US universities and those with work experience in high-tech companies such as IBM, Intel and National Semiconductor. They were lured to Samsung with an attractive compensation package, rapid promotion opportunities and a sense of mission to contribute to Korea's technological development. They played a critical role in technology transfer and the development of new products and technologies, and many of them were promoted to top executive positions. When developing the 64K DRAM and 256K DRAM microchips, Samsung created two competing product development teams, one in Korea and the other in Silicon Valley (Kim, 1997). Both the internal competition and collaboration between the R&D sites created intense pressure to deliver results and shortened development time. Active interaction between the teams through joint research, consulting, and training quickly transferred knowledge from Silicon Valley to the Korean team.

While the 64K DRAM and 256K DRAM chips were developed with licensed technologies, Samsung developed the next-generation 1M DRAM chip with its own design and process technologies. Its R&D investment increased from US$10 million in 1981 to more than US$1 billion in 1995. As the cost of semiconductor R&D grew exponentially, the Korean government formed a national R&D consortium consisting of Samsung, LG and Hyundai to develop the next-generation 4M DRAM microchip. While the consortium spent US$110 million on R&D over three years, the government contributed 57 percent of the total R&D budget (Kim, 1997). Samsung was the first of the three companies to complete the design of a 4M DRAM microchip and was only six months behind Japan. Samsung caught up with the Japanese in the race to develop the 16M DRAM, and finally overtook them in the development and mass production of the 64M DRAM in 1992. In 1994, after investing US$150 million in R&D over the previous three years, Samsung successfully developed the world's first 256M DRAM microchip. Since then, Samsung has been at the forefront of DRAM chip design and process technology, maintaining the world's number one position for more than 20 years.

Samsung's concurrent development process has been a key factor in shortening the development time to market. When the 4M DRAM microchip was launched on the market, technology and product development plans were already set up for 16K DRAM and 64K DRAM microchips. To narrow the gap with technology leaders, Samsung began mass production of DRAM chips concurrently while working on R&D. Samsung effectively used cross-functional teams to enhance collaboration among R&D, product design and production. Design and production engineers participated in all phases of the development process, sharing information and resolving problems quickly by carrying out activities simultaneously rather than sequentially (Shin and Chang, 2006). The co-location of R&D and production at a single site in Giheung facilitated close interaction and collaboration, significantly reducing communication and coordination costs (Siegel and Chang, 2009).

Samsung leveraged its resources and capabilities in DRAM to expand into the flash memory market. As the technology and production process for flash memory were similar to DRAM, it could be produced using DRAM fabrication lines with only small adjustments in equipment, thereby saving significantly on the cost of building a new production line (McKern and Tayan, 2009). It made a bold move to overtake the leading player, Toshiba, and succeeded in developing a

NAND flash memory chip at the same time as Toshiba. By developing new product applications for USB drives, MP3 players, and mobile phones, and through relentless cost and productivity improvements, Samsung eventually overtook Toshiba in 2002.

Resources and capabilities developed in the semiconductor business were effectively deployed to develop the liquid crystal display (LCD) business. In particular, new product and process development capability, quality control and operations management skills, investment decision know-how, and human resource management systems were all transferred from the semiconductor business to the LCD business, resulting in significant synergies (Park *et al.*, 2008). In 1998, just three years after it started its LCD business, Samsung had captured the largest market share in the world and was introducing new products faster than the Japanese competitors.

Relentless innovation to achieve global market leadership

After becoming Chairman of the Samsung Group, Lee Kun-Hee emphasized the need for change and innovation in response to rising global competition. He grew increasingly worried that Samsung was losing its competitiveness and becoming complacent. In June 1993, he urgently convened a meeting of 200 executives in Frankfurt, Germany, where he unveiled Samsung's "New Management" initiative. The "New Management" was a comprehensive change program in product, process and people that reflected Chairman Lee's deep thinking and sense of urgency. His famous statement, "Change everything except your wife and children," conveyed his strong commitment to fundamental change. One of the main goals of Samsung's "New Management" was to raise the quality of Samsung's products to the world-class level.

The "New Management" was first applied to the mobile phone business, which was struggling with poor quality and disappointing sales performance. In 1993, Motorola was the dominant player in the Korean market with 65 percent market share, while Samsung's market share was only 10 percent. Chairman Lee gave the wireless division an ultimatum: "Develop a world-class mobile phone comparable to Motorola's, or Samsung will exit from the mobile phone business." The development team worked around-the-clock, disassembling Motorola's phones and conducting hundreds of comparison tests to identify areas for improvement. In October 1994, a new model was unveiled and introduced under the brand name "Anycall." The model was compact, weighed less than Motorola's, and its reliability, voice quality and durability were substantially improved over previous models. The new product was carefully tested in Korea's mountainous regions to ensure connection quality, as this was determined to be the key differentiator against Motorola's. Any defective products were destroyed and burned in so-called a "burning ceremony" to remind people that quality is of the utmost importance and could not be compromised. With an aggressive marketing campaign emphasizing its premium quality and excellent suitability for Korea's mountainous topography, Samsung overtook Motorola in the domestic market, its market share doubling from 26 percent in 1994 to 52 percent in 1995 (Lee and Lee, 2004).

Samsung pioneered the development of Code Division Multiple Access (CDMA) cellular phones through early investment in CDMA technology. The emerging CDMA technology had the advantage of high efficiency in frequency utilization and better quality in voice transmission, and was designated as a national R&D project in 1989. Samsung participated in the R&D consortium with LG, Korea Telecom, Qualcomm, and ETRI (Electronics and Telecommunications Research Institute), and was able to produce most of the core chips required in CDMA phones. In 1996, it developed the first CDMA-based cellular phones with voice recognition features and captured more than 57 percent of the domestic CDMA cellular phone market. It expanded into the global market by supplying CDMA phones to Sprint, a US telecom carrier, and developed customized phones for its network under the co-branded name "Sprint-Samsung." After this first export success, Samsung expanded into Hong Kong, Brazil and other emerging markets, capturing more than 50 percent of the global CDMA cellular market (ibid.).

Next, Samsung focused on the Global System for Mobile Communications (GSM) market, which accounted for more than 70 percent of the global cellular phone market. But the hurdle was quite significant, as the Big Three (Nokia, Motorola, and Ericsson) were well established in the market. To differentiate against its competitors, Samsung took the offensive and created new trends in mobile phones, instead of just following the industry leaders. For example, in 2002, it developed the world's first TFT-LCD phone with a unique folder-type design and, in 2007, it led the trend in camera function by introducing the world's first 350,000-pixel camera phone (Lim, 2009). In 2009, it introduced the world's first AMOLED screen-based full touch-screen phone, leading the global trend in user interface. In 2003, the company was ranked third in the world in terms of unit sales of mobile phones. In 2012, it overtook Nokia to become the world's largest vendor of mobile phones, with 25.1 percent market share worldwide.

Despite a late start in the smartphone market, Samsung overtook Apple in 2012 to become the world's largest smartphone manufacturer, capturing 30.4 percent of the global smartphone market, according to research firm Strategy Analytics. The company recorded a series of hits with its flagship models, the Galaxy S range of smartphones and Galaxy Note devices. It adopted Google's Android operating system and offered a variety of innovative models that appealed to a wide range of user segments and price points. It refreshed its product lines more quickly and efficiently than its competitors, delivering leading-edge features and larger screen sizes that appealed to consumers looking for an alternative to Apple's iPhone. Samsung's ability to produce its own key components, such as application processors, memory chips, display panels and batteries, through its vertically integrated structure and efficient supply chain, was considered a key competitive advantage in delivering new products faster and more efficiently than its competitors.

Samsung recognized the importance of design and introduced new models with eye-catching designs that created emotional bonds with consumers. In 1996, Chairman Lee emphasized the strategic importance of design by declaring the "Year of Design Revolution." The design organization was upgraded into the Corporate Design Center which reported directly to the CEO. Foreign consultants were hired to provide training and stimulate creative thinking about design concepts. Designers were empowered to participate in the entire product development process and play a central role in the formulation of product/market strategies. The company established an international design network in the world's major cities including Milan, London, Tokyo, Shanghai, San Francisco and Los Angeles to monitor the latest design trends and develop customized designs for international markets reflecting local tastes and life-styles (Freeze and Chung, 2008). Since 2006, Samsung has won more than 300 design awards from internationally recognized institutions such as the Industrial Design Excellence Awards (IDEA) and iF (International Forum).

Samsung's global marketing and brand-building initiatives helped improve the company's image as a high-tech, innovative company. To unify its marketing communications globally, it consolidated its advertising under one agency, and launched a series of corporate branding campaigns such as "Samsung DigitAll, Everyone's Invited," positioning the company as a leader in the digital convergence era. To market its new mobile phones, it held global launch events in three continents simultaneously and aroused the curiosity of mobile phone users through innovative pre-release marketing on its website (Lim, 2009). Samsung effectively used Olympic sponsorships and sports marketing to build its global brand. In 1996, Chairman Lee was selected as an International Olympic Committee (IOC) member, and since the 1998 Nagato Winter Olympics, Samsung has been an official sponsor of the Olympics in the wireless communications category. Samsung has also been active in supporting sporting events such as the LPGA (Ladies Professional

Golf Association) and Chelsea Football Club in the English Premier League. It developed a high-end luxury phone in collaboration with fashion designer Giorgio Armani and a premium music phone with Bang & Olufsen. Samsung's premium market positioning allowed the company to command a price premium and helped raise its brand image. In 2005, Samsung surpassed Sony to become the 20th ranked global brand as measured by Interbrand. In 2012, it moved to ninth place with an estimated brand value of US$32.9 billion.

Shedding resources through corporate restructuring is another way of exercising dynamic capability (Eisenhardt and Martin, 2000; Danneels, 2010). In 1997, Samsung's financial situation deteriorated as a result of the huge decline in the price of memory chips and the onset of the Asian financial crisis. The net profits of the company decreased from US$2.8 billion in 1995 to US$87 million in 1997. Chairman Lee viewed the crisis as an opportunity to improve competitiveness and accelerate change. In 1998, Samsung launched a bold restructuring initiative aimed at rationalizing its business portfolio, streamlining costs and reducing debt. Some 47 marginal or unprofitable businesses were divested or spun-off to generate cash flow. More than 30 percent of the workforce was laid off through early retirements, spin-offs and outsourcing arrangements. Process innovation was systematically implemented to streamline overheads and administrative costs, reduce inventory and account receivables, and improve productivity. As a result of this total restructuring initiative, the company's net profits increased by 254 percent and the debt/equity ratio fell from 300 percent in 1997 to 85 percent in 2000 (Samsung Electronics, 2010). By divesting itself of underperforming resources through timely restructuring, Samsung was able to turn the crisis into an opportunity to improve its competitiveness and refocus on its core semiconductor, LCD and mobile phone businesses to achieve global market leadership.

As of 2013, Samsung Electronics was organized into four major businesses: Consumer Electronics, Information Technology & Mobile Communications, Semiconductors, and Display Panels. The company had a well-balanced business portfolio in terms of growth and profitability, and maintained a strong synergistic relationship among the businesses in line with the company's vision of digital convergence. In 2012, the company had a global network of 24 research and development centers, invested about 5.9 percent of its revenues in R&D, and registered a total of 5,081 patents in the USA, ranking second after IBM on the list of top US patent assignees.

Despite the remarkable growth and transformation of Samsung Electronics, Chairman Lee is constantly worried about the future. He believes Samsung cannot afford to rest on its laurels since most of its businesses today will become obsolete within ten years. In 2009, the company developed a new vision for the future with the goal of reaching US$400 billion in revenues by 2020 and becoming one of the top five global brands. It will develop new growth engines by investing US$20 billion in new businesses such as solar cell, electric vehicle batteries, LED, biopharmaceuticals and medical equipment. Whether Samsung can achieve the new vision and sustain its global leadership remains to be seen, but Chairman Lee's constant vigilance and perpetual sense of crisis have been a key driver of its dynamic capabilities by creating a culture of relentless innovation and change.

Conclusion

This chapter has examined the successful growth and transformation of Samsung Electronics and how it has achieved global leadership by exercising various modes of dynamic capabilities. It highlighted the importance of entrepreneurial insights and bold investment, rapid technology catch-up through dynamic learning and resource leverage, and relentless innovation to achieve global market leadership as key drivers of Samsung's success. The following summarizes the key findings and insights from this case study.

First, top management's entrepreneurial insights and bold investment decisions play a critical role in the development of a firm's dynamic capabilities. In the case of Samsung, its founder/Chairman, Lee Byung-Chul was able to recognize and seize the opportunities in the semiconductor industry by developing insights into market trends and government policies, benchmarking Japanese companies and accurately assessing Samsung's capabilities and resource gap based on two feasibility studies. Chairman Lee Kun-Hee's deep insights and commitment to the semiconductor business enabled Samsung to invest heavily in economic downturns and reap the benefits in the long term. Such bold investments were possible due to the leader's strong commitment and entrepreneurial insights, and a corporate governance system which enabled a long-term investment horizon and rapid decision-making by top management.

Second, the Samsung case shows that it is possible for a late-mover to catch up and leapfrog established competitors through dynamic learning and resource leverage. Samsung was able to rapidly catch up with established competitors by leveraging external sources of technologies through multiple channels such as joint ventures, acquisitions, technology licensing, strategic alliances, equipment suppliers, consultants, as well as large-scale investment in R&D, production and people development. Having achieved global market leadership in DRAM, Samsung leveraged its resources and capabilities to enter related businesses, such as flash memory, LCDs and mobile phones. In both the flash memory and LCD businesses, it was able to achieve global leadership quickly by sharing and transferring technological capabilities, operational know-how and human resources from the established DRAM business.

Third, to achieve and sustain global market leadership, relentless innovation and a perpetual sense of crisis are needed throughout the organization. Stimulated by Chairman Lee's "New Management" initiative, Samsung's mobile phone business embarked on a major transformation and developed a series of world-class products through relentless innovation in technology, design and marketing, capturing the number one position in the global mobile phone and smartphone market. Samsung's ability to develop its own key components through its vertically integrated structure and efficient supply chain has been a key success factor in delivering a broad range of innovative smartphone models more quickly and efficiently than its competitors.

Fourth, shedding resources through timely corporate restructuring can be an effective way of exercising dynamic capabilities. Samsung viewed the Asian financial crisis of 1997 as an opportunity to improve its competitiveness and accelerate change. By releasing resources through timely restructuring, it was able to refocus on its core businesses and achieve global market leadership. Despite its remarkable success, Chairman Lee's constant vigilance and sense of insecurity about Samsung's future have been key drivers of its dynamic capabilities by creating a culture of continuous innovation and change.

This chapter has examined the growth and transformation of a Korean electronics company that has achieved global market leadership from the perspective of dynamic capabilities. Future research could analyze the key drivers of dynamic capabilities using large sample data and empirically test its relationship to firm performance. Case studies that compare and contrast the growth strategies and dynamic capabilities of innovative Asian companies would be another fruitful area for future research.

References

Chang, S.J. (2008) *Sony vs Samsung: The Inside Story of the Electronics Giants' Battle For Global Supremacy,* Singapore: John Wiley & Sons.

Chang, S.J. and Podolny, J. (2002) "Samsung Electronics' semiconductor division (A)," *Stanford Graduate School of Business Case,* IB-24A.

Cho, D.S., Kim, D.J. and Rhee, D.K. (1998) "Latecomer strategies: evidence from the semiconductor industry in Japan and Korea," *Organization Science,* 9(4): 489–505.

Danneels, E. (2010) "Trying to become a different type of company: dynamic capability at Smith Corona," *Strategic Management Journal,* 32: 1–31.

Eisenhardt, K.M. and Martin, J.A. (2000) "Dynamic capabilities: what are they?" *Strategic Management Journal,* 21: 1105–1121.

Electronics Industry 50-Year History Publishing Committee (2009) *The Miraculous Time,* 50, Seoul: The Electronics Newspaper (in Korean).

Freeze, K.J. and Chung, K.W. (2008) "Design strategy at Samsung Electronics: becoming a top-tier company," Design Management Institute Case Study, DM1021.

Harreld, J.B., O'Reilly, C.A. and Tushman, M.L. (2007) "Dynamic capabilities at IBM: driving strategy into action," *California Management Review,* 39(3): 21–43.

Khanna, K., Song, J. and Lee, K. (2011) "The paradox of Samsung's rise," *Harvard Business Review,* 89(7/8): 142–147.

Kim, L. (1997) "The dynamics of Samsung's technological learning in semiconductors," *California Management Review,* 39(3): 86–100.

Lee, B.Y. and Lee, S.J. (2004) "Case study of Samsung's mobile phone business," KDI School Working Paper, 04–11.

Lee, S.J. (2011) "Dynamic capabilities at Samsung Electronics: analysis of its growth strategy in semiconductors," KDI School Working Paper, 11–07.

Lim, T. (2009) "Samsung mobile phone beats recession," *SERI Quarterly,* October: 86–93.

McKern, B. and Tayan, B. (2009) "Samsung Electronics global flash memory market," Stanford Graduate School of Business Case, IB-70.

Mathews, J. (2002) "Competitive advantages of the latecomer firm: a resource-based account of industrial catch-up strategies," *Asia Pacific Journal of Management,* 19: 467–488.

Mathews, J. and Cho, D.S. (1999) "Combinative capabilities and organizational learning in latecomer firms: the case of the Korean semiconductor industry," *Journal of World Business,* 32(2): 139–156.

Michell, T. (2010) *Samsung Electronics and the Struggle for Leadership of the Electronics Industry,* Singapore: John Wiley & Sons.

Park, T.Y., Choung, J.Y. and Min, H.G. (2008) "The cross-industry spillover of technological capability: Korea's DRAM and TFT-LCD industries," *World Development,* 36(12): 2855–2873.

Samsung Electronics (1999) *Samsung Electronics 30-Year History,* Seoul: Samsung Electronics (in Korean).

Samsung Electronics (2010) *Samsung Electronics 40-Year History,* Seoul: Samsung Electronics (in Korean).

Shin, J.S. and Chang, S.W. (2006) *Anatomy of Samsung Semiconductor's Global Leadership,* Seoul: Samsung Economic Research Institute (in Korean).

Siegel, J. and Chang, J. (2009) "Samsung Electronics," Harvard Business School Case, 9–705–508.

Teece, D.J. (2007) "Explicating dynamic capabilities: the nature and microfoundations of (sustainable) enterprise performance," *Strategic Management Journal,* 28(13): 1319–1350.

Teece, D.J., Pisano, G. and Shuen, A. (1997) "Dynamic capabilities and strategic management," *Strategic Management Journal,* 18(7): 509–533.

Wang, C. and Ahmed, P. (2007) "Dynamic capabilities: a review and research agenda," *International Journal of Management Review,* 9(1): 31–51.

28

SM Entertainment and Soo Man Lee

John Lie and Ingyu Oh

Introduction

The phenomenal popularity of "Gangnam Style" in 2012—a number one hit in virtually every OECD country and the most watched YouTube video of all time as of 2013—laid to rest the prevailing skepticism regarding K-pop, a shorthand term for a new style of South Korean popular music (Lie, 2012). Although few could plausibly deny K-pop's appeal across Asia in the early 2010s, Psy's viral video demonstrated that the globalization of South Korean popular music may not be a pipe dream. Bracketing the question of global appeal, especially in North America and Europe, K-pop's penetration is indisputable not only in the neighboring countries of China, Japan, and Taiwan, but also across much of South-east Asia (Siegel and Chu, 2010). Before the late 1990s, the few South Korean singers with name recognition abroad cultivated markets with similar sensibilities and tastes: Japan and Taiwan. By the early 2010s, K-pop was an indelible presence, part and parcel of the larger South Korean popular cultural export called the Korean Wave (*Hallyu* in Korean) (Lie and Oh, 2012).

The South Korean music industry comprises virtually every imaginable genre in world music. European classical music retains a small but strong share. It is possible to find everything from jazz and blues to reggae and hip hop as well as Korean traditional music and "world music." Yet what defines the leading edge of the South Korean music industry is K-pop. It is in turn usually characterized by ensemble performance of attractive boy and girl groups, whose songs have catchy refrains (hooks) and signature dance moves. The proximate musical influences stem largely from African-American-dominated US pop music, especially dance pop and hip hop. Although K-pop is produced and promoted by numerous agencies, three groups—SM Entertainment, JYP Entertainment, and YG Entertainment—are dominant. In particular, SM Entertainment which produced and promoted perhaps the leading girl group (Girls' Generation) and the most popular boy band (Dong Bang Shin Ki or TVQX) remains something of a *primus inter pares.*

In this chapter we focus on SM Entertainment and its founder Soo Man Lee. It is a case study of entertainment entrepreneurship that reveals a great deal about contemporary South Korean political economy. It also suggests that it is much less a vision for the future but rather for the present that is a key to navigating successfully the changing fashion of pop music listeners.

Before K-pop

Soo Man Lee came of age in the 1970s, a time of turbulent political struggles in South Korea (Lie, 1998). Matriculating at the prestigious Kyungbock High School and Seoul National University, he spent much of his university years cultivating his musical interest rather than his professed major in agriculture. The prevalent musical genre among left-leaning, anti-government students was folk music, and Lee achieved modest success as a folk singer and also as a radio disc jockey. Running foul of the authoritarian regime, he pursued studies in Southern California from 1980.

Lee's time in Southern California coincided with a massive transformation of the US pop music industry. He became enamored of music videos in general and MTV in particular, and the indisputable star of the new medium was Michael Jackson and what came to be known as dance pop. Combining vocal prowess with dancing virtuosity, Jackson and other dance-pop stars, including Madonna, defined the era. Lee jettisoned his earlier infatuation with folk music and embraced the new, vibrant genre and the new technology (just as he shifted his studies from agriculture to computer science). His American interlude would provide the template for his future success.

It is not that South Korea did not have an inchoate form of dance pop in the 1970s (on South Korean popular music, see Lie, 2015). The rock star and impresario Shin Joong-hyun (aka Jacky Shin) had produced a number of dynamic young female singers who also danced, such as the Pearl Sisters and Kim Ch'u-ja. However, the dominant genre in South Korea then was "trot," a Japanese-influenced style of slow, often soulful, ballads. Just as the government censored trot music for being Japanese (to counter the suspicion that the regime was pro-Japanese, it proscribed Japanese cultural imports), it also banned rock and pop-rock music for being "immoral." It should be noted that the other popular genre at the time, folk, was also often suppressed for its putatively "communist" (anti-government) tendency. Consequently, the musical genres that dominated South Korea in the 1980s and beyond were the aforementioned trot and pop ballads, hardly the stuff of export.

Returning to Seoul in 1985, Lee sought to revive his career as a performer. Finding only limited success, he turned increasingly to the promotion and production of other pop-music performers. Yet in both endeavors Lee's time had clearly not arrived. South Korean musical tastes still yearned for trot and ballads, with very little demand for pop, rock, or dance pop. Critical in this regard was the underdevelopment of youth culture—both as a relatively independent demographic group and as a source of spending power. Had he ended his musical career in 1990, Lee would be remembered as a minor figure from the 1970s music scene.

The rise of the youth

Almost all the preconceptions about the South Korean music scene were overturned by the overnight success of Seo Taiji wa Aidul (Seo Taiji and the Boys) in 1992 (Lie, 2012). The group's debut single sold 1.7 million copies (the population of South Korea then was about 40 million). Incorporating rap, hip-hop, and break dancing, the group defined a new reality for South Korean popular music. Pop music in South Korea became almost contemporaneous with the trends in the United States. A new and rapidly growing slice of pop music consumers eagerly followed the South Korean renditions of the latest American style, such as rap and reggae, hip hop and techno pop. The ascent of Seo's group also signaled that South Korean youths were now a central player in the music market. By the early 1990s, South Korea had become a democratic and affluent society, with a growing middle class. Cultural liberalization and economic affluence arrived with the proliferation of inexpensive and private means of musical reproduction, such as portable listening devices from miniature radios to MP3 players. Young South Koreans had the means, both financial and technological, to become the dominant demographic in the pop music industry.

Lee was quick to seize on the opening suggested by Seo Taiji wa Aidul. The MTV revolution he had witnessed in Southern California in the early 1980s converged with his long-standing interest in Japanese pop music, especially in teen idols. At first, he sought to replicate the formula of Seo's group, recruiting Hyun Jin Young in a nightclub. Hyun was one among many Korean Americans who brought back the latest in music and dance in the United States to South Korea, emulating in his case the then popular Bobby Brown and his Rabbit dance. Hyun, though popular, failed to reach superstardom or to spawn immediate imitators.

In seeking a more mainstream and hence a more profitable niche, Lee then turned to producing boy bands. Backstreet Boys in the United States and Shonentai in Japan were extremely successful in the 1980s and Lee sought to replicate the formula—attractive boys who sing and dance well—in South Korea. His first act was H.O.T. Debuting in 1996, the group was a sensation. Following in its stead, Lee, who had incorporated the forbearer of SM Entertainment in 1995, quickly produced SES, SHINHWA, and other groups, almost all of which proved to be successful. These proto K-pop groups marked a new era in South Korean pop music in which largely single-sex groups sang and danced ensemble to a mixture of US pop music genres. Rather than employing South Korean names, the norm became to use Roman alphabet, usually English, names and words. In part, the change reflected the government's globalization policy in which English became a quasi-official language in some circles. In short, South Korean pop music became less Korean and more global (or American). Both in terms of music and extra-musical dimensions, South Koreans by the late 1990s had reached the global (largely American) standards. That is, South Korean pop music stars by 2000 did not sound (or seem) all that distinct from their counterparts in OECD countries.

The export imperative

The possibility of export was not planned. Unexpectedly H.O.T. attracted throngs of young fans not only in South Korea but also in China. Lee considers it the beginning of the Korean Wave (South Korean popular culture export), though the fan base remained restricted numerically and geographically. Be that as it may, the unintended popularity of H.O.T. in China brought to fore the very possibility of exporting South Korean popular culture. As we mentioned, few if any had anticipated that South Korean pop music would find receptive audiences beyond South Korea. Beyond the more traditional genres of trot, which was popular in Japan, the only other major exception was the "Madonna of South Korea," Kim Wan-son who had achieved limited fame in Taiwan in the late 1980s. However, what H.O.T. signified was by no means an exception but became very much a rule: other South Korean pop groups also found followings in China, Taiwan, and elsewhere from the late 1990s.

SM Entertainment pursued two distinct paths. First, it began to expand its operations to China and elsewhere, staging "SM Live in China" in December 2001. In this pathway, SM Entertainment largely exported performers and records as they were produced in South Korea. Second, and more ambitiously, Lee sought to crack the Japanese pop music market by recruiting and cultivating promising talent. The first major project was BoA, who spent a considerable time in Japan learning the language and mores and went on to register a number one hit in 2002. She may have been aided by the bonhomie generated by the joint hosting of the 2002 World Cup by Japan and South Korea. Yet the more salient factor is that BoA was presented as a J-pop (a new style of Japanese popular music that emerged in the late 1980s) star. Not only did she cultivate a Japanese look and manners, but she also spoke Japanese fluently. That is, she was to all intents and purposes a J-pop star who happened to hail from South Korea (which was not widely publicized). In effect, SM Entertainment pursued a strategy of localization. Following BoA's success, SM Entertainment released TVQX's (Toho Shinki in Japan) Japanese-language debut song in 2006. The group proved to be a sensational success, not only in Japan but also across East Asia.

In the early 2000s, SM Entertainment focused on cracking and cultivating the Japanese market. The reason is not difficult to fathom. However great the future potential of the Chinese market, its earnings were a fraction of what the Japanese market commanded. More significantly, the decision to export was not merely due to H.O.T.'s unexpected success or the foresight of Lee and other top decision-makers at SM Entertainment. Rather, SM Entertainment and the South Korean music industry in general experienced a potentially catastrophic crisis in the late 1990s. On the one hand, the Asian currency crisis hit South Korea as hard as the IMF crisis by 1997. The economic downturn was a profound shock to the music industry in particular and the South Korean economy in general. On the other hand, the more problematic for the long-term profitability was the introduction of mp3 players in 1996 and the ensuing digital revolution in music. Given the relatively weak copyright protection in South Korea, illegal downloading drastically cut CD sales. Export, in short, was the only plausible solution for the South Korean music industry to survive and thrive, aided by the South Korean penchant for export to solve economic problems.

Thus, SM Entertainment's turn to export was largely a reaction to the looming external constraints. In spite of the popularity of SM Entertainment's performers in China, its initial export effort to China was a disaster. Not only did the agency know little about the Chinese music industry but it was also unaware of China's notorious disregard for copyright protection. To rectify its misadventure in China, Lee hired Youngmin Kim, who was raised in Japan and spoke fluent Korean and Japanese, to work the Japanese market (Oh and Park, 2012). Japan was much more attractive because it not only possessed the world's second largest pop music market but also protected copyright.

There are other salient factors at work in the presumed profitability of the export market. We would be remiss to ignore the rapidly enriching North-east and South-east Asia, the post-Cold War relaxation of geopolitical tensions and the concomitant rise in regional trade and interaction, and the maturing of the South Korean popular music industry. Just like their counterparts in automobiles and semiconductors, South Koreans were beginning to produce globally competitive pop music products by the turn of the millennium. In this regard, it is important to stress the proliferation of foreign-trained professionals—musicians, composers, choreographers, and so on—and the ready availability of diasporic Koreans, especially Korean Japanese and Korean Americans. These twin sources of human capital propelled South Korean popular music to absorb readily the latest trends in the United States, Japan, and elsewhere, and to generate their own innovation. Finally, what proved fortuitous for SM Entertainment and other new companies in the mid to late 1990s was the progressive government's anti-monopolistic measures, which allowed smaller start-ups to thrive, rather than the large conglomerates that had dominated the South Korean economy. That is, a major entrepreneurial opening was created by the government's limit on the power of South Korean conglomerates, such as Samsung and Hyundai. To be sure, CJ Entertainment grew out of the Samsung Group to become the largest domestic entertainment company in South Korea but its focus has been on expanding its domestic market share.

The K-pop formula

The current modal K-pop is dance pop music, with considerable techno and hip hop influence, featuring same-sex groups. K-pop groups are usually idol groups that stress physical attractiveness and appeal to younger listeners. There are older genres and styles that survive, as well as solo performers, but in the early 2010s the acts that define K-pop within and outside South Korea are boy and girl groups, including SM Entertainment's Super Junior and Girls' Generation.

SM Entertainment is the largest and the best-known K-pop agency. Nonetheless, it was far from the first to seek export and external success or to incorporate the latest American rhythms and beats to South Korean pop music. Even in the creation of the K-pop formula, it is difficult to say that SM Entertainment has been the most innovative. Probably the first group to assemble all the elements of the early 2010s K-pop style—a hook or a catchy refrain and a signature dance move that goes with the lyrical hook—was the group Wonder Girls in 2007. This is the style that propelled the viral success of "Gangnam Style" in 2012. Yet what SM Entertainment does extremely well is to practice and perfect the formula. Whether we look at Super Junior or Girls' Generation, the formula is realized to near perfection.

The principal source of the perfectionist performance is the rigorous recruitment and training process. SM Entertainment selects the most promising youths and trains them for three to seven years. The training regime is nearly a total institution, especially toward the latter phase. Not only do the aspirants receive training in singing and dancing but also in languages (to be able to communicate with fans outside of South Korea) and other skills essential to pop stardom. The studio system that SM Entertainment and others have created is a veritable star factory, which has also received a great deal of negative publicity in the wake of several high-profile suicides and lawsuits (Oh and Park, 2012).

K-pop is predicated on an extreme division of labor. Although pop stars who compose their own songs and perform instruments do exist in South Korea, almost all K-pop stars focus on their singing and dancing. Every aspect of production is assigned to an in-house professional or outsourced to a major foreign expert. That is, SM Entertainment recruits and trains the stars but it also assembles a vast variety of constituent skills that go into the making of pop music stars and hits. For example, it works with about 400 composers and producers around the world. In short, it is explicitly a culture industry, a business dictated to making money by making music (Lie, 2012; Oh, forthcoming).

K-pop is notable not only for its distinctive production regime but also for its marketing. SM Entertainment has learned from the experiences of export-oriented conglomerates, such as Samsung and Hyundai, as they entered foreign markets. In part, the experiences and the knowledge are widely disseminated in South Korea via newspaper articles, social networks, and books and lectures. Heeding Hyundai's initial failure to crack the US market and its later success, SM Entertainment not only seeks to manufacture excellent products but also to rely on local business people. For example, it provides a favorable margin of profit to enlist local support and enthusiasm, which in turn leads to a favorable promotion for its performers. At the same time, SM Entertainment seeks to adapt K-pop groups. Girls' Generation, for example, includes members fluent in English, Japanese, and Chinese, in order to communicate with local fans. The group maintains different national and language websites, and routinely releases songs sung in Japanese. It also sustains fan groups across the world. As Lee put it, "We must fit talent to each market that demands different products." As noted, in addition to Soo Man Lee's extended stay in the United States, the CEO of SM Entertainment, Youngmin Kim, spent his childhood in Japan. Although indisputably South Korean in origin and identification, SM Entertainment and its peers operate as enterprises geared to the export-market. In so doing, the music is perhaps pan-Asian or even global in character but almost completely denuded of Korean cultural tradition (Lie, 2012).

SM Entertainment has embraced not only new trends but also new technology. SM Entertainment's CEO Youngmin Kim apparently noticed YouTube on the first iPhones marketed in Japan and seized on its potential to market its performers. Relying on free but transnational means of

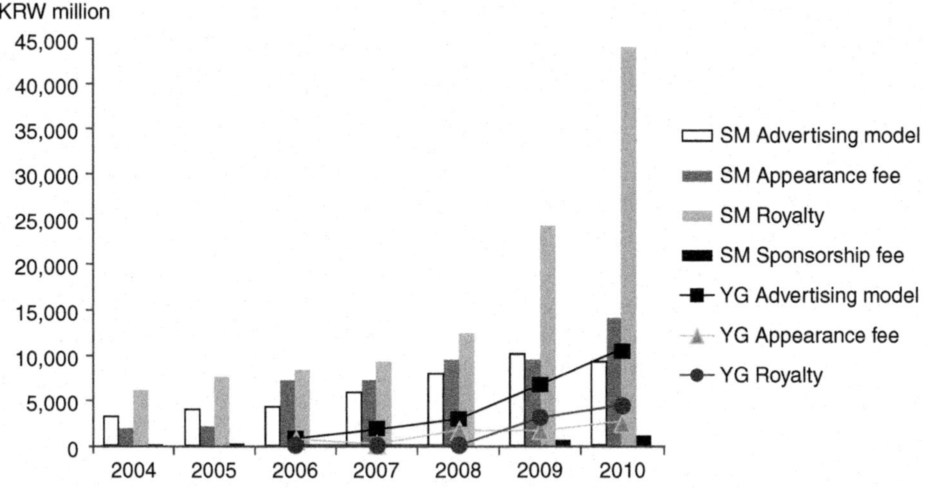

Figure 28.1 Rising royalty income (SM Entertainment)

Source: Oh and Park (2012).

advertising, SM Entertainment therefore banked on the aftermath of the MTV revolution that the founder Lee had witnessed first-hand in the early 1980s. Particularly noteworthy is the role of YouTube as a major source of revenue as it is about the only means by which royalty can be collected from countries where copyright protection is weak. SM Entertainment's attempts to be apprised of the latest global trends in pop music and different country's musical audiences and tastes, as well as keeping up with the newest technology, have allowed them to succeed where their Japanese counterparts in particular have failed.

Finally, K-pop is notable as a post-record pop music industry. Historically music promoters and record companies generated revenues from record sales above all, supplemented by royalty income and appearance fees. Figure 28.1 discloses not only the growing revenues of SM Entertainment and YG Entertainment (which promotes Psy) but also their increasing reliance on appearance fees. The K-pop business model was born of the catastrophic decline in record sales (largely due to the appearance of digitized music and the possibility of illegal downloading) and is therefore well-prepared to deal with emerging markets in which copyright protection remains lackluster.

Rethinking entrepreneurship

In business folklore, there is a tendency to celebrate the genius and the foresight of a successful entrepreneur. The perfect 20–20 hindsight allows a heroic and triumphant narrative. In the realm of economic theory, Joseph Schumpeter (1934) waxed poetic about the dynamic role of entrepreneurship in economic development. Yet these narratives and theories often exaggerate the foresight and the insight. Rather, the reality is more murky and complex.

In the case of Soo Man Lee, it was not so much that he had foresight but that he was at the right place at the right time. Although it would be easy to draw a straight line from the MTV Revolution and the dance pop turn he witnessed in the early 1980s to the YouTube Revolution and the rise of K-pop two decades later, he had in fact tried other genres and styles. It is not that he hit upon the boy band formula out of the blue but rather attempted something different before its limited success had turned him to try something that was explosively popular in the United States and Japan. He did not foresee H.O.T.'s success abroad. BoA and Toho Shinki (TVQX) were produced as J-pop acts, and not presented as K-pop. The current modal style of K-pop was created in conjunction or competition with other agencies and we cannot identify SM Entertainment as a pioneer in terms of music, dance, or even the very idea of exporting K-pop. In short, we cannot see heroic foresight or a simple line from the early 1980s to the present. Rather, his success owes a great deal to the fact that he was able to learn what was popular at the time and to seek to replicate it as a high-quality product.

Tracing each of the major shifts in Lee's career, rather than imposing his own vision, he made largely ad hoc and incremental decisions and changes. After all, he went to the United States to study agriculture and then computer science, not music or entrepreneurship. Yet he was able to transmogrify his study abroad into a successful career as a pop impresario. Here again it is important to stress that he did not insist on his newfound enthusiasm. When he sensed the time was ripe for a boy band or an idol group, he looked around—principally to the United States but also to Japan—for models and inspirations. Even then, his initial success in Japan owed more to his and his firm's ability to meet the current demand of the Japanese youth market. The eventual emergence of the current K-pop formula also rests less on his innovative and far-sighted conception and more on his willingness to make incremental improvements and to learn from his rivals and competitors. That is, he muddled through the messy reality of the popular music industry (cf. Hirschman and Lindblom, 1962). The messiness of muddling through does not deny the imperative of preparation, including the establishment of a star factory, and business savvy, especially in the realm of marketing and creativity outsourcing to the US and Europe.

Lee's entrepreneurial career is akin to riding the successive waves of pop music fashion. Like a good surfer, he had prepared meticulously even if the preparation was unplanned both in the long run (his long-standing interest in popular music and his exposure to the market leader, the United States and also Japan) as well as the short run (making adjustments based on the current reality). What is undoubtedly true is that he did not foresee the future but he apprehended the present. That is, he saw a wave or a fashion come when it did, and he was prepared to ride it. There is probably no golden rule for entrepreneurship, as in life, but surfing the wave is not a bad way to go.

References

Hirschman, A. and Lindblom, C.E. (1962) "Economic development, research and development, policy making," *Behavioral Science,* 7: 211–222.

Lie, J. (1998) *Han Unbound,* Stanford, CA: Stanford University Press.

Lie, J. (2012) "What is the K in K-pop?," *Korea Observer,* 43: 339–363.

Lie, J. (2015) *K-pop,* Berkeley: University of California Press.

Lie, J. and Oh, I. (2012) "Introduction," *Korea Observer,* 43: 333–337.

Oh, I. (forthcoming) "Mass media technologies and popular music genres: K-pop and YouTube," *Korea Journal.*

Oh, I. and Park, G.-S. (2012) "From B2C to B2B: selling Korean pop music in the age of new social media," *Korea Observer,* 43: 365–397.

Schumpeter, J.A. (1934) *The Theory of Economic Development,* Cambridge, MA: Harvard University Press.

Siegel, J. and Chu, Y.K. (2010) "The globalization of East Asian pop music," Harvard Business School Case Study 9–708–470.

Mainland China

29

Capability accumulation and the growth path of Lenovo

Zhongjuan Sun, Wei Xie, Kuanrong Tian and Yanyu Wang

Introduction

Lenovo Group is one of the leading IT companies in China and the second-largest PC provider in the world. Founded in 1984 by 11 computer scientists in Beijing, as the New Technology Developer Inc., it was soon renamed as Legend and started a new era of consumer PCs in China. In 2004, aspiring to expand its business globally with a more global-like brand, the company changed the brand name "Legend" to "Lenovo," taking "Le" from Legend, and adding "novo" the Latin word for "new," to reflect the spirit of innovation at the core of the company. The current CEO, Yang Yuanqing, joined Lenovo in 1989 as a salesman, and rose rapidly through its ranks to CEO in 2005. In less than three decades, with his predecessor, Liu Chuanzhi, Yang Yuanquing has spearheaded Lenovo's ascent to its current position (Kirkland and Orr, 2013). We will try to answer the question how Lenovo has achieved such a prominent success in less than three decades. In this chapter we draw on the concepts of entrepreneurship and capability accumulation to explain the competitive strategies adopted in the growth path of Lenovo.

Entrepreneurship has been perceived as an important factor in the creation and growth of firms (Kirzner, 1979; Shane and Venkataraman, 2000; Eckhardt and Shane, 2003; Langlois, 2007). In order to compete in a dynamic and ever-changing market, an entrepreneurial firm has to accumulate capabilities, which is usually defined as the capacity to recognize, conceive, create and exploit opportunities in order to generate competitive advantages (Mitchelmore and Jennifer, 2010; Jyotsna and Ananda, 2011; Zahra and Wright, 2011). The path of accumulation of entrepreneurial capabilities includes creation, integration and renewal. These three segments can operate separately, but also integrated as one unit. The creative capabilities include the ability of exploration and utilisation (March, 1991; Levinthal and March, 1993), such as developing new markets, innovating new technology, building organizational culture, constructing a management mode and establishing international operational ability. Integration capability means the integration of internal resources and external resources, accessing external resources requires valuable complementary resources (Harrison *et al.*, 2001). Renewal capability is defined as freeing inappropriate assets, building new thinking and bringing new resources from external sources to build new core competitive advantages (Danneels, 2002), such as creating markets for the new products, innovating new products and technology, building a new culture, constructing leadership capability, and adjusting international operations. The three capabilities influence each other, reflecting the coincidence of the timing and display pattern. Additionally, the three accumulation paths are dynamic and are improved, integrated, and reconstructed continuously.

The entrepreneurial act needs to have competitive strategies to cultivate its capabilities, and thereby to create competitive advantages. Unlike most high-tech companies, which begin with core proprietary technology and gradually develop downstream capabilities in manufacturing, marketing, sales and distribution, Lenovo followed a reverse development process from downstream to upstream (Xie and White, 2004). As a result, Lenovo first adopted market extension as the competitive strategy. Marketing capabilities have direct and complementary effects on both revenue and profit margin growth rates (Rust *et al.*, 2004; Morgan *et al.*, 2009) and sustained competitive advantages (e.g., Slotegraaf and Dickson, 2004; Vorhies and Morgan, 2005; Krasnikov and Jayachandran, 2008). After generating a large amount of capital, Lenovo shifted its focus on developing technology. Economic theory suggests that the performance outcomes relate to innovation. New technology may change the routine or use new systems. New technology can be an enabler of product or service innovations to offer a new service or to deliver products to customers in a way that is new to the enterprise (Koellinge, 2007). It is worth noting that a firm's competitive strategies can shift the focus and intensity of business activities while strategies are influenced by a firm's existing set of resources and capabilities. Dynamic capabilities stipulated by Teece *et al.* (1997) are further emphasized in a view of a world that is complex, changing, and uncertain. Therefore, to sustain competitive advantages, firms need to alter strategies to adapt to this ever-changing environment.

This chapter explores the entrepreneurial activities and the growth path of capabilities accumulation in Lenovo Group Limited. Lenovo began as a spin-off of a leading R&D institute in computer science. Lenovo followed a reverse development process from downstream (sales and distribution) to upstream (innovation) and its accumulation of dynamic capabilities is created through two key competitive strategies: market expansion and technology development. These strategies help generate competitive value, such as technology upgrading, market distribution, capital advantages and financial performance. We describe Lenovo's capabilities accumulation process in terms of three phases: (1) the distribution and sale phase (1984–1990); (2) the manufacturing and technology developing phase (1991–2004); and (3) the branding and global deployment phase (2005–present).

The rest of this chapter is structured as follows: the next section is the introduction to the Lenovo Group. Lenovo's development stages and capabilities accumulation paths are then presented, while the managerial implications are included in the next section. The final section offers the conclusion.

The Lenovo Group

Lenovo is a US$30 billion technology company and the world's second-largest PC vendor (official website of Lenovo: www.lenovo.com/). They have more than 30,000 employees in more than 60 countries, serving customers in more than 160 countries. Lenovo was founded in Beijing and incorporated in Hong Kong under its previous name, Legend. The company begins by distributing and installing PCs produced by foreign manufacturers before expanding into own production of PCs and launching its own PC brand. In 1988, Lenovo (called Legend before 2004) received the highest National Science-Technology Progress Award in China for its invention of a Chinese-character computer input device. Lenovo now is the largest PC company in China. Table 29.1 documents the critical events in the growth pathway of Lenovo.

Table 29.1 Critical events in Lenovo's history

Year	*Events*
1984	Established in 1984 as ICT Co., a government-funded R&D institute under the Chinese Academy of Sciences
1987	Became a distributor for AST, and later for HP and other foreign branded PCs
1988	Established Hong Kong Computer Group, a joint venture with a Hong Kong partner to produce PC motherboards and add-on cards and operated a trading business
1989	Renamed as Legend Group Co.
1990	Legend changed its role from that of an agent for imported computer products to that of a producer and seller of its own branded computer products
1993	Became the largest local PC manufacturer in China, behind AST and Compaq
1996	Legend became the market share leader in China for the first time and controls over 30% of the country's market share
1998	Legend establishes the first Legend Shop
1999	Legend became the first Chinese PC manufacturer to be the top seller (by units) in the Asia-Pacific region (excluding Japan) and heads the Chinese national Top 100 Electronic Enterprises ranking
2000	Legend becomes a constituent stock of the Hang Seng Index-HK. Legend ranked in top 10 of world's best managed PC vendors.
2001	Legend successfully spun off Digital China Co. Ltd, which is separately listed on the Hong Kong Stock Exchange
2002	Changed its English name from Legend Holdings Limited to Legend Group Limited
2004	Changed its English name from Legend to Lenovo. Lenovo decided to develop the rural market
2005	Lenovo completed the acquisition of IBM's Personal Computer Division and became the third-largest personal computer company in the world
2006	The first Lenovo-branded products outside of China debut worldwide
2007	Lenovo became the partner of the 2008 Olympic Games in Beijing
2008	Lenovo entered the worldwide consumer PC market with new Idea brand
2009	Lenovo led PC industry in using recycled material
2010	Lenovo achieved its highest ever worldwide market share and became the world's fastest growing major PC manufacturer
2011	Forbes names Lenovo one of the world's "100 Most Reputable Companies"
2012	Lenovo became the world second-biggest PC manufacturing firm

Sources: Lenovo official website and Xie and White (2004).

In 1994, Lenovo became a public company, listed on the Hong Kong Stock Exchange. In 1997, it overtook both IBM and Compaq as the leading PC supplier in China, and since then has remained in first place and expanded its share to over one-third of the Chinese market since 2012 (see the market shares of the top four PC manufacturers in China in Table 29.2).

Legend Holdings changed its name to Lenovo in 2004 and, in 2005, acquired the former Personal Computer Division of IBM. For 8 years from 2005 to 2012, Lenovo enjoys faster growth in PC sales than its competitors. Its PC market share rose to 14.8 percent from 6.9 percent globally (see Figure 29.1). In 2012, Lenovo became the world's second-largest personal computer vendor by unit sales.

Table 29.2 Market shares of top four PC manufacturers in China (%)

Rank	*1992*	*1996*	*1997*	*1998*	*2002*	*2006*	*2011*	*2012*
1	AST (26.9)	COMPAQ (9.2)	Lenovo (10.7)	Lenovo (21.5)	Lenovo (27.3)	Lenovo (27.6)	Lenovo (29.5)	Lenovo (35.5)
2	COMPAQ (18.5)	IBM (6.9)	IBM (7.5)	IBM (6.2)	IBM (9)	Founder (13%)	Acer (10.9)	Acer (9.5)
3	Greatwall (11.2)	Lenovo (6.9)	COMPAQ (6.7)	Founder (5.9)	Founder (5)	HP (9)	Dell (10.4)	Dell (9.4)
4	IBM (5.2)	HP (6.7)	HP (6.5)	HP (5.6)	Dell (5)	Dell (9)	HP (8.5)	HP (5.3)

Sources: Xie and White (2004) and public information.

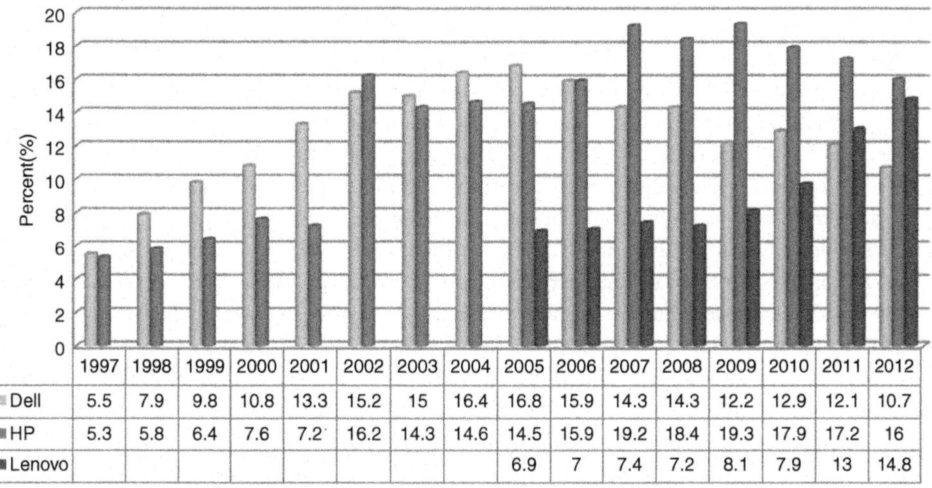

	1997	1998	1999	2000	2001	2002	2003	2004	2005	2006	2007	2008	2009	2010	2011	2012
Dell	5.5	7.9	9.8	10.8	13.3	15.2	15	16.4	16.8	15.9	14.3	14.3	12.2	12.9	12.1	10.7
HP	5.3	5.8	6.4	7.6	7.2	16.2	14.3	14.6	14.5	15.9	19.2	18.4	19.3	17.9	17.2	16
Lenovo									6.9	7	7.4	7.2	8.1	7.9	13	14.8

Figure 29.1 Global PC market share by units, 1997–2012

Sources: Lenovo's official website, public information and annual report.

Development stages and capability accumulation

Rather than beginning with core proprietary technology and gradually developing downstream capabilities in manufacturing, marketing, sales and distribution, Lenovo followed a reverse development process from downstream (sales and distribution) to upstream (innovation) (Xie and White, 2004). This section describes this process in terms of three phases that include the initial stage of distribution and sale (1984–1990), the ensuing manufacturing and technology developing stage (1991–2004), and the third stage of branding and global deployment (2005–present). At each stage, we link changes in the market and technology activities to Lenovo's resources and capabilities accumulation as competitive strategies.

Distribution and sale phase (1984–1990)

Competitive strategies

During the 1980s, second-tier foreign producers, such as California-based AST Research, occupied the leading market shares, because PC sales in China were negligible. From 1987, Legend expanded its activities to trade and distribution and became the first distributor for AST (the leading foreign brand in China at that time). These activities soon became its primary source of revenue, and also generated capital that Lenovo invested in a joint venture in Hong Kong to trade and then manufacturer motherboards and add-on cards.

Legend gained technology capability and market knowledge by trial-and-error before 1990. For instance, Lenovo tried to sell televisions and failed. However, Legend successfully developed Chinese-language computer input devices (the Legend Hanka-Chinese character card) in 1987 and established its key technology. In 1990, the first Legend PC was launched on the Chinese market. Legend completed its transition from an agent for imported computer products to a producer and seller of its own branded computer products. These events mark the start of the manufacturing and technology development phase of Lenovo (see Table 29.3).

Learning and capability development

Lenovo started as a distributor for AST (the leading foreign brand in China at that time), and then other foreign brands like Hewlett-Packard. By distributing foreign-made PCs, Lenovo accumulated a considerable amount of financial resources and marketing and distribution capabilities. The former CEO, Liu Chuanzhi, said "Our earliest and best teacher was Hewlett-Packard" (Gold *et al.*, 2001). Through these activities, Lenovo also began to build up its understanding of its Chinese customers and their PC purchasing habits. In the meantime, taking the opportunity as a distributor of Hewlett-Packard, Toshiba and IBM PCs at the early stage of production of its own Legend brand PC, enables Lenovo to closely scrutinize foreign products designs and customers' feedback. Lenovo made extensive efforts to create its national distribution network, which was extremely valuable to a manufacturer (see Figure 29.2). In 1990s, only the state-owned distribution organizations had distribution networks. The central planning system is responsible for fulfilling the State Planning Commission and relevant industrial bureaux's allocation directives for manufacturing inputs, intermediary products, and final goods. In contrast, Lenovo was geared towards its customers' needs, not the state's plan. Therefore, Lenovo could only survive by satisfying customers' needs.

Manufacturing and technology developing phase (1991–2004)

Competitive strategies

In 1990, Legend PC was launched on the domestic market. Legend became a publicly traded company after being listed on the Hong Kong Stock Exchange in 1994. Since 1997, Legend has overtaken both IBM and Compaq and became the leading PC supplier in China, and since then has remained in the leading position and expanded its Chinese market share to over one-third since 2012 (see Table 29.2). In 1998, Legend opened its first Legend exclusive store in Beijing, started its exclusive store system, and formed its domestic market strategy. In 1999, Legend became the top PC vendor in the Asia-Pacific region and heads the Chinese national Top 100 Electronic Enterprises ranking. At the end of this stage, Legend authorized 50 distributors in each of the seven regions, into which it divided the Chinese market, and each distributor had its own reseller network. Altogether, there were approximately 2,000 resellers in Lenovo's distribution system, in addition to Lenovo's 130 home-PC franchised store branded as "Lenovo 1+1." Lenovo identified the different market segments in terms of commercial use and personal use. Hence, the "Lenovo 1+1" home PC range is designed to satisfy the needs of the individual consumer. The "Lenovo 1+1" franchised store is set to offer services to personal customers. This system is known as the "Lenovo 1+1" retail network.

Table 29.3 The technology development of Lenovo

Year	*Events*
1987	Innovate Chinese-language computer input devices (Legend Hanka-Chinese character card)
1990	The very first Legend PC is launched on the market
1993	Legend Chinese-Western language graphic terminal on the market
1993	Legend enters the Pentium era, producing China's first "586" PC. Legend establishes 1+1 retail network
1995	Legend introduces the first Legend-brand server
1997	Legend signs an Intellectual Property agreement with Microsoft, the most valuable deal ever made in China at the time
1998	The millionth Legend PC comes off the production line. Intel Chairman Andy Grove attends the ceremony, and takes the PC for Intel's museum collection
1999	Legend launches pioneering Internet PC, with its "one-touch-to-the-net" feature, which enables millions of Chinese PC users to easily access the Internet
2001	Legend first introduces the "digital home" concept and launches accessories-enabling PC
2002	Legend Sureye intelligent monitoring and controlling system, Legend's DeepComp 1800, Legend Tianqi 9220 and Kaitian 680 on the market
2003	Legend successfully develops DeepComp 6800 in November 2003. It ranks 14th in the Top 500 list of the world's supercomputers
2004	Lenovo decides to develop the rural market by launching the "Yuanmeng" PC series designed for township home users
2005	Lenovo introduces the industry's thinnest, lightest and most secure Tablet PC, the ThinkPad X41 Tablet
	Lenovo introduces the first widescreen ThinkPad with embedded wireless WAN, the ThinkPad Z60, available for the first time with a titanium cover
2006	Lenovo introduces the first dual-core ThinkPad notebook PCs, improving productivity and extending battery life for up to 11 hours
	The first Lenovo-branded products outside of China debut worldwide
	Establishes Center of Excellence (COE) located in Singapore
2007	Lenovo introduces first EPEAT Gold Monitor with new visuals portfolio
	Microsoft China and Lenovo establish a joint innovation center in China
2008	Lenovo becomes the first PC manufacturer to announce a client virtualization platform
2009	Lenovo debuts Enhanced Experience for Windows 7, delivering significantly better performance for the new operating system
2010	Lenovo introduces LePhone, its first smartphone
2011	Lenovo forms Mobile Internet Digital Home (MIDH) business unit to attack growing opportunity in consumer devices such as smartphones, tablets and smart TV
2012	Lenovo acquires Stoneware, a software firm focused on cloud computing

Sources: Lenovo official website and public information.

Considering the development in technology between 1990 and 2000, Lenovo had to develop a large-scale and low-cost manufacturing capability to ensure its cost competitiveness in the face of the foreign and domestic fierce competition. In 1993, Legend entered the "Pentium Era," producing China's first "586" PC. Legend established the "1+1" retail network, and five years later, the millionth Legend PC came off the production line. Legend entered the stage with the capacity of mass production. In 2002, Legend launched its first technological innovation convention, "Legend World 2002," which opened its "Technology Era." In that year, Legend's R&D input reached CN¥800 million, more than double that of the previous

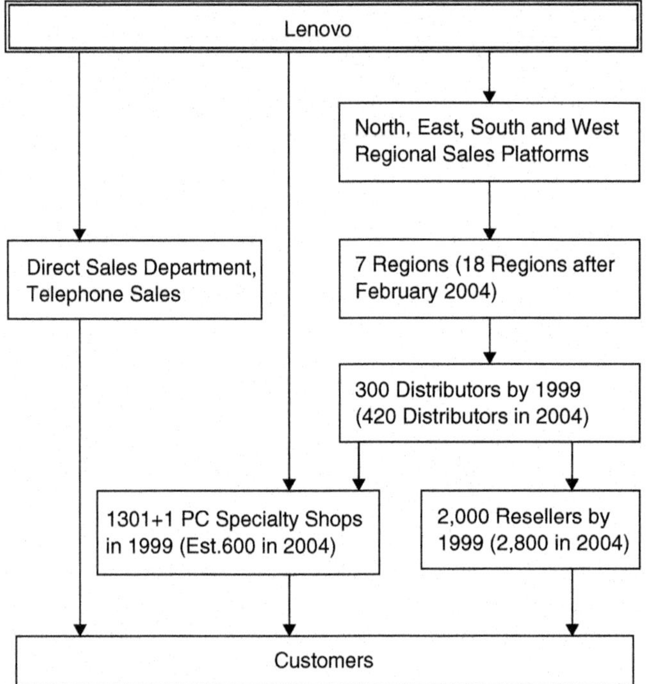

Figure 29.2 Lenovo's distribution network

Sources: Xie and White (2004) and the publicly available interviews of key decision-makers in Lenovo from newspapers and business magazines.

year. These funds were mainly invested in infrastructure construction, laboratory construction, wages of technicians, R&D of materials' input. What's more, Legend launched its Collaborating Applications project. Through cooperation with a few large companies and the Chinese Ministry of the Information Industry, Legend promoted the formation of the industrial standard in 2003. As a result, Legend innovated a series of new products that year, including Legend's DeepComp 1800, the Legend Sureye intelligent monitoring and controlling system, the Legend Tianqi 9220 and Kaitian 680. It is worth mentioning that Legend's supercomputer, the DeepComp 1800 is China's first computer with 1,000 GFLOP (floating point operations per second) and China's fastest computer for civilian use, ranked 43rd in the Top 500 list of the world's fastest computers.

Learning and capability development

At this stage, Lenovo adopted several important strategic approaches to satisfy customers' needs and to accumulate market knowledge. First, it offered Chinese customers PCs with the latest processors at a low price (*Business Week*, 1999). Lenovo offered leading technology specially tailored to Chinese customers (Gold *et al.*, 2001) by designing products for different market segments, different customer groups, and used different distribution channels based on its awareness of customer preferences and behaviours. The third element of Lenovo's strategy was to compete on the basis of price. For comparable products, Lenovo priced its products at about two-thirds of foreign-made PCs (*Wall Street Journal*, 1997). For example, in August 1996, Lenovo was selling its 75MHz Pentium-based PC for US$1,520, compared to similar models by AST and IBM selling for US$2,000 or more (*Upside*, 1996). During the period of expanding global markets, the acquisition of IBM's PC division marked an important step. Through this acquisition, Lenovo immediately gained IBM's sales channel and market.

Internal R&D is an important path of capability accumulation that supported Lenovo's cost-based and customer-focused strategy. Successful implementation of this strategy requires R&D activities that bring marketing, product design and engineering, and manufacturing together. Therefore, Lenovo has successively set up a two-tier research structure and three-point research centers in the manufacturing and technology developing phase. Lenovo's management has settled on a two-tier structure (see Figure 29.3) corresponding to what they term "technology for today" and "technology for tomorrow and the day after tomorrow."

The first tier, charged with developing today's technology for PCs, is located with the IT Business Cluster, which includes the server, notebook, consumer IT, commercial desktop and several other business units. These are served by more specific labs, for example, the Desktop PC Development Center based on five supporting labs that are responsible for parts and components, consumer systems, commercial systems, architecture and standards, and application software. These

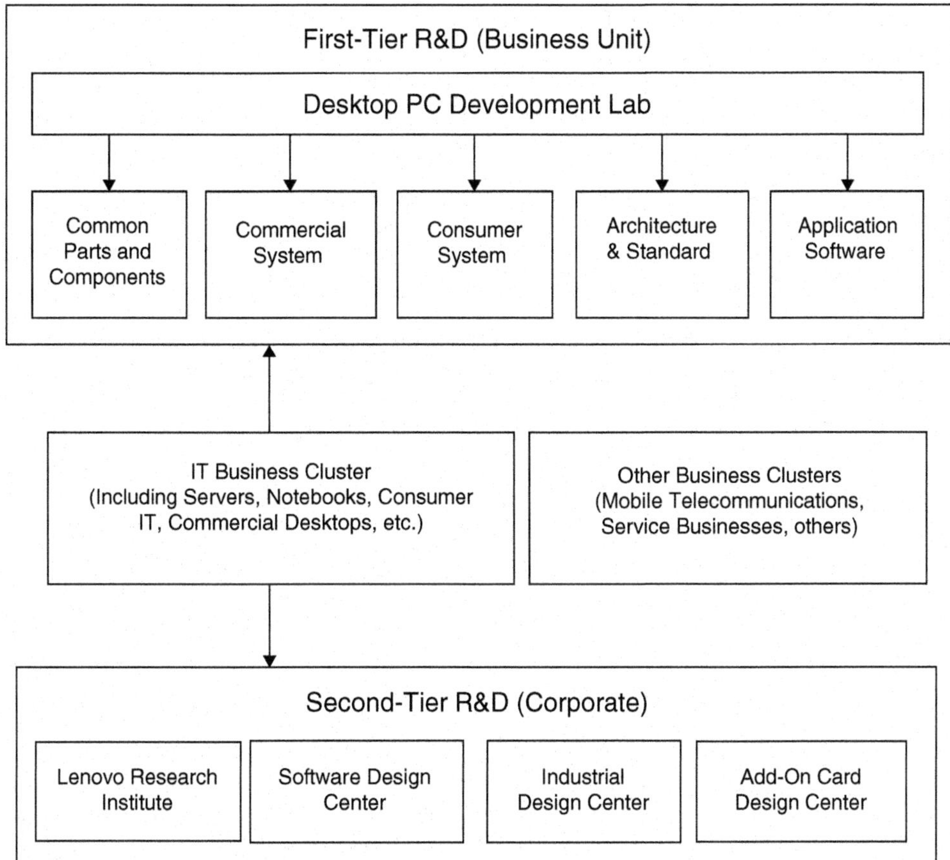

Figure 29.3 Lenovo's two-tier R&D organization structure

Source: Xie and White (2004).

labs are responsible for engineering systems and components based on needs identified in current operations, though in some cases they may subcontract research work to second-level R&D centers. In any case, these labs need to cooperate with the production engineering departments in Lenovo's three manufacturing plants, ensuring that their solutions are cost-effective to manufacture (interview with Mr. Yuhai Ou of Lenovo on 27 March 2004).

Second-tier R&D, under a deputy director, is corporate-level and includes four centers. The first, the Lenovo Research Institute, is at the heart of Lenovo's development of future key technologies. It focuses on coordinating applications, to develop the technologies and protocols that will make it possible to exploit opportunities for coordinating different information devices, including home appliances, telecommunications and computers. The other three centers are charged with developing technologies and platforms for all business units within Lenovo. The Software Design Center develops application software, the Industrial Design Center focuses on product appearance and attractiveness; and the Add-On Card Design Center develops motherboards and other parts and components to optimize the performance of Lenovo's products. These centers are designed to support the first-level R&D units, and relationships between the first- and second-tier centers are governed by internal contracting agreements. Because of the breadth of technologies and capabilities relevant for PCs, Lenovo recognizes that it must supplement internal R&D activities, especially those targeting the future, with cooperative activities with other firms. To this end, it has formed alliances with China Telecom, IBM, National Semiconductor and D-Link, among others. In August 2003, for example, it co-founded with Intel the Lenovo-Intel Future Technology Advancement Center. This center is charged with building reliable computation environments and key technologies for the next-generation Internet, and designing leading-edge products that fuse computers and telecommunications.

Branding and global deployment phase (2005–present)

Competitive strategies

In 2004, Legend announced the adoption of its new "Lenovo" logo in an bid for global expansion. In 2005, Lenovo completed the acquisition of IBM's Personal Computer division. This acquisition marked the official starting point for the company's global expansion. Lenovo entered into overseas markets, and integrated domestic and overseas markets accordingly by accessing the external resources. Through this process, Lenovo built up a strong presence in the international market. In the same year, Lenovo became the world's largest provider of biometric-enabled PCs by selling its one-millionth PC with an integrated fingerprint reader. Lenovo renewed its overseas market and business strategy, in such as the China regions covering Hong Kong and Taiwan from 2006. Russia and other 12 nearby countries were also included in 2007. On January 27, 2011, in order to boost Lenovo's Japanese sales share, Lenovo formed a joint venture with the Japanese electronics firm NEC to produce personal computers. At that time, NEC had 20 percent of the Japanese PC market, while Lenovo barely had 5 percent market share. In the same year, Lenovo acquired Medion, a German electronics manufacturing company and got 14 percent of the German computer market. Lenovo set up a new production factory and distribution center in the Legnica Special Economic Zone in Poland. With the integration of the business coverage, the international business layout was constructed. In 2012, Lenovo acquired the Brazil-based electronics company Digibras. From 2005, Lenovo started focusing on innovation, drawing internal and external resources together to speed up the technology upgrade. In particular, Lenovo paid attention to external sources, For example, after Lenovo acquired IBM's Personal Computing Division, Lenovo introduced a series of new technologies, including the industry's thinnest, lightest and most secure Tablet PC, the ThinkPad X41 Tablet, and the first widescreen ThinkPad with embedded wireless WAN, the ThinkPad Z60. Lenovo established a Center of Excellence (COE) located in Singapore, to develop advanced technology for international expansion in 2006. In the next year, Microsoft China and Lenovo set up a joint innovation center in China, initiating the new dimension for cooperation and innovation between enterprises. Lenovo maintained its lead position in technology innovation. Between 2008 and 2009, Lenovo sold and bought back the mobile business, and promoted the speedy growth of its mobile technology and business. As of 2009, the mobile division ranked third in terms of unit sales in China's mobile handset market. Lenovo invested CN¥100 million providing seed funding for mobile application development for its LeGarden online app store. As of 2010, LeGarden had more than 1,000 programs available for the LePhone. In May 2012, Lenovo announced an investment of US$793 million to construct a mobile phone manufacturing and R&D facility in Wuhan, China (Lee, 2012).

Learning and capability development

The speed of Lenovo's growth was accelerated by the acquisition of external distribution channels. In 2005, Lenovo smoothly entered the overseas market by acquiring IBM's Personal Computer division. This acquisition brought Lenovo US$10 billion potential sales per year (before acquisition, IBM PC sales were US$10 billion per year, see Figure 29.4) and improved both its branding and technology (Stephen, 2012). Another example is Lenovo EMC, a joint venture formed by Lenovo and EMC, offering network storage solutions. It offers a more robust range of products to serve small and medium-sized businesses than Lenovo previously offered.

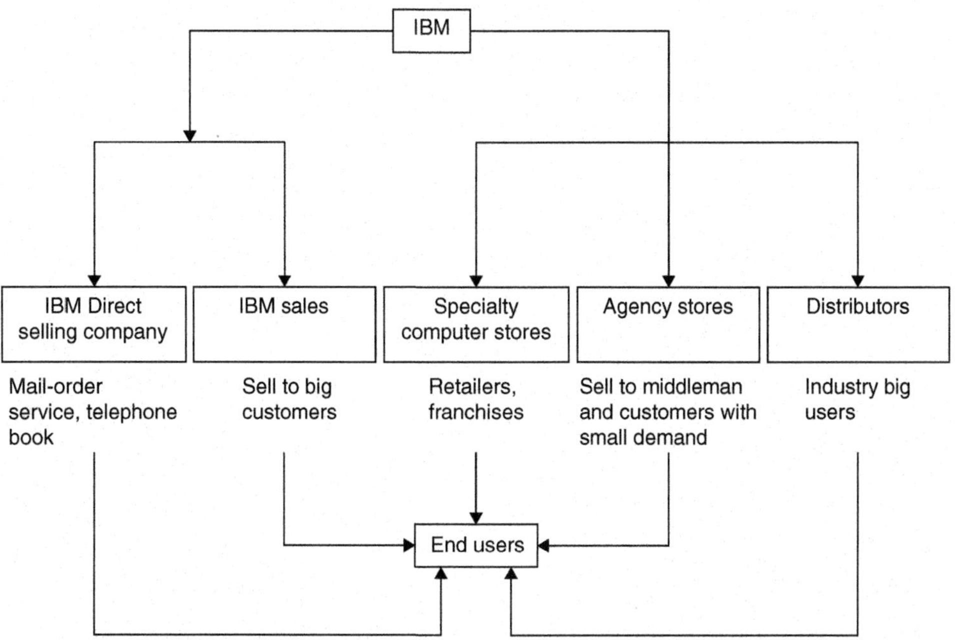

Figure 29.4 IBM's distribution channel

Sources: Lenovo official website and interviews of Lenovo's key decision-makers from newspapers and business magazines.

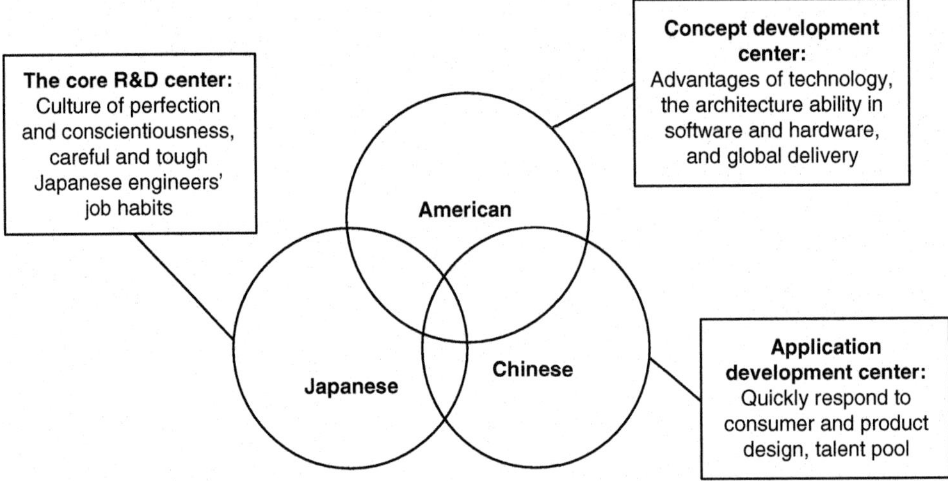

Figure 29.5 A global collaborative, efficient innovation system

Sources: Lenovo official website and the publicly available information from interviews of key decision-makers of Lenovo from newspapers and business magazines.

In 2005, Lenovo acquired IBM's PC business for US$1.25 billion. The takeover provided the company with American know-how to expand globally. The acquisition gave Lenovo's PC business a major boost. Liu Chuanzhi, former board chairman of Lenovo, said:

> We benefited in three ways from the IBM acquisition. We got the ThinkPad brand, IBM's more advanced PC manufacturing technology and the company's international resources, such as its global sales channels and operation teams. These three elements have shored up our sales revenue in the past several years.
>
> *(Zhou, 2012)*

Lenovo built a global collaborative, efficient innovation system after the purchase of IBM's PC division. In addition, three R&D centers in Japan, China and America helped Lenovo take full advantage of different capabilities to improve technology and productions invention (see Figure 29.5). This innovation system has created a series of new productions, such as the world's thinnest full-featured notebook in 2008. Research centers of software and hardware in the United States have strong research capabilities. The global research and development management system in the US research centers is well equipped for global operation. The Japan R&D center is good at compact notebook designing and manufacturing. The research center in China responds quickly to customer needs, and there are many talented team members to be allocated to future research projects.

Managerial implications

We now focus on market expansion and technology development as the main competitive strategies and in turn how they enhance the organizational capabilities. In a dynamic and complex market, demand and supply are constantly in flux, knowledge which used to be valuable could quickly be obsolete. As a result, in order to maintain competitive advantage, the firm needs to keep unlearning the outdated knowledge and learning new knowledge. Put differently, the firm needs to create, maintain and expand capabilities through relentless learning (Chandler, 1992). Lenovo's development history and the conceptual elements in the market and technology are worth learning for managers. In this section, we discuss some of the conceptual resources and capabilities accumulation paths in the process of Lenovo's development:

- *The reverse development process.* Lenovo represents the way in which a new entrant may challenge incumbents, especially foreign competitors, by developing resources and capabilities that are especially adapted to the local market. On the one hand, the payoffs of innovation activities are determined by the market process that involves not only the activities of the innovator, but also the reactions of the customers and competitors (Koellinge, 2007). Lenovo strives to maintain its market-focused product innovations that prove hard for domestic competitors to replicate. Lenovo has maintained this strategy as it has extended its capabilities into manufacturing and R&D, namely, a major objective of Lenovo's ongoing activities is to develop products that target specific customer segments. This clearly illustrates how the nature and direction of business activities evolve in the firm's accumulation of relevant resources and capabilities.
- *Leverage internal and external resources to raise capabilities.* The case of Lenovo also shows changes in the capabilities and domains in which a firm competes and also illustrates ways to acquire new resources and capabilities. Initially, Lenovo competed in a number of sales markets by selling other firms' products or technology. In recent years, even the largest innovative organization cannot rely solely on internal resources, they must also acquire knowledge and capability from external sources. Therefore, in the branding and global deployment phase, Lenovo gained external markets and technology capability through mergers and acquisitions, collaboration and joint R&D centers. After acquiring IBM's global PC and forming a strategic alliance with IBM, Lenovo integrated the skills from both sides and acquired a world-class distribution network with global reach, and R&D sources.
- *Relentless learning.* The customer is the first source of Lenovo's learning, with which it had direct contact through its extensive PC distribution network. Lenovo actively sought customer input for its product development activities. For instance, Lenovo incorporated six "hot keys" on the keyboard, so the users can access six of the most frequently used functions by clicking the "hot key." This implementation of a new design was based on customers' survey. This model proved to be a great success, and sold 900,000 units within a year of its launch (*Asia Week*, 2001). Experiences as a distributor of leading foreign brand computers were also valuable to Lenovo. Lenovo accessed first-hand data on customers' feedback and products' repair issues through this approach.

Conclusion and future research

Lenovo began as a spin-off of a leading R&D institute in computer science. Rather than beginning with core proprietary technology and gradually developing downstream capabilities in manufacturing, marketing, sales and distribution, Lenovo started business in distribution and sales by allocating its resources to the sales and customer services. The wealth accumulated through those activities helped fund Lenovo's development for the next phase as a manufacturer. Similarly, its experience in manufacturing not only generated revenues, but also provided insight for R&D opportunities. The transition of each development phase is associated with business opportunities and enabled Lenovo to compete directly with leading firms in the industry.

In this chapter, we have described this process in terms of three development phases to investigate Lenovo's progress. By focusing on the two competitive strategies of market expansion and technology innovation in each phase, this chapter explores the capabilities accumulation path of Lenovo Group Limited. As Lenovo became a global enterprise, its product lines have expanded from PCs to tablets and mobile devices. In order to outstrip its competitors, and to make three-pronged investments in manufacturing, marketing, and management, it is essential to exploit cost advantages from the economies of scale and scope, as Chandler (1992) suggested. In this chapter, we focus only on demonstrating two of these three-pronged investments in Lenovo, namely marketing (distribution) and production (technology). As Lenovo grows into a giant corporation with a global brand, the previous production-centric business model needs to change. Lenovo needs to change the mindset, as rightly asserted by Yang Yuanqing, "we must consider the whole package: hardware, software, services, and content" (Kirkland and Orr, 2013). The internal structure of the organization has to change in sync with the growth of the corporation. How to manage the organizational reengineering on its pathway of growth is equally important. Organizational change is a double-edged sword. It can establish a more focused business, and also it can unleash a backlash of unrest and rupture. How Lenovo manages its organizational change, such as dealing with cultural differences when merging with foreign companies, is a topic worth further study.

Acknowledgments

The research on which this chapter is based was financially supported by the National Natural Science Foundation of China (Research Project Reference: No. 71073092, No. 71372051 and No. 71121001) and British Academy Awards (Reference: SG122404).

References

Asia Week (2001) "The stuff of Lenovo," 25 May.

Business Week (1999) "How Lenovo lives up to its name," 5 February.

Chandler, A.D. (1992) "Organizational capabilities and the economic history of the industrial enterprise," *Journal of Economic Perspectives,* 6(3): 79–100.

Danneels, E. (2002)'The dynamics of product innovation and firm competences," *Strategic Management Journal,* 23(12): 1095–1121.

Eckhardt, J.T. and Shane, S.A. (2003) "Opportunities and entrepreneurship," *Journal of Management,* 29: 333–349.

Gold, A.H., Malhotra, A. and Segars, A.H. (2001) "Knowledge management: an organizational capabilities perspective," *Journal of Management Information Systems,* 18: 185–214.

Harrison, J.S., Hitt, M.A., Hoskisson, R.E. and Ireland, R.D. (2001) "Resource complementarity in business combinations: extending the logic to organizational alliances," *Journal of Management,* 27(6): 679–690.

Jyotsna, M. and Ananda, M. (2011) "Entrepreneurial drivers and entrepreneurial abilities: a conceptual and integrative framework," *Competition Forum,* 9: 429–435.

Kirkland, R. and Orr, G. (2013) "Thriving in a'PC-plus' world: an interview with Lenovo CEO Yang Yuanqing," *McKinsey Quarterly,* 6: 1–7.

Kirzner, I.M. (1979) *Perception, Opportunity and Profit,* Chicago: University of Chicago Press.

Koellinge, P. (2007) "Why are some entrepreneurs more innovative than others?," *Small Business Economics,* 31: 21–37.

Krasnikov, A. and Jayachandran, S. (2008) "The relative impact of marketing, research-and-development and operations capabilities on firm performance," *Journal of Marketing,* 72: 1–11.

Langlois, R.N. (2007) "The entrepreneurial theory of the firm and the theory of the entrepreneurial firm," *Journal of Management Studies,* 44: 1107–1134.

Lee, M.,(2012) "Lenovo to launch mobile devices facility in Central China," Reuters, www.reuters.com. Retrieved 7 May.

Levinthal, D.A. and March, J.G. (1993) "The myopia of learning," *Strategic Management Journal,* 14(S2): 95–112.

March, J.G. (1991) "Exploration and exploitation in organizational learning," *Organization Science,* 2(1): 71–87.

Mitchelmore, S. and Jennifer, R. (2010) "Entrepreneurial competencies: a literature review and development agenda," *International Journal of Entrepreneurial Behaviour & Research,* 16: 92–111.

Morgan, N.A., Vorhies, D.W. and Mason, C.H. (2009) "Market orientation, marketing capabilities, and firm performance," *Strategic Management Journal,* 30: 909–920.

Rust, R.T., Ambler, T., Carpenter, G.S., Kumar, V. and Srivastava, R.K. (2004) "Measuring marketing productivity: current knowledge and future directions," *Journal of Marketing,* 68:76–89.

Shane, S. and Venkataraman, S. (2000) "The promise of entrepreneurship as a field of research," *Academy of Management Review,* 25: 217–226.

Slotegraaf, R.J. and Dickson, P.R. (2004) "The paradox of a marketing planning capability," *Journal of the Academy of Marketing Science,* 32: 371–385.

Stephen, C. (2012) "China's Lenovo may be one-off success," *Market Watch,* www.marketwatch.com/story/chinas-lenovo-may-be-one-off-success-2012-18-19. Retrieved 20 August.

Teece, D.J., Pisano, G. and Shuen, A. (1997) "Dynamic capabilities and strategic management," *Strategic Management Journal,* 18(7): 509–533.

Upside (1996) "China enters the computer age," August.

Vorhies, D.W. and Morgan, N.A. (2005) "Benchmarking marketing capabilities for sustained competitive advantage," *Journal of Marketing,* 69: 80–94.

Wall Street Journal (1997) "China's personal-computer industry is starting to beat out U.S. companies," 19 November.

Xie, W. and White, S. (2004) "Sequential learning in a Chinese spin-off: the case of Lenovo Group Limited," *R&D Management,* 34: 407–422.

Zahra, S.A. and Wright, M. (2011) "Enterpreneurship's next act," *Academy Management Perspective,* 25(4): 67–83.

Zhou, X.Y. (2012) "Lenovo, on top of the PC World," *People's Daily,* 19 November.

30

Zong Qinghou and the Wahaha Group

Fangqi Xu and William R. Nash

Introduction

The Wahaha Group is the number one maker of soft drinks in China and was founded by Zong Qinghou in 1987. Wahaha did not have any capital for business registration at the time. Thus, they borrowed 140,000 RMB (about US$22,000) from the local government agency for registration and started their business of consignment sale. The main goods were notebooks, pencils, and ice-lollies.

The Wahaha Group has experienced prodigious expansion and reported a sales volume of 63.6 billion RMB (US$10.09 billion) in 2012 and continuously kept its position in China. How did the company achieve its growth so rapidly? This chapter attempts to answer that question and was written based on literature research and an interview with Zong. The authors conclude and explain Wahaha's success from the perspective of management innovation, including innovations of product development, marketing, and managerial methods.

Who is Zong Qinghou?

Zong's family

Zong Qinghou was born in 1945 in a house on East Street in Suqian City, Jiangsu Province, China. Several years later, he had one younger brother and three younger sisters.

According to Zong's genealogy, a great man named Zong Ze was his ancestor in the eleventh century. He was Governor of Kaifeng, which is thought to be one of the seven ancient capitals of China. Since he achieved many military exploits in the fight against the invasion of a counter-attacking northern nation, he became a national hero. Regarding his ancestry, Zong Qinghou is the direct descendant of the 36th generation of Zong Ze. From Zong Ze through Zong Qinghou's father, there were many government positions held by members of the clan. Thus, Zong Qinhou is a descendant of a noble family.

However, such a family did not provide Zong Qinghou with any honor or help. In fact, this family name gave him much difficulty. After the birth of socialist China, the family background of the workers, poor peasants and the People's Liberation Army were regarded as the "red family," while those born in families of landlords, rich peasants, capitalists and the

Kuomintang (KMT) soldiers were considered the "black family." A person who was born in the "red family" received help from the government for education and employment, while someone born in the "black family" did not receive any help from the government for those activities. Zong Qinghou's father was a servant of the old regime. Needless to say, he belonged to a "black family," and that was the source of considerable hardship when Zong was young.

Zong's early career

Since Zong Qinghou was born in a "black family," he lived a hard life and did not eat three meals a day from an early age. After graduating from middle school, he wanted to attend a normal school that did not require payment of any fees for tuition, meals and accommodations. However, he was refused entry to the school on the grounds that he was born in the "black family." He choked back tears and decided to work outside the home, because he did not want to increase the financial burden on his family. He was 16 years old, and he worked at various menial jobs for about two years. Whether repairing a car, carrying a large bag, or a sizeable container of popcorn, he did any work he could find. This was during the beginning of the era of the planned economy and included three consecutive years of natural disasters, and the lives of the people were marked by great poverty. Thus, it was impossible to save a little money as a part-time worker.

In 1963, when Zhoushan Mamu Fisheries, a state-owned company, started recruiting in Hangzhou, Zong was attracted by the posters and applied for a position and did not talk about his parents, since he wanted to escape from his painful life. However, once he entered the fisheries, he discovered it was a reform-through-labor farm, but it was too late to get out of it. The so-called reform-through-labor farm was actually a camp of people who were assigned there based on convictions for political reasons. These camps mainly imposed hard labor, such as the development of farmland and creating landfills. Zong was not a prisoner, but he did the same work as those who were. Moreover, his remuneration was unbelievably low. For example, he pulled a large flatbed tricycle with 500 kg of soil to a place that involved a 15 km round trip and received only 0.15 RMB (about 93 cents, US$1 equivalent to about 6.3 RMB). While engaged in the heavy labor, he did not give up, but worked harder than many others.

In 1966, the so-called Great Cultural Revolution began, and China fell immediately into disarray. Many held a naïve hope that they could leave the rural areas somehow, if they worked hard enough, but they ended up very sad, because their hopes were dashed. Zong did not, as he looked at the situation around him dispassionately. Of course, he did not know whether or not he could leave the rural area and go back to his hometown.

In 1976, after more than 10 years, the Great Cultural Revolution finally was over. In order to resume production, the city's labor shortage became a growing problem, so the Chinese Government began to implement a new policy of decentralization by allowing young people to move back to their hometowns. Thanks to this policy, Zong was transferred to the family register of Hangzhou in his hometown after 15 years. In China, it was impossible for someone to freely move their household registration from a rural to an urban area.

When Zong looked back on his rural life of 15 years, he always said indifferently, "Because of the lot of trouble in the bottom layer of society, I trained my own willpower." What can we make of his words? Since he was born in a "black family," he was unable to control his destiny, but it is better to push forward than to look backward or to do nothing. The past was bitter, but Zong did not deny his experiences and thought of it as the basis of a future life, so he envisioned a happy future developing from a bitter past. This characteristic distinguishes Zong from many others.

Zong's business life

The Hangzhou Government started a policy called "Heir," in order to solve the problem of labor shortage in 1978. That is, if an old man or woman retired, his or her one child could enter the same organization and do the same work. As the result, a banker's son became a banker, a public official's daughter became a public official, and a cleaner's son became a cleaner. It was a very strange policy, but in its time, nobody thought of it as unfair, because his or her career depended on the occupation of their parents.

Zong Qinghou's mother was a teacher in a primary school, so he should have become a school teacher. But since he had only the educational background of middle school, he could not become a primary school teacher. Thus, he became a staff member at Hangzhou Gongnong Corrugated Paper, a small factory that had been established by the school. His daily routine was to visit customers and take orders. It was his first step as a salesman and also was the first point of contact with the market and customers. However, even today a company established by a primary school is not recognized in society, because its technology, quality, and credit are lacking. Therefore, one can imagine the difficulty of taking an order from customers 30 years ago. In the early stage, he did not get any orders when he visited customers. But he was not discouraged. He repeatedly visited the same customers and finally gained the trust of each one and gained orders. The joy of his first success became the foundation of his lifetime. He became a top salesman, because he knew the joy of the selling.

Since continuity of management was difficult, and the tempo of economic reform was accelerating, Hangzhou Gongnong Corrugated Paper Factory decided to introduce an operating contract system in the Spring of 1987. This so-called system is a method that involves paying predetermined profits to the factory, and any remaining income would become the salesman's remuneration. The factory held a meeting for the employees and announced the system. But the employees felt there was considerable risk, and nobody responded positively. As a last resort, the factory lowered the payment to 20,000 RMB, and Zong raised his hand and said in a loud voice, "Let me do it. I will pay 100,000 RMB first year!" Everyone thought he was stupid! In general, though, he saw the lowered payment as a clear advantage to him. Why did he claim he would pay five times the lowered payment? Zong saw things differently than other employees and thought of it as a big opportunity for him and took advantage of it, given his drive for success.

On May 1, 1987, a new sign was hung in the Qintai Street 160, announcing the Sales Department of Shangcheng Schools Factory. In fact, it was a small shop, but it is the origin of the Wahaha Group. Zong was appointed manager of the shop, and that year he was 42 years old.

Since the shop did not have any capital to apply for a business license, Zong borrowed 140,000 RMB (US$22,000) from the Shangcheng Education Office, and several years later, he repaid the debt. On the other hand, because Zong did not invest any of his own funds in this shop, it was recognized as a state-owned enterprise. Now Wahaha is a private enterprise, but it was a big problem when Zong wanted to change the company's character from a state-owned enterprise to a private enterprise.

Initially, the shop's main business was to sell pencils, note pads, soft drinks, and so on to students in the Shangcheng area. When orders came, Zong would deliver the products on his bicycle. He was the manager, but he had only two staff members who were retired teachers. His management position was really considered blue-collar. However, the small shop produced sales of 1.51 million RMB in just nine months. Zong received a net profit of 172,300 RMB, after paying the money owed to the factory. Zong laughed out loud for the first time.

The next year, Zong introduced a production line with 100,000 RMB and began to produce pollen nutrients. At the time, pollen nutrients were very popular in China, thus Zong also joined the boom. However, the rumor that the pollen nutrients contained an ingredient harmful to health was soon so widespread that Zong was forced to stop production. Zong was never one to be set back by temporary failure, and he started to look for his next product to sell. His observations in supermarkets and food shops led him to the realization that though pollen nutrients had disappeared, other nutritional supplements were being sold with adults as the target audience. It occurred to him that a nutritional supplement for children should be developed, and he took action immediately.

In order to procure professional advice, Zong visited Zhu Shoumin, who was a professor at Zhejiang Medical University and a nutritionist. Professor Zhu had been researching the nutritional status of children and was thinking about doing something, because the malnutrition in children was increasing since the government had implemented the policy of "one-child" families. For Professor Zhu, Zong's visit was an opportunity for industry–university cooperation. Professor Zhu described some of the conditions to Zong. Having a single child who is loved by both parents and grandparents resulted in pampering, and they overlooked the importance of a balanced diet from a nutritional standpoint. If someone were to develop a nutritional supplement that appealed to children's appetite, it might attract a large market. Zong was enlightened on the spot and realized the business chance. He invited Professor Zhu to serve as technical advisor, and he hired experts from Hangzhou Yu Qingtang, where the famous Chinese medicine maker of Yaoshan (the mixed product of Chinese medicine and food) originated, and he began the R&D on a children's nutritional supplement. Professor Zhu designed the product formula for Zong, and Zong developed the prototype bases for it. One year later, the first product was successful.

Zong's honors and worth

Zong has received many honors, not only from the Chinese government, but from other sources as well. Some examples in China are the "National Model Worker," "China Economic Person of the Year," "National Outstanding Entrepreneur," "China Business Master," "China Charity Award," and so on. However, the one that is most important to him is the Representative of the National People's Congress (NPC). Since being elected as Representative of the NPC for the first time in 2003, he has been elected three other times and travels to Beijing to attend the NPC Conference each year, and before each meeting, Zong always prepares proposals that are based on surveys focusing on industry or social problems. He presents his proposals at the conference. Overall, he has presented 11 motions, comments and proposals, including "A motion about improvement of trademark law," "A comment on *The Basic Housing Protection Ordinance (draft)*," which was a proposal for the government to provide economic housing to urban residents, and "A proposal about exempting the working-class from personal income tax," at the 2013 conference. Because his proposals are closely related to the interests of ordinary people, he was held in high esteem by both the mass media and the citizenry.

Of course, because of Zong's honors, his monetary worth always became a hot topic both in China and overseas. According to *Forbes*, Zong Qinghou was ranked the number one billionaire in mainland China in 2013. In fact, it was second time for him (see Table 30.1).

Zong has not been satisfied with his increase of wealth and wants to catch up with Li Ka-shing, who is the founder and chairman of Cheung Kong (Holdings) Limited, which is based in Hong Kong. He is considered the richest Chinese man in the world. Zong once said he created his wealth in 15 years, while Li Ka-shing created his in 20 years. This statement may make one recognize that Zong is viewed as someone who is the equivalent of extremely focused and hard-working ordinary people. In fact, in addition to his reading, drinking tea, and smoking, he has almost no other hobbies. For example, he never plays golf and does not enjoy attending banquets. This is obviously related to his simple habits that developed in his rural life of 15 years.

Table 30.1 Wealth ranking of Zong Qinghou in China, 2004–2013

Year	*Net worth*	*Rank in Mainland China*
2004	$157.0 million	58
2005	$192.0 million	64
2006	$119.0 million	213
2007	$1.9 billion	22
2008	$1.1 billion	63
2009	$2.4 billion	16
2010	$4.8 billion	3
2011	$7.0 billion	1
2012	$6.5 billion	5
2013	$11.6 billion	1

Source: Forbes.

What is Wahaha?

Wahaha's naming and logo

In 1988, Zong introduced a manufacturing line that produced a nutrient for children. He placed an advertisement in the *Hangzhou Daily* to identify a good name for his product. As a result of this endeavor, Zong chose the name of Wahaha. It means a laughing voice in Chinese and is known widely as the title of a children's song. Thus, Zong named the product the Wahaha Children's Nutrient and registered a series of trademarks (Luo, 2008). Because this product has an effect on the appetite, parents wanted their children to drink it, and the nutrient products became an instant hit. Zong then changed the company name to Hangzhou Wahaha Children's Nutrient in 1989, and it was the first unification of the name and the trademark (Zuo and Liu, 2008). However, the production facilities needed to expand, as market demand had been increasing every day. Thus, Zong searched for an opportunity for M&A.

At the same time, Hangzhou Canned Foods, which was a state-owned company, had been suffering from a deficit operation. It was a bigger company than Wahaha and was authorized by the Chinese Government as one of the exporters in the canned foods industry. Due to its failing operations, the Government of Hangzhou City decided to force the company to go bankrupt or be sold off. Zong decided to take over the company for the purchase price of 80 million RMB (US$12.6 million). In the end, it became one of the unusual cases of a small fish (Wahaha only had 200 employees) eating a big fish (Canned Foods had 2200 employees) in the business history of China. After that, the Wahaha Group was abbreviated to Wahaha and was officially born in 1991 (Zuo and Liu, 2008).

As indicated above, Wahaha's history was that of a state-owned company, but several years later, Zong and WAES (Wahaha Association of Employee Stock-ownership) bought a great deal of stock back from the Shangcheng District. Now, the composition of stock ownership is as follows: Shangcheng District has 46 percent; Zong, 29.8 percent; and WAES, 24.2 percent (F. Xu, personal communication, March 30, 2010). While the district is the largest stockholder, basically 54 percent is private holdings, while 46 percent is national capital. Also, Zong and WAES have established a number of companies thus far. Such companies do not include any government funds. Therefore, the Wahaha Group is now a private company.

Wahaha's trademark includes a boy's head, which not only shows his kindness and innocence, but also has the features of a naughty boy (see Figure 30.1). It suits the name Wahaha.

Figure 30.1 Wahaha's trademark
Source: Wahaha's homepage.

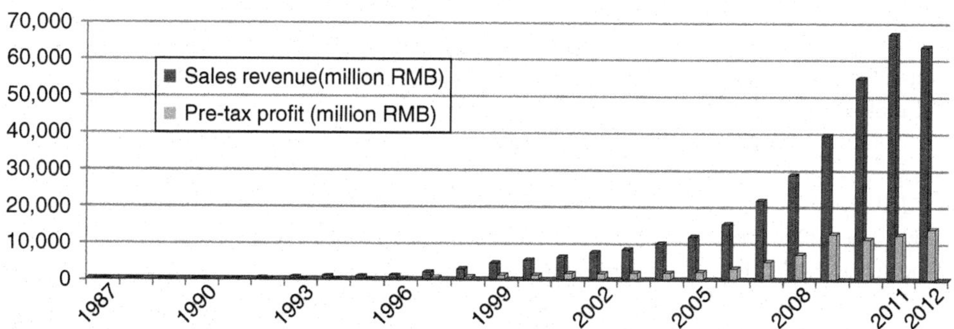

Figure 30.2 Trends in sales revenue and pre-tax profits of Wahaha
Source: F. Xu, personal communication with Zong Qinghou.

Wahaha's scale and achievements

Wahaha is the largest beverage maker in China. In fact, this record has been sustained for 14 years. Its sales revenue reached 63.6 billion RMB (US$10.09 billion) and pre-tax profit of 14 billion RMB (US$2.22 billion) in 2012. According to Figure 30.2, we know Wahaha's sales revenue decreased last year, but the pre-tax profit is still increasing.

Wahaha's products includes nutrients, canned foods, milk, drinking water, fruit juice, carbonated drinks, tea, plant drinks, sports drinks, fruit milk, milk powder, nutrition noodles, and so on.

In order to seek new profit growth, Wahaha entered the retail business and opened a shopping center in Hangzhou in November 2012. The shopping center was named WAOW Plaza, and was designed to sell European brands exclusively, including Castangia dal, GROC, Carmen Melero, ANNA, and the like. At the opening ceremony, Zong said he wanted to open 100 WAOW Plazas within five years in China (Sina net, 2012).

Wahaha's innovations

Wahaha's product development innovation

When Wahaha was a small company, it mainly targeted its competitors' goods and added some ideas for improvement. For example, a competitor developed a new milk drink, which became a hit. Wahaha added vitamin A and vitamin B to it and identified it as nourishing milk. In the end, Wahaha's sales volume was larger than the competitor's. In negative terms, we can basically think of it as "imitation." However, if the product involved only simple imitation, it would never have become a hit. Adding something to the product and including the popularity of the Wahaha name provided qualities that emphasized the notion of imitation with modification. Since this aspect of innovation built on a competitor's action, Zong called it "Following Type Innovation" (Xu, 2010).

When Wahaha became a medium sized company, it had been doing what was identified as "innovation by importation," including that of new technology and equipment. For example, when a competitor developed a mineral water from mountain springs and advertised the characteristics of natural water, Wahaha developed Chunjing Water by using the newest manufacturing facility and measurement instruments, and advertised the quality of the water. In Chinese, the word Chunjing means water that is pure and clean. Now Wahaha has the top consumer share of the water market in China. According to Zong, such innovation is "Import Type Innovation" (Xu, 2010).

In recent years, Wahaha has been doing "original innovation" by itself, indicating a desire to develop goods that do not yet exist in the world. "Nutri-Express," a mixture of fruit juice and milk, is a good example. This product has now become one of Wahaha's best sellers. The sales volume was 9 billion RMB (US$1.42 billion) in 2009. Zong explained such innovation is "Original Type Innovation" (Xu, 2010).

Underlying these three types of innovation are two basic characteristics of Wahaha product development. One involves starting from a simple case and gradually building up to higher levels of difficulty. The other focuses on meeting the demands of consumers, i.e., innovations do not always use high levels of technology, but always attempt to gratify their customers' thirst for new goods.

Wahaha's marketing innovation

There are many unique cases of Wahaha's marketing entry. In the middle of the 1980s, local makers entered the cola market one after another. There were many brands of cola in China, such as Tenfu Cola, Shaolin Cola, Happy Cola, etc. But once the two cola giants, Coca-Cola and PepsiCo, started to counter-attack, the local cola brands were soon driven out of the cola market. The same situation may be found in many countries around the world. Consumers naturally associate Coca-Cola and PepsiCo with the word "cola." In fact, for these two cola giants, there have not been many competitors anywhere, if any at all, who have achieved success without some sort of co-operator or partnership arrangement.

It was big news in China when Zong decided to enter the cola market. Everyone who knew the cola history opposed his decision, because Coca-Cola and PepsiCo seemed too powerful. But Zong did not alter his intention. His competitive strategy became that of "farm areas and small towns surrounding cities," which some might trace back to the thinking of Mao Zedong during China's guerrilla age (Wang, 2010). Mao was the first socialist president in China and implemented a "rural and small town" policy that reflected his strategic thinking. From a marketing and capitalist approach that developed in later years, this strategy might suggest that a new cola company should not try to compete initially with the Coca-Cola and PepsiCo giants in the big cities, but, rather, should focus on servicing the vast farm areas and small towns, and then attempt the big cities after building a consumer base in areas near the big cities.

Wahaha developed a cola with more Chinese characteristics, in order to meet the needs of customers who live in farm areas and small towns. For example, it was sweeter than general cola, and was initially offered at a price about 10 percent cheaper than Coca-Cola and PepsiCo.

Figure 30.3 Wahaha Future Cola
Source: Wahaha's homepage.

Promotion was started on a large scale through TV commercials, newspaper advertisements, and so on.

Through attentive supervision and mass promotion, Zong's strategy succeeded, contrary to a lot of expectations. Wahaha put its Future Cola (Figure 30.3) on sale in 1998, and it gained a 14 percent share of the cola market in China by 2001, although Coca-Cola and PepsiCo had 42 percent and 23 percent shares respectively in the same year (Bagchi, 2009). While this ratio has not changed greatly over subsequent years, it is still an indicator of Zong's vision and strategic planning.

Moreover, this innovative business venture demonstrates a very important concept of differentiation, which was developed by Professor Michael E. Porter of the Harvard Business School (Porter, 1980). If we interpret Wahaha's competitive strategy in terms of Porter's conceptualization, Wahaha's activities clearly demonstrated that they used a differentiation strategy. Concretely, their differentiation strategy included five factors:

1 *Differentiation of area.* Coca-Cola and PepsiCo focused on big cities, but Wahaha targeted farm areas and small towns, where about 70 percent of the Chinese people live, providing the potential of a very large market.
2 *Differentiation of customer.* Coca-Cola and PepsiCo appealed to white-collar customers living in bigger cities, while Wahaha sought to appeal to blue-collar workers, as well as the common people living in farm areas and small towns.
3 *Differentiation of taste.* Coca-Cola and PepsiCo used their traditional taste recipe as they expanded globally, but Wahaha developed a cola with Chinese taste characteristics.
4 *Differentiation of price.* There are no differences in price between Coca-Cola and PepsiCo, but Wahaha Future Cola is 10 percent cheaper than they are.
5 *Differentiation of advertising medium.* Coca-Cola and PepsiCo primarily use each city's advertising medium, i.e., local TV, radio, and newspapers, because most people who are living in cities do not watch National TV (CCTV). However, Wahaha uses mainly CCTV for advertising, which is popular in rural areas and small towns.

Wahaha's managerial method innovation

Wahaha's management innovation sometimes appears not only as product development, but also as management methodology. For example, it is very difficult in China for a production company to collect their accounts receivable. Wahaha had tackled the problem without exception, and their accounts receivable remain at almost zero. How was this achieved?

In fact, Zong had been troubled by this for several years after he started the business. So, he decided to solve the problem fundamentally through quality and trust. He paid a lot of attention to quality improvement and made sure quality was up to both national standards and ISO standards. At the same time, he visited a lot of dealers and proposed mutual trade principles, making it necessary for the dealer to pay a percentage in advance. The amount of money is about 10 percent of expected turnover in one year. Once the payment was confirmed, Wahaha shipped the goods quickly. For his part of the trade agreement, Zong guarantees the dealer's profit. Needless to say, it is almost impossible for the dealer not to trust Zong. However, swindlers do appear anywhere in China. For example, in one instance a dealer paid in advance to a company, but the company disappeared suddenly after receiving the advance payment. Such risks do exist, but Zong never compromises and keeps his side of the bargain. Only a few dealers believed him at the start. But now, Wahaha has over 2,000 primary dealers, and the number has been increasing every year in China (Li and Zou, 2009). Competitors have attempted to introduce the same method, but it has not gone well. Why? Apparently, they were unable to develop a trust relationship, as did Zong. Personal contact and years of business relationships have helped him develop a reputation based on his integrity.

Also, we can provide another case to explain Wahaha's innovation of management methodology. For example, there is no "vice-chairman position" in Wahaha. Zong is Chairman and President. Nobody has been appointed to be vice-chairman or vice-president thus far. The mass media often considers Zong to be a despot and is sometimes critical of him. However, Zong has stated that:

> Why I did not prepare a vice-president so far? The main reason is I want to make decisions rapidly. We have twenty heads of departments as well as competitors' vice-president. But since their position is not equal [to mine], they will follow me and not negotiate with me. It is necessary to concentrate the power in China. However, it is not a problem to appoint some people in vice positions, because my prestige has been established and Wahaha has become a big company today. But vice positions would not have been useful for competitiveness at the time.
>
> *(F. Xu, personal communication, March 30, 2010)*

What factors contributed to Wahaha's rapid growth in its brief history?

The external factors

We think the external factors include three aspects. The first is the reform of the economic system for the farm areas, i.e., a policy change regarding the farm and city relationships. The second involves the acceleration of opening China to the outside world. Finally, the third is the development of a market economy.

As noted earlier in this chapter, the policy of reform of the economic system started with the farm areas in China in 1987, by liberating the productivity of the farm areas. Since a series of policy changes (for example, the system of land contracting, tax exemption, lease of agricultural land, working away from home, etc.) were enforced, the peasants' standard of living improved quite rapidly. As a result, the purchasing power of the peasants increased, and a consumer market was established and has continued to develop.

Next, the acceleration of opening China to the outside world provided outstanding business opportunities to individuals who have strong entrepreneurship propensities, such as Haier's Zhang Ruimin, Lenovo's Liu Chuanzhi, and, of course, Zong Qinghou.

Needless to say, a so-called planned economy had been enforced in China until 1978. There were no private companies at that time. After the 1978 policy change, private companies sprung up like mushrooms. Moreover, thanks to the transition to a market economy, many private companies were able to grow and prosper. Of course, it has taken a number of years to make progress in this transition, and many companies, both state-owned and private, have gone bankrupt.

The internal factors

The internal factors are based primarily on Zong. In other words, Wahaha would not have existed without Zong. Although he has a limited formal educational background, having left school after middle school, he has become a lifelong learner, and, thus, he has been able to overcome poverty and a modest beginning in life. An analysis of his personal characteristics would also define him as a creative entrepreneur, who displays outstanding abilities with regard to a tendency for reflective thinking, the art of persuasion, decision-making, taking action to seize opportunities, endurance during difficult times, and a focus on uniting those with whom he chooses to develop relationships. Further elaboration of what might appear to be the 'mystery of Zong' is presented below:

1 Zong once said:

> I like reading and have read a variety of books. Even now, this custom has never changed. If I have some time, for example, on a business trip, I will buy a book or magazine. It made me learn much knowledge. And since I was living in the lower level of society, I am able to understand deeply the social present condition.
>
> *(F. Xu, personal communication, March 30, 2010)*

This comment is quite revealing of Zong's drive, ambition, and desire to improve his mind; it probably is the basis of his development of his ability to think through issues and reflect on a variety of possibilities; and it seems to come neither naturally nor by accident, but, rather is based on his constantly seeking to educate himself through reading and taking risks to experience possibilities.

2 It is obvious that Zong is not an ordinary entrepreneur, but, rather, a brilliant one who leads through the ability to sincerely articulate his vision and lead by persuasion. Outstanding entrepreneurs understand that they rarely achieve great success by acting alone. They know that they have to provide persuasive narratives of their visions to their employees to enable them to gain their trust and commitment to goals. It also involves more than just being a good talker, particularly when the ability to act is weak; no one will believe him/her. At the same time, if an entrepreneur has the ability to act but is unable to articulate his/her vision, nobody will follow him/her. Zong never uses flowery expressions, but his sincerity seems to charm others.

3 Zong is sensitive to business opportunities and is willing to take calculated risks, particularly with regard to changing government policy and the resultant evolution of economic conditions. As indicated near the beginning of this chapter, he realized what was transpiring with the change in economic conditions and decided and acted quickly when the Contract and

Responsibility System presented him with a management opportunity with the cardboard box company. He didn't miss that opportunity and risked a higher offer than others. Later, he realized a new business opportunity when he started the consignment venture, even though it involved great hardship and endurance.

4 It is also obvious that when Zong decided something, he took action quickly. Sometimes, his subordinates are unable to follow his vision, but still show respect for their boss' actions. His entrance into the cola market, when most thought the endeavor would fail due to large company competition, is a good example. Few thought he would succeed, but Wahaha Future Cola was born and became a huge success.

5 Zong's ability to unite others is remarkable. During his lifetime, he has experienced all social levels and finds it easy to associate with everyone. For example, politicians, bureaucrats, scholars, journalists, suppliers, dealers, employee, competitors, agencies, customers, etc., all seek to cooperate with him. So, he is not a lonely entrepreneur. To the contrary, he has built trusting relationships with so many in such a variety of endeavors that he has built an incredible network that provides him with a great deal of insight.

What have we learned from this case study?

After reforming the economic system and opening up to the outside world, numerous enterprises were born and foreign companies expanded their operations in China every year. One initial result was that many Chinese enterprises suffered bankruptcy because they were unable to compete. However, some enterprises like Haier, Lenovo, and Wahaha became stronger through competition with foreign giants. Studying such successful enterprises leads to some common findings. Although these Chinese entrepreneurs' educational backgrounds are modest, i.e., none have an MBA degree, they have developed outstanding management skills, and they have distinctive Chinese characteristics. Wahaha's Zong certainly is a typical case.

Many Westerners were unable to understand such Chinese enterprises' competitive strategy in terms of Western management theory. This is certainly understandable, since Chinese entrepreneurs had not read any Western books on management nor studied Western management theory during their student days.

However, they were able to succeed, the main reason being the ability to innovate by combining what they were observing as Western management practices with Chinese conditions. In Chinese, innovation is *Chuangxin*, and it is accompanied by a common awareness that "the only *Chuangxin* is our company's core competence." A Western creativity researcher, Robert Sternberg, has proposed that creativity is a decision, and he asserts, "People are creative largely by dint of their decision to go their own way. They make decisions that others lack the will or even the courage to make . . ." (2003, p. 5). Sternberg additionally provides a list of 10 creativity items; for example, "To define problems in ways different from those in which their colleagues define them" (ibid., p. 5). These 10 items seem to be involved in this decision to be creative (see the web address on p. 379 for his column when he was President of the American Psychological Association, the APA). Sternberg's proposition that "creativity is a decision", along with his list of 10 items, could possibly be used to describe Zong, as well as other innovative Chinese entrepreneurs. In any event, these Chinese entrepreneurs certainly seem to intuitively understand the creative and innovative process.

Bibliography

Bagchi, R. (2009) "Wahaha: posing a threat to Coca Cola and Pepsi in China," IBS Research Center.
Gao, C. (2004) *The Wahaha Method,* Beijing: China Workers Press.

Li, Y. and Zou, J. (2009) *Zong Qinghou tan Yingxiao,* Hangzhou: Zejiang People's Publishing House Press.
Luo, J. (2008) *Wahaha and Zong Qinhou,* Beijing: China Machine Press.
Porter, M.E. (1980) *Competitive Strategy,* New York: The Free Press.
Sina net (2012), http://finance.sina.com.cn/roll/20121129/131713840927.shtml (accessed 14 July 2014).
Sternberg, R. (2003) "Creativity is a decision," *American Psychological Association Monitor,* 34(10): 5.
Wang, L. (2010) *Zong Qinghou Rushi Shuo,* Beijing: China Economic Publishing House.
Xu, F. (2010) "Wahaha Group's management innovation," in *Proceedings of the 13th Annual Conference of the Japan Academic Society for Ventures and Entrepreneurs,* pp. 34–37.
Zuo, Z. and Liu, H. (2008) *The Chinese Divorce of Wahaha and DANONE,* Beijing: China CITIC Press.

Web addresses

APA, Sternberg column: www.apa.org/monitor/nov03/pc.aspx.
Wahaha's website: www.wahaha.com.cn/.

31
The Alibaba Group and Jack Ma

Mark J. Greeven

From today midnight onwards, I won't be CEO. From tomorrow business will be my hobby. I'm very proud of my 14 years in business . . . If you trust the young, you will trust the future.

(Jack Ma, opening speech of 10th Anniversary celebration of Taobao in Huanglong Stadion, Hangzhou, May 10, 2013)

Introduction

The Alibaba Group is China's leading e-commerce company and operates 25 business units employing 24,000 people, including the world's largest online business-to-business (B2B) platform, Alibaba.com, and China's largest online consumer marketplace, Taobao.com. Alibaba.com debuted on the Hong Kong Stock Exchange in 2007, raising US$1.7 billion, the world's largest internet IPO since Google in 2004. As the leading small business e-commerce platform in the world, it has over 110 million registered users worldwide (December 2012). Taobao Marketplace, China's most popular consumer-to-consumer marketplace, has more than 800 million product listings and more than 500 million registered users as of June 2012. It is one of the world's top 20 most visited websites. Taobao's business-to-consumer (B2C) brother, Tmall, features over 70,000 multinational and Chinese brands, thereby being the largest B2C platform in China. Together with Taobao Marketplace, the gross merchandise volume of these two platforms is more than US$1 trillion in 2012. As the lifeblood of Alibaba Group, Alipay is China's most widely used third-party payment system with more than 800 million registered accounts (December 2012).

The Alibaba Group was established only 14 years ago in June 1999 by Jack Ma and 18 other founders. The main founder, Jack Ma, comes from Hangzhou, the capital city of Zhejiang Province, which is the booming heart of private entrepreneurship in China. Within a year the Alibaba Group had raised US$25 million from Softbank, Goldman Sachs, Fidelity, and other institutions. Two years later, in 2002, Alibaba.com became profitable and in the subsequent years the Alibaba Group developed into a multi-billion dollar comprehensive e-commerce ecosystem. Jack Ma was the first Mainland Chinese to appear on *Forbes* Magazine's cover. How did the Alibaba Group succeed in creating sustainable value to suppliers, partners and customers within such a short time frame?

In what follows, this chapter discusses the development of Alibaba Group, its business ecosystem and its founder Jack Ma, aiming to provide fresh insights and inspiration for researchers and students, practitioners, entrepreneurs and policy-makers through the fascinating story and experience of Alibaba Group and Jack Ma. I draw on my colleagues' and my ongoing research on Alibaba's ecosystem business model, knowledge sharing within the ecosystem, Taobao and Koubei. The chapter is based on our publications in the *Financial Times* (Greeven *et al.*, 2012), an ECCH teaching case (Greeven *et al.*, 2009), interviews with various managers in the Alibaba Group, video material and published English and Chinese reference materials. Please note that Alibaba Group's development is so fast that by the time of this publication we can probably add a few new Alibaba ventures. Nevertheless the main trends and development over the last 14 years remain insightful!

The Alibaba Group: 14 years of growth

Jack Ma started China's first internet website called China Business Pages in 1995, initially competing and later cooperating with China Telecom. After a China Telecom buyout and several other short assignments in 1999, he got 18 friends together and raised US$60,000 to establish Alibaba.com in his hometown Hangzhou.

Alibaba.com, frequently quoted as one of the top five websites in the world along with Yahoo, Amazon, eBay and AOL, is the flagship of the Alibaba Group. Launched in 1999, Alibaba.com now has two platforms: Alibaba.com International and Alibaba.com China. Alibaba.com International is the leading global e-commerce platform for small businesses around the world. The platform has around 36 million registered users from more than 240 countries and regions and almost 3 million stores (Alibaba.com, June 2013). SMEs remain the major clients of Alibaba.com International. Alibaba.com China is the leading domestic e-commerce platform for Chinese small businesses. As of December 31, 2012, the platform had around 78 million registered users and more than 8.5 million supplier storefronts. Key in the development of Alibaba.com was the introduction of a fee-paying membership package that gave priority placement to stores and products. Furthermore, in collaboration with leading credit service companies, Alibaba.com provides TrustPass profiles to reliable partners. With the exclusive focus on SMEs and a combination of a clever strategy of immediately monetizing the user base and very selective international expansion (such as Japan, India), Alibaba.com quickly became a premier brand in e-commerce.

In May 2003, Jack Ma launched Taobao.com. Taobao.com offers a comprehensive range of products from collectibles and hard-to-find items to consumer electronics, clothing and accessories, sporting goods and household products. In less than 10 years Taobao has become one of the world's most popular e-commerce marketplaces. In 2008, the Group announced a further investment of RMB 50 billion (US$7.35 billion) in Taobao for the next five-year period to upgrade the company's software and hardware systems and to construct the "Taobao City"—a high-tech park West of Hangzhou, where Taobao would have its own Internet data centers. Jack Ma founded Taobao.com also as a defensive move to protect the Group from eBay's entry into China. When eBay launched in China, it had global revenues of more than US$2 billion. As a young, domestic entity, Taobao was taking on a huge rival while also fending off many similar small competitors in the sector, where barriers to entry were low. Key success factors include the choice of free listings, changing the apparent weakness of being a small Chinese company into a strength (for instance, emphasizing Chinese culture by using Kongfu names for moderators) and developing an innovative customer service in which customers can have instant communication with sellers via instant messenger Aliwangwang (Greeven *et al.*, 2012). Moreover, trust has been crucial for the business transactions, as Jack Ma is so aware. The shop assessment and review system and instant communication in combination with strict reviewing and policy for new shopkeepers aim to safeguard trust and vouchsafe the authenticity of the sellers. However, a fraud incident did arise in 2011, when the Group identified 2000 fraudulent Chinese sellers. Understanding the crucial importance of trust in the e-commerce business, three top executives left the company, taking responsibility for the fraud. Lastly, the online payment system Alipay has been instrumental in the success of Taobao.com, not only differentiating it from its competitors but revolutionizing the payment market in China (Greeven *et al.*, 2012).

Alipay.com was introduced shortly after the founding of Taobao in 2004. It is China's leading third-party online payment platform, with a market share of over 50 per cent. In 2008, it facilitated nearly US$20 billion in online payment volume and had 48 million users, compared to 33 million credit card holders in China. Unlike other services, Alipay takes payments from the buyer directly and puts it in an escrow account, thereby creating the necessary safeguard that Chinese buyers and sellers need. Sellers can then be sure that the payment delivery will be honored. As proudly stated on the website, on November 11, 2012, Alipay set a record for the highest daily number of transactions, processing 105.8 million payments during a 24-hour period. As a first mover in the online payment market, it currently has partnerships with 170 financial institutions in China and abroad (including 14 foreign currencies).

In 2005 Alibaba Group formed a partnership with Yahoo! China with the aim of making it the number one Chinese search engine, competing against its international rival Google.com and local rival Baidu.com. Yahoo! China provides Chinese-language portal services like email, a search engine, an interactive cyber community and information on finance, sports, lifestyle and entertainment. Its customers are advertisers who buy banners, text-links and auction-based pay-for-performance marketing services on its website. The search engine, however, was not the Group's specialty. Yahoo! China lost its market share from the start and lagged behind Baidu and Google. Then, in 2006, the Alibaba Group acquired Koubei.com, a local online listing site. Koubei.com, founded in 2004, offers classified listings services. It has 2 million registered users in over 2,000 cities accessing information on daily lives, including restaurants, housing, childcare, employment, travel and entertainment. Two years later, Yahoo! China merged with Koubei.com. The new company, Yahoo! Koubei, provides regional listing services powered by search, map and social networking technology.

Alibaba.com has always focused on serving the needs of its clients, the SMEs, and realized that many of the small online stores were growing larger. Using primitive ordering, procurement and inventory systems may delay deliveries and restocks. Therefore, in 2007, Alisoft.com was founded. Alisoft.com specializes in developing and trading internet-based business management solutions. Alisoft.com is like a giant supermarket where customers can browse for all kinds of software. It commands over 40 per cent of China's Software as a Service (SaaS) market and was the first company in Asia to launch a "software store" platform integrating advanced internet, telecommunication and software applications. Besides email, inquiries, bookkeeping and invoicing, Alisoft provides customers with software for communication, customer relations, marketing information, sales force, inventory and financial management among others. Realizing that online shops also need online advertising and marketing strategies, Alibaba Group developed Alimama in 2007, initially independent from the Group, to become China's leading internet advertising company with close to half a million media publishers as partners. Alimama.com was integrated into Taobao in October 2008. The Alibaba Group R&D Institute was established in September 2008 to study the latest global and Chinese market trends. Although Alibaba Group was already successful in understanding the dynamic and diverse Chinese market, Jack Ma wanted to stay on top of developments. The research reports generated by the 100-person staff are fed to company managers to help them make decisions. Alibaba Group R&D Institute merged with Alisoft.com in July 2009.

Recent years have seen a boom in foreign luxury brand sales and rising brand awareness in China. Taobao.com took the opportunity to become an online shopping landmark in China with an extensive brand selection and launched Tmall.com in April 2008. Tmall.com aims to be the online platform for quality, brand-name goods serving the needs of increasingly sophisticated Chinese consumers. In June 2011, it separated from Taobao's consumer-to-consumer (C2C) marketplace and became an independent platform. It offers several digital malls, such as a consumer electronics mall, a book mall, a beauty mall and so on. Brands with flagship retail storefronts on Tmall.com include UNIQLO, L'Oréal, Bjorn Borg, Adidas, P&G, Unilever, Nike and Levi's.

In 2009 the Group focused on the development of IT services and support infrastructure. Alibaba Cloud Computing was founded to serve as a developer of platforms for cloud computing and big data management. Alibaba Cloud Computing provides the necessary data and infrastructure support for the growth of Alibaba Group and the whole e-commerce ecosystem. It provides a comprehensive suite of internet-based computing services, including e-commerce data mining, high-speed massive e-commerce data processing, and data customization. Alibaba Cloud Computing was part of the bigger plan of the Alibaba Group to create a Big Taobao strategy. The Big Taobao strategy shows the Group's ambition to become a provider of e-commerce infrastructure services for all e-commerce market participants. Alibaba Group created a cross-business team comprising senior managers from Taobao, Alipay, Alibaba Cloud Computing and Yahoo! China to execute a full-scale roll-out of the Big Taobao strategy.

In 2010 and 2011, Alibaba Group extended its consumer services considerably. Reaching out to international markets, the Group built a global e-commerce marketplace made up of small business sellers in 2010: AliExpress. It offers a wide variety of consumer products in 40 major categories. At the moment it lists over 50 million products and has buyers in more than 200 countries. In 2011 Alibaba Group announced it was going to build a network of warehouses. In March 2011, Juhuasuan was launched as a group buying platform but became independent in 2011, reaching a gross merchandise volume of US$3 billion in 2012. Taobao's first offline mall appeared in Beijing in May 2011: Taobao Mall iFengChao Furniture Showroom. In October of the same year, the Group opened shopping search engine eTao, which provides information about products, sellers and discounts across the various Alibaba Group platforms, including group buying. In 2011, this platform became independent and aims to help Chinese consumers make online purchase decisions. The search results currently include, among others, Taobao Marketplace, Tmall.com, Amazon China, Dangdang, Gome, Yihaodian, Nike China and Vancl.

Alibaba.com delisted from the HK Stock Exchange only five years after listing and in September 2012 the Group completed the initial repurchase of shares from Yahoo! and restructured its relationship. In 2013, Alibaba Cloud Computing merged with HiChina. Recently, the Alibaba Group announced the development of a partnership with Sina, another internet giant in China. In particular, the Group acquired an 18 per cent stake in the Twitter-like Weibo that currently serves over 350 million users in China. Weibo is not only China's most popular Twitter, short message service, it is also a key marketing tool for word-of-mouth strategies and other online marketing tools. Moreover, observers suggest that the acquisition can also be seen as a defensive move against the rise of Alibaba Group's competitor Tencent and its popular social media tool Weixin, that has an increasingly large group of followers (close to 300 million) and serves an international market via WeChat. In May 2013, Jack Ma announced his retirement as CEO of the Alibaba Group and during the 10th year anniversary ceremony of Taobao.com, he formally handed over the leadership to Lu Zhaoxi. Many observers expect the company to go IPO soon; the recent reorganization into 25 business units may be a forewarning. As Gordon Orr from McKinsey commented recently in *The Economist* (2013a): "It could become one of the world's most valuable companies five years from now." Further directions are likely to be in (big) data analytics, integration in global markets and supply chain and warehousing networks. In particular, emerging economies and other low-trust countries may be next steps for Alibaba (*The Economist*, 2013b). Alibaba is there to stay and grow.

The business model of Alibaba: building an innovative ecosystem

I asked Jack Ma a question during the Family Day in 2006 in Hangzhou. The family that brought me was a good friend in the marketing department of Taobao and by joining him as a friend of the family, I could sit in on the interactive social meeting that Jack Ma was hosting with about a 100 employees. I had the pleasure of meeting him and asking what he thinks makes his company innovative. His answer was simple and straightforward: while innovation from the outside looks radical and suggests immediate big changes, the reality is that they are continuously improving each part of the business process; many small improvements that when you take a snapshot at the beginning of the year and at the end of the same year, would suggest a huge change. He noted that innovation is a process of continuous improvement and seeing the bigger picture, a comprehensive view of the business process that not only includes the company but also its partners and clients.

Building a business ecosystem

> An economic community is supported by a foundation of interacting organizations and individuals—the organisms of the business world. The economic community produces goods and services of value to customers, who are themselves members of the ecosystem. The member organisms also include suppliers, lead producers, competitors, and other stakeholders. Over time, they co-evolve their capabilities and roles, and tend to align themselves with the directions set by one or more central companies. Those companies holding leadership roles may change over time, but the function of the ecosystem leader is valued by the community because it enables members to move toward shared visions to align their investments, and to find mutually supportive roles.
>
> *(Moore, 1996, p. 26)*

The Alibaba Group has built a business ecosystem in which the company is deeply embedded in the business environment and coevolves with its partners and clients. The Alibaba Group has been actively developing mutually beneficial relationships with its partners in the ecommerce value chain, customers and suppliers. The Group consists of a wide variety of smaller companies that are split to keep the company small and flexible. The management believes that smaller entrepreneurial companies are more likely to remain innovative. More importantly, the emerging business network is built on synergy and even allows external partners to benefit from participating and contributing.

The Alibaba Group has become a facilitator and engine of the ecosystem. For instance, Etao.com is a competitor of the search engine Baidu and allows the user to search beyond the Alibaba Group companies, giving consumers the best deal across a variety of websites. Another example is the marketplaces the Group built for software providers outside of the Group via Alisoft and online advertisers and media companies outside of the Group via Alimama. Moreover, Alipay deals with all the e-commerce transactions and operates as an intermediate between the bank of the seller and the bank of the buyer. Alipay has become a frequently used online payment system, also outside the Alibaba Group. The product management and enterprise software solutions provided by Alisoft to SMEs take care of the management of SME business processes. Product delivery is part of the Group in terms of AliXpress (physical products) and Alibaba Cloud (digital products). Thereby a whole ecosystem is created in which the Group companies form a spider's web that links the digital platforms, enabling businesses to meet consumers directly, facilitate online payment, software and advertisement services. The Alibaba Group has evolved from a rudimentary e-commerce platform to a business network that satisfies all the basic needs of Chinese SMEs.

While the core of the ecosystem is Alibaba.com and Taobao.com, the middle layer of supporting companies directly assists the core services, including not only, among others, Alipay, Alisoft, eTao, Alimama, but also third-party transportation and warehousing firms. Moreover, the ecosystem further connects to outer layers with partners in the business process, with companies that serve other needs, such as resource planning, customer relationship management, business intelligence, mobile service, storage, printing and packaging, and training and education. In this way, external service providers can offer more services than the Group itself could.

The ecosystem model that Alibaba Group has created has several interesting features (Greeven *et al.*, 2009):

- The use of advanced information technology allows customers to search for anything they want from a wide range of products in an electronic marketplace. The reputation and feedback mechanism in combination with live-chat communication between the buyer and seller ensures reliability and trust. Due to the comprehensive ecosystem of services, clients can negotiate prices, transactions, logistics and delivery time, all at low cost. Creating mutual benefit at low cost, any new partner can join this business network.
- All the necessary tools to run an SME are available in the Alibaba Group's ecosystem, generating large complement advantages. From establishing the virtual shop to finding out the most economic logistics service; from waiting for potential customers to proactively promoting his or her products in the network. All these complementary services are available at low cost either within the Group or within the ecosystem.
- The Alibaba Group benefits from an enormous variety of products in their listings, a long tail effect. Not only traditional commodities can be found but also online advertisements, software products and digital products.
- Since the business units are synergistic, value and business can be created for one another. Opening a Taobao shop may be only the first step, one can then conveniently develop an online advertisement via Alimama and search for alternative suppliers on Alibaba.com. Economies of scale are created by shared services such as Alipay and Aliwangwang.

The company culture of interaction and knowledge sharing between the Group companies is facilitating problem solving and building of relevant new technologies (Driem, 2011). As one manager in Tmall told us:

> You must stand on strong shoulders. You cannot solve problems only by yourself. Society is changing very fast; you need to share knowledge because you cannot solve all the problems by yourself. The Internet industry is very open. We can find some technological documents from other companies so we can improve. We learn from these companies so we must share our knowledge with them. We must help others and they help us.
>
> *(ibid.)*

Moreover, a manager responsible for knowledge sharing within Alibaba Group emphasized the role of internal knowledge sharing in being innovative:

> Knowledge sharing is very important for innovation. There is a famous saying in Chinese that: "exchange an apple for another apple will get you one apple, exchanging ideas or

> opinions with another will get you two ideas." Innovation always comes from an easy environment in which employees exchange and ideas will automatically come out.
>
> *(Alibaba Group manager, cited in Driem, 2011)*

The importance of an open and interactive atmosphere within the Group is clear from the beginning for every new employee. A manager at Alipay stated "The first thing when a new employee starts working for us, we will tell him the importance of knowledge sharing. We organize a conference to share their knowledge" (cited in ibid.).

Employees of Alibaba are called Aliren ("Ali-people") and are part of a very close network. There is a strong sense of shared vision and employees feel committed. Entrepreneurship is deeply embedded inside the Alibaba Group and forms an important part of the culture of the Alibaba Group. There is an open and friendly atmosphere inside the Group, allowing employees to exchange ideas. All in all, the Group has succeeded in building an innovative and adaptive ecosystem that is responsive to the context of China's ecommerce market.

The context of the Alibaba Group's growth

The Alibaba Group's business ecosystem is embedded in the Chinese business environment. It evolves while solving problems for Chinese SMEs, a key driving force in China's economic boom. The number of SMEs in China has risen to 50 million in 2012 with average growth of above 7 percent annually. China's private enterprise sector is generally more productive and profitable than its state-owned enterprise (SOE) sector. Bold reforms under the Ninth Five Year Plan (5YP) 1995–2000 led to a greatly expanded role for the private sector. The private sector has become not only the main generator of output (an estimated 70 percent of GDP) and employment, and strongest growth engine, but also the most active sector for innovation in China in 2011 (World Bank, 2012).

Over 75 percent of those Chinese SMEs are using third-party e-commerce services in 2012, up from 25 percent in 2006. The Boston Consulting Group (2012) reports that the Chinese Internet economy is growing to a size of US$850 billion (cf. in the USA, US$1,000 billion and in the EU, US$1,100 billion) in 2016. Thereby it is becoming one of the top industries in China, getting larger than traditional industries such as real estate, education and logistics. Online retailing is expected to grow from US$72 billion (2010) to an astonishing US$422 billion (2016). There are many other strong players in the e-commerce market, such as Tencent, Baidu and Sina, but Taobao.com is dominant in the C2C market with an 80 percent market share. One possible explanation for the enormous potential of China's internet industry is the size and diversity of the Chinese market. Where top physical retailers just cannot reach enough customers via physical stores in hundreds or thousands of cities, internet access is widespread. Of the more than 500 million internet users today, already 150 million are buying products online. Alibaba Group understands and shapes these developments through creating value for all partners involved in the business ecosystem.

Jack Ma: innovator with a dream and passion

> I have never put myself on a moral high ground. I just consider which things I do are right and which things I do are wrong. When it comes to doing business, I fear others put me as a paragon of virtue. However, all men want to do bad things, and I also want to. Don't be hypocritical, don't talk nonsense. I am an ordinary person, I'm just doing business.
>
> *(Jack Ma in an interview in* Esquire China, *2013)*

One of the drivers of the success of Alibaba is its founder, Jack Ma, or Ma Yun in Chinese. There is no shortage of Chinese language books on Jack Ma and Alibaba. Books such as *Alibaba: There's No Difficult Business* (Zheng, 2007), *Ma Yun Talks about Management* (Zhu, 2008), *Ma Yun Talks about Entrepreneurship* (Li and Zhou, 2009) and *An Investigation on Alibaba Group: Study on Alibaba's Business Model* (Chen, 2009) discuss Jack Ma's passionate entrepreneurship, Alibaba's corporate culture and business model. The sheer amount of publications on him and, for instance, his participation in TV shows suggest his charisma and reach and influence on young entrepreneurs in China. One such show is *Win in China*, a CCTV2 national reality television show in which entrepreneurs compete for investment in their project or company. The show is produced by Wang Lifen and is a modified version of the American show *The Apprentice*, and besides Jack Ma also Hugo Xiong of IDG Venture Capital is on the judging panel. An astonishing 150,000 entrepreneurs competed in 2008 for an extended audience (via TV, internet, DVD) of 200 million people.

Jack Ma was born in 1964 in Hangzhou, the capital city of Zhejiang Province in the southwest of Shanghai. He grew up during the Cultural Revolution and at an early age became interested in learning English. For eight years, since he was 12, he went every morning to a hotel near the West Lake to give free tours to foreign tourists to improve his English. Nevertheless, he failed the university entrance exam twice, but eventually attended Hangzhou Teacher's Institute (Hangzhou Normal University, 1984) and graduated in 1988 with a bachelor's degree in English. Afterwards he became an English teacher in the Hangzhou Dianzi University (1988), founded his first company, Hangzhou Hope Translation Agency (1994) but not long afterwards he tried his hand at China's first website (1995): China Business Page. In fact, Jack Ma had limited knowledge of the internet at that time. One of the first times he used a computer and the internet was on a trip to Seattle, Washington. There he tried to search for "China" and did not get any search results. So upon return he started the China Business Page. The website had a similar vision as Alibaba.com, to list Chinese companies on the internet and help foreigners find Chinese websites. However, China Telecom, after first being his competitor and later his business partner, bought his share and in 1998 he took the job as general manager at an information technology company established by the China International Electronic Commerce Center, a department of the Ministry of Foreign Trade and Economic Cooperation. Over the years, he never got rid of the idea of setting up a company to achieve his vision and a year later he established Alibaba.com.

Throughout the past 14 years, Jack Ma has kept the entrepreneurial and innovative spirit alive, as is clear from their culture statement: "Our business success and rapid growth are built on the spirit of entrepreneurship, innovation, and an unwavering focus on meeting the needs of our customers." In particular, every new employee goes through extensive training in which the core values of Alibaba are discussed: customer first, teamwork, embrace change, integrity, passion, commitment. To put it more explicitly: "customer first, employee second and shareholder third." Jack Ma's vision is clear. Moreover, as an article in *The Financial Times* (2005) reports, Alibaba's employees tend to experience what Jack Ma's vision is intended to accomplish. The report mentions that employees see him as a leader with charisma and credibility, that Alibaba provides the opportunity to make a difference by developing new ways of doing business, and that employees have a sense of ownership and entrepreneurial spirit. Moreover, people grow under pressure to change, while Jack Ma is often available on their internal BBS to discuss issues, giving a sense of transparency and open communication.

Drawing on various Chinese language books and publications (e.g. Zheng, 2007; Zhu, 2008; Li and Zhou, 2009; Chen, 2009), including broadcasts of speeches made at Columbia University and Stanford University, we can start to paint an insightful and interesting picture of Jack Ma and Alibaba's company culture. Jack Ma's experience is unlike other successful entrepreneurs who graduated from top business schools. His education experience was very ordinary but he was always aware of his strengths. He had an interest in English and could speak it well from early age, so he chose it as his major in university. He went abroad and found the opportunities of doing business online so he started to build a website for Chinese companies to be known abroad, which also used his English language capability and his international vision.

Jack Ma is a passionate entrepreneur and he knows how to pass on such passion to the people around him. His speeches are always impressive and influence a lot people. He began his business with nothing but a dream and passion. His dream is not only about himself but about the whole country and society. He is proud that his website helps a lot of Chinese small companies to find clients online and has enabled many Chinese families to live from e-commerce. The dream makes him never give up and the passion makes people around him believe the dream like he does.

Regarding Jack Ma's entrepreneurial path, there is more criticism than praise. At first, he was regarded as a madman. When Chinapage.com started, he tried to convince Chinese companies to post their business information on the website abroad and he charged an advertisement fee. He sent a photo and 2000 words information about the company to the USA by UPS and the US company would help him post the information online and then they printed the website pages and sent them back by UPS. Chinapage.com is the first Chinese business website. At the start of the business, most Chinese companies had never heard of a website; few companies would believe a product and service they had never seen. Jack Ma was not believed for quite a long time until the website slowly gained popularity in China. Nevertheless, Jack Ma never gave up. He thought that he did the right thing and he kept trying. Observers contend that because Jack Ma was distrusted by others, he paid more attention to how people create trust and he knew more about how to make people trust each other; Alipay and Taobao are based on the trust network he has created.

Compared to other company executives, Jack Ma does not have many shares in Alibaba. He doesn't want people to listen to him because he has a controlling stake in the company. He wants to run the company with his wisdom, strategy and vision. He doesn't want the employees to feel that they are working for Jack Ma but wants them think they are working for the same dream. Here we see a core element of Alibaba's company culture. As he said in various sources, we cannot create a country but we can create a company culture.

Jack Ma likes Chinese Kongfu novels. People can find him under the name of Swordsman of a novel, chatting with employees online. He may bring a sword and go for a stroll in the company. He may suddenly stand behind you with an ice-cream in his hand for you. He is not good at board role-playing games but he likes to have fun with his employees and allow others to laugh at him. At company parties, he may dress up as a fisherman. Being happy at work has become corporate culture and in that way employees have a good time at work.

Jack Ma retired as the CEO in May 2013, but remains executive chairman and took up the job as Director General of the China Trustee Council of The Nature Conservancy, of which he was already a member. The Alibaba Group announced in May 2010 that it will begin in 2010 to earmark 0.3 percent of its annual revenues to fund efforts designed to spur environmental awareness and conservation in China and around the world.

Conclusion

Alibaba has many challenges ahead and it is up to the new CEO, Lu Zhaoxi, and the over 24,000 employees to tackle them. First, to what extent is the current business model sustainable? Global and domestic competition but also the threats of changing government policies with regard to the Chinese internet are possible challenges to the business model. Second, the global economic climate is changing and the effects of the financial crisis and shock in the financial markets have not yet fully reached China. Moreover, the risks and uncertainties in the domestic real estate market and the insecurity of social and health services may at a certain stage affect spending and other economic behavior in the domestic market. Third, technological changes are ever more frequent. In particular, recent developments in data analytics and big data science are happening fast. Alibaba Group is sitting on top of what may be the world's largest consumer behavior database but it has yet to be seen to what extent they can monetize its value.

Fourth, as a highly diversified business group, the challenges of coordinating the 25 business units with an overall corporate strategy are not to be underestimated. Alibaba Group is building an empire that is trying to do everything but can it be the best at everything? Fifth, is it possible to expand Alibaba's business model across national borders and gain market share abroad? Even though the Chinese internet market is very large, the EU and US markets are equally interesting and full of potential. In particular, those markets are more sophisticated and demanding and may challenge the Chinese internet business model. Lastly, Jack Ma recently retired from his position as CEO and as in any large company found by an entrepreneur with strong charismatic leadership qualities; the challenges for his successor Lu Zhaoxi are significant.

It was in 2004 when I first heard about Alibaba and Jack Ma. By slowly understanding what this new company was doing, I started to feel confident about my PhD research project idea to study innovation in China. Alibaba is an entrepreneurial firm of an unusual kind with a strong innovative capability, not only building a successful e-commerce firm but at the same time building an entire industry and providing a breeding ground for young entrepreneurs. The case of Alibaba provides rich insights and possibilities for further research on business model innovation, knowledge sharing, innovation capability, strategy in emerging markets and leadership. Furthermore, the insights provided in this chapter may provide inspiration for managers in the global internet industry, current and nascent entrepreneurs and policy-makers.

Acknowledgments

The author gratefully acknowledges the insights and editorial work by Yuan Ming, Zhejiang University, Hangzhou, China. Moreover, the insights developed in this chapter rely on discussions with various Alibaba Group managers, Frido van Driem and Tao Yue, Shengyun Yang, and Eric van Heck of the Erasmus University Rotterdam, The Netherlands.

References

Alibaba.com (2013) "Company overview." Available at: http://news.alibaba.com/specials/aboutalibaba/aligroup/index.html (accessed June 2013).

Boston Consulting Group (2012) "The internet economies," paper, Boston Consulting Group, March.

Chen, J. (2009) *An Investigation on Alibaba Group: Study of Alibaba's Business Model,* Economy & Management Publishing House (in Chinese).

Driem, F. (2011) "Intrafirm knowledge sharing in a transitional environment," unpublished Master of Science thesis, Erasmus University, Rotterdam.

Esquire China (2013) "Jack Ma: I'm afraid other people put me on a moral high ground," (in Chinese). Available at: www.iheima.com/archives/24170.html (accessed 7 January 2013).

Financial Times (2005) "Alibaba.com: a smiling community with a dream." Available at: www.ft.com/intl/cms/c6aba388–74a6–11db-bc76–0000779e2340.pdf (accessed June 2013).

Greeven, M.J., Yang, S., Van Heck, E. and Krug, B. (2009) "The ecosystem of the Alibaba Group: how is Alibaba Group's strategy and implementation in China creating sustainable value for suppliers, partners and customers?" European Case Clearing House (ECCH), 310–125–1–2.

Greeven, M.J., Yang, S.Y., Yue, T., Van Heck, E. and Krug, B. (2012) "How Taobao bested eBay in China," *Financial Times,* March 12.

Li. X. and Zhou, J. (2009) *Ma Yun Talks about Entrepreneurship,* Zhejiang People's Publishing House (in Chinese).

Moore, J.F. (1996) *The Death of Competition: Leadership and Strategy in the Age of Business Ecosystems,* New York: HarperBusiness.

The Economist (2013a) "The world's greatest bazaar: Alibaba, a trailblazing Chinese internet giant, will soon go public," *The Economist,* March 23.

The Economist (2013b) "China's ecommerce giant could generate enormous wealth provided the country's rulers leave it alone," *The Economist,* March 23.

World Bank (2012) *China 2030: Building a Modern, Harmonious, and Creative High-Income Society,* the World Bank, Development Research Centre of State Council, the People's Republic of China, Conference edition.

Zheng, Z. (2007) *Alibaba: There's No Difficult Business,* Zhejiang People's Publishing House (in Chinese).

Zhu, F. (2008) *Ma Yun Talks about Management,* Haitian Publishing House (in Chinese).

32

Entrepreneurial learning and capabilities development of a manufacturing firm in China

The case of the Haier Group

Diana S. Kwan and Fu-Lai Tony Yu

Introduction

> First we observe and digest [a new method] then we imitate it. In the end, we understand it well enough to design a new product independently.
>
> *(Zhang Ruimin, CEO of Haier Group)*[1]

Since Deng Xiaoping carried out economic reform in 1979, China has developed into a manufacturing powerhouse. China has transformed itself from an extremely poor country into the largest exporter and the second largest economy in the world (World Bank, 2010). Associated with this export growth has been a rapid shift in the composition of its export basket, from simple labor-intensive products to more diversified products, including many high-technology products (Martin and Manole, 2004). This dazzling economic performance has triggered the interest of scholars in economic development. Neoclassical development economists adopt new growth theories and total factor productivity to explain China's industrialization process. The weaknesses of the neoclassical paradigm lie in the aggregation approach. In particular, the neoclassical economic approach does not explain how manufacturing firms in China learn and innovate. This chapter attempts to show how manufacturing firms in China learn and enhance their capabilities. More specifically, it adopts an entrepreneurial learning and capabilities framework to explain the development path of latecomer firms in China in general and the Haier Group, a consumer goods manufacturer in China, in particular. Moreover, this chapter focuses on uncertainty and coordination problems faced by the entrepreneur during the production process. In what follows, a theoretical framework of entrepreneurial learning and innovation capabilities for manufacturing firms in latecomer economies will be presented. Then, a case study of the Haier Group, a world-renowned refrigerator and home appliances brand in China, follows. Finally, the conclusion and implications will be given.

Entrepreneurial learning and capabilities development for latecomer firms in China

It is argued that Asian latecomer firms acquire and assimilate foreign technologies to grow and compete (Hobday, 1994; Kim, 1997; Yu, 1997, 2005; Mathews, 2001). From imitation to innovation, latecomer firms are able to catch up with and even leapfrog the market leaders. Based on Hobday (1997), Yu (1998) and Mathews (2002), this chapter argues that manufacturing firms in China go through three stages of technological learning, namely, (1) building up basic production skills; (2) consolidating production capabilities; and (3) enhancing innovative capabilities.

Stage 1: building up production capabilities

Kirzner (1973) argues that the role of entrepreneurship lies in its alertness to opportunities. Having identified a profit opportunity, the entrepreneur puts capital resources together in the firm to produce the goods for sales in the market in order to reap the profit. Entering a particular business implies that the entrepreneur has the confidence to produce a product for profit. To do so, the entrepreneur needs to possess some basic technical skills. The technical knowledge of the entrepreneur may come from schooling or training from previous employments. With some basic production skills, the entrepreneur continues to learn and improve his or her knowledge.

In China, most entrepreneurs learn by imitation. One form of imitation is reverse engineering. Kim (2001) argues that reverse engineering is a duplicative imitation of existing mature foreign products. Latecomer firms in China buy a unit of foreign product, take it back to the factory and try to understand the designs and functions of the components. Through reverse engineering, latecomer firms learn how to duplicate a product (Kim and Nelson, 2000). They usually target popular foreign products for imitation. Nonetheless, the entrepreneur and the team may encounter difficulties during replication. If the business is small, the latecomer firm cannot afford to hire foreign engineers to solve the problems. The entrepreneur may rely on professional handbooks, trade magazines, the internet and/or information exchange with equipment suppliers. Latecomer firms acquire knowledge by mixing and matching different components by trial and error. With poor technological capabilities, they use native methods to produce no-brand products to compete in low-end value market by price. These products are poor in quality. They also encounter the threat of being driven out of the industries if cheap and good quality foreign products are allowed to penetrate local markets.

Stage 2: consolidating production capabilities

As latecomer firms in China obtain some basic skills in producing a product, they try to get some orders from overseas so as to expand their businesses. Original Equipment Manufacturer (OEM) business is crucial for latecomer firms to survive and grow. In OEM production, latecomer firms manufacture products according to the specifications laid down by transnational corporations (TNCs). Although products are sold to overseas markets with TNCs' brand names and distribution channels, latecomer firms need to understand product specifications according to the world's standard. Latecomer firms in China, as OEM suppliers, are able to learn and acquire product development knowledge from the foreign customers. Furthermore, foreign corporations often provide training, technical specifications and advice on engineering and capital goods (Hobday, 1997). Over time, latecomer firms in China meet quality requirements from overseas markets. They then further build up production capabilities by expanding the production scale, reducing the production costs by pooling production orders and increasing the production capacity from other foreign OEM customers. They also learn how to adopt product quality control for the sake of capturing larger market shares. In short, being OEMs, latecomer firms in China learn foreign technologies and raise their production capabilities.

Stage 3: enhancing innovative capabilities: from sheer imitation to creative imitation

Latecomer firms in China simply cannot compete by low labour costs with firms in other countries with the lowest cost of production. In order to survive, latecomer firms move away from sheer imitation and produce innovative products. As production capabilities improve, many latecomer firms in China are able to produce something different from the market via double-loop learning (Argyris, 2002).[2] Double-loop learning means that people who frequently encounter stimuli or receive impressive rewards for controlling a situation to enrich their knowledge can move towards a higher level of complexity (Yu, 1998, p. 14). Applied to production capabilities, firms can accelerate learning by analyzing and selecting the prototype to create new products and then combine different ideas to become a new model. Accordingly, latecomer firms in China, after obtaining basic technological know-how, are able to produce high value products and sell in the niche market where there is high profit margin. To promote their own brand products overseas, they form strategic alliances with foreign firms.

(i) Strategic alliances

Latecomer firms in China enhance their innovative capabilities by sharing technologies with foreign firms via strategic alliances. Zollo *et al.* (2002) argue that a strategic alliance is a form of cooperative venture to handle general alliance management knowledge, new product development knowledge and partner-specific knowledge. Parties in a strategic alliance cooperate with a common objective and share their own resources. Using strategic alliances, China's latecomer firms enter the foreign market rapidly. Sharing technological knowledge encourages product innovation, including an improvement in the manufacturing process and maintains the product innovation-based competitiveness (Imai, 1986; Murray *et al.*, 2005).

(ii) Moving up from OEM to ODM and/or OBM

Many Asian manufacturing firms such as Samsung from South Korea and BenQ from Taiwan obtain advanced knowledge from multinational corporations through original design manufacturers (ODM) (Hobday, 1995; Yan, 2012). Likewise, latecomer firms in China (e.g. Lenovo) which originally served as OEM suppliers transform into original design manufacturers (ODM) and original brand manufacturers (OBM). Being an ODM, firms carry out product design and process according to general design layout supplied by the foreign buyer (Hobday, 1997). Latecomer firms in China thus build up competence through modifying mature technology. However, moving from OEM to OBM is not as simple as it seems. It requires a substantial commitment of time and resources to establish channel relationships and share-of-mind in target markets (Wreden, 2004). As an OBM in global business, the firm needs to "tackle . . . the difference of culture, regulation, language, and ways of practicing business between local and foreign subsidiaries" (Yan, 2010, p. 22). For example, in the 1990s, Taiwan's Acer launched Aspire personal computer in the US market. However, after losing around US$200 million since 1996 in the USA, Acer withdrew from the US market in 1999 (*Business Week*, 2000). The setback forced Acer to undertake a serious of radical organizational reengineering plans,[3] which included slashing its unprofitable own-brand operation, shifting own-brand sales away from the USA to concentrate more on the Asian and Chinese market (Shih, 2005).

(iii) Research and development (R&D) and problem-solving

Problem-solving brings changes in production procedures, product components, and product designs. Apart from strategic alliances and OEM subcontracting, latecomer firms in China solve technical problems in innovation and upgrade their technological capabilities by R&D activities (Hobday, 1995). Studies in the management of technology have observed that firms invest in R&D and utilize information which is available externally. R&D provides in-house technical capability which keeps firms informed of the latest technological development and facilitates the assimilation of new technology (Tilton, 1971, p. 71; Cohen and Levinthal, 1989, p. 569). Cohen and Levinthal (1989, p. 569) further argue that R&D develops the firm's "absorptive capability," i.e. the firm's ability to identify, assimilate and exploit outside knowledge. Hence, through investment in R&D activities, latecomer firms in China learn and create imitative products with a performance that may be significantly better or where the production costs are considerably lower than the original (Kim and Nelson, 2000; Yan, 2012). In other words, these firms move away from single-loop learning to double-loop learning, resulting in incremental innovation.

The case of the Haier Group

Haier Group (hereinafter Haier) has been chosen as a case study because it reflects the technological learning of typical manufacturing firms in China. As a latecomer firm in China, Haier managed to upgrade its technological learning, transforming itself from the production of simple goods, generally as an OEM subcontractor, into new product lines through its own design and branding capabilities (Fukasaku, 2007). Its products have successfully penetrated overseas markets and become a world brand.

Haier's background

Haier is a consumer electronics and home appliances company headquartered in Qingdao city, Shandong Province, China. Its products include air conditioners, mobile phones, computers, microwave ovens, washing machines, refrigerators and televisions. Haier was formerly a refrigeration factory under the name of Qingdao Refrigerator Co. which was founded in the 1920s. In 1949, the firm was nationalized by the Communist government. As a state enterprise, it performed poorly and the factory was close to bankruptcy. In desperation, the Qingdao government appointed Mr. Zhang Ruimin as the managing director of the factory in 1984. Under Zhang's management reform, Qingdao Refrigerator Co. returned to profitability and sales growth averaged 83 percent per year by 1986. Having diversified its product line covering other consumer products, the company adopted a new name, Haier, in 1991. By the end of the 1990s, Haier had become a well-known brand in China with products ranging from mobile phones to computers. It had also captured a dominant market share in its core white goods division. Having had success in the domestic market, Haier moved on to the international stage with the goal of building a global brand name. It opened a production plant in Indonesia in 1996, and the Philippines and Malaysia in 1997. It entered the US market in 1999 and competed directly with established American giants such as General Electric (GE), Whirlpool, Frigidaire and Maytag. In 2008, Haier surpassed its rival, Whirlpool, as the world's top refrigerator producer in terms of sales. Haier continued to expand the business in other international markets. It entered Pakistan in 2002 and Jordan in 2003. In Africa, it had plants in five countries, namely Tunisia, Nigeria, Egypt, Algeria and South Africa. It also purchased a factory in Italy so as to enter the European market. In 2010, Haier had the world's largest market share in white goods, with 6.1 percent. It became the world's largest manufacturer of domestic appliances and the fifth largest manufacturer of consumer goods in the world (www.haier.com, retrieved on 29 Dec. 2011; Liu and Li, 2002, pp. 699–706; Sun, 2002, pp. 266–282; Yi and Ye, 2003; Yu, forthcoming).

Native and naïve production methods in the early days

In the 1920s, a refrigerator factory was built in Qingdao. After the establishment of the People's Republic of China in 1949, the factory was then taken over by the central government and turned into a state-owned enterprise. The plant was manually operated and was an old workshop run by a Communist cadre, Ms. Yang Mianmian, who had studied at the Shandong Institute of Technology. Through learning-by-doing, a site visit to the Beijing Snowflake refrigerator factory and the help of consultants from Shanghai, the technicians and workers of the Qingdao Refrigerator Co. learnt and acquired the knowledge and skills to make refrigerators. The manufacturing methods they acquired were native and naïve. Under the socialist regime, the market was strictly closed and protected. All production facilities were controlled by the government. Competition was shielded off from the outside world. Qingdao's production enjoyed full protection from the government. All Yang needed to do was to follow the instructions of the central planning committee and produce according to the central orders. As a result, both the production and innovation capabilities of the Qingdao Refrigerator Co. remained low. The enterprise suffered from worn-out infrastructure, poor management and lack of quality control. Production rarely reached 80 refrigerators a month. By the 1980s, the enterprise had incurred a debt of over ¥1.4 million[4] and was close to bankruptcy.

1984–1994: the enterprise reform and consolidating production capabilities

Following Deng Xiaoping's economic reform in 1984, Zhang Ruimin[5] was appointed the managing director of the factory by the Qingdao government. Zhang's entrepreneurship and vision brought life back to the firm. Before Zhang joined the firm, the factory could only produce 80 refrigerators per month. The manufacturing equipment was inferior and the refrigerators were produced with poor quality control. More devastatingly, there was no market demand for poor quality refrigerators selling at a price of ¥800 at that time. Zhang realized that inadequate production skills, low technological standards and poor quality control were impairing the firm's capabilities. After Deng's government embarked on the "Four Modernizations" policy in 1983, state enterprises were allowed to initiate a "responsibility system." Zhang then undertook a radical reform of the structure of the firm, particularly raising the firm's capabilities in order to compete. After receiving many customer complaints about the faulty fridges, Zhang had 76 faulty refrigerators lined up on the factory floor and ordered his employees to destroy them with hammers in 1985. He preached to his workers, "Destroy them! If we sell these refrigerators, we'll continue making mistakes and the company will go bankrupt!" Zhang determined to restructure the company. He introduced radical reform through a strict staff performance evaluation system called the OEC (i.e., Overall: Every day/Everyone/Everything; Control and Clearance). Under the system, every task was controlled. Each employee was given a target work (both quantity and quality) before the work started. Employees finished the target work every day and received full salary. Any employee who earned more points in the system would receive a bonus or promotion. Those who failed to finish the target work would be fined or demoted. A key feature of the OEC system was that employees were evaluated according to their daily job performance. Another feature was that the factory floor was painted in yellow, green and red footprints. Poorly performing employees had to stand on red footprints and explain why they did not do their work well. Zhang's reform provided a major incentive for employees to perform well every day (Hawes and Chew, 2011, pp. 67–83).

Licensing from the German Liebherr Company

In order to stay in the market, Zhang focused on producing high quality products. He attempted to acquire foreign technologies from leading global firms through direct purchases or strategic alliances. In 1984, Haier acquired new technology from refrigerators that were manufactured abroad. After conducting an assessment of 32 potential cooperative partners, Haier established an alliance with the Liebherr Company of Germany. Liebherr had 70 years of experience in producing high quality refrigerators. Its refrigerators were generally regarded as the leading ones in the world. Compared to Liebherr's refrigerators with four-star technology, Haier performed the very old-fashioned two-star technologies with a freezing capability of -12°C. The freezing capability of a four-star refrigerator was -18°C. When cooperating with Liebherr, Haier was licensed to import Liebherr's four-star refrigerator production technology and equipment to China. Haier became the only company in China which produced this modern refrigerator. In other words, the technological capabilities of Haier were greatly enhanced. After establishing an R&D department, Haier sent more than 40 top engineers and managers to Liebherr to master the technological skills required to develop advanced refrigerators. In 1985, a year after licensing Liebherr's technology, Haier introduced its first four-star refrigerator onto the Chinese market and became the leading refrigerator producer in China (Duysters *et al.*, 2009: 329–330). Haier now upgraded its capabilities. New skilled workers replaced outdated unskilled workers. The installation of Liebherr's equipment and technology was accompanied by a new and rigorous commitment to quality. As Zhang's disciplined management techniques broke away from the tradition of the iron rice bowl in Chinese state-owned enterprises, the company began to turn around. By 1986, Haier had returned to profitability and sales growth were averaging 83 percent per year. As a result, sales increased from ¥3.5 million in 1984 to ¥40.5 billion by 2000.

Original Equipment Manufacturer (OEM)

Zhang benefited from OEM business with the company US Appliance to manufacture refrigerators in the 1990s. Haier produced household appliances according to the general design layout supplied by the US Appliance. The sales channels were distributed in US chain stores such as Wal-Mart. The sales volume of Haier continued to rise over the next five years. In particular, Haier understood the US customers' demand for mini-fridges and met their needs in university dormitories and hotel rooms. OEM became value-added for Haier to enable them to learn by understanding product engineering and how to enter the world's market. Haier pursued quality control with zero error detection and total quality management. As Zhang said, "A defective product is a waste." So, it was possible for Haier to keep a portion of the market share in the USA. In addition, it achieved the ISO 9001 quality certification for its refrigerator production in 1992. Its basic production capabilities were thus recognized. Zhang quickly realized that being an OEM supplier and selling low-priced products, Haier could not significantly increase its market share in the industry. He determined to establish a brand name.

Renamed Haier

With the German Liebherr Company serving as its partner, Haier built up its production capabilities and gradually conducted innovations. In 1992, it formally changed its name to Qingdao Haier. The name "Haier" was finalized in 1993 to promote its brand. In Chinese, Haier means "it likes a blue ocean." The use of the pun "Haier/higher" is obvious (Yi and Ye, 2003, p. 8). Haier is a high quality brand name that "goes global."[6] As Zhang states, "Our purpose in exporting is to establish a brand reputation overseas. We have created an important brand in China, and we are taking that brand to other markets" (quoted in Wu, 2003).

From 1995 onwards: enhancing innovative capabilities and go-global

From OEM to ODM/OBM

After acting as an OEM for foreign companies, Haier established its own brand products in overseas markets in 1999. To establish brands in foreign markets, many latecomer firms in China first export products to developing economies such as South-east Asia where there are no strong competitors. However, Haier did otherwise. Taking an unconventional path, Haier entered the US market where the largest global competitors with top quality products were found. There were two reasons for this decision. First, Haier regarded it as a challenge to enter developed markets. In advanced countries such as the United States, the firm had to meet demanding requirements from customers and retailers. Zhang believed that if Haier could succeed in entering markets in advanced nations, it would then be easier for Haier to expand their business in other emerging markets. If Haier could compete in the US market with other brands such as GE, Matsushita and Philips, it would then take on the markets in the developing countries without much difficulty. Second, if Haier successfully launched branded products in the United States, then its products would easily be accepted by the customers in the emerging markets because Haier had already gained a reputation in an advanced nation (Palepu *et al.*, 2006, pp. 10–12).

Although Haier had performed well in the domestic market, going global was another story. It was a huge challenge for Haier to enter the US market. The US market was flooded with top competitors. If Haier wanted to share the pie, it needed a strategy. Haier could not afford to go into head-to-head competition with its brand rivals. Instead, it would enter the market in a segment that was not adequately served. Zhang discovered that the US market lacked good refrigerators for college dormitories and offices. Haier saw this golden opportunity and produced mini-fridges with a design that can double as a computer desk. The product was suitable for college students living in dormitories. After being successful in selling products such as compact refrigerators and wine cellars in the United States, Haier was able to attract the attention of the major US retail chains like Wal-Mart and Best Buy. It established a good relationship with them and held a strong position to sell its other appliances such as standard refrigerators, apartment refrigerators, air conditioners, and washing machines in the market. In 2005, Haier had a 26 percent share of compact refrigerators, over 50 percent of wine cellars and 17 percent of air conditioner sales in the United States (Palepu *et al.*, 2006, pp. 10–12).

R&D to enhance innovative capabilities

To enhance its innovative capabilities, Haier appreciated the importance of R&D. In 1995, it set up a technology research center and overseas design centers (Duysters *et al.*, 2009). In the United States, Haier established a design center and developed in-house R&D capabilities that used skilled local labor. Through R&D, Haier was able to produce appliances to meet the demands of American households. For example, it produced a convertible bottom drawer refrigerator with a spacious drawer at the bottom for storing fruit and vegetables or frozen foods.

Internationalization via joint ventures and strategic alliances

Zhang noted, "[Profit] margins are low here [in China]. If we don't go outside, we can't survive"[7] (Bonaglia *et al.*, 2007). Haier started to form joint ventures and strategic alliances with foreign partners in order to reach the overseas markets. With continuous stimuli from strategic partners, Haier experienced double-loop learning and enhanced its innovative skills. This can be illustrated by two examples.

Example 1. Haier formed a joint venture with the Japanese company Sanyo, in 2002. After understanding the needs of the Japanese market, Haier successfully introduced mini-fridges with a good appearance and product design and a proper product structure. In 2011, Haier acquired Sanyo's washing machines, refrigerators and other consumer electric goods.[8] About 3,000 employees were transferred from Sanyo to Haier. The acquisition enhanced their technological and innovative capabilities and expanded the markets in South-east Asia.

Example 2. Haier established a series of strategic alliances with global firms including Mitsubishi, ESS, Lucent, Metz and Philips to strengthen brand building and innovative capabilities. In particular, Haier formed strategic alliance with Ericsson which was the leading provider of wireless technologies. It incorporated Ericsson's Bluetooth technology into its household appliances and encouraged new product development.[9] It absorbed market information and diffused the technological knowledge to manufacture high value products through cooperation.

Conclusion

This chapter has constructed an entrepreneurial learning and capabilities framework to explain the development path of latecomer firms in China in general, and Haier in particular. This study argues that Haier, as a latecomer firm in China, went through three stages in their technological paths, namely, stage 1, the acquisition of basic production skills; stage 2, the consolidation of production capabilities; and stage 3, the enhancement of innovative capabilities.

Under the leadership of Zhang Ruimin, Haier has gone through drastic enterprise reforms and transformation. To rescue Haier from bankruptcy, Zhang introduced a strict employee performance evaluation process which provided a major incentive for workers to perform well. Furthermore, by forming a collaboration network with a top German firm in home appliances and acting as OEM suppliers for multinational corporations, Haier was able to enhance its production capabilities in making consumer appliances.

As the qualities of Haier's products improved, Haier then tried to sell its own branded products overseas by using the US market as a testing ground. Haier also enhanced its innovative capabilities via R&D. In 1995, Haier established a design center in the United States and developed in-house R&D capabilities that utilized skilled local labor. Through R&D, Haier was able to produce home appliances which benefited American households.

Like other Chinese multinational firms, Haier went global by forming joint ventures and strategic alliances with foreign partners. With continuous stimuli from its strategic partners overseas, Haier experienced double-loop learning and enhanced its innovative skills. In particular, Haier formed a joint venture with Sanyo and successfully introduced the mini-fridges with a good appearance in product design and proper product structure. Haier's home appliances were distributed through Sanyo's sales channels which enhanced its reputation and Sanyo batteries were sold in China through Haier's distribution network. Haier also entered a series of strategic alliances with global firms including Ericsson, Mitsubishi, ESS, Lucent, Metz and Philips to strengthen brand building and innovative capabilities. Through a process of entrepreneurial learning from imitation to innovation, Haier was able to "go global" and catch up with the firms in advanced countries.

In 2008, Haier was ranked number 1 on "Overall Leadership of Mainland China Corporations" by the *Wall Street Journal Asia*. In the same year, R&F and Beijing Famous-Brand Evaluation Co. announced that Haier had topped the list for seven consecutive years as the "China Most Valuable Brand" with a brand value of US$11.7 billion. In 2009, the China National Household Electric Appliances Service Association ranked Haier number 1 in the Year Customer Satisfaction Survey. In 2009, Haier was the only Chinese household appliances enterprise to win *Business Week*'s Top 10 Chinese and Foreign Enterprises in China "Green Economy Award" (Lin, 2009, p. 47).

Notes

1 Quoted in Paine (2001, p. 7).
2 According to Argyris (2002, p. 206):

> Single-loop learning occurs when errors are corrected without altering the underlying governing values. For example, a thermostat is programmed to turn on if the temperature in the room is cold, or turn off the heat if the room becomes too hot. Double-loop learning occurs when errors are corrected by changing the governing values and then the actions. A thermostat is double-loop learning if it questions why it is programmed to measure temperature, and then adjusts the temperature itself.

3 For a detailed discussion of the organizational reengineering in Acer since 2000, see Yan (2010, pp. 21–22).
4 ¥ is the Chinese currency, yuan: US$1 = ¥6.314 on 19 January, 2012.
5 Zhang Ruimin was born into a working family in Qingdao, China, in 1949. After finishing his high school education, Zhang went to work in the Qingdao Construction Hardware Factory for 12 years. In 1980, he was promoted to be the Deputy Director of the factory. He then became the Deputy Manager of the Household Appliance Division of the Qingdao municipal government the next year. He was responsible for technology control and approval of new products. In 1984, Zhang was appointed Director of the Qingdao Refrigerator Factory after the resignation of three directors in that year. Under Zhang's leadership, Haier was transformed from a traditional home appliance manufacturer to a global innovator. Zhang is known as the "Jack Welch of China." For further information on Zhang Ruimin, see Tang (2005) and Zhang (2011).
6 From www.forbes.com/global/2001/0806/039.html (accessed 14 August, 2013).
7 Quoted in *The Economist*, "Haier's purpose," 18 March 2004.
8 See www.haier.com/my/newspress/announcement/201203/t20120330_120921.shtml (accessed 26 June, 2013).
9 See www.haier.cn/ (accessed 10 October 2010).

Bibliography

Argyris, C. (2002) "Double-loop learning, teaching, and research," *Academy of Management Learning & Education,* 1(2): 206–218.

Bonaglia, F., Goldstein, A. and Mathews, J. (2007) "Accelerated internationalization by emerging markets' multinationals: the case of the white goods sector," *Journal of World Business,* 42(4): 369–383.

Business Week (2000) "Another about face for Acer," April 23. Available at: www.businessweek.com/stories/2000–04–23/another-about-face-for-acer (accessed 14 August 2013).

Cohen, W.M. and Levinthal, D.A. (1989) "Innovation and learning: the two faces of R&D," *The Economic Journal,* 99(397): 569–596.

Duysters, G., Jacob, J., Lemmens, C. and Yu, J.T. (2009) "Internationalization and technological catching up of emerging multinationals: a comparative case study of China's Haier Group," *Industrial and Corporate Change,* 18(2): 325–349.

Fukasaku, K. (2007) *Business for Development: Fostering the Private Sector,* Paris: OECD.

Hawes, C. and Chew, E. (2011) "The cultural transformation of large Chinese enterprises into internationally competitive corporations: case studies of Haier and Huawei," *Journal of Chinese Economic and Business Studies,* 9(1): 67–83.

Hobday, M.G. (1994) "Export-led technology development in the four dragons: the case of electronics," *Development and Change,* 25(2): 333–361.

Hobday, M.G. (1995) "East Asian latecomer firms: learning the technology of electronics," *World Development,* 23(7): 1171–1193.

Hobday, M.G. (1997) *Innovation in East Asia: The Challenge to Japan,* Cheltenham: Edgar Elgar.

Imai, M. (1986) *Kaizen,* New York: Random House.

Kim, L. (1997) *Imitation to Innovation: The Dynamics of Korea's Technological Learning,* Boston: Harvard Business School Press.

Kim, L. (2001) "The dynamics of technological learning in industrialization," *International Social Science Journal,* 53: 297–308.

Kim, L. and Nelson, R. (2000) *Technology, Learning and Innovation,* Cambridge: Cambridge University Press.

Kirzner, I.M. (1973) *Competition and Entrepreneurship,* Chicago: University of Chicago Press.

Lin, T.W. (2009) "Haier is Higher: a Chinese company's roadmap to success via its reengineering system," *Strategic Finance,* December: 41–49.

Liu, H. and Li, K.Q. (2002) "Strategic implications of emerging Chinese multinationals: the Haier case study," *European Management Journal,* 20(6): 699–706.

Martin, W. and Manole, V. (2004) "China's emergence as the workshop of the world," Working Paper No. 216, Stanford Center for International Development, June.

Mathews, J.A. (2001) "National systems of economic learning: the case of technology diffusion management in East Asia," *International Journal of Technology Management,* 22(5/6): 455–479.

Mathews, J.A. (2002) "Competitive advantages of the latecomer firm: a resource based account of industrial catch-up strategies," *Asia Pacific Journal of Management,* 19: 467–488.

Murray, J.Y., Kotabe, M. and Zhou, J.N. (2005) "Strategic alliance-based sourcing and market performance: evidence from foreign firms operating in China," *Journal of International Business Studies,* 36(2): 187–208.

Paine, L.S. (2001) *The Haier Group (A), Harvard Business Case Studies,* 9–398–101, July 27.

Palepu, K., Khanna, T. and Vagras, I. (2006) "Haier: taking a Chinese company global," *Harvard Business School Case,* 9–706–401.

Shih, S. (2005) *Millennium Transformation: Change Management for New Acer,* Taiwan: Aspire Academy. Available at: www.stanshares.com.tw/StanShares/upload/tbBook/1_20100817144639.pdf (accessed 14 August 2013).

Sun, J. (2002) *The Corporate Strategy of Haier,* Beijing: Enterprise Management Press, pp. 266–282.

Tang, I.Y. (2005) "A case study of a leader: Zhang Ruimin." Available at: www.runsky.com/homepage/dl/spec/2004/usa4/guo/userobject1ai551524.html (accessed 30 December 2011).

Tilton, J.H. (1971) *International Diffusion of Technology: The Case of Semiconductors,* Washington, DC: Brookings Institution.

World Bank (2010) *Op-ed: A Constructive Role with China.* Available at: http://web.worldbank.Org/WBSITE/EXTERNAL/NEWS/0,contentMDK:22699125~pagePK:64257043~piPK:437376~theSitePK:4607,00.html (accessed 1 October 2010).

Wreden, N. (2004) "From OEM to OBM: crossing the chasm", October. Available at: www.fusionbrand.com/pdf/from_oem_to_obm_crossing_the_chasm.pdf (accessed 15 August 2013).

Wu, Y. (2003) "China's refrigerator magnate," *McKinsey Quarterly,* 3: 106–115.

Yan, H-D. (2010) "Entrepreneurship, strategic leadership and firm transformation: the case of the Acer Group," paper presented at the 6th Annual Meeting of the Chinese Hayek Society, Hong Kong Shue Yan University, 6–7 August.

Yan, H-D. (2012) "Entrepreneurship, competitive strategies and transforming firms from OEM to OBM in Taiwan," *Journal of Asia-Pacific Business,* 13(1): 16–36.

Yi, J.J. and Ye, S.X. (2003) *The Haier Way: The Making of a Chinese Business Leader and a Global Brand,* Dumont, NJ: Homa & Sekey Books.

Yu, T.F.-L. (2005) "Technological strategies and trajectories of Hong Kong's manufacturing firms," *International Journal of Technology and Management,* 29(1/2): 21–39.
Yu, T.F.-L. (forthcoming) "Entrepreneurial leadership, capital structure and capabilities development of the firm: the case of the Haier Group," *International Journal of Economics and Business Research.*
Yu, T.F.-L. (1997) *Entrepreneurship and Economic Development in Hong Kong,* London: Routledge.
Yu, T.F.-L. (1998) "Economic development in latecomer economies: an entrepreneurial perspective," *Development Policy Review,* 16(4): 353–372.
Zhang, X. (2011) *Ruimin Zhang's Wisdom of Confucian Entrepreneurs,* Hangzhou: Zhejiang University Press.
Zollo, M., Reuer, J.J. and Singh, H. (2002) "Inter-organizational routines and performance in strategic alliances," *Organization Science,* 13(6): 701–713.

Hong Kong

33

The strategies of real estate companies in Hong Kong

The case of Hongkong Land Holdings Ltd

Jianfu Shen, Adrienne La Grange and Frederik Pretorius

Hongkong Land Holdings Ltd (HKL), founded in 1889, is the real estate investment and development subsidiary of the Jardine Matheson Group (JMG), a Hong Kong conglomerate founded as a trading enterprise in 1832 and currently controlled by the Scottish family Keswick. The group is involved in several industries in Hong Kong and Asia and has various subsidiaries, including six listed companies that occupied 10.75 percent of total market value of the Hong Kong Stock Exchange at the beginning of 1990 (Mok *et al.*, 1992) before the group moved its listings elsewhere (see below).[1] JMG's real estate arm, HKL, is a leading real estate investment, management and development company in Hong Kong, with a substantial real estate portfolio concentrated in prime commercial areas in Hong Kong, and some interests elsewhere in major Asian cities including Singapore. HKL is possibly best known for its large (dominant) portfolio of commercial properties in Central, the prime central business district of Hong Kong, acquired during the colonial era, amounting in the mid-1990s to some 40 percent of the total stock of Grade A office space in Central.

HKL's contemporary history and present state are largely defined by its strategic actions during the lead-up to the return of Hong Kong's sovereignty to the People's Republic of China (PRC) in 1997, and events as they unfolded afterwards. Its present trajectory began on 31 March 1995, when HKL was delisted from the Hong Kong Stock Exchange and its listing was transferred to Singapore, together with the other subsidiaries in the Jardine Matheson Group. Yet HKL's major business remained in Hong Kong and its real estate portfolio was not altered by the listing switch. It was still the leading landlord in Central, Hong Kong, but at the time it also seemed obvious that the strategies and decisions behind delisting in Hong Kong were expected to have at least a mixed, but probably negative, impact on HKL's decisions to expand its business and might cause it to lose opportunities in Hong Kong and Mainland China. Its dominant position as a commercial landlord in Central Hong Kong has certainly been eroded since then, as other companies, notably Henderson Land and Cheung Kong, have captured many commercial investment/development opportunities in Central after 1997.

Political uncertainty and the delisting decision

HKL was established in 1889 by two prominent businessmen in Hong Kong—Sir Paul Chater and James Johnstone Keswick. Their political background and lobbying ability yielded a prime reclaimed site in Hong Kong after its formation, which provided a starting point for HKL's development of "Central" as Hong Kong's primary business district. After that, HKL built and redeveloped commercial buildings on its Central sites through the decades. In 2000, it was estimated that HKL's holdings represented about 40 percent of total Grade A office stock and some 45 percent of total prime retail space in Central (Sito, 1999). Residential properties accounted for a negligible portion of the group's portfolio.

Although there were great early successes from JMG and HKL's commercial activities in Hong Kong and China, the relations between JMG and China were not always good. After the founding of the People's Republic of China in 1949, JMG was compelled to abandon most of its business interests in Mainland China, and concentrated on its remaining interests in Hong Kong (Sender, 1993). After 1949, Jardines and Hong Kong Land prospered along with Hong Kong, as the Territory developed rapidly from an entrepot and mainly agricultural economy, through light manufacturing to a higher-order trade and financial services economy by the mid-1990s. However, JMG and HKL's image and standing in Hong Kong society, and ultimately their prosperity, were always seen as intimately associated with Jardine's presence in the lead-up to the Opium Wars and the establishment of Hong Kong in 1842, and subsequently with the British colonial government and its machinations (rightly or wrongly) (Tate, 1995). Moreover, it all occurred against the increasing uncertainty created by the looming change of sovereignty in Hong Kong in 1997, as Hong Kong's colonial era drew to its end, and uncertainty over the approach to Hong Kong's freewheeling capitalism that would be adopted by the new sovereign, the PRC.

Despite the assurances of the 1984 Joint Declaration and adoption of The Basic Law, Hong Kong's mini-constitution, which enshrined capitalism at least until 2047, there remained general uncertainty in the business community and lack of confidence in the takeover of Hong Kong by China after 1997. For JMG and HKL matters came to a head between 1984 and 1994. From the early 1980s, HKL had been subject to a serious takeover challenge led by some of Hong Kong's most powerful business interests, who sought to unlock the group's shareholder value in its commercial real estate assets, which were often considered to be underused by analysts and other real estate companies. Challenges centered around Li Ka-Shing, the Chairman of Cheung Kong (Holdings) Limited. To counter these challenges, JMG first established a new company, Jardine Matheson Holdings, incorporated in Bermuda in 1984. After failure in seeking an exemption from the Hong Kong Stock Exchange's takeover code, Jardine Matheson moved its primary stock exchange listing from Hong Kong to London in 1991. Then, in 1994, Jardine Matheson delisted six companies, including HKL, in Hong Kong and moved their listings to Singapore. The group's actions had a significant detrimental effect on business sentiment in Hong Kong, as it was viewed as a major insult to the PRC government and its already declared intention to adopt a hands-off approach to managing Hong Kong, and, given the political climate of the time and JMG's history, led to rapid deterioration in relations between Jardine Matheson and China. These strategic actions came to affect Hongkong Land's fortunes detrimentally for much of the following decade. In the 1990s, JMG's participation in business in China and Hong Kong was impeded by the Chinese Government (Shameen, 2007). Realizing this as a grave error, the managing director of Jardine Matheson issued a general apology to China in 1995 (Davies and Ridding, 1996); and somewhat improved relations gave HKL opportunities to invest in Mainland China which it only managed to bring to fruition meaningfully through joint ventures with local developers a decade later (from 2005 onwards), particularly in the residential sector.

It was clear that JMG and HKL were at an important strategic impasse as 1997 approached, despite its apparent reconciliation with China. In Hong Kong's dynamic commercial environment others took the opportunity to make gains from the Group's malaise, and JMG and HKL were confronted again with competition and takeover threats from local conglomerates in Hong

Kong. These were not from new actors—in 1997 and 1998 the Li Ka-Shing flagships, Cheung Kong and Hutchison Whampoa moved again by accumulating through two companies owned by Li Ka-Shing 3.03 percent of Jardine Matheson Holdings and 3.06 percent of HKL. After reaching 3 percent, any further bid to take over HKL would be expensive, and effectively stopped the bid, essentially the result of the defensive, cross-shareholding structure established between Jardine Matheson Limited and Jardine Strategic Holdings Limited, all as part of the 1984 Bermuda incorporation.[2] By 2000, HKL was 32.9 percent directly held by Jardine Strategic Holdings Limited, while Cheung Kong (Holdings) Limited and Hutchison Whampoa Limited together held a 4.7 percent interest in HKL (Pretorius and Ho, 2009), enough to remain a strategic takeover threat.

By 1997, it was clear that HKL was in a tenuous situation, albeit in no financial difficulty, and that without firm strategic action it was simply managing the decline of a portfolio of prime real estate assets that was in need of significant attention and investment. It needed more than simply countering takeovers based on corporate structure and peculiar shareholder voting classes to maintain control of the company, the company's health and future investment also mattered. HKL (and JMG) adopted interim strategies to address the persistent takeover threats and rumors, and to maintain stability while attempting to develop a post-1997 direction for the company. The actions followed by the company in effect concentrated on highly prudent and effective financial management, and could be interpreted as aimed at maintaining HKL in excellent financial health while it addressed its strategic impasse. Table 33.1 presents historical trends of some measures of HKL's finances for selected years since 1995. From 1995 onwards HKL maintained relatively conservative financial leverage ratios. The average ratios of Net Debt to Equity, Long-Term Debt to Total Assets, and Total Debt to Total Assets are 33 percent, 25 percent and 33 percent, all conservative for a company generating strong and stable cash flow.[3] While low debt ratios possibly prevented the company from suffering financial distress and provided the controlling Keswick family with the

Table 33.1 Key financial statistics for HKL

Measure	*1995*	*2000*	*2005*	*2010*	*2012*	*Mean*	*Volatility*
Capital structure							
Net debt to equity (%)	4.6	74.4	25.7	12.1	12.5	33	
Long-term debt to total asset (%)	13	33.1	33.6	12.5	12.7	24.7	
Total debt to total assets (%)	22.2	75.2	38.9	19.3	17.6	32.9	
Liquidity and financial flexibility							
Current ratio	1.6	1.1	2.1	1.7	2.5	2.4	
Short-term debt to total debt (%)	41.4	56	13.7	35.4	27.9	24.4	
Profitability (%)							
Operating margin	95.6	68.1	66.3	63.1	68.4	45.6	72.2
EBITDA margin	96.1	74.4	62.8	65.4	71.9	45.6	71.9
Return on common equity	3.1	11	33.2	27.6	5.7	10.7	15.9
Return on assets	2.5	6.2	20.3	21.7	4.7	7.3	9.6
Return on capital	2.6	8.9	24.4	23.3	5.2	12	8.4
Dividend and growth rate							
Dividend payout ratio (%)	75.3	65.9	8.6	7.6	27.8	59.2	
Sustainable growth rate (%)	0.8	3.7	30.3	25.5	4.1	8.7	

Note: The data come from Bloomberg. Mean is the average value from 1993 to 2012. Volatility is the standard deviation of these ratios from 1993 to 2012.

potential resources to fight off takeover threats, it also may have meant that the company missed investment opportunities due to its limited use of external capital. Although it had the financial capacity to act quickly when opportunities arose, it often appeared reluctant to do so.

Besides a conservative capital structure, HKL also preserved liquidity and financial flexibility over this time. The average Current Ratio over the period was 2.4 and the average ratio of Short-Term Debt to Total Debt was 24 percent. The profitability ratios indicate that HKL has stable income over the period, clearly its well-located portfolio of assets was still attractive enough to the business community to command good rentals. Dividend Payout ratios were high throughout the time, thus keeping shareholders reasonably comfortable despite the relatively passive strategic position in the late 1990s. Overall, however, the financial status of HKL from 1993 to 2012 suggested that the company had a strong preference to avoid debt financing and retain flexibility, while distributing a large portion of its profits as dividends. In the late 1990s, while financially healthy and with no immediate critical problems looming, there were cracks showing in HKL's edifice as growth rates were shown to be relatively low, and asset management without reinvestment could not be expected to substitute for significant reinvestment for much longer.

While different opinions exist about the nature of these matters, it may be argued that HKL's single most important asset in the 1990s, and the structural factor that allowed them to overcome the political and public sentiment problems that they faced for most of the 1990s, was the quality and stability of cash flows generated by the well-located (but aging) asset portfolio, particularly in Central. This facet of HKL's performance deserves special attention. Most HKL income was (and still is) generated by its asset portfolio in Central, linked by the highly convenient elevated walkways. Table 33.2 breaks down total revenues by components year by year from 1998 to

Table 33.2 Structure of HKL's revenue

Year	*Revenue from commercial and residential properties (US$m)*					*Revenue from commercial properties (US$m)*			
	Total	*Commercial*	*(%)*	*Residential*	*(%)*	*Rental*	*(%)*	*Management services*	*(%)*
1998	527.4	525.3	99.6	2.1	0.4	469.8	89.1	55.5	10.5
1999	418.9	418.1	99.8	0.8	0.2	364.8	87.1	53.3	12.7
2000	386.5	385.7	99.8	0.8	0.2	327.5	84.7	58.2	15.1
2001	396.5	396.5	100	0	0	336.9	85.0	59.6	15.0
2002	396.6	396.6	100	0	0	336.4	84.8	60.2	15.2
2003	383.7	363.7	94.8	20	5.2	303.8	79.2	59.9	15.6
2004	409.1	338.9	82.8	70.2	17.2	278.5	68.1	60.4	14.8
2005	367.6	347.8	94.6	19.8	5.4	279.4	76.0	61.4	16.7
2006	555.9	441.7	79.5	114.2	20.5	346.4	62.3	95.3	17.1
2007	933.2	535.6	57.4	397.6	42.6	440.5	47.2	97.7	10.5
2008	1022.3	676.2	66.1	346.1	33.9	574.1	56.2	104.6	10.2
2009	1322.6	764.4	57.8	558.2	42.2	669	50.6	95.4	7.2
2010	1340.6	784	58.5	556.6	41.5	681.8	50.9	102.2	7.6
2011	1223.7	804.2	65.7	419.5	34.3	700.3	57.2	103.9	8.5
2012	1114.8	862.7	77.4	252.1	22.6	745.5	66.9	117.2	10.5

Note: The data come from Bloomberg and Annual Reports. Revenues from commercial real estate include rental income and service income; and revenues from residential real estate include sales of residential properties and trading properties. Most revenues of residential real estate are from the sales of residential properties.

2012. Its commercial assets in Central continue to contribute the bulk of revenues. Before 2003, residential properties rarely contributed to HKL's revenues, but since then some diversification is evident. Overall it indicates that HKL did diversify somewhat from commercial letting and real estate management to residential properties and residential real estate development. It seemed that after a long time the focus on its Central Portfolio was relaxed somewhat to include cautious ventures into residential development activities, but this is of secondary importance to their major strategic initiative, i.e., repositioning of and adjusting HKL's key Central office and retail real estate portfolio, and diversifying activities geographically and sectorally to make up for time lost during the politically troubled 1990s.

Strategic response: repositioning and adjusting HKL's asset portfolio

In realizing that HKL had fallen behind its principal rivals as far as market share was concerned, particularly in its historical heartland, Central, it also understood that this is with little doubt where the company's strength continued to lie. This is thus where it focused its efforts to re-establish HKL as Hong Kong's landlord of choice to discerning commercial tenants that valued a distinctive address. Also, Hong Kong's financial and legal sectors continued to grow and cluster in Central, many in HKL's office properties, and to these companies comparatively cheaper rental was not always a deciding factor in their location decisions but often proximity to key clients and businesses. But though the distribution of office locations within Hong Kong had changed over the previous two decades, Central still remained the traditional prime office location in Hong Kong. But while HKL owned approximately 40 percent of high-end office space in early 1990, other than 9 Queens Road Central which was eventually subdivided and sold, it had not added any assets to its portfolio. Table 33.3 shows the key buildings that were completed in Central since 1990—HKL's only contribution in effect was a redevelopment of an existing asset—Chater House. This was the problem at the end of the 1990s: the Company's properties remained attractive in terms of location, but they were relatively old compared with new completions such as International Finance Centre, the Cheung Kong Center, the Man Yee Building, AIA Central and The Center.

Table 33.3 Commercial buildings in Central, Hong Kong

Building	*Completed*	*Owner/developer*
9 Queen's Road Central	1991	S E A Holdings Ltd, subdivided ownership, HKL development
AIA Central	2005	Lai Sun Development, others
Cheung Kong Center	1999	Hutchison Whampoa Ltd/ Cheung Kong
Citibank Plaza	1992	Great Eagle, Champion REIT
Entertainment Building	1993	Hysan Development Co. Ltd
Man Yee Building	1999	Man Hing Hong Lands Investment Ltd
The Center	1998	Cheung Kong (Holdings) Ltd
The Centrium	2001	Sino Group Limited
One International Finance Centre	1998	Henderson, Sun Hung Kai
Two International Finance Centre	2003	Henderson, Sun Hung Kai
Hing Wai Building	1998	Hing Wai Investment Co Ltd
New World Tower: Tower 2	1991	New World Development Co. Ltd
Chater House	2003	HKL

Source: www.skyscrapers.com.

It was clear that firm action was required to counter the increasing gravity in Central of companies like Henderson Land and Cheung Kong. The age of its properties had, however, affected HKL's ability to attract new tenants, and long-established tenants were faced with substantial new and enticing choices. For example, in 1999, HKL failed to attract the high profile Mandatory Provident Fund Authority (MPFA) as an anchor tenant in the Landmark's office towers, even though it had offered the lowest rents of the three proposals put to the Authority; and similarly, the Hong Kong Monetary Authority chose to purchase several floors in Henderson/Sun Hung Kai's International Financial Centre. As tenants looked to save costs during the Asian financial crisis by relocating to new properties with long rent-free periods in a market with a substantial vacancy rate, HKL's older and more established buildings in Central saw a rise in their vacancy rates.

At the end of the 1990s, HKL realized that it could not afford to delay action to renew its assets, and embarked on an aggressive marketing campaign to regain the ground it had lost through its period of political paralysis. It moved on several fronts: to reposition its aging office buildings, HKL demolished and redeveloped its oldest building in the Central portfolio in 1998. The new building, named Chater House, comprised an office tower and a retail podium. The shape of the site allowed HKL to offer large modern-style column-free floor plates, missing from its older properties and offered by all newer buildings. Also for the first time in Hong Kong, the building would offer a shell and core finish option that allowed tenants to create their own layouts to suit specific business needs. Upgrading the overhead walkways connecting the building to HKL's other buildings was also part of the redevelopment programme. It was originally suggested that the Company should consider redeveloping some of the older buildings in the Central portfolio, in order to compete with the new stock on offer from other companies, exemplified by buildings such as the Cheung Kong Centre. Although there had been criticisms that much of HKL's aging stock would not be suitable for banks and brokers, the Company was also aware of the need to maintain in Central a range of buildings with different characteristics in order to serve different tenants. Many of the existing tenants of HKL, for example, were lawyers, accountants and doctors who valued their location but did not need upgraded facilities to conduct their business, and were thus not keen to pay for it. Occupancy rates of the Central portfolio remained fairly stable from around 1995–2000 (average 95 percent), and the cash flow it generated, coupled with low leverage, allowed the company to adopt a measured approach to its actions.

However, the office portfolio was only one part of the problem; HKL also had a large portfolio of prime retail properties in Central. It made sense to have an integrated strategy to its retail and office portfolios, as they were all retail podium/office tower buildings, all interlinked with the walkway system that facilitated pedestrian access that greatly advantaged HKL's retail properties. As with the office properties, though, the retail properties, such as The Landmark, Prince's Building and Alexandra House, also faced competition in the Central district and other districts in Hong Kong from newer shopping precincts such as the Galleria and the International Finance Centre Mall, with designer shops and exclusive brand names in abundance. Although located on Central's periphery, situated between Central and Wanchai, Pacific Place in Admiralty was famous for its brand-name luxury goods and became a shopping destination in its own right. In Tsim Sha Tsui, the Harbor City similarly became a focal point and attracted many tourists from Mainland China. A counterweight had to be developed to these competing retail attractions.

As new and modernized retail centers in other business districts increasingly provided a better shopping environment for consumers and tourists, HKL first had to find ways to improve marginal returns and stay competitive in Central. Knowing that rental discount offers would not attract or retain tenants in the long term, nor allow long-term retail tenant portfolio planning, the group started to invest systematically but vigorously in maintaining and improving its Central retail portfolio to enhance marketability and attractiveness. The basement of the retail arcade of the Landmark was the first structure to be refurbished, and was completed in 1999. Second, in April 1998, HKL commenced refurbishment of the Prince's Building retail podium. Externally, the main feature of the refurbishment was the creation of attractive, new double-storey shop units at street level. The old, concrete canopy was removed and replaced by a metal-and-glass canopy. Internally, the refurbishment work involved new designs for shopfronts, new finishes for floors, walls and ceilings and special architectural lighting. New directional signage and retail directories were also installed to complement the improved ground-floor access. Further, HKL continued to upgrade the telecommunications infrastructure of its whole portfolio. In 2000, all of HKL's office buildings were fully wired, providing all tenants with access to a full range of satellite TV, cable TV, broadband, internet, fixed-line and mobile-telephony services. It also upgraded its real estate management standards.

Possibly the most creative, but intuitively logical, component of HKL's repositioning of its Central assets was its "Brand Central" campaign (see Pretorius and Ho, 2009). With a high concentration of its real estate assets in Central, HKL's name was closely linked to the district's locational attractiveness, and the Brand Central campaign aimed to embed "Central" and "HKL" as synonymous in the public's mind. The Brand Central market awareness campaign highlighted the attraction of Central as a prime office and shopping location and promoted HKL's association with Central. The group made initial investments to develop a community website known as "centralhk.com," which would provide information on the latest promotional, cultural and musical events in Central, and would highlight dining privileges and the trendiest items on offer. To further strengthen the image of The Landmark as the focus of community life in Central, HKL staged regular cultural events and exhibitions. It segmented its Central portfolio further by differentiating The Landmark further, with its own marketing imagery, in 2012. Through the launch of these campaigns, HKL had redefined its role as a landlord and combined strategic marketing of its commercial property assets as partner to the business of its tenants.

The Central portfolio was always the core asset in HKL and its principal source of value, and for a long time the Company thus continued to focus its attention on Central district in Hong Kong. While the repositioning of its Central assets followed its unstable domicile commitment of the mid-1980s to the late 1990s, it also addressed the concentration risk associated with its asset portfolio in Central and Hong Kong. After incorporating in Bermuda and delisting from Hong Kong, the company tried to diversify its business geographically to reduce its exposure to Hong Kong. An earlier series of attempts since the 1970s had proven unsuccessful, however. One example was the investment in Trafalgar House, a British conglomerate in real estate investment, real estate development, construction, shipping and more, where HKL eventually took a loss of about £100 million by selling its shares to Kvaerner in 1996. The company then attempted to diversify its portfolio by investment in commercial properties in Asia. Its activities in the Marina complex in Singapore were particularly successful. In 1998 and 1999, revenues generated outside Hong Kong were negligible, at around 4.5 percent between 2000 and 2005. In these years the company held investment properties in Hanoi and Singapore; and after 2006, HKL launched various residential and commercial projects in Singapore, Macau, Bangkok and Jakarta (see Table 33.4). Since then non-Hong Kong revenues have been at levels mostly exceeding 10 percent, as can be seen from Table 33.5 (though fairly volatile). The strategy of broadening its commercial investments regionally did yield rewards in that it enabled HKL to diversify its earnings geographically and allowed participation in the growth of important Asia cities, but possibly of greater importance was that it created a presence for HKL outside Hong Kong.

The last highly visible piece in HKL's repositioning strategy was to increase its activities in the residential sector. Since repositioning, the company commenced its first residential development

Table 33.4 Geographic composition of HKL's revenue

Revenue	*Hong Kong, Macau and China (US$m)*	*(%)*	*South-east Asia and others (US$m)*	*(%)*	*Total*
1998	525	99.5	2.4	0.5	527.4
1999	415.8	99.3	3.1	0.7	418.9
2000	374.2	96.8	12.3	3.2	386.5
2001	378.8	95.5	17.7	4.5	396.5
2002	378.3	95.4	18.3	4.6	396.6
2003	365.8	95.3	17.9	4.7	383.7
2004	391.4	95.7	17.7	4.3	409.1
2005	349.2	95.0	18.4	5.0	367.6
2006	427	76.8	128.9	23.2	555.9
2007	517.8	55.5	415.4	44.5	933.2
2008	648.7	63.5	373.6	36.5	1022.3
2009	834.4	63.1	488.2	36.9	1322.6
2010	935.9	69.8	404.7	30.2	1340.6
2011	937.6	76.6	286.1	23.4	1223.7
2012	999.7	89.7	115.1	10.3	1114.8

Note: The data come from Bloomberg and Annual Reports. According to annual reports, starting from 2007, HKL generated revenues from Macau and Mainland China.

project in Hong Kong in 2001 and realized profits from its residential activities in 2003. In 2006, the company had 11 residential projects in Singapore; in the same year the residential sector contributed approximately 20 percent of total revenues. In 2007, this portion increased to 42 percent, from zero in 2002. With more residential projects launched and completed in Mainland China and Singapore, it appears as if HKL has indeed set about becoming more active in development activity, the most profitable (and risky) real estate sector of all. This is some way indeed from the image of the staid and static portfolio investor of the 1980s and somewhat directionless and politically unpopular company of the 1990s.

Conclusion

The case of Hongkong Land Holdings Ltd well illustrates several important facts of the state of business, governance, strategy and the influence of governments. While HKL remains a Hong Kong company, albeit listed in Singapore, its ill-fated political judgments particularly at the end of the 1980s and during the early 1990s and its delisting from Hong Kong, harmed relations between HKL and its parent company and the Chinese government. The company took many years to re-establish its good faith in Hong Kong and repair the relations with the Chinese government, which required significant public acts of contrition. The company itself has worked steadily since the late 1990s to reposition the company, renew and partially redevelop its portfolio of prime commercial property assets in Hong Kong, but also to diversify increasingly into profitable development activities, all effectively backed by strong recurrent cash flows from its now better performing Central portfolio. This strategy further still has substantial potential, with untapped redevelopment scale in several of its prime Central assets. HKL also deserves credit for commencing a two-pronged diversification strategy, geographic and sectoral (residential), notably with activities in China that have largely come to fruition after 2010. Possibly least tangibly, it has to be credited

Table 33.5 HKL's investment properties and development projects

Year	*Commercial property holdings*		*Commercial developments*	*Residential holdings*	*Residential developments*
1999	Central Portfolio	Hanoi: 2 properties	Hong Kong: 2 projects; Singapore: 1 project	Hong Kong: 1 property	
2000	Central Portfolio	Singapore: 1 property; Hanoi: 2 properties	Hong Kong: 1 project	Hong Kong: 1 property	
2001	Central Portfolio	Singapore: 1 property; Hanoi: 2 properties	Hong Kong: 1 project	Hong Kong: 1 property	Hong Kong: 1 project
2002	Central Portfolio	Singapore: 1 property; Hanoi: 2 properties		Hong Kong: 1 property	Hong Kong: 1 project
2003	Central Portfolio	Singapore: 1property; Hanoi: 2 properties		Hong Kong: 1 property	Hong Kong: 1 project
2004	Central Portfolio	Singapore: 1 property; Hanoi: 2 properties			Hong Kong: 2 projects
2005	Central Portfolio	Singapore: 1 property; Hanoi: 2 properties			Hong Kong: 2 projects
2006	Central Portfolio	Singapore: 1 property; Hanoi: 2 properties			Hong Kong: 2 projects; Singapore: 11 projects
2007	Central Portfolio	Singapore: 1 property; Hanoi: 2 properties			Hong Kong: 2 projects; Singapore: 11 projects
2008	Central Portfolio	Singapore: 1 property; Hanoi: 2 properties			Hong Kong: 2 projects; Singapore: 12 projects
2009	Central Portfolio	Singapore: 1 property; Hanoi: 2 properties			Hong Kong: 1 project; Singapore: 9 projects

(Continued)

Table 33.5 (Continued)

Year	*Commercial property holdings*		*Commercial developments*	*Residential holdings*	*Residential developments*
2010	Central Portfolio	Singapore: 3 properties; Macau: 1 property; Jakarta: 2 properties; Bangkok: 1 property; Hanoi: 2 properties	Singapore: 1 project; Jakarta: 1 project	Hong Kong: 2 properties; China: 1 property; Macau: 1 property	Singapore: 10 projects; China: 7 projects
2011	Central Portfolio	Singapore: 3 properties; Macau: 1 property; Jakarta: 2 properties; Bangkok: 1 property; Hanoi: 2 properties	Hong Kong: 1 project; Singapore: 1 project; Jakarta: 1 project	Hong Kong: 2 properties; China: 1 property; Macau: 2 properties	Singapore: 10 projects; China: 8 projects
2012	Central Portfolio	Singapore: 3 properties; Macau: 1 property; Jakarta: 2 properties; Bangkok: 1 property; Hanoi: 2 properties	Hong Kong: 1 project	Hong Kong: 2 properties; China: 1 property; Macau: 2 properties	Singapore: 9 projects; China: 8 projects

Source: HKL Annual Reports, various years. China refers to Mainland China.

for establishing a most creative "Brand Central" marketing strategy to raise awareness of its ubiquitous position in Central, and in particular the prominence of its retail portfolio. In all, HKL has made up for the strategic ground it lost, but, possibly irrevocably, it has also lost critical market share: from being the undisputed dominant commercial landlord in Central until the mid-1990s, it no longer has this beneficial position and has now to compete much harder for new business against newer assets and competitors with deep pockets.

With respect to corporate governance, however, JMG and HKL do not represent what may euphemistically be described as international "best practice." It is almost impossible to acquire some of HKL's still underused prime commercial properties, because cross-shareholding ensures that the controlling status of Jardine Matheson and its subsidiaries, including HKL, stays with the Keswick family. Not without some irony, here in Asia is a company controlled by a British family, and Asia is where Asian corporate governance is so often criticized for being overly family-centric, detrimental to minorities, and also against the development of a market in corporate control (Claessens *et al.*, 2000). Nevertheless, it seems as if HKL has adapted to the business environment and overcome its political problems in post-handover Hong Kong. Questions still remain, however. In the future, is there a programme to redevelop some buildings in the Central portfolio given that some are aging, have redevelopment potential, and that there is now more intensive competition in Central? How should the company approach its retail portfolio as retailing in Hong Kong marches relentlessly up-market and with the competition of more retail centers? How would HKL and JMG handle the takeover threat in the future?

Notes

1 Five of these companies (Jardine Matheson, Jardine Strategic, Dairy Farm, Hongkong Land and Mandarin Oriental) belonged to 33 constituent stocks in the Hang Seng Index before they were delisted on the Hong Kong Exchange.
2 See Pretorius and Ho (2009).
3 In 2000 and 2001, the ratios of Total Debt to Total Assets were 75.19 percent and 82.17 percent, which are exceptionally high. According to its annual reports, HKL raised debt financing by "taking advantage of the favorable debt market environment for high-quality borrowers to source fresh funding facilities." The ratios in these two years increase the average ratio of twenty years.

References

Claessens, S., Djankov, S. and Lang, L.H. (2000) "The separation of ownership and control in East Asian corporations," *Journal of Financial Economics,* 58(81): 112.
Davies, S. and Ridding, J. (1996) "Taipans who missed the boat," *Financial Times,* March 2/March 3, 1996, p. 7.
Hongkong Land Holdings (1998–2012) *Company Annual Reports.* Hong Kong: author.
Mok, H.M., Lam, K. and Cheung, I. (1992) "Family control and return covariation in Hong Kong's common stocks," *Journal of Business Finance & Accounting,* 19(2): 277–293.
Pretorius, F. and Ho, M. (2009) "Hongkong Land Holdings Limited: strategic repositioning of real estate assets," The Asia Case Research Centre, The University of Hong Kong, Ref. 03/157C.
Sender, H. (1993) "Fixed assets: British Hongs still tied to the colony," *Far Eastern Economic Review,* July 8, p. 22.
Shameen, A. (2007) "Can Jardine Matheson remake itself into a growth story?" *Edge,* (Singapore), October 8.
Sito, P. (1999) "Hongkong Land upgrades Central portfolio," *South China Morning Post,* March 22.
Tate, M. (1995) "House of horrors: how Jardine's bolt hole became a black hole?" *The Observer,* November 5.

34

Entrepreneurship in the food and catering industry

A case study of Maxim's Group

David F.K. Ip and Richard Cheung Lam

Introduction

Few can dispute that Hong Kong Maxim's Group is the largest food and beverage corporation and restaurant chain in Hong Kong. According to its official webpage (www.maxims.com.hk/en/about/cat_01_a.asp), it now "operates over 810 outlets in Hong Kong and China", offering such a wide array of services and products that few can stay unimpressed. This includes a chain of Chinese, Asian and European restaurants, fast food outlets, bakeries and cafés, Japanese restaurants that offer sushi and *donburi* as well as Starbucks. Moreover, it also operates air catering services at 11 cities in China (including Beijing and Shanghai) with Chinese partners in addition to its partnership with the Hong Kong Hospital Authority to provide food services to in-patients of the New Territories West Cluster and the Queen Elizabeth Hospital. At the same time, it is also the caterer for over 60 institutions and local schools in Hong Kong, while providing special catering services for special events (such as the International Exposition and opening ceremony for the Hong Kong International Airport). Furthermore, its presence in the Chinese festive products market should not be overlooked—the moon cakes (for the Mid-Autumn Festival), dumplings (for the Dragon Boat Festival), Chinese sausages, and Chinese puddings (for the Chinese New Year), as well as the wedding cakes it produces, are particularly popular, even on the Mainland.

What is remarkable about the Hong Kong Maxim's Group is not how successful its current operation is, but how it has managed, in only a few decades, to expand from only a small local restaurant serving Western food in 1956 into a leading cross-border giant corporation in the food and beverage sector. In particular, we are interested not only in how it was started, but also the process by which its owners developed and nurtured the business, applying their creativity and determination to exploring the opportunities in the market, taking on the risks and committing the resources required to realize their goals, and the innovations and strategies they devised to respond to and overcome the challenges in growing their operations. In short, it is their entrepreneurship that should deserve our attention and this is precisely what this chapter intends to do—a case study of the founders of the Hong Kong Maxim's Group, Dr James Wu and his elder brother, S.T. Wu, and their entrepreneurship.

Other than what is specified, most of the data in this chapter is derived from our personal interviews with Dr James Wu, conducted in April 2013.

In the beginning

The first Maxim's Restaurant was founded in 1956 and it was a major departure from what James Wu and his elder brother, S.T. Wu, had been doing. S.T. Wu was an economics graduate of Lingnan University in Guangzhou. Upon his graduation in 1935, he was snatched up by Luk Hai Tong (LHT) Limited, a business consortium that started in 1923, whose business involved properties, mortgages, life insurance and pharmaceuticals,[1] to be the accountant for one of its major hotels, the Gloucester Luk Kok, one of grandest, if not the tallest, buildings in Hong Kong.

In 1945, when James Wu returned to Hong Kong after completing his tertiary education in Lingnan University, he worked as an assistant manager to his brother running the Queen's Theatre, a posh cinema managed by LHT, where his grandfather and father were also shareholders. Given the nature of their work, they often had to entertain movie stars, producers and bankers in Western restaurants. At the time, there were only two major Western restaurants in Hong Kong—the Peninsula in Kowloon and the Hong Kong Hotel on Hong Kong Island. Yet the latter closed its door in 1953 and that left a noticeable gap in the Hong Kong restaurant market. This left James thinking about running his own Western restaurant, not merely to take advantage of the opportunity left open by the closure of the Hong Kong Hotel, but more importantly, he thought it was time to have a Western restaurant operated by Chinese and serving clients who were not exclusively Westerners.

James first began to experiment by running a coffee lounge for the more up-market cinema-goers at the Queen's Theatre—those who paid higher admission charges for the Dress Circle. It was called the Savoy, and perhaps one could say this was the beginning of the Maxim's.

In 1956, the time seemed right for James and S.T. to open their Western restaurant. A small Western restaurant located in Lane Crawford Building, one of the prime office buildings in Hong Kong's CBD (Central Business District), decided to close down because the owners were unhappy about the profit-sharing arrangements with the building management. Given the availability of a prime location, and the support from a few classmates at Lingnan University, the two brothers established Hong Kong Caterers Ltd to establish Maxim's, a French restaurant cum nightclub with live band music in the winter of 1956, with an investment of HK$300,000, a sum that could have bought them two properties or ten flats at the time.

It has to be noted that, however, when James entered the restaurant business, he was not exactly a total layman. When he was a student at the Lingnan University, he in fact had some experience of the canteen catering service in the student canteen, particularly in terms of learning how important it was to control costs, delivering food and services as well as management.

Growth and the first major challenge

James was very proud of the risks Maxim's took between 1956 and 1958. As a way to build the image of the restaurant, Maxim's hosted a number of food festivals featuring international cuisine, and it also pioneered a children's menu specifically catering for kids, with food served on plates decorated with the images of Mickey Mouse. It was also the first restaurant in Hong Kong serving strawberries imported from Japan and served with fresh cream, with a price tag of HK$8 per serving, that made its reputation as a classy restaurant in the colony. But most importantly, as a strategy to impress its clientele further, James decided to host two performances given by the then famous pop group, The Platters, whose recordings of "Only You", "Smoke Gets in Your Eyes", and other hits had been top of the charts the world over. This was an immediate success; not only were the 200 seats in the restaurant booked out days before the performances, but also on the night of the performance, police had to be called in to control the crowds who were outside the restaurant trying to get in, giving the restaurant the publicity it needed to enhance its position as an exclusive, top-class restaurant.

However, in 1962, Maxim's faced its first major challenge when the major international hotel chains, Hilton, Mandarin Oriental and others, opened their restaurants and nightclubs, one by one, making it more and more difficult for Maxim's to compete in the business particularly when the competitors were offering more grandiose club designs, classier menus, bigger live bands and more popular acts. The profits of Maxim's began to nosedive and this called for new strategies in response.

Both James and S.T. had to make a critical decision whether Maxim's should confront their rivals head-on or whether they should seek a different approach to running their restaurant/nightclub altogether. In the end, they decided that, given their financial capacity and experience, it would be wise to adopt a strategy of broadening their clientele base, turning Maxim's into smaller restaurants and placing them in various locations in Hong Kong as a way to expand its business without having to take the unnecessary risk of losing out to the giant hotel chains. In 1966, Maxim's decided to launch its first café, Maxim's Boulevard, and a cake shop, Maxim's Cakes, at the Ocean Terminal, Hong Kong's first major shopping centre and terminal for cruise ships, which immediately captured an upmarket clientele who enjoyed having tea, coffee and Western pastries. Its success helped Maxim's to redefine its future pathways—in the following two years, a total of 20 Maxim's cafés and bakeries proliferated, moving away from its earlier high-end market but paving the way for its eventual expansion into a fast-food restaurant chain in 1972.

Development by innovation

The 1970s were an important watershed decade for business for Maxim's. In 1970, Japan was the host of Expo '70 (*Nihon bankoku hakuran-kai*, or *Ōsaka Banpaku*, as it was held in Osaka between March 15 and September 13). This was the first World's Fair held in Japan and Hong Kong was also a participant with its own pavilion showcasing the culture and attractions of the city. As part of the package, the pavilion required a canteen, not only to provide food and meals to the staff working in the pavilion, but also to promote Chinese food to the Expo visitors from all over the world. The Hong Kong government subsequently called for quotations for the provision of catering services, yet few responded. This was because many companies were scared off by the demonstrations being staged by striking workers in the streets in Japan, which often led to violent, open conflicts with the police, especially during spring and autumn. However, for James, behind every risk there was always an opportunity. He estimated that, as an international exposition being held in Asia for the first time, within six months the number of visitors should be around 32 million, of which 30 million would be from Japan. To him, this represented a huge, captive market demanding to be accessed. Finally, Maxim's submitted a quotation and was awarded the contract for the exposition catering.

For James, what followed was the bigger challenge of devising a management plan for the canteen first and foremost to serve effectively and smoothly a huge, international clientele, of which Maxim's had little previous experience, while at the same time assuming the role of ambassador to promote Hong Kong's Chinese food. To this end, James and one of his business partners spent half a year in Japan visiting canteens serving fast foods. He was particularly impressed by what he saw in the canteen located on the top floor in the popular department store Matsusakaya, where each customer could get and finish their meal within a short 26 minutes with the help of a ticketing system and a menu board clearly listing the prices of the available food items of the day. Based on the management ideas he had learned from the Japanese canteen and his own ideas as to what would suit the taste of international visitors, he planned three set menus of different prices for Chinese lunches, that included Chinese dim-sum, pickles and barbequed pork as well as a more sophisticated Cantonese food dinner menu for both visitors and the Hong Kong pavilion staff who had little chance of finding other canteens open on the Expo site in the evening. Moreover, as a measure to ensure the quality of the food it served, James decided to offer his chefs double the salaries they normally received, plus two months' extra bonus, and two trips for their family members to visit them in Japan. Assisted by his daughter, Annie, who applied the public relations skills and language ability she had gained from studying at the Armstrong Business College in Berkeley, California, the success at the Expo turned out to be a turning point for Maxim's, not only in terms of the financial gain (about one million Hong Kong dollars), but also the inspiration it provided for James to experiment further in serving Chinese food and advancing Maxim's.

In 1971, building on the insights gained from the Japanese operation, Maxim's decided that conceptually Chinese restaurants could be run drastically different from the traditional practice. The first major departure was the decor of the restaurant. Traditionally, Chinese restaurants were usually adorned with traditional Chinese cultural motifs, including the use of bright red and gold colors, as well as the ubiquitous symbols of dragons and phoenix, lanterns and hard floors. What Maxim's decided to offer was a completely new concept—Chinese food, but Western service. As part of the Western service, the decor of its Chinese restaurants was reimaged and redesigned. A great deal of thought went into creating a less boisterous or bustling but more intimate and serene ambience for serving a Chinese meal—the colour scheme of the decor was toned down with the absence of loud colours; instead beige and other pastel colours were employed. Likewise, all its restaurants were carpeted to minimize the annoying clacking and distracting noises coming from customers walking on hard surfaces. Waiters working in these restaurants also had a complete makeover—they were required to appear well groomed and well-mannered, aided by their simple yet well designed uniforms. Even the plates and bowls and cutlery used were deliberately simple—white, unadorned as opposed to the traditional ones often embossed with motifs of longevity and good fortune. Nonetheless, the one major decision Maxim's determined to make and stick to was its absolute refusal to allow its diners to share a table, a practice which many successful traditional Chinese restaurants considered suicidal for business at the time.

These new ideas were introduced to Maxim's first Chinese restaurant, Jade Garden, managed by James Wu's daughter, Annie Wu. In addition to the new practices described, the restaurant was also known for a number of bold moves. The first was its location. Instead of being on the street level, according to tradition, it was located on the fourth floor of Star House. Furthermore, while most traditional Chinese restaurants tended to display their barbequed meat and foods at the front near the entrance, they were placed in the middle section of the restaurant, making it easy for diners in every corner of the restaurant to see while the waiters now had to walk a shorter distance to deliver these dishes from this section of the restaurant.

Thereafter, the company launched a number of Cantonese restaurants based on this concept, of which Maxim's Palace was known to be one of the Chinese restaurants occupying the largest floor space in Hong Kong, and the others were known for serving regional Chinese cuisines (including Chiuchow Garden, Peking Garden, Hunan Garden, Shanghai Garden and Sichuan Garden). Indeed, the model provided by Maxim's practically revolutionized and institutionalized how Chinese restaurants are run and how Chinese food could be served to upper middle-class diners in Hong Kong. It is not an overstatement by saying that in every "modern" Chinese restaurant in Hong Kong, one can see the imprint of Maxim's. And when Maxim's became the normal, standard benchmark for the industry, it is easy for many to overlook how original and innovative Maxim's was.

Partnership

If the Expo '70 was a major milestone for Maxim's, two years later, the addition of Hongkong Land of the Jardine Matheson Group as its partner or major shareholder was even more critical in shaping growth and development. According to James Wu, Jardine Matheson had been planning to get into the Chinese restaurant business for a while but they lacked the knowledge and expertise. After the success in Japan, Maxim's was quite determined to continue to expand its cafés and restaurants, but it also realized that a major problem it had to overcome was getting the right premises in the right locations. Knowing that Hongkong Land, a subsidiary of Jardine Matheson, owned quite a few properties in Tsim Sha Tsui, Causeway Bay as well as the Central Business District in Hong Kong, Maxim's believed that joining forces with Jardine would be the most strategic move for its growth. In doing so, Maxim's agreed to sell off 50 per cent of its shares to Jardine in 1972, allowing half its profits to go to its new partner while, in return, it gained easy access to the premises in prime properties owned by Hongkong Land.

At the time, the joint venture with Jardine Matheson Group was regarded by many as very risky because the common perception of forming a partnership with a Western/foreign partner meant the automatic subordination of the Chinese partner. However, James was able to convince Jardine that his elder brother, S.T. Wu, should be the Chair of the board of directors, which would be the best way to demonstrate trust between the working partners. Also, should conflicts arise, it would be better to settle things within the board rather than leave decisions to the shareholders meeting, where consensus would normally take more time and effort to reach.

After more than 40 years of partnership with Jardine Matheson, it became clear that the trust and decision made then have been central to continued success of Maxim's even until the present: throughout the period of this partnership, not only was there no argument over profit-sharing, most importantly, this partnership has guaranteed that Maxim's will continue to open new branches in Hong Kong's most strategic prime locations in the Central Business District.

Diversification: airplane catering

Jardine Matheson Group, however, is not the only business partner Maxim's has. A bigger and even more important partner, in fact, emerged in 1979 when Deng Xiao Ping, who was the Vice Premier of China at the time, decided to sign a bilateral aviation agreement with the USA for a US–China air service, with the first direct flight scheduled to take off on May 1 in 1980 between San Francisco and Beijing. However, this also posed another monumental problem for the Civil Aviation and Administration of China (CAAC) because meals had to be served during the long-haul flight without any stopover, as dictated by Deng. At the time the airplane catering service was practically non-existent in China. While Japan Air Lines and Swiss Air were happy to assist, they also made harsh demands—the former demanded priority rights for Japanese planes to land in return for a US$4 million loan, and the latter demanded high interest payments and a 50/50 profit-sharing deal. Both options were considered by CAAC as unacceptable but there were few alternatives. In the end, Shen Tu, the then Director of CAAC, contacted the Chief of China News Agency in Hong Kong, Wang Kang, for help. Wang Kang had met and befriended James Wu through its annual China National Day banquets and receptions, where catering was provided by Maxim's. With encouragement and assistance from his daughter, Annie Wu, James decided to accept the challenge but the obstacles encountered were numerous.

Four were in particular significant. The first was the CAAC's lack of understanding and hence the rejection of the business framework to set up a limited company for the catering business; and the second was the issue of shareholding—CAAC simply could not understand why it should hold 51 per cent while Maxim's held 49 per cent. Third was the final approval by the central Chinese government, and fourth was that the embargo imposed on China by the USA since the Korean War in the 1950s still remained valid at the time, and this meant no air-catering kitchen equipment was allowed to be exported to China directly unless someone was willing to re-ship the entire shipment to China and pay for the expenses, which amounted to US$2 million. In the end, it took James and his daughter rounds of negotiation, a great deal of perseverance, patience, and determination to overcome these problems. In the process, James invited Dairy Farm Limited, which was the only caterer providing in-flight meals at the Hong Kong Kai Tak Airport, and the East Asia Bank to set up a new company, Hong Kong-China Air-Catering Company Limited (HKCAC), to provide air-catering and act as a guarantor responsible for any losses incurred should the business deal with CAAC fall through. He also took charge of transporting the entire kitchen for air-catering from the USA to Hong Kong, then shipped it to Tianjin via cargo and to Beijing by trucks. And on April 21, 1980, less than two weeks before the first direct flight between San Francisco and Beijing took off, approval from the Foreign Investment Management Committee finally came through, enabling CAAC (Beijing Air-Catering Company Limited) and HKCAC to operate legally as the first ever Sino-Foreign Joint Venture No. 1 in China. Its success not only opened up opportunities for Maxim's to expand its operation to Shanghai and other airports, but it also has become the benchmark for other air-caterers in China thereafter.

Reinvention of Maxim's

At the time when Maxim's was expanding its Chinese restaurants using its unique model, its first fast food outlet was also established in 1972. Like its Chinese restaurants, immediately the fast food operation became so popular that other caterers began to copy it. However, after almost a quarter of a century's service, as observed by Michael Wu, one of the members of the third generation of the Wu family who joined Maxim's at the age of 21, Maxim's seemed to have grown old-fashioned and tired, to the point that even OLs (office ladies), a Hong Kong term referring to women working in white-collar jobs in business, were so embarrassed to let others know that they had bought something from Maxim's fast food store that they wanted to hide its shopping bag, while they did not mind showing what they had bought from McDonald's (*Hong Kong Economic Journal*, July 15, 2013: A11). Yet the General Manager of Maxim's did not see any need for change and held on to the philosophy that no change was necessary as long as the business was making a profit. It was not until after 1997 when the restaurant sector as a whole was encountering greater pressures from rising costs and tough competition, that Maxim's decided to continue to diversify further through a complete makeover of its branding and identity.

In 1998, it started a new line of contemporary restaurants and cafes under m.a.x. concepts, characterized by their insistence on offering great food, genial ambience and attentive service in delivering Chinese and a wide variety of cuisines from different corners of the world, including modern Continental, Japanese, Vietnamese, Thai and fusion cuisine. The most notable success in this line of restaurants is Thai Basil, which was regarded by Condé Nast Traveler as one of the 60 best restaurants in the world in 2000. The success spurned another concept of a more affordable South-east Asian restaurant in 2005, Rice Paper.

Meanwhile, in 2000, a number of their flagship Chinese restaurants also underwent a makeover under another new management framework of "jade concepts", delivering a new Chinese cuisine that highlighted delivering fresh, flavourful and healthy Chinese cooking which was not greasy, with no MSG (monosodium glutamate) added, while being tastefully presented and supplemented with an appropriately selection of premium grade Chinese teas. This included the higher-end restaurants whose names were associated with the word "jade", but later in 2005, with the success of a new Chinese restaurant, Jasmine, operating under the m.a.x. concepts, some of the "jade concepts" Chinese restaurants were further "modernized".

In many ways, all these changes were initiated by Michael Wu who had been working his way up his ladder within the Maxim's Group to become the Managing Director and one of the board members. But that was not the only new changes he made to the company. In 2000, he also introduced Starbucks to Hong Kong, which currently has over 130 outlets located in Hong Kong and Macau.

However, how Starbucks are run in Hong Kong deserves further attention. In every other country, cooked foods are not allowed to be served in Starbucks because the owner insisted that the smell of cooked food would ruin the aroma of the coffee. However, knowing that it had its own bakeries and patisseries, Maxim's boldly requested Starbucks to allow it to serve cakes, sandwiches and pies using warmers, and this met with little objection. Not surprisingly, within the first two months of operation, the Starbucks outlets were already making a profit and over 30 new branches were subsequently added throughout Hong Kong within the following two years before more Starbucks were opened in Macau.

Three years later in 2003, the Chinese restaurant, Peking Garden, was re-opened in Hong Kong's CBD after more than a year of renovation headed by a Chilean architect, and provided a new eclectic look, featuring bronze and dark wooden touches as well as walls painted an unmistakably Latin shade of red, signalling the total reinvention of the image and branding as bold, innovative, fresh, up-to-date and youthful, targeting specifically an up-and-coming, young, middle-class clientele.

In 2005, against popular belief that only fast food would be profitable in theme-parks like Disneyland, it opened a Chinese restaurant there because "not every visitor would enjoy having hamburgers, hot dogs and pizzas" (*Hong Kong Economic Journal*, July 15, 2013: A11). In the following year, the Group also brought Genki Sushi and Sen-ryo, the former a popular Japanese conveyer-belt sushi restaurant chain, the latter a Japanese restaurant dedicated to serving traditional Edo-style handmade sushi from the Tochigi-ken prefecture in Kanto Region. In the same year, another well-known American steak house, Lawry's the Prime Rib, was also brought to Hong Kong.

If these were attempts to remake Maxim's and give it a totally new image, all the fast food outlets under its wings were not exempt. A new concept, Maxim's MX, was launched at the same time to rebrand these shops. Two well-known Hong Kong designers, Alan Chan and Steve Leung, were selected to complete the remodelling mission—with Chan responsible for offering the fast food chain a new dynamic logo with Leung taking charge of interior design that ultimately received a Gold Award from the New York magazine, *Hospitality Design*, in the fast food design category.

In 2007, a new line of bakery-cafés called simplylife serving freshly baked, handmade European-style breads, pastries and light meals was created, targeting yet another distinct set of young upwardly-mobile clientele. So far 11 of these outlets have been established since then. In March 2008, Maxim's acquired Arome, a bakery that was established in the 1980s specializing in cakes and pastries with a Japanese twist and aiming at the higher-end market. Maxim's also made another expansion into the new supermarket chain, Market Place by Jasons, that aims to carve out a niche in the affluent food market. Then, in a more recent move in 2012, when the supermarket chain opened its latest branch in Causeway Bay, a shopping magnet frequented by tourists, and the fashionable post-1980s and in general, upper middle-class consumers, Maxim's introduced its latest Urban Bakery, featuring freshly baked croissants and other European breads. It was an instant success in that despite its price tag (HK$13 each, as opposed to what is normally charged by other bakeries of HK$9), the number of croissants sold exceeded 2,000 a day.

In 2010, the makeover of Maxim's continued with another new Japanese concept store, Dondonya, serving *donburi* (bowls of rice) using top quality Akitakomachi rice and premium ingredients, making its presence felt. It was later extended further and turned into Dondonya Shokudo (cafeteria), catering specifically to the growing youth market that seems to continually embrace any new Japanese flavour. Similarly, the influence of Maxim's on the Mainland China market increased. In addition to its expansion of cafés (simplylife) and Genki Sushi in Shenzhen, Guangzhou and other cities, a swanky, modern Shanghainese restaurant, Wu Tong Ju, was opened in March 2011, in the very popular and very chic Xintiandi, an entertainment and shopping district in Shanghai.

It must be noted, however, that Maxim's Group was not immune from setbacks. For instance, in 1992, Maxim's did try to extend its market into Guangzhou but with little success. In 1999, at the height of the Hello Kitty craze in Hong Kong, Maxim's went into a joint venture with Sanrio and opened a number of Hello Kitty Cafés but as soon as the fad faded, the cafés were closed down. Likewise, according to an interview with Michael Wu in the *Hong Kong Economic Journal* (15 July 2013), he admitted that: "Some years back, we had our eye on a shop front in Festival Walk in Kowloon Tong for a restaurant, but the landlord [was less than interested] and told us bluntly that our Chinese restaurants were just too behind the times."

Entrepreneurship

There are many ways to define what an entrepreneur is. In many early studies of entrepreneurs, the main focus was on the personal attributes that make them different from waged workers or non-entrepreneurs. For example, some suggested that entrepreneurs were particularly effective in dealing with ambiguous or uncertain situations, especially in the way they made decisions, frequently resisting conformity and favouring taking risks because they enjoyed and were ready to make changes (Sexton and Bowman, 1985). Likewise, others believed that they were focused, creative, egocentric and adept at seizing advantages (Low and MacMillan, 1988; Gartner, 1990; Bolton *et al.*, 2003; Thompson, 2004). In more recent times, entrepreneurs were treated more as individuals who behaved differently rather than having different personal characteristics. For example, Renko *et al.* (2012) highlighted in particular entrepreneurs' ability to seek out and take advantage of business opportunities which others had failed to recognize while Sarasvathy and Venkataraman (2011) opined that they were especially skilled at problem-solving. Although these are well-established and accepted observations, it is more appropriate for this case study to treat the success of Maxim's Group as a process of the growth and development of an organization. For this reason, the framework developed by Wang (2013) of looking at entrepreneurship as a process of identifying, evaluating and pursuing opportunities, and creating new variations, such as products, services and values, by virtue of resources and innovative activities, is also most relevant for illustrating what Maxim's has achieved over the years.

Identification, evaluation and pursuit of opportunities

At first glance, how Maxim's was first started seemed simple, according to the way it was described by James Wu. However, on closer inspection, what was interesting was in fact the market for a Western restaurant for the privileged or elite Chinese clientele had always been there. However, had it not been because of the discrimination he had experienced—that is, "being a Chinese customer I was always told to sit at the table next to the restaurant's washroom"—he would not have been motivated to pursue the notion of having his own Western restaurant with a Chinese clientele base, especially considering that he had little prior professional knowledge of catering except for a very brief period, when he and a group of classmates decided to run their own canteen in protest at the sudden price increase by the caterer while studying at Lingnan University in Qujiang District in Shaoguan. More interesting still was that even when he was able to identify the business opportunity, now looking back, James Wu admitted that it was not possible for the first Maxim's to get off the ground without capital, especially social capital.

In one of his interviews, he confessed that his job as an assistant manager running the posh Queen's Theatre in Hong Kong Island's CBD had enabled him to get to know quite a number of influential people (including Sir Kan Yuet-keung, who was a senior partner of the famous local law firm, Lo & Lo, and who successively served as the chairman of the Law Society of Hong Kong and was later appointed Senior Unofficial Member of the Legislative Council and Executive Council in the 1960s and 1970s). It was they who gave him and S.T. Wu legal and other advice that made it possible for Maxim's to open.

Creation of new variations: products, services and values

It was James Wu and his elder brother, S.T. Wu, who were a major force and were instrumental in creating many new products and services in Maxim's, ranging from its switch from serving an elite to a middle-class clientele, its quick expansion into the pastry market, to its pioneering efforts in adapting attentive service characteristics of Western restaurants to serve Chinese food, then to its more recent diversification into serving Chinese regional and South-east Asian cuisines in its fleet of restaurants, in addition to the continual upgrade of its fast food chains. However, the key guide to the operation of Maxim's, according to Wu, has been his business philosophy or values, which he calls the "three benefits principles" (Yin, 2008).

In short, the three main principles refer to the ways Maxim's as a business deals with its employees, customers and shareholders. Of these three groups, Wu insisted on giving top priority to his employees. In his view, "Catering is a people-centred business that relies on team work. Only good employees can provide good services without which shareholders would not get good returns." Moreover, "Even with the most delicious food, or having the best location, the business would suffer if staff performances are poor." Hence, when Maxim's first started, Wu made a point of driving his kitchen staff home because "they worked till one or two in the morning when buses or trams stopped running".

As an added incentive, in contrast to many Chinese employers in the restaurant business, he wanted Maxim's to offer its employees a salary higher than the normal market rate for the same type of work performed, and that was on top of allowing its employees a day off entitlement each week, which was something unheard of in the 1950s, when almost every Chinese employer wanted to squeeze as much time as possible from their workers as a rule. As well, he believed it was necessary to promote his employees whenever there was a chance, as a way of fostering and consolidating staff morale and as an incentive to encourage better performance. Most importantly, he also pledged he would not sack his staff as long as they were productive, and he made it a principle that every staff member would be paid at the end of the month with no delays, because "every worker in the organization has their family obligations—there are rents and school fees to be paid, and cash is needed to buy food."

Notwithstanding, James Wu preferred to recruit staff who had little previous work experience in the catering/restaurant business. It was his view that "many restaurant workers in the previous generations had developed poor work habits and attitudes" and "bringing them into your own business would run the risks of exposing other staff to bad role models". Having new inexperienced staff members, for him, was not a problem at all as "Maxim's will provide them with proper training and they will learn the culture of the organization."

To James Wu, the organizational culture must be based on merit, and this was to be the only criterion for staff promotion and dismissal. If this sounds a bit too demanding, he in fact has made strong demands of himself. For one thing, he did not consider himself the "big boss" but likes to see himself as a regular staff member who enjoys no special privilege. "Every employee in the organization is entitled to a 15% discount on the foods produced or served by Maxim's and I am no exception," he emphasized strongly in his interview. "I do not get more discounts because I own the business, nor do other members of the board, because I believe it is bad practice for the business when the CEO gets more fringe benefits and especially when these benefits are not accountable."

On Maxim's 50th anniversary, the company held a four-day buffet event for over 12,800 staff members from every rank and file, as a way to show their appreciation of the dedication and hard work they had contributed to Maxim's. The event served a total of 560 different dishes and it set a Guinness Record as the world's largest buffet meal ever served.

As for the second principle, he felt strongly that customers are the cornerstone of business success. For this reason, the Wu brothers firmly believed that a successful business must be attentive to the needs as perceived by the consumers. And this is also where detail and innovation are the most important. In reviewing how Maxim's coped with a few major crises, his wisdom was that "little things made all the difference". The following are a few illustrative examples:

1 When Maxim's first opened its fast food outlet for business, like most other popular fast food joints, the best-selling items were BBQ pork and steamed chicken with rice. However, Wu observed that instead of offering only meat, a few stems of fresh vegetables should be added not only because it would make the meal nutritionally more balanced, it would also make the fast food served in Maxim's stand out from others, especially when none of the competitors were offering fresh vegetables with their meals.
2 When SARS (Severe and Acute Respiratory Syndrome) hit Hong Kong in 2003, business for most food caterers and restaurants suddenly crashed as everyone was overly anxious about health and safety and unwilling to eat out, even to the point of stopping shopping for bread in bakeries. Maxim's Cakes immediately reacted by repackaging their bread and pastries and put them in individually sealed plastic/cellophane bags, making them looked much more hygienic and appealing. In the end, while the business of Maxim's as a group suffered, the volume of sales in its bakeries actually rebounded dramatically.
3 For many Chinese, the mid-autumn festival is not only a major celebratory occasion when moon-cakes are consumed. It is also the time when moon-cake producers, ranging from bakeries to restaurants and hotel chains, are battling one another to claim fame and a significant market share. Determining to win a bigger share of the local market, Maxim's strategy focused on using the best duck eggs as one of its ingredients. As Wu explained, "Many Chinese moon-cake connoisseurs consider the egg yolk to be the key determinant of whether a moon-cake is of good quality. If the moon-cake is cut in half, with its yolk oozing a bright, orangey glow, people would consider it is most desirable and of superior quality." To this end, Wu spent a long time searching for the perfect egg yolk for quality moon-cakes for Maxim's. Indeed, the egg yolk became a major selling point for Maxim's and it also strengthened their reputation as a reliable and quality cake producer.

As for the third principle regarding the shareholders, he made it clear that when the organization had accumulated enough surplus, 80 per cent must be given to the shareholders because that was what they had expected. And he also insisted that contrary to traditional Chinese practice, no shareholder in the company, regardless of how large or small the amount of shares one holds, could exercise any personal influence in hiring or firing staff members because "the merit system must be upheld at all costs". In his view, if the personnel management system fails, ultimately the business will also fail. After serving the company over 50 years, Dr James Wu retired in 2008 and is now the Honorary Chairman.

Michael Wu, the current Chairman and Managing Director of Maxim's Group, did not attain his position simply because of any privilege he derived as part of the Wu family. Instead, when he graduated in 1992 at the age of 21, like everyone else, he worked his way up from the bottom, doing jobs as delivery boy and waiter. When he first joined Maxim's, he was in internal communications. Similarly, Wilson Wu, the current Executive Director of Maxim's Group, also worked his way up from a junior clerk position at CAAC after graduating from Wharton School of the University of Pennsylvania in the USA with his MBA.

Creativity and innovations

In reviewing the history of Maxim's Group, one readily observes that it is also a process of the application of creativity and innovations—specifically, applying creative solutions to problems, enhancing and improving the efficiency and effectiveness of its business, especially through developing new ways of doing things as well as heading off in new directions.

In the early development of Maxim's Group, the Wu brothers' creativity was unmistakable: its success in redefining its position from a trendy club targeting the elites in town to operating a series of French/European-inspired cafés catering for a less prestigious but taste-conscious middle class is indicative of their creativity in resolving the first major crisis of survival. Later on, their decision in taking on the challenge of operating a canteen at the Osaka International Exposition likewise demonstrates not only their willingness to take risks, but also their vision, determination and commitment to find new ways to manage the daily operation of their business by applying techniques that proved to give the Japanese fast food outlets greater efficiency and effectiveness. The incorporation of a formal management system in the operation of Chinese food catering may now seem common and is something that people take for granted, but when seen in its historical context, it was a bold and innovative move that required leadership, dedication and committed investment, particularly in developing and managing human resources. Its continued experiments of fusing "Western [restaurant] services [in style and standards] and Chinese food [presentation]" in its up-market Chinese restaurant chains have further shown that their approach to innovation has been more enterprising than that of other people, especially in terms of focusing on active learning, generating knowledge to lead, and not just responding to the needs of their customers.

Similarly, how James Wu decided to take on the challenge of diversifying into the air catering sector in China and how, in the end, Maxim's came to deliver the final product against all the odds also testifies to Wu's creativity in problem-solving not only in terms of "know-how" but also "know-who" (Gibb, 1996).

Some people in the catering sector in Hong Kong think that the success of Maxim's is due to its luck because of its association with Jardine Matheson, or more specifically, its subsidiary, Hongkong Land, which has provided Maxim's with every opportunity to start a restaurant/bakery in all the buildings it owns, particularly in the CBD. However, those in the know would insist that the sale of half of the shares in Maxim's to Jardine, in fact, was less about luck but more illustrative of the Wu brothers' foresight and creative strategy for planning and consolidating their future expansion (http://realblog.zkiz.com/greatsoup38/22343). Without the injection of financial and property resources, Maxim's rapid expansion and growth would have been much less impressive.

In all fairness, however, the remarkable comeback of Maxim's as an iconic brand in Hong Kong's food and catering sector in recent years must be attributed to the entrepreneurship of its current Chairman and Managing Director, Michael Wu. Much of the makeover from being a tired, safe and conventional business to a renewed, re-energized, young, vibrant, cosmopolitan and diversified operation, typified by its recent acquisition of a franchise to operate Starbucks, Genki Sushi, Lawry's The Prime Rib, and the inauguration of a host of South-east Asian eateries and lifestyle-based cafés not only in Hong Kong, but also in China, in many ways, is based on Michael's own vision of revitalizing a family business, giving it a fresh identity through different personas. His ultimate ambition is to turn Maxim's into an international icon that embodies the quality and experience which consumers find special and unique. And as part of the makeover, a notable convergence of views between Michael and his grand-uncle, James, is for Maxim's to be respected also as an enterprise with corporate social responsibility.

As a social entrepreneur, since 1988 James has been donating his time and money generously to Lingnan University in Guangzhou, as his way of showing his appreciation of what he learned from Lingnan Primary School in Hong Kong, Lingnan University Affiliated Secondary School and Lingnan University in Guangzhou. S.T., however, focused his charity work mostly in his hometown, Taishan (http://realblog.zkiz.com/greatsoup38/22343). In 1987, he persuaded the Ministry of Education of the People's Republic of China to reopen Lingnan University in Guangzhou at its original location for the purpose of "reviving Lingnan education". In 1989, when Lingnan (University) College was established as a business school, he became the first Chairman of the Board of Trustees, leading it to become one of the top business schools in China.

As a business, Maxim's has also been one of the top ten donors in Hong Kong's Community Chest Fund, as well as an active supporter of the Chest's other philanthropic activities. In 2009, it pioneered the idea of donating breads that were not sold daily to charity organizations but it did not work well as NGOs then were not as supportive as in recent times. With participation from its staff and public volunteers, over 200 of Maxim's bakeries have been giving away surplus breads. It is estimated that over 1,000,000 pieces of bread will be given to over 70 charity organizations in 2013. Although Maxim's is not a social enterprise or a non-profit organization that applies entrepreneurial strategies to sustain itself financially, at least it is involved in an innovative use of its own resources and trying to make an impact on their social mission and addressing social needs.

Conclusion

Entrepreneurship has emerged as an area of intense interest in the past few decades not only in the field of management, but also in economics (Kihstrom and Laffont, 1979; Douglas and Shepherd, 2002), psychology (Shane *et al.*, 1991; Kolvereid and Isaksen, 2006), sociology (Lever-Tracy *et al.*, 1996; Thornton, 1999) and other social sciences (Hofstede, 1980; Thomas and Mueller, 2000; Audretsch, 2012; Wiklund *et al.*, 2011). For this reason, the studies conducted span a wide range of foci that include the personal attributes, motivations, skills, behaviours, strategies, leadership, innovation and development of entrepreneurs. However, what this chapter has aimed to accomplish is not so much a case study of one of the individual biographies of one of the founders of Maxim's Group, Dr James Wu, or its current heir in the business, Michael Wu. Rather, it is a study of how the ideas, values and visions of these two key figures have illustrated what entrepreneurship is all about—not merely a process of business survival, but one that involves insights in identifying, seeking, assessing and committing opportunities, finding new ways to enhance, renovate, transform, or invent, create, expand and diversify its products, services as well as reshaping its business vision and values through leadership, especially in taking on challenges, managing risks, and commending resources and innovative activities to inject new energy and synergies to the business. In doing so, the changing contexts and environments that helped to explain the business activities of Maxim's and its directions are also provided. It is hoped that in adopting not a singular perspective, but a developmental and its process-oriented approach for this case study, we could illustrate the diverse and heterogeneous nature of entrepreneurship research, and that by analyzing the experiences of Maxim's, the social learning aspect of entrepreneurship research, i.e., how we can learn from experiences of others, could continue to provide inspirations in this dynamic field of study of human actions.

Note

1 http://huaqiaogp.com/zyrw_show.asp?guid=20100722180144157.

References

Audretsch, D. (2012) "Entrepreneurial research", *Management Decision,* 50: 755–764.

Bolton, B.K., Thompson, J. and Thompson, J.L. (2003) *The Entrepreneurs in Focus: Achieve Your Potential,* London: Thompson Learning.

Douglas, E.J. and Shepherd, D.A. (2002) "Self-employment as a career choice: attitudes, entrepreneurial intentions, and utility maximization", *Entrepreneurship Theory and Practice,* 26: 81–90.

Gartner, W.B. (1990) "What are we talking about when we talk about entrepreneurship?" *Journal of Business Venturing,* 5: 15–28.

Gibb, A.A. (1996) "Entrepreneurship and small business management: can we afford to neglect them in the twenty-first century business school?" *British Journal of Management,* 7: 309–321.

Hofstede, G. (1980) "Motivation, leadership and organization: do American theories apply abroad?" *Organizational Dynamics,* 9: 42–63.

Kihstrom, R.E. and Laffont, J.J. (1979) "A general equilibrium theory of firm formation based on risk aversion", *The Journal of Political Economy,* 87: 719–748.

Kolvereid, L. and Isaksen, E. (2006) "New business start-up and subsequent entry into self-employment", *Journal of Business Venturing,* 21: 866–885.

Lever-Tracy, C., Ip, D. and Tracy, N. (1996) "Diaspora capitalism and the homeland: Australian Chinese networks into China", *Diaspora: A Journal of Transnational Studies,* 5: 239–273.

Low, M.B. and MacMillan, I.C. (1988) "Entrepreneurship: past research and future challenges", *Journal of Management,* 14: 139–161.

Renko, M., Shrader, R.C. and Simon, M. (2012) "Perception of entrepreneurial opportunity: a general framework", *Management Decision,* 50: 1233–1251.

Sarasvathy, S.D. and Venkataraman, S. (2011) "Entrepreneurship as method: open questions for an entrepreneurial future", *Entrepreneurship Theory and Practice,* 35: 113–135.

Sexton, D.L. and Bowman, N. (1985) "The entrepreneur: a capable executive and more", *Journal of Business Venturing,* 1: 129–140.

Shane, S., Kolvereid, L. and Westhead, P. (1991) "An exploratory examination of the reasons leading to new firm formation across country and gender", *Journal of Business Venturing,* 6: 431–446.

Thomas, A.S. and Mueller, S.L. (2000) "A case for comparative entrepreneurship: assessing the relevance of culture", *Journal of International Business Studies,* 31: 287–301.

Thompson, J.L. (2004) "The facets of the entrepreneur: identifying entrepreneurial potential", *Management Decision,* 4: 243–258.

Thornton, P.H. (1999) "The sociology of entrepreneurship", *Annual Review of Sociology,* 25: 19–46.

Wang, Q. (2013) "Constructing a multilevel spatial approach in ethnic entrepreneurship studies", *International Journal of Entrepreneurial Behavior and Research,* 19: 97–113.

Wiklund, J., Davidsson, P., Audretsch, D.B. and Karlsson, C. (2011) "The future of entrepreneurship research", *Entrepreneurship Theory and Practice,* 35: 1–9.

Yin, X. (2008) "James Wu, Maxim's 'three benefits' makes new experiences in food and beverages". Available at: www.hotels263.com/magazine/Article/ShowArticle.asp?ArticleID=911. (accessed September 16 2013).

35

Entrepreneurship as a global coordinator

The Li & Fung Group

Fu-Lai Tony Yu and Diana S. Kwan

Introduction

> [Li & Fung] focuses on designing the best possible processes across a global network for delivering the right product to the right place at the right time at the right price.
>
> *(Fung* et al., *2008, p. 20)*

Li & Fung is an exemplary multinational enterprise based in Hong Kong since 1949. The company deals with a wide range of products including apparel, household goods, furnishings, toys, health and beauty products. Today, it coordinates the manufacture of goods through a network of 70 offices in more than 40 countries. In 2009, Li & Fung was ranked 27th in the World's Best Companies by *Business Week*, 26th in *Asia's Fabulous*, 50th by *Forbes Asia*, and 888th in the World's Biggest Public Companies by *Forbes.*[1]

In what business is the Li & Fung business group involved? Is it an exporter, a merchandiser, manufacturer, retailer, customer or supplier? Interestingly, the answer can be any one of them. In other words, Li & Fung performs all these functions. However, when viewed from the Austrian perspective of market process, Li & Fung is properly regarded as an international entrepreneur. It earns profits via global coordination. This chapter attempts to use the Austrian theories of entrepreneurship in economics to explain the operations and practice of Li & Fung's business. Specifically, this chapter integrates the contributions of Ludwig von Mises, I.M. Kirzner and F.A. Hayek to entrepreneurship and market process to obtain a theory of global coordination. This theory is then applied to re-interpret Li & Fung's dynamic success.

The literature review

Because Li & Fung are so successful as an international empire, studies on them are not lacking. Materials on the Li & Fung Group can be found from interviews of Victor and William Fung, the third generation of the business empire (for example, see Slater, 1999; Holstein, 2002; Fung, 2007; *CNN*, 2009). In an interview conducted by Magretta (1998), Victor Fung shares the concepts and strategies of borderless manufacturing and supply chain management. Fung's brothers explain the management of supply chain business (Fung, 1997; Fung *et al.*, 2008; Wind *et al.*, 2009). Hutcheon (1992) and Feng (2007) have written the biography of Li & Fung. In particular,

Feng (2007) portrays the transition from traditional Chinese family business to multinational enterprise in terms of business strategy, entrepreneurship and cultural values in the last century. Li & Fung collaborates with their trading partners and adapt to each other through coordination, learning and innovation (Wind *et al.*, 2009: 300–301). Hagel and Brown (2005) further define Li & Fung's role as a network orchestrator which enhances flexibility and connects the best capabilities in the world. Chang and Phi (2007) analyze the acquisition of the Integrated Distribution Services Group Limited (the IDS Group). Case studies of Li & Fung conducted by Harvard Business School include Loveman and O'Connell (1995), Long and Seet (1996), Yoshino and George (1998), Hagel (2002), McFarlane and Young (2002).[2] Despite extensive studies of biography, economic analysis and supply chain management, an entrepreneurial explanation of Li & Fung's operation is still missing. This chapter fills that gap. More specifically, an Austrian theory of global coordination is called for. This chapter starts with an Austrian theory of international entrepreneurship and global coordination, followed by the case study of Li & Fung. The background of Li & Fung is then presented. Li & Fung's global coordination from an Austrian economic perspectives will be presented in the next section. The final section is the conclusion.

The Austrian theory of international entrepreneurship and global coordination

The most important role of international entrepreneurship is to coordinate global economic activities. Austrian economics argues that in the market, no individual is homogeneous.[3] Each market participant has his/her own experience and stock of knowledge, and hence, each thinks and foresees the future differently. As a result, plans in the market often mismatch. F. Von Hayek (1945) calls the compatibility of plans a coordination problem. For example, computer producers in Taiwan (say, ASUS) today need to estimate what consumers (say, JC Penney) in the United States want tomorrow. Likewise, American producers are also keen to know their rivals' plans so that they can formulate their selling or pricing strategies. Charging a wrong price or producing a wrong product (i.e. mismatches of plans) can be disastrous and leads to business failure.

In the Austrian economic perspective, entrepreneurs attempt to coordinate economic activities for profits. In von Mises' words (1949, p. 328):

> The driving force of the market process is provided neither by the consumers nor by the owners of the means of production—land, capital goods, and labor—but by the promoting and speculating entrepreneurs. These are people intent upon profiting by taking advantage of differences in prices. Quicker of apprehension and farther-sighted than other men, they look around for sources of profit. They buy where and when they deem prices too low, and they sell where and when they deem prices too high. They approach the owners of the factors of production, and their competition sends the prices of these factors up to the limit corresponding to their anticipation of the future prices of the products. They approach the consumers, and their competition forces prices of consumers' goods down to the point at which the whole supply can be sold. Profit-seeking speculation is the driving force of the market as it is the driving force of production.

I.M. Kirzner adds further insight into Hayek's and von Mises' arguments. Using Kirzner's ground-breaking insights in 1973 (Kirzner, 1973), we argue that the role of international entrepreneurs lies in their ability to identify global profit opportunities. They discover and exploit global opportunities according to their hunches. International entrepreneurs, with their superior ability of reading market data, exploit profit opportunities around the world. According to

Martin (2007, p. 6), profit opportunities in the world market come in three ways. The first is the recognition of previous errors or mismatches of plans. The second is the introduction of new opportunities. The third is the uncertainty of the future.

International entrepreneurs are able to integrate "innumerable scraps of existing information that are present in scattered form" throughout the world (Kirzner, 1985, p.162). The international coordination process is thus "the systematic plan changes generated by the flow of market information released by market participation—that is, by the testing of plans in the market" (Kirzner 1973, p. 10). Increased coordination means that entrepreneurs' plans are made more compatible (Martin, 2007, p. 4).

Knowledge transmission in a global market

If economics is a coordination problem (Hayek, 1945), then it is of utmost importance to analyze how knowledge is created and transmitted during the process of international exchange. Assuming two individuals, Mr. A and Ms. B, living in England and Hong Kong respectively, each possesses their own stock of knowledge and subjectively interprets incoming events each day. Mr. A wishes to attain end X and Ms. B wishes to attain end Y. Each person will do economic calculations and make a judgment on his or her project with respect to the external environment. Assume Mr. A would like to achieve his end but he does not have the means at his disposal. Furthermore, he does not know where and how to obtain such means. On the other hand, Ms. B owns abundant resources/the means for which she has no use for her purpose, though the resources are suitable for Mr. A to attain his end. The economic problem is that Mr. A and Ms. B do not know each other. Obviously, in this case, international trade cannot be carried out for both lack the knowledge required for trade. According to the subjectivist theory of knowledge (Kirzner, 1979: 137–153), for these two parties, the opportunity simply does not exist.[4]

Even if merchants of two nations accidentally discover that both have the intention to trade, international transaction may not be carried out, for both parties' thinking and actions are socially embedded. Traders' minds are governed by a set of habits, traditions, institutions, norms, customs and legal rules which make them follow these guides without being asked. This knowledge is taken for granted and socially constructed. Each trading party, with different cultures and values, will accordingly interpret the social world differently. Specifically, it takes a lot of effort to find out if the trading partner is trustworthy. This can be illustrated by the first occurrence of trade between the English and the Chinese during the late Ch'ing Dynasty. Their trade encounter unfortunately ended with a conflict, the Opium War. The cultural content of the Sino-British conflict can be seen by the fact that the British referred to this war as a "trade war." For the British, the purpose of the war was to demand free trade with China and eliminate unfair treatment laid down by the Ch'ing government officials. However, the Chinese referred to the conflict to as an "opium war" because of the enormous amount of opium shipped to China, leading to moral degradation and loss of foreign exchange (silver).[5] Hence, knowing your trading parties, making an entrepreneurial move, learning and testing foreign markets by trial and error are the main elements in international trade. However, such important elements are missing from the neoclassical paradigm.

The issues of culture and knowledge justify the role of the middleman in international trade. To be sure, the role of the middleman is well documented in the mainstream price and transaction costs theories (for example, see Casson, 1982; Reekie, 1984). However, from a human agency perspective, a middleman is more than just a person who links both parties together. The middleman, in our case, is also an entrepreneur as well as a knowledge creator. He or she transmits knowledge and performs entrepreneurial discovery, and hence, raises the well-being of both trading parties.

In the above example, assume Mr. A and Ms. B do things routinely each day, and a third person, Mr. C, practises as a middleman.[6] Person C discovers that there is an opportunity in the international market. He contacts Ms. B in Hong Kong and offers to buy the resource which Ms. B has in abundance and sells it to Mr. A in England. As a consequence of Mr. C's entrepreneurial action, all three parties gain. This is essentially the case of Kirznerian entrepreneurship (Kirzner, 1973) which conducts arbitrageurship.[7] The neoclassical economic analysis argues that trade would continue until the marginal rate of substitutions between two goods for all parties is equal. Their analysis would end at the optimal equilibrium. Unfortunately, such technical analysis, though elegantly presented, loses the insight of how human agents behave and how knowledge is created and transmitted. According to de Soto (1995, pp. 234–237), there are at least three significant implications due to the result of entrepreneurial arbitrageurship.

First, by performing as a middleman, entrepreneur Mr. C creates new information which did not exist before. An entrepreneurial act implies the creation of information which takes place in the agent's mind. In our case, information is created by Mr. C. Moreover, as soon as Mr. C enters into the international transaction with Mr. A and Ms. B, new information is also created in the minds of Mr. A and Ms. B. As a result of Mr. C's action, Mr. A in England becomes aware that the resource that he lacks is available in another part of the world. Hence, Mr. A takes a new action that he had not considered before. On the other hand, Ms. B in Hong Kong becomes aware that the abundant resource she possesses can now be sold overseas at a good price too. Therefore, Ms. B also takes a new action previously not taken before. In short, Mr. C's entrepreneurial action gives rise to a chain of new knowledge in the world market.

Second, entrepreneurial creation of knowledge implies the simultaneous transmission of knowledge in the global market. Knowledge transmission means that people learn from others and create new knowledge in their minds as a result of learning. In our example, new ideas have been created in the minds of Mr. A and Ms. B respectively at the same time as a result of Mr. C's entrepreneurial action: (1) trader Mr. A now may proceed to pursue his desired goal which could not be attained due to the lack of a specific kind of resource owned by Ms. B. (2) Trader Ms. B now realizes that her resource is useful and valuable, and therefore should not be wasted. It can be conceived that in general, through the prices signal, such knowledge (received by both Mr. A and Ms. B) will be spread to the entire global community in the market process.

Third, through learning, trading parties revise their plans, formulate new expectation (Lachmann, 1956) and make an economic judgment (Knight, 1921) on the new situation. Hence, economizing resources or more precisely, the coordination of actors' expectations or plans will be possible. In our case, as a result of Mr. C's entrepreneurial action, both Mr. A and Ms. B will revise their plans in accordance with the new messages they perceive. In particular, Mr. A, now having the resource at his disposal, can attain his end and undertake action that he could not take previously. On the other hand, Ms. B is not wasting her resource any more, but keeps and conserves it in order to sell it in the international market. Therefore, all the trading parties in the market will learn, revise their plans, and modify their actions accordingly, thereby economic coordination is made possible. More importantly, each party adjusts to the world market in the best possible way without knowing that they are actually learning. As Schutz and Luckmann (1989, p. 8) note, "one learns both to 'adjust' one's own conduct appropriately to the goal of action and also to improve one's interpretation of the conduct of others." This interactive market process, a simple and effective way of coordinating economic activities and improving human welfare, is precisely Adam Smith's concept of the invisible hand. In what follows, we shall adopt the Austrian theory of international coordination to understand the success of Li & Fung in global markets.

Background of Li & Fung

Li & Fung was first established in Guangzhou, China, by Mr. Fung Pak-Liu and Mr. Li To-Ming in 1906. As a former teacher of English, Fung spoke fluent English and was competent to be an intermediary between Chinese manufacturers and Western buyers. In the beginning, Li & Fung exported porcelain and silk from Mainland China before diversifying into bamboo and rattan ware, jade, ivory handicrafts, and fireworks. In 1937, Fung Hong-Chu, Fung Pak-Liu's second son, moved the company to Hong Kong where there was a deep harbor and a stable political situation.[8] When Fung Pak-Liu passed away in 1943, Li To-Ming retired and sold all his shares to the Fung family. Fung Hong-Chu then took over the business.[9] After 1949, a large influx of immigrants came from Mainland China to Hong Kong. They worked in labor-intensive manufacturing industries such as toys, garments, electronics and plastic flowers. Li & Fung sought good trading opportunities and shipped these products from Hong Kong around the world.

During the early 1970s, the US-educated third generation of the Fung family, Victor and William Fung, joined Li & Fung. They transformed the company from a traditional Chinese family business into a modern enterprise. They restructured the two core businesses, namely, export trading and retail. Li & Fung expanded the business and established regional offices in Taiwan, Singapore and Korea. In 1979, when Deng Xiaoping's Open Door policy was implemented in Mainland China, manufacturing factories in Hong Kong were relocated to the mainland. The headquarters in Hong Kong focused on design, sales, logistics and banking. From 1995 onward, the company has transformed itself from being a regional sourcing company into an international coordinator. It acquired Inchcape Buying Services (Dodwell), Swire & Maclaine Ltd, Camberley Enterprises Ltd and Colby Group Holdings Ltd. Sales grew sevenfold between 1998 and 2008 and totaled US$14.3 billion in 2008 (*CNN*, 2009, December 9). In 2009, it had 13,400 staff, of which 3,045 were based in Hong Kong and 10,357 around the world (Li & Fung Limited, 2009). It generated a net income of HK$3.37 billion[10] with a network of nearly 11,000 suppliers served by over 80 offices in 40 countries (ibid.). It is one of the biggest apparel providers to such companies as Abercrombie & Fitch (A&F) and Tommy Hilfiger. It is also successful in the business of consumer goods such as homeware, toys and sports equipment. Despite its achievements in export trading, Li & Fung does not own any raw material, factory or machine. Instead, it surveys the manufacturing process and finds the best-in-class supplier for each stage of production. Li & Fung coordinates economic activities around the world to meet the expectations in a changing market.

Li & Fung as an international coordinator

Li & Fung not only adapts but also anticipates the changing market situation. Victor Fung agrees with his father that "change is inevitable and that change is often for the good because the old way is not necessarily the best" (Fung, 1997, p. 225). However, change brings uncertainty and opportunity. Li & Fung people are on constant alert for profit opportunities in the global market and are "able to pre-empt the market" (Fung, 1999, quoted in Slater, 1999, p. 13). For William Fung, it is absolutely essential for the company to "anticipate change, strive for constant improvement and be prepared to reinvent the company, to start from zero base if necessary, and above all, institutionalize the change" (Fung, 2003). Li & Fung exhibits its capabilities of global coordination. As an international coordinator, Li & Fung is capable of "drawing out the talent and creativity of the network, coordinating all the individual elements, and ensuring the success of the overall process" (Fung *et al.*, 2008, p. 37). While it understands its partners' visions, strategies, organizations and needs, it does "actually *anticipate* customer needs and the needs of their end consumers" (Fung *et al.*, 2008, p. 121, italics original). It creates a market and enables business parties to meet the demands in the market.

Dynamic global networking

Li & Fung believes that "companies don't compete against other companies. Networks compete against networks" (Fung *et al.*, 2008, p. 16). Global networking enhances "the capability to connect to competencies—the capability for network orchestration—and the capability for learning might be becoming as important as any firm-specific capabilities" (ibid., p. 208). Li & Fung exhibits capabilities in international coordination by: (1) understanding the capabilities of the market participants; (2) building mutual trust; (3) ensuring quality and on-time delivery; (4) constructing a global information network; and (5) internal organization and incentive system (Cheng, 2001).

Li & Fung "dissects" manufacturing beyond national borders. The company itself does not employ any factory worker, or own raw materials, a factory or machinery. Yet, it matches the best-in-world capabilities and offers a one-stop shop or assortment package for its customers around the world (Fung, 1998, quoted in Magretta, 1998, p. 104). When a client thinks about a new product, Li & Fung customizes and assembles the components from all over the world. The "suppliers supply the raw materials, the manufacturers manufacture the goods, and we [Li & Fung] handle all the logistics. No one in our supply chain is asked to do more than what he is capable of doing" (Long and Seet, 1996). Li & Fung matches manufacturers and suppliers to meet the customer's requirements on design, production, quality assurance and delivery schedule. Its role is to "orchestrate the production, come up with samples and feed them [suppliers] information. All that is going way, way beyond that original matching function" (Fung, 1999, quoted in Slater, 1999, p. 11). That is to say, Li & Fung integrates scattered knowledge and synchronizes "the best possible processes across a global network for delivering the right product to the right place at the right time at the right price" (Fung *et al.*, 2008, p. 20).

Li & Fung as a knowledge broker

Li & Fung can be regarded as a global knowledge broker who transmits, assimilates and creates knowledge around the world. It acts as a knowledge hub to share knowledge and collaborate with other market participants. Each specialized division in the company is an independent small business headed by an expert in a specific product. Li & Fung provides administrative support, infrastructure, facilities, finance and human resources. These experts are empowered to act entrepreneurially but free from administrative duties to maximize their capabilities. They have "immediate access to the knowledge and resources of the larger parent organization, while maintaining their individual identities . . . to build creatively and rebuild flexibly, to respond to customers better and improve the operation of the business" (Fung *et al.*, 2008, p. 96). In this way, these intrapreneurs, "mini-John Waynes," develop capabilities and maintain flexibility and innovation.

> [They] take their wagon trains out into new business areas in search of opportunities, and they stand independently. They build and orchestrate networks. They are able to respond quickly to changes on the ground. On these frontiers, they live or die by their own abilities.
> *(ibid., p. 83)*

They catch up with the latest market trends and pursue profit opportunities with other entrepreneurs around the world. Li & Fung coordinates flexible and diverse capabilities to quickly respond to the expectations of the market.

On the other hand, Li & Fung coordinates capabilities around the globe by "filling in the mosaic" (Yoshino and George, 1998). It makes partial acquisitions and receives priority attention from the partner while the partner is not dependent on Li & Fung for business. For instance, the acquisition of Inchcape Buying Services (Dodwell) in the Asia-Pacific region in 1995 transformed Li & Fung from a regional trader to a multinational virtually overnight.[11] To promote "acting locally and thinking globally," Li & Fung encourages working teams to bring in local culture and diversify the international perspective. It develops a knowledge-based environment. In collaborating with entrepreneurs around the world, Li & Fung believes that "local solutions are often distinctly tailored to the needs of a specific region" (Fung *et al.*, 2008, p. 200). In the acquisition of the Inchcape, Li & Fung empowers Inchcape to keep

> very high retention rates of managers after acquisitions and creates opportunities to learn from the best practices of the acquired firm . . . gives some freedom to local offices . . . allows overseas offices to develop their own management model that fits local circumstances.
>
> *(ibid., p. 90)*

To enhance the effectiveness of global coordination, Li & Fung promotes mutual understanding, trust and tolerance, in contrast with traditional top-down Chinese family business. The company facilitates monthly English-speaking meetings and a twice-yearly international conference. It encourages the staff to express their ideas and share information with their fellow partners all over the world. In this way, Li & Fung integrates Chinese values and Western culture so that

> a totally new Chinese management model is in the making; such a model not only embraces traditional values like industry, thriftiness, and social harmony, but also borrows from the West qualities such as flexibility and innovation in doing things, as well as the readiness to assimilate foreign elements.
>
> *(Fung, 1993, quoted in Feng, 2007, p. 95)*

Li & Fung provides the incentives of experimentation and diversity. It understands and compares the performance of business parties. Each business party is designated the roles, job specifications and performance benchmark. Good performers are rewarded by a bonus but poor performers are designated other assignments. A policy committee is established to ensure quality assurance. In the committee, a group of product managers meet once every five to six weeks. They share information and carry out the policies regarding business ethics, monitoring, compliance and corporate social responsibility. Rigorous factory inspection and continuous training programs are carried out to develop entrepreneurial knowledge and capabilities (Loveman and O'Connell, 1995). The Three-Year Strategic Plan enables the company and its partners to "anticipate changes and adjust or initiate reforms ahead of the others" (Feng, 2007, p. 237) and "find gaps in the business and come up with new areas to develop" (*Telegraph*, 1 June 2008). Li & Fung encourages business parties to adopt a new way of thinking and to discover profit opportunities in the market.

Online capabilities in knowledge coordination emerge in the modern digital world. Information technology, digital communication and the internet facilitate a fast and reliable means of knowledge coordination. Li & Fung develops an online communication network of product development and order fulfillment among their trading parties. Electronic data exchange accommodates direct communication with the customers. Admittedly, while information technology increases the effectiveness and efficiency of decision-making, human experience and knowledge are still complex and indispensable. Li & Fung recognizes the importance of human experience and knowledge:

> Technology is not the technology itself, but how important human judgment and experience continues to be . . . Advanced management science tools are important in addressing the complex challenges of managing global networks, but the decisions are so complex that they cannot be entirely entrusted to machines. Skilled experts, supported by information systems, make decisions about where to manufacture and how to design each chain.
>
> *(Fung* et al., *2008)*

Li & Fung integrates information technology, human experience and knowledge. It maintains a "close and deep" relationship with partners and customers (Li & Fung Research Center, 2003, p. 154). It coordinates customer-oriented knowledge and enhances online capabilities on "boosting efficiency, improving coordination . . . creatively rethinking" (Fung *et al.*, 2008, p. 148). In a sophisticated telecommunication network, entrepreneurs are able to understand market trends, anticipate demand and capture more value after a product leaves the factory. For example, in the retail business, Li & Fung shares sales and consumer data with manufacturers, distributors and retailers to prevent stockouts, excess inventory, ensure quality, and so forth (Quelch and Bartlett, 2006, p. 61). Along with modern technology, Li & Fung's global coordination emphasizes understanding and collaboration, assimilates best-in-class knowledge, and shares new insights with partners around the globe.

Case study: Gymboree and Li & Fung[12]

Gymboree, a US-based children's wear retailer, plans to stock 10,000 fleece-lined puffer jackets for next winter. The company initially contacts manufacturers in the United States because of close proximity, high quality and efficiency. However, manufacturing costs are very high. Gymboree then considers sourcing from suppliers overseas. Although manufacturers in Pakistan produce good and cheap jackets, terrorism is Gymboree's main concern. In many regions in East Asia, the costs of manufacturing garments are low due to abundant cheap raw materials and workforces. Hong Kong was once a famous place for garment manufacturing. Knowing that Li & Fung is one of the biggest apparel providers for other American brands such as Tommy Hilfiger, as well as an Asian-based agent with an extensive network of suppliers and manufacturers around the globe, Gymboree approaches Li & Fung and says, "Our company usually makes orders four or five times every year, including more than 2000 styles per season. For this winter, this fleece-lined puffer jacket is what we are thinking about—such a layout, fabric, lining and quantities. Each jacket will be sold at US$40. Can you come up with a production program?" Li & Fung accepts the deal and forms a working team for Gymboree. The team is responsible for sourcing the best manufacturing capabilities around the globe in the cheapest way for Gymboree. As a result, all parties, including Gymboree, Li & Fung, suppliers and manufacturers from developing economies, gain. We take the fleece-lined puffer jacket as an example (Figure 35.1).

For each fleece-lined puffer jacket sold at US$40, Li & Fung notices that there is a profit opportunity of "soft $4" which is achieved by the difference of manufacturing costs and retail price (Fung *et al.*, 2008, p. 146). Li & Fung estimates that the cost of cloth accounts for between 35–45 percent of the retail price, and accessories between 5–7 percent (Li & Fung Research Center, 2003). Li & Fung uses the cheapest and best quality resources all over the world. For example, it uses shell from a Korean producer, 100 per cent polyester thermal fleece from China, reserves a factory in Taiwan for weaving and dying, and orders front zippers from YKK in Shenzhen, China (Figure 35.1). Finally, Li & Fung calculates that if the costs of designing, sourcing, manufacturing and logistics are kept at below US$10, it will make a profit. Since clothing techniques, such as insulation, waterproofing, inserting the zip are complex, Li & Fung frequently discusses

Figure 35.1 Borderless manufacturing
Source: Li & Fung Research Center (2003, p. 121).

production with Gymboree and factories around the world. An extensive global network significantly shortens the production time. Five weeks before the delivery, Li & Fung receives the specification of the product from Gymboree and informs the factory in Taiwan of the style and colour of garments. For an abundant workforce and cost-efficient production capabilities, China is the best place to do "cut, make and trim," the final stage to make jackets. To meet the tight deadline, all materials are shipped and assembled in three factories in Guangdong and Zhejiang, China. Li & Fung designates each manufacturer to assemble jackets between 30 percent and 80 percent of its own total productivity. In this way, Li & Fung controls sourcing and manufacturing costs, increases the efficiency of manufacturing and ensures cost-effectiveness and high profit margins for Gymboree.

In each listed factory, Li & Fung assigns a team of technicians and quality-control officers to monitor the manufacturing process and ensure the products meet the minimum testing requirement. Defective products are flagged and will not be sold. The first batch of puffer jackets are made and checked by Li & Fung. They are then sent to Gymboree for approval. Li & Fung ensures the manufacturing process is at the right place at the right time. Each puffer jacket looks exactly the same as if it were produced in the same factory. Despite being labelled "Made in China," each jacket "*moves the world*" (Fung *et al.*, 2008, p. 184, italics original). It is "made by Hong Kong." Li & Fung also provides a replenishment service to eliminate market mismatch such as buying the wrong products and overstocking obsolete products (Li & Fung Research Center, 2003, p. 123). Jackets then have a price tag attached before being packed in standard-sized containments and transported to over 600 retail stores and 140 outlet stores in North America right before the new season starts (www.gymboree.com/, accessed 28 January 2011).

Gymboree is astonished by the high quality, and efficient and cost-effective global coordination given by Li & Fung. Gymboree regards Li & Fung as its "eyes and ears."[13] Li & Fung keeps up to date of the latest data on raw materials, technology and fashion trends by regular on-the-job training and overseas visits to fashion capitals such as London and Paris. It helps Gymboree to forecast fashion trends in the coming year. With Li & Fung's international entrepreneurship, suppliers, manufacturers and customers around the globe are linked and coordinated. For the next few years, Gymboree continues to collaborate with Li & Fung to expand its businesses in markets such as shoes, hair accessories, umbrellas and children's non-garment items. Mike Mayo, a senior vice-president of Gymboree, says:

> We are able to send all our products over to one agency. They go into the Li & Fung's computer system and then are sent out to all of their locations throughout the world, whether they are in Indonesia, Bangkok, New Delhi, or Seoul. The different factories compete and get their costs as sharp as they can for a particular area.
>
> *(Fung* et al., *2008, p. 117)*

Li & Fung coordinates each stage of the production process conducted by suppliers, manufacturers and Gymboree. In short, Li & Fung removes the hassles in sourcing, manufacturing and distribution and henceforth reduces the information cost for all the trading parties involved.

Conclusion

This chapter develops the Austrian theory of international coordination which can be used to understand the business dynamics of Li & Fung. In the global market, mismatches of plans and mutual distrust are common. International entrepreneurs coordinate global economic activities. These international entrepreneurs are not only middlemen but also knowledge creators. They transmit and create knowledge and perform entrepreneurial discovery around the globe, and hence, improve the well-being of humankind.

Li & Fung is one of the biggest providers of consumer goods in the world. It does not employ any factory worker, or own raw materials, machinery or a factory for manufacturing household products. However, by adopting and linking up the most efficient and cheaper manufacturing process in different parts of the world, Li & Fung is able to gain pure entrepreneurial profit. As a result of the dynamic entrepreneurship of Li & Fung, Hong Kong has evolved into a knowledge hub which integrates knowledge scattered in every corner of the world.

Acknowledgments

An early version of this chapter was presented at the Seventh Annual Conference, Asian Studies Association, Hong Kong, held at Hong Kong Shue Yan University on 2–3 March 2012, and published in the *Journal for Global Business Advancement*, Special Issue on Global Business Advancement and Competitive Advantage, 4(4) (2011): 387–400.

Notes

1 For the details of achievements made by Li & Fung, see www.lifung.com/eng/newsroom/lifung_news/news100205.pdf (accessed 27 July 2010).

2 Both Victor and William Fung graduated with MBAs from Harvard Business School. Victor Fung taught in the Business School after completing his PhD in Economics at Harvard University. Since the Fung brothers' return to Hong Kong in the early 1970s, they have maintained a close relationship with Harvard Business School.

3 Mainstream neoclassical economics assumes market participants, firms and products in the market are homogeneous.

4 The subjectivist approach does not stress knowledge itself, but rather what people know about knowledge. This approach focuses on the kind of knowledge about which people know nothing at all. It follows that "things about which men are completely ignorant are things that simply do not exist" (Kirzner, 1979, p. 138). See also Yu (2001, pp. 47–63).

5 For a further discussion of the Sino-British conflict, see Yu and Kwan (2003, pp. 76–78).

6 Adopted from de Soto (1995, pp. 228–253). Using simple stickmen as an illustration, de Soto is able to demonstrate the essence of the Austrian entrepreneurial process.
7 White (1976, p. 4) argues that Kirzner does not distinguish arbitrageurship from entrepreneurship.
8 When the Second Sino-Japanese War broke out between 1937 and 1945, Hong Kong was comparatively inaccessible, immune from the Japanese invasion and in a stable political situation.
9 Although the Li family are no longer active in Li & Fung, the name of Li & Fung has been kept until now. In Chinese, the characters of Li and Fung mean profit and abundance respectively.
10 Currently, US$1 = HK$7.8.
11 Inchcape was a traditional British trading *Hong* (company) led by Western managers. It has a large pool of customers in Europe and established sourcing offices in Europe, South Asia, the Mediterranean and Latin America.
12 Adapted from Magretta (1998) and Fung *et al.* (2008).
13 Laura Willensky, the vice-president of merchandising and design for Gymboree, says: "They [Li & Fung] are our eyes and ears" (*Time*. Available at: www.time.com/time/magazine/article/0,9171,1115648,00.html, accessed 3 August 2010).

Bibliography

Casson, M. (1982) *The Entrepreneur: An Economic Theory*, Oxford: Blackwell.

Chang, B. and Phi, J. (2007) "The IDS story: reinventing distribution through value-chain logistics," in H.L. Lee and C.-Y Lee (eds) *Building Supply Chain Excellence in Emerging Economies*, New York: Springer, pp. 367–390.

Cheng, L.K (2001) "Li & Fung Ltd: an agent of global production," in L.K. Cheng and H. Kierzkowski (eds) *Global Production and Trade in East Asia*, Boston: Kluwer Academic, pp. 317–324.

CNN (2009) "The unstoppable Fung Brothers," December 9. Available at: http://money.cnn.com/2009/12/07/news/international/li_fung.fortune/ (accessed 21 July 2010).

de Soto, J.H. (1995) "Entrepreneurship and the economic analysis of socialism," in M. Gerrit (ed.) *New Perspectives on Austrian Economics*, London: Routledge, pp. 228–253.

Feng, B.-Y. (2007) *100 Years of Li & Fung: Rise from Family Business to Multinational*, Singapore: Thomson Learning.

Fung, V.K. (1997) "Evolution in the management of family enterprises in Asia," in W. Gunwu and W. Siu-Lun (eds) *Dynamic Hong Kong: Business and Culture*, Hong Kong: The University of Hong Kong, pp. 216–229.

Fung, V.K. (2007) "How to compete in a borderless world: eliminating borders with global networks," *Knowledge Leadership*, Winter: 28–31.

Fung, V.K., Fung, W.K. and Wind, Y.J. (2008) *Competing in a Flat World: Building Enterprises for a Borderless World*, Upper Saddle River, NJ: Wharton School Publishing.

Fung, W.K. (2003) *'Talking to CEOs' Show: Anticipate Change and Reinvent Yourselves Is Key to Survival*. Available at: www.cuhk.edu.hk/ipro/pressrelease/030417e.htm (accessed 22 July 2010).

Hagel, J. (2002) "Leveraged growth: expanding sales without sacrificing profits," *Harvard Business Review*, October: 69–77.

Hagel, J. and Seely Brown, J. (2005) *The Only Sustainable Edge: Why Business Strategy Depends on Productive Friction and Dynamic Specialization*, Boston: Harvard Business School Press.

Hayek, F.A. (1945) "The use of knowledge in society," *American Economic Review*, 35: 519–530.

Holstein, W.J. (2002) "Middleman becomes master," *CEO Magazine*, 182: 53–56.

Hutcheon, R. (1992) *A Burst of Crackers: The Li & Fung Story*, Hong Kong: Li & Fung Ltd.

Kirzner, I.M. (1973) *Competition and Entrepreneurship*, Chicago: University of Chicago Press.

Kirzner, I.M. (1979) *Perception, Opportunity, and Profit*, Chicago: University of Chicago Press.

Kirzner, I.M. (1985) *Discovery and the Capitalist Process*, Chicago: University of Chicago press.

Knight, F.H. (1921) *Risk, Uncertainty, and Profit*, New York: Houghton Mifflin.

Lachmann, L.M. (1956) *Capital and its Structure*, Kansas City: Sheed Andrews and McMeel, Inc.

Li & Fung Limited (2009) *Annual Report 2009*. Available at: www.irasia.com/listco/hk/lifung/annual/ar55263-e00494.pdf (accessed 23 July 2010).

Li & Fung Research Center (2003) *Supply Chain Management: The Practical Experience of the Li & Fung Group*, Hong Kong: Joint Publishing (H.K.) Ltd (in Chinese).

Long, D. and Seet, R. (1996) "Li & Fung (A)," Harvard Business Case Studies, 9–396–107.

Loveman, G.W. and O'Connell, J. (1995) "Li & Fung (Trading) Ltd," Harvard Business School Case, 9–396–075.

McFarlane, F.W. and Young, F. (2002) "Li & Fung (A): Internet issues," Harvard Business School Case, 9–301–009.

Magretta, J. (1998) "Fast, global, and entrepreneurial: supply chain management, Hong Kong style: an interview with Victor Fung," *Harvard Business Review,* September–October: 102–114.

Martin, A. (2007) "Mises, Kirzner and Knight on uncertainty and entrepreneurship: a synthesis," Working Paper. Available at: http://mises.org/journals/scholar/martin.pdf (accessed 26 September 2011).

Quelch, J.A. and Bartlett, C.A. (2006) *Global Marketing Management: A Casebook,* Mason, OH: Thomson/South-Western.

Reekie, W.D. (1984) *Markets, Entrepreneurs, and Liberty: An Austrian View of Capitalism,* Brighton: Wheatsheaf Books.

Schutz, A. and Luckmann, T. (1989) *The Structures of the Life World,* vol.II, Evanston, IL: Northwestern University Press.

Slater, J. (1999) "Masters of the trade," *Far Eastern Economic Review,* July 22: 10–13.

Telegraph (2008) "Li & Fung—the Made in China giant you have never heard of," June 1. Available at: www.telegraph.co.uk/finance/newsbysector/retailandconsumer/2790870/Li-and-Fung-the-Made-in-China-giant-you-have-never-heard-of.html (accessed 3 August 2010).

Time (2007) "Exports: trading up," November 15. Available at: www.time.com/time/magazine/article/0,9171,1115648,00.html (accessed 3 August 2010).

von Mises, L. (1949) *Human Action,* 3rd edn, Chicago: Contemporary Books Inc.

White, L.H. (1976) "Entrepreneurship, imagination and the question of equilibrium," in S. Littlechild (ed.) *Austrian Economics,* vol. III, Aldershot: Edward Elgar (1990), pp. 87–104.

Wind, Y., Fung, V. and Fung, W. (2009) "Network orchestration: creating and managing global supply chains without owning them," in P.R. Kleindorfer and Y.J. Wind (eds) *The Network Challenge: Strategy, Profit, and Risk in an Interlinked World,* New Jersey: Wharton School Publishing, pp. 209–315.

Yoshino, M.Y. and George, A. (1998). "Li & Fung (A): beyond 'filling in the mosaic'—1995–98," Harvard Business School Case 9–398–092.

Yu, T.F.-L. (2001) "Entrepreneurial alertness and discovery," *Review of Austrian Economics,* 14(1): 47–63.

Yu, T.F.-L. and Kwan, D.S.M. (2003) "Learning, catching up and the international economic order: the trilateral relationship between China, Britain and Hong Kong in the entrepreneurial perspective," in T.F.-L. Yu (ed.) *East Asian Business Systems in Evolutionary Perspective: Entrepreneurship and Coordination,* New York: Nova Science Publishers, Inc., pp. 67–88.

Index